Humanistic Botany

Humanistic Botany

by

OSWALD TIPPO

University of Massachusetts
Amherst

and

WILLIAM LOUIS STERN

University of Maryland
College Park

with illustrations by

Alice R. Tangerini

Smithsonian Institution
Washington D.C.

W·W· NORTON & COMPANY · INC·
New York

ACKNOWLEDGMENTS:

Pages 2–3: GREEN LAURELS by Donald Culross Peattie, copyright © 1936, copyright renewed © 1963 by Donald Culross Peattie. Reprinted by permission of Simon & Schuster, Inc.

Pages 3–4: From UNIVERSITY DAYS in MY LIFE AND HARD TIMES Copyright © 1933, 1961, James Thurber. Published by Harper and Row, New York. Originally printed in THE NEW YORKER. And from VINTAGE THURBER by James Thurber copyright © 1963, Hamish Hamilton, London.

Page 117: THE DOUBLE HELIX by James D. Watson, New York, Atheneum Publishers, 1968. Reprinted by permission of Atheneum Publishers.

Page 218: NARCOTIC PLANTS by William A. Emboden, Jr., 1972, The Macmillan Company, New York. British rights granted by Studio Vista, c/o Cassell & Collier Macmillan Ltd., London.

Pages 256–257: From PHANTASTICA, NARCOTIC AND STIMULATING DRUGS by Louis Lewin, translated by P.H.A. Wirth. Copyright © 1964 by Routledge & Kegan Paul Ltd. Reprinted by permission of the publishers, E. P. Dutton & Co., Inc. British Rights granted by Routledge & Kegan Paul Ltd., London.

Pages 314–315: THE CONQUISTADORS by Jean Descola, New York, The Viking Press, Inc., 1957. Malcolm Barnes, tr. British Rights granted by George Allen & Unwin Ltd., London.

Pages 315–316: ADMIRAL OF THE OCEAN SEA by Samuel Eliot Morison, Little, Brown and Company in association with The Atlantic Monthly Press.

Page 355: YANKEE FROM OLYMPUS by Catherine Bowen, Little, Brown and Company in association with The Atlantic Monthly Press.

Pages 399–400: FLOWERING EARTH by Donald Culross Peattie, 1939, G. P. Putnam's Sons. Reprinted by permission of Noel R. Peattie and his agent, James Brown Associates, Inc. Copyright © 1939 by Donald Culross Peattie.

Pages 528–529: THE GRAPES OF WRATH by John Steinbeck. New York, The Viking Press, Inc., 1939. Copyright © 1939 by John Steinbeck. Copyright renewed. British rights granted by McIntosh and Otis, Inc.

Pages 540–543: Based on material appearing in THE CLOSING CIRLCE, by Barry Commoner (Alfred A. Knopf, Inc.).

Pages 543–545: A SAND COUNTY ALMANAC AND SKETCHES HERE AND THERE by Aldo Leopold. London, Oxford University Press, 1949.

ISBN 0 393-09126-0

4 5 6 7 8 9 0

Give me truths,
For I am weary of the surfaces,
And die of inanition. If I knew
Only the herbs and simples of the wood,
Rue, cinquefoil, gill, vervain and agrimony,
Blue-vetch and trillium, hawkweed, sassafras,
Milkweeds and murky brakes, quaint pipes and sundew,
And rare and virtuous roots, which in these woods
Draw untold juices from the common earth,
Untold, unknown, and I could surely spell
Their fragrance, and their chemistry apply
By sweet affinities to human flesh,
Driving the foe and stablishing the friend,—
O, that were much, and I could be a part
Of the round day, related to the sun
And planted world, and full executor
Of their imperfect functions.
But these young scholars, who invade our hills,
Bold as the engineer who fells the wood,
And travelling often in the cut he makes,
Love not the flower they pluck, and know it not,
And all their botany is Latin names.
The old men studied magic in the flowers,
And human fortunes in astronomy,
And an omnipotence in chemistry,
Preferring things to names, for these were men,
Were unitarians of the united world,
And, wheresoever their clear eye-beams fell,
They caught the footsteps of the SAME. Our eyes
Are armed, but we are strangers to the stars,
And strangers to the mystic beast and bird,
And strangers to the plant and to the mine.
The injured elements say, "Not in us;"
And night and day, ocean and continent,
Fire, plant and mineral say, "Not in us,"
And haughtily return us stare for stare.
For we invade them impiously for gain;
We devastate them unreligiously,
And coldly ask their pottage, not their love.
Therefore they shove us from them, yield to us
Only what to our griping toil is due;
But the sweet affluence of love and song,
The rich results of the devine consents
Of man and earth, of world beloved and lover,
The nectar and ambrosia, are withheld ...

Ralph Waldo Emerson

Contents

Preface

1 The Nature of Botany   1

Definition of Botany   4
Definition of Plant   5
Definition of Living, or Life   6
Plants versus Animals   8
Summary   9
Suggested Readings   9

2 Form and Function   11

A Flowering Plant   11
Photosynthesis   14
Internal Structure of the Leaf   15
Roots   19
Internal Structure of the Stem   22
What Happens to the
    Carbohydrates Produced in
    Photosynthesis?   23
The Unique Chemistry of Plants   26
Organic Gardening   27
Some Special Highlights of Form
    and Function   29
General Botany Textbooks   40
Suggested Readings   41
Plant Names   43

3 On Names and Naming   45

Folk Names for Plants   45

Botanical Names   50
The Species   58
The Order of Plants   60
Summary   65
Suggested Readings   65
Plant Names   66

4 Linnaeus   69

The "Prince" Is Born   70
Lapland Journey   72
Achievements in Holland   73
Physician in Stockholm   78
Professor at Uppsala   79
Mature Years   83
Contributions   85
Suggested Readings   86

5 The Cell   89

Finding the Cell   90
Position of the Cell in Life   94
The Anatomy of Cells   96
Transition to the Electron
    Microscope   104
New Cells from Old   108
Inheritance and DNA—Mystery
    of Mysteries   113

Summary   120
Suggested Readings   123
Plant Names   125

6   *Wood*   127

Value and Uses of Wood   128
Wood Is a Plant Product   129
An Attractive Figure   144
Properties of Wood   145
Wood Destroyers   147
The Age of Trees and the Ages
    of Man   151
Suggested Readings   161
Plant Names   163

7   *Poisonous Plants*   165

What Is a Poisonous Plant?   166
Types of Poisonous Plants   168
What to Do in Case of
    Suspected Poisoning   183
Suggested Readings   184
Plant Names   185

8   *Marijuana*   187

Botany of Marijuana   187
Uses by Man   189
History   191
Types of Cannabis   192
The Effects of Cannabis   196
A Few Essential Terms   197
Major Studies of the Marijuana
    Problem   198
Books on Marijuana   204
A Final Personal Note   204
Suggested Readings   205

9   *Medicinal Plants*   209

Plants, Botany, and Medicine   209

A Few Representative and
    Important Medicinal Plants   216
Conclusions   250
Suggested Readings   252
Plant Names   253

10 *Plant Hallucinogens*   255

Definition of Hallucinogens   255
History   257
Hallucinogens and Psychiatry   259
The Major Plant Hallucinogens   261
Suggested Readings   275
Plant Names   277

11 *Food Plants*   279

Hunting and Agricultural Periods   280
What Is Food?   281
Twelve Plants Standing between
    Man and Starvation   284
Edible Wild Plants   296
The Improvement of Cultivated
    Food Plants   296
Suggested Readings   301
Plant Names   303

12 *Spices*   305

The Great Disguisers   305
Flavor Comes of Age   307
Companion to Exploration   308
Spices the World Over   320
Suggested Readings   333
Plant Names   334

13 *Algae*   337

Blue-Green Algae   338
Green Algae   338
Brown Algae   344
Red Algae   350
Diatoms   351

Impact of Algae on Man 351
Summary 358
Suggested Readings 358

14 *Fungi* 361

Plant Body 362
Reproduction 362
Groups of Fungi 363
Harmful Activities of Fungi 373
Useful Aspects of Higher Fungi 380
Plant Pathology 384
Suggested Readings 386

15 *Mosses and Ferns* 389

Mosses and Liverworts 389
Vascular Plants 390
Life History of a Fern 391
Origin of Land Plants 396
Suggested Readings 400

16 *Seed Plants* 403

Place in the Plant Kingdom 404
Gymnosperms 404
Angiosperms 410
Suggested Readings 426
Plant Names 427

17 *Genetics* 429

Why Study Genetics? 429
What Is Genetics? 430
Mendel's Basic Crosses 433
Summary of Mendel's Four
  Laws of Genetics 440
A Few Problems 440
Meiosis, or Reduction Division 441
Similarity between Mendel's
  Factors (Genes) and
  Chromosome Behavior 443

Developments in Genetics since
  Mendel 443
Plant Breeding 447
Scientific Method as Illustrated
  by Genetics 450
Suggested Readings 452

18 *Mendel* 455

Formative Years 455
Mendel Becomes a Monk 456
Botanical Research 457
His Later Years 457
Contributions 458
Suggested Readings 459

19 *Evolution* 461

The Evolution Controversy 461
Evidence for Evolution 466
Course of Evolution 471
Causes of Evolution 471
Types of Evolution 476
Impact of Evolution on Society
  and the Intellectual World 477
Suggested Readings 481

20 *Darwin* 483

Forebears 483
Early Life 484
University Days 484
The Voyage of the *Beagle* 485
London 487
Down 487
The Evolution Project 489
Other Books 490
Qualities of the Man 491
Contributions 492
Suggested Readings 493

21 *Ecology*   495

    Understanding Our Environment:
    Vital Cycles of Life   496
    Links of Life: The Food Chain   512
    Plant Succession   515
    Summary   519
    Suggested Readings   522
    Plant Names   523

22 *Man's Influence over His
    Environment*   525

    Despoiling the Land   528
    Food Chains and Poisoned Food   531
    The Car and the Air   536
    Rules and Ethics for Ecology   539

    Suggested Readings   546
    Plant Names   549

23 *Exploring for Plants*   551

    The Breadfruit Voyages   554
    Tea, the Gentle Brew   560
    Royal Lily   564
    The Future   569
    Suggested Readings   570
    Plant Names   572

    Glossary   575

    Index   595

Color illustrations follow pp. 208, 240, 352, and 384.

Preface

This text is intended for the undergraduate course in botany elected by nonscience majors—by students who plan to concentrate in the humanities and fine arts, in the social and behavioral sciences, in the various preprofessional curricula leading to careers in law, business, and the like. This book is not written for botany courses enrolling majors in botany, plant science, and biology, or majors in one of the other natural sciences such as chemistry or physics. For such professional or preprofessional botany courses there are available a number of good, solid scientific texts of imposing comprehensiveness and alarming bulk. Courses and books of this type necessarily presuppose some sophistication in chemistry, physics, and even mathematics.

Since the present text is designed for the generalist, we have purposely avoided the extremely technical and have deliberately included little or no chemistry and physics. No mathematics is required for the intelligent reading of this book. We have endeavored to restrict ourselves to a minimum of technical terms, trying instead to place the emphasis on concepts and ideas. We have eschewed detailed anatomical descriptions and the usual plethora of life histories.

Our aim is not to offer a comprehensive book in botany covering all aspects of the several subdisciplines of plant science, and certainly not to provide the usual extensive survey of the plant kingdom. We have rather elected to deal with a few selected topics which we consider of interest and of some lasting importance to anyone. We are persuaded that a botany course planned for nonscience majors should be—at least, might be—different from the standard course for science majors. In the words of Pistol in Shakespeare's *Henry V,*

> Discuss unto me; art thou officer?
> Or art thou base, common, and popular?

This book is intended to be "base, common, and popular"—popular, that is, in the sense that it is intended for people—lay people.

One of us has been experimenting with such a course during the last few years. Some of his colleagues have good-naturedly referred to the course as botany for poets. A more accurate title, we think, would be *humanistic botany,* for it is intended to present botany of interest and appeal to the nonspecialist. We think such a course should place major emphasis on plants and topics that have an impact on people: plants useful to us; poisonous plants; medicinal plants, including narcotic and hallucinogenic plants; food plants and population problems; organic gardening; ecology—the great cycles of nature and their alarming abuse by man. We have included chapters on genetics and evolution because of their profound impact on society and intellectual history.

Occasionally we mention the modes of inquiry or ways in which botanists and other scientists carry on their investigations. And from time to time we include information about the people who have made major contributions to botany. Who were they? What motivated them? And so we have written chapters specifically about such great botanists and biologists as Linnaeus, Mendel, and Darwin. We have succumbed occasionally to the temptation to include references to botany in literature. What have the great writers, humorists, poets, savants said about plants and botany? Where appropriate we have called attention to the aesthetic qualities of plants.

In sum, our emphasis is on plants and man—their impact on civilization, history, religion, and human thought. In other words, we have tried to present a small segment of ethnobotany, literally, "people botany." Again, our object is not to be encyclopedic or exhaustive; rather our intent is to open windows and to present vistas which we hope will inspire some readers to pursue these subjects further.

At the ends of several chapters we have listed the common names of plants together with their appropriate scientific names. We have followed this practice because frequently the Latin binomials have a special significance and thus add meaning to the plant referred to. Also, if we were to use common names alone, there would be numerous cases where the reader could not be sure of the identity of the plant to which we refer—for example, bittersweet, nightshade, snakeroot, and vetch. In the chapters on the plant groups, we have employed scientific names in the text, for often there are no common names, particularly for the lower plants. In a few places, we have cited alternative scientific names, for these may be encountered in the books listed under Suggested Readings.

We are indebted to the following colleagues for their critical reading of certain chapters: Allen V. Barker, C. Ritchie Bell, Howard E. Bigelow, Margaret E. Barr Bigelow, Paul J. Bottino, Murray F. Buell, Edward L. Davis, David E. Fairbrothers, Sidney R. Galler, Lester Grinspoon, Charles B. Heiser, Jr., Francis W. Holmes, John M. Kingsbury, William J. Koch, George H. M. Lawrence, Richard E. Schultes, Paul B. Sears, Solomon H. Snyder, Carl. P. Swanson, Frederick S. Troy, Warren H. Wagner, Jr., Peter L. Webster, and Robert T. Wilce.

It is a pleasure to acknowledge the assistance and many courtesies provided by the Smithsonian Institution, Longwood Gardens, and the Division of Photographic Services, University of Maryland. On many occasions our library work was smoothed by Ruth F. Schallert of the Smithsonian. Frederic Rosengarten, Jr., rendered encouragement and help with the spices and directed us to sources of information and illustrations. James A. Duke's visits to the coca lands of South America resulted in his special help with our photographic portrayals of this important drug plant. Color pictures and chapter facing photographs were taken by Walter H. Hodge, to whom we are grateful. We are indebted to Philip and Effie Tanis for their many kindnesses during the gestation of this book and especially for Phil's patience with his two "professors."

We wish to record our appreciation to Faye E. Leonard, Karen Nelson, and Janet M. Weaver for their painstaking and professional typing of several versions of the manuscript.

Finally, the authors express their gratitude to Flory, Susan, and Paul Stern, and to Emmie, Denis, and Ray Tippo for their perceptive reading of the text, their proofreading and their many other contributions, including their constant encouragement.

February 1976   Oswald Tippo
                                                   William Louis Stern

Humanistic Botany

Fallen column at the Temple of Olympian Zeus, Athens. The acanthus leaves carved on the top of the column characterize the Corinthian capital.

1
The Nature of Botany

Since this book is devoted to plants, to botany, and to the impact of plants on people, let us begin by examining just what is meant by the two terms **botany** and **plants.** But before attempting a formal definition of botany it may be of interest to see what several laymen, general writers, and nonbotanists have had to say about the meaning and content of botany.

Ambrose Bierce, short-story writer, satirist, and journalist, defines botany in his *The Devil's Dictionary* (1906) as "the science of vegetables—those that are not good to eat, as well as those that are. It deals largely with their flowers, which are commonly badly designed, inartistic in color, and ill-smelling."

Thomas Jefferson (1743–1826), third president of the United States, founder of the University of Virginia, and a man greatly interested in the sciences, indeed, in all learning, writes, "Botany I rank with the most valuable sciences, whether we consider its subjects as furnishing the principal subsistence of life to man and beast, delicious varieties for our tables, refreshments from our orchards, the adornments of our flower borders, shade and perfume of our groves, materials for our buildings, or medicaments for our bodies."

In a text used in schools and colleges in the nineteenth century, *Familiar Lectures in Botany* (1829), Almira H. Lincoln writes,

The objects of [botany's] investigation are beautiful and delicate; its pursuits, leading to exercise in the open air, are conducive to health and cheerfulness. It is not a sedentary study which can be acquired in the library, but the objects of the science are scattered over the surface of the earth, along the banks of the winding brooks, on the

1

borders of precipices, the sides of mountains, and the depths of the forest. . . . Animals, though affording the most striking marks of designing wisdom, cannot be dissected and examined without painful emotions. But the vegetable world offers a boundless field of inquiry, which may be explored with none but the most pure and delightful emotions.

Another interesting point of view with respect to botany appears in *Green Laurels* (1936), an account of the lives of the great botanists and other naturalists, written by Donald Culross Peattie, a botanist trained at Harvard, who devoted his life to the interpretation of botany to laymen:

And what more natural, you ask, than that botanists should collect plants? The public conception of a botanist is little other than a man with a vasculum, who can name on sight any and all plants. Alas, what antiquated notions one may retain! Modern botany has almost ceased to concern itself with living plants. In many places, particularly in Germany and in the Germanized American universities, the "amiable science," as Goethe called it, is become an affair of titration tubes, spectroscopes, microtomes, chromosomes, and the mathematics of genetics. The botanical faculty are practically vassals of the physics and chemistry departments. Through their mills, vegetable tissue passes as the raw materials of the laboratory. It is in many cases of so little apparent moment to know the names or the life habits of the living plant which furnishes forth the experimental material, that it is possible now to be a bespectacled young doctor of botany without having a speaking acquaintance with half a dozen living plants and where they grow.

In fact, it is a matter of some pride, especially to the young instructors, to profess a joking ignorance of Linnaean science. "Linnaeus could not now be considered a botanist at all," is a statement that I have recently read. Its author doubtless conceives of Linnaeus as the one who invented Latin names, a man who betrayed the essential frivolity of his character by devising the floral clock—a plot where diurnal and nocturnal flowers, opening at their different and appointed times, told off the hours in the garden of his country estate at Hammerby. And there was an emotional strain in Linnaeus's character, a candid love of beauty, an impetuous enthusiasm for Nature (whose very name is now in poor repute), and a partisan insistence upon his great artifact of a schema, that intensely embarrass the thin-lipped and the ardorless.

Who that has passed through college has not had the pleasure of one or two field trips with a grey-cheeked biologist of today? You must surely remember it—how the class straggled behind, harkening listlessly, feeling as ill at ease out in the open, in all that sweet natural chaos, as the instructor looked in his business suit with his Phi Beta Kappa key sparkling unnaturally on his vest, while he pointed out a few organisms that it is not feasible to bring into the laboratory.

A more personal evaluation of botany comes from the pen of James Thurber, reporter, humorist, and famed contributor to the *New Yorker* magazine. For reasons which will become obvious, perhaps we should add that Thurber lost an eye in a boyhood accident with a bow and arrow. Because this passage, taken from Thurber's autobiography, *My Life and Hard Times* (1934), portrays one beginning student's attitudes toward and difficulties with botany, it should be of some interest to other beginners:

I passed all the other courses that I took at my University, but I could never pass botany. This was because all botany students had to spend several hours a week in a laboratory looking through a microscope at plant cells, and I could never see through a microscope. I never once saw a cell through a microscope. This used to enrage my instructor. He would wander around the laboratory pleased with the progress all the students were making in drawing the involved and, so I am told, interesting structure of flower cells, until he came to me. I would just be standing there. "I can't see anything," I would say. He would begin patiently enough, explaining how anybody can see through a microscope, but he would always end up in a fury, claiming that I could *too* see through a microscope but just pretended that I couldn't. "It takes away from the beauty of flowers anyway," I used to tell him. "We are not concerned with beauty in this course," he would say. "We are concerned solely with what I may call the *mechanics* of flars." "Well," I'd say, "I can't see anything." "Try it just once again," he'd say, and I would put my eye to the microscope and see nothing at all, except now and again a nebulous milky substance—a phenomenon of maladjustment. You were supposed to see a vivid, restless clockwork of sharply defined plant cells. "I see what looks like a lot of milk," I would tell him. This, he claimed, was the result of my not having adjusted the microscope properly, so he would readjust it for me, or rather for himself. And I would look again and see milk.

I finally took a deferred pass, as they called it, and waited a year and tried again. (You had to pass one of the biological sciences or you couldn't graduate.) The professor had come back from vacation brown as a berry, bright-eyed and eager to explain cell-structure again to his classes. "Well," he said to me cheerily, when we met in the first laboratory hour of the semester, "we're going to see cells this time, aren't we?" "Yes, sir," I said. Students to right of me and to left of me and in front of me were seeing cells; what's more, they were quietly drawing pictures of them in their notebooks. Of course, I didn't see anything.

"We'll try it," the professor said to me, grimly, "with every adjustment of the microscope known to man. As God is my witness, I'll arrange this glass so that you see cells through it or I'll give up teaching. In twenty-two years of botany, I—." He cut off abruptly for he was beginning to quiver all over, like Lionel Barrymore, and he genuinely wished to hold onto his temper; his scenes with me had taken a great deal out of him.

So we tried it with every adjustment of the microscope known to man. With only one of them did I see anything but blackness or the familiar lacteal opacity, and that time I saw, to my pleasure and amazement, a variegated constellation of flecks, specks, and dots. These I hastily drew. The instructor, noting my activity, came back from an adjoining desk, a smile on his lips and his eyebrows high in hope. He looked at my cell drawing. "What's that?" he demanded, with a hint of a squeal in his voice. "That's what I saw," I said. "You didn't, you didn't, you *didn't*!" he screamed, losing control of his temper instantly, and he bent over and squinted into the microscope. His head snapped up. "That's your eye! he shouted. "You've fixed the lens so that it reflects! You've drawn your eye!"

Definition of Botany

With the foregoing in mind, we now ask the question, What is botany? Simply put, **botany** is the study, or the science, of plants. These few words do not, however, convey an adequate conception of the breadth of the field of botany, for it concerns itself with all aspects of plants: their structure, names, classification; the chemical and other processes which go on in plants; the distribution of plants over the face of the earth; the relationship of plants to other plants, animals, and the environment (**ecology**); and their diseases, inheritance, evolution, and fossils, as well.

These aspects are sometimes referred to as the basic, or pure, phases of plant study. It is important to note, however, that botany also includes those aspects of plant study which place major emphasis on the use of plants by man. Thus **horticulture** (the study of vegetables, fruit-bearing plants, and ornamental plants) with its subdivisions of **olericulture** (study of vegetables), **pomology** (study of fruits), and **floriculture** (study of ornamental plants), as well as **forestry** (the study of trees which produce timber and other wood products) and **bacteriology** (the study of bacteria), are all divisions of botany, or plant science. But they have become so important in their own right, that usually they are segregated as distinct disciplines. Properly speaking, however, anything about plants is grist for the mill of botany and should be included in the definition.

Definition of Plant

We have said that botany is the study of plants, but we might well ask, What is a plant? This is not an idle question as we shall see. Note the statement of a student who wrote on his pretest administered on the first day of his botany course, before any of the course work had begun, that "plants cannot walk, swim, or make noise." In point of fact plants do move (sensitive plant, Venus's flytrap, walking fern, tumble weed), plants do swim (simple aquatic plants known as algae), and some plants also make a noise (the tropical sandbox tree makes a loud clatter when the seeds shoot out from the exploding fruit; corn plants can literally be heard to grow on a hot July night; and the she-oak, indeed, derives its name from the fact that the sound made by the wind blowing through its branches supposedly resembles the babble of human tongues).

Most people when asked the question, What is a plant? reply that a plant is something with roots, stems, leaves, flowers, fruits, and seeds. Actually, there exist plants which lack one or more, or even all, of these listed structures. Lower, or primitive, plants in particular show little or no differentiation, are microscopic in size, and often have but one cell; others are in the form of delicate threads or filaments or are spherical in shape. Indeed, there is an endless diversity of plant forms and shapes and many plants lack the usual structures we associate with a typical plant.

How then can we define a plant? In the first place, we can say a plant is living. Frequently this simple but fundamental fact is overlooked. For example, we have all heard some vegetarians explain that they do not eat meat because as a matter of principle they will not eat anything living or anything from a creature which has to be killed. Often such persons are surprised to learn that the lettuce, carrots, and other vegetables they consume are indeed living. There may be good reason for vegetarianism but it cannot be justified on the grounds that animals are living whereas plants are not.

Definition of Living, or Life

So we can agree that plants are living things, but you may ask, what is a living thing? And here we have to admit that we cannot give a satisfactory definition of life for it is a very elusive concept. Indeed there are those who hold that we are here confronted by one of the fundamental limitations of science. **Science,** you should bear in mind, is knowledge which is acquired through our various senses such as seeing, hearing, smelling, and feeling. Our brains then work with and rework the data obtained through our sense organs, organizing these sensory impressions or collective experiences into the generalizations, principles, and laws of science. There are those who insist that life and the state of living possess attributes beyond the ken of sense organs, and that to obtain an adequate or complete concept of life we must look to the poet and philosopher. In any case, scientists, whether admitting the inherent limitations of science or not, in attempting to define living have to settle for a catalogue of the characteristics of living things which can be perceived by our sense organs.

1. **Organic compounds:** All living things are made up of substances which contain the element carbon (C). As you have doubtless learned, organic compounds occur in **organisms** (living things) as
   a. **carbohydrates:** compounds of carbon, hydrogen (H), and oxygen (O) in which the ratio of hydrogen to oxy-

gen atoms is 2:1, as in water; hence the name carbohydrate.

b. **fats:** compounds of carbon, hydrogen, and oxygen, but in which the ratio of hydrogen to oxygen is not 2:1 but usually much greater.

c. **proteins:** compounds with carbon, hydrogen, oxygen, and nitrogen (N).

These three classes of organic compounds are termed **foods,** which are defined in biology as organic compounds which furnish energy or form living cells. You will note that biologists make a distinction between foods and **raw materials** such as mineral salts, which are sometimes popularly referred to as "plant food," as in commercial fertilizers. Although all living things contain carbon, not all objects with carbon are living; for example, there is the gas carbon dioxide (CO_2) in the air and marsh gas (CH_4).

2. **Responsiveness:** Living things exhibit the ability to react to stimuli or changes in the environment such as a flash of light or a touch. A sensitive plant responds to touch by closing its leaves; plant stems grow toward light, while roots grow toward the pull of gravity.

3. **Growth:** It will suit our present purpose to describe growth as an irreversible increase in size. But not all objects which increase in size are living; a snowball rolling down a hill comes to mind.

4. **Absorption of energy** and **expenditure of energy:** Plants absorb light energy from the sun and then use this energy to build complex organic compounds or they use it in movement. In the process of **respiration** foods are broken down and energy is released. Respiration is a chemical process and is not to be confused, as it often is, with breathing which is the forceful inhalation and exhalation of air requiring lungs or gills. Plants do not breathe but they do respire, as indeed all living things carry on respiration.

5. **Reproduction:** In reproduction the organism duplicates itself, it forms similar offspring.

6. **Cells:** These microscopic compartments contain protoplasm, the living stuff of the cells.

In practice we use a combination of these attributes to characterize life and living things; as has been pointed out, any one of these attributes may be found in something nonliving. Admittedly, simply by listing these several characteristics we have not provided a very satisfactory or complete description of the complex of phenomena known as life. Certainly this definition would not satisfy the poet or philosopher, nor, for that matter, a reflective scientist. But, given the limitations of the scientific method, perhaps we shall never be able to do better.

Plants versus Animals

A while ago we stated that a plant is a living thing; but you may say that animals are also living things. How do we distinguish between the types of organisms? Although scarcely anyone confuses a higher plant such as an oak tree with a well-developed animal such as a horse it is more difficult to distinguish between some of the lower or more primitive plants and animals, for plants and animals share many characteristics. One of our colleagues, in a moment of inspiration, once remarked that plants do everything animals do, but they do it quietly and with great dignity. And so again we have to resort to a list of the typical characteristics of plants, admitting, as in the case of defining life, that no one attribute is sufficient. Consequently we must employ the totality of characteristics to provide even a half-decent definition of a plant. Features which characterize plants include:

1. **Chlorophyll:** the green pigment usually located in leaves. Yet, fungi (i.e., mushrooms, molds, bacteria) are considered plants although they have no chlorophyll.
2. **Ability to manufacture food:** the process of **photosynthesis,** specifically the process in which water and carbon dioxide react in the presence of light and chlorophyll to form sugar (carbohydrate) and oxygen. All green plants carry on photosynthesis, yet fungi, lacking chlorophyll, do not.
3. **Continuous growth:** Higher animals generally grow during a youthful period then reach adult size, after which they remain pretty much the same size for the rest of their lives. Plants, at least in such seed plants as our common trees, continue to grow year after year, adding not only to their length but to their girth as well. Thus we have the giant West Coast redwoods which have attained a length of 380 feet or the Australian eucalyptus trees which may grow even taller.
4. **Localized growth:** In general, animals grow all over; there is no special growth zone in the body, but rather, all parts of animals increase in size. In plants growth is localized in the tips of stems and their branches; in the tips of roots and their branches; and, in some plants such as trees, in special growth layers located between the wood and bark. This latter growth layer is called the **cambium** which,

through its activity each year, adds new wood cells on the inside and new bark cells on the outside.

5. **Cellulose:** a carbohydrate elaborated from the sugar manufactured in photosynthesis and deposited in cell walls. It is the structural framework of plant cell walls and does not occur in animals, except for the marine animals known as tunicates. Animals in fact do not have cell walls in the sense in which we use the term in botany. It is the cellulose of plant cell walls which is exploited by man to furnish cellulose in the making of paper and in the production of clothing from cotton and flax.

6. **Fixed position:** Although there are numerous exceptions, as in the instance of swimming algae and fungi, the fixed location is a fact of life for most higher plants, such as flowering plants. They cannot move from these positions, although their branches, leaves, and flowers may move. Being fixed in place profoundly affects their structure and behavior: Their roots grow out in all directions in the soil exploring for the raw materials water and mineral salts; their leaves and branches reach out in all directions to obtain carbon dioxide and the oxygen necessary for life; male reproductive cells, to reach the female plants or structures must be carried by wind, water, insects, or by some animal; and their seeds, to achieve wide distribution, must be borne by the wind, water, insects, birds, or by other animals.

Summary

Botany is the study of plants, all aspects of plants. **Plants** are living things, defining **living things** as those with **carbon, responsiveness, growth, absorption** and **expenditure of energy, respiration, reproduction,** and **cells.** Plants differ from animals in that the former typically have **chlorophyll, photosynthesis, continuous growth, localized growth, cellulose** in cell walls, and **fixed position.**

Suggested Readings

Knobloch, Irving W. *Selected Botanical Papers.* Englewood Cliffs, N. J.: Prentice-Hall, 1963. A collection of essays on general aspects of plants and their importance to civilization.

Peattie, Donald C. *Green Laurels.* New York: Simon and Schuster, 1936. The lives and achievements of the great naturalists, such as Linnaeus, Lamarck, Darwin, Wallace, and Goethe, by a botanist turned popular writer.

Veins on the underside of a leaf of the
Queen Victoria water lily (*Victoria
regia*).

2
Form and Function

Our objective in this chapter is to give a brief description of the salient features of plant structure and of the basic processes which take place in plants, calling attention to the manner in which plants meet the various problems of existence confronting them, given their fixed positions anchored in the soil. Plant form is molded by the functions the plant performs, making due allowance for the legacies provided by past history or evolution.

We do not intend to go into any great detail about either structure or function; if you wish to probe more deeply into either **plant morphology** (the study of form and structure) or **plant physiology** (the science which deals with functions and processes), we call your attention to the several comprehensive textbooks of general botany which are listed at the end of the chapter. In general, we will limit ourselves here to those topics and facts which are basic to understanding the rest of the book. Occasionally we shall include a topic because of its human relevance.

A Flowering Plant

We realize, of course, that there is no such thing as a typical plant among the hundreds of thousands of different flowering plants, any more than there is a typical or average person. However, it will be useful if we begin with a quick review of the salient features of a generalized flowering plant.

In the first place, you know that a flowering plant (Figure 2.1) consists of several parts—root, stem, leaf, and flower. The first

11

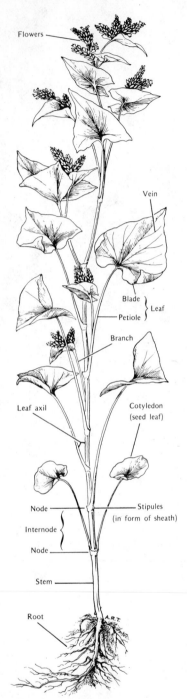

Flowers

Vein

Blade } Leaf
Petiole }

Branch

Leaf axil

Cotyledon
(seed leaf)

Node ——— Stipules
(in form of sheath)

Internode {

Node

Stem

Root A.R.T.

Figure 2.1 Buckwheat, a flowering
plant with root, stem, leaves, and flowers.

three parts are sometimes called **organs;** the **flower** is a collection of a number of organs.

The **root,** usually composed of a primary, or main, root and
branch roots, absorbs water and mineral salts from the soil; it
anchors or supports the plant; it conducts materials; and it
stores food and other substances, particularly those roots which
are enlarged, as carrot, beet, and turnip roots.

The **stem** is made up of the main axis (or trunk in a tree) with
side, or lateral, branches. The points on the stem where the
leaves are attached are called **nodes** and the segments of the
stem between nodes are termed **internodes.** Since only stems
have nodes and internodes, these features become important
diagnostic characteristics when identifying certain questionable structures, such as underground stems, which are often
confused with roots. Stems provide support for leaves and flowers, conduct materials, store food, and, if green, as in a grass,
manufacture food.

The **leaf** may consist of three parts: the thin, broad expanse of
green tissue, the **blade;** the **leaf stalk,** or **petiole,** which attaches
the blade to the stem; and, in some plants, two little flaps of tissue at the base of the petiole called **stipules.** The upper and
acute angle between the petiole and stem is designated the **leaf
axil;** this is a very significant region, for it is here that normally
a **bud** originates which later may develop into a branch.
Because of their location in leaf axils and on the sides of stems,
these buds are called **axillary,** or **lateral, buds,** to distinguish
them from the **terminal buds** borne at the tips of the main stems
and at the tips of side branches. Infrequently a bud may be initiated elsewhere, as in the instance of a wound, in which case
the bud is termed an **adventitious bud** (literally, "a bud arising
in a foreign place"). If you hold a leaf blade to the light, you will
see the **veins,** which not only support the soft green tissue of
the leaf but also conduct materials. The chief function of the leaf
is food manufacture, or **photosynthesis.**

A leaf with a single blade is a **simple leaf** (Figures 2.1, 2.2, and
2.3); if the blade is divided into parts, the leaf is a **compound
leaf** (Figure 3.5), and each of the individual units is a **leaflet.** If
the leaflets are arranged along the petiole in the fashion of a
feather, we have a **pinnately compound leaf** (Figure 3.5) as in
the sumac, the tree of heaven, and walnut. On the other hand, if
the leaflets all take their origin at the tip of the petiole, like the
fingers of the hand, we have a **palmately compound leaf** (Figure 8.2), as in the horse chestnut and buckeye.

Figure 2.2 Alternate, pinnately veined leaves of sassafras.

The main veins in a leaf may form a feather pattern (**pinnately veined leaves,** Figure 16.24), or the chief veins may spread out from the tip of the petiole like the fingers of the hand (**palmately veined leaves,** Figure 2.1). Pinnate and palmate leaves are characteristic of the group of flowering plants known as **dicotyledons,** such as oaks, geraniums, and elms. If the main

See photograph on page 10, Queen Victoria water lily.

Figure 2.3 Opposite, palmately veined leaves of maple.

veins run parallel with one another, we have a **parallel-veined leaf,** characteristic of the other group of flowering plants called **monocotyledons,** such as corn and other grasses, lilies, irises, tulips, and orchids.

There may be only one leaf attached to a node with successive leaves arranged in a spiral fashion around the stem; this is the **alternate,** or **spiral, arrangement** (Figure 2.2). If there are two leaves at each node, facing one another across the stem, we call it the **opposite arrangement** (Figure 2.3). When there are three or more leaves attached to a node, we have the **whorled arrangement.** These various arrangements, coupled with differential lengths of petioles, insure equitable weight distribution and, even more important, a minimum of shading of leaves.

The **flower** (Figure 16.13) is made up of an outer cycle, or whorl, of green or otherwise colored, leaflike structures called **sepals;** next in order is a whorl of brightly colored members called **petals;** then a group of clublike objects which are **stamens** and which bear sacs at their tips containing dustlike **pollen;** and, finally, in the center of the flower there are one or more structures resembling small bowling pins, the **carpels** or **pistils.** Each carpel or pistil consists of an enlarged base called the **ovary,** inside of which are borne the tiny **ovules** destined to become **seeds;** a neck, or **style;** and an inflated tip, the **stigma,** the spot where pollen is received. The flower is a reproductive structure, but we will postpone to later chapters a consideration of the actual reproductive process.

Photosynthesis

As mentioned in Chapter 1, an important difference between most plants and animals is that plants are able to carry on **photosynthesis,** the process by which plants manufacture food. Unquestionably it is the most important chemical reaction in plants, indeed, in the entire organic world, for if it ceased, all mankind and all animals would die. Plant leaves contain special structures which make it possible.

A simplified description of photosynthesis shows that water and carbon dioxide react in the presence of light and chlorophyll at a suitable temperature to yield sugar and oxygen:

$$\text{water} + \text{carbon dioxide} \xrightarrow[\text{suitable temperature}]{\text{light and chlorophyll}} \text{sugar} + \text{oxygen}$$

Water for the reaction comes from the soil, from which it is absorbed by the roots and then conducted to the stem, and thence to the leaves in a specialized tissue known as **wood,** or **xylem.** The **carbon dioxide** of the air (where there are but 3 parts per 10,000 parts of air) diffuses into the leaf through pores, usually located on the lower surface of the leaves. By **diffusion** we mean that a substance in a gaseous or liquid medium moves from a region where there is a higher concentration of the substance to a region where there is less of it. **Light** comes from the sun in nature, but light energy also may be furnished by artificial illumination. It should be emphasized that some form of energy is always required in a chemical reaction involving any type of synthesis.

The green pigment, **chlorophyll,** is located in the cells of leaves in special structures, the **chloroplasts.** As you will learn in Chapter 5, on cells, chlorophyll molecules are spread over the surfaces of **plates, or lamellae,** in chloroplasts. Chlorophyll absorbs and collects light, or radiant energy, from the sun and the pigment becomes activated. In a series of rather complex steps, light energy is converted into chemical energy which is then stored in sugar (glucose) molecules.

Some of the **sugar** produced in the photosynthetic process may be used in the leaf to build up new cells or it may be used in the process of respiration which yields energy. Some, if not most, of the sugar is transported to the stem, root, fruit, or seeds where it is converted for storage into insoluble carbohydrates such as starch. The sugar which is transported from the leaf is conducted in a special tissue called the **phloem,** which is continuous from the veins of the leaf down through the stem and root.

A small quantity of the **oxygen** produced during photosynthesis may be used by the leaf in respiration, but most of the gas diffuses out of the leaf through the pores on the lower surface of the leaf.

Internal Structure of the Leaf

Now we turn to the internal anatomy of the organ which is responsible for photosynthesis. Let us see how it provides the necessary water and carbon dioxide and how it disposes of the sugar and oxygen produced in the process.

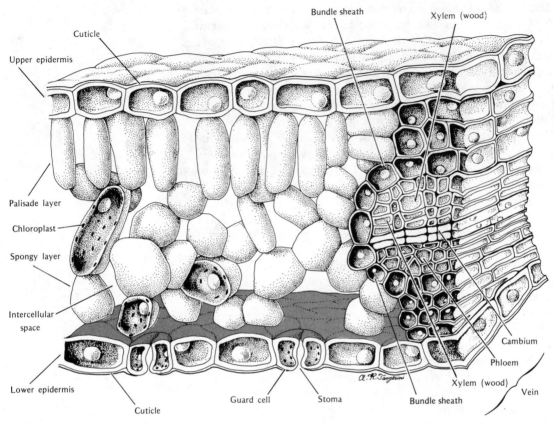

Figure 2.4 Three-dimensional view of sectioned leaf.

As you can see in Figures 2.4 and 2.5, the top surface of the leaf is composed of a single layer of **upper epidermis cells** covered with a waterproofing layer of wax called the **cuticle,** which minimizes water loss. The next layer, made up of long cells, is designated the **palisade layer** because of its resemblance to the old palisade forts of colonial times. Below the palisade layer is a zone of cells placed rather loosely; this is the **spongy layer** which has many relatively large **intercellular spaces** among the cells which permit the various gases involved in the process of photosynthesis to circulate. Both the palisade and spongy layers are well supplied with chloroplasts hence these two layers carry on photosynthesis. Here and there in the spongy layer are groups of cells making up the **veins** comprised of **xylem cells** (at

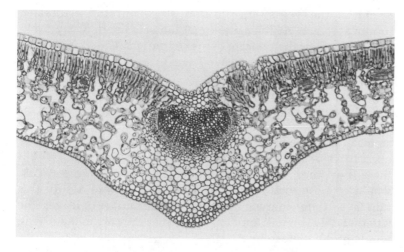

Figure 2.5   Cross-section of a privet leaf. [Courtesy Carolina Biological Supply Co.]

the top of the vein) and **phloem cells** (at the bottom of the vein). As mentioned, the veins not only give support to the leaf, but also the xylem in them conducts water to the manufacturing cells and the phloem transports the elaborated food away.

The lower surface of the leaf is composed of the **lower epidermis** in which there are small pores, or **stomata** (Figure 2.6). Each **stoma** is flanked by two **guard cells** which control the opening and closing of the stoma. In face view, the guard cells look like two beans with a space in between, the stoma. The guard cells are valvelike structures which cause the stomata to open in light and close in the dark. The stomata permit gases to diffuse in and out of the leaf—during the day carbon dioxide diffuses in and oxygen diffuses out. Although the stomata are very small, about the size of a pin prick, they are exceedingly numerous: 10,000 to 20,000 per square centimeter, with a total of 140 to 240 million on a single corn leaf. Finally, the lower epidermis is covered with a **cuticle.**

As you read the last two paragraphs and examined Figures 2.4 and 2.5, you must have been impressed with the thought that the leaf is a beautifully designed machine for the job of photosynthesis. The blade is a flat expanse of green tissue held out by the petiole in such a way that it intercepts the maximum amount of light from the sun. Yet the leaf is thin so that light penetrates to the chloroplasts in the manufacturing cells of the spongy and palisade layers. Water, a raw material in the process, is delivered to the manufacturing units by means of the

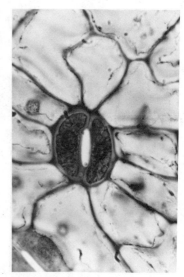

Figure 2.6   Stoma flanked by two guard cells.

xylem in the veins; the phloem ships out the elaborated product—sugar. At the same time, the veins supply the backbone to support the delicate tissues of the leaf. Gases are important in the process of photosynthesis—carbon dioxide is a raw material and oxygen is a product. These two gases are able to circulate in and around the manufacturing cells by virtue of the fact that the leaf is honeycombed by a ramifying system of intercellular spaces. Gases enter the leaf by means of pores, or stomata, whose portals are controlled by guard cells which may open or close the orifices. All this is impressive enough, but there is another minor detail without which the whole system would collapse—we refer to the cuticle. If it were not for this thin layer of transparent wax covering the surface of leaves, the latter would soon wilt and die, exposed as they are to the drying winds of the atmosphere.

Transpiration

Effective as the cuticle is in waterproofing the leaves, there is still one vulnerable aspect in the make-up of leaves—the stomata, which interrupt the otherwise continuous cuticle. One unfortunate consequence of the circumstance that stomata are open in light is that water vapor is lost from the leaves. (In the parlance of the day, this situation would be called a trade-off, one supposes.)

This process, in which there is evaporation of water from the plant, is called **transpiration.** Incredibly large quantities of water are lost in this fashion; one single corn plant in one growing season may take up and lose as much as 50 gallons of water through transpiration. If all the water lost by transpiration accumulated on the ground in a field of corn, at the end of the growing season there would be a pool of water seven inches deep. It has been estimated that an acre of corn may transpire 300,000 gallons of water in one summer. Calculations have been made on an acre of beech-maple trees which result in the incredible estimate of 10,000 barrels of water lost in one day for that acre. Small wonder that one of our colleagues a few years ago, overcome by the magnitude of water lost in transpiration, announced dramatically to his botany class that "transpiration may be defined as a damn shame." And then came the final examination in which the inevitable question on the definition of transpiration appeared. Half the class defined it "as a damn shame."

Figure 2.7 Root system of blackjack oak. [Courtesy U.S. Department of Agriculture.]

Roots

Earlier we said that water is transported to the leaves by means of xylem tissue which is continuous from the veins through the stem and to the root. Accordingly, we should now turn our attention to the organ which is responsible for the absorption of water and mineral salts such as nitrates, phosphates, and sulfates from the soil. We refer, of course, to the root. It is sometimes convenient to refer to the total **root system** of a plant, by which we mean the main root, or main axis, together with its extensive and ramifying branches. In general, the root system of a plant is equivalent in size and extent to the **shoot system** (that part of the plant above ground, i.e., the stem with its attached branches and leaves). In other words, the trunk of a tree and its branches above ground are roughly equivalent in extent to the root and its branches underground (Figure 2.7). A single corn plant may have roots which penetrate to a depth of eight feet and spread four feet to all sides; a sugar-beet root system may grow down six feet (Figure 11.10); and an arid-land plant, such as a mesquite tree, may have roots as long as sixty feet. These extensive, ramifying root systems are effective in anchoring the plant in the soil and in giving support to the entire plant. Furthermore, in view of the fact that roots absorb water and mineral salts from the soil, it is obviously an advantage to have these organs penetrate the soil thoroughly and widely.

To study the extent of roots in a squash plant, Colonel William Clark, first professor of botany at the Massachusetts Agricultural College (now the University of Massachusetts), carefully removed (in 1874) all the roots and found that the roots if placed end to end would reach a distance of 15 miles. Incidentally he was also interested in the forces developed by actively growing plants—he had noted that heavy stone sidewalks are sometimes lifted by vigorously growing roots. He rigged up a harness on a young developing squash fruit and then placed weights on it. He found that the expanding squash fruit lifted a weight of 2.5 tons before the harness broke.

The extensive nature of root systems has profound ecological significance, for the intermeshing root systems of plants hold the soil in place, a feature which is particularly important on a hillside or mountain slope. Hence, when all the trees on such sites are cut, **erosion** develops allowing the soil, including the nutrients, to wash away, thereby exposing the bare subsoil.

The same result is produced by overgrazing, a situation which occurs when too many cattle are pastured in a given area. The animals eat the shoots and even part of the roots, leaving only the bare soil. Winds then blow off the topsoil (**wind erosion**). In the 1920s, in the Southwest, because of widespread overgrazing extensive wind erosion produced what was called a dust bowl. The botanist Paul Sears wrote of this castastrophe in ecological terms in his *Deserts on the March*, while John Steinbeck in his novel, *The Grapes of Wrath*, depicted the human tragedy of families being forced to leave their windswept Oklahoma farms and ranches to migrate to the promised land of California—only to have their descendants face another ecological disaster, the smog of the decades following 1940.

Root-Hair Cell

The actual root structures responsible for the absorption of water from the soil are **root-hair cells** (Figure 2.8) on the surfaces of roots. These are located only on a short zone near the

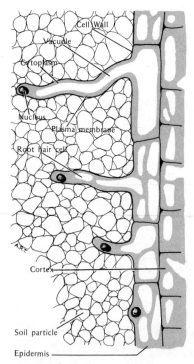

Figure 2.8 Root-hair cells growing among soil particles.

tips of roots. Root-hair cells are T-shaped, with long projections penetrating the soil. Previously we commented on the extensive branching nature of the root system which makes it possible for the roots to penetrate the soil environment for many feet on all sides. The root-hair cells, by their shape and length, add to the absorptive capacity of roots. It is estimated that the projection of the root-hair cell increases its surface over an ordinary surface cell by a factor of 12. The principle of increasing the surface of absorptive structures is one which is often encountered in the organic world; for instance, the villi of the intestines and the internal folds of mitochondria do this as well.

In addition to the vast increase in the absorptive surface provided by the unique shape and length of the root hairs, their absorptive capacity is also enhanced by the very great numbers of these cells. A few years ago an enterprising botanist estimated that a single rye plant has approximately 14 billion root-hair cells; if placed end to end, the total length of the root-hair cells on a single plant is 6,600 miles. (You will note that botanists are fond of placing things end to end.) Another interesting point is that usually these root-hair cells last for only a day or two, so they are constantly being replaced; it is estimated that about 100 million new ones are formed each day on a single rye plant.

Now all this has practical significance: When you pull a plant from the soil, you break off the root hairs, with the result that the plant cannot take in all the water it needs, so it wilts and finally dies. Therefore you are told that when transplanting you should always take up a clump of undisturbed earth around the plant—a ball of earth in the case of a tree or shrub. In this way the root hairs remain intact and continue to absorb water, and the plant survives. You might consider the root hairs to be the life line of the plant—at least the water line.

Internal Structure of the Root

The water absorbed by the root-hair cells passes into the conducting cells of the root and then to the stem. Figure 2.9 is a diagram of a cross-section of a root showing the main regions of this organ. At the surface is the **epidermis** with its root-hair cells which have the function of absorption. The next zone, a fairly extensive one, is the **cortex** which stores food. In the very center there is a region forming a cross, the **wood**, or **xylem**, which conducts water and mineral salts. Alternating with the points of the cross (Figure 2.10) are islands of tissue known as **phloem** which conducts soluble foods.

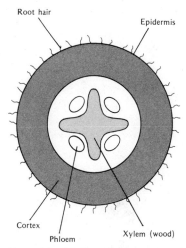

Figure 2.9 Diagram of cross-section of a root.

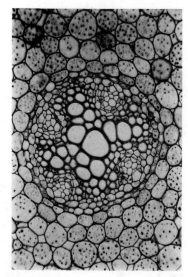

Figure 2.10 Cross-section of buttercup root.

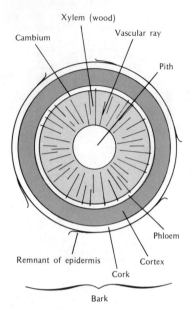

Figure 2.11   Diagram of cross-section of a stem.

We should note that the root we have just described is merely one of many different types, but it will serve as an illustration of the general features of all roots. In all root types there is the same striking division of labor among the tissues—root hair cells absorbing water; cortex storing starch and other foods; xylem conducting water and dissolved mineral salts; and phloem transporting soluble foods.

Internal Structure of the Stem

We have already made the point that the conducting tissues—xylem and phloem—of the root are continuous with those of the stem. They do, however, have a somewhat different configuration in the stem, as you can see in Figure 2.11, a cross-section of a stem. Starting from the outside, we encounter successively the following zones: At the periphery is the **cork,** a layer which replaces the epidermis in older stems and protects this organ from excessive water loss; the **cortex** which stores food, as in the root; a continuous ring of **phloem** which conducts the soluble foods; a thin layer of **cambium;** a thick ring of **xylem,** or **wood,** which offers support and conducts water and mineral salts; and in the very center a small region called the **pith** where food may be stored. Running radially through the xylem, cambium, and phloem are thin bands, the **vascular rays** (Figure 6.6), which conduct materials in a horizontal direction and store food. The term **bark** is a collective term which includes the epidermis (if present), the cork, the cortex, and the phloem; in other words, everything outside of the cambium.

Wood or Xylem

This complex tissue, which conducts water and mineral salts from the root to the stem, is made up of two types of special conducting cells known as **tracheids** (Figure 6.11) and **vessel cells.** The tracheids are long spindle-shaped cells, whereas the vessel cells resemble pieces of pipe or tile with holes or perforations at the top and bottom. The individual vessel cells fit together to form a pipeline, or **vessel,** (Figure 6.14), as it is called.

Phloem

This tissue, which conducts soluble food from the leaf to the stem and root, is composed of **sieve-tube cells** (Figure 6.8), whose end walls are perforated with a number of small holes, and thus resemble a kitchen sieve, hence the name. The individual sieve-tube cells fit together to form a pipeline, designated a **sieve tube,** comparable to the vessel in the xylem.

Cambium

The cambium, composed of a single layer of cells, is an extremely important zone in the plant, for it is a growing layer. By the division of its cells, it forms new wood cells on the inside and new phloem cells on the outside; in this manner it adds to the diameter and girth of the stem.

What Happens to the Carbohydrates Produced in Photosynthesis?

Having described some of the tissues involved in the transport of materials to and away from the photosynthesizing leaf, we now turn to the fate of the food manufactured. Some of the sugar synthesized in the process of photosynthesis may be used up in respiration and hence yield energy for other processes of the plant. Or, by forming chains, sugar molecules may be converted into starch and then stored as a reserve food in the root, stem, fruits, or seeds. Sugar may be transformed into cellulose, another type of carbohydrate chain, which forms the basic framework of cell walls. Sugar may also be converted into fats or into amino acids with the addition of nitrogen and sometimes sulfur. The resulting amino acids may form chains called proteins, some of which function as **enzymes,** or **organic catalysts,** substances which facilitate chemical reactions, often speeding up the reactions, while not themselves being used up in the process.

You will note that the synthesis of sugar, or photosynthesis, is the basic synthesis—all other syntheses depend on it.

Humus Theory

We have said that plants obtain their raw materials—water and mineral salts—from the soil and carbon dioxide from the air. From the water and carbon dioxide, the plant manufactures food, specifically sugar, through the process of photosynthesis. It has taken several hundred years of painstaking experiments to establish these facts. More than two thousand years ago Aristotle (384–322 B.C.) suggested the humus theory; that is, that the food in plants is derived from humus or organic material in the soil. And strangely this belief still persists in certain quarters. A curious distortion of this ancient belief is found in the reference to commercial fertilizer as plant food; commercial fertilizer is not plant food, but is made up of mineral salts (i.e., raw materials). True foods, on the other hand, are organic compounds belonging to the three categories of carbohydrates, fats, and proteins.

Van Helmont's Willow

A classic experiment designed to reveal the fundamental facts of plant nutrition was conducted by the Belgian physician Jean-Baptiste Van Helmont in 1630. He planted a willow sapling weighing 5 pounds in a metal pot with soil weighing 200 pounds. He covered the top of the pot around the willow. For the next five years he watered the plant but added nothing else. At the end of the five-year period, he found that the willow now weighed 169 pounds and the soil had lost 2 ounces. What valid conclusions would you draw from this simple experiment? Van Helmont came to two conclusions:

1. The weight increase in the willow did not come from the soil, for only 2 ounces were lost and yet the willow gained 164 pounds.
2. The weight increase came from the water added.

His first conclusion is correct and the second is correct as far as it goes. However, he was not aware of the role, established later, of carbon dioxide in photosynthesis, so he failed to appreciate that this gas also contributes to the weight increase.

This experiment illustrates the halting way in which progress is made in science; it led to a partial answer, but subsequent research provided additional data which forced a modification of the original explanation or hypothesis.

Significance of Photosynthesis

In summarizing the role of photosynthesis in nature, we should repeat that it is unquestionably the most important process in the organic world, for all life depends on it because ultimately all food is derived from this process. This dependence on plants includes all animals as well as human beings. Botanists are fond of quoting the Bible in this connection: "All flesh is grass." Or as the bacteriologist Hans Zinsser put it in his *Rats, Lice, and History*, "Man may be defined as a parasite on a vegetable."

Most people do not recognize this fundamental fact, or if they are vaguely aware of it, they do not fully comprehend its great significance. To appreciate the magnitude of our dependence on plants and specifically on photosynthesis, suppose that some new virus developed which destroyed chloroplasts—and this is not beyond the realm of possibilities, for destructive diseases such as chestnut blight have virtually eliminated our chestnuts in this country, Dutch elm disease is decimating our American elms, and potato blight was responsible for the deaths of millions of people in the nineteenth century. You can imagine the havoc and panic produced by this chloroplast-destroying virus as it gradually leads to the death of all plants in one area of the country and then spreads to all other regions of the United States and finally to the rest of the world. (Perhaps you will be reminded of similar catastrophic events described in Michael Crichton's novel, *The Andromeda Strain*.) As the plants disappear, animals die of starvation, and eventually all mankind is eliminated. Such is our dependence on these microscopic structures known as chloroplasts and such is our absolute dependence on the process of photosynthesis.

There are other ways as well in which man is beholden to plants: Much of our fuel is traceable to the process of photosynthesis. When we burn wood we are burning plant cell walls composed of cellulose and **lignin,** both compounds which are produced from the carbohydrates manufactured in photosynthesis. The same is true of the fossil fuels—peat, coal, oil, and gas. Peat is clearly of vegetable origin, as is coal which was formed from the plants growing in the Carboniferous period, some 350 million years ago. Oil and gas are likewise thought to have been produced by ancient microscopic plants. Much of the clothing we wear comes from plant material produced from the products of photosynthesis—the fibers of cotton and linen, and even such synthetics as rayon are derived from the cellulose in wood.

Finally, all mankind and all animals are dependent on the oxygen produced in the process of photosynthesis. Not only do man and animals use up oxygen in respiration, but this vital gas is further depleted by the burning of fuel and by various industrial processes. So, if the green plants were not constantly replenishing the oxygen of the air and using up the accumulated carbon dioxide from animal respiration, fuel burning, and from factories, all living creatures, including man, would suffocate and die. Already it is reported that at certain times in Japan, because of the oxygen deficit produced by the concentration of industries, people are forced to wear oxygen masks.

The Unique Chemistry of Plants

Not only are plants unique in that they are the only organisms which carry on photosynthesis, manufacturing food from the simple raw materials water and carbon dioxide, but only plants can make the eight essential **amino acids** required by man and other organisms to be able to synthesize proteins. Even if man were supplied all the carbohydrates and, hence, all the calories he needed, he still would require these eight essential amino acids from plants to survive.

Only plants can make most of the **vitamins** (minute quantities of organic substances which must be added to some organisms for proper **metabolism,** the collective name for all the chemical reactions which go on in the body). For example, the carotenes, or vitamin A, which all animals need, are synthesized exclusively by plants. (Although the body of man cannot produce vitamins, his mind can, in the sense that chemists are able to synthesize most of the vitamins in their laboratories.)

Finally, only plants, of all living things (we include bacteria as plants), and then only certain ones such as the legumes, some algae, lichens, and a few others, can take nitrogen from the air where it is not available for use by most plants or by animals and combine it with certain other elements so that it can be absorbed by plant roots. This process is called **nitrogen-fixation.**

Thus, it can be said that plants carry on the basic syntheses in nature—that plants hold the basic patents for the fundamental chemical processes in nature.

Mineral Nutrition

We have said that plants need water from the soil and carbon dioxide from the air for photosynthesis. In addition, they require certain elements, such as nitrogen and sulfur, for the manufacture of amino acids and proteins and other elements (potassium, calcium, magnesium, iron) for other purposes. These essential elements are present in the soil in the form of mineral compounds or salts (nitrates, phosphates, and sulfates), and are absorbed in modified form (ionic) by the roots.

Organic Gardening

Currently there is widespread interest in plant nutrition in the guise of organic gardening. Perhaps we should begin with a statement on precisely what is meant by the term. **Organic gardening** means that no commercial or manufactured fertilizer is used in the growing of crops. Instead compost, garbage, manure, and other organic materials are employed. Pulverized rock is permitted. In addition, the plants are not sprayed with synthetic pesticides, such as DDT, to control insects, fungi, and other disease-producing agents. Pest and disease control is accomplished by the maintenance of good health in the plants, the manual removal of insects, the use of natural insect repellants such as marigolds and tansy and of such natural insecticides as rotenone and pyrethrum, both of which are derived from plants, and the application of **biological control.** By biological control we mean the use of other organisms which are natural enemies to combat insect pests and other parasites; for example, bacteria, viruses, and ladybugs are used to destroy certain pests. Finally, no manufactured or synthetic herbicides, such as 2-4-D, are applied to control weeds; weeds are removed by hand or by hoe or are controlled by **mulching** (placing a layer of organic material such as bark chips or lawn clippings over the surface of the soil).

Obviously there is much to recommend the practices advocated by organic gardeners. By not spraying pesticides and herbicides on plants there is less poisonous residue to contend with which might be toxic to human beings. Sprays kill good insects as well as the pestiferous types, not to mention birds and earthworms, both of which play a useful role in nature. Another danger of constantly employing synthetic pesticides is that the insects and parasitic fungi will, over time, mutate into more resistant types, which means that higher and higher concentrations of a chemical may have to be applied to combat the resistant pests. Higher concentrations of poison, of course, increase the danger to human beings when they consume the vegetables and fruits.

There are further benefits and positive aspects to organic gardening: Since no commercial fertilizers are applied, there is less potential for excessive runoff and leaching losses of nitrates and the resultant pollution of water supplies as happens with the large-scale, excessive use of commercial fertilizers. Then, too, organic gardeners place the proper emphasis on the quality of the product—fruit or vegetable—and not on its superficial appearance. Finally, organic gardening is good, solid ecology, for its practices are in harmony with the great cycles of nature—materials are recycled, for one thing.

Sometimes the proponents of organic gardening, in their understandable enthusiasm, forget that the practice of applying humus—compost, dead plants, kitchen refuse and manure, including human feces—is an ancient agricultural procedure which long ago was recognized as beneficial from a number of standpoints: It loosens the soil and hence there is better air circulation around roots, especially in heavy or clayey soils—roots require oxygen to live; organic material increases the water-holding capacity of soils, particularly of sandy soils; and the organic materials provide bacteria with food. These bacteria break down complex organic compounds into simpler, usable compounds such as nitrates, sulfates, and phosphates.

The criticism which botanists have of organic gardening is not of its many virtues and advantages but of its use of language and its theory. With respect to the first of these, organic gardeners make the distinction between a **chemical fertilizer** and an **organic fertilizer,** such as compost and manure. Clearly both classes of materials are chemical. Rather than speaking of chemical fertilizer, it would be more accurate to say commercial or manufactured fertilizer. But more serious is the apparent lack of recognition by some organic gardening enthusiasts that the organic materials in manure, compost, and garbage have to be broken down by bacteria into inorganic substances such as nitrates, sulfates and phosphates (actually into ionic form) before living plants can absorb these materials and use them. It makes no difference to the plant whether these inorganic salts come from commercial fertilizers or from garbage. To paraphrase Gertrude Stein, chemical is a chemical is a chemical.

Furthermore, there is no scientific evidence that the vegetables or fruits resulting from organic gardening are more nutritious or have more or better vitamins than those grown with commercial fertilizers. Finally, while it is entirely feasible to adhere strictly to orthodox organic gardening principles in the small home garden, there is a real question whether such methods can be applied to the extensive acreages of commercial agriculture. A nation faced with mass starvation and needing to maximize output is likely to choose to ignore some of the precepts of organic gardening.

Some Special Highlights of Form and Function

The topics included in this section give a further dimension to several aspects of form and function already discussed in this chapter: They illustrate some of the complexity of development in both plant form and function.

Herbs, Shrubs, and Trees

It is convenient to refer to three different types of plant forms:

1. **Herbs** (Figure 2.1), which are soft-stemmed plants with little wood, low in stature—only a few inches or a few feet tall—and usually they live a year or a few years at most (examples: buttercup, grasses, daisy).
2. **Shrubs** (Figures 3.9 and 3.10), which have more wood, are taller—up to 10 to 15 feet—live longer, and usually have not one trunk but several arising from the ground line (examples: forsythia, privet, lilac).
3. **Trees** (Figures 2.7 and 16.11), which have a good deal of wood, are much taller—may reach 100 or more feet—live sometimes hundreds of years, and usually have one main trunk arising from the root (examples: pine, oak, elm).

You will note that there is no sharp line of demarcation among the three types; rather one type grades into the other, which is exactly what you would expect if evolution has taken place. Nevertheless, these three terms are convenient descriptions and you will note that subsequently, whenever we introduce a new plant, we will almost invariably classify it as an herb, or a shrub, or a tree.

A Branch of a Tree in the Winter Condition

In the temperate zone most trees of the group known as flowering plants are **deciduous,** that is, they shed their leaves in the autumn. This is doubtless an adaptation to the conditions produced by winter during which little or no water is absorbed from the soil. If the typical broad leaves of flowering plants remained on the tree in winter, much water would be lost and the tree would probably die. Trees which do not shed all their leaves at one time are called **evergreens.** Their leaves are usually small or needlelike, covered with a heavy cuticle and with stomata sunken in cavities, thereby giving some protection from excessive transpiration.

Figure 2.12 is a drawing of a twig from a horse chestnut tree. You will observe at the tip of the stem the **terminal bud.** It is made up of resin-covered **bud scales** surrounding some wooly material. In the very center of the bud there is the delicate growing region, the **meristem.** In the spring the meristem will add to the length of the stem and will also form such lateral appendages as leaves.

Along the sides of the stem you will see smaller buds, the **lateral,** or **axillary, buds.** Note that they are invariably above triangular scars, which are the **leaf scars** left by the petioles of leaves when they dropped off in the fall. If you look closely at the leaf scars you will observe small dots; these are the **bundle scars** left by the conducting strands in the petiole. Each leaf scar, or rather each pair of leaf scars, for they occur in couplets in the horse chestnut, marks a node, and you will recall that the segment of the stem between two successive nodes is an internode.

Note that the terminal bud is large whereas the lateral buds are smaller. Usually the lateral buds do not grow and form branches unless the terminal bud is removed. The latter produces **hormones** which inhibit the development of the axillary buds. (**Hormones** are organic chemical substances manufactured in small quantities in one part of the plant and then [usually] transported to another part where they exert their special effects.) If the terminal bud is removed, no inhibiting hormones reach the lateral buds so they grow out and form lateral branches. Horticulturists employ the technique of pinching off the terminal buds of flowering plants if they wish to have a full, bushy growth with many flowers.

The surface of the twig is covered with a protective coating known as the **bark,** the outer region of which is the **cork,** a layer which is more or less impervious to the passage of water and hence protects the stem from excessive water loss. Slightly raised dots on the cork represent pores, the **lenticels,** which permit gaseous exchange to take place between the outside air and the interior of the stem.

At intervals along the length of the stem, there are bands of small and compressed triangular scars. Each band of scars consists of several **terminal-bud scale scars,** and represents the place where the terminal bud was at one time before the stem

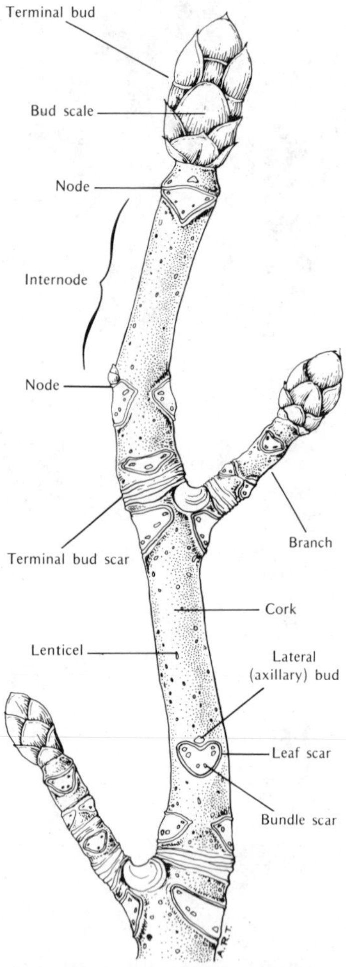

Figure 2.12 Horse chestnut stem in winter condition.

Terminal bud

Bud scale

Node

Internode

Node

Terminal bud scar

Lenticel

Branch

Cork

Lateral (axillary) bud

Leaf scar

Bundle scar

grew out as a result of the activities of the terminal meristem (Figure 5.9). Thus, the age of a young twig can be determined by counting the stem segments between these bands of terminal-bud scale scars.

Plant Hormones

Plant **hormones** like those produced in the terminal bud can be regarded as chemical messengers. Most of them are growth-regulating substances, such as the **auxins** and **gibberellins** which promote cell enlargement and the **cytokinins,** which incite cell division. In general these substances are manufactured in actively growing tissues, as in shoot and root apices and in young leaves and fruits, and they then migrate from these apices and young organs to regions of elongation, which may be some distance from the point of synthesis.

One of the most widely occurring auxins is indoleacetic acid (IAA) which is responsible for the apical dominance of the terminal bud (a phenomenon already alluded to), promotes the initiation of roots on the bases of stem cuttings, stimulates the initiation of cambial activity in the spring, and in general promotes stem growth, but inhibits root elongation. Even in the case of the stem, at one concentration auxin may promote growth while at a different concentration it may slow growth. Furthermore, in the control of growth, several hormones may interact to promote elongation, while others inhibit growth (i.e., ethylene). Thus hormonal balance is significant in achieving coordination among the various cells and tissues of the plant.

During the last few years several synthetic growth substances (indolebutyric acid, naphthaleneacetic acid, etc.) have been manufactured and these compounds have some of the same effects as the naturally occurring auxins.

Gibberellins, which occur naturally in plants, stimulate elongation of stems and leaves. Indeed, dwarf varieties of some plants may be dramatically converted into tall plants by proper treatment with gibberellins. The effects of these substances were first noticed by farmers in Japan who observed certain extraordinarily elongated rice seedlings. This condition came to be called the "foolish-seedling" disease of rice. We now know that it is caused by an infestation of the fungus *Gibberella*. The fungus produces the gibberellin which in turn induces the wild, abnormal growth of rice seedlings.

Cytokinins stimulate cell division, and are commonly found in young fruits and in the food-storing tissue (endosperm) next to the young embryo in the seed. For some time it has been known that coconut milk (which is liquid endosperm) promotes the growth of fungi and plant tissues in culture. The reason for this enhancement of growth is the presence of cytokinins, as well as auxins and other substances.

Hormones and related synthetic growth substances are used widely in agriculture for a number of different purposes. Plant propagators in greenhouses and in nurseries apply auxins to cuttings to achieve better root growth. Hormones are used to obtain seedless fruits (e.g., tomatoes); gibberellins are employed to increase the size of fruits (e.g., grapes). Ethylene gas, which is usually regarded as an inhibitory hormone, for it slows stem elongation, also promotes the ripening of fruit. To prevent the premature fall of fruits such as apples, pears, and oranges, the appropriate trees are sprayed shortly before harvest with a synthetic growth regulator such as naphthaleneacetic acid. This substance slows the formation of the separation layer at the bases of the stalks bearing the fruits and the fruits remain attached to the parent plants. Synthetic **herbicides** (weed killers) such as 2,4-D are employed to eradicate weeds and other undesirable vegetation. It is a remarkable fact that 2,4-D kills broad-leaved plants (mostly dicotyledons) but is relatively nontoxic to narrow-leaved monocotyledons. Thus, 2,4-D is used widely to control weeds in lawns, golf courses, and in fields of corn, wheat, and other grains.

Annuals, Biennials, and Perennials

Other terms which are useful in describing plants are those relating to the length of the life cycle of the plants. *Annual, biennial,* and *perennial* are all terms which are employed in everyday parlance, but let us be sure we know what they signify in botany. An **annual** is a plant which completes its life cycle in one year, during that year the seed germinates and forms a plant with root, stem, leaves, and, eventually, flowers which produce fruit and new seeds. The plant then dies and winters over in the form of seeds (examples: petunia, marigold, ragweed). A **biennial** completes its life cycle in two years; during the first year the seed forms the plant with root, stem, and leaves, and in the second year the flowers appear and new seeds are produced (examples: carrot, beet). A **perennial** is a plant whose life cycle is three or more years long. After one year, or many years (in trees, for example), flowers and seeds may be produced annually but the **vegetative body** (root, stem, and leaves) persists year after year (examples: elm, maple, dandelion, iris, peony).

Weeds

Weed is a term we shall use constantly and which we had better define forthwith. In its broadest sense, a **weed** is merely a plant which is growing in a place where it is not wanted. A dandelion growing in a lawn is a weed; an oak seedling growing in a potato patch is a weed; a corn plant growing in a soybean field is a weed; and an orchid growing in the wrong place in the tropics is a weed. Theoretically any plant may become a weed simply by growing in a place it is not welcome. It happens that there are certain aggressive plants which always seem to grow where they are not wanted; these plants are customarily branded as weeds; for example, dandelions, ragweed (Figure 7.1), pigweed, chickweed, witch or quack grass, bindweed, water hyacinth (Figure 16.2), kudzu (Figure 22.9), and poison ivy (Figure 7.7).

We have given a simple, yet broad, definition of a weed. The specialist, of course, will think of other attributes of weeds; for instance, they colonize disturbed habitats (bulldozed roadsides, plowed fields, etc.), they are not regular members of the original community of plants (they are foreign to a particular group of plants or location), they are abundant, they are noxious or troublesome, and, finally, they are usually of little or no economic value.

Grafting

Earlier, mention was made of the central role of the cambium in the growth of the stem. This layer is of special significance in the practice of **grafting** (Figure 2.13), in which a small twig—the **scion**—of one plant is affixed to the stem and root system of another—the **stock**—in such a way that the cambial layers of both are in contact. A number of precautions should be observed if one wishes to achieve a successful graft:

1. The cambial layers of stock and scion must be together.
2. The stock and scion must be of the same kind of plant, or at least closely related.
3. The union of stock and scion should be secured with tape or twine.

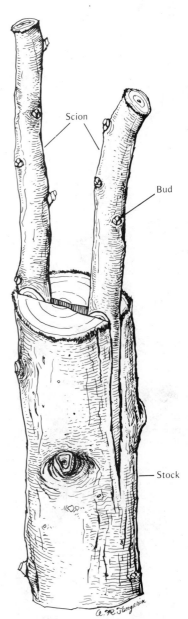

Figure 2.13 One type of grafting in which scions with wedge-shaped tips are inserted in the notch or cleft of the stock.

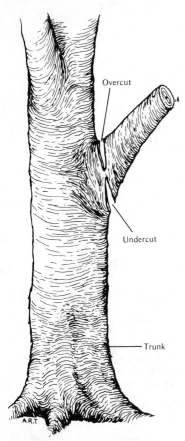

Overcut

Undercut

Trunk

A.R.T.

Figure 2.14A Good and poor pruning practices: The tree above is
pruned properly, for the cuts are
made close to the main stem. An undercut is made first, followed by an
overcut, so that when the limb falls
the bark of the main stem will not be
torn by its weight.

4. The union of the two should be covered with wax to
   prevent drying out.

Grafting is performed for a number of reasons: to propagate a
desirable type of plant, for example, a fruit tree, whose own root
system is very susceptible to root rot; to perpetuate the characteristics of a particularly fine plant which might be lost in the
usual process of sexual reproduction and seed formation, in
which the plants often do not breed true, as in apple varieties;
and to speed up propagation, rather than waiting for a seed to
germinate and a tree to flower and fruit, which may take years.

Pruning

Likewise, the practice of **pruning** (Figure 2.14), of cutting off
stems and branches, eventually involves the cambium in
wound healing. Too often people faced with a decaying or
broken limb, cut it off several inches or even several feet from
the main stem in a mistaken effort to play it safe. Actually, the
limb should be cut flush with the bark of the main stem; in this
way the food conducted by the adjacent phloem will be close at
hand to aid in the wound-healing process. When a stub of a
branch is left the food in the phloem of the main stem will not
be conducted up to the wound and hence the wound will not be
covered by the activities of the cambium. As a result, decay may
set in at the tip of the stub and this decay subsequently may
spread down to the main trunk. (Incidentally, in removing a
branch, especially if it is large, a cut should be made from the
bottom closer to the main stem then a second cut made at the
top. Then the weight of the limb will not strip the bark from the
main trunk.) Finally, wounds should be covered with a protective pruning compound to prevent drying out and attacks from
fungi and insects.

Autumnal Coloration

See Plate 1a, autumnal coloration.

Turning to leaves, an especially dramatic aspect of their function manifests itself in the fall when they regale themselves in
golden yellows, bright oranges, and brilliant reds. There is still
much that is unknown about **autumnal coloration,** but we do
know that this marvelous phenomenon is favored by bright,
short days and cool nights.

During the growing season, the chlorophyll of the leaf is
disintegrating constantly; but is also continually being replaced

from the raw materials conducted to the leaf. In the fall, the conducting cells in the xylem (vessel cells) leading into the leaves become plugged, so that raw materials, such as minerals, are no longer readily transported to the blades. Thus, in the autumn, when the chlorophyll disappears, no new pigment can be synthesized for lack of raw materials. As a result, other pigments which have been there all along but masked by the green chlorophyll now show up; for example, the yellow and orange pigments, **carotenoids** (called this because they give carrots their yellow-orange color). Carotenoids, located in the chloroplasts along with chlorophyll, are not readily disintegrated by light or heat and so we have the pleasure of admiring the golden yellows and bright orange colors in the autumn.

Many of the reds and violet-reds of the fall season are caused by **anthocyanins** (these same pigments are responsible for the reds, blues, and violets in flowers) which are dissolved in the cell sap. For some reason in the fall the sugar accumulating in the leaf is transformed into anthocyanin. We know that bright days and cold nights promote this conversion.

Someone has said that castles reach their peak of beauty when touched by decay; in a sense, the brilliant autumnal coloration is likewise a phenomenon of death and disintegration.

Carnivorous Plants

Among the most bizarre modifications of leaves are those of a fascinating assemblage of approximately 500 species of plants known as **carnivorous** or **insectivorous plants.** They are able to capture insects and other small animals by means of leaves modified into passive traps or active spring devices which capture prey. The plants then digest the foods in the soft parts of the animals; thus, in a small way, they reverse the usual procedure in which animals eat plants.

The pitcher plant (Figures 2.15 and 2.16), native to the bogs and swamps of Eastern North America, has hollow, tubular leaves which form urn- or trumpet-shaped receptacles in which insects are captured. The upper portion of the pitcher, which itself may measure up to a foot in length, is colored red and purple, resembling a bright flower. The colors plus the nectar the plant produces attract insects to an opening at the top with a very slippery lip. When insects crawl over the lip, they slide into the receptacle which contains water. It is difficult if not impossible for the insects to crawl out because the side walls of the

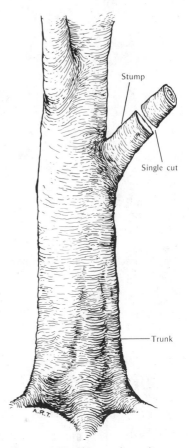

Figure 2.14B The tree above shows poor pruning, for the cut is made some distance from the main stem, thus leaving a stump which may decay.

Figure 2.15 Pitcher plant (*Sarracenia purpurea*). [Courtesy Donald E. Schnell.]

pitcher are lined with stiff, sharp spines, all pointing downward. After the insects have exhausted themselves in repeated attempts to climb out, they fall into the liquid where enzymes secreted by the plant digest the soft parts of the animals. The digestive process also may be aided by the bacteria which reside in the pitcher.

There are even more dramatic pitcher plants growing in the moist rain forests of the Philippines, Indo-Malaya, and Australia. These species (belonging to the genus *Nepenthes*, Figure 2.17), often grown in northern conservatories, have large, urn-shaped pitchers which sometimes measure as much as twenty inches long, although the average lies somewhere between four and six inches. The leaf blades narrow down to long tendrils by means of which these plants cling and even climb over other plants. The tips of the tendrils form large pitchers which may hold a quart or more of water. Otherwise these tropical pitcher plants operate very much as does the one already described.

Another group of pitcher plants, called cobra plants, or cobra lilies (Figure 2.18), grows in the wet meadows and marshes of western Oregon and northern California. The modified leaves bear a striking resemblance to snakes—even to a forked, tonguelike projection thrust out from the mouth near the top of the hooded leaf—hence the name of the plants. Insects are at-

Figure 2.16 Pitcher plants (*Sarracenia flava*). [Courtesy U.S. Department of Agriculture.]

tracted to the slitlike opening on the side of the pitcher by bright colors and nectar. Once the insect enters the darkened chamber, it has difficulty in retracing its steps, for the entrance is screened from the outside light by the overhanging hood. Furthermore, the insect is distracted by the light shining through thin, transparent places in the roof which resemble skylights. After repeated attempts to escape, the insect falls exhausted into the liquids of the receptacle where it is digested through the activities of bacteria. Any attempts to scale the walls of the receptacle are repelled by extremely slippery places and by numerous down-thrust spines. The prey found in these pitchers is like that of the other pitcher plants already described—ants, beetles, flies, small toads and frogs, and centipedes. There is no reliable evidence to confirm the occasional reports that pitcher plants, even the large tropical *Nepenthes*, capture prey of the size of pigeons, rats, rabbits, or man.

Sundews (Figure 2.19), distributed in western North America from Alaska to northern California and in the Great Plains region as well as on the Atlantic coastal plain, are tiny swamp plants (measuring an inch or two). One species, the round-leaved sundew, has leaf blades covered with hairs whose tips are globular and sticky. When an insect lands on a leaf, it is held in place by the sticky substance on the hairs it touches, while other hairs fold inward and also adhere to the prey. Enzymes are secreted which digest the insect, whereupon the hairs unfold and assume the receptive stance, ready for the next juicy visitor. The hard parts of the insect are blown away by the wind or are washed off by rain.

Probably the most remarkable of all these fascinating plants is the Venus's flytrap (Figure 2.20) which grows on the coastal plain of North and South Carolina. It is found nowhere else in the world and, therefore, is a good example of an **endemic species.** The leaves have blades which are hinged in the middle and each of the two halves of the blade bears three sensitive trigger hairs. If an insect chances to touch two of these hairs or perhaps brushes against a hair twice, the leaf halves fold together and the spines which line the margins of the blade fasten together like interlocking fingers. While the insect is held tight in this fashion, enzymes are secreted and the foods in the animal are digested and absorbed by the plant. After a few days, the leaf reopens, the chitinous exoskeleton of the insect is blown or washed away, and the plant is ready for another tidbit.

Figure 2.17 Tropical pitcher plant (*Nepenthes dicksoniana*). [Courtesy Donald E. Schnell.]

Figure 2.18 Cobra plant (*Darlingtonia californica*). [Courtesy Donald E. Schnell.]

Figure 2.19 Sundew (*Drosera capillaris*). [Courtesy Donald E. Schnell.]

Figure 2.20 Venus's flytrap (*Dionaea muscipula*). [Courtesy Donald E. Schnell.]

People often have Venus's flytraps in their homes, where they delight in springing the plant's traps with a pencil or other object. The plants may be fed flies, raw meat—small quantities, not whole steaks—and egg white. You will have noted in our description of the operation of the trigger mechanism that in order to spring the trap two hairs must be touched or a single hair must be touched twice. Occasionally it has been suggested whimsically that this is an indication that the plant can add. In any case, it is rather interesting that this plant has established such a threshold for its response.

You may wonder why carnivorous plants have evolved the various devices for capturing insects and other small animals. Whether it is the complete explanation or not, we do know that these plants usually grow in swamps and bogs where available nitrogen is scarce. It may be that the several devices for trapping insects are adaptations which permit the plants to supplement their nitrogen-poor intake from the soil with the nitrogenous compounds from digested animals.

For nearly 200 years insectivorous plants have attracted the attention not only of lay people but also of scientists, including the great evolutionist Charles Darwin who wrote one of the masterly books on the subject. Because of the considerable attention they have commanded and their widespread collection, combined with the fact that their swampy habitats are fast disappearing before the onslaughts of civilization, these remarkable plants face the danger of extinction. Obviously we need to take steps to conserve these bizarre plants.

Carnivorous plants are remarkable enough in their own right, but because of their unusual structure and fascinating behavior, there appear periodically stories in the press about the discovery or existence of tropical man-eating trees whose massive tentacles reputedly fasten onto humans—usually females—crush their bodies in their viselike clasp, and then leisurely digest their succulent bodies (Figure 2.21). As a fair representative of this kind of science fiction we offer the following wire-service news story which appeared a few years ago, datelined London:

SCIENTISTS SEEK
MAN-EATING TREE

Madagascar Tribes Worship It, Giving
It Young Girls as Living Sacrifice,
Explorer Says

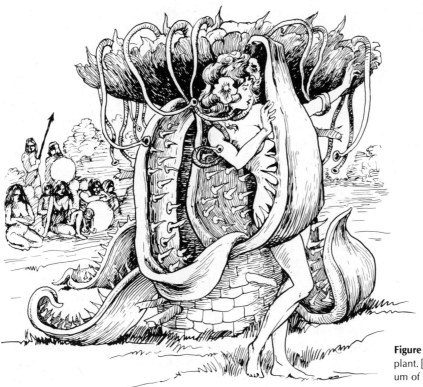

Figure 2.21 Fanciful human-eating plant. [Redrawn; courtesy Field Museum of Natural History.]

A band of British explorers, including one woman, will land on the islands of Sinbad the Sailor in a few weeks to search for the mysterious Madagascar "Sacrifice Tree," which devours human beings.

The so-called man-eating tree, which actually is said to take the lives of young girls rather than men, is not a product of the imagination, high authorities declare.

Captain V. De La Motte Hurst, a Fellow of the Royal Geographical Society, has been convinced that it not only exists, but that each year it devours several of the most beautiful maidens of the island. The superstitious tribes offer the girls to the tree as sacrifices, he said.

"I have been told about the tree by many chiefs of the island and I have no doubt of its existence," Captain Hurst said. "It eats human beings, but since the natives worship it, they are reluctant to reveal its location."

The tree, as described to the captain, is similar to a colossal pineapple. It is about eight feet tall and six feet around the base. It has long tendrils, which reach upward, each about as thick as the arm of a man.

The leaves are large and concave, and are lined with "claws." From the tree comes an intoxicating liquid, which the natives drink to arouse the hysteria which leads up to the sacrificial ceremony.

"While the natives dance around the tree, a young girl is forced to drink the liquid," Captain Hurst said. "Then she is compelled to get up into the middle of the tree.

"The tree's tendrils and leaves are hyper-sensitive and as soon as the weight of the sacrificial maiden is pressed against them, the tendrils entwine her. The leaves raise slowly and completely hide the girl.

"The pressure of the tendrils and leaves is like a vise and it is said the body of the girl is crushed. I am told that the leaves remain in that formation for five or six days and then slowly reopen. Only the bones of the victim are found."

Captain Hurst's expedition will land at Morundava, a small village on the coast of Madagascar. It will pass through the territories of half a dozen tribes, some of which are hostile.

The expedition hopes to take a motion picture of the tree sacrifice.

Needless to say, no motion picture nor further report of the expedition has appeared in the years since this story was published.

General Botany Textbooks

The following is a list of good, comprehensive textbooks of general botany, any one of which would be a useful supplement to *Humanistic Botany*, especially in the areas of plant morphology and plant physiology.

Cronquist, Arthur. *Introductory Botany*. 2d ed. New York: Harper & Row, 1971.

Fuller, Harry J., Zane B. Carothers, Willard W. Payne, and Margaret K. Balbach. *The Plant World*. 5th ed. New York: Holt, Rinehart and Winston, 1972.

Fuller, Harry J., and Oswald Tippo. *College Botany*. 2d ed. New York: Henry Holt, 1954.

Jensen, William A., and Frank B. Salisbury. *Botany*. Belmont, Calif.: Wadsworth, 1972.

Neushul, Michael. *Botany*. Santa Barbara, Calif.: Hamilton, 1974.

Raven, Peter H., Ray F. Evert, and Helena Curtis. *Biology of Plants*. 2d ed. New York: Worth, 1976.

Weier, T. Elliot, C. Ralph Stocking, and Michael G. Barbour. *Botany*. 5th ed. New York: Wiley, 1974.

Wilson, Carl L., Walter E. Loomis, and Taylor A. Steeves. *Botany*. 5th ed. New York: Holt, Rinehart and Winston, 1971.

Suggested Readings

Darwin, Charles. *Insectivorous Plants*. New York: Appleton, 1875. A classic, early study on the structure and behavior of insect-eating plants by the great evolutionist. It remains one of the best books on the subject.

Emboden, William A. *Bizarre Plants*. New York: Macmillan, 1974. A popular account of many of the most fascinating and extraordinary plants.

Gabriel, Mordecai L., and Seymour Fogel, eds. *Great Experiments in Biology*. Englewood Cliffs, N.J.: Prentice-Hall, 1955. Excerpts from some of the great scientific papers of the past, such as those of Hooke on cells, Fleming on the discovery of the action of penicillin, van Helmont on his classic experiment with the willow tree, Mendel's letter to Nägeli, as well as some of the original writings of Wallace, Darwin, Schwann, Pasteur, and Weismann.

Galston, Arthur W. *The Life of the Green Plant*. 2d ed. Englewood Cliffs, N.J.: Prentice-Hall, 1964. A brief, lucid paperback on plant nutrition, and the physiological aspects of growth and development.

Hartmann, Hudson T., and Dale E. Kester. *Plant Propagation*. 3d ed. Englewood Cliffs, N.J.: Prentice-Hall, 1975. A comprehensive manual on propagation, including material on cuttings and grafting.

Pendergast, Chuck. *Introduction to Organic Gardening*. Los Angeles: Nash, 1971. A useful introduction to organic gardening.

Ray, Peter M. *The Living Plant*. 2d ed. New York: Holt, Rinehart and Winston, 1972. A general, albeit sophisticated, treatment of plant physiology, including photosynthesis, water transport, mineral nutrition, food conduction, growth, development, and reproduction.

Rodale, Robert, ed. *The Basic Book of Organic Gardening*. New York: Ballantine, 1971. A good introduction to the subject by an advocate of organic gardening.

Salisbury, Frank B., and Robert V. Parke. *Vascular Plants: Form and Function*. 2d ed. Belmont, Calif.: Wadsworth, 1970. An advanced text in which plant physiology is integrated with plant structure.

Sears, Paul B. *Deserts on the March*. 3d ed. Norman: University of Oklahoma Press, 1959. An early classic on the role of plants in stemming erosion and dust storms by a distinguished plant ecologist.

Shetler, Stanwyn G., and Florence Montgomery. *Insectivorous Plants*. Information Leaflet No. 447. Washington, D.C.: Smithsonian Institution, 1965. Concise, informative pamphlet with excellent illustrations.

Steward, F. C. *About Plants*. Reading, Mass.: Addison-Wesley, 1966. A useful, scholarly discussion of such physiological topics as inorganic nutrition; metabolism, including respiration; water economy; movement of materials; growth; development; and reproduction—by a leading researcher in plant physiology.

Plant Names

Common name	Scientific name	Family
cobra plant	*Darlingtonia californica*	Sarraceniaceae
pitcher plant	*Sarracenia purpurea*	Sarraceniaceae
tropical pitcher plant	*Nepenthes* spp.*	Nepenthaceae
sundew	*Drosera capillaris*	Droseraceae
Venus's flytrap	*Dionaea muscipula*	Droseraceae

*Spp. = plural of species; sp. = singular of species.

The bushy form of the horsetail plant
(*Equisetum*) has suggested both its English vernacular name and its botanical
name.

3
On Names and Naming

Torn between her passion for Romeo and her family's scorn of the Montagues, Juliet cries,

"Tis but thy name that is my enemy;
Thou art thyself, though not a Montague.
What's a Montague? it is nor hand, nor foot,
Nor arm, nor face, nor any other part
Belonging to a man. O! be some other name:
What's in a name? that which we call a rose
By any other name would smell as sweet;
So Romeo would, were he not Romeo call'd.

Thus Shakespeare points out the arbitrariness of names as he describes the attachment of names to family honor and pride; he questions the value of names, queries their application and meaning, and asks if they must always be affixed to the same entity. The intrinsic nature of a person, plant, animal, or event, is not altered by the name which we happen to apply to it. Yet, names, even with their deficiencies, are indispensable guides to the order of any realm. Names are abbreviated histories, they have dimension in time; they are the beginning points of classification, the designations by which things are known. These are some of what *is* in a name.

Folk Names for Plants

Almost everyone grows up knowing the names of some plants: maple, oak, iris, violet, lettuce, dandelion, coconut, coffee, chocolate, black pepper, clove. These names which we learn during childhood are **vernacular, common,** or **folk names;** that is, des-

45

ignations for plants in our own language, easy to learn and to recall. In many cases their origins stretch back to other times, to other countries, and to other languages. Vernacular names have been applied to plants of special interest, and naming has been motivated because of the value of the plant to man and the need, therefore, for a name. But most plants are not of special interest or use to people and so we find that most of the plants in the world do not have names derived from vernacular speech. All plants which are known, however, do have **botanical names.** These appear in Latin form. Many botanical names come directly or indirectly from the actual names applied to certain plants familiar to the ancients, from the Greeks and Romans, their contemporaries and predecessors. Vernacular names are not to be despised and discarded in favor of botanical names. They should be recognized for what they are and looked upon as potentially pithy sources of plant lore antedating in many cases the modern use of botanical names.

Source and Substance

Some vernacular names come directly from a conspicuous feature of the plant itself. What could be more natural than to apply the name arrowhead to a plant having arrow-shaped leaves or cattail to a marsh plant with a stiff fruiting stalk like the rigid tail of a feline at bay? Blueberry is a good name for a plant having blue fruits, and the sunflower, too, is aptly named for its golden disc resembles the sun. The tropical tree called fry wood has long pods which clickety-clack incessantly in the wind and reminded someone of a crackling fire. Smell and taste have played their roles in naming plants such as stinkhorn, skunk cabbage, and bittersweet. Plant names can be rude, too; pissabed is another name for dandelion and bluet. Plants grow in almost every conceivable place on earth; mountain laurel, marsh mallow, wallflower, bog rosemary, water hyacinth, sandbur, and sea grape provide clues to habitats. Some plants flower during different seasons of the year or at different times during the day; these have been noted in Christmas cactus, Easter lily, spring beauty, four-o'clock, morning-glory, and night-blooming cereus.

Our ancestors had a good eye for plants which they hoped would relieve some of their sufferings, and the names they gave to these plants indicated their real or hoped-for medicinal virtues. Gravel root was used to dissolve stones in the urinary bladder, black-eye root to remove discoloration in tissues caused by bruises, and wormwood to expel intestinal parasites. Birthroot was an American Indian remedy employed to ease and promote parturition. A firm belief in the goodness of God who put everything on earth for his people gave rise to the **doctrine of signatures** which held that the key to man's use of plants was hidden in the form of the plant itself; one had only to look closely. From the multitude of plants to which healing properties were assigned by the herbalists (botanist/physicians) of the Renaissance and before, it is evident that these ancients must have had powerful insights and fertile imaginations. John Gerard, an English herbalist of the late sixteenth century, noted that viper's bugloss bore seeds shaped like the head of a snake and that "the herbe chewed and the juice swallowed downe is a most singular remedy against poyson and the biting of any venemous beast." Certainly the dotted leaves of lungwort resemble a piece of consumptive lung tissue and must be beneficial in curing pulmonary diseases. Bloodroot has orange-red sap and must be useful, therefore, in alleviating diseases of the blood. Hemorrhoids could be cured by taking an infusion concocted from the knobby roots of pilewort. Some plants, as the mandrake, which resembled the whole of the human body, were considered as panaceas and were treated almost reverentially.

Kiss-me-Dick but touch-me-not? Names can be playful, humorous, whimsical, and sometimes fanciful. Origins of these names may be obvious; other times we can only surmise what they meant to some shepherd or herdsman who may have coined them aptly hundreds of years ago. But they still excite our curiosity, and who would not wonder at the secret meaning that might lie in love-in-idleness, kiss-me-at-the-garden-gate, welcome-home-husband-though-never-so-drunk, or widow's tears? And the quaint "language of flowers" comes from a gentler age when certain human qualities were imputed to different flowers, when bachelor's button signified single blessedness, yellow chrysanthemums indicated a slighted love, and forget-me-not told of true love.

Over the centuries, as the peoples of England and Europe traveled about the world, they carried with them the homely names of familiar plants which they commonly adapted to the new plants of new lands without regard for botanical meaning. Among the colonists there were few who were scientifically trained and it was a completely natural thing for them to

Figures 3.3, 4 Tree and branchlet of *incense cedar*.

Figures 3.1, 2 Young trees and branchlet of eastern *red cedar*.

Figure 3.5 Compound leaves of *Spanish cedar*.

transfer these old, friendly names. The evening primrose of North America has only its yellow color in common with the garden border plants called primrose in England; the mountain laurel of northeastern North America has stiffish glossy green leaves like the laurel of the Old World, but that is where the similarity ends; and the white beech of Australia is far removed from the stately beech of Europe, except for its gray-barked trunk.

Science Can't Rely on Vernacular Names

At this point, you might ask, then, why don't botanists use vernacular names which have such a rich heritage and may be so full of meaning? Reasons for the interest in and fascination with vernacular names are precisely the ones which forbid their use in scientific language. Vernacular names are not botanically precise, they are not universally accepted and used, and they are rarely subject to uniformity. Two examples might help to show why vernacular names have these built-in deficiencies.

The same vernacular name is sometimes given to different plants. Cedar may refer to eastern red cedar (Figures 3.1 and 3.2), incense cedar (Figures 3.3 and 3.4), western red cedar, Atlantic white cedar, Spanish cedar (Figure 3.5), and banak cedar, as well as to the biblical cedar of Lebanon (Figures 3.6 and 3.7). The name cedar in each of these appellations would lead us to believe that these were all similar plants, but the fact is they are more or less diverse botanically. On the other hand, different vernacular names are also applied to the same plant. The European white water lily, a garden favorite, has at least 245 local names in four different languages: 15 English, 44 French, 105 German, and 81 Dutch. Marsh marigold has over 80 local names in Britain, about 60 in France, and at least 140 in Germany, Austria, and Switzerland. And what is more, some of these names may also apply to other kinds of plants as well as to the marsh marigold. This would be a hopeless situation in an international science; nobody would know for sure what kind of plant was being discussed. Pharmacognosists (drug scientists) writing about a potentially new drug plant would certainly be perplexed; agricultural and horticultural scientists would not know to which crop and fruit plants their colleagues were referring; botanists would wonder about the sanity of their overseas correspondents. The Babel of the Bible would pale by comparison. Surely more exact and universally understood names for plants are called for and, with their limited utility, vernacular names do not fit the bill.

Figures 3.6, 7 Tree and cone-bearing twigs of the biblical *cedar of Lebanon.*

[**Figures 3.1**–7 Four distinct species of trees—belonging to four different genera, to three separate plant families, and to the two major groups of the seed plants—each one of which is called *cedar.*]

49

Figure 3.8 Picking coffee "cherries" in Costa Rica. [Courtesy U.S. Department of Agriculture.]

Botanical Names

The botanical name with its unfamiliar Latin ring is often tossed off as too difficult to pronounce, long, meaningless, pedantic, or even snobbish. Yet we do use many botanical names in everyday speech without thinking of them as such. Rhododendron, hydrangea, chrysanthemum, asparagus, amaryllis, geranium, fuchsia, and petunia are all botanical names. Like vernacular names they have meaning and historical interest. Unlike vernacular names, however, they can be applied precisely and uniformly; they are universally understandable and there is only one valid name for each kind of plant.

Two Words in Each Plant Name

For the sake of discussion we can consider the botanical name of the plant (Figure 3.8) from which coffee comes: *Coffea arabica.* Complete botanical names (and animal names) consist of two parts, and for this reason they are called **binomials.** The first name in the binomial is the **genus** (plural, **genera**). It is always capitalized and may stand alone. The second is the **species,** or **specific name;** it is usually decapitalized and may not be used alone. The generic name is a noun and the specific name is an adjective or a genetive (possessive) which must agree with the noun in number and in gender. *Coffea,* the genus name, is a Latinized form of the Arabic word for the beverage, *kahwah.* The specific name, *arabica,* indicates that the plant was thought to originate in Arabia by the botanist who named it. *Coffea arabica,* then, refers to only one kind of plant; it is a name which is intelligible regardless of where it is used, regardless of the native language of the user; it is universally understood and universally applied only to one kind of plant. *Homo sapiens* is the binomial for man; *homo* is a Latin word for a "human being" or "mankind"; *sapiens* means "wise" or "prudent" in Latin. Carolus Linnaeus, who coined the binomial, used *sapiens* to distinguish intelligent man from the other animals. Binomials may be likened to names of chemical elements. The name of a chemical element locates it in a unique position in the periodic table of the elements; the binomial, likewise, locates a plant, or animal, in a particular position; it suggests the characteristics of the plant and indicates its relationship in the scheme of plant life.

Binomials are followed by the name or an abbreviation of the name of the botanist who first coined the binomial and who first described the plant: in *Coffea arabica* L., L. stands for the renowned eighteenth-century Swedish botanist Carolus Linnaeus; in *Crataegus submollis* Sarg., Sarg. stands for Charles Sprague Sargent, founder of Harvard University's Arnold Arboretum; in *Quercus velutina* Lam., Lam. stands for Jean Baptiste Lamarck, French evolutionist and botanist; in *Cornus nuttallii* Audub., Audub. stands for John James Audubon, ornithologist, naturalist, and painter.

Botanical names were not always in binomial form and old-time botanists referred to plants in lilting Latin phrases. Even as late as the eighteenth century we find botanists corresponding with each other in ponderous phraseology. When the German botanist Johann Jakob Dillenius wrote to his friend Linnaeus, he said, "In your last letter of all, I find a plant gathered on the coast of Gothland, which you judge to be a *Polygonum erectum angustifolium floribus candidus* of Mentzelius, and *Caryophyllum saxatilis foliis gramineis umbellatus corymbis* of C. Bauhin; nor do I object. But, it is by no means Tournefort's *Lychnis alpina linifolia multiflora perampla radice*." Linnaeus called the latter plant simply *Gypsophila fastigiata* (baby's breath). Small wonder then that Linnaeus finally adopted a consistent **binomial system of nomenclature** (naming) as a concise and uniform way to refer to plants. Whereas catnip had been *Nepeta floribus interrupte spicatis pedunculatis*, Linnaeus just called it, *Nepeta cataria* (*cataria* being a Latin word referring to cats). With the tremendous influx of new plant specimens from explorations associated with the expanding overseas empires of the eighteenth and nineteenth centuries, the utility of Linnaeus's binomial system could not long be denied.

The event which regularized the binomial system of nomenclature was the publication in 1753 by Linnaeus of his two-volume study, *Species Planatarum* (The species of plants). In this work, Linnaeus scrupulously adhered to the principle of binomialism in naming and describing the 5,900 plants included. This monumental publication has had a profound and continuing influence on modern botany, even though it is over 200 years old. *It is the starting point for the modern naming of plants.* When questions arise about which of several names applied to a plant is correct, usually the earliest name must be chosen. This is called the **principle of priority.** Also, botanists who name plants new to science are required to be absolutely certain that the names they choose have not been used before. Considering that there are now hundreds of thousands of plant names in use, it is no trivial task to search for a name which has not been employed previously. Among the first tasks which must be carried out in this search is reference to the first edition of Linnaeus's *Species Plantarum* of 1753, the base line of nomenclature for plants. In this way, the selection and use of botanical names avoid one of the pitfalls of vernacular names, which is use of the same name for different kinds of plants.

Generic Names

The plebians and patricians who wandered the byways of ancient Rome had names for the common Italian plants of field and wood, and our generic names for pine (*Pinus*, Figures 3.9 and 3.10), maple (*Acer*, Figures 3.15, 3.16, and 3.17), juniper

Figures 3.9, 10 Shrub and twig of the mountain pine, *Pinus mugo*.

(Juniperus, Figures 3.1 and 3.2), wheat *(Triticum,* Figures 11.2 and 11.3), oak *(Quercus,* Figure 3.11), and ivy *(Hedera)* are derived directly from the Latin. In the classical writings of Virgil, Columella, Pliny, and Ovid, these plants seem to have been well known. We have just borrowed their names and adapted them to modern botanical usage. Similarly, we have taken ancient Greek names, Latinized them, and formed them into modern botanical names. Our garden plants *Daphne, Scilla,* and *Anemone* are named from the Greek. Names of Roman and Greek gods and goddesses have been used for plants; the little wild *Calypso* orchid and the deadly nightshade *Atropa* are loan-words of this kind. *Tagetes,* the genus name of the marigold, is based on Tages, the Etruscan deity of divination.

Personal names are found in many generic names—royalty, scientists, poets, gardeners, patrons. Mostly the names are honorific; sometimes they are subtly derogatory; frequently they are odd. Take, for example, the generic name *Sinowilsonia,* a combination which means Chinese Wilson. This was the nickname of Ernest H. Wilson, one of the great plant explorers who spent so many years in China that he indeed became "Chinese Wilson" to his colleagues. Johann Georg Siegesbeck was one of Linnaeus's most severe critics and a keen personal animosity

Figure 3.11 A leafy branchlet of white oak, *Quercus alba*.

TAB: XXIII.

SIGESBECKIA. *Hort. Cliff.* 412. *sp.* 1.
a *Ramulus cum flore.*
b *Flos lente inspectus.*

J. WANDELAAR del. & fecit.

Figure 3.12 Reproduction of the plate from Linnaeus's *Hortus Cliffortianus* showing *Sigesbeckia*. Linnaeus chose this lowly nondescript plant as the namesake of his bitter adversary, botanist Johann Georg Siegesbeck.

developed between these two botanists. There is, no doubt, a hidden barb in Linnaeus's name *Sigesbeckia* for the weedy, small-flowered unattractive member of the sunflower family (Figure 3.12). *Galinsoga* is a pesty, widespread garden weed with diminutive flowers. It was named by Hipólito Ruiz and José Antonio Pavón, two botanical explorers of the eighteenth century, after Mariano Martinez Galinsoga, a doctor of Madrid whose botanical accomplishments are said to match the smallness of the flowers.

The celebrated French chemist Joseph Louis Gay-Lussac, whose name is associated with his law concerning the volume of gases, is commemorated in *Gaylussacia,* a relative of the blueberry. Similarly, *Linnaea* (Figure 3.13) was named after Linnaeus. This plant was dearly loved by Linnaeus and he is frequently pictured holding a flowering branchlet. With tongue-in-cheek humility, he wrote, ''*Linnaea* was named by the celebrated Gronovius and is a plant of Lapland, lowly, insignificant, disregarded, flowering but for a brief space—from Linnaeus who resembles it.'' Robert Fitzroy, captain of H.M.S. *Beagle,* the ship which carried Charles Darwin on his epochmaking voyage of discovery, is commemorated in *Fitzroya,* an evergreen tree of Chile. And *Nicotiana,* the tobacco genus, is named for Jean Nicot, French ambassador to Lisbon, who introduced the weed into France.

Figure 3.13 Twinflower, *Linnaea borealis.*

Modern generic names may be formed from Latinized vernacular names and from geographic places—countries, rivers, mountains, states. Other generic names come from combinations of Latin and Greek words which describe some character of the plant itself. *Trifolium,* the genus of sweet clover, comes from *tri-,* ''three,'' and *folium,* a ''leaf.'' It refers to the three leaflets characteristic of clover. *Hydrangea* is derived from Greek origins and comes from *hydor,* ''water,'' and *aggos,* a ''jar.'' It probably refers to the cup-shaped fruit of these shrubs. The blue dye indigo is extracted from plants of the genus *Indigofera* and the word is compounded of indigo plus the Latin, *fero,* to ''bear.'' *Rhododendron* is from the Greek for ''rose tree,'' a reference no doubt to the red flowers borne by some kinds of rhododendrons. The sunflower is *Helianthus,* a Greek combination which means ''sun flower.''

Specific Names

Like generic names, specific names are derived from a wealth of sources and we have to marvel at the diversity of these epithets and the flexibility of the Latin language base which permits such adaptations. At this point, it might be useful to recall that specific names are descriptive, they tell us about the generic name, or they are possessives. Probably, most often, specific names describe some feature of the plant—color, shape, size, habitat, aroma, taste. Thus, *rubrum* means ''red''; *album,*

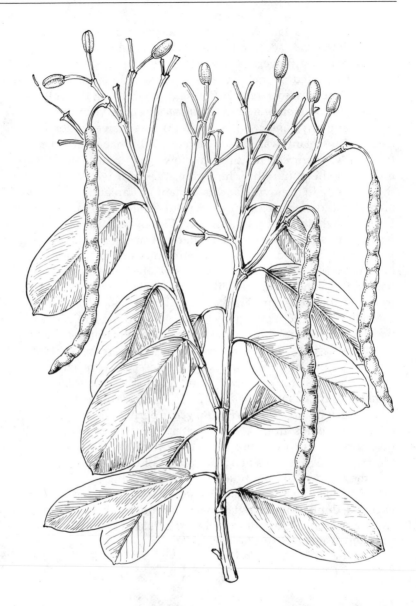

Figure 3.14 Fruit-bearing branchlet
of *Capparis cynophallophora.*

"white"; *nigrum,* "black"; *foetidus,* "bad smelling"; *mellitum,*
"honey scented"; *dulce,* "sweet"; and *acidum,* "sour." *Folium,* as
noted above, is Latin for "leaf." *Latifolium* means "broad
leaved"; *angustifolium,* "narrow leaved"; *sagittifolium,* "arrow-
shaped leaf" (after Sagittarius, the Archer); and *longifolium,*
"long leaved." Specific names are frequently commemorative in

the same manner as generic names. Liberty Hyde Bailey, renowned American horticulturist, is honored by *baileyi*; David Douglas, plant hunter after whom the Douglas fir is named, is noted in *douglasii*; and Prince Metternich of Austria is remembered in *metternichii*. The adjectives *canadense*, *virginianum*, *malayanum*, *britannicum*, and *philippinense* are derived from place names; *rivale* means "growing by streams"; *petraeum*, "rock loving"; *seclusum*, "hidden"; and *palustre*, "marsh loving."

Naming Plants

The binomial then, is usually a combination of a generic noun and a specific adjective. Together they should tell us something about the kind of plant with which some botanist has associated them. The binomial is a kind of abbreviated language form and, with the helpful guides which you should now have, it ought to be possible to understand and enjoy, and even to have fun with, what may have previously seemed mere drudgery. *Capparis cynophallophora* is the pornographic binomial of a little white-flowered tree (Figure 3.14) which grows on some of the Florida Keys and Caribbean islands. It was named by Linnaeus, probably in one of his more inventive moods. *Capparis* is the old Greek name of these shrubs, and the flower buds of another species, *Capparis spinosa*, are pickled, salted, and sold as capers. *Cynophallophora*, the specific name, is formed from three Greek words: *kyon*, a "dog"; *phallos*, a "penis"; and *-phor*, a suffix meaning "to bear" or "to carry." Thus, our Caribbean caper is the one which bears a dog's penis, and it is aptly named, for the fruit is long, cylindrical, and somewhat tapering. The specific name must have seemed particularly fitting to Linnaeus and one can see him chuckling over the reaction of some future generation to his sly name. The garden sunflower is *Helianthus annuus*. The generic name is Latinized from the Greek for the "sun," *helios*, and *anthemon*, a "flower." *Annuus* means "annual" and refers to the fact that this plant lasts only one season and must be planted anew each year. *Rosa carolina* is the rose from Carolina, *Rosa* being the old Latin name for the rose. *Lilium catesbaei* is Catesby's lily. *Lilium* is the Latin name for the lily and Mark Catesby was an English artist/naturalist who visited the New World in the early eighteenth century and returned home to write *A Natural History of Carolina, Florida and the Bahama Islands*.

A paramount advantage of botanical over vernacular names then is that there is only a single valid name for each kind of plant. This name is universally accepted and understood and the rules for naming plants are set forth in the *International Code of Botanical Nomenclature.* By mutual agreement all botanists adhere to the provisions recommended in this document. There is no United Nations armed force which compels botanists under penalty to carry out the regulations. Success of the Code rests on good faith and the realization of common benefit.

The Species

Botanical names, as we know them, were devised to bring order to the world of plants. Each plant has its own handle, a unique title not held by any other plant. Naming does not alter the intrinsic quality of each plant any more than Romeo's quality was changed because he happened to be surnamed Montague. However, since a name is attached to a plant quality called a **species,** we ought to know what a species is. Characterization of this one concept, has probably been the subject of more inquiry, midnight-oil-burning, symposia and seminars, trivializing, and endless debate than any other single topic in the whole realm of modern biology—and it is still unresolved. Even to attempt to bring a stop to all this wrangling would be presumptuous of us and we can only hope to give a brief idea of what others have thought about species and to tell you what we think it ought to mean.

Changing Concepts of the Species

John Ray, English botanist and clergyman, wrote in 1704 that "plants which differ as species preserve their species for all time, the members of each species having descended from the seed of the same original plant." Linnaeus in 1737 held essentially to the same idea and said that "species are as many as the Supreme Being produced diverse forms at the beginning." An early writer of American botany books, Almira H. Lincoln, stated in 1840 that "a *Species* includes such individuals as agree in certain circumstances of the roots, stems, leaves, and inflorescences [flowers or groups of flowers]." In the sixth edition (1872) of *The Origin of Species,* Charles Darwin looked "at the term species as one arbitrarily given, for the sake of convenience, to a set of individuals closely resembling each other." And in 1905, Hugo de Vries, Dutch botanist and geneticist, felt that "species are, at the present time, for a large part artificial, or stated more correctly, conventional groups," and every biologist "is free to delimit them in a wider or in a narrower sense, according to his judgment." Somewhat humorously (we hope), another botanist asserted that a species is an entity which can be recognized from a train going 30 miles an hour.

A recent and somewhat technical definition has it that a species is a group of individuals that closely resemble one another because of their descent from common ancestors, and that have become more or less sharply separated from all other coexisting species by the disappearance of intermediate forms. Analyzed in the light of current thinking and experimentation, it appears that the concept of species has two components, one based on structural characteristics—the older idea—and one based on breeding behavior—a newer notion. According to this newer view, members of the same species are supposed to be able to interbreed freely to produce fertile offspring.

Implicit in all modern characterizations of species is the principle of evolution; that is, species which are present on earth today are related through ancestral pathways to earlier forms of plants. There is evidence that some of the pre-Darwinian naturalists were aware of evolution and questioned the rigid application of the doctrine of special creation; that is, that God created all species and these species, unchanged in number or kind, now populate the earth. The church-dominated society of Linnaeus's time, for example, precluded any outright statement by him to this effect. Nevertheless, in 1912 Edward L. Greene presented arguments to support his thesis that Linnaeus was a secret evolutionist; that hidden among the mundane descriptive phrases of *Species Plantarum* is proof that Linnaeus suspected the origin of one species from another.

Just What Is a Species?

So what can we glean from all of this that will help us to understand what a species is?

1. A species is a **kind** of plant (or animal). White oak (*Quercus alba*, Figure 3.11), red maple (*Acer rubrum*, Figure 3.15), white pine (*Pinus strobus*, Figures 16.9 and 16.10), coconut palm (*Cocos nucifera*, Figure 11.12), tobacco (*Nicotiana tabacum*), are species or kinds of plants.
2. Each individual of a species is related to other individuals of the same species because they have common ancestors; they have evolved from the same sources.
3. Individuals of the same species are similar in structure, more so to each other than to other kinds of plants.

4. Species maintain themselves in nature; they do not change appreciably from generation to generation over short periods of time.

5. Individuals of a species interbreed and produce fertile offspring.

All of this is not very practical, you might say. How can I recognize my garden flowers? How can I tell poison ivy from English ivy? Do I have to perform breeding experiments on plants? How can I know the ancestry of the plants I have? So, we say to you, depend on what you can see. Select what have proven to be reliable features, primarily those from the reproductive structures—flowers and fruits—and secondarily from the vegetative characters—leaves, stems, and roots. Do as Linnaeus did. Follow the biblical precept of Matthew when he taught how to recognize false prophets: "You will recognize them by the fruits they bear. Can grapes be picked from briars, or figs from thistles?" This same principle can be applied to species.

The Order of Plants

Most people know some plant genera, probably without even realizing it. The idea of the genus comes naturally, even while we are children. Almost casually we learn that there are several kinds of oaks and different kinds of maples. Oak and maple are just the vernacular names for *Quercus* and *Acer,* two genera of plants. We grasp the essence of genus without trying. A genus is simply a grouping of allied or similar species. Whether species are alike enough to be lumped within the same genus is a judgment for the botanist. *Quercus alba* (white oak, Figure 3.11), *Quercus virginiana* (live oak), and *Quercus suber* (cork oak); *Acer rubrum* (red maple, Figure 3.15), *Acer saccharum* (sugar maple, Figure 3.16), and *Acer palmatum* (Japanese maple, Figure 3.17); *Rosa canina* (dog rose), *Rosa gallica* (French rose), and *Rosa cinnamomea* (cinnamon rose) are each a group of species within which the features of the plants are similar enough to persuade someone of their over-all generality. "Rose is a rose is a rose is a rose."

Figures 3.15, 16, 17 The three different maples shown (*Acer rubrum, A. saccharum, A. palmatum*) are easily recognized as of the same genus by the over-all similarity of their leaves.

The same strategy used to bring similar species together in the genus operates in forming the plant **family;** a plant family is a collection of similar genera. Oaks of all kinds, all the species of quercuses, belong to the beech (*Fagus*) family. There are botanical similarities between all oaks and all beeches which are so cogent as to have induced some botanists to place them together in the same family. The family of oaks and beeches is Fagaceae; the -*aceae* ending tells that the group in question is a plant family. Use of this ending for plant family names is dictated by the *International Code of Botanical Nomenclature.** Similar families are placed together into groups called **orders,** and similar orders are gathered into units called **classes.** Each of these groups—genera, families, orders, classes—can be expected to be more inclusive than those which precede it. Classes are more inclusive than orders, orders are more inclusive than families, families than genera, and genera than species.

Such a steppingstone arrangement of units is called a classification. In plants, and animals, the basic unit of classification is the species which is represented by a two-word name, the binomial. When species are characterized and named, the initial step in the classification process has been completed. Someone has decided, based on a chosen series of characteristics, that the members of a group of plants or animals (a population) are sufficiently alike among themselves to comprise a species.

Classification is the science of **taxonomy** and persons who are specially adept in this field are **taxonomists.** Taxonomy is the science which concerns order and system; without it there would be no regular way to organize and arrange the vast numbers of organisms on earth, both plant and animal; there would be no orderly way to locate and retrieve information about these plants and animals. Our knowledge of plants and animals, once learned, could be lost—to science and perhaps more importantly, to mankind. It has been estimated, for ex-

*There are eight legitimate exceptions to the consistent use of the -*aceae* ending for plant family names. These names, not ending in -*aceae*, are classical family names. In the list which follows alternative names which do end in -*aceae* are shown in parentheses: Palmae (Arecaceae), palm family; Gramineae (Poaceae), grass family; Cruciferae (Brassicaceae), mustard family; Leguminosae (Fabaceae), bean, or pulse, family; Guttiferae (Clusiaceae), mangosteen family; Umbelliferae (Apiaceae), carrot family; Labiatae (Lamiaceae), mint family; and Compositae (Asteraceae), sunflower family. In the lists of scientific names after each chapter, we have used the traditional family names.

ample, that there are well over 800,000 species of plants, most of which are yet to be discovered, characterized, and named. New plants (that is, new to man) are still being discovered all the time through exploration and study. A keen plant taxonomist might learn—perhaps—5,000 plants during a lifetime of study. Most botanists know far fewer. Some even spend a lifetime studying a single species. David Starr Jordan, a famous ichthyologist (a specialist in fishes) who became president of Stanford University, was once asked if he remembered the names of all the Stanford students. He replied that he "used to, but found that for every student's name I remembered, I forgot the name of a fish. So I gave up." Classification provides us with an order of ranked compartments or pigeonholes for the kinds of plants so that we do not have to depend upon our memory; all we need to know is the system upon which the classification rests.

Changing Concepts of Order

Satisfying the compulsion to set things in order has been one of the major preoccupations of mankind. "Order," asserted Edmund Burke, is "the eternal fitness of things." Alexander Pope described order as "Heav'n's first law; and, this confest,/Some are and must be greater than the rest." It has been said that Linnaeus believed himself to have been divinely commissioned to make an inventory and an orderly arrangement of all the realms of nature. Indeed, there has been a continuing search in botany for rational principles upon which plant order, or classification, could be founded. Theophrastus of Lesbos (ca. 374–287 B.C.), the Father of Botany, pupil and friend of both Aristotle and Plato, produced a system of classification which took advantage of elementary plant form. He considered plants as herbs, undershrubs, shrubs, and trees. These are perhaps the almost inevitable views that someone might have had about plants, especially in the ancient classical world; yet, they would have appeared to be a completely rational and practical classification. Probably owing to the enormous and continuing influence of Aristotle, this system persisted in use until the eighteenth century and the advent of Linnaeus upon the botanical scene. Coexisting with the Theophrastian method during the Middle Ages and Renaissance were a series of purely utilitarian classifications based on the uses of plants: medicine, food, poison, beverages, clothing, construction, magic. These systems were the handmaidens of the botanist/physicians of the time, the herbalists or herb doctors.

Other attempts to classify plants were developed in the seventeenth century, and the systems of the Frenchman Joseph Pitton de Tournefort and the Englishman John Ray brought an understanding of the fundamental properties of flower, fruit, and seed to the construction of their classifications. But it was Linnaeus who devised a practical system of plant classification in 1735 based on the structure, arrangement, and number of the so-called sexual parts in the flower. Linnaeus's system was a numerical classification and its use was avowedly to help people identify plants readily. A supreme advantage of Linnaeus's classification was that it was simple and easily committed to memory.

Linnaeus's is usually called a sexual system of classification because it relied on the so-called sexual parts of the flower. In eighteenth-century Europe, this was naughty indeed and Linnaeus was roundly castigated by a few of his more prudish contemporaries. Johann Siegesbeck, the St. Petersburg botanist after whom Linnaeus named the pesty *Sigesbeckia*, doubted "very much if any Botanist will follow his lewd method." He attacked Linnaeus's system as "loathsome harlotry" and asked how anyone could teach without offense "so licentious a method" to studious youth. Nevertheless, his system of classification was a great success and was in wide use until the middle of the nineteenth century.

Following the publication in 1859 of the *Origin of Species* by Charles Darwin, botanists began to search for evolutionary clues in the structure of plants, evidence they hoped would reflect the unifying principles of evolution and the relationships among plants as propounded by Darwin. In the construction of modern systems of classification, taxonomists attempt to arrange plants in a three-dimensional evolutionary tree (Figure 19.4). Branches portray the various paths of evolution. Plants thought to be closely related are placed nearer to each other on the same path than plants which seem to be more distantly related. Evolutionary theory more or less influences every newly proposed system of plant classification today.

A Convenient Arrangement of Plants*

It is appropriate now to show you one arrangement of plants, to give you a framework within which to associate them, and to provide a basis for the discussions to follow. We chose the groupings below for their simplicity and usefulness, not

*These plants will all be discussed in detail in Chapters 13–16.

because they reflect the latest breakthroughs in evolutionary findings—they do not. You will see at a glance that the simpler and generally smaller plants appear first (thallophytes) and the more complex and larger appear later in the sequence (embryophytes). There are fewer species of these simpler plants than the more complex. Also you will be more familiar with the complex than with the simple plants since the former are larger, easier to see and recognize, and are frequently and knowingly encountered in your daily experiences.

I. Thallophytes: Plant body relatively simple (*thallus:* a combination of cells not organized into roots, stems, or leaves); dissemination by spores.
   A. *Algae:* Seaweeds, pond scums, water blooms. Plants contain chlorophyll, manufacture own food. In addition, they may have brown, red, blue, and other pigments; mostly aquatic. About 21,000 species described.
   B. *Fungi:* Molds, mushrooms, yeasts, bacteria. Plants lack chlorophyll, do not manufacture own food, exist on nonliving and decaying organic matter or are parasitic; mostly terrestrial. About 100,000 species described (250,000 *estimated*).
II. Embryophytes: Plant body relatively complex; embryo present.
   A. *Bryophytes:* Mosses, liverworts, hornworts. Plants comparatively small with leaflike, stemlike, and rootlike structures; no xylem or phloem; disseminated by spores.
   B. *Vascular plants:* Plants comparatively large with true leaves, stems, and roots; xylem and phloem present.
      1. Seedless vascular plants: Ferns, horsetails, club mosses. Disseminated by spores. About 10,000 species described.
      2. Seed plants: Disseminated by seeds.
         a. Gymnosperms: Pines, spruces, firs, hemlocks, cycads, ginkgo. Plants usually have cones, not flowers; seeds naked, not enclosed in a fruit. About 800 species described.
         b. Angiosperms: Plants have flowers; seeds covered, enclosed in a fruit. About 250,000 species described (500,000 *estimated*).
            i. Dicotyledons: Maples, marigolds, beans, coffee, daisies. Leaves have netted veins; floral parts in fours or fives or in multiples of four or five; two seed leaves present.

ii. Monocotyledons: Palms, grasses, orchids, lilies. Leaves have parallel veins; floral parts in threes or multiples of three; one seed leaf present.

Summary

Plant names are written or verbal designations for kinds of plants. They are applied in vernacular language or in the botanical sense. A plant name is a convenience which permits us to pinpoint a given kind of plant with more or less accuracy. Vernacular names, though sometimes meaningful and interesting, are variable and imprecise; hence botanical names, which are subject to regulation and are universally understood by botanists, have become the nomenclatural language of reference in science. **Botanical names** consist of two words in Latinized form, a **genus name** followed by a **specific epithet,** which taken together comprise the **binomial.** Binomials are applied to kinds of plants and only one binomial can be used validly to denote a given **plant species.** A **species** may be characterized as follows: It represents a kind of plant, all the individual members of a given species are related, all individuals of a species are similar in structure, species maintain themselves in nature, and individuals of a species interbreed with each other and produce fertile offspring. Groups of similar species make up **genera;** similar genera make up **families;** similar families make up **orders;** similar orders make up **classes.** Genera, families, orders, classes, and other more inclusive groups arranged in an orderly manner comprise a **classification.** The species is the basis of all classification of plants. Botanists who classify plants are **taxonomists** and **taxonomy** is the science of classification. The bases for constructing systems of classification have changed from early ones based on superficial plant form, to others depending on the utilitarian values of plants, to those reflecting structure and function of floral parts. Modern systems of classification follow **Darwinian principles of evolution** and attempt to show relationships among plants.

Suggested Readings

Bailey, L. H. *How Plants Get Their Names.* New York: Macmillan, 1933 (reprinted New York: Dover Publications, 1963). Popular account of plant naming by the late dean of American horticulture.

Blunt, Wilfrid. *The Compleat Naturalist: A Life of Linnaeus*. New York: Viking, 1971.

Lawrence, George H. M. *Taxonomy of Vascular Plants*. New York: Macmillan, 1951. A scholarly text on plant classification, descriptions of plant families, and the history of taxonomic botany.

Smith, A. W. *A Gardener's Dictionary of Plant Names*. London: Cassell, 1972. Revised, enlarged, and annotated by William T. Stearn with a wealth of anecdotal notes on the scientific names of most garden plants.

Thiselton Dyer, T. F. *Folk-lore of Shakespeare*. London: Griffith & Farran, 1883 (reprinted New York: Dover Publications, 1966). Contains a chapter on plant names and their meanings as used in the Great Bard's plays.

———. *The Folk-lore of Plants*. New York: D. Appleton and Company, 1889 (reprinted Detroit: Singing Tree Press, 1968).

Plant Names

Common name	Scientific name	Family
arrowhead	*Sagittaria* spp.	Alismataceae
Atlantic white cedar	*Chamaecyparis thyoides*	Cupressaceae
bachelor's button	*Centaurea cyanus*	Compositae
banak cedar	*Virola koschnyi*	Myristicaceae
birthroot	*Trillium* spp.	Liliaceae
bittersweet	*Celastrus scandens*	Celastraceae
black-eye root	*Tamus communis*	Dioscoreaceae
black pepper	*Piper nigrum*	Piperaceae
bloodroot	*Sanguinaria canadensis*	Papaveraceae
blueberry	*Vaccinium angustifolium*	Ericaceae
bluet	*Houstonia caerulea*	Rubiaceae
bog rosemary	*Andromeda glaucophylla*	Ericaceae
cattail	*Typha* spp.	Typhaceae
cedar of Lebanon	*Cedrus libani*	Pinaceae
chocolate	*Theobroma cacao*	Sterculiaceae
Christmas cactus	*Zygocactus truncatus*	Cactaceae
clove	*Eugenia caryophyllus*	Myrtaceae
coconut	*Cocos nucifera*	Palmae
coffee	*Coffea arabica*	Rubiaceae
dandelion	*Taraxacum officinale*	Compositae
Easter lily	*Lilium longiflorum*	Liliaceae
eastern red cedar	*Juniperus virginiana*	Cupressaceae
European beech	*Fagus sylvatica*	Fagaceae
European white water lily	*Nymphaea alba*	Nymphaeaceae
evening primrose	*Oenothera* spp.	Onagraceae

forget-me-not	*Myosotis* spp.	Boraginaceae
four-o'clock	*Mirabilis jalapa*	Nyctaginaceae
fry wood tree	*Albizia lebbek*	Leguminosae
gravel root	*Eupatorium purpureum*	Compositae
incense cedar	*Libocedrus decurrens*	Cupressaceae
iris	*Iris* spp.	Iridaceae
kiss-me-at-the-garden-gate	*Viola tricolor*	Violaceae
kiss-me-Dick	*Euphorbia cyparissias*	Euphorbiaceae
laurel	*Laurus nobilis*	Lauraceae
lettuce	*Lactuca sativa*	Compositae
love-in-idleness	*Viola tricolor*	Violaceae
lungwort	*Pulmonaria officinalis*	Boraginaceae
mandrake	*Mandragora officinarum*	Solanaceae
maple	*Acer* spp.	Aceraceae
marsh mallow	*Althaea officinalis*	Malvaceae
marsh marigold	*Caltha palustris*	Ranunculaceae
morning-glory	*Ipomoea purpurea*	Convolvulaceae
mountain laurel	*Kalmia latifolia*	Ericaceae
night-blooming cereus	*Hylocereus undatus*	Cactaceae
oak	*Quercus* spp.	Fagaceae
pilewort	*Ranunculus ficaria*	Ranunculaceae
primrose	*Primula* spp.	Primulaceae
sandbur	*Cenchrus* spp.	Gramineae
sea grape	*Coccoloba uvifera*	Polygonaceae
skunk cabbage	*Symplocarpus foetidus*	Araceae
Spanish cedar	*Cedrela* spp.	Meliaceae
spring beauty	*Claytonia virginica*	Caryophyllaceae
stinkhorn	*Phallus impudicus*	Phallaceae
sunflower	*Helianthus annuus*	Compositae
touch-me-not	*Impatiens biflora*	Balsaminaceae
violet	*Viola* spp.	Violaceae
viper's bugloss	*Echium vulgare*	Boraginaceae
wallflower	*Cheiranthus cheiri*	Cruciferae
water hyacinth	*Eichhornia crassipes*	Pontederiaceae
welcome-home-husband-though-never-so-drunk	{ *Euphorbia cyparissias* or *Sedum acre*	Euphorbiaceae Crassulaceae
western red cedar	*Thuja plicata*	Cupressaceae
white beech	*Gmelina* sp.	Verbenaceae
widow's tears	*Tradescantia* spp.	Commelinaceae
wormwood	*Artemisia absinthium*	Compositae
yellow chrysanthemum	*Buphthalmum salicifolium*	Compositae

Linnaeus honored on a Swedish
fifty-kroner bill.

4

Linnaeus

Prince of Botanists

The Enlightenment which engulfed Western Europe after 1750
was slow in reaching Sweden. Its overtures, which began in
England and in the Dutch republic in the seventeenth century,
had left Sweden almost totally untroubled. Not until 1730 did
the Swedish universities at Uppsala and Lund begin to yield to
the forces from abroad. The libertarian teachings of the Enlightenment were carried back to Sweden by those zealous students
who were fortunate enough to study overseas. The divinely
sanctioned monarchy, a privileged state-supported church and
hereditary aristocracy, a legal system which encouraged con-
ventionality at the expense of individuality, and the encouragement of local autonomy and tradition—hallmarks of a built-in
conservatism—were slow to disappear from Sweden. Since the
early 1700s Sweden had been involved in a series of fruitless
wars, and internal political and economic disruption continued
throughout most of the century.

On the Continent and in England there was intellectual ferment in philosophy, politics, literature, art, and science.
France's leading satirist, playwright, and philosopher, François Voltaire, was at the peak of his influence, as was the philosopher and author, Jean Jacques Rousseau. Franz Joseph Haydn,
Johann Sebastian Bach, and Georg Friedrich Händel were revo-
lutionizing music. The deistic philosophers criticized religious
revelation and often argued against a personal god, for they in-
sisted that God revealed Himself in the order of nature rather
than in the words of the Bible. Immanuel Kant was bent on his
crusade against rationalism. The painter, William Hogarth, sa-
tirized on canvas the corruption then rampant in the boroughs
of London and Thomas Gainsborough produced his memorable

portraits and vivid landscapes of the English countryside. Modern chemistry was founded and the properties of oxygen explained by England's Joseph Priestley and France's Antoine Laurent Lavoisier. And James Watt invented the first practical steam engine in 1765. Louis Antoine de Bougainville commanded the first French expedition around the world between 1766 and 1769 and James Cook spent the years between 1768 and 1780 on his unparalleled discoveries in navigation, geography, astronomy, and natural history. Physically isolated from but intellectually immersed in this sea of furor and ferment, Carolus Linnaeus, son of an impecunious Swedish pastor, sought to bring order and sense to the kingdom of nature.

The "Prince" Is Born

Småland is a farming district in the south of Sweden, and it was in the poor town of Råshult (Figure 4.1) that young Nils Ingemarsson Linnaeus became assistant minister of the congregation. In 1705 Nils Linnaeus married the minister's daughter Christina and a son, whom they named Carl after the reigning king, was born on May 22, 1707. Later Carl Linnaeus inscribed at the head of one of his biographical essays, *"Potest e casa vir magnus exire"* (A great man can come forth from a cabin). The great Linnaeus was of course referring to the modest circumstances of his birth in a not so modest manner. He romanticized the season of his birth as, "the fairest time of spring when the cuckoo is heralding summer, between the unfolding of the leaf and the opening of the blossom."

It was in the tiny garden of the minister's home (Nils succeeded his father-in-law as minister) that Nils introduced young Carl to the wonders of plant life. Nils was a remarkably sensitive man, especially when it came to the beauties of nature, and we may suppose that Carl was filled with the excitement of it all by his father. His first toys were said to be flowers. The Latinized name "Linnaeus," which Nils adopted during his years as a theological student, is symbolic of his appreciation of nature and it was chosen from that of the linden tree (*Tilia*) which grew in the farmyard of Nils's father. The Swedish name of the linden is *lind*.

Carl was first educated at his father's side, but when he was seven years old Nils hired a tutor. At ten years of age, Carl was admitted to the elementary school at Växjö. There, according to

Figure 4.1 This humble cabin at Råshult, Sweden, was the birthplace of Carl Linnaeus. [Courtesy Swedish Information Service.]

Linnaeus, "Crude teachers endeavored to instill in the children a liking for the sciences with such crude methods that it made their hair stand on end." Carl subsequently lost interest in formal schooling and in desperation his father once again hired a tutor for his reluctant son. In 1724, at the age of 17, Carl was enrolled in the secondary school at Växjö in a curriculum essentially designed to prepare students for the ministry. His success was uneven in his various subjects: He was among the best students in physics and mathematics and among the poorest in rhetoric, metaphysics, ethics, Greek, Hebrew, and theology. He found botany his most loved subject and managed to acquire a few well-known books about plants. His teachers were aware of his special interest and he was teased as "the little botanist." Nils inquired of Carl's teachers about the progress of his son and his abilities. Discouragingly, Papa Linnaeus was told that his son was not very bright, that he was not suited for higher learning, and that he ought to learn a trade.

One day when Carl's father was visiting the physician Johan Rothman about a medical matter, the conversation turned to Carl's progress at school. Rothman urged Nils not to withdraw his son from school but to allow him to complete the final year. It so happened that Dr. Rothman, besides doctoring, taught natural sciences at the secondary school; he agreed to take a personal interest in young Carl and to help exploit his unusual talents for the natural sciences. Rothman took Carl under his wing and in a fatherly spirit instructed him privately in physiology and botany. This special education was so successful that Carl received a certificate of completion of the school course. Without Rothman's kindly interest and help, Linnaeus might have ended up as a tailor or tinsmith with an uncommon love for flowers.

In 1727, when Linnaeus was 20 years of age, he entered the university at Lund and a year later transferred to the University of Uppsala. At Uppsala, while still a student and under the guidance of Dr. Olof Rudbeck (for whom Linnaeus later named the genus *Rudbeckia*, the black-eyed-Susan), Linnaeus published an enumeration of the plants of the Uppsala Botanical Garden, *Hortus Uplandicus*. In this treatment he followed Tournefort's system, but since the number of plants in the garden soon exceeded the kinds contained in Tournefort's classification, Linnaeus produced a new edition of *Hortus Uplandicus* with a classification of his own making. This was the first time that the sexual system of plants, later refined by Linnaeus, was used.

Lapland Journey

By decree the Royal Society of Sweden had been directed to carry out a research expedition to Lapland, the northernmost of the Swedish provinces. Because of this directive, Linnaeus promptly sought financial support for a trip to Lapland and the opportunity to undertake this potentially rewarding journey. In his proposal of 1731 to the Royal Society he pointed out that Lapland was one of the last frontiers and "now after all Europe and almost the whole world has been investigated as far as natural sciences are concerned, Lapland still lies almost as if shrouded in a state of darkest barbarism." He expressed the hope that in Lapland there would be an unusual opportunity to make significant discoveries in natural history and he explained why he, of all people, would be the best person to make these discoveries. After all, he was a citizen of Sweden, healthy, indefatigable, was unemployed (!), had no wife, and was a naturalist. Linnaeus was successful in his application and on May 12, 1732, he commenced his arduous five-month trek through Lapland. He described himself at departure as having "a short sword hung at my side, and I had a small fowling-piece between my thigh and saddle; I also had a graduated 8-sided rod for taking measurements. In my pocket was a wallet containing my passport from the Governor of Uppsala and a letter of recommendation from the Society. Thus equipped I left Uppsala . . . . I was twenty-five years old, all but about half a day."

During his journeys in Lapland Linnaeus went almost everywhere by foot; he was alone most of the time and traveled 2,500 miles (Figure 4.2). His various comings and goings through icy streams and swampy meadows should have dampened his botanical ardor. He wrote at one point about his exhaustion from great exertions and long trips and "from carrying my own baggage [for the Lapp carried the boat], from sleepless nights, from having no cooked food and from drinking too much water [since there was nothing else to drink and nothing to eat but unsalted and often maggoty fish]." Nevertheless, Linnaeus's enthusiasm with this new world was unbounded and he imagined the small flowers to wave at him in friendship. All of nature seemed personified to him and he delighted in making rough sketches of those plants, animals, and Lapps that met his fancy. Linnaeus returned in October to Uppsala burdened with the booty of his trip, a suit of Lapland dress in which he delighted to strut around Uppsala, and many real and some farfetched tales of adventure. The journey itself produced the *Flora Lapponica* in 1737, a listing of Lapland plants with their descriptions and habitat notes, and the *Iter Lapponicum* (Lapland journey), an account of the travels which was published posthumously.

More important, perhaps, than the published accounts which resulted directly from his trip to Lapland, was the solitude Linnaeus enjoyed—the opportunities he had to examine unadorned nature, to cogitate on the scheme of things. The journey has been described by Edward L. Greene, one of Linnaeus's biographers, as "one of the most fruitful seasons of his whole life, though he was now but twenty-five years of age." Some compare the Lapland visit as a "brooding period" akin to Darwin's five years of searching for the meaning of life while a passenger aboard H.M.S. *Beagle*.

Figure 4.2 Landscape at Aktse, Lapland, as it might have appeared to the young Linnaeus in 1732. [Courtesy Swedish Information Service.]

Achievements in Holland

Linnaeus's education was continued in the Netherlands between 1735 and 1738, a period that was to prove exceedingly important in his life. His main purpose for visiting Holland was to secure a degree in medicine from the university at Harderwijk. The university, though of no great distinction, was a favorite with Swedish students of the eighteenth century for seeking the M.D. Harderwijk must have been the diploma mill of its time, for it was known that the M. D. could be secured relatively rapidly with little expense. For example, the day after his arrival, Linnaeus passed the medical examination and on the very next day the director of the university granted him permission to print his dissertation which he had taken with him, already written, from Sweden. The dissertation was entitled, *Hypothesis nova de febrium intermittentium causa* (A new theory concerning the cause of intermittent fevers). Four days later, on June 12, 1735, little more than ten days after his arrival in Holland, Linnaeus defended his dissertation in formal disputation. The University of Harderwijk was closed by Napoleon in 1818.

After receipt of the M.D., Linnaeus took his manuscript of *Systema Naturae* (System of nature) and visited Dr. Johann Friedrich Gronovius, physician and botanist at Leiden in the Netherlands. Gronovius was a man of considerable personal wealth whom Linnaeus described as, "the most intellectually inquisitive Dutchman" he had ever met. Gronovius was so favorably impressed with Linnaeus, that he offered to publish Linnaeus's manuscript immediately. Thus Gronovius must be credited with having recognized the potentially epoch-making character of this work which provided a foundation for the classification of all plants, animals, and minerals. The manuscript, expanded in a few places, was given to the printer on June 20, 1735; it appeared at the end of the year in Latin on only 14 crowded pages in giant folio. Today only 29 copies of the first edition are known to exist.

Systema Naturae: *The Realms of Nature*

The sexual system of plants, which was introduced in full to the learned world in *Systema Naturae*, provided a simple but ingenious arithmetical method of arranging plants. There were 24 major groups arranged according to the number of stamens (so-called male floral parts), their relative lengths, their distinction or fusion with each other, or their absence. Thus groups were called Monandria (Greek: *monos*, "one"; *andros*, "man" or "male"; i.e., "one stamen"), Diandria ("two stamens"), Triandria ("three stamens"), and so on. Within each of the major groups, subordinate units were based on the number of carpels (so-called female floral parts): Monogynia (Greek: *gyne*, "woman" or "female"; i.e., "one carpel"), Digynia ("two car-

pels"), Trigynia ("three carpels"). Only a simple knowledge of
floral structure and a good eye were necessary to place an unknown plant into one of Linnaeus's groups and to find its
name.

Linnaeus's sexual system, or as he called it, *"Nuptiae plantarum"* ("marriages of plants"), was written in metaphorical
form and the phraseology of its lines falls quaintly on our modern ears: "Husband and wife have the same bed," "husband
and wife have different beds," "husbands related to each
other," "five husbands in the same marriage," "husbands live
with wives and concubines," and "equal polygamy, consists of
many marriages with promiscuous intercourse"! Small wonder
that there was some tongue-wagging and head-shaking about
Doctor Linnaeus's licentious method. Even Erasmus Darwin,
Charles's grandfather, in his "The loves of the plants," con-
torted Linnaeus's system into fanciful verse:

Three blushing maids the intrepid nymph attend,
and *six* gay youths, enamour'd train! defend.

and

Thy love, Callitriche, *two* Virgins share,
Smit with thy starry eye and radiant hair.

and

Two brother swains, of Collin's gentle name,
The same their features, and their forms the same.

Really!

Still, as botanist Leon Croizat has written, Linnaeus's system
had "an instantaneous and enormous appeal to the mind of the
public. . . . By a bold stroke of the pen the nebulous world of
plants was made to act like husbands and wives in unconcerned
freedom, and everybody was prepared to grasp the meaning . . . without effort. The educational value of [Linnaeus's sys-
tem] . . . was tremendous, for it dispensed with musty tomes,
learned verbiage, pompous trappings, and the like, to appeal
directly to the flowers in the field." Linnaeus was one of the
very first popularizers of nature. "Very few works may compete
with the *Systema naturae* in purposefulness and power of well-
meant vulgarization."

In August 1735 Linnaeus met George Clifford, a director of
the Dutch East India Company and one of the very wealthy men

of Europe. Clifford, a hypochondriac, hired Linnaeus to serve as his personal physician and also to identify all the plants growing on his vast estate at the Hartekamp, situated not far from Leiden and Haarlem. Linnaeus had his first opportunity here to see the splendor of tropical plants. He reported that he was treated "like a prince," was loved "like a son of the house," and "had everything that he could wish for, lodgings than which none more magnificent could be imagined, splendid gardens and greenhouses, a complete botanical library." What could be better? The two years Linnaeus spent at the Hartekamp were probably the most comfortable and carefree of his whole life. Not only was Linnaeus treated regally, but Clifford put at Linnaeus's disposal sufficient funds to enlarge the botanical garden with new plants and to procure books for the library.

During the summer of 1736, Linnaeus traveled to England under the financial sponsorship of Clifford. He visited the botanical gardens in Chelsea and at the University of Oxford; he met the famous and renowned of the botanical world in England. Nor did he neglect to tramp the English countryside. Oscar Wilde, Irish wit and dramatist, envisioned that Linnaeus "fell on his knees and wept with joy when he saw for the first time the long heath of some English upland made yellow with the tawny aromatic blossoms of the common furze [*Ulex*, a spiny shrub also called gorse]."

Books published during Linnaeus's sojourn at the Hartekamp between 1735 and 1737 included *Fundamenta Botanica* (Foundations of botany; an ingenious book of 12 chapters in which the science of botany is reduced to 365 aphorisms), *Bibliotheca Botanica* (The botanical library; a compilation of 1,000 botanical books by almost as many authors), *Genera Plantarum* (Genera of plants), *Critica Botanica* (Rules for botanical naming), and *Flora Lapponica* (Flora of Lapland). *Hortus Cliffortianus* (Clifford's garden), a splendid, richly illustrated catalogue, appeared in 1738 (Figures 4.3 and 4.4).

In October 1737, at 30 years of age, having published 12 major books and received the M. D. degree, Linnaeus left the gilded halls of the Hartekamp. He spent the winter in Leiden moving on equal terms in the professional circles of one of Europe's most respected educational institutions, the University of Leiden. While there he helped in the rearrangement of the botanical garden and gave assistance to Professor Gronovius in his preparation of the *Flora Virginica*. Early in 1738 Linnaeus could no longer postpone his return to Sweden. No other period

Figure 4.3   Title page of Linnaeus's *Hortus Cliffortianus.*

Figure 4.4 Frontispiece of *Hortus Cliffortianus* showing the crowned goddess, Mother Earth, with the keys to Nature's realms in her right hand, and a wreathed bust, probably of Linnaeus's mentor, Clifford.

in Linnaeus's life was as productive of botanical work as the three years spent in Holland.

During the Holland years, Linnaeus did not learn to speak Dutch. Although he was president of a select organization of Dutch scientists, and a lecturer on many occasions, he consistently delivered his talks in Latin—the language then well understood and used professionally by all academically educated people. Even in his autobiographical notes Linnaeus comments about his lack of talent in languages and he himself thought it remarkable that he did not learn English, German, or French. "Time is never so dearly bought as when people go abroad for the sake of languages only," Linnaeus wrote.

Physician in Stockholm

After his return to Sweden, he traveled to Falun and later married his fiancée of four years, Sara Elisabeth Moraea. Linnaeus, now a married man, needed a ready source of income with which to set up a household and begin the next stage of his career, so, he established a medical practice in Stockholm as the quickest means to these ends. "Stockholm received Linnaeus in the month of September 1738 like an outsider. He had the intention of earning his living there as a physician. Since, however, he was unknown to everyone at that time, there was no one who would entrust his precious life to the hands of an untried doctor nor indeed even that of his dog." Actually, Linnaeus had no intention of spending the rest of his life ministering to other people's aches and pains and he confided to a Swiss friend, "Should I come to Uppsala I will completely renounce medical practice and devote myself exclusively to plants." But Linnaeus made significant personal associations in Stockholm which were to be of great importance for his future.

Generally speaking, no doctor in Linnaeus's times could make a decent living from an independent medical practice and physicians sought, therefore, some official affiliation with the court or municipality. But he could not wait for this eventuality and, after a period, he seems to have become a very popular physician. One biographer of Linnaeus describes his method of rapidly gaining a medical practice:

When he saw no way to acquire a medical practice, he began to frequent popular restaurants where young cavaliers who had been wounded *in castris Veneris* [in the pursuit of Venus] sat about. He encouraged them to be of good cheer, to have a glass of Rhine wine, and gave assurances that he would cure them in two weeks. When finally two who had hitherto been treated unsuccessfully placed their lives in his hands and were promptly cured, he had within one month most of the young people under his care. Through this his credit began to rise so that by early March he had a most respectable practice due to the prevailing pox and fevers.

Thus young Dr. Linnaeus became a specialist in the treatment of venereal diseases as a means of opening a successful and lucrative medical practice.

In 1739 Linnaeus was appointed medical officer to the admiralty for the naval base at Stockholm with a salary of 200 silver talers a year. The hospital, attached to the naval base at Stockholm, had between 100 and 200 sick, among whom were quite a number suffering from the "French evil" and who were kept isolated in special rooms. Linnaeus was very proud of his accomplishments during his first year as a physician in Stockholm, at the age of 32. As he wrote in his autobiography, "Within a single month Linnaeus becomes public lecturer at the Knights' Hall with a stipend, physician to the admiralty with a salary and first president of the Academy." He remained in Stockholm until 1741 when he was called to the University of Uppsala to become professor of theoretical and practical medicine. In 1747 he was given the rank and title of archiater (chief physician) by the king and in 1762 was elevated to the nobility and entitled to use the appellation, von Linné.

Professor at Uppsala

At Uppsala Linnaeus taught botany, symptomology, dietetics, materia medica, and natural science; he was also in charge of the Botanical Garden. He gave up general medical practice, although he did continue to treat friends and occasionally the poor. Giving up his medical practice in Stockholm caused him no grief and he wrote, "By the grace of God I am now freed from the miserable drudgery of that practice in Stockholm; I now hold the position that I have long hoped for." Linnaeus—as might be imagined—went on to rearrange the Botanical Garden, and in 1742 he applied to the university for funds to build an orangery (a greenhouse, originally for growing orange trees)

Figure 4.5 Linnaeus's original garden at Uppsala with his orangery in the background as it looks today. [Courtesy Swedish Information Service.]

so that he could raise tropical plants (Figures 4.5 and 4.6). He was successful and a year later the building was ready to receive tropical plants.

Linnaeus was a very successful teacher (23 of his pupils became professors) and his field trips into the country were eagerly anticipated and well attended by his students. They were gay outings and well disciplined. Benjamin D. Jackson, Linnean specialist, wrote that Linnaeus was always at the head of the troop followed by an "Annotator" or secretary to take his dictation as directed. Another of the students was designated "Fiscal" and his job was to maintain discipline among members of the assemblage. Others were marksmen to shoot birds for specimens. When the foray was over, the group marched back to town with Linnaeus leading like a general. French horns and kettle drums accompanied the singing and banners flew in the breeze. At the Botanical Garden, following shouts of *"Vivat Linnaeus,"* the day's enjoyment was closed. After about 20 years, however, his popularity as a teacher waned considerably; he no longer continued to attract the number and quality of students as he had before.

During the years 1747, 1759, and 1772, Linnaeus served as rector of the university, but he continued his teaching schedule unabated except for his later years. In a letter to the Austrian botanist Nikolaus Joseph von Jacquin, he described his usual daily routine:

Every day I give a one-hour public lecture, then I hold a kind of private seminar with a number of students. After

Figure 4.6 An ornamental onion in Linnaeus's garden at Uppsala. [Courtesy James W. Walker.]

that I spend one hour with Danish students and two with Russians. And so, having talked for five hours before lunch, in the afternoon I read proof, write manuscripts for the printers and letters to my botanical friends, visit the garden and see those who come to visit me; I also look after my bit of land, and this means that on many days I barely have time to eat. If you saw me you would certainly pity my lot, for here am I, surrounded by a large family, and yet I must make time to visit with both my compatriots and foreigners arriving here. While my colleagues can constantly enjoy the amenities of life, I have to work day and night on the investigation of a science that a thousand men will not be able to complete, to say nothing of the time I squander every day on scientific correspondence and so bring upon myself a premature old age. If the Almighty grants me a few more years I will release the aging horse from the yoke so that he will not entirely collapse and end up being a laughing stock. If then I succeed in having my garden and a few rare plants, I shall rejoice in them.

But Linnaeus really seemed to enjoy his busy life, even though the passage above shows him as a man who could feel sorry for himself and indulge in a bit of self-pity.

Species Plantarum: *Cornerstone of Botany*

The *Species Plantarum* (Species of plants) did not arise full-blown in the mind of Linnaeus, rather genesis took place only after years of reflection and experience. Many of the events in Linnaeus's early career prepared the way for final crystallization of the work: identification of his Lapland plant collections, writing *Hortus Cliffortianus* from living plants on Clifford's estate and access to Clifford's fine library, helping Gronovius with his *Flora Virginica*, preparation of his own *Flora Zeylanica* (Flora of Ceylon). Linnaeus estimated that by 1736 he had probably a firsthand acquaintance with some 8,000 plants, more than any other person of his time. *Genera Plantarum*, first published in 1737, had established a satisfactory generic framework. It now remained for Linnaeus "to achieve his mission of recording the works of the Creator by publishing an orderly survey of the species according to the principles expounded in his *Critica Botanica* (1736)," the work in which he outlined the rules and methods for naming plants.

Origin of the binomial system as used by Linnaeus appears

almost to have been an accident. It started out as an indexer's shorthand. In 1741 Linnaeus journeyed through to the Baltic islands of Öland and Gotland under the auspices of the state, assigned to record the natural resources of these places. He was to prepare a report of findings upon his return. Plants (and animals) were described in the text using phrase-names—*Pyrola scapo unifloro, Pyrola racemis unilateralibus, Pyrola staminibus adscendentibus pistilis declinatis, Pyrola floribus undique racemosis*—as had been the custom. These names, however, do not appear in the index in this fashion. Rather, names such as *Pyrola irregularis, Pyrola secundiflora, Pyrola umbellata*, and *Pyrola uniflora* appear, each standing for one of the phrase-names in the text. The report of his observations on these islands appeared in 1745 in Swedish as *Öländska och Gothländska Resa* (Journey to Öland and Gotland). Another important first in this work is that Linnaeus lists the plants as they grew, by habitat, ecologically rather than taxonomically. William T. Stearn, Linnean scholar, remarks, "The journey described was undertaken primarily as an economic survey, in accordance with the spirit of the times in Sweden during the 'Age of Liberty'; the exigencies of indexing led him to devise a nomenclature suitable to it. Thus his binomial system arose from the impact of everyday life upon an academic problem."

From 1745 on Linnaeus tried out his new system in several works, meanwhile seeking to perfect it. The first edition of *Species Plantarum* appeared in 1753 and in it the binomial system of nomenclature, first used as a convenience in 1745, was consistently applied to the names of all plants. This is not to say that everyone at the time embraced binomial nomenclature. In England, for example, the method was at first coldly received, "Men versed in the classification and nomenclature of the learned, modest and revered John Ray saw no advantage in discarding them for Linnaeus's untried system." Significantly, by 1830, whereas Linnaeus's sexual system had outlived its usefulness and domination of world botany, the binomial method in the *Species Plantarum* was firmly anchored and remains the keystone of nomenclature of both plants and animals. In botany this work and the date 1753 are the bases for establishing priority of publication for names; the starting point for animal names stems from the tenth edition of Linnaeus's *Systema Naturae* of 1758.

The purpose of *Species Plantarum* was to provide a practical survey of all plants known at the time of Linnaeus together with

Figure 4.7 Hammarby, Linnaeus's country home near Uppsala. [Courtesy Swedish Information Service.]

references to earlier literature, brief descriptions of the plants, and notes on their geographical range. Linnaeus did not write the work to introduce the binomial system to the world; this was only an incidental, though highly significant, by-product. *Species Plantarum* contains descriptions with nomenclatural synonymies of 5,900 plants arranged according to the sexual system of classification. In this single work Linnaeus succeeded in returning plant nomenclature to the simplicity, brevity, and usefulness of vernacular names, while at the same time he introduced order and uniformity to the application of names.

Mature Years

In 1758 Linnaeus acquired his country estate at Hammarby (Figure 4.7), situated six miles from Uppsala. He enlarged the buildings in 1762 "when he noticed that he was weak and wished his children to have shelter." Linnaeus spent his summers at Hammarby and gave private instruction there to visitors from abroad. A garden was laid out with foreign plants, many of them from Siberia. On a hill behind the manor house Linnaeus had a small stone structure built for storing his collections. He had decided to build this "museum on the hill" after his valuable collections in Uppsala had only barely been rescued from a fire (Figure 4.8). In 1780 Linnaeus's country estate was acquired by the Swedish government, and today it is a Linnaeus memorial where many mementos gathered by the

Figure 4.8 "Museum on the hill" at Hammarby, built by Linnaeus for the safekeeping of his precious collections. [Courtesy James W. Walker.]

Figure 4.9 Library desk from which Linnaeus lectured when in residence at Hammarby. [Courtesy Swedish Information Service.]

Swedish Linnaean Society are exhibited (Figure 4.9). The main residence has been extensively restored to its state during Linnaeus's lifetime. A visit allows one to set the clock back 200 years and to picture the great naturalist there with his family and students.

When Linnaeus acquired Hammarby he was the father of an imposing family. Of seven children, five survived. The first child was born in 1741 and was named for his father. The numerous descendants of Linnaeus in Sweden today are the offspring of daughters Sophia and Elisabeth Christina.

Twilight

Throughout his lifetime Linnaeus was frequently ill and indisposed. He suffered from migraine and begged his medical correspondents for advice from their own experience. During one period of his life he complained of excruciating pains and sleepless nights owing to attacks of "sciatic gout." These were alleviated, finally, by eating great quantities of fresh wild strawberries. But Linnaeus's attacks did not always coincide with the fruiting season of the strawberry, and during certain seasons he simply suffered on. The queen, learning of Linnaeus's predicament, ordered wild strawberries to be grown in the royal hothouses exclusively for his use. It is said that the demand for strawberries forced their price to ten times normal when the news of Linnaeus's use of this remarkable medication became known.

In 1764 Linnaeus came down with a feverish illness which cannot now be diagnosed with certainty but it appears to have been paratyphus or influenza. It must have been serious, however, for Linnaeus wrote that he was close to death. Surprisingly, the tough old man outlived the two doctors who treated him during this illness.

The closer Linnaeus came to the last decade of his life, the more frequent and debilitating were his illnesses. A stroke in 1774, which he described as a first "message of death," resulted in paralysis which gradually, though only partially, subsided. A painting by Linnaeus's contemporary, Alexander Roslin, shows how he looked in 1775 (Figure 4.10). In 1776 a second stroke came and this was to be the last year of his autobiographical notes. He wrote of the results of this seizure, "Linnaeus limps, and hardly walks, speaks indistinctly, can scarcely write." The last summer of his life, that of 1777, was spent at his beloved Hammarby where, when weather permitted, he would have himself taken into the garden or up to his little museum on the hill where he could enjoy the sight of all the precious things he had brought together during his immensely productive life. Autumn that year brought with it a rapid decline in his mental and physical condition. Semiconsciousness ensued and his phenomenal memory lapsed so that he did not even know his own name at the end. Linnaeus died in early January 1778. His ashes lie under a flat stone near the entryway to the cathedral in Stockholm. Nearby, according to his instructions, is a bronze medallion inscribed with his name, the dates of his birth and death, and the words, *"Princeps Botanicorum"* (Prince of Botanists).

Figure 4.10   Linnaeus at age 68. The original painting was executed by Alexander Roslin and it now hangs in the Swedish National Gallery, Stockholm. [Courtesy Swedish Information Service.]

Contributions

As Charles Darwin was to dominate nineteenth-century biology, Linnaeus was preceptor of eighteenth-century biology. Linnaeus had enormous self-confidence and a prodigious ego. After all, singlehandedly he had created order where formerly chaos had reigned. *Deus creavit, Linnaeus disposuit* (God creates, Linnaeus arranges). He sent his student-disciples to the far corners of the earth on hazardous expeditions to bring or send back the botanical bounty for the master to study. Five of his apostles never returned, having been lost in the performance of the master's directives.

Linnaeus himself possessed great tenacity and single-mindedness of purpose. He was an intuitive organizer whose sights were clearly set on the job to be done. This intensely focused concentration accounts for his enormous output. His major books number 87 and there are seemingly innumerable shorter and less important works, dissertations, poems, and scholarly articles. Commenting on Linnaeus's prolificacy, Wilfrid Blunt has remarked that Linnaeus, like John Ruskin (1819–1900), wrote a book when he wanted to learn about a subject. Linnaeus named 7,700 species of plants and was said to have had an incomparable memory. His reaction to the stimuli of nature was both emotional and personal.

As a man Linnaeus was a paradox: He showed humility before God on the one hand, and (sometimes) arrogance before his contemporaries and peers on the other. His contributions to natural history are legion. Those achievements of special botanical significance are:

1. He founded the binomial system of nomenclature as we know and use it today.
2. He established a successful and popular system of classification.
3. He named and described all plants known up to 1753.
4. He instituted clear terminology for plant description.
5. He provided rules and regulations for naming plants.

Linnaeus was the great botanical encyclopedist.

Linnaeus's influence extended beyond the boundaries of botany. Both Jean Jacques Rousseau and Johann Wolfgang von Goethe (1749–1832) acknowledged their indebtedness to Linnaeus, particularly to concepts expressed in his *Philosophia Botanica*. Goethe acknowledged late in life that "with the exception of Shakespeare and Spinoza, I do not know anyone [other than Linnaeus] among those no longer living who has so strongly influenced me." This is exceptional tribute from one as learned as the immortal Goethe.

The main body of Linnaeus's personal plant collections and manuscripts, as well as his collections of dried fishes, insects, shells, botanical and zoological libraries, were sold by his widow in 1784 to James E. Smith of England. They were subsequently purchased from Smith's widow in 1829 by the Linnean Society of London and now reside in air-conditioned splendor in Burlington House, Piccadilly, London, where they may still be consulted.

Suggested Readings

Blunt, Wilfrid. *The Compleat Naturalist: A Life of Linnaeus.* New York: Viking, 1971. A charmingly written, profusely illustrated account of the major events in and persons affecting the life and work of Linnaeus; nontechnical; an appendix by William T. Stearn lists Linnaeus's important publications and analyzes his contributions to natural history.

Goerke, Heinz. *Linnaeus.* New York: Scribner's, 1973. The author is a medical historian and there is a chapter on Linnaeus as a practicing physician.

Stafleu, Frans A. *Linnaeus and the Linnaeans: The Spreading of Their Ideas in Systematic Botany, 1735–1789.* Utrecht: A. Oosthoek's Uitgeversmaatschappij N.V., 1971. Botanical lives, travels, and contributions of Linnaeus's student disciples.

Stearn, William Thomas. "An Introduction to the *Species Plantarum* and Cognate Botanical Works of Carl Linnaeus" in *Carl Linnaeus Species Plantarum: A Facsimile of the First Edition 1753.* London: The Ray Society, 1957, pp. xiv–176. A scholarly analysis of the contributions of Linnaeus.

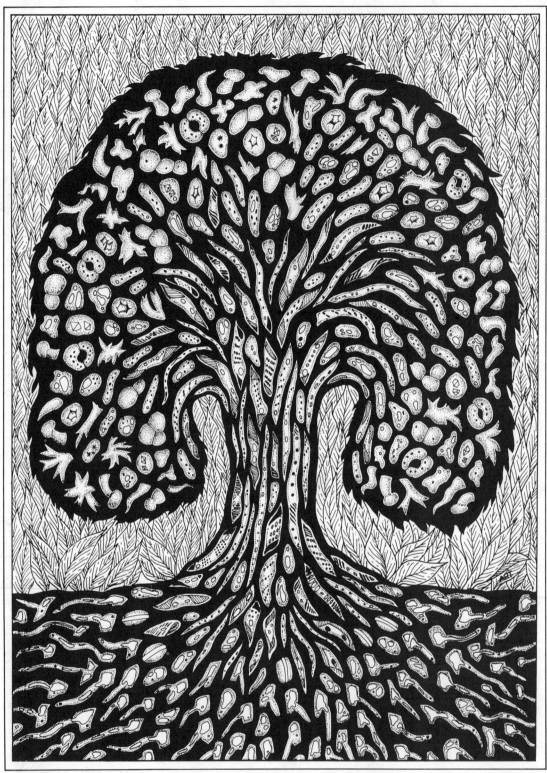

Cells, basic structural units of the plant
body.

5
The Cell
Unit of Life

Any understanding of the processes of life must necessarily be grounded in an understanding of the cell, for all of life, in the final analysis, begins as a cell. Appreciation of the mechanisms and modes of cell division, cell structure, cell chemistry, and cell physics underlie any real comprehension of the processes of growth, inheritance, reproduction, and disease. And the form and style of each kind of organism is set by the structure and arrangement of the cells of which it is made. Time and time again, even the popular press refers to matters of social, medical, and moral concern in which knowledge of the cell is central to understanding and judgment: planned inheritance or genetic engineering, inherited disease, chromosomal aberrations, DNA, artificial implantation of human sperm, sperm banks, congenital drug addiction, and such cellular abnormalities as benign overgrowths and malignant or cancerous tumors.

As intelligent, concerned citizens it is our responsibility to influence deliberations in legislatures which affect our social welfare and which will affect the social welfare of our children and our fellow citizens. We should attempt to persuade our legislators from the vantage point of strength founded on personal knowledge rather than from the weakness of ignorance and hearsay. With the growing expertise of scientists and medical practitioners, new potentials for cellular manipulation are being explored and it is already theoretically possible, through a combination of sperm implantation and detailed knowledge of the hereditary make-up of parents, to engineer a human organism with particular characteristics or traits. It has been possible for years to breed animals with desired characteristics, and plants with specific properties can be developed with considerable accuracy.

You might ask at this point, but what does a knowledge of the plant cell have to do with the possibility of genetic engineering in human beings, or with cancer, or with chromosomal aberrations, or genetic disease? Most of the fundamental properties of cells in plants and in animals are exactly the same. Our task then is to tell you something about cells and their position in the life of the plant and to provide you with an outline at least for understanding cellular behavior. To accomplish much more than this would require that you have an understanding of biochemistry and biophysics.

Finding the Cell

Cells are the structural units of plants and animals and, as already noted in Chapter 1, all living things are composed of cells; they are one of the characteristics of life. In the main, cells are tiny and cannot be seen without considerable magnification. Thus the discovery of the cell had to await the invention of a proper instrument, namely, the **microscope.** Credit for the invention of the microscope is given to several lens-grinders, in different countries, and at somewhat different times. But it is agreed that the microscope was developed during the waning years of the sixteenth century, apparently first by the Dutch spectacle makers, Hans and Zacharias Janssen. It is thought that the invention was accidental, that Hans and his son Zacharias fortuitously placed two lenses in proper relative positions in a tube so that the device acted as a true compound microscope. An excellent account of the long and fascinating history of the microscope—from glass lenses full of built-in aberrations to the modern electron microscope—is given in the book by S. Bradbury listed in the Suggested Readings at the end of the chapter.

For many years the microscope was the plaything of the wealthy and leisured classes: As a diversion following dinner, a host might entertain and amuse his guests in the salon with a newly purchased microscope. These were often highly ornamented and filigreed, more admired for their curlicues than for the curious images produced by their lenses. It was not until the second half of the seventeenth century that serious work with the microscope began; soon there were recorded observations in writing and illustrations, although the frivolities in the salons continued.

Among the pioneer microscopists was the inimitable draper of Delft, Antony van Leeuwenhoek (1632–1723), who communicated his observations by letter to the prestigious Royal Society in London. These letters, written in old-fashioned Dutch, appeared as a series of 112 articles (over a 50-year period, 1673–1723) in the *Philosophical Transactions of the Royal Society*, a scholarly journal which is still being published today. It was this talented Dutchman who, with his tiny homemade microscopes (Figure 5.1), revealed to the world for the first time the teeming minutiae of single-celled life which exists in droplets of water and who first described what we now know are bacteria and protozoa. Clifford Dobell has written a charming story about the life, times, and works of Leeuwenhoek and his book, listed at the end of this chapter, we commend for pleasurable reading.

Robert Hooke *and* Micrographia

More important to our present discussion is Robert Hooke (1635–1703), English experimental philosopher, physicist, and mathematician, discoverer and namer of the cell. Hooke was a genius who even as a child displayed his intellectual gifts by mastering six of Euclid's mathematical treatises in one week. He taught himself to play the organ and learned Greek, Latin, some Hebrew, and several other Oriental languages. He was graduated M.A. from Christ Church College, Oxford, in 1663.

In 1662, Hooke was invited to join the newly formed Royal Society and was appointed curator of experiments. A year later, at age 28, he was elected a fellow. Today, by the time scholars are elected fellows of the Royal Society, they are usually doddering graybeards, hardly able to enjoy the honors and perquisites of fellowship in the time left to them on earth.

Hooke was apparently a bundle of energy, performing his own experiments in physics and mathematics, preparing demonstrations for other fellows (part of his duties as curator), examining all manner of things with his microscope, and tending to his academic responsibilities as professor of geometry at Gresham College where he read astronomical lectures in 1664 and 1665. In 1677 he shared the secretaryship of the Royal Society with his contemporary Nehemiah Grew. Hooke was made a doctor of physic in 1691, probably an equivalent of today's honorary doctoral degree. His later years were marred by exceedingly poor health, culminating in blindness. He became

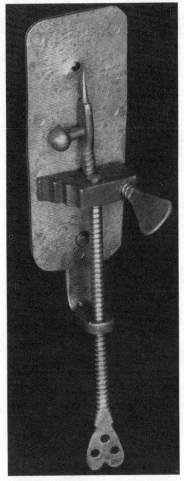

Figure 5.1 Replica of one of Leeuwenhoek's tiny microscopes. This one is about three inches long. The lens is visible at the top of the picture near the pointed specimen holder.

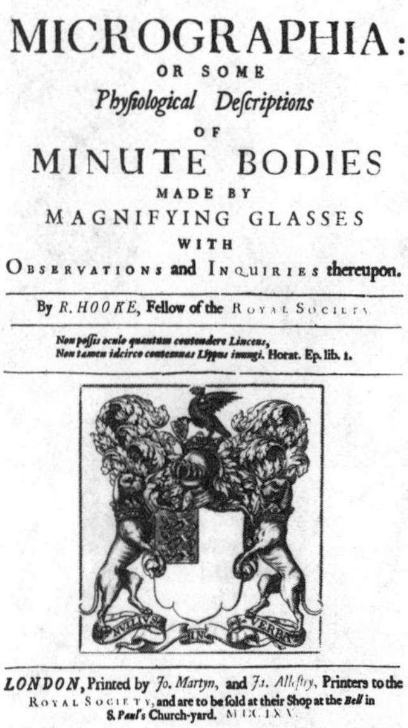

MICROGRAPHIA:

OR SOME

Physiological Descriptions

OF

MINUTE BODIES

MADE BY

MAGNIFYING GLASSES

WITH

OBSERVATIONS and INQUIRIES thereupon.

By R. HOOKE, Fellow of the ROYAL SOCIETY.

Non possis oculo quantum contendere Linceus,
Non tamen idcirco contemnas Lippus inungi. Horat. Ep. lib. 1.

LONDON, Printed by Jo. Martyn, and Ja. Allestry, Printers to the
ROYAL SOCIETY, and are to be sold at their Shop at the Bell in
S. Paul's Church-yard. M DC LXV.

Figure 5.2 Title page from Hooke's 1665 *Micrographia*. [Courtesy National Library of Medicine.]

quarrelsome and jealous and it is said that his vibrant spirit was warped by consuming illnesses.

In 1665 Hooke published an extensive summary of his observations with the microscope under the auspices of the Royal Society. It is known by the ponderous title, *Micrographia: or Some Physiological descriptions of Minute Bodies made by Magnifying Glasses, with Observations and Inquiries Thereupon* (Figure 5.2). The title is usually abbreviated, *Micrographia* and as such it constitutes one of the great classics of biology. In words and pictures Hooke detailed his methods, his specimens, his instruments (Figure 5.3), and his observations, culminating for our present purposes, in his delineation of the cell.

Hooke's drawings are exquisite and some would rank today with the very finest of scientific illustration. Everything conceivable came within the scope of his insatiable curiosity and we find such quaintly titled chapters as "Of the Point of a sharp small Needle," "Of the Edge of a Razor," "Of the fiery Sparks struck from a Flint or Steel," "Of an Ant or Pismire," "Of the curious texture of Sea-weeds," "Of a Louse," "Of the beard of a wilde Oate," and "Of gravel in Urine." All told, there are 60 of these observations or chapters.

Of greatest historical interest to biologists is Hooke's "Observ. XVIII. Of the Schematisme or Texture of Cork, and of the Cells and Pores of some other such frothy bodies." It is in this momentous Observation that the cell is first described and drawn (from the tissue of cork). For your enjoyment, read aloud the words of this seventeenth-century savant while you ponder the diligence, persistence, and tolerated frustrations that must have been required, because of what would be considered today a dim light source, a primitive cutting instrument, and most importantly, horrible lens aberrations for which there was then no remedy:

I took a good clear piece of Cork, and with a Pen-knife sharpen'd as keen as a Razor, I cut a piece of it off, and thereby left the surface of it exceeding smooth, then examining it very diligently with a *Microscope*, me thought I could perceive it to appear a little porous; but I could not so plainly distinguish them, as to be sure that they were pores, much less what Figure they were of: But judging from the lightness and yielding quality of the Cork, that certainly the texture could not be so curious, but that possibly, if I could use some further diligence, I might find it to be discernable with a *Microscope*, I with the same sharp Pen-knife, cut off from the former smooth surface an exceeding thin piece of it, and placing it on a black object Plate, because it was it self a white body, and casting the light on it with a deep *plano-convex Glass*, I could exceeding plainly perceive it to be all perforated and porous, much like a Honey-comb in these particulars. . . .

Next in that these pores, or cells, were not very deep, but consisted of a great many little Boxes, separated out of one continued long pore, by certain *Diaphragms*. . . .

I no sooner discern'd these (which were indeed the first *microscopical* pores I ever saw, and perhaps, that were ever seen, for I had not met with any Writer or Person, that had made any mention of them before this) but me thought I had with the discovery of them, presently hinted to me the true and intelligible reason of all the *Phaenomena* of Cork. . . .

[The mathematician in Hooke now comes to the fore: He is curious about the number and size of these bodies.] I told [counted] several lines of these pores, and found that there were usually about threescore of these small Cells placed end-ways in the eighteenth part of an Inch in length, whence I concluded there must be neer eleven hundred of them, or somewhat more than a thousand in the length of an inch, and therefore in a square Inch about a Million, or 1166400. and in a Cubick Inch, about twelve hundred Millions, or 1259712000. a thing almost incredible, did not our *Microscope* assure us of it by ocular demonstrations. . . .

Nor is this kind of Texture peculiar to Cork onely; for upon examination with my *Microscope*, I have found that the pith of an Elder, or almost any other Tree, the inner pulp or pith of the Cany hollow stalks of several other Vegetables: as of Fennel, Carrets, Daucus, Bur-docks, Teasels, Fearn, some kinds of Reeds, *&c.* have much such a kind of *Schematisme*, as I have lately shewn that of Cork. . . .

But though I could not with my *Microscope*, nor with my breath, not any other way I have yet try'd, discover a passage out of one of those cavities into another, yet I cannot thence conclude, that therefore there are none such, by which the *Succus nutritius* [nutritive juice], or appropriate juices of Vegetables, may pass through them; for, in several of those Vegetables, whil'st green, I have with my *Microscope*, plainly enough discover'd these Cells or Poles [*sic*] fill'd with juices, and by degrees sweating them out: as I

Figure 5.3 One of Hooke's several microscopes. It was manufactured in London by Christopher Cock but was designed and used by Hooke. Presently it is in The Billings Microscope Collection of the Medical Museum, Armed Forces Institute of Pathology, Washington, D.C. [Courtesy Armed Forces Institute of Pathology.]

have also observed in green Wood all those long *Microscopical* pores which appear in Charcoal perfectly empty of anything but Air.

Hooke tells us in these passages of several characteristics of cells which can be summarized as follows:

1. Cells are small and are revealed only with the use of a microscope.
2. They are boxlike and appear as though partitioned from a larger structure by "Diaphragms."
3. They occur in great numbers in the materials at which he looked.
4. They are the common property of all the plants he examined.
5. They do not appear to have communication with each other.
6. Fresh cells from green plants are filled with juices and cells from burned wood (charcoal) are filled with air.

Although by today's standards there are several misconceptions here, nevertheless, the essential form of the cell and its ubiquitousness in plants (at least) are clearly stated. Also Hooke foresaw the presence of protoplasm and cell sap in his "juices of Vegetables" and realized that these were only present in green, fresh plant parts. He attributed to plants a *Succus nutritius*, a nutritive juice, which he seems to have realized was a product of the living organism. Even though he was unable to demonstrate how the nutritive juice was transported from cell to cell, nevertheless, he discounted the absence of some means of passage just because he could not see these means. He understood the limitations of his instruments. There is no doubt of Hooke's skill as an observer nor of his veracity in faithfully recording what he saw. His interpretations and opinions are clearly distinct from his observations.

Position of the Cell in Life

The Cell Theory

Great ideas seldom spring full-blown from the mind of one person. In almost all cases profound generalizations from among the fields of man's intellectual pursuits are born slowly, assembled through a long gestation period, steeped, as it were in the broth of time. Celebrated scholars, scientists, philosophers, and artists—Charles Darwin, Ludwig van Beethoven, Niels

Bohr, Michelangelo Buonarroti, Frank Lloyd Wright, Marja Sklodowska Curie, James D. Watson, and Francis Crick—all are beholden to their predecessors (and contemporaries) for having laid the groundwork from which their own endeavors could arise. We all build upon foundations set down by our forebears. And so it was with what has come to be known as the **cell theory** or **cell doctrine**, linked so closely with the names of Matthias Jakob Schleiden (1804–1881) and Theodor Schwann (1810–1882). These two Germans, botanist and zoologist respectively, were the right people at the right time.

The assemblage of concepts for which Schleiden and Schwann are remembered came about through the publication of two scientific papers, "Contributions to Phytogenesis" by Schleiden in 1838 which was followed in 1839 by Schwann's "Microscopical Investigations on the Agreement of Structure and Growth of Animals and Plants." Schwann, the zoologist, extended Schleiden's theory to encompass animal cells, thus demonstrating the fundamental parallelism in the composition of animals and plants, indeed, the concordance at the cellular level of all life. There are three basic ideas bound up in the cell theory and these have been interpreted in a modern manner by Carl Swanson in his book, *The Cell:*

1. *Life exists only in cells.* All organisms, plant and animal, are made up of cells and the activities of organisms are dependent upon the activities of cells, both individually and collectively. The collective attributes of life are the collective attributes of cells: organic composition, responsiveness or irritability, growth and reproduction, absorption and expenditure of energy.
2. *The continuity of life has a cellular basis.* All cells come from other cells, and all parts of cells owe their existence to parts of pre-existing cells.
3. *There is a relation between structure and function in cells.* The cell is the structural and functional unit of plants and animals. The form of a cell is correlated with its function. Chemical activities of cells, which are outwardly reflected by form and function, occur within and are determined by certain submicroscopic cellular components arranged in a specific manner. We will have more to say about this later in the chapter when discussing DNA and RNA.

Sizes of Cells

Hooke was first to give us some idea of the sizes and numbers of cells in plants. He was so impressed with the great numbers and smallness of cells, that he could hardly believe his eyes. For purposes of comparison biologists who study cells **(cytologists)** use a unit of measure called the **micron (micrometer).** There are 1,000 microns in a **millimeter** and about 25 millimeters in an inch. So, you can appreciate how small some cells are if microns—about $1/25,000$ of an inch—must be used to measure them.

The smallest plant cells are those of bacteria, some of which are only .5 of a micron in diameter and only barely visible with the conventional glass-lensed microscope. At the other limit are some fiber cells of the nettle family which may reach a length of 200,000 microns (about 8 inches). Bacterial cells and nettle fiber cells are extremes, however; most plant cells fall within a range of 10 to 100 microns (between $1/2,500$ and $1/250$ of an inch). Between 40 and 4 such cells would just cover the period at the end of this sentence.

Some impression of the number of cells in a large plant can be gained using an ordinary apple tree as an example. It has been calculated that there are about 50 million cells in the leaf of an apple tree. Even a small apple tree, say one with only 6,000 leaves, would have 300 billion cells in the leaves alone. Now if we were to count the cells in the whole tree—leaves, fruits, flowers, branches, trunk, and roots—we would reach the altogether staggering amount of 25 trillion cells. Apple trees are relatively small as trees go, and one shrinks from the prospect of estimating the number of cells which must be present in those most massive of seed-bearing plants, the giant sequoias of California. (The General Sherman giant sequoia is estimated to weigh over 6,000 tons.) On the other hand, many entire plants consist only of one cell: bacteria and certain algae and fungi. If the number of cells in an apple tree is startling, we should be astounded to learn that a volume of one cubic inch would contain nine trillion entire organisms (cells) of *Eberthella typhosa,* the medium-sized bacterium which causes typhoid fever.

The Anatomy of Cells

Continuing improvement in the microscope, coupled with refinements in methods of preparing biological specimens for study, have increased our capacity to understand the structure of the cell and its vital role in plants and animals. During the first decades of the nineteenth century, following the early work in organic chemistry by the Swede Jöns Jakob Berzelius (1779–1848), biologists began to concern themselves more

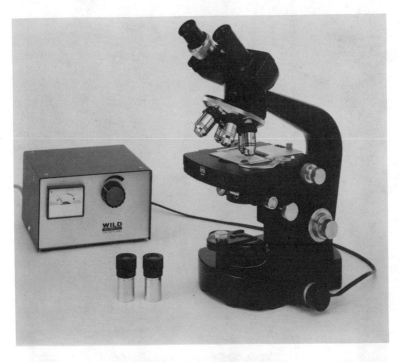

Figure 5.4 Modern, highly sophisticated light microscope such as would be used to study plant cells. The light source is enclosed in the base of the instrument and light intensity is controlled by the rheostat to the left. [Courtesy Wild-Heerbrugg Instruments.]

seriously with the chemistry as well as with the structure of cells. Probably the German botanist Hugo von Mohl (1805–1872)—coiner of the term **protoplasm** for the living substance of the cell—can be said to have moved cell chemistry to the forefront of biological inquiry. More recently, the use of polarized light and X-ray diffraction microscopy have strengthened our understanding of cell form and molecular construction.

The contemporary biologist has several investigative levels from which to approach the study of cells (**cytology**) depending upon his or her objectives. Each level of inquiry has its limitations and no single thrust can reveal everything about the cell. No longer, however, are we entirely dependent on one basic instrument—the microscope with glass lenses. But even with the sophisticated and elaborate modern laboratory apparatus—transmission and scanning electron microscopes and various other physical and chemical instrumentation—we still do not know all the answers about the functions and structure of cells. (After all, we have been studying cells for only 300 years.) And there is still much to learn with that relatively uncomplicated instrument, the conventional, or **light microscope** with glass lenses (Figure 5.4). The light used to illuminate the specimen in

Figure 5.5 An electron microscope. The magnetic fields are produced in the cylindrical vertical housing with the viewing screen at its base. Built into the left and right consoles are instruments, controls, and the camera for electron photomicrography. [Courtesy JEOL.]

this instrument usually comes from the beams of a tungsten filament electric lamp, hence the name light microscope. By contrast, beams of electrons are directed toward the specimen in the **electron microscope** (Figure 5.5). We ought to stress, however, that the light microscope has an effective maximum magnification of about 900 to 1,000 times and that some of the important requirements for its successful use are not in the optics of the instrument itself; rather, they are "a good *Eye*, a clear *Light*, and a *Rasor*, or very keen *Knife*, wherewith to cut them ['Bladders' and 'Aer-Vessels'] with a smooth surface, and so, as not to Dislocate the *Parts*" (from *The Anatomy of Trunks* . . . by Nehemiah Grew, 1682).

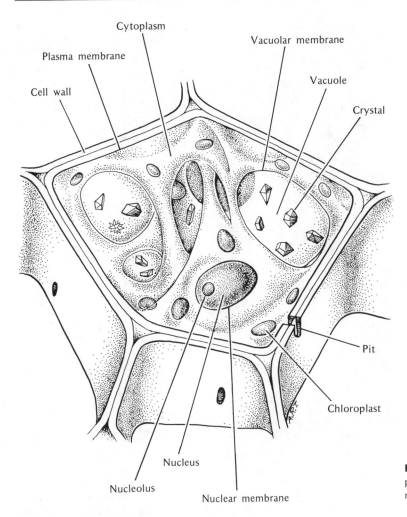

Cytoplasm

Vacuolar membrane

Plasma membrane

Vacuole

Cell wall

Crystal

Pit

Chloroplast

Nucleus

Nucleolus

Nuclear membrane

Figure 5.6 Green plant cell showing parts which can be seen with the light microscope.

With the Light Microscope

All cells are three-dimensional and many-sided (Figure 5.6). In the bodies of seed-bearing plants, ferns, mosses and liverworts (see Chapters 15 and 16), similar kinds of cells are cemented together in clusters or layers where they act as a group to perform certain functions. Such aggregations of cells are called **tissues** (Figure 5.7). Tissues are of various kinds and may comprise thick-walled cells, thin-walled cells, water-conducting cells, food-storage cells, or gamete-producing cells, for example. Cells in tissues are surrounded by other cells and we know now

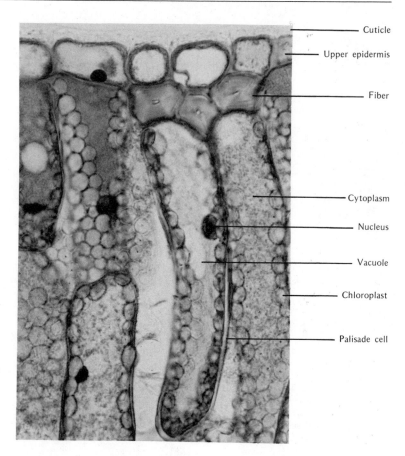

Cuticle

Upper epidermis

Fiber

Cytoplasm

Nucleus

Vacuole

Chloroplast

Palisade cell

Figure 5.7 Magnified view of leaf tissues of podocarpus, a tropical gymnosperm with broad, thick leaves, showing several different kinds of specialized cells and their parts. [Courtesy W. John Hayden.]

that there is communication between and among them, just as Hooke probably guessed though he could not prove it. While each cell contributes a share to the life processes of the tissue of which it is a part, it continues, simultaneously, to act as an independent unit of life. Cells thus have "dual personalities," as Schleiden pointed out in 1838. For example, **cell division**—the production of new cells from pre-existing cells—takes place independently of the tissue of which the dividing cell is a part; at the same time, the newly produced cell becomes a part of the tissue, adding to its bulk and form, and contributing to its overall activities.

As mentioned before, in plants each cell is enveloped in a more or less stiff **cell wall** composed of **cellulose,** a carbohydrate consisting of long-stranded molecules each made of many small particles of **glucose,** a kind of sugar. Almost all plants have cellulose cell walls, in contrast to most animals where cellulose does not usually occur. Cotton cloth, for example, consists of fibers from the seeds of the cotton plant, and it is almost pure cellulose. In trees and shrubs—woody plants—cellulose in the walls of wood cells is combined with a hardening substance, **lignin,** and it is lignin which gives wood many of its characteristic properties. The cell wall supports and protects the inner parts of the cell and it provides channels for intercellular communication without weakening its role in support.

Von Mohl noted that some of the substances within the cell displayed the properties of life (and we know from Chapter 1 that life is a condition which is not subject to rigid definition nor can it be characterized simply). To this living stuff of the cell von Mohl gave the name **protoplasm,** which means "first form." Two of the several components enveloped by the cell wall comprise the whole of the protoplasm. These two parts, visible with the light microscope, are the **cytoplasm** and **nucleus** (plural, **nuclei,** Figures 5.6 and 5.7). Each of these parts is an essential element in the living cell, for without the presence of either, cellular life eventually ends. Because of this, we must take a moment to reflect on these cell parts for they make up the very substance of life and embody all of its basic characteristics.

Cytoplasm. The cytoplasm (Figure 5.6) is bounded on its outer surfaces, those surfaces which closely adhere to the cell wall, by a living, ultrathin "skin" (about $1/_{100}$ micron), or **plasma membrane** (Figures 5.6 and 5.8), which is too thin for a cross-section to be seen with the light microscope. All materials passing into or out of the cell must cross the plasma membrane which exercises control over what substances may enter and leave the cell. The cytoplasm of adjacent cells is continuous through minute pores localized in thin places (**pits**) in the cellulose cell wall; that is, tenuous strands of cytoplasm connect all living cells through pores in these pits. The cytoplasmic strands are only barely visible with the light microscope.

Cytoplasm is a viscid-appearing fluid—often likened to uncooked egg white—which contains some particles which can be seen with the light microscope. These particles include **plastids,** disklike, membranebound bodies which may store starch, oil, or protein and which, in green plant cells, contain the pigment **chlorophyll.** The starch in potatoes, for example, occurs in plastids in living cells of the tuber. Chlorophyll-containing plastids

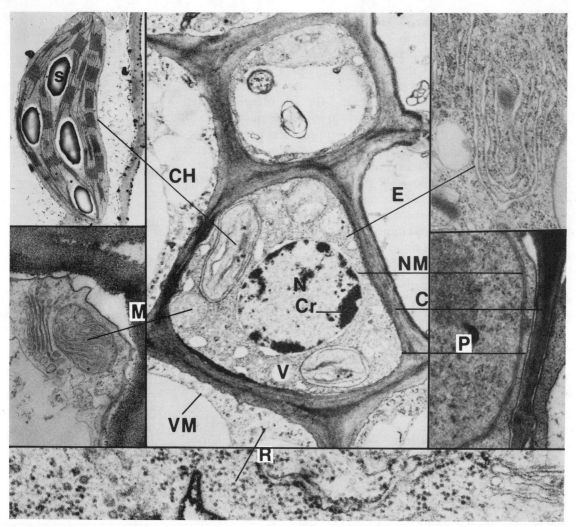

Figure 5.8 Electron micrographs of green plant cell and parts showing various submicroscopic structures; all parts are greatly magnified. C = cell wall; CH = chloroplast; Cr = chromatin; E = endoplasmic reticulum; M = mitochondrion; N = nucleus; NM = nuclear membrane; P = plasma membrane; R = ribosome; S = starch grain; V = vacuole; VM = vacuolar membrane. [Courtesy M. Kenneth Corbett and Roy W. Vickery.]

are **chloroplasts** (Figures 5.6, 5.7, and 5.8) and it is in these bodies that photosynthesis occurs. Chloroplasts are the factories of the cell. Indeed, they are the assembly lines where most of the energy available on earth today is converted into food. Fossil fuels—coal, gas, and oil—are repositories of energy captured and transformed by chloroplasts and stored in plants hundreds of millions of years ago. Cytoplasm also contains soluble components (sugars, for example) which are converted through chemical reactions into structural parts of the cell or are utilized as sources of energy to fuel the activities of the cell.

Nucleus. Probably the most vital of the bodies embedded in the cytoplasm (which can be seen with the light microscope) is the nucleus (Figures 5.6, 5.7, and 5.8). The nucleus is the center for the control of all cellular activities. In particular, it controls heredity. As Carl Swanson has written, "a cell without a nucleus [or nuclear material] is a cell without a future, because it cannot give rise to viable progeny." The nucleus in plant cells is usually spherical. Like the cytoplasm, the nucleus is enclosed in an ultrathin "skin," the **nuclear membrane** (Figures 5.6 and 5.8), a cross-section of which is invisible with the light microscope. This separates the nucleus from the cytoplasm and it regulates movement of materials into and out of the nucleus. With the light microscope, one or more small globular bodies might be seen in the nucleus; these are the **nucleoli** (singular, **nucleolus,** Figures 5.6 and 5.12), a word which means "little nuclei." The nucleoli give rise to the protein-forming bodies **(ribosomes)** of the cell. The nucleus also contains a network of strands which stains deeply when colored with certain biological dyes. For this reason, the network (Figure 5.8) is called **chromatin,** meaning a colored substance. *It is in the chromatin that the mechanism of heredity resides.*

Vacuole. Plant cells have liquid-filled regions in the cytoplasm called **vacuoles** (Figures 5.6, 5.7, and 5.8). In young, newly formed cells, there may be many small vesicles of this kind; as the cell ages, however, the vesicles fuse to form one large vacuole and the cytoplasm is pushed up against the cell wall. The vacuole is separated from the cytoplasm by another membrane, the **vacuolar membrane** (Figures 5.6 and 5.8). It has properties similar to the plasma and nuclear membranes in that it regulates the kinds of materials which move from the cytoplasm into the fluid of the vacuole **(cell sap)** and from the vacuolar fluid into the cytoplasm. The fluid-filled vacuole helps to maintain the turgidity (dilation) of the cell and at the same time it acts as a depot for stored materials and as a repository for waste products excreted from the cytoplasm. Analyses of cell sap have shown it to contain a great variety of substances: water, salts, acids, tannins, sugars, alkaloids, latex, and pigments, for example. Flower color and the red pigment which oozes from cut beet roots are contained in the vacuolar sap. Tannic acid, used in tanning leathers, and natural rubber are useful products derived from the cell sap of certain plant species. Sometimes, the concentration of certain salts in the cell sap is so high that crystals (Figure 5.6) are actually deposited.

Cell cavity. When a cell dies—and all plant cells eventually die—the cellulosic cell wall and its components remain in place and, unless they decompose, they stand as a sign to tell us that here there was once a living cell. All the protoplasm and cell sap dry up or otherwise deteriorate. These processes leave a **cell cavity** enclosed by the cellulosic shell which once contained the living cell substance.

Most of the cells in the wood of a tree trunk are dead, the contents having died and been lost in one way or another. But, as you will read in Chapter 6 on wood, dead cells are not necessarily functionless, for though the active, water-conducting cells of wood are dead, as are most of the fibrous cells, they still continue to conduct water and support the tree. As a matter of fact, if the water-conducting cells of wood were stuffed full of protoplasm, they would conduct little water because the cell cavities through which the water moves would be plugged up.

Transition to the Electron Microscope

It was apparent toward the end of the nineteenth century that the optical limits of the light microscope had been reached. The very finest lenses were being manufactured and the cytoplasm, nucleus, vacuoles, and cell cavities could easily be seen and studied with the magnifications produced. But gaining increased magnification in itself proved not to be a problem in seeing finer detail, since by combining the proper lenses it was theoretically possible to increase magnification ad infinitum. The problem was to increase **resolution** at the same time magnification was increased. Resolution is simply the ability to distinguish two separate points of light or points of detail in a specimen. The principle of resolution was clearly understood in the seventeenth century and Robert Hooke was well aware of it. But then interest in this principle was applied to telescopes and it was treated in relation to astronomy and the observation of the so-called double stars. Hooke, as a matter of fact, was the first to conclude that in order to see those stars as double—that is, as two distinct points of light—they had to be resolved or separated by the lenses. "Empty amplification [magnification] is a folly of lenses of the past," notes Bradbury, as he stresses that increasing resolution must accompany increasing magnification if we are to see any detail. The head of a pin is still the head of a pin regardless of how much we enlarge it.

Owing to the intrinsic properties of glass lenses and the light used to illuminate specimens, the very best limit of resolution which can be achieved with the light microscope (Figure 5.4) is $^1/_4$ of a micron. This means, that any two points of detail in a specimen under observation which are closer than $^1/_4$ of a micron cannot be seen as two points—regardless of the magnification of the lenses. Thus cytologists using light microscopes were stymied in their search for the ultimate structure of the cell and it was impossible, until the advent of the first electron microscopes in the early 1930s, to gain much more understanding of the fine structure of the cell than we have already told you about.

Through research in Germany during the 1920s, it was discovered that certain negatively charged atomic particles called **electrons** could be generated by a device called an **electron gun.** Soon after, it was learned that an electron beam could be produced with the gun. Using this information electron microscopes were designed in a manner somewhat parallel to the light microscope except, instead of an ordinary light source, an electron gun was substituted and a series of magnetic fields replaced the glass lenses. The specimen image is projected onto a screen in the electron microscope and you look at this much as you would a television screen.

The greatest advantage of the electron microscope is not so much in the tremendous increase of magnification which it allows (more than 500,000 times), but rather in the parallel increase of resolving power. The very best electron microscopes (Figure 5.5) can distinguish detail between two points on a specimen which are only three angstroms apart (an angstrom unit is $^1/_{10,000}$ of a micron and a micron, you will remember, is $^1/_{25,000}$ of an inch).

Use of the electron microscope to reveal the fine structure of the cell was made possible only through a parallel development in techniques for cutting ultrathin slices of cells. Electron beams cannot penetrate thick specimens. Cells for viewing with the light microscope can be cut as thin as four or five microns. Ordinary light can easily penetrate sections of this thickness, but they are much too thick for electrons to pass through. Thus a special instrument **(ultramicrotome)** for ultrathin slicing was devised and, with new slicing techniques, it was possible to cut sections of cells between $^1/_{20}$ and $^1/_{100}$ of a micron thick. When you realize that sections of the plasma membrane are invisible with the light microscope because they are only $^1/_{100}$ of a micron thick but that they can be seen with the electron microscope, you will have some idea of the importance of the technological developments necessary to produce the ultrathin sections and the increased resolution and magnification afforded by the electron microscope.

The Fine Structure of Cells

With the electron microscope now at our disposal, let us take another look at some of the cell structures (Figure 5.8) we examined before with the light microscope. The plasma membrane, which we could not see in section with the light microscope, turns out to be a three-layered envelope. It is composed of molecules of protein and fat arranged in layers. The protein molecules, through their ability to fold and unfold, stretch and contract, are probably related to the special selective properties of this membrane which regulates the kinds of substances entering and leaving the cell. It ought to be pointed out that the plasma membrane is not like a simple, thin plastic bag holding the cell contents; on the contrary, it is elastic and changeable, pliable in some cells and rigid in others. Nuclei, plastids, and vacuoles are also enclosed in similar laminated membranes. The plasma membrane is intimately connected with the internal membrane systems of the cell.

   Mitochondria. One of the cytoplasmic particles which we could have mentioned above under the discussion of cell particles, is the **mitochondrion** (plural, **mitochondria,** Figure 5.8). Mitochondria are just at the limit of visibility with the light microscope and their internal structure has only been accurately determined with the electron microscope. Mitochondria range from $^1/_5$ to seven microns in diameter; they vary in shape from spheres to rods to branching rods. Each mitochondrion is bounded on its external surface by a several-layered membrane. Internally mitochondria consist of a series of folded membranes similar to the laminated membranes of other cell particles. The mitochondrion is concerned with the capture, conversion, and transfer of energy to other cell parts. The chemical reactions involved in these processes take place on the surfaces of the internal membrane system. Mitochondria are the major sites of respiration in the cell.

Chloroplasts. The process of photosynthesis is driven by energy derived from light—in nature, the light of the sun, or solar energy. Trapping the sun's light, converting it into chemical energy, and storing it in molecules (sugar) derived from carbon dioxide and water—all this takes place within the cytoplasmic particle called the **chloroplast** (Figures 5.7 and 5.8). Chloroplasts are easily seen with the light microscope; they are variously shaped and may be disklike, spiral, star-shaped, or cup-shaped, and cells may have one or many in the cytoplasm. With the electron microscope we can see that each chloroplast is surrounded externally by a several-layered membrane and internally it is organized into stacks of disks which are connected to each other. The **chlorophyll** molecules are organized within these stacks, sandwiched between layers of proteins, enzymes, and other compounds. This arrangement is efficient for trapping light and for converting it into chemical energy through **photosynthesis.** It was thought that if chlorophyll could be extracted from green plant cells—which it can—then it might be possible to induce photosynthesis in the laboratory using solutions of chlorophyll. Imagine the benefits derived from such a system; we could manufacture food in the laboratory and eventually in factories. But this has never been accomplished and photosynthesis is only carried on in intact chloroplasts (except for blue-green algae which lack true chloroplasts and in purple bacteria).

Other kinds of plastids, those that store starch, oil, and protein, are membranebound as is the chloroplast. However, they do not possess the layers of disks characteristic of chloroplasts, nor, of course, do they contain chlorophyll. All plastids, however, are derived from a common type of precursor plastid and what each becomes at maturity depends upon external factors (exposure to light, for example) and upon the kind of cell in which it is found.

Ribosomes and **endoplasmic reticulum. Ribosomes** are among the smallest of the cytoplasmic particles and range in diameter from 200 to 250 angstroms (Figure 5.8). They are generally spherical and composed of a nucleic acid and protein. Ribosomes are found in every kind of cell and are intimately concerned with the manufacture of proteins. The formation of ribosomes is initiated in the nucleus (by the nucleoli) but they are assembled in the cytoplasm.

In almost all cells there is an elaborate membrane system in the cytoplasm which is related to the manufacture of cellular products. This is the **endoplasmic reticulum** (Figure 5.8), a membranebound complex of flattened tubules extending through the cytoplasm from pores in the nuclear membrane to connect with the plasma membrane. Membranes of the endoplasmic reticulum are three-layered as is the plasma membrane. During the later stages of cell division, when daughter nuclei are formed, the new nuclear membranes are derived in part from remnants of the endoplasmic reticulum. Ribosomes are frequently seen adhering to the endoplasmic reticulum giving it a rough appearance. In other instances, the endoplasmic reticulum is smooth and there are no ribosomes attached to it. Enzymes appear to function as an integral part of the endoplasmic reticulum and so various beneficial reactions take place there. There is some thought too that the endoplasmic reticulum, through its connections with the plasma membrane, provides canals for materials to reach the interior of the cell and thus it acts as a transportation system.

New Cells from Old

Now that we have some idea about the structure of cells it is logical next to find out where new cells come from and how they are produced. In seed-bearing plants, like pines, palms, cabbages, and apples, the first cell of a new plant is formed by the union of sperm and egg in a process to be described later in some detail. This cell divides many times to form the embryo which is present in all seeds. It is this embryo, through the production of new cells resulting in growth, which finally becomes the green leafy familiar plant of our fields, forests, and gardens.

Plant Meristems

For the most part, new cells are produced in certain regions of the plant body called **meristems,** a word coined from the Greek, **meristos,** "divided or divisible." You will recall that these are localized growing places, sites where during the growing season cells are produced at a rapid rate. One kind of meristem is situated at the apices of stems (Figure 5.9), roots (Figure 5.10), and their branches. Production of new cells in such **apical meristems** and the subsequent elongation of these cells are responsible in large measure for the lengthening (growth) of plant

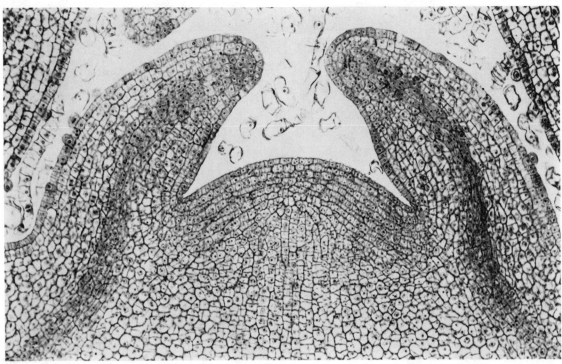

Figure 5.9 Longitudinal section of the apical meristem in the ash stem as magnified with the light microscope. A region in the dome is responsible for production of new cells which lengthen the stem. The two lobes which overarch the dome are developing leaves. [From C. L. Wilson, W. E. Loomis, and T. A. Steeves, *Botany,* 5th ed., New York: Holt, Rinehart and Winston, 1971. Courtesy Carl L. Wilson and Augustus E. De Maggio.]

parts in the spring and early summer. Another meristem where new cells are regularly formed is the **vascular cambium** (see Chapter 6), the special cell-producing layer between the bark and wood. Cells produced by the vascular cambium cause plant parts to thicken, that is, to grow in diameter.

Temporary meristems may be formed when a plant is wounded or when it is affected by disease. Such meristems continue to produce new cells until the wound is healed or the disease contained, after which the meristem cells revert to a stable condition. Certain horticultural practices, such as budding and other types of grafting, rely on the ability of plants to form temporary meristems and to produce new cells. The new and highly successful asexual method of rapidly growing desirable orchid species, called "meristemming," involves the culture of orchid tissue (the meristem) in a sterile nutrient medium.

Higher animals do not have regions comparable to meristems and consequently the growth of their bodies is fixed in form and size. Because of the presence of meristems, a perennial

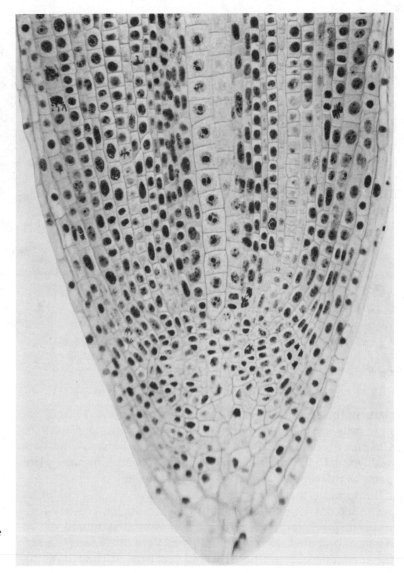

Figure 5.10 Longitudinal section of the apical meristem in the onion root as magnified with the light microscope. The initiation of new cells begins in a region about one-third the way up from the root tip. [Courtesy W. John Hayden.]

plant like a tree can grow to great size over a long period of time and develop a rather free and constantly expanding form compared with a dog, a cow, or a hog. However, as discussed earlier in the chapter under the cell theory, the processes by which new cells are formed in plants and animals are essentially identical. They can be seen with the light microscope and under special optical conditions it is usually possible to follow the entire process of cell division and new cell formation in living cells. Cell division and new cell formation are two of the most exciting and profound of all biological phenomena.

Cell Division

In line with our aim of reducing excessive terminology and detail, the following description of the process of cell division (Figure 5.11A–L) is quite simplified. Before a cell divides, the nucleus is fairly homogeneous in appearance and the chromatin seems to be a well-dispersed network. At the onset of cell division, however, the chromatin network begins to gather together (actually a coiling process) to form a number of discrete, more or less shortened and thickened strands (Figure 5.11A–D). These are the **chromosomes** which at this stage already show evidence of a longitudinal doubling or duplication. The nuclear membrane disappears and the chromosomes lie directly in the cytoplasm. The chromosomes migrate toward the middle of the cell and line up along what would be the cell's equator (Figure 5.11E–G). Each original chromosome has now completely doubled lengthwise into two new chromosomes, called daughter chromosomes, which separate and move away from the equator of the cell toward opposite ends, or toward the poles (Figure 5.11H–J). At about this time, a new cell wall begins to appear (Figure 5.11J, K) across the middle of the original cell and the daughter chromosomes begin to arrange themselves into two clumps, one in each new cell that is being cut off by the forming cell wall (Figure 5.11L). In each group the chromosomes gradually become less distinct, thinner, and more elongated. A chromatin network forms in each new cell surrounded by a re-formed nuclear membrane (Figure 5.11L). The new cell wall completes its formation and two complete new cells make their appearance (Figure 5.12).

It is important to remember that as a result of this process each new cell contains the same numbers and kinds of chromosomes which were present in the original cell. As you probably already know from your general reading, **genes,** the ultimate hereditary units (the "factors" of Gregor Mendel; see Chapters 17 and 18), occur in linear fashion, one after the other, along the lengths of chromosomes. During chromosomal duplication, each gene on each chromosome is replicated exactly so that these bearers of hereditary traits are equal in number and

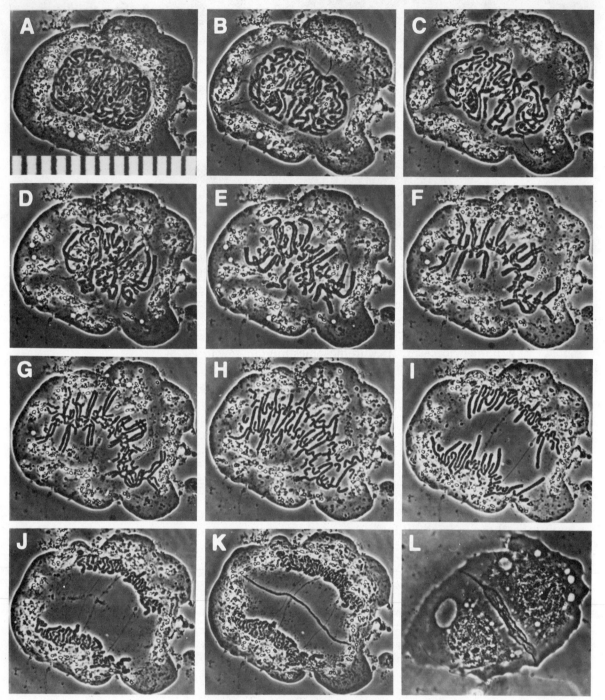

Figure 5.11 A–L.   Sequence of activities involved in the division of a single living endosperm cell of the African blood-lily (*Haemanthus katherinae*). The complete cycle of division took about five hours. [Courtesy William T. Jackson.]

identical in kind in each of the newly formed nuclei. Thus the hereditary potential of the original cell is transmitted unimpaired and unaltered to the two new cells which are formed. In this manner, the hereditary continuity of life is maintained.

Chromosome Number

The number of chromosomes in cells of each species of plant and animal is fixed; that is, chromosome number is one characteristic of a species (Figure 5.13). In the body cells of man (*Homo sapiens*) there are 46 chromosomes. Among the flowering plants, the most frequently encountered chromosome numbers are 14, 16, and 18; maize has 20, onion 16, trillium 10, sunflower 34, and zinnia 24. The highest chromosome numbers are found in the ferns; cells of *Ophioglossum vulgatum* (adder's-tongue fern) have over 500 chromosomes; in the related *Ophioglossum petiolatum*, there are more than 1,000 chromosomes, the largest number reported in any vascular plant. It is somewhat startling to realize, however, that the chromosome number is known for only about 10 percent of all seed plants and for other groups of plants, the percentage is even lower.

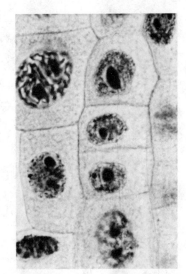

Figure 5.12   Final stage in cell division involves production of the cell wall between daughter cells. The central two cells in this highly magnified section of onion root tip tissue are the result of a recent cell division. A nucleolus is visible in each of them. [Courtesy W. John Hayden.]

Inheritance and DNA—Mystery of Mysteries

The **gene,** or unit of heredity, is the term first applied to Mendel's "factors" (see Chapters 17, 18) by Wilhelm Ludvig Johannsen (1857–1927), a Danish geneticist. That genes occur as particles was established through experiments many years ago, but we have yet to see what a gene actually looks like. Nevertheless, we do know much about the behavior of genes and we may be very close to discovering their ultimate structure.

Although many scientists had been engaged in studies of gene structure, investigations at King's College (University of London) and at Cambridge University's Cavendish Laboratories just after World War II, particularly by Rosalind Franklin (Figure 5.14), Maurice Wilkins, James D. Watson, and Francis Crick (Figure 5.15), culminated in a series of experiments and molecular model building which moved us to the brink of a thorough understanding of the gene. For their work in unraveling this mystery of mysteries, Wilkins, Watson, and Crick were awarded Nobel Prizes in Medicine and Physiology in 1962. The

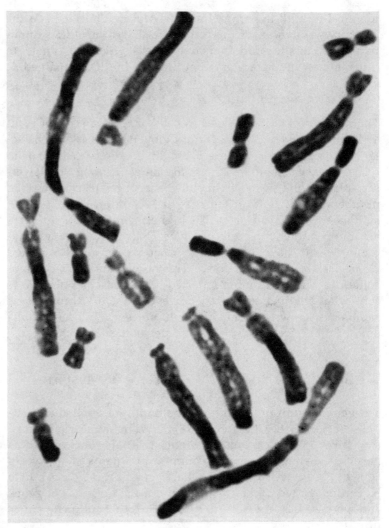

Figure 5.13   Sixteen chromosomes of the African blood-lily (*Haemanthus coccineus*). [Courtesy Delbert T. Morgan, Jr.]

Figure 5.14   Rosalind Franklin in the Laboratoire Central des Services Chimiques de l'État, Paris, 1947 or 1948. [Courtesy Anne Sayre.]

inside story of these studies is contained in a frankly written and very readable book by Watson entitled, *The Double Helix: A Personal Account of the Discovery of DNA*. A subsequent book by Anne Sayre, *Rosalind Franklin and DNA*, has added an unexpected dimension to the story of the search for the structure of

Figure 5.15 James D. Watson and Francis H. C. Crick in the Cavendish Laboratory, Cambridge University, with their model of the DNA molecule. [Courtesy James D. Watson.]

DNA. Aside from the narrative of discovery, these books show the human side of how scientific discoveries are made; the jealousies and misunderstandings that arise among gifted people plunging headlong toward the same goals; the competition, real and imagined; and how the intense desire to be first affects their behavior toward one another.

In a 1934 textbook on cytology by the late Lester W. Sharp, professor of botany at Cornell University, there is a statement which will help you to understand recent developments in our knowledge of how genes work. First, you must realize that the gene, like so many other biological phenomena, is a system (or at least one intrinsic part of a system), an assembly of activities or units which act together to produce a given result or to shape a given form. Sharp said, ''The operation of any system, living or lifeless, depends upon the materials of which it is made up (its chemical composition), the arrangement of these materials (its physical organization), and the set of surrounding conditions under which it acts (its environment)." Beginning with the chemical investigations of protoplasm during the last decades of the nineteenth century, it has been determined that the uniqueness of cells and organisms is a function of the uniqueness of the proteins of which they are composed. Therefore, if we could find a way to determine why certain proteins occur in certain organisms, we would be at least on the threshold of understanding why organisms differ from each other. And if we could find out what it is in the cell or organism that regulates or gives the signals for the formation of specific proteins, we might even have a big toe over that threshold.

Because it was suspected that the nucleus regulated the activities of the cell, scientists focused their attentions on learning its chemical and physical make-up. They found that basically the nucleus consisted of **nucleic acid**—which they were able to define empirically—and some simple form of protein. As we know now, this nucleic acid has proven to be critical in understanding the mechanisms by which genes exert their influence and this is the story of **DNA—deoxyribonucleic acid.**

As a starting point, we could hypothesize that since proteins are the keystones of uniqueness, there must be some relationship between genes—the bearers of hereditary characters—and proteins. Further, we might say that genes actually exercise their control through the medium of certain kinds of proteins called **enzymes** and that the presence in the cell of this or that enzyme is actually a biochemical trait or character. (Remember, an enzyme is an organic catalyst; it facilitates chemical reactions without being used up in the process.) Are genes, then, proteins? Some scientists thought so.

During subsequent investigations on nucleic acids, DNA was isolated and it was shown to occur in the chromosomes (hence, nuclei) of all cells. Certain experiments suggested that all genes were composed of DNA. If this were to be proven, it might mean that DNA itself would provide the key to open the treasure chest containing the secrets of life. But what was the physical structure of DNA? How were its components organized? And more to the point, what was the bearing of DNA on the regulation and transmission of hereditary characters?

Francis Crick leaned toward the DNA hypothesis and, as James Watson wrote,

> There were scientists who thought the evidence favoring DNA was inconclusive and preferred to believe that genes were protein molecules. Francis [Crick], however, did not worry about these skeptics. Many were cantankerous fools who unfailingly backed the wrong horses. One could not be a successful scientist without realizing that, in contrast to the popular conception supported by newspapers and mothers of scientists, a goodly number of scientists are not only narrow-minded and dull, but also just stupid.

Watson recounts how after considerable thought about changing his research program from protein chemistry to DNA, about fair play and the probability of stepping on the scientific toes of Maurice Wilkins who had already staked a large claim on DNA study, and after a series of stimulating discussions on the subject with Watson, Crick, working with Watson, proceeded to crack the structure of DNA—with the help of Wilkins's X-ray diffraction pictures.

Sayre's book, however, throws additional light on the events portrayed by Watson. It appears that Rosalind Franklin, working at King's College, though in isolation from Maurice Wilkins, had presented what later proved to be crucial data on one aspect of the probable DNA structure during a seminar attended by Watson. Watson, in his book, disparages Franklin's studies and Franklin herself. He refers to her as Wilkins's "assistant," which, as an independent scientist, she was not; he calls her "Rosy," a name by which she was not known to anyone; he criticizes her physical appearance: "She was not unattractive and might have been quite stunning had she taken even a mild interest in her clothes. . . . There was never lipstick to contrast with her straight black hair. . . her dresses showed all the imagination of English blue-stocking adolescents."

In any event, after attending Franklin's seminar, Watson and Wilkins discussed her report over dinner that same evening and, according to Watson, Wilkins allowed that "little real progress had been made by Rosy since the day she arrived at King's. . . . Maurice had doubts about whether she was really measuring what she claimed." In short, Watson gives Franklin and her X-ray diffraction data, from which he and Crick later borrowed liberally, short shrift. In an exhaustive documentation of Rosalind Franklin's investigations, Sayre demonstrates convincingly that Franklin, in reality, was well on the way toward solving the DNA structural puzzle herself.

Rosalind Franklin died at 37 years of age in 1958, a victim of cancer. Sayre and many of Franklin's scientific contemporaries believe that had she been alive in 1962 "when the Nobel Prize committee was considering its awards, she could hardly have been overlooked." But, Nobel Prizes are not awarded posthumously. In an epilogue to his book, Watson admitted that his "initial impressions of her, both scientific and personal (as recorded in the early pages of this book), were often wrong." Although Watson drew a jaundiced portrait of Rosalind Franklin and her scientific contributions for us, this does not detract from his and Crick's genius in designing a model of the DNA molecule (Figure 5.15) nor from the incredibly valuable advancement this was to biological science.

The Double Helix and DNA

Watson and Crick were able to show that the DNA molecule is a **double helix,** or coil, which may be viewed as a twisted ladder (Figure 5.16A). The basic chemical groupings of which the twisted ladder is composed are three-part molecular structures called **nucleotides.** These each contain a sugar called **deoxyribose,** a **phosphate,** and a **nitrogen-containing (nitrogenous) base** (Figures 5.16A and 5.17). In each nucleotide, the sugar and phosphate components are of the same kind, but there are four different kinds of nitrogen-containing bases designated by the biochemical shorthand $A, T, G,$ and C. Nucleotides are the main building blocks of DNA. To return to our DNA/double helix/ladder analogy, sugars and phosphates alternate in long rows to make up the backbone of each ladder upright; attached to each sugar molecule is one of the four kinds of nitrogen bases. The nitrogen bases from opposite ladder uprights pair with each other to form the ladder rungs (Figure 5.16A). However, only certain pairs of nitrogen bases (called **complementary pairs**) will bond to form rungs (A will only join with T and C only with G [Figure 5.17]). The AT and CG bonds hold together the two uprights. Variations in the arrangement and sequence of the pairs of bases along each spiral of the double helix are crucial to the action of the DNA system.

During the early stages of cell division, the duplication of

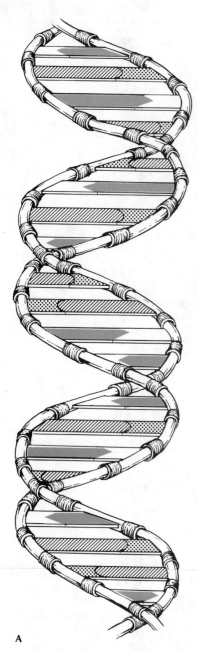

A

Figure 5.16 A–C Models of the DNA double helix and manner of DNA replication. (A) Double helix of a DNA molecule comprising two spiral backbones of alternating sugar and phosphate molecules and connecting rungs

each chromosome is coincident at the molecular level with the unwinding of the double helix and the separation of the two backbones from each other by the pulling apart of the ladder rungs (Figure 5.16B). As the spirals unwind, the bonds are ruptured between the members of each pair of nitrogenous bases and the nucleotide strands separate. Along each single old nucleotide strand, a new and complementary strand is synthesized (Figure 5.16C). Each new strand is a mirror image of the parental strand. Copying of DNA is based upon the formation of correct specific pairs of nitrogen bases, *AT* and *CG*. Members of incorrect pairs cannot form bonds and so do not fit the growing strand of parental DNA.

Thus two double helix molecules result, one of which passes to each of the daughter chromosomes during cell division. In this way, the DNA molecule reproduces, or **replicates,** itself exactly, just as we have known that during cell division each gene reproduces itself exactly and each chromosome reproduces itself exactly.

The Cellular Cryptogram

The DNA molecules are the ultimate data banks of genetic information and now that you have an idea of the way in which DNA molecules can duplicate themselves to form other DNA molecules, we ought to tell you about how this process is related to the production of proteins. In a way the biochemist is not too unlike the student of evolution or the comparative morphologist (although we imagine that some would cringe at the thought); both are on the lookout for similarities. It was not long after the details of the DNA molecule became known that biochemists saw parallels in structure between DNA and proteins. Both, of course, occur in cells and are nitrogen-containing compounds. Proteins are composed of subunits called **amino acids** just as DNA molecules are composed of subunits called nucleotides. These amino acids are arranged in a precise order in proteins, as nucleotides are in DNA, and they are linked to one another just as nucleotides are linked to each other. Amino acids, as a matter of fact, are called the building blocks of proteins. Thus there appeared to be considerable chemical and physical similarity between protein molecules and DNA molecules. Was this similarity only a coincidental biological parallel or was there some basis, some underlying phenomenon, responsible for these resemblances?

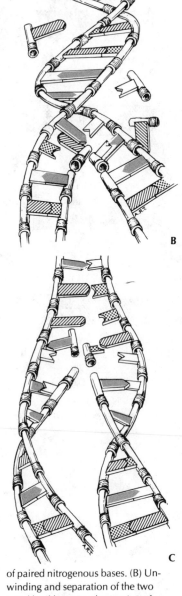

B

C

of paired nitrogenous bases. (B) Unwinding and separation of the two spiral backbones and rupturing of rungs. (C) Reconstitution through replication of two molecules of DNA, each identical to the parent double helix.

119

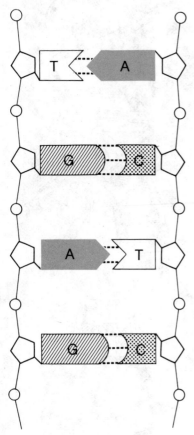

Figure 5.17 Nucleotides, basic chemical groupings of the DNA molecule.

DNA, the storehouse of genetic information, occurs principally in the nucleus (or in the nuclear material of bacteria and blue-green algae) of the cell, but proteins are formed in the cytoplasm. Was it possible that DNA in some way transmitted coded instructions that could be read in the cytoplasm, telling it to produce a particular kind of protein or enzyme? If so, was there a system for carrying that code from the nucleus to the cytoplasm and could the code be translated there into instructions for protein formation? Answers to these questions were forthcoming when it was learned that not only could DNA replicate itself but it could also, by a process called **transcription,** form another kind of nucleic acid, **RNA—ribonucleic acid.** As a matter of fact, DNA was shown to produce three kinds of RNA. RNA transcription is accomplished by one of the two strands of DNA.

A strand of RNA differs only slightly from a strand of DNA; RNA strands are also composed of nucleotides arranged in a specific manner. One kind of RNA, **ribosomal RNA,** made in the nucleus is transferred to the ribosomes in the cytoplasm. Another kind of RNA, **transfer RNA,** also made in the nucleus, contains a specific code consisting of an arrangement of bases such that amino acids—the building blocks of proteins—can be attached. These two kinds of RNA assist in the assembly of proteins. But the sequence of amino acids in the proteins (and this is basically what determines the kind of protein) is fixed by the message carried from the DNA to the ribosomes by a third kind of RNA, **messenger RNA.** Protein synthesis then takes place in the ribosomes. When the manufacture of the protein is completed in the ribosome, the protein is released to take its proper place in the cytoplasm where it may act as an enzyme and enter into chemical reactions or where it may become the structural material of membranes, plastids, or other cell parts.

Summary

Cells are the structural units of plants and animals. Owing to their small size, their discovery awaited the invention of the **microscope** in the late sixteenth century. Cells were first seen by the Englishman **Robert Hooke** and described in his book, *Micrographia,* in 1665. It remained for the synthetic work of

Schleiden and Schwann (1838, 1839), botanist and zoologist respectively, to place the cell in its proper perspective within plants and animals. From this work came what today is called the **cell theory** or **cell doctrine.** Its essential features are:

1. Life exists only in cells, the structural units of both plants and animals.
2. The continuity of life has a cellular basis and new cells arise from pre-existing cells.
3. There is a relation between structure and function in cells at all levels.

Cells in plants are bounded on their external surfaces by walls composed of **cellulose,** a complex carbohydrate. The living portion of the cell is **protoplasm** and it has two essential components: a **nucleus** and **cytoplasm.** Cytoplasm is enveloped by a three-layered **plasma membrane,** visible in cross-section only with the **electron microscope.** It is composed of layers of fat and protein and regulates passage of all materials into and out of the cell. **Plastids** are particles embedded within the cytoplasm. The most important plastid in green plants is the **chloroplast** in which **photosynthesis** (food manufacture) occurs and which contains the green pigment **chlorophyll.** Chloroplasts can be seen with the light microscope but their layered, enclosing membrane, only with the electron microscope. Similarly, **mitochondria,** centers of respiration, can be seen with the light microscope but their minute structure has only been revealed by the electron microscope. Visible with the electron microscope are **ribosomes,** sites of protein synthesis, and the **endoplasmic reticulum,** a network of tubules concerned with manufacturing and enzymatic activities in the cell. **Vacuoles** are fluid-filled **(cell sap)** sacs in the cytoplasm easily demonstrated with the light microscope. These sacs act as dumping grounds for cellular wastes and as places of food storage.

By far the most important part of the living cell is the **nucleus,** the control center and seat of all hereditary activities. The nucleus is visible with the light microscope but the details of its surrounding laminated membrane, only with the electron microscope. The nucleus contains a network of strands called **chromatin** which is the material that makes up the **chromosomes. Nucleoli,** small globular bodies concerned with the formation of ribosomes, are also present in the nucleus.

When a cell dies, its internal components dry up leaving the

cell cavity, an internal space formerly occupied by protoplasm and enclosed by the cell wall.

Cells divide to produce new cells. In plants, dividing cells are concentrated in **apical meristems** at the tips of stems and roots and in the **vascular cambium** between the bark and wood. **Cell division** includes two major stages:

1. Division of the cytoplasm and the formation of a new cell wall across the old, or parent, cell.
2. Nuclear division.

Nuclear division entails the duplication of each chromosome and component **gene** and the subsequent movement of the **daughter chromosomes** into the two newly forming nuclei. Thus newly produced cells have the same genetic potential—in terms of numbers and kinds of chromosomes and genes—as the parent cell. The number of chromosomes in cells of each species is fixed and **chromosome number** is a characteristic of species, both plant and animal.

The genetic mechanism of all organisms is contained in the nucleus. A nucleus consists of two main chemical fractions: **nucleic acid** and **protein.** Genetic information is stored in a nucleic acid called **DNA (deoxyribonucleic acid).** Molecules of this compound occur as a **double helix,** each coil of which is composed of a row of smaller molecules called **nucleotides.** The unique component of each nucleotide is the **nitrogen-containing base.** Pairs of these bases are linked across the coils of the double helix. Before cell division, the helices unwind, the bonds between the bases are broken, and each separated strand of DNA then replicates itself, making two double helices. During cell division, each of the newly formed double helices moves into one of the newly formed nuclei. Thus activity at the molecular level parallels activity at the visible level represented by the equal duplication of chromosomes during nuclear division. The genetic information contained in each DNA molecule is transmitted unchanged to each newly constituted nucleus.

DNA molecules, besides being able to duplicate themselves, can produce another nucleic acid, **RNA (ribonucleic acid).** Ribonucleic acid is manufactured in the nucleus but moves out into the cytoplasm, carrying with it coded genetic messages from the DNA molecule. This information is transmitted to the ribosomes, which manufacture proteins. Since differences in proteins are responsible for differences in organisms, and since information on what kinds of proteins to build are contained in the DNA molecule, it appears that the essential components of genes are DNA molecules. Thus the DNA/RNA system is the fundamental mechanism for the production of proteins unique to certain organisms and of specific **enzymes** (a kind of protein) which regulate certain chemical reactions in the cell. These unique proteins and specific enzymes are the biochemical traits upon which the genetic constitution of organisms is based.

Suggested Readings

Bradbury, S. *The Evolution of the Microscope.* London and New York: Pergamon, 1967. History of the development of the microscope.

Crick, F. H. C. "The Genetic Code." *Scientific American 207* (October 1962): 66–74. Written by Nobel laureate and co-model-builder of the DNA molecule.

———. "The Genetic Code: III." *Scientific American* 215 (October 1966): 55–62.

Dobell, Clifford. *Antony van Leeuwenhoek and his "Little Animals."* New York: Harcourt, Brace, 1932 (reprinted New York: Dover Publications, 1960). The appealing story of Leeuwenhoek told through his letters with notes on his birthplace, family and friends, and his position in the history of biology.

Dubos, Rene. *The Unseen World.* New York: Rockefeller Institute Press, 1962. Popularized account of the cell and those who studied disease-producing microorganisms.

Grew, Nehemiah. *The Anatomy of Plants with an Idea of a Philosophical History of plants. . .* 2d ed. London: W. Rawlins, 1682 (reprinted with an Introduction by Conway Zirkle, New York: Johnson Reprint Corp., 1965). Classical foundation of plant structure by one of the fathers of plant anatomy.

Hooke, R. *Micrographia: or Some Physiological Descriptions of Minute Bodies Made by Magnifying Glasses. . .* London: Jo. Martyn and Ja. Allestry, 1665 (reprinted Weinheim, Germany: J. Cramer, 1961). One of the great books of biology; first description and naming of the cell.

Jensen, William A., and Roderic B. Park. *Cell Ultrastructure.* Belmont, Calif.: Wadsworth, 1967. Atlas of excellent electron microscope pictures of cell particles with associated text.

Kornberg, Arthur. "The Synthesis of DNA." *Scientific American* 219

(October 1968): 64–78. Received Nobel Prize for demonstrating that a specific enzyme catalyzed the synthesis of DNA in vitro.

Merrell, David J. *An Introduction to Genetics.* New York: Norton, 1975. Comprehensive textbook with several clearly written but technical chapters on DNA, RNA, the genetic code and their influence on heredity.

Mirsky, Alfred E. "The discovery of DNA." *Scientific American 218* (June 1968): 78–88. Mirsky was a codiscoverer of RNA in chromosomes and contributed to information about RNA regulation in the nucleus.

Nirenberg, Marshall W. "The Genetic Code: II." *Scientific American* 208 (March 1963): 80–94. Nobel Laureate at National Institutes of Health who contributed to breaking the genetic code by determining how the DNA/RNA system determined protein synthesis in vitro.

Olby, Robert. *The Path to the Double Helix.* London: Macmillan, 1974. A historian of science's view of the long road to the double helix; a series of scientific histories; scholarly but lively; based partly on personal interviews with the participants in the adventure; absorbing; partly technical.

Pfeiffer, John, and the editors of Time-Life Books. *The Cell.* 2d ed. New York: Time-Life Books, 1972. An easy-to-read, very well-illustrated, broad view of the cell and its niche in the structure of organisms, theory of disease, embryology, and genetics.

Sayre, Anne. *Rosalind Franklin and DNA.* New York: Norton, 1975. Sayre's personal narrative of events in the life of Rosalind Franklin and her critical role in determining the structure of the DNA molecule.

Swanson, Carl P., and Peter L. Webster. *The Cell.* 4th ed. Englewood Cliffs, N.J.: Prentice-Hall, 1977.

Thomas, Lewis. *The Lives of a Cell: Notes of a Biology Watcher.* New York: Viking, 1974. Series of essays which appeared in the *New England Journal of Medicine* between 1971 and 1973; semitechnical.

Watson, James D. *The Double Helix.* New York: Atheneum, 1968. Frankly written, highly personalized tale of the plots and persons working to solve DNA structure; read with, but before, Anne Sayre's book for insight into the private biases of some scientists.

————. *Molecular Biology of the Gene.* 2d ed. Menlo Park, Calif.: W. A. Benjamin, 1970. Authoritative; comprehensive; definitely not bedtime reading.

————, and F. H. C. Crick. "Molecular Structure of Nucleic Acids: A Structure for Deoxyribose Nucleic Acid." *Nature* 171 (1953): 737, 738. The classic paper which first described the molecular pattern of the double helix.

Plant Names

Common name	Scientific name	Family
apple	*Pyrus malus*	Rosaceae
beet	*Beta vulgaris*	Chenopodiaceae
cotton	*Gossypium* spp.	Malvaceae
giant sequoia	*Sequoiadendron giganteum*	Taxodiaceae
maize	*Zea mays*	Gramineae
onion	*Allium cepa*	Liliaceae
sunflower	*Helianthus annuus*	Compositae
trillium	*Trillium* spp.	Liliaceae
zinnia	*Zinnia* spp.	Compositae

In addition to its functional utility,
wood has natural ornamental value as
this Japanese garden gate shows.

6
Wood

Most Humanly Intimate
of All Materials

From the fantastic totem of the Alaskan—erected for its own sake as a great sculptured pole, seen in its primitive colors far above the snows—to the resilient bow of the American Indian, and from the enormous solid polished tree-trunks upholding the famous great temple roofs of Japan to the delicate spreading veneers of rare exotic woods on the surfaces of continental furniture, wood is allowed to be wood.

It is the most humanly intimate of all materials. Man loves his association with it, likes to feel it under his hand, sympathetic to his touch and to his eye. Wood is universally beautiful to Man.

With fine sensitivity expressed in a kind of prose poem, Frank Lloyd Wright extolled wood, not as an object to be "joined and glued, braced and screwed, boxed and nailed, turned and tortured," and subjected to other indignities, but rather, as a product of nature, to be molded with tenderness and understanding in making man's home a more beautiful place in which to live. And yet, even though most of the world's human population lives in wooden houses, sits on wooden chairs, eats at wooden tables, smokes wooden pipes, cooks on and is warmed by wood fires, humans have little real understanding of wood's structure and properties and even less appreciation for its inherent beauty.

Unlike other structural materials—metals and plastics—wood is a highly complex natural product, used by man long before

127

he ever discovered how to smelt metals and concoct synthetic plastics. Wood is unique among all raw materials, and as Egon Glesinger has stressed in his *The Coming Age of Wood*, it is universal, abundant, and potentially inexhaustible. These are his "big three of wood."

Value and Uses of Wood

Wood and wood products are of enormous commercial importance and they appreciably benefit mankind. In all industrialized nations these commodities account for a significant proportion of the total national consumption of goods. In nations with little industrial activity, wood is often one of the few readily obtainable materials which provide for the nonfood necessities of life: shelter, warmth, and tools. The position of wood in the economy of the United States may be taken as an example for an industrial nation. Consumption of industrial timber products reached a peak of 13.7 billion cubic feet in 1972. For this year, average per capita consumption of all timber products was 67.9 cubic feet. Of this, 35.1 cubic feet were used as lumber, 20.5 as pulp products, 7.7 as plywood and veneer, 2.3 as miscellaneous forest products (classed as cooperage logs, poles and piling, fenceposts, hewn ties, round mine timbers, box bolts, excelsior bolts, chemical wood, shingle bolts), and 2.3 cubic feet were consumed as fuel wood. And this does not account for some of the lesser forest products: naval stores (turpentine and rosin), bark, tannins, sugar, volatile oils, and dyes. Sale of timber products provides a major source of income for some regions of the United States. Oregon, Washington, and California earned $800 million, $545 million, and $340 million respectively from their forests in 1972.

A recent report by United States Forest Service economists indicates that "timber supplies are not likely to rise significantly unless forest management, utilization, and research programs are substantially expanded. The longrun outlook is thus one of increasing competition for the available timber and high prices." This skeptical view of future timber resources could improve sharply since "U.S. forests have the capacity, in time, to grow substantially more timber than is currently being produced. In addition, there are opportunities for improvement in the utilization of the timber that is harvested." Forests are one of the world's few renewable natural resources; unlike mineral reserves and fossil fuels, they can be regrown and replaced; their products are often reusable and can be recycled easily and relatively inexpensively as compared with metals and some other mineral resources. Thus a combination of wise forest management, efficient utilization of forest products, and extensive reutilization of these products could result in a continuing source of these natural botanical resources for years to come.

The uses of wood are as varied as its structure and properties, and it would seem almost superfluous to tabulate them here so well are they known. But, perhaps an abbreviated list might not be out of order nor overly redundant. Aside from its obvious uses in house construction and furnituremaking, pulp and paper manufacture, and in fabricating multitudes of wooden articles for day-to-day living, wood is also used for poles and pilings, mine timbers, flooring, railroad ties, shakes and shingles, boxes and barrels, tanks and vats, baskets, pallets, composition board (Masonite is a kind of composition board), sawdust and shavings, tool handles, musical instruments, sporting goods, synthetic fibers (rayon and cellulose acetate), transparent films (Cellophane), explosives (nitrocellulose), cellulose sponges, tar and charcoal, naval stores, plastics, chemical flavorings (vanillin), tannins, and dyes. Even in the construction of modern concrete and steel skycrapers, thousands of board feet of lumber and layer upon layer of plywood are used in temporary construction—forms for pouring concrete, scaffolding, guardrails. New steel ships glide into the water guided on greased ways of timber. Decking is often of wood, as are the decorative appointments and trim in the saloons of ocean liners. The vaulted roofs of avant-garde church architecture soar skyward on gracefully curved trusses of resin-bonded, laminated layers of wood.

Wood Is a Plant Product

Wood occupies an important position and plays a critical role in the form and functioning of all vascular plants. It is the structural framework of trees and shrubs; yes, and even of the tiny garden herbs and weeds which look as though they had no backbone at all. The fibers in wood have much to do with the strength of the plant; they hold it upright, allow it to be flexible in wind and rain, to be tough and resilient, and to withstand mechanical damage. And yet there are of course differences: perennial plants such as trees and shrubs, with large amounts of

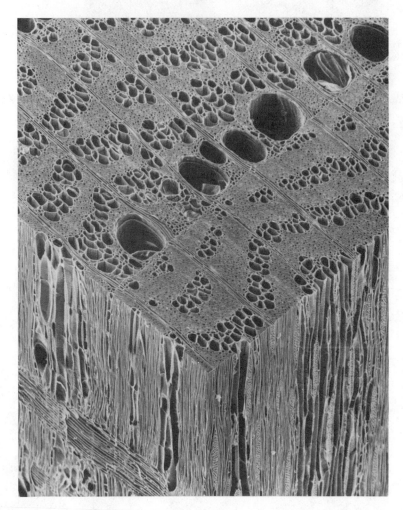

Figure 6.1 Block of elm wood exposing three sides to view. This magnified picture was taken with a scanning electron microscope. The enormous depth of field gives three-dimensional reality which allows us to see into the cells and to appreciate their intricate design and structural relationships. [Courtesy Wilfred A. Côté.]

wood, are more noted for these properties than annual garden herbs which contain little wood and few fibers. Then too, it is through certain kinds of cells in wood that the water and dissolved minerals from the soil are transported and delivered to other parts of the plant, to the leaves, flowers, and developing fruits and seeds (see Chapter 2).

The botanist who studies woody tissues has a rare opportunity to view an unseen world, one which is visible only through the microscope. The tissues of wood are among the most beautifully intricate and delicately patterned of all the works of nature (Figure 6.1). To have been among the first to see these

designs, to have looked down the tube of a microscope at a
thinly sliced section of wood during the seventeenth century,
not knowing what would be revealed by the lenses, must have
been a profound experience for the early microscopists, men
such as Nehemiah Grew (1641–1712) and Marcello Malpighi
(1628–1694). Indeed, we have Grew's own words to go by—we
know how he was struck by the fineness of the woody tissues
he saw: "The Staple of the Stuff is so exquisitely fine, that no
silkworm is able to draw anything near so fine a thread. So that
he who walks about with the meanest stick, holds a piece of Nature's Handicraft, which far surpasses the most elaborate Woof
or Needle Work in the World" (from, *The Anatomy of Plants with
an Idea of a Philosophical History of Plants . . .* , 1682).

Today we are able to use the findings of microscopic wood
study (**wood anatomy**) in several ways: We can provide helpful
information for the taxonomist in his quest to identify plants,
we can predict the physical and mechanical properties of wood,
and we have been able to learn much about the evolution of
plants through analyses of the cells and tissues of wood. Wood,
being less liable to decay than the tissues of succulent herbs, is
frequently found preserved in fossil deposits. We have a-
vailable for evolutionary study then, records from ancient
specimens of wood, concrete evidence of plant life in the past,
physical documents of botany from previous geologic epochs.
Annual layers in wood provide the archeologist and ethnog-
rapher with guideposts for dating prehistoric human cultures.
It is even possible to aid in questions of law and criminology,
and wood study is now a mainstay of investigations in the foren-
sic laboratory. In this field, wood has evoked considerable popular interest.

Sleuthing with Wood

In 1932 Charles A. Lindbergh was the celebrated hero whose
first solo flight from New York to Paris in 1927 had captured the
imagination of the world. His airplane, the "Spirit of St. Louis,"
was known to everyone and even today it hangs like an echo of
the past in the Smithsonian's Air and Space Museum, a
reminder of that marvelous voyage. Lindbergh's wife was the
former Anne Morrow, daughter of Dwight W. Morrow, partner
in the investment firm of J. P. Morgan & Company and U.S. ambassador to Mexico between 1927 and 1930. On March 1, 1932,
the 21-month-old son of the Lindberghs was kidnapped from
the nursery of their remote country home near the little village

of Hopewell, New Jersey. This kidnapping and the subsequent murder of the baby stirred the emotions of the American public as no other crime had ever done. Because of the fame of the Lindberghs, fathers and mothers from one end of the country to the other identified with the distraught parents while the tales of ransom notes, cruel hoaxes, and telephone calls unfolded in newspapers and on the radio.

Evidence surrounding the kidnapping was slim and insubstantial. In part it consisted of handwriting on ransom notes, marked money from the pay off, a wooden ladder hidden in a clump of bushes about 60 feet from the house, footprints of stocking-clad feet beneath the second floor nursery window, indentations of ladder rails in the soft earth beneath the window and two marks made by the upper ends of the rails on the whitewashed walls of the house, and a $^1/_4$-inch carpenter's chisel on the ground near where the ladder had been placed (Figure 6.2). There were no eyewitnesses nor were there any identifiable fingerprints.

The case was placed in charge of Colonel H. Norman Schwarzkopf, superintendent of the New Jersey State Police; later the Federal Bureau of Investigation was called in. But what concerns us here is the wooden ladder, for this provided crucial information which led to the conviction of Bruno Richard Hauptmann for the kidnap-murder of the Lindbergh infant (Figure 6.2). The case is a landmark in the annals of criminology because of the extraordinary testimony of the state's chief witness, Arthur Koehler (Figure 6.3), the expert on wood, and for its suggestion to legal officers of the growing importance of the application of science to trial problems.

It was because of the wooden ladder that Colonel Schwarzkopf called in Arthur Koehler, wood technologist with the U.S. Forest Products Laboratory in Madison, Wisconsin. He was asked to examine the ladder and to report on it to see if he could discover any promising clues. To anyone else this would have seemed an impossible request. The ladder was a homemade affair, full of individual characteristics; there were no others like it. This was a boon to Koehler. On the basis of the cell structure of the wood, Koehler was able to determine the kinds of wood of which it was made. The ladder was a hodgepodge, such as one might make from scraps: rungs of soft ponderosa pine and Douglas fir, rails partly of hard North Carolina pine and Douglas fir; dowels used to fasten the several sections of rail together were of birch.

Figure 6.2 The reassembled kidnap ladder by which Bruno Richard Hauptmann climbed to the nursery of the Lindbergh home in Hopewell, New Jersey, to abduct Charles A. Lindbergh, Jr.

Figure 6.3 Arthur Koehler, "expert on wood," whose testimony helped convict Bruno Richard Hauptmann of the kidnap-murder of Charles A. Lindbergh, Jr. [Courtesy U.S. Forest Products Laboratory.]

Two parts of the North Carolina pine rails were dressed on a machine planer. Planer knives leave telltale grooves on surfaces of dressed boards. These marks can be seen with oblique lighting and it is possible from the markings for an expert to determine the kinds of planer cutter heads which smoothed the board and the rate at which the boards passed through the machine. Koehler found that the North Carolina pine rails had been planed on a machine which had eight knives in the cutter heads that dressed the wide surfaces and six in the cutter heads that dressed the edges of the boards. Koehler saw that one of the cuts made by the knives in the planer head was defective, that is, knicked. From this he was able to calculate the number of knife cuts per revolution of the cutter heads and the rate at which the lumber passed through the planer.

Using these data, by questionnaire and telephone, Koehler canvassed 1,600 mills in the Atlantic states where North Carolina pine grew and was manufactured into wood products. In answer to his queries, Koehler learned that there were 25 mills which had machine planers of the type employed to fashion the pine rails in the ladder. Koehler requested samples of planed lumber from each of the mills and he examined these painstakingly in his laboratory in Madison, Wisconsin. Then, he saw it—a lumber sample from a machine like that which had planed the boards in the ladder, with grooves indicating the same style of cutter heads and the same rate of passage through the planer. The sample had been submitted from the mill of M. G. and J. J. Dorn of McCormick, South Carolina. Koehler visited the mill personally to verify his findings; he came away somewhat disappointed because he could not find any boards in the storage yard of the mill with the characteristic marks. Successful mill operators do not allow dull or knicked planer knives to stay that way very long. However, Koehler was convinced that he was on the right track; diligently and patiently he traced shipments of Dorn lumber up and down the land and finally identified a shipment sent from McCormick to the National Lumber and Millwork Company in the Bronx, New York. It was found shortly thereafter that Hauptmann had worked for this company and on December 29, 1931, had bought $9.31 worth of lumber from them.

Further evidence involving wood came to light when Koehler found that a rather dull hand plane was used to smooth two edges of one of the ladder rails. The planed board had characteristic ridges, identical with those left by a hand plane later found

Figure 6.4 Model showing how nail holes in ladder rail were matched with those in the floor joists of the Hauptmann attic.

in Hauptmann's tool box. When Koehler appeared on the stand as a witness, with the permission of the court, he clamped a vise on the judge's bench, secured a piece of wood in it, and in the presence of the court and jury, planed it with Hauptmann's plane. The resulting markings matched exactly with the markings on the ladder rail.

Police officers investigating the case had found that one of the floor boards in Hauptmann's attic had been sawed out, that a section was missing. Koehler was able to show that one section of ladder rail had been part of a longer board. There were nail holes in it as well and these bore no relation to the construction of the ladder. Furthermore, there was no rust around the nail holes. This told Koehler that the wood had been in a protected place. It was thus Koehler's contention that the section of ladder rail had been cut from the flooring in Hauptmann's attic and he proceeded to demonstrate this to the court.

First, when the ladder rail section was placed over the floor joist in Hauptmann's attic, the nail holes in the ladder rail corresponded perfectly with the nail holes in the joists (Figure 6.4). Second, when the ladder rail and the sawed floor board were joined where they had been sawed apart, the figure (see page 144) of the wood in each piece connected and matched completely (Figure 6.5). Third, the annual rings (see page 151) of the two pieces were identical with respect to width and curvature (Figure 6.5). Fourth, sawdust from the upper side of the ceiling plaster below where the floor board had been cut was from the same species of tree as the wood of the ladder rail. And fifth, the width of the saw cut was between .035 and .037 of an inch and Hauptmann had two saws in his tool chest which made just such cuts.

All of these bits and pieces of evidence from wood, added to other information on handwriting and marked money, were sufficient to convict Hauptmann of the crime. No further evidence in Hauptmann's behalf came to light after several appeals and writs of review and Hauptmann was executed on April 3, 1936. Koehler had made good his early boast, that he would "hang the ladder right around Hauptmann's neck."

Framework and Function

We ought to return now to wood as a plant product so that we can appreciate its structure and understand something of its formation. Figure 6.6 is a photograph of the cross-section of an

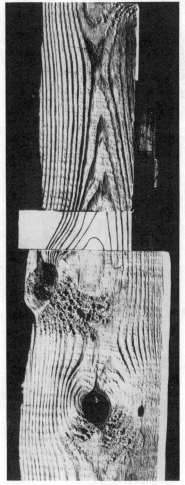

Figure 6.5 Actual section of wood from the ladder rail and from floor board in Hauptmann's attic showing the corresponding pattern of the wood and annual rings of both pieces. The inserted central section represents wood lost during the manufacture of the ladder. [Courtesy U.S. Forest Products Laboratory.]

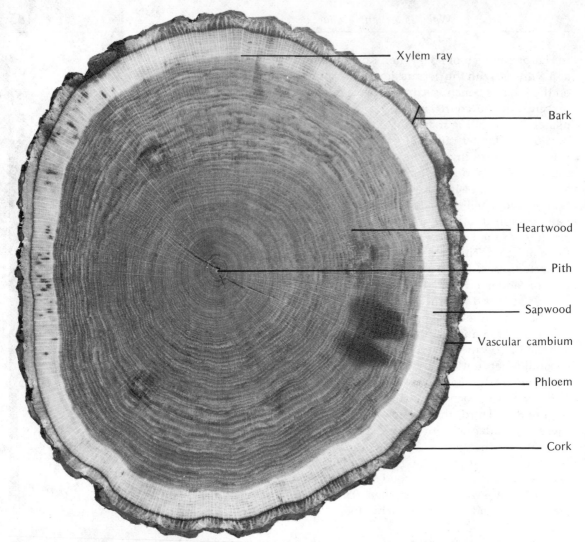

Xylem ray

Bark

Heartwood

Pith

Sapwood

Vascular cambium

Phloem

Cork

Figure 6.6 Cross-section of an oak tree trunk. The dark central portion making up most of the wood, is the nonconductive heartwood; the outer, lighter zone is the conductive sapwood. [Courtesy U.S. Forest Products Laboratory.]

oak tree trunk. As we have already explained in Chapter 2, in the very core of the trunk of a tree is the **pith,** a spongy narrow straw of tissue. Surrounding the pith is the wood (**xylem**); the wood comprises the vast bulk of the tree trunk. The wood is covered by the **bark,** the outermost layer of the tree trunk. Between the bark and the wood, where they adjoin one another, is an exceedingly thin sheath of tissue, the **vascular cambium** (Figure 6.7). The cambium has peculiar and very necessary properties, for it is a **meristem** and its cells are thus able to divide to produce new cells. Cambial cells are responsible for producing additional wood cells toward the inside and bark cells on the outside. More wood cells are always produced than bark cells. Through this action—the production of cells by the cambium—the tree trunk increases in diameter during each growing season. Wood cells are retained for the life of the tree, but the outer bark cells are eventually forced off the tree trunk by the inexorably accumulating wood underneath. The flaking off of bark is easily seen in certain kinds of trees, notably the sycamore or plane tree. The outer bark is soft and scaly in many trees and easily detached, evidence of its transient connection with the trunk. Wood is the mast of the tree; it supports the branches and its parts. It is also the pipeline which brings water from the well of the soil, through the roots and trunk, and it disperses the water to all parts of the plant. It even stores some food.

The innermost part of the bark, near the cambium, contains cells which also have conductive properties (**phloem;** Figure 6.8). This conduction system, however, carries sugars made in the leaves and other soluble foods to places in the tree where they are used for energy or for making cellular substances—cell walls and protoplasm. Phloem also stores food. The outer part of the bark is usually thicker, more spongy and corky than the inner conductive part. It protects the tree from mechanical damage, browsing animals, insect attack, loss of water through evaporation, and from the inroads of disease-producing organisms.

Softwoods. The cells in wood are variously modified to perform the functions of support, conduction of water and dissolved minerals, and food storage. In the wood of pine and in other conifers (cone-bearing trees and shrubs; Figures 6.9, 6.10, and 6.11)—popularly called **softwoods**—there are two kinds of fundamental cells. One is the **tracheid,** a cigar-shaped, elongated cell (Figure 6.11) with thickish pitted walls enclosing a **cavity** in the middle. The other is the **ray cell.** Practically all of the wood of a pine tree trunk consists of a mass of closely packed tracheids (Figure 6.9). The tracheid performs two of the major jobs in trees: It conducts water and supports the trunk at the same time. **Pits** (Figures 6.10 and 6.11) in the cell wall are part of a hydraulic communication system which connects tracheid with tracheid, and it is through these pits that the cell cavity of one tracheid is interconnected with that of the next. Water and dissolved minerals move upward through the wood in the tree trunk threading a circuitous course from one tracheid to another. Tracheids in the wood of the trunk are attached to those in the wood of the root, and a complete, remarkably efficient fluid transportation system carries water right up to the

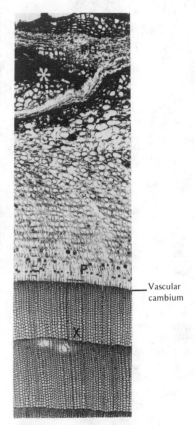

Vascular cambium

Figure 6.7 Magnified view of a radial strip through wood (bottom), vascular cambium, and bark (top) of white pine stem. [Courtesy Lalit M. Srivastava and *Arnoldia*.]

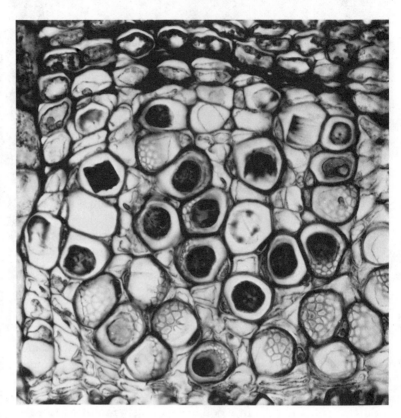

Figure 6.8 Cross- (right) and longitudinal (p. 139) sections (magnified) through the food conducting tissues of the phloem. Pores occur at the ends of the elongated cells and it is through these that food passes from cell to cell. [Courtesy Ray F. Evert and Susan E. Eichhorn.]

ends of the tiniest green needles. Simultaneously, the tracheids, with their thickened cell walls, strengthen the trunk and its branches and give them a quality of limberness which enables the tree to hold up during the stresses of storms and under the weight of ice and snow.

Almost everyone knows that the sawed surfaces of some tree stumps show lines that look like the spokes of a wheel. These are the **vascular rays** (Figure 6.9), a part of the wood which consists of flat ribbons or sheets of cells (**ray cells**) organized into tissues which are inserted along and between rows of tracheids. Just as the tracheid cell system conducts fluids from the bottom to the top of a tree trunk, so the system of rays can conduct fluids laterally across the tree trunk, from the pith toward the bark and from the bark toward the pith. Unlike tracheids, all of which carry water and dissolved minerals, some ray cells carry soluble food and others transport water. Sugars which have been manufactured in the leaves are transported downward

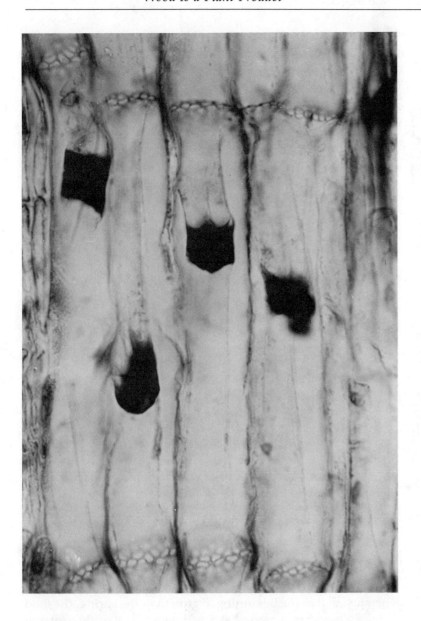

through the phloem cells of the inner bark to be switched off into the food-carrying cells of the rays for conduction across the wood and bark to places of need. Water from the tracheids is shunted into water-transporting ray cells for movement into the cambium, phloem, and associated cells of the bark. Toward the end of the growing season in temperate and cold climates, food

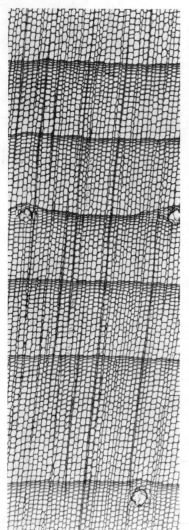

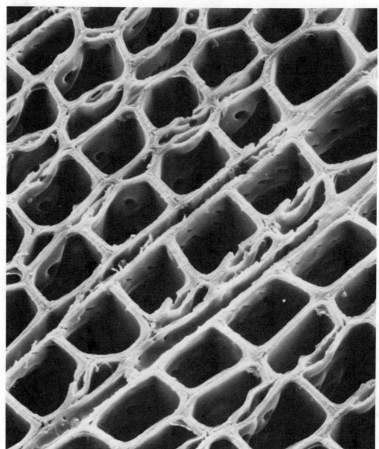

Figure 6.10   Scanning electron micrograph of tracheids in wood of larch, a conifer (softwood). Pits, by means of which water passes from tracheid to tracheid, are clearly visible. [Courtesy Wilfred A. Côté.]

Figure 6.9   Magnified cross-section of white pine wood. The numerous small openings are tracheids; horizontal bands are annual rings; vertical lines are the vascular rays; large openings are resin ducts, tubes into which resin is secreted. [Courtesy U.S. Forest Products Laboratory.]

may be concentrated in ray cells for storage over the winter. Then just before the beginning of growth in the spring, the food is released and transported across the rays to actively growing plant parts, especially to the reactivated vascular cambium which is now producing new cells of xylem and phloem at a great rate.

Hardwoods. The structure of **hardwoods** (woods of dicotyledons) is similar to that of softwoods and there are cells that perform the same basic functions—support; conduction of water,

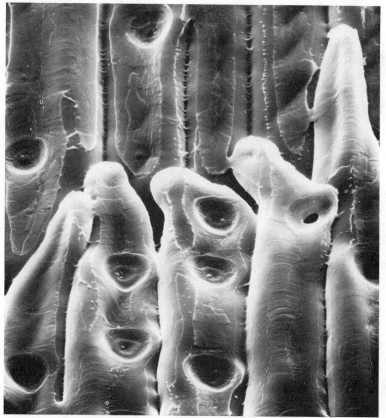

Figure 6.11 Scanning electron micrograph of a softwood showing intact tips of tracheids with bordered pits in their walls. [Courtesy Wilfred A. Côté.]

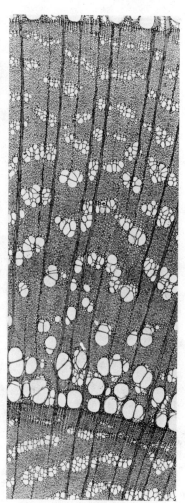

Figure 6.12 Magnified cross-section of American elm wood. The large openings are vessels. These are embedded in a groundmass of thick-walled fibers. The band of wood across the photograph represents one annual ring; vertical lines are vascular rays. [Courtesy U.S. Forest Products Laboratory.]

dissolved minerals, and food; and food storage—for the hardwood tree (Figures 6.12, 6.13, and 6.14) as for the softwood tree. There are also some very important and fundamental differences between the woods of these two categories of plants. The primary water-conducting cell in dicotyledons is the **vessel cell** (Figure 6.13). It looks like a tiny pore to the naked eye on the smoothed-off end of a piece of wood (Figures 6.1 and 6.12). The vessel cell is shortened and flat- or slope-ended, rather than being elongated and taper-pointed like a tracheid. Also, instead of the water passing from cell to cell through pits in the walls as it does in tracheids, vessel cells are attached end to end, one on top of another, to form an elongated pipeline in the wood called

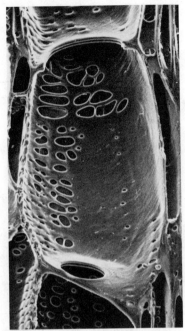

Figure 6.13 Scanning electron micrograph of a single complete vessel cell and parts of two others at the top and bottom in a hardwood species. The opening at the lower end of the intact vessel cell is the perforation through which water moves from cell to cell. [Courtesy Brian G. Butterfield and Brian A. Meylan.]

a **vessel** (Figure 6.14). Each tree trunk contains many thousands of vessels. The ends of vessel cells are perforated and open (Figure 6.13) and each cell in the series is continuous with the next one through these openings and through the cell cavity, not unlike a series of threaded segments of iron pipe.

Vessels are surrounded by elongated tapering cells, **fibers,** which look much like tracheids, but the walls of these cells are very thick by comparison and the pits are minute, too small for any significant intercommunication and water conduction. Fibers in hardwoods, like the tracheids in softwoods, comprise the greatest bulk of the wood mass (Figure 6.12). Fibers are specialized to perform a single function—support—just as vessel cells are specialized to perform a single function—conduction.

Whereas in softwoods the tracheid carries water and supports the tree trunk and its branches, in hardwoods these two jobs are distributed to two different kinds of cells, the fiber and vessel cell, respectively. It would seem that the broad open-ended vessel cells, united one above the other to form vessels, are more efficient water carriers than a similar row of tracheids in which the water is conducted tortuously from tracheid to tracheid through a series of pits in the walls. Also the thick-walled fiber with tiny pits, which does not conduct water, seems to provide stronger mechanical support than the thinner-walled, larger-pitted tracheid.

Dicotyledonous woods also have **vascular rays** and these function much as do those in conifer woods. But the rays in dicotyledons may be quite broad sheets of cells, while rays in conifers are always very narrow. The broad rays of dicotyledons, because of their greater volume, would seem to be more effective food repositories and food transporters than the narrow rays of conifers.

Conifers, however, do not seem to suffer from any of these apparent deficiencies of food storage, food and water transport, and xylem strength and they are quite able to thrive and to cope with the conditions of growth and development each season. As a matter of fact, as will be pointed out later in this chapter, the oldest trees are not the efficient dicotyledons, but the struggling conifers.

Botanically, the terms hardwood (dicotyledon) and softwood (conifer) are not very accurate. There are woods like balsa, which is classed as a hardwood, which are very much softer than some of our pines which are classed as softwoods. The terms have a popular and commercial utility, but it ought always to be remembered that they may have little or no bearing on the actual physical hardness of the wood.

Wood Grows Old

As the wood in the trunk of a tree ages there are certain changes which affect life processes, much as increasing age in humans takes its toll of vigor and responsivity. Progressively, from the core of the tree outward, the wood begins to die so that in an old tree only the outermost few inches of wood continue to conduct water and to store food. The center section, however, is still effective in supporting the tree, since support only depends on the presence of cell walls and not on living cytoplasm. Old trees in which the center has rotted out may continue to live for many years because the outer layers of wood still continue to perform the vital activities of water conduction and food storage. Wood from the dead center of a tree is **heartwood;** the conductive outer layers of wood comprise **sapwood** (Figure 6.6).

During the formation of heartwood, the center wood of the trunk becomes a garbage dump for waste or excess organic materials produced in the outer portions of the wood by cells in the heartwood itself, and perhaps even by other parts of the tree. Plants, unlike animals, have no excretory system by which superfluous substances can be voided externally. Waste, that is, discarded or unused products of cellular activity, are probably conducted into the center of the tree by the ray cells, converted there into insoluble compounds, and deposited permanently. Tree wastes may consist of tannins, gums, resins, dyes, and volatile oils, all or some of which may color the heartwood distinctively. In many trees, the heartwood is dark-colored and the sapwood, by contrast, is light-colored (Figure 6.6). It is the variously colored heartwood of trees which is desirable for many kinds of decorative purposes. The black walnut which has a chocolate-purple heartwood has a whitish and not particularly attractive sapwood. Only the heartwood of mahogany has the characteristic red-brown color so desired for furniture manufacture, and you would not want veneered paneling made from the white sapwood of the black cherry. Heartwood, too, is more resistant to decay than is the sapwood and for this reason it is desired for timbers which are used in contact with the ground for fence posts and poles (as black locust and osage orange). The wastes of trees are valuable products to man.

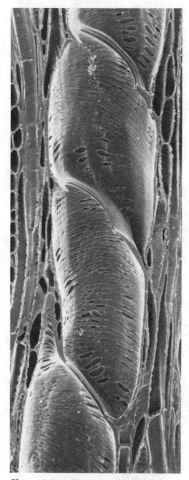

Figure 6.14 Scanning electron micrograph of a portion of a vessel in a hardwood. Four vessel cells are shown one above the other; the upper and lower ones are incomplete. [Courtesy Brian G. Butterfield and Brian A. Meylan.]

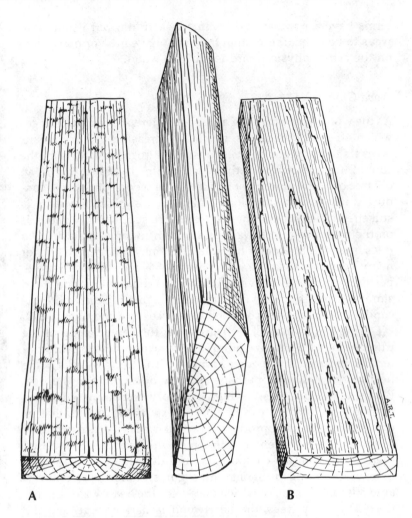

Figure 6.15   The direction in which logs are sawn into boards partially determines the appearance and pattern of wood. Board *A* is quarter-sawn; board *B* is plain-sawn. [Redrawn from U.S. Forest Products Laboratory photograph.]

A

B

An Attractive Figure

The appearance of wood used for furniture manufacture and for trim depends on several factors, only one of which is color. The patterns we associate with wood surfaces comprise **figure**—not grain as it is often called. **Grain,** properly used, refers to the prevailing direction of the fibers and tracheids in wood and it only contributes to the over-all pattern, or figure. Other features which influence figure are presence or absence of annual rings (see page 151), differences between early wood and late wood (see page 154), prominence of vascular rays, size of vessels, position of wood in the tree, and the direction in which boards are cut.

Boards are sawn from logs in two ways with reference to the diameter of the log (Figure 6.15). **Quarter-sawn** boards result from cuts which are approximately parallel to a radius or diameter of the log. Quartered boards are distinguished on the broad surface by the appearance of the annual rings which are approximately parallel to the length of the board and by the vascular rays which cross the annual rings at right angles (Figure 6.16). If the vascular rays are light reflecting and very large, as in species of oak and sycamore, a so-called silver grain results. On the other hand, if the saw cuts are perpendicular to a radius or diameter of the log, **flat-cut** or **plain-sawn** boards result. Annual rings on flat-cut boards look like a series of hills and valleys or wavy lines (Figure 6.17).

If you stop to think for a moment, you will realize that it is possible to saw out many more plain-sawn boards than quarter-sawn boards from a log since there are relatively few boards which can be cut out parallel to a radius. The figure in quartered boards is more attractive and therefore more desirable to some purchasers than to others. For these reasons, quarter-sawn lumber is more expensive than plain-sawn lumber from the same tree species.

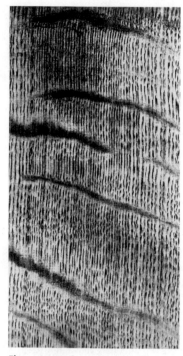

Figure 6.16 Quarter-sawn oak board. The irregular bands which run from left to right are broad vascular rays characteristic of oak; vertical lines are annual ring boundaries. [Courtesy U.S. Forest Products Laboratory.]

Properties of Wood

The physical and mechanical properties of wood do not directly affect its figure nor influence its appearance. Nevertheless, the uses of wood are also governed by its material properties and these in turn may be traced to the tracheids and fibers which comprise most of the cells in wood. The physical properties of wood include such characteristics as hardness, weight, and thermal and electrical conductivity. Mechanical properties are an expression of the behavior of wood under applied forces. Strength, for example, is a mechanical property. Mechanical properties are influenced by physical properties. These, along with the working qualities of wood (for example, ability to take finishes; ease of sawing, planing, nailing, splitting, and turning) and durability in the environment, are among the factors which help to determine the uses of wood.

The **specific gravity** of wood is the ratio of the weight of a

Figure 6.17 Plain-sawn oak board. The wavy lines are annual ring patterns. [Courtesy U.S. Forest Products Laboratory.]

Figure 6.18 The smaller block of lignum vitae wood on the left weighs the same as the larger block of balsa wood. The specific gravity of lignum vitae is 1.32 vs. 0.20 for balsa. [Courtesy Chicago Museum of Natural History.]

piece of wood in air to the weight of an equal volume of water. Thus, if a cubic inch of wood weighed twice as much as a cubic inch of water, the specific gravity of the wood would be two. The extreme range of specific gravities of woods native to the United States is from 0.21 for corkwood to 1.04 for black ironwood. Black ironwood weighs more than an equivalent volume of water and we could predict that this is not the kind of wood with which to build a raft. Most commercially useful woods of the United States have specific gravities between 0.35 and 0.65. A number of tropical woods are exceedingly heavy; bannia from Surinam has a specific gravity of 1.30, lignum vitae from the Caribbean, Mexico, Central and South America, is 1.32 (Figure 6.18), and greenheart from Guyana is 1.06. Some of the lightest woods also come from the tropics; the specific gravity of balsa from Ecuador is 0.20 (Figure 6.18) and quipo from Panama is 0.14. Specific gravity is determined by size of cells, thickness of cell walls, and the ratio between cell size and wall thickness.

Strength of wood is measured by the different kinds of

primary stresses to which it is subjected. These are **compressive stress, tensile stress,** and **shear stress.** Different kinds of wood will respond differently to the forces of these three primary stresses. However, the specific gravity of wood is the best index that exists for predicting the strength properties of wood because it is a measure of the relative amount of cell wall material present. Compressive strength, for example, is directly proportional to the specific gravity of wood; the higher the specific gravity, the greater the compressive strength.

Hard woods are also strong woods since hardness, like strength and specific gravity, depends upon the amount of cell wall material present. Woods having cells with thick walls—that is, with much cell wall material per unit of volume—will be stronger, heavier, and harder than woods with thin-walled cells. It is possible, therefore, to predict the relative strength, weight, and hardness of wood by looking at the structure of woody cell walls with a microscope.

Wood Destroyers

While wood has great utility for many purposes, its very organic composition, the cellulose and lignin of the cell walls (see Chapter 5), makes it susceptible to several kinds of deterioration during use after removal from the forest. There are three main agencies of wood deterioration: **wood-inhabiting fungi, wood-boring insects,** and **marine borers.** Together these destroy or render useless for structural and decorative purposes enormous quantities of forest products annually.

Fatal Fungi

Wood is frequently invaded by fungi, usually colorless plants which do not manufacture their own food as do green plants. Rather they exist through their ability to digest organic matter and incorporate it into their own cells for use as energy and for building new cellular materials—for their own growth. Some fungi can live on dead and decaying wood and others, the **parasites,** can attack wood in the living tree. Wood-inhabiting fungi are of three kinds, depending upon the nature of their development in and on wood and the type of deterioration which they cause: **wood-destroying fungi, wood-staining fungi,** and **molds.** Wood-destroying fungi can actually destroy the cell walls of tracheids and fibers, drastically alter the physical

Figure 6.19 The rotten log, evidence of the activities of decay-producing fungi.

properties of wood, and profoundly change the mechanical properties. Disorganization of the cell wall substance produces **decay.** Decay is familiar to us in the rotting log (Figure 6.19), the punky outdoor stair tread, the powdery rafter under the leaky roof. The staining fungi and the molds are superficial and they exist on easily digested residues and organic compounds stored in the cells of wood: sugars, starch, and other simple carbohydrates. Activities of these fungi usually do not result in any appreciable loss of strength in wood, but their presence causes unsightly discolorations which are classed as defects in lumber and prevent its use for decorative purposes. Different kinds of wood vary in their natural resistance to decay and staining. The place where wood is used, whether protected or exposed to rain, snow, and the soil, also affects the durability and resistance of wood to attack by fungi.

The most important factors in preventing decay by fungi are adequate drying (seasoning) and proper handling and storage of lumber before it is put into use. Design of structures to avoid unnecessary exposure of wood to conditions favorable to decay is important in protecting wood. Where this is impossible, wood must be treated to impede or prevent decay. This is accomplished by application of a variety of weather-resistant coatings, varnishes, paints, and stains. Wood which is severely imperiled by exposure to the soil (poles, posts, building footings, floor joists, and sills) must be treated with chemical preservatives that are toxic to fungi. To apply these we take advantage of the natural porosity of wood; preservatives can be painted on, absorbed into the wood by soaking, or injected under high pressure (Figure 6.20). Creosote, Wolman salts (fluoride-phenol mixtures), copper naphthenate, and other poisonous mixtures are used. Coal-tar creosote, patented as a wood preservative in England by John Bethell in 1838, is still the most effective chemical known for protection against fungal decay, insects, and marine borers. However, none of these is permanent or guaranteed forever; eventually timbers in contact with the soil will decay as the preservatives lose their effectiveness or leach out and the wood will have to be replaced.

Figure 6.20 Cylinders for pressure-treating timbers with preservatives. Timbers shown will be impregnated with "Wolman" salts, a poisonous mixture containing fluorine and phenol. [Courtesy Koppers Company.]

Insects

Insect damage to forest products may occur in the standing tree, in the green saw log, in unseasoned lumber, in stored and seasoned lumber, and during use. In most cases, damage by wood-boring insects is done by insect larvae, immature forms such as worms and grubs. Larvae burrow into the wood to secure both food and shelter and they leave characteristic tunnels or galleries. In some cases, the adult insects are responsible for wood deterioration. This group includes the subterranean termites (Figures 6.21 and 6.22), ambrosia beetles, and carpenter ants. Holes which result from the ravages of insects are not only unsightly but, by destroying the continuity of the tracheids and fibers, they reduce the structural strength of the wood. Poisonous preservatives are used to protect wood from insect damage although in some instances repellents are effective.

Marauders of the Sea

Among the most unlikely destroyers of wood are the marine borers. Some of these creatures, the *limnorias*, are crustaceans, specialized relatives of lobsters, shrimps, and crabs. In their larval stages, they are free-swimming, however, as adults they

Figure 6.21 "Business end" of subterranean termite, one of the many insect enemies of wood. [Courtesy Koppers Company.]

Figure 6.22 Remains of wooden house supports following severe termite attack. [Courtesy Koppers Company.]

bore into wooden structures immersed in sea water: dockage, pilings, and the hulls of wooden boats (Figure 6.23). *Teredos* or shipworms are mollusks closely related to clams, oysters, and scallops. They too have a free-swimming larval form but settle as adults into a sedentary existence chewing into underwater wooden structures with their modified shells which are part of the boring mechanism (Figure 6.23). Marine borers are devastatingly effective in reducing solid, untreated timbers to meshwork in short order. In 1969 it was estimated that damage caused by borers to marine installations of the United States was in the neighborhood of $200 to $250 million. But this destruction is nothing new. Ships of Christopher Columbus's little fleet were riddled by shipworms toward the end of his fourth and last voyage to the New World. As they crossed the Caribbean from Panama to the island of Hispaniola, his ships sank deeper and deeper into the sea and Columbus lamented, "the ships pierced by borers worse than a honeycomb, the people [crew] spiritless and desperate." Columbus was forced to beach his porous ships on Jamaica where he was marooned for many months, for on the night of June 22, 1503, the water almost reached the deck of his flagship.

The most effective treatment for timbers against marine borders is creosote, but this is not completely protective against some species of limnoria. In certain tropical waters where the organisms are active throughout the year even creosoted timbers are destroyed in just a few years. Other protective measures involve sheathing of pilings with plastics, concrete, and metal. Such coverings are effective only as long as they are intact; the slightest opening allows the borer larva access and damage may then proceed undetected until the timber falls away completely destroyed.

Another approach to the problem of protecting marine-exposed timbers, is to take advantage of the natural resistance to these organisms inherent in some timber species. That greenheart and angélique from the Guianas have been marketed throughout the world as marine-borer-resistant timbers is well known, for example. Although one might think that some of the very heavy, hard, and dense tropical woods would show high resistance to attack, many of these are heavily damaged in service. Woods with a high natural content of silica (silicon dioxide, the chemical basis of glass and the mineral quartz) are resistant to some kinds of borers but not to others. Ironically cocobolo, a timber which shows high natural resistance to all

Figure 6.23 Teredos and limnorias are marine animals which infest underwater timbers. Upper specimen shows the result of a combined attack by both groups of animals on susceptible pine wood; lower specimen represents resistant cocobolo wood which was immersed in sea water next to the pine wood over the same period of time. [Courtesy John D. Bultman and U.S. Naval Research Laboratory.]

classes of borers, is unsuitable for structural use because of the small size and poor form of the tree (Figure 6.23).

The Age of Trees and the Ages of Man

In certain parts of the world, where the climate breaks the year into seasons, trees respond by alternately growing and ceasing to grow season by season throughout their lives. This cycling can be detected in the wood of the trunk which reflects the alternating periods of growing and ceasing in the formation of layers of growth (Figure 6.24). In the temperate regions of the world where there is only a single growing season during the year one of these layers of growth is formed each year; it becomes a mirror of the age of the tree. We can call each yearly layer of growth an **annual ring,** and even school children know what fun it is to count these on a stump and come up with the age of the tree.

Late wood

Early wood

Annual ring

Figure 6.24 Cross-section of conifer trunk showing distinct annual rings. Dark parts of the rings are late wood, light parts are early wood. [Courtesy U.S. Forest Products Laboratory.]

The captive audience at Oliver Wendell Holmes's breakfast table was treated one time to the story of a hemlock which blew down in Holmes's woods. He took time out to count the annual rings and by figuring backward, he impressed his listeners with the periods of history that the patriarch tree had withstood. With a slice of the hemlock wood in his hand, in good pedagogic fashion, he caught the attention of his breakfast companions: "Look here. Here are some human lives laid down against the periods of its growth, to which they corresponded. This is Shakspeare's. The tree was seven inches in diameter when he was born; ten inches when he died . . . . Here is the span of Napoleon's career;—the tree doesn't seem to have minded it. I never saw the man yet who was not startled at looking on this section. I have seen many wooden preachers,—never one like this."

From what we can tell, by actual records and by implication, man has always associated rings in the trunks of trees with the growth of the tree. Surely people who lived close to nature—when nature was everything there was—developed some feeling for tree growth even if they did not understand the details. But there are writings too.

Theophrastus, who lived in Greece during the third century B.C., recognized layers in the trunk of the silver fir and likened these to the layers of an onion. It is uncertain, however, whether he referred specifically to the bark or to the wood or if he realized that the rings were annual. We read that about 850 A.D., the Caliph Motewekkil cut down all the sacred cypresses of the Magians and found one that is said to have shown 1,450 rings of growth. Further details are absent. Albertus Magnus (1193?–1280), who knew all there was to know in his time, noted ringlike layers of wood in the alder but it is doubtful if he related them to tree growth. Leonardo da Vinci (1452–1519) who, among numerous other pursuits and talents, was a structural engineer recognized the annual character of the rings in wood from trees and timbers. It is thought likely that in Leonardo's time, this information was passed on to artisans who worked in wood. Alexander von Humboldt (1769–1859), in his many-faceted essays in *Views of Nature*, felt that it was Michel Montaigne (1533–1592), French essayist and courtier, who first showed in 1581 the relationship between annual rings and the age of trees. Supposedly Montaigne picked up the information from a skilled worker engaged in crafting astronomical instruments. Perhaps knowledge of tree rings was kept alive during the sixteenth century by instrument makers and artisans rather than in the learned writings of savants.

In any event, the knowledge seems to have been rediscovered in the seventeenth century by the pioneer plant anatomists Nehemiah Grew and Marcello Malpighi. It seems too, that the great Dutch microscopist, Antony van Leeuwenhoek (1632–1723), the first to see and describe bacteria, also wrote on tree rings. There is little doubt that he understood the association between the rings and their annual character in terms of tree growth. Thus, since about the middle of the seventeenth century, there has been a general understanding of annual rings and tree growth, although the many variations and exceptions are still not fully explained, even today.

Growth by the Year

An annual ring (Figure 6.24) is a layer of wood produced in trunks, roots, and their branches in trees and shrubs in those parts of the world where there is normally only one growing season each year. Each ring, then, represents one annual increment, or layer, of woody tissue. The layer of wood results from the production of wood cells toward the center of the tree by the vascular cambium. It is this activity which causes the trees to grow wider each year. It will be recalled that the cambium which is located between the bark and wood also produces layers of bark cells, but toward the outside during each growing season. However, the layers of wood cells are permanent fixtures of the tree while the outermost layers of bark are continually pushed off the tree as new bark is formed underneath the old and as new wood is produced by the cambium each season. Hence, ordinarily there are no persistent annual rings in bark.

It is important to emphasize that an annual ring is a **layer** of wood, not a line or circle. Better still, if you think of the trunk of a tree as a cone, then each of the annual rings becomes one of a series of nested cones, the younger ones of which are always formed on top of or outside of the older ones. It is the fact of periodic seasonal stoppage of growth that produces a mark, or ring, around the circumference of the tree trunk and which makes the successive layers of growth become visible so that they can be counted on a stump or in a log.

Each annual layer of growth consists of two parts. Because during springtime there is abundant moisture in the soil, cells of wood produced then **(early wood)** are usually more abundant, thinner-walled, and larger in diameter than those cells produced toward the end of the growing season **(late wood)** when there is not so much moisture available for growth. Cells of the late wood are usually fewer, thicker-walled, and sometimes smaller in diameter than those of early wood. The change in appearance between the band of late wood cells (relatively dark colored) of one year and the band of early wood cells (relatively light colored) of the next year, produces a circular mark around the tree trunk and its branches (Figure 6.24). This mark is the boundary of the annual ring; that is, the margin between the wood formed during one year and that produced in the next year.

In some tropical regions where there is little seasonal interruption of growth during the year no distinct rings are formed. Also, in other tropical regions where rings of growth are produced, they are not strictly associated with annual increments and several may be formed each year. By and large, rings of growth in trunks of tropical trees are not reliable indicators of annual enlargement and the age of the tree.

Growth and Environment

Increase in diameter of tree trunks, with or without the production of annual rings, is one result of growth (see Chapters 1 and 2). Some other results are lengthening of twigs, formation of leaves, and production of flowers, fruits, and seeds. The amount and kind of growth are governed and influenced by a complex of internal and external conditions some of which are very obvious and others not. Soil moisture, mineral nutrients in the soil, intensity and duration of sunlight, temperature, and competition of plants with surrounding plants for moisture, minerals, and sunlight, are all factors which have a direct and apparent bearing on growth. It is reasonable to assume, and it can be proven, that abundant moisture and mineral nutrients coupled with ample sunlight and warm temperatures will produce maximum growth if we consider other growing conditions not to be limiting. We could expect that with the above conditions in force, tree growth would proceed at a favorable rate. On the other hand, if one or more growing conditions is less than suitable, tree growth would be somewhat or greatly curtailed, depending upon the degree and kind of limitations to growth.

Like the chain which is no stronger than its weakest link, any one of the conditions of growth may limit the growth of a tree. In most forest zones no one of the conditions of growth is so stringent as to control growth in and of itself. However, there are a few forest regions where this is true, where a single condition may be so strained as to affect the growth of trees seriously. Temperature in Alaska and northern Sweden and soil moisture in certain arid lands of the American Southwest may alone control tree growth in these places. Soil moisture as a limiting factor in growth has proven immensely important in several fields of inquiry: anthropology and archeology, climatology, botany, forestry, astronomy, ecology, and hydrology.

In those tree species which normally produce annual rings as an accompaniment to growth, the width of each ring—the combined band of early wood and late wood—indicates relative growth for a particular season. The annual ring is a summary of all factors or conditions under which growth for any period proceeds. In some arid regions of Arizona, Colorado, and New Mexico, for example, where all conditions except soil moisture are favorable for growth, the relative width of annual rings is directly proportional to available moisture—the more moisture, the wider the annual ring. Precipitation, absorbed by trees from

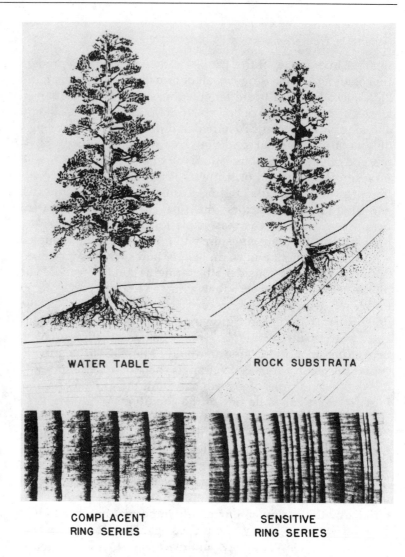

WATER TABLE   ROCK SUBSTRATA

COMPLACENT
RING SERIES

SENSITIVE
RING SERIES

Figure 6.25 Complacent and sensitive ring series. The former are useless in studies of dendrochronology. [Courtesy Laboratory of Tree-Ring Research, University of Arizona. From M. A. Stokes and T. L. Smiley, *An Introduction to Tree-ring Dating,* Chicago: University of Chicago Press, 1968.]

the soil, varies from year to year, often appreciably, and the relative amount is reflected in the widths of annual rings.

Also tree species vary in their sensitivity to available soil moisture; the piñon pine, Douglas fir, ponderosa pine, and Rocky Mountain juniper are especially responsive. The slightest variations in soil moisture are transmitted to the cambium and are mirrored in the relative width of the annual ring of wood produced for any given growing season. Trees of this kind, growing in places where soil moisture is the limiting factor in growth, produce **sensitive ring series** (Figure 6.25), sequences of annual rings which vary in width proportionately to the moisture available for growth. On the other hand, trees (even these same species of trees) which grow in places where all conditions of growth are favorable from season to season, produce annual rings which vary little over long periods of time. Rings of this kind tell us that growth has proceeded leisurely, without any pronounced stress. Sequences of rings in these trees are **complacent ring series** (Figure 6.25).

Annual Rings, Sunspots, Dendrochronology

Ring sequences which are valuable for other than just telling how old a tree is or for estimating rates of growth in forest mensuration are those which are sensitive, or responsive. Ring series which distinguish delicately between successively moist and dry seasons or periods have stories to tell if we can but interpret their silent messages. That kind of interpretation was begun in the United States toward the very beginning of the twentieth century by Professor Andrew Ellicott Douglass (1867–1962), astronomer and director of the Steward Observatory of the University of Arizona in Tucson (Figure 6.26).

Douglass's original interest in tree rings arose from his several years' residence in the dry country of Arizona and his observations of the formidable tenacity of trees to exist and grow in such a sere environment. As an astronomer he reasoned, "Since in a general way it is the sun's heat that evaporates the ocean water and causes winds to bring that water over the continents to fall as rain, it seemed possible or even likely that we would find in the variation of ring thickness some traces of variation in the sun, perhaps some indication of the 11-year sunspot cycle. The characters in any sort of climatic changes which could most easily be identified with a solar source would be cycle length and similar time of coming of the maxima [of solar cycles]." This hypothesis of about 1901 was the basis of an intensive sally into tree-ring study which is now being carried on with even greater refinements at the Laboratory of Tree-Ring Research, University of Arizona, by Professor Douglass's successors. The science, or study, of the chronological sequence of annual growth rings in trees, founded by Douglass, is termed **dendrochronology,** literally, "the study of telling time with trees."

Figure 6.26 Andrew Ellicott Douglass, astronomer and pioneer dendrochronologist. [Courtesy Smithsonian Institution.]

Ancient Sites and Tree Rings

The most imaginative and perhaps useful outcome of the work originated and pursued by Douglass is the application of tree-ring study to the dating and chronological sequencing of the migrations, civilizations, and culture of prehistoric inhabitants—Indians (or better, native Americans)—of the arid American Southwest. In the 1920s, during three expeditions led by Dr. Douglass himself, the golden age of Pueblo Bonito, New Mexico, was set at 1067, one year after the Battle of Hastings which resulted in the Norman conquest of England. The great Cliff Palace, now in Mesa Verde National Park, Colorado, dates to 1073. White House Ruin in Arizona's Canyon de Chelly, contains timbers cut in 1060, 25 years before the famous *Domesday Book* of William the Conqueror was compiled. These discoveries pushed back the historical horizons of the Southwest to about 400 years before the birth of Columbus.

The key to dating Indian dwelling places is in the timbers used in construction, the sticks used in cooking fires, and in the wooden artifacts used to haft stone axes and knives. Materials for tree-ring dating come from several types of habitation sites among which are the hogan (a lodge composed of logs originally covered with earth or sod; Figure 6.27), the pueblo (an apartmentlike adobe dwelling in which timbers formed the rafters or roof poles), and from fireplaces containing intact bits and pieces of charcoal. Wood showing annual rings from any of these artifacts can serve as a basis for dating. There are four requirements for dating specimens and, by association, the time they were put into use by prehistoric people.

1. Trees used for dating purposes must add only one layer of wood each year; that is, the growth rings must be truly annual.
2. Tree growth must be limited by a single environmental factor.
3. The single environmental factor must vary in intensity from year to year and the resulting annual rings must faithfully reflect this variation by their width.
4. The single environmental factor must be effective over a wide geographical area.

These four requirements are satisfied only in a few places in the world, the foremost being certain regions of the American Southwest.

Figure 6.27 Ancient Indian hogan from which timbers were taken for use in cross-dating. [Courtesy Laboratory of Tree-Ring Research, University of Arizona. From M. A. Stokes and T. L. Smiley, *An Introduction to Tree-ring Dating,* Chicago: University of Chicago Press, 1968.]

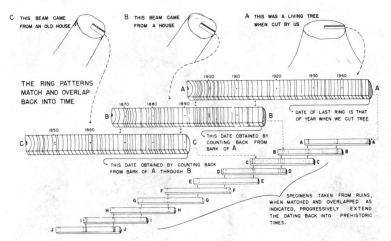

Figure 6.28 Diagram illustrating the method of cross-dating, a technique used to extend dates backward in time. [Courtesy Laboratory of Tree-Ring Research, University of Arizona. From M. A. Stokes and T. L. Smiley, *An Introduction to Tree-ring Dating*, Chicago: University of Chicago Press, 1968.]

Time Marches Back with Trees and Timbers

A **master chronology**—the Rosetta Stone of dendrochronology —of tree rings from the general area must be constructed. Master chronologies built up by the method of **cross-dating** have been established for several areas in the American Southwest. Briefly, master chronologies and cross-dating techniques, as outlined in Figure 6.28, begin with aged living trees (A) which show annual ring sequences of the sensitive type. The series of ring patterns in these is studied, interpreted, mapped, and permanently recorded for future use. These activities are followed by matching successively the annual ring patterns of timbers from prehistoric ruins which may at least in part predate the age of the living tree. Taken together, these operations constitute cross-dating. The inner rings of the living tree may match the outer rings (later formed during the life of the tree) of a prehistoric timber (B). Similarly, other prehistoric timbers (C) in the area may have outer rings which match the inner rings of timber B. Thus time is extended back through an unbroken succession of telltale tree rings.

Through such painstakingly careful comparisons and correlations one master chronology dating back 8,200 years has been worked out. This chronology is based on ring sequences in bristlecone pines from the White Mountains of California, discovered and studied by the late Edmund Schulman (1908–1958) of the Laboratory of Tree-Ring Research. Many of these White Mountain bristlecone pines, which cling tenuously to life, are

Figure 6.29 Ancient bristlecone pine sculptured by the elements. This tree is growing at 11,000 feet elevation in Utah's Dixie National Forest. [Courtesy U.S. Department of Agriculture and Lee Prater.]

over 4,000 years old and at least one of them is more than 4,600 years of age, surpassing the oldest known giant sequoia by several centuries. These venerable plants sprouted as seedlings in the early decades of the twenty-sixth century B.C. They are unquestionably the oldest living things on earth (Figure 6.29).

But to return now to our problem. With an appropriate master chronology of annual rings in hand it is a relatively simple matter—requiring patience, much care, and considerable experience—to match the annual ring sequence in a prehistoric timber with the master chronology built up for an area. It becomes possible, with confidence and accuracy, to date prehistoric culture using timber or charcoal. The message of the tree has been outlined in a unique and characteristic diary of annual rings produced under a severe and demanding environmental taskmaster. And there are other messages to read as well as those of age and chronology.

Other Tree-Ring Stories

Even in Douglass's time, other information than chronology was deduced from a study of tree rings. Besides recorded observations of recurrent 11-year intervals during which sunspots were most numerous and Douglass's hypothesis that these solar changes affect the weather which in turn affects tree growth, using annual ring width as a basis, he was able to demonstrate this cyclic 11-year interval over a period of 500 years. Centuries-long weather records have been compiled in this manner giving rise to the subdiscipline of **dendroclimatology,** the study of climate using data stored in tree rings.

Years of fat and lean, of good moisture conditions and poor moisture conditions, are recorded in the wide and narrow tree rings. This story is correlated with the existence of prehistoric Indians, some of whom built permanent adobe apartment houses and farmed the surrounding areas. Abandonment of these centers, the presumed migration of their inhabitants, and perhaps even drastic cultural changes can be associated with periods of prolonged drought reflected in consecutive series of narrow annual rings. We know, for example, of an extended dry period between 1276 and 1299, and of shorter ones in 840, 1076, 1379, and 1632. Forest fires and lightning strikes, too, have left their charred scars sealed up inside the trees. Disease, insect devastations, and unusually early and late frosts are recorded in tree rings as well. Resources of dendrochronology are being turned into new avenues now, to historical studies of hydrology and stream flow, ecology and forest succession. The history of the impact of man on the environment seems also to be approachable through tree-ring study.

Results of even the latest dating methods using radioactive carbon 14 (C_{14}) have been called into question and have been shown to be less accurate and more variable than time-telling through annual rings. Measurements from annual rings have shown that some of the C_{14} dates from prehistoric sites in Europe are as much as 700 years in error. "As a result," writes Colin Renfrew in "Carbon 14 and the Prehistory of Europe," "the view that cultural advances diffused into Europe from the east is no longer tenable." The redoubtable A. E. Douglass would be pleased to learn of this modern success story for his storytelling tree rings.

Suggested Readings

Albion, Robert Greenhalgh. *Forests and Sea Power: The Timber Problem of the Royal Navy 1652–1862.* Cambridge, Mass.: Harvard University Press, 1926. Scholarly study of importance of America's trees to Britain's mastery of the seas.

Busch, Francis X. "The Trial of Bruno Hauptmann for the Murder of Charles Lindbergh, Jr. (1935)." In *Prisoners at the Bar.* Indianapolis and New York: Bobbs-Merrill, 1952.

Carroll, Charles F. *The Timber Economy of Puritan New England.* Providence, R. I.: Brown University Press, 1973.

Dobell, Clifford. *Antony van Leeuwenhoek and his "Little Animals."* New York: Harcourt, Brace, 1932 (reprinted New York: Dover Publications, 1960).

Douglass, Andrew Ellicott. "The Secret of the Southwest Solved by Talkative Tree Rings." *National Geographic Magazine* 56 (December 1929): 736–770. Good reading; stories of some of Douglass's early work on dating prehistoric Indian culture through annual ring study.

———. "Tree Rings and Climate." *University of Arizona, Physical Science Bulletin* no. 1 (1937), pp. 1–36. Somewhat technical.

Fritts, Harold C. "Tree Rings and Climate." *Scientific American* 226 (May 1972): 92–100.

Glesinger, Egon. *The Coming Age of Wood.* New York: Simon and Schuster, 1949. Popularly written chapters on the contributions of technology to forest products; a how-do-we-get thus and so from trees and how to make them last.

Horn, Stanley F. *This Fascinating Lumber Business.* Indianapolis and New York: Bobbs-Merrill, 1951. This might be entitled "from forest to you"; a popular account of how trees are logged and manufactured into usable products.

Koehler, Arthur. "Technique Used in Tracing the Lindbergh Kidnapping Ladder." *American Journal of Police Science* 27 (1937): 712–724. Personal story of how ladder was traced to kidnapper.

Panshin, A. J., and Carl de Zeeuw. *Textbook of Wood Technology,* vol. 1. *Structure, Identification, Uses, and Properties of the Commercial Woods of the United States and Canada.* 3d ed. New York: McGraw-Hill, 1970. Comprehensive; technically written.

Panshin, A. J., E. S. Harrar, J. S. Bethel, and W. J. Baker. *Forest Products, Their Sources, Production, and Utilization.* New York: McGraw-Hill, 1962. Standard text for college and reference; technical.

Renfrew, Colin. "Carbon 14 and the Prehistory of Europe." *Scientific American* 225 (October 1971): 63–72. Semitechnical article about use of radioactive carbon and dating of prehistoric cultures in Europe.

Schulman, Edmund. "Bristlecone Pine, Oldest Known Living Thing." *National Geographic Magazine* 113 (March 1958): 354–372. The discovery and dating of these trees from California's White Mountains; beautiful colored pictures.

Southwell, C. R., and J. D. Bultman. "Marine Borer Resistance of Untreated Woods over Long Periods of Immersion in Tropical Waters." *Biotropica* 3 (1971): 81–107. Technical article outlining exhaustive studies on woods with reputed natural resistance to marine borers.

Stallings, W. S., Jr. "Dating Prehistoric Ruins by Tree-Rings." *Laboratory of Anthropology, Santa Fe, New Mexico, General Series,* bulletin no. 8 (1949), pp. 1–18.

Stokes, Marvin A., and Terah L. Smiley. *An Introduction to Tree-Ring Dating.* Chicago: University of Chicago Press, 1968. A nontechnical primer on the methods of dendrochronology; nicely illustrated.

Studhalter, R. A. "Tree Growth I. Some Historical Chapters." *Botanical Review* 21 (1955): 1–72. Technical monograph.

Wright, Frank Lloyd. "In the Cause of Architecture IV. The Meaning of Materials—Wood." *Architectural Record* 64 (1928): 481–488.

Plant Names

Common name	*Scientific name*	*Family*
alder	*Alnus* spp.	Betulaceae
angélique	*Dicorynia paraensis*	Leguminosae
balsa	*Ochroma pyramidale*	Bombacaceae
bannia	*Swartzia bannia*	Leguminosae
birch	*Betula* spp.	Betulaceae
black cherry	*Prunus serotina*	Rosaceae
black ironwood	*Krugiodendron ferreum*	Rhamnaceae
black locust	*Robinia pseudoacacia*	Leguminosae
black walnut	*Juglans nigra*	Juglandaceae
bristlecone pine	*Pinus aristata*	Pinaceae
cocobolo	*Dalbergia retusa*	Leguminosae
corkwood	*Leitneria floridana*	Leitneriaceae
cypress	*Cupressus* spp.	Cupressaceae
Douglas fir	*Pseudotsuga menziesii*	Pinaceae
giant sequoia	*Sequoiadendron giganteum*	Taxodiaceae
greenheart	*Ocotea rodiei*	Lauraceae
hemlock	*Tsuga canadensis*	Pinaceae
lignum vitae	*Guaiacum officinale*	Zygophyllaceae
mahogany	*Swietenia* spp.	Meliaceae
North Carolina pine	*Pinus* spp. (The name North Carolina pine comprises a group of pines of southeastern United States.)	Pinaceae
oak	*Quercus* spp.	Fagaceae
osage orange	*Maclura pomifera*	Moraceae
pine	*Pinus* spp.	Pinaceae
piñon pine	*Pinus edulis*	Pinaceae
plane tree	*Platanus* spp.	Platanaceae
ponderosa pine	*Pinus ponderosa*	Pinaceae
quipo	*Cavanillesia platanifolia*	Bombacaceae
Rocky Mountain juniper	*Juniperus scopulorum*	Cupressaceae
silver fir	*Abies alba*	Pinaceae
sycamore	*Platanus* spp.	Platanaceae

The early spring-flowering false hellebore (*Veratrum viride*), some of whose
alkaloids make it a toxic plant but its
alkaloid veratrine is used in medicine
to reduce blood pressure.

7

Poisonous Plants

The Herbs in Dr. Rappaccini's Garden

You will perhaps recall Nathaniel Hawthorne's vivid, tragic story, *Rappaccini's Daughter*, in which he describes the awesome plants grown in the doctor's garden for his diabolic experiments. While we would not wish to suggest that toxic plants, whether cultivated or wild, have all the extraordinary properties of Dr. Rappaccini's amazing vegetable products, they are in truth a remarkable group of organisms which have fascinated people for centuries. Indeed, almost everyone encounters poisonous plants sometime in his life. And it would seem that these contacts will increase with more and more people returning to the land or each year spending at least vacations in wild, rural, or unfamiliar areas. In time of war, of course, hundreds of thousands of our youth characteristically serve in the tropics where they are exposed to poisonous species in strange **floras** (plants of a specific area or region).

In a recent year (1972), the poison control centers of the United States reported that plants were fourth in a list of emergencies involving supposed poisoning, preceded only by aspirin, detergents, and vitamins in that order. Plants, exclusive of mushrooms or toadstools, were responsible for some 4,700 of the cases, over 4.5 percent of the total. These figures do not include the millions who suffer from hay fever and who receive a rash from such plants as poison ivy. In addition, hundreds of thousands of domestic animals are poisoned each year. And yet, considering the total number of plant species—variously estimated as 500,000 to 800,000—a relatively small number—700 species—are now known to be toxic to man or animals.

165

What Is a Poisonous Plant?

A poisonous plant is one containing some substance which produces a deleterious or harmful reaction in man or animal.

General Observations

In general, it is well to beware of plants with white, milky juice, although this does not mean that all such plants are toxic. Plants growing in the temperate United States which are unknown to a person and which bear white or red fruits should be regarded with suspicion. Finally, avoid plants with an unpleasant, bitter taste. It is also a fact that there is a concentration of toxic plants in certain families: spurge or euphorbia family (castor bean, poinsettia [controversial]), tomato or potato family (deadly nightshade, jimson weed), and carrot family (poison hemlock, water hemlock).

Fortunately most poisonous plants must be consumed in rather large amounts to be toxic. Humans and wild animals characteristically do not eat large quantities of any one plant; rather they nibble here and there, thus poisoning is not too frequent. Domestic cattle, on the contrary, are often poisoned for they have a tendency, especially after a long winter confinement with its attendant diet of dry hay, to feed voraciously in spring pastures on any green, succulent plant. All too often they chance upon toxic species.

Man enjoys another advantage; namely, he vomits easily and so rids himself of objectionable substances, whereas domesticated animals—cattle, sheep, goats, and horses—do not vomit effectively and thus are more vulnerable to toxic plants. Children represent a special danger, for being curious by nature they put objects into their mouths, particularly bright objects such as berries which may be toxic. Thousands of children are thus threatened each year.

It is well to remember that poisoning depends on the quantity of a plant consumed and that even with such common vegetables as spinach, cabbage, turnips, and rutabagas, poisoning may result if any one of these food plants is eaten in large quantities over an extended period of time to the exclusion of other foods. Then, too, a plant which is toxic for one species of animal may be eaten with impunity by another; horses, for example, are readily killed by eating the leaves of yews, while deer strip the trees or shrubs of foliage with no apparent adverse effect.

Further, individuals of the same species, for example, man, differ in their reactions to toxic plants; some people are very susceptible to poisoning by certain plants while others are more or less immune. The same individual may show differences in sensitivity to the same plant at different times depending on the state of his health and other factors.

Role of Poisons in Plants

In some plants the presence of toxic substances may discourage browsing animals and thus they serve a protective function. In other plants, perhaps in most plants, the occurrence of toxic substances is more or less a chemical or physiological accident; that is, plants synthesize all sorts of chemical compounds which accumulate in their tissues because they, unlike animals, do not have excretory systems. These stored chemicals may have no specific function in the plant nor offer any survival advantage, but since they may also have no negative effect on survival, the property of forming such toxic compounds is perpetuated from generation to generation by the mechanisms of heredity.

No! noteument thinking.

History

Prehistoric man early identified toxic plants and used their poisons on his spears and arrows to bring down game as well as his enemies. By placing the poisons in pools and ponds, he stunned fish which rose to the surface, making fishing a pleasant chore.

The Greeks and Romans of the Classical period hired expert poisoners to destroy their rivals and enemies. This common practice necessitated a counteroffensive in the form of employing tasters of food and drink to protect the wealthy and powerful. In the Middle Ages poisoning became a flourishing art in which the Borgia and Medici families earned special notoriety. Plant poisons were commonly used to remove the competition and to promote succession to royal thrones and to other positions of power. These poisons thus came to be referred to as "succession powders." If an heir apparent stood in the way in a royal family, if the eldest son in a wealthy family became a troublesome obstacle, or if there was a need to remove an unwanted husband, wife, or lover, it was a simple thing to slip a bit of poison into food or drink, to pour a little poison in a sleeper's ear, or if one wished to be especially romantic and reckless, to smear a little poison on the lips before kissing the person to be eliminated. In addition, poisons were used in the biological warfare of the day: In military campaigns mass poisoning was achieved by sprinkling toxic substances in the water supply of rival forces.

Special note was made of poisonous plants in **herbals,** the botany books of the Medieval and Renaissance periods which consisted of illustrations of plants accompanied by descriptions with particular emphasis given to the utility of the plants— whether edible, medicinal, or poisonous.

Types Of Poisonous Plants

It is sometimes useful to classify poisonous plants according to the symptoms produced, while at other times it is convenient to group plants which have similar toxic substances. In the pages which follow, we discuss the most important poisonous plants under one or the other rubric.

Allergy-Producing Plants

Over 13 million people in the United States suffer from so-called **hay fever,** or **allergic rhinitis,** caused by wind-blown pollen as well as by spores of fungi. In general, there are three main periods of suffering during the year, and an individual may experience anguish in one or more of them. In the early spring the wind-pollinated trees such as the oaks, elms, maples, birches (Figure 16.24), and walnuts are the culprits. In midsummer the grasses are responsible for the hay fever which is sometimes called rose fever since it occurs when roses are blooming and quite naturally the conspicuous flowers of the rose are blamed for the trouble rather than the inconspicuous small, green flowers of the grass family. (In other words, we have here a kind of guilt by association.) In the fall, the period during which the largest number of persons is affected, the ragweeds (common ragweed, tall ragweed, and other species of this genus belonging to the composite or daisy family; Figures 7.1, 7.2, 7.3, and 7.4) are usually the cause of autumnal allergic rhinitis, although pollen from such weeds as lamb's-quarter and pigweed may also irritate some persons. The troublesome ragweeds are plants which flourish in disturbed areas such as along roadways, construction sites, and similar spots where the native plant cover has been removed. For many years the

Figure 7.1 Tall (*Ambrosia trifida*) and common (*A. artemisiifolia*) ragweeds.

Figure 7.2 Common ragweed (*Ambrosia artemisiifolia*).

Figure 7.3 Common ragweed (*Ambrosia artemisiifolia*).

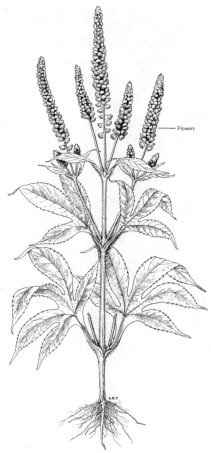

Figure 7.4 Tall or giant ragweed (*Ambrosia trifida*).

handsome insect-pollinated goldenrods (Figure 7.5) which happen to flower at the same time as the ragweeds were blamed for hay fever even to the extent of barring them from public places.

The disease known as allergic rhinitis is caused by the proteins in pollen (Figure 7.6) or in fungal spores which irritate and inflame the membranes of the nasal passage of those persons who are susceptible. The damaged membranes produce **histamines** (organic bases with carbon, hydrogen, and nitrogen;

See Plate 1b, goldenrod.

Figure 7.5 Goldenrod (*Solidago*).

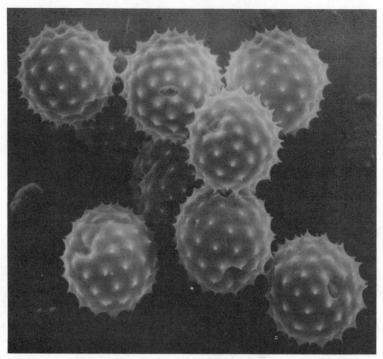

Figure 7.6 Ragweed (*Ambrosia trifida*) pollen photographed with scanning electron microscope. [Courtesy Willard W. Payne.]

the amino acid histidine yields histamine) which cause the glands of the nose and adjacent regions to secrete fluids as well as to relax the muscles of the blood vessels thus changing the permeability of the membranes so that there is more secretion of fluids. **Antihistamines** are drugs used to slow the release of histamines and thus decrease the discharge of liquids from nose and eyes. Unfortunately some antihistamines produce drowsiness and other undesirable side effects. Various inhalators containing benzedrine, ephedrine (originally derived from the plant *Ephedra*), and other substances shrink and soothe the membranes.

Plants Which Cause Dermatitis

Among the common plants which on contact produce **dermatitis** (skin disease manifested by irritation and skin rash) are several species of the genus *Toxicodendron*, poison ivy (Figures 7.7 and 7.8), poison sumac (Figure 7.9), and poison oak. Each

Figure 7.7 Poison ivy (*Tox-icodendron radicans*).

Figure 7.8 Poison ivy (*Tox-icodendron radicans*) climbing on tree trunk.

Figure 7.9 Fruits of poison sumac (*Toxicodendron vernix*). [Courtesy U.S. Department of Agriculture.]

year some two million people in the United States develop dermatitis as a result of contact with one of these. Actually, it is estimated that one out of every two people is susceptible, for many who claim to be immune are not and in some instances a person immune at one time may subsequently develop a rash.

The three poisonous species, poison ivy, poison sumac, and poison oak, should not be confused with other nonpoisonous members of the related *Rhus* genus such as staghorn sumac, the common roadside shrub or small tree, whose large pinnate leaves are a brilliant red in autumn.

The ubiquitous poison ivy which may occur as a low-growing constituent of the ground cover or as a robust vine climbing on trees and walls (Figure 7.8), has three shiny leaflets and white berries. In the words of an old rural verse:

> Leaves of three, quickly flee
> Berries white, poisonous sight!

The toxic principle or chemical, is a sticky, oily substance produced in canals that run through the plant body. Apparently the oily substance is absent from the pollen. To develop dermatitis a person must come in contact with the plant or some object which has had contact with the plant, such as a dog or shovel. However, droplets of the substance may be carried by smoke and people have developed the characteristic skin rash after burning poison ivy plants. If one of these poisonous *Toxicodendron* species is touched, one should immediately wash all contacted surfaces of the body with a strong soap. To get rid of the plants, they should be dug out or sprayed with an appropriate **herbicide** such as 2, 4-D.

An oriental *Toxicodendron,* the lacquer tree, provides the lacquer used to coat furniture and trays with a resistant, often beautiful finish. Some people have received skin rashes from handling such objects.

While not a *Toxicodendron* but a close relative in the sumac family, the poisonwood tree or shrub of the West Indies and south Florida, including the Keys, causes severe poisoning.

A quite different type of skin irritation is induced by the stinging nettles, or wood nettles, common in shady, wet woodlands. Here the poisonous substances (which include a histamine) are located in epidermal hairs whose tips break off upon contact and the broken ends act like hypodermic needles injecting the poison into the body.

Another kind of skin rash is brought about by the weed called wild parsnip. Gardeners frequently acquire this rash in the course of weeding. In order for the condition to develop there must be a combination of contact, a moist skin (as from sweating), and exposure to the sun.

Plants Poisonous Because of Alkaloids

In the early part of this chapter it was noted that poisonous plants are often bitter in taste. In many cases this bitter taste as well as toxicity is due to the presence of **alkaloids**—chemicals which are alkalilike (hence the name) or basic in reaction rather than acid, bitter in taste, organic, nitrogenous, and finally have a marked physiological effect on animals including man. This effect is usually exerted on the nervous system. To assist in the recognition of alkaloids, they are given names ending in *ine* as in caff*eine*, morph*ine*, nicot*ine*, and coc*aine*. Alkaloids are not only important in **toxicology** (the study of poisons) but also in human medicine, for many of our drugs are alkaloids. Over 5,000 alkaloids have been discovered in plants.

One of the earliest plants to appear in the spring is the false hellebore, or *Veratrum*, a member of the lily family. It has several alkaloids which act on the nervous system.

See illustration page 164, hellebore.

Yews (*Taxus*)—the commonly cultivated English and Japanese yews planted around houses as well as the wild species —possess the alkaloid taxine. All parts of the plant including the seeds are toxic, except for the bright red covering of the berries. Yews have been responsible for the poisoning of humans as well as of horses and cows, but, as was remarked earlier, for some reason deer are able to eat the leaves without harmful effect.

See Plate 1c, yew.

A famous poisonous plant is the poison hemlock (Figure 7.10), also known as fool's parsley, whose juice was responsible for the death of the Greek philosopher Socrates who was condemned to death for the alleged crime of corrupting the youth of Athens. For the Greeks of that period the use of hemlock was the regal way of dying. A crown of flowers was placed on the head of the victim who would then manage a brave smile and an appropriate speech. The alkaloids in the plant cause paralysis of the muscles, including the breathing muscles, and death ensues. Incidentally, poison hemlock, a herbaceous member of the carrot family, is not to be confused with the hemlock tree, an evergreen gymnosperm.

Flowers

Figure 7.10   Poison hemlock or fool's parsley (*Conium maculatum*).

Another toxic plant which is not without its historical significance is the thorn apple (*Datura*; Figure 7.11) also known as Jamestown weed and jimson weed, and a member of the potato-tomato family. It has a whole battery of alkaloids including atropine, hyoscyamine, and scopolamine. The latter mixed with morphine induces a twilight sleep and is used for women in labor. These alkaloids produce **hallucinations** (perceiving objects which have no reality; or seeing, hearing, smelling, and feeling things which are not present). Someone has said that the jimson weed may make one "hot as a hare, blind as a bat, red as a beet, dry as a bone, and mad as a wet hen." It derives its name from the fact that in the seventeenth century troops

Figure 7.11 Jimson weed or thorn-apple (*Datura stramonium*). [Courtesy U.S. Department of Agriculture.]

were sent to Jamestown, Virginia, to quell an uprising. Some of the soldiers ate the fruit of the plant and became very ill. Robert Beverly's *History of Virginia* gives this beguiling account:

> Some of them ate plentifully of it, the effect of which was a very pleasant comedy, for they turned natural fools upon it for several days: one would blow up a feather in the air; another would dart straws at it with much fury; and another, stark naked, was sitting up in a corner like a monkey, grinning and making mows at them; a fourth

would fondly kiss and paw his companions, and sneer in their faces, with a countenance more antic than any in a Dutch droll. In this frantic condition they were confined, lest they should, in their folly, destroy themselves,—though it was observed that all their actions were full of innocence and good nature. Indeed, they were not very cleanly. A thousand such simple tricks they played, and after eleven days returned to themselves again, not remembering anything that had passed.

Another member of the potato-tomato family is the common roadside deadly nightshade or climbing nightshade, with purple flowers and bright red berries whose unripe, or green, fruits are toxic. Other members of this same family are the thoroughly edible tomatoes and potatoes. But it is interesting that the leaves and vines of tomatoes have killed cattle and that potato sprouts, spoiled potatoes, diseased potatoes, and potatoes with green spots have all led to severe poisoning of humans. Animals have died from eating potato vines. The alkaloid in potatoes, tomatoes, and nightshade is solanine (after *Solanum*, the genus to which these plants belong).

See Plate 1d, nightshade.

Plants Poisonous Because of Glycosides

Nearly as important as the alkaloids in producing poisoning by plants are the **glycosides,** chemical compounds consisting of one or more sugar molecules attached to one or more nonsugar molecules. Like alkaloids they are often bitter, they may have a marked physiological effect on animals and man, and they are important in toxicology and in medicine.

Children sometimes eat black or wild cherry fruits with their enclosed seeds. If the seeds are crushed, the glycoside amygdalin produces hydrocyanic acid (HCN) which is poisonous. The same process occurs when animals eat the leaves of the wild cherry. It is important to emphasize that hydrocyanic acid is only produced from the glycoside amygdalin when the leaves of the wild cherry are wilted, crushed, or frosted, or when seeds of cherries are crushed. The hydrocyanic acid inhibits a respiratory enzyme which in turn leads to asphyxiation.

The important tropical food plant manioc, or cassava (Figures 11.7 and 11.8), from which we derive our tapioca is a plant which contains hydrocyanic acid in its fresh condition. The acid must be removed by squeezing out the juice or by

Figure 7.12 Oleander (*Nerium oleander*). [Courtesy U.S. Department of Agriculture.]

evaporating, otherwise cyanide poisoning will occur. Fortunately not all cultivars, or races, of manioc produce hydrocyanic acid.

If large quantities of certain members of the mustard family (cabbage, rutabagas, turnips) are consumed over an extended period of time to the exclusion of other foods, goiter may develop. There are glycosides in these plants which when present in large amounts in the human body will prevent the thyroid gland from accumulating iodine and hence inhibit the formation of the thyroid hormone which will result in goiter.

The discovery of the glycoside **dicoumarin** in sweet clover is a fascinating illustration of how scientific research leads to quite unexpected results. In the early 1920s a bleeding disease was observed in Wisconsin. Cattle so affected had large, raised blisters on their bodies, sometimes several feet in circumference and as much as a foot high, filled with blood. The animals gradually bled to death. Subsequent investigation revealed that the animals had eaten wet or moldy sweet clover. In examining the moist sweet clover hay, Dr. K. P. Link of the University of Wisconsin noted the presence of **coumarin**, a glycoside commonly found in freshly cut vegetation. Then Link discovered that two coumarin molecules combine to form **dicoumarin** which is a substance that prevents the clotting of blood. Later, it was suggested that since dicoumarin is an anticoagulant it could be used in human medicine to prevent the formation of blood clots.

This series of events is a good illustration of **serendipity**, the discovery by chance or accident. (The word was coined by Horace Walpole and is derived from a tale entitled "The Three Princes of Serendip" in which the princes are repeatedly discovering by chance things they did not seek.) The original investigation in Wisconsin was focused on ascertaining the cause of the bleeding in cattle but ultimately this research led to the discovery of a valuable medicine which is effective in preventing blood-clotting in humans. Another by-product of this research has been the use of dicoumarin as a rodent killer under the name of Warfarin. It causes internal bleeding and eventual death in rats and mice.

Cardiac glycosides which stimulate the heart are another type of glycoside found in some toxic plants. Children are sometimes poisoned by ingesting a bit of the foxglove or digitalis (Figure 9.7) in the garden, or perhaps some wild dogbane. One of the deadliest plants in this group is the oleander (Figure 7.12), a common houseplant and a favorite hedge plant in Florida, California, and Hawaii where it is grown for its attractive white, pink, or red flowers. The plant is so toxic that one leaf may kill an adult. There have been cases of serious poisoning resulting from someone using an oleander twig as a skewer to roast a hot dog or to mix a cocktail.

Plants Poisonous Because of Other Toxins

Some plants contain plant poisons, or **toxins,** other than alkaloids and glycosides. One of the most dangerous is the precatory bean (Figure 7.13), or rosary pea, of Florida and the West Indies, which is grown in greenhouses in the North. The seeds of this plant are an attractive red with a black tip, and are often made into strings of beads or rosaries. The whole, intact seed is not harmful but if a seed is crushed, that single

See Plate 2a, precatory bean.

Figure 7.13 Precatory bean or rosary pea (*Abrus precatorius*).

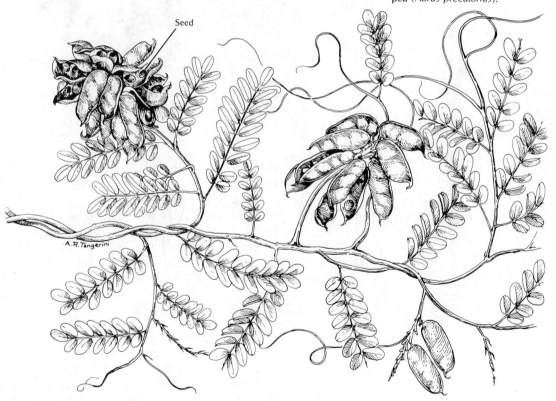

Seed

A.R. Tangerini

Figure 7.14 Castor bean (*Ricinus communis*). [Courtesy U.S. Department of Agriculture.]

seed is enough to kill a child. The toxin causes the agglutination of the red-blood cells.

Another very poisonous and yet fairly common plant is the castor bean (Figures 7.14 and 7.15), a member of the spurge, or euphorbia, family, whose seeds are highly toxic. One of the seeds is sufficient to kill a child, a half dozen, to kill an adult. The old-fashioned purgative castor oil is made from the oil extracted from the seeds of the castor oil bean.

Plants Poisonous Because of Oxalates

A number of plants cause trouble because they have rather large concentrations of oxalic acid which combines with calcium to form calcium oxalate crystals which may block kidney tubules. A familiar plant in this class is the sorrel, or sour-weed. Rhubarb is an interesting case. We customarily eat the leaf stalks, or petioles, and discard the leaf blades which have oxalic acid and are poisonous. During World War I, an overzealous bureau of the British government made the mistake of urging citizens not to waste the rhubarb blades but to eat them. As a consequence there were numerous poisonings and some deaths in England.

An old country joke is to persuade a green city slicker to eat a piece of the corm (enlarged underground stem) of the Jack-in-the-pulpit. The victim almost at once experiences a hot burning sensation in his mouth caused by the action of needlelike crystals of calcium oxalate. This may prove to be a very dangerous prank, for we now know that some people react so violently that the tissues of their mouths swell up and can block breathing and lead to death if immediate medical help is not provided. Other plants in this category are the early spring skunk cabbage and the widely used office and houseplant *Dieffenbachia*, called dumb cane because the action of an enzyme on the tongue makes one speechless.

Figure 7.15   Spiny fruits and seeds of castor bean (*Ricinus communis*). [Courtesy U.S. Department of Agriculture.]

Plants Poisonous Because of Accumulations of Minerals

Some plants absorb certain minerals—copper, lead, selenium, molybdenum, and several others. They may accumulate these minerals in such concentrations that when the plants are eaten they are toxic to man and animals. Some of the soils in Australia are high in copper content. In the United States because of the use of tetraethyl lead in high-test gasoline, there are indications that some plants are accumulating lead in toxic amounts. Crop plants such as oats, corn, and sorghum may take up large quantities of nitrogen in the form of nitrates (NO_3) as a result of the excessive use of fertilizers. In the digestive process the nitrates are converted into nitrites (NO_2) which are ten times as toxic as nitrates. Hundreds of cattle and sheep have been lost because nitrites impair the ability of the blood to transport oxygen.

In the West there are sizable stock losses as a result of cattle having eaten plants which accumulate selenium. They develop a disease called blind staggers which causes them to wander about aimlessly, even to run into fences and other solid objects. Or they have alkali disease which makes them become lame, emaciated, their hooves deformed, and eventually they fall into a kneeling position from which they are unable to rise. There are some 15 western states whose rocks and soils have soluble selenium.

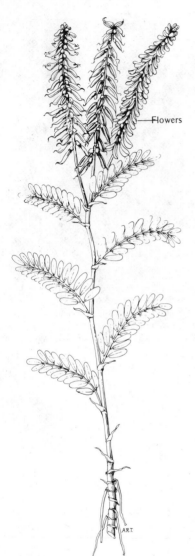

—Flowers

Some plants require selenium and will not grow elsewhere; these are called **selenium indicator plants.** By coincidence uranium is found in the same geological formations, so uranium prospectors look for selenium indicator plants to lead them to valuable uranium deposits. There are approximately 24 species of poison vetch (Figure 7.16) belonging to the genus *Astragalus* (a legume) which require selenium and therefore have proven to be useful indicators. There are still other species of poison vetch which will accumulate selenium if they happen to be growing in soils with selenium though they do not require it. Whereas plants with high concentrations of selenium have caused serious stock poisoning, there is no evidence thus far that such plants have been toxic to humans.

Finally, the conditions of blind staggers and alkali disease should not be confused with loco disease which impels horses to act in a wild and crazy fashion. This malady, caused by alkaloids, is also produced by some species of *Astragalus*, the so-called loco weeds (Figure 7.17), but they are different species from those leading to blind staggers and to alkali disease.

Figure 7.16 Poison vetch (*Astragalus bisulcatus*).

Figure 7.17 Locoweed (*Astragalus mollissimus*).

Plants Poisonous Because of the Presence of Resins

A few plants possess resins (amorphous substances usually derived from essential or volatile oils) or resinoids which irritate nerve and muscle tissues. Water hemlock (Figure 7.18), related to poison hemlock, is one of the most toxic of plants, for as little as one mouthful of the root will kill a man. Mountain laurel (Figure 7.19) and the related sheep laurel, or lambkill, have toxic resinoids which kill browsing sheep and cattle. The Delaware Indians apparently used laurel to commit suicide. The attractive white-flowered Mayapple has a toxic resinoid and children have been poisoned by eating the unripe fruit.

Plants Which Produce Photosensitivity Leading to Poisoning

Some plants produce **photosensitivity** in some animals—in other words, some substance from the plant becomes poisonous to the animals upon exposure to light. In order to have animal poisoning of this type there must be a combination of three conditions:

1. The animal must be unpigmented or lightly pigmented with little or no hair.
2. The animal must eat one of a particular group of plants.
3. The animal must then be exposed to sunlight.

When unpigmented, or blond, pigs eat buckwheat (*Fagopyrum*) (Figure 2.1), they may develop a disease called fagopyrism in which the skin becomes red, blisters appear, and the skin may slough off. There may also be liver damage. The roadside St. John's wort is another plant which induces photosensitivity and hence is poisonous under the described conditions.

Figure 7.18 Water hemlock (*Cicuta douglasii*). [Courtesy U.S. Department of Agriculture.]
See Plate 2b, St. John's wort.

Other Poisonous Plants

In addition to those already discussed, there are many other poisonous principles in plants with deleterious effects on man. When white snakeroot (Figure 7.20), a member of the daisy, or composite, family, is eaten by cows they develop a condition known as trembles and when people drink milk from such cows they get milk sickness which can be fatal. During the colonial period in this country milk sickness was one of the most important causes of death. It was a terrifying disease for the cause was not known. Various bizarre theories were suggested, for instance, that spider webs or poison ivy were responsible for the

Figure 7.19   Mountain laurel (*Kalmia latifolia*). [Courtesy U.S. Department of Agriculture.]

Figure 7.20   White snakeroot (*Eupatorium rugosum*). [Courtesy U.S. Department of Agriculture.]

malady. In the early nineteenth century there were serious epidemics in Appalachia and in the Midwest. Nancy Hanks, Abraham Lincoln's mother, apparently died of the disease. In some localities the population was reduced by as much as 50 percent and whole villages were abandoned. In North Carolina there is a Milk Sick Ridge, a grim reminder of this dread disease. The causative principle is trematol, a complex alcohol present in white snakeroot. All parts of the plants are poisonous.

Pokeweed, or pokeberry (Figure 7.21), a purple- to red-stemmed rank herb of roadside and empty lot, is poisonous, particularly the root. In spring the young leaves are frequently used as a pot salad, a practice which cannot be recommended because evidence is accumulating that a substance in the plant causes quiescent, or adult, white-blood cells to become rejuvenated and to divide again. The result is similar to a kind of leukemia. The shiny purple berries with a grapelike juice are occasionally eaten by children and, while less toxic than the roots, they can be poisonous. Interestingly birds eat the fruit without suffering ill effects.

The traditional Christmas decorative plant poinsettia, with its brilliant red leaves (not flowers), is a member of the spurge or euphorbia family. It exudes a white, milky juice which has been reported as poisonous. This is disputed by some who point to experiments with rats in which no poisoning occurred. But reports of poinsettia poisoning still come in to poison control centers.

See Plate 2c, poinsettia.

Horsetails (*Equisetum*; Figure 15.13) and the bracken fern when eaten by horses can be poisonous. These plants have an enzyme, thiaminase, which breaks down thiamine (vitamin B_1). The animals, deprived of vitamin B_1, eventually die.

Some mushrooms and the ergot fungus are also poisonous but they will be dealt with in other chapters of this book.

What to Do in Case of Suspected Poisoning

The first thing to do when plant poisoning has or is thought to have occurred, of course, is to call a doctor or a poison control center. Be sure to identify the plant which provoked the condition or at least save the plant or plant part for the doctor's examination and for confirmation by a botanist. A third suggestion is that you induce vomiting in the afflicted person. You should know that there are poison control centers in all major cities, usually associated with hospitals, which keep up-to-date information on the common poisonous plants and the latest curative procedures.

As prevention, however, you would be well-advised never to

Figure 7.21   Pokeweed or pokeberry (*Phytolacca americana*).

eat any plant or part of a plant which you do not recognize as safe. Fortunately there are a number of good books on toxic plants: the authoritative work *Poisonous Plants of the United States and Canada* is by Professor John Kingsbury of Cornell University. He also has a popular and very readable guide, *Deadly Harvest.* The book *Human Poisoning from Native and Cultivated Plants* by James Hardin and Jay Arena is also recommended as a concise, well-illustrated manual.

Suggested Readings

Evers, Robert A., and Roger P. Link. *Poisonous Plants of the Midwest and Their Effects on Livestock.* Special publication 24. Urbana-Champaign: College of Agriculture, University of Illinois, 1972. Handsome bulletin with copious illustrations, some of these in color. Emphasis on plants poisonous to livestock, with notes on toxic principles, symptoms, and treatment. Written jointly by a botanist and a professor of veterinary medicine.

Hardin, James W., and Jay M. Arena. *Human Poisoning from Native and Cultivated Plants.* 2d ed. Durham, N.C.: Duke University Press, 1974. This compact book, coauthored by a botanist and a physician, emphasizes the plants poisonous to man. It provides notes on toxic principles and treatment, and is well illustrated with both drawings and photographs—some of the latter in color.

Howard, Richard A., Gordon P. DeWolf, Jr., and George H. Pride. "Guide to potentially dangerous plants." *Arnoldia* 34, no. 2 (1974), pp. 41–96. A recent pamphlet prepared for popular use by professional botanists. Publication is illustrated and contains notes on the parts of the plants which are poisonous and on symptoms produced by the toxic plants. An excellent movie based on the same material is also available from the Arnold Arboretum, Harvard University.

Kingsbury, John M. *Deadly Harvest: A Guide to Common Poisonous Plants.* New York: Holt, Rinehart and Winston, 1965. A popular guide to the common poisonous plants by the leading American authority on the subject. Highly recommended for the beginner.

———. *Poisonous Plants of the United States and Canada.* Englewood Cliffs, N. J.: Prentice-Hall, 1964. The authoritative, comprehensive treatise, or Bible, on poisonous plants by the outstanding expert on toxic plants.

Muenscher, Walter C. *Poisonous Plants of the United States.* Rev. ed. New York: Macmillan, 1951. Concise with excellent drawings of toxic plants. Briefer but older than Kingsbury's *Poisonous Plants.* Now available in a paperback edition (1975).

Plant Names

Common name	Scientific name	Family
bracken fern	*Pteridium aquilinum*	Polypodiaceae
buckwheat	*Fagopyrum esculentum*	Polygonaceae
castor bean	*Ricinus communis*	Euphorbiaceae
common ragweed	*Ambrosia artemisiifolia*	Compositae*
deadly nightshade, bittersweet	*Solanum dulcamara*	Solanaceae
dumb cane	*Dieffenbachia seguine* and other species	Araceae
false hellebore	*Veratrum viride*	Liliaceae
foxglove	*Digitalis purpurea*	Scrophulariaceae
horsetail	*Equisetum arvense*	Equisetaceae
Jack-in-the-pulpit	*Arisaema triphyllum*	Araceae
loco weeds	*Astragalus,* certain species	Leguminosae*
manioc, cassava, tapioca	*Manihot esculenta*	Euphorbiaceae
Mayapple	*Podophyllum peltatum*	Berberidaceae
mountain laurel	*Kalmia latifolia*	Ericaceae
oleander	*Nerium oleander*	Apocynaceae
parsnip	*Pastinaca sativa*	Umbelliferae*
poinsettia	*Euphorbia pulcherrima*	Euphorbiaceae
poison hemlock	*Conium maculatum*	Umbelliferae
poison ivy	*Toxicodendron radicans* (= *Rhus toxicodendron*)	Anacardiaceae
poison oak	*Toxicodendron quercifolium* (= *Rhus quercifolium*)	Anacardiaceae
poison sumac	*Toxicodendron vernix* (= *Rhus vernix*)	Anacardiaceae
poison vetch	*Astragalus,* several species	Leguminosae
poisonwood tree	*Metopium toxiferum*	Anacardiaceae
pokeweed, pokeberry	*Phytolacca americana*	Phytolaccaceae
precatory bean, rosary pea	*Abrus precatorius*	Leguminosae
rhubarb	*Rheum rhaponticum*	Polygonaceae
St. John's wort	*Hypericum perforatum*	Hypericaceae
sheep laurel, lambkill	*Kalmia angustifolia*	Ericaceae
skunk cabbage	*Symplocarpus foetidus*	Araceae
sorrel	*Oxalis* species	Oxalidaceae
stinging nettle	*Urtica dioica*	Urticaceae
sweet clover	*Melilotus alba, M. officinalis*	Leguminosae
tall ragweed	*Ambrosia trifida*	Compositae
thornapple, jimson weed	*Datura stramonium*	Solanaceae
water hemlock	*Cicuta maculata*	Umbelliferae
white snakeroot	*Eupatorium rugosum*	Compositae
wood nettle	*Laportea canadensis*	Urticaceae
yew	*Taxus cuspidata, T. baccata, T. canadensis*	Taxaceae

*In a few cases we use the older family names, for they are often encountered in the books listed in the Suggested Readings and elsewhere.

A dump heap which has accumulated
outside the crude shelter of ancient
man. Note the *Cannabis* plants growing on the discarded refuse.

8
Marijuana
Man's Ancient Camp Follower

If you were to examine the eight or nine leading textbooks of general botany, you would find that most make no reference to marijuana, Indian hemp, or cannabis (Figure 8.1); the few that do have only a line or two and this usually some innocuous mention of its use as a fiber plant. Yet for the general public marijuana is probably one of the plants best known and most frequently mentioned in conversation and discussion. It is attracting an enormous amount of attention; scarcely a day goes by without a reference in the daily paper to some new medical finding or to some legal aspect relative to the use of the plant. Furthermore, Indian hemp is one of man's oldest plant companions, initially as a weed growing in the rich nitrogenous dump heaps around his campsites and later as one of his earliest cultivated plants, grown for its fibers and its stimulating properties.

Botany of Marijuana

This ancient plant and its products are known by literally scores of common names, among the most widely used of which are marijuana, marihuana, Indian hemp, hemp, cannabis, hashish, hash, grass, pot, Acapulco gold, bhang, charas, and ganja.

It is an annual herb which may reach a height of 18 feet but is usually shorter. The leaves are compound with 3 to 15, but mostly 5 to 11 toothed leaflets arranged in a palmate fashion (Figure 8.2). The fruit is one-seeded (an **achene**). Unlike most flowering plants which have stamens and carpels in the same flower, cannabis has flowers with stamens on one plant (so-

Figure 8.1 Marijuana or hemp (*Cannabis sativa*). [Courtesy U.S. Department of Agriculture.]

187

Figure 8.2 Close-up of marijuana (*Cannabis sativa*) showing palmately compound leaves with marginal teeth.

called male flowers) and flowers with carpels on a different individual (so-called female flowers; Figure 8.3), a condition described as **dioecious.** Maleness or femaleness or sexuality is not too firm a character in these plants for they occasionally undergo sex reversal; that is, male plants sometimes bear flowers with carpels and conversely female plants develop male flowers.

The female plants are usually taller and stockier and have a fuller aspect because they have more leaves near the flowers. Cannabis is a native of central Asia but it has spread as a weed to or is cultivated in all temperate and dry tropical regions of both hemispheres. The flower organs and adjacent parts bear glandular hairs which exude a light, amber-colored oleoresin (a more or less liquid resin) containing the intoxicant, tetrahydrocannabinol (THC).

Cannabis is extremely polymorphic; that is, it shows great variability in its appearance and in its various structures. There are many races or types depending on the geographical origin of the plants—whether they are from India, Mexico, or from the Midwest of the United States. Then, too, it should be remembered that hemp has been cultivated for centuries, and in different parts of the world it was selected for different desirable

Figure 8.3 Female marijuana (*Cannabis sativa*). [Courtesy U.S. Department of Agriculture.]

characteristics which made it better or more suited for one of its several uses. So the plants vary a good deal in the amount of intoxicating principle, or THC, from virtually none to fairly high concentrations. Further, because of widespread global migration, plants of all types or races may grow in the same region in adjacent fields.

In view of its polymorphic nature it is not surprising that authorities differ with respect to the taxonomy applied to the plants. Some botanists hold that although there may be different types or races, all these plants belong to the same species, *Cannabis sativa*, the binomial Linnaeus gave it in 1753. In the judgment of other taxonomists there are three species: *Cannabis sativa*, of temperate United States and most of the rest of the world; *Cannabis indica* (named by the great French evolutionist Lamarck), of central Asia; and *Cannabis ruderalis*, a more northern species growing in Russia and Siberia, described by Russian botanists in 1924.

Cannabis is placed in the Cannabaceae, or hemp, family which includes not only hemp but curiously enough another economic plant, hop, which looms large in connection with another intoxicant—alcohol. Hops, the clusters of flowers, are used to flavor beer.

Uses by Man

For thousands of years cannabis has been grown by man as a useful plant. The striking point is that cannabis has so many different uses: for fibers in making rope, cordage, twine, sailcloth, sacks, bags, and oakum to caulk boats; for oil (from the seeds) which is edible and is used as a lamp oil and in the manufacture of paints, varnishes, and soaps; for birdseed which, in times of famine in Eastern Europe, has been utilized as a human food; for its stimulating or intoxicating properties; and for medicine.

Cannabis has long been employed as a medicine in various parts of the world such as Asia—including India, Turkey, Malaya, Burma—and in Egypt, South America, and South Africa. It figured importantly as a medicine in the herbals of the Middle Ages. Renewed interest was initiated in the medical virtues of cannabis in 1839, when an Irish physician, serving in India, published a paper on the medicinal uses of cannabis as he observed them in Asia. During the period 1840–1900 considerable attention was given to cannabis as a medicine with about 100 scientific papers published on the subject. It was recommended as an **analgesic** (substance which allays pain), for such conditions as neuralgia, rheumatism, asthma, pain in labor, gastric ulcers, and painful menstruation. The great physician Sir William Osler (1849–1919) considered it a "most satisfactory remedy" for migraine headache. It was used as an **anticonvulsant** (muscle relaxant, or remedy for convulsions) in cases of menstrual cramps, tetanus, and epilepsy. Some doctors prescribed cannabis as a **soporific** or **hypnotic** (sleep-producing) for senile insomnia, as an appetite stimulant, and, more recently, as an **antibiotic** (biological agent which kills or retards the growth of bacteria and fungi). It has been used to facilitate withdrawal from addiction to opium, alcohol, and similar drugs. Cannabis has been found to be useful as a tranquilizer or antidepressant in connection with the treatment of psychiatric diseases such as melancholia.

Other virtues of cannabis as a medicinal drug include its extraordinary low toxicity—no deaths have ever been authenticated for the medicinal use of cannabis or, for that matter, for any ingestion or smoking of cannabis. Compare this record with that of aspirin which is said to be responsible for 500 to 1,000 deaths each year in the United States. Furthermore, the claim is made that there is no reliable or unquestionable evidence of any cellular damage resulting from the use of cannabis. Contrast this with tobacco and its role in lung cancer and with alcohol with its deleterious effects on the brain and liver. In spite of these two important qualities—low toxicity and no demonstrated tissue destruction—cannabis has virtually disappeared as a medicinal drug for the reason that it is insoluble in water and so cannot be injected intravenously. The introduction of the hypodermic syringe into American medicine made this lack of solubility an important drawback. Also, because cannabis as it is derived from different plants varies in potency, it is difficult to obtain standard dosages for medicinal purposes. The development of synthetic analgesics such as aspirin and of hypnotics (i.e., barbiturates and other sleep-inducing drugs) replaced cannabis in these spheres of medicine. Then, too, morphine came to be used as a more powerful drug and hence more effective for serious and painful wounds. Until 1941 cannabis was included in the U.S. *Pharmacopeia* and the *National Formulary*—treatises listing officially approved drugs. It continues to be listed in the pharmacopoeias of Great Britain, Germany, and Japan.

Recent reports based especially on research with synthetic tetrahydrocannabinols, a few of which are water soluble, indicate some promise for the future use of cannabis derivatives as analgesics, for hypertension (high blood pressure), and as therapeutic agents in such psychological conditions as extreme anxiety and depression. There are now known some 29 cannabinolic constituents in *Cannabis*. Some of these are under intense study in the hope that from this veritable chemical factory we may discover a new medicinally valuable agent.

History

Attention has already been directed to the fact that cannabis is an ancient cultivated plant and thus has been associated with man from his historic beginnings. Records indicate that the plant was known in China 8,500 years ago and that by 900 B.C. the Assyrians burned it as incense. There are even older archeological remains documenting this close relationship between man and cannabis. The Sanskrit *Zend-Avesta* first mentions its use as an intoxicant in 600 B.C. Herodotus, Greek historian of the fifth century B.C., reports that the Scythians of southeast Europe and Asia burned the seeds and inhaled the smoke as a stimulant, a curious report that has recently been substantiated by archeological finds in Scythian tombs. In the Egyptian city of Thebes the inhabitants used it as a stimulating drink. Galen, Greek physician of the second century A.D., records that it was made into cakes and warned that if eaten to excess the cakes had intoxicating qualities. Marco Polo reports that in the eleventh century in Asia Minor there lived a Moslem religious leader, Hasan-Ibn-Sabbah, who sent out his men to murder the Christians of the Crusades. For their grim deeds they were rewarded with hashish. In the words of Marco Polo,

See illustration on page 186.

> He [Hasan] kept at his court a number of the youths of the country, from twelve to twenty years of age, such as had a taste for soldiering. . . . Then he would introduce them to his garden, some four, or six, or ten at a time, having first made them drink a certain potion [hashish] which cast them in a deep sleep, and then causing them to be lifted and carried in. So when they awoke they found themselves in the garden. . . .

When therefore they awoke, and found themselves in a place so charming, they deemed that it was paradise in very truth. And the ladies and damsels dallied with them to their hearts' content. . . .

So when the Old Man would have any prince slain, he would say to such a youth: Go thou and slay so and so; and when thou returneth my angels shall bear thee into paradise. And shouldst thou die, natheless even so I will send my angels to carry thee back into paradise.

These young murderers came to be called **hashishins** and there is a suspicion that the word *assassin* is derived from hashishin or else that both assassin and hashish are derived from Hasan. In any case, cannabis has long been used as an inebriant. In Africa and in India it has had an ancient role in religion and magic. The ancient *Veda* refers to the plant as the "liberator of sin" and "heavenly guide." In some regions of India the plant is still regarded as sacred and some temples have it growing in their gardens.

Types of Cannabis

In the United States we have two kinds of cannabis:

1. **Marijuana,** dried crushed leaves and flowering tops; usually smoked in cigarettes.
2. **Hashish,** resin from the flowers; smoked, eaten or drunk.

The marijuana of the United States, derived from local weeds or cultivated plants and made up, as it often is, of crushed leaves, stems, twigs, and tops of the plant not to mention the adulterants that are sometimes added, is usually low in THC and hence sometimes almost lacking in the intoxicating principle. The marijuana which is brought in from Mexico and other dry, hot regions is stronger. Some of this stronger type may come from *Cannabis indica*. The hashish used in this country is smuggled in from North Africa and the Near East.

In India there are three kinds of cannabis products:

1. **Bhang,** the weakest, is from dried plants; gathered green, powdered, and made into a drink with water or milk or made into candy with sugar and spices.
2. **Ganja,** two to three times as strong as bhang, comes from

dried tops with the exuded resin from cultivated female plants; is smoked with tobacco or eaten or drunk.

3. **Charas** (hashish), ten times as strong as bhang; pure resin gathered (according to a possibly fanciful story) by laborers wearing leather garments or else naked, streaking through the fields of cannabis; the resin sticking to the sweaty bodies or to the leather is then collected and the material is normally smoked or eaten mixed with spices.

In India and in other parts of Asia cannabis is used widely by the poor as a tonic, especially for those who have jobs requiring endurance and considerable physical work. It not only has religious significance but it is highly valued as a folk medicine, particularly as it is commonly assumed that cannabis is an **aphrodisiac** (sexual stimulant).

Literary Associations

In the course of the last four or five centuries various western literary figures have been attracted to cannabis. François Rabelais (1494?–1553), French novelist, humorist, satirist, physician, and monk, wrote *The Herb Pantagruelion* in which he refers to the antibiotic properties of marijuana and mentions that the seeds are much sought after by birds. Rabelais, although quite knowledgeable in the botany of the day, confuses the sexes of cannabis—an unforgiveable error for a Frenchman. The source of his error was the assumption that the larger and more robust plants must be male even though they bear seeds.

In the nineteenth century a number of literary figures in and around Paris experimented with marijuana and hashish as well as with other drugs. In this group were such men as Théophile Gautier, Bayard Taylor, Charles Baudelaire, and Fitz Hugh Ludlow. The cannabis was largely ingested or eaten, not smoked. The written accounts of their cannabis experiments are often distorted and excessive for they used alcohol, opium, and other drugs at the same time, so we cannot accept these literary accounts, often written in beautiful prose, as dependable descriptions of the effects of cannabis. In Paris Gautier founded *Le Club des Haschischins* (The hashish club), whose other members were Victor Hugo, Honoré de Balzac, Baudelaire, and Alexandre Dumas. Among the literary works inspired by cannabis are those by Fitz Hugh Ludlow, an American who wrote *The Hashish Eater: Being Passages from the Life of a Pythagorean* (1857); by Théophile Gautier whose *The Hashish Club* is a gaudy account of the effects of eating hashish (Gautier records the remark of a psychiatrist who has experimented with hashish and in referring to someone's expression of pleasure over the reverie says, "This will be subtracted from your share in Paradise"); and by Charles Baudelaire's *Les Paradis Artificiels* (The artificial paradises, 1860) in which he describes in charming prose the psychological reactions of the hashish eater. There is every indication that these literary works were inspired by Thomas De Quincey's *Confessions of an English Opium Eater* (1821). More recently (1966), Allen Ginsberg wrote "First Manifesto to End the Bringdown" for the *Atlantic Monthly* in which he refers to cannabis as the "metaphysical herb." The first half of this essay was written while Ginsberg was smoking marijuana. Most of these books and articles are readily available since they have been reprinted in David Solomon's *The Marihuana Papers* and in George Andrews and Simon Vinkenoog's *The Book of Grass*, both of which are cited in the Suggested Readings at the end of this chapter. Lester Grinspoon's *Marihuana Reconsidered* also gives a useful summary of the relationship between cannabis and certain men of letters.

The United States Experience

Cannabis was first planted in 1611 near Jamestown, Virginia and from this early date to the Civil War it was an important cash crop, for its fibers were essential for the manufacture of rope and cordage, very important supplies for navies consisting entirely of sailing ships. George Washington tells us in his diary of 1765 that he raised hemp for fiber. (Henry VIII required that English farmers cultivate cannabis so that the royal navy would not lack for rope and sail.) Cannabis fiber was also used in the manufacture of the best grades of paper, ironically for the paper used in printing Bibles. In this early period cannabis was prescribed as a drug. During World War II, because our supply of manila hemp (derived from a species related to the banana cultivated in the Philippine Islands) was cut off, the United States government did everything it could to encourage the cultivation of cannabis for hemp fiber, including subsidization of production. So, during the first 300 years after its introduction to the United States cannabis was known and grown primarily for its fiber but, as discussed earlier, secondarily as a source of medicine.

Around 1900 cannabis was reintroduced in another guise: It

was brought into the Gulf States from Mexico by workers and sailors who smoked marijuana. This use spread to the rest of the population, particularly to musicians in the cities. Before 1937 only 16 states had laws on marijuana; after 1937 virtually all states adopted such regulations. Some sociologists have suggested that one of the stimuli for enactment of these laws was provided by the pressure of the liquor lobby which did not welcome the competition from a rival intoxicant.

In the 1930s there developed a major wave of crime in New Orleans. The police and the newspapers attributed the increase in crime to persons who smoked marijuana. A good deal of emotion bordering on mass hysteria, not to mention racism, manifested itself. The United States Bureau of Narcotics claimed that marijuana incited crime and such alarmist warnings as the following were issued by the Federal Bureau of Investigation: "He really becomes a fiend with savage or 'cave man' tendencies. His sex desires are aroused and some of the most horrible crimes result. He hears light and sees sound. To get away from it, he suddenly becomes violent and may kill." There ensued further distortion as well as lurid, sensational testimony before Congress, all followed by the passage of the Federal Marijuana Act of 1937. The Act's provisions included:

1. Persons employing cannabis for approved industrial or medical purposes must register and pay a tax of $1 per ounce.
2. Other users must pay a tax of $100 per ounce.
3. Violators of the preceding regulations were subject to penalties for tax evasion or a fine of up to $2,000 and/or a prison term of not more than five years.

The federal government used the tax approach because it was feared that the direct approach would be considered an unconstitutional invasion of the rights of states. In any case, largely because of this particular approach, marijuana smokers resorted to the underground market. Incidentally, in the hearings in Washington which preceded the passage of the Act of 1937, Dr. William Woodward appeared for the American Medical Association to argue against the bill on the basis of a lack of solid evidence, and he further urged the importance of continuing medical research with cannabis. Despite these efforts the law was enacted.

Upon the urging of the Federal Bureau of Narcotics, most states passed similar restrictive legislation. In Georgia, until quite recently the penalty for the first offense for the transfer or sale by an older person to a minor was life imprisonment and the death penalty for the second offense. In Texas a few years ago simple possession brought a minimum sentence of two years and a maximum penalty of life imprisonment. In Rhode Island, next to first-degree murder, the sale of marijuana is the most harshly punished crime, earning more severe penalties than second-degree murder, armed robbery, or rape. The sale to a minor may result in a 30-year term in jail.

Recently there has been a movement to relax the severity of the punishment, particularly for mere possession of the drug. In Nebraska possession has been reduced to a misdemeanor and the penalty for a first offense is seven days in jail. In Oregon and California possession of less than an ounce is treated as a violation rather than as a crime and suspects get a ticket as with a parking violation. The maximum penalty is a $100 fine. The federal government modified its draconian stance with respect to marijuana in the Comprehensive Drug Abuse Prevention and Control Act of 1970. Possession for personal use is defined as a misdemeanor punishable by up to one year in jail and a $1,000 fine for the first offense and up to $2,000 and two years for the second offense. Selling, growing, and importing are all classified as felonies with stiff penalties.

The Effects of Cannabis

We should now turn to a brief consideration of the **pharmacology** (science of the action of drugs on animals) of cannabis. It is well to bear in mind that there is great variation in response—with the strength of the dose, whether marijuana or hashish, with the particular person, with the physical and mental state of the person at the time of use, and with the social setting in which the material is used. In general, smoking of marijuana may produce some or perhaps nearly all of the following effects:

1. Increased heart beat and initially there may be a slight rise in blood pressure in some people.
2. Red eyes.
3. Sense of euphoria or a feeling of well being.
4. Sometimes a feeling of anxiety, even panic, particularly in beginners.

5. A floating sensation (you may remember the Persian and Arabian tales of flying carpets—these tales no doubt arose from the experiences obtained from the use of hemp which gives one the sensation of floating in air and traveling through space).
6. Feeling of thirst—the mouth feels dry.
7. Increase in appetite.
8. Laughter, even a giggly feeling of hilarity.
9. The desire to speak more freely.
10. Altered sense of time—ten minutes may seem like hours.
11. Hallucinations—flashing lights, constant changing color forms and patterns.
12. Heightening of the keenness of senses.
13. Drowsiness.
14. Stimulating or depressing feeling, or both.
15. Ataxis, or inability to coordinate movements.
16. Vertigo or dizziness.

A Few Essential Terms

Before discussing marijuana further, we should pause to consider the numerous terms which are used and unfortunately used in different senses in the general drug field. The word **drug** itself is employed in a variety of ways. To the physician it is any substance employed as a medicine in the treatment of physical or mental disease (e.g., aspirin); to the layman, it means a medicine, or it often connotes a material which is habit-forming or leads to addiction (e.g., heroin). We shall use the term *drug* in its wider sense, meaning any chemical substance which alters structure or function in a living organism: a biodynamic agent.

The word **narcotic** has even more diverse usages than the term *drug*. The popular or newspaper meaning refers to dangerously addictive agents or those presumed to be addictive. The broad, etymologically correct definition signifies any agent capable of causing a depressive state (narcosis) in the central nervous system, either slight, as with tobacco, or intense, as with morphine. Legally it may be defined in terms of specifically listed drugs (which may or may not be addictive) rather than in terms of any common action. Some authorities follow a strict definition; according to them, a true narcotic would be one which produces addiction. **Addiction**, in turn, involves three elements: tolerance, withdrawal symptoms, and intense craving. **Tolerance** means that progressively larger doses of a drug must be taken in order to achieve a given effect (e.g., morphine, heroin, alcohol). **Withdrawal symptoms** refer to the severe physical reactions, usually nearly unbearable, sometimes even fatal, which occur when a person who has developed tolerance to a drug abruptly stops taking the drug. The physical reactions may include weakness, shivering, vomiting, loss of bowel and bladder control, as in the case of withdrawal from opium or its derivatives, or delirium tremens (DTs) in alcoholic withdrawal. **Craving,** or **psychological dependence**, of course, refers to the intense hunger for the drug and is often termed **habituation.** This overpowering craving may be characteristic of a drug and yet not be accompanied by either tolerance or withdrawal, as in the case of cocaine. Some tobacco smokers and some coffee drinkers develop a psychological dependence or irresistible craving for the alkaloids nicotine and caffeine and manifest nervousness and anxiety if they are not available. In this book we shall use *narcotic* in the strict sense; that is, a substance which produces addiction which in turn involves tolerance, withdrawal symptoms, and craving.

Major Studies of the Marijuana Problem

Report of the Indian Hemp Commission

In 1894 the British government published the massive report (8 volumes with 3,000 pages) of the Indian Hemp Commission. The report was the result of investigations over a two-year period of the mental, moral, and physical effects of cannabis, and it involved interviewing approximately 800 doctors, heads of asylums, clergymen, army officers, tax collectors, hemp dealers, peasants, fakirs, smugglers, coolies, and others knowledgeable in this sphere. The cynics of the time predicted that the findings would be hostile to cannabis, for they were confident that the powerful Scotch whiskey interests would not tolerate anything which might compete with their products. However, the Commission reached some opposite conclusions:

1. There is no substantial evidence that moderate use will produce mental and moral injury.

2. There is no proof of any connection between moderate use of cannabis and disease.
3. Moderate use does not lead to excess any more than it does in the case of alcohol.

U.S. Army Panama Study

In 1925 a U.S. Army Board of Inquiry made a study of marijuana use by soldiers stationed in the Panama Canal Zone. The report, published in 1933, concluded

1. There is no evidence that marijuana is a habit-forming drug in the sense of alcohol, opium, and cocaine.
2. No evidence could be found of any appreciable deleterious effects on users.

LaGuardia Report

In the 1930s the New York newspapers carried a rash of lurid news accounts about marijuana and its putative dangers. This induced Fiorello ("The Little Flower") La Guardia, colorful mayor of the city, to ask the New York Academy of Medicine to appoint a panel of experts to study the medical, sociological, and psychological aspects of marijuana. The Academy appointed 31 eminent physicians, psychiatrists, clinical psychologists, pharmacologists, chemists, and sociologists. The report was released in 1944 with, among others, the following findings:

1. No proof was found that major crimes are caused by smoking marijuana.
2. Marijuana smoking does not lead to aggressive or antisocial behavior.
3. Marijuana smoking does not alter the basic personality structure of the smoker.
4. Marijuana smoking does not cause sexual overstimulation.
5. There is no evidence that marijuana smoking leads to addiction in the medical sense of the word, that is, there is no evidence of tolerance.
6. Marijuana smoking does not lead to morphine or heroin or cocaine addiction.
7. The use of marijuana is not associated with juvenile delinquency.

Subsequently the LaGuardia report was denounced by the

American Medical Association and by the Federal Bureau of Narcotics. Despite the report, the Bureau still continues to insist that marijuana is a dangerous drug and that it may lead to the use of heroin and other hard drugs.

Report of the National Commission on Marihuana and Drug Abuse

The most recent extensive report on marijuana is that of the National Commission on Marihuana and Drug Abuse published in 1972. The document points out that whereas in the 1900s marijuana was used primarily by minority groups, by the 1960s its use had spread to middle- and upper-class college youths and to the high schools, including those in the affluent suburbs. It is estimated that approximately 24 million Americans have tried marijuana with nearly 8.5 million current users. Forty percent of the college population has experimented with the drug. There is evidence that many lose interest in it after some experimenting. One of the noteworthy features of the use of marijuana is that to a large extent it is a symbol of protest—of protest aimed at parents, schools, communities, society, business, government, and particularly the Establishment.

The report makes some interesting comparisons among marijuana and alcohol and tobacco. Alcoholism afflicts some 9 million Americans. It is estimated that the annual cost of alcoholism and alcohol abuse is about $15 billion, and that alcohol is the cause or is associated with half of all homicides and about a quarter of all suicides. Additionally, alcohol is a factor in half of the 30,000 highway fatalities each year. As for tobacco, approximately 550 billion cigarettes are smoked in the United States each year. According to the Surgeon General of the United States (*The Health Consequences of Smoking, 1972*) cigarette smoking is the major cause of lung cancer in men and a significant cause of lung cancer in women. Approximately 250,000 to 300,000 deaths are attributed to tobacco smoking each year in this country.

One of the questions raised in the report is, Why the marijuana fad? The answer the report offers is: The widespread use of marijuana is related to the increase in leisure or, in other words, to boredom, to the loss of a sense of community, and to a loss of a vision of the future. And it is noted that these changes are taking place in an environment of affluence. The investigators found that for a high percentage of young users there is a relationship with a common life style of the parents, a life style characterized by medicine taking (sleeping pills, tranquilizers, laxatives, etc.), cigarette smoking, and alcohol drinking.

In order to write intelligently about the effects of marijuana the report felt it necessary to define five types of users:

1. Experimenters—those who have used the drug in the past but not currently.
2. Intermittent users—those who smoke two to three cigarettes per month to one per week.
3. Moderate users—those who smoke several a week to one per day.
4. Heavy users—those who smoke more than one per day.
5. Very heavy users—those who are constantly intoxicated with high THC preparations, usually hashish, over a long time.

The Commission observes: "From what is now known about the effects of marijuana, its use at the present level does not constitute a major threat to public health. However, this statement should not lead to complacency. Marihuana is not an innocuous drug. The clinical findings of impaired psychological function, carefully documented by medical specialists, legitimately arouse concern.... Unfortunately, these marijuana-related problems, which occur only in heavy, long-term users, have been overgeneralized and overdramatized. Two percent of those Americans who have used marijuana are now heavy users and constitute the highest risk group." Among the other conclusions of the Commission are the following (individual items quoted verbatim):

1. Any psychoactive drug is potentially harmful to the individual.
2. Looking only at the effects on the individual, there is little proven danger of physical or psychological harm from the experimental or intermittent use of the natural preparations of cannabis, including the resinous mixtures commonly used in this country. The risk of harm lies instead in the heavy, long-term use of the drug, particularly of the most potent preparations.
3. The experimenter and the intermittent users develop little or no psychological dependence on the drug. No organ injury is demonstrable.
4. Some moderate users evidence a degree of psychological

dependence which increases in intensity with prolonged duration of use.

5. The heavy user shows strong psychological dependence on marijuana and often hashish.

6. The weight of the evidence is that marijuana does not cause violent or aggressive behavior, if anything, marijuana generally serves to inhibit the expression of such behavior.

7. Neither informed current professional opinion nor empirical research, ranging from the 1930's to the present, has produced systematic evidence to support the thesis that marijuana use, by itself, either invariably or generally leads to or causes crime, including acts of violence, juvenile delinquency or aggressive behavior.

8. Recent research has not yet proven that marijuana use significantly impairs driving ability or performance.

9. A careful search of the literature and testimony of the nation's health officials has not revealed a single human fatality in the United States proven to have resulted solely from ingestion of marijuana.

10. Minimal abnormalities in pulmonary function have been observed in some cases of heavy and very heavy smokers of potent marijuana preparations (ganja or hashish).

11. No objective evidence of specific pathology of brain tissue has been documented. This fact contrasts sharply with the well-established brain damage of chronic alcoholism.

12. Although evidence indicates that heavy, long-term cannabis users may develop psychological dependence, even then the level of psychological dependence is no different from the syndrome of anxiety and restlessness seen when an American stops smoking tobacco cigarettes.

13. The fact should be emphasized that the overwhelming majority of marijuana users do not progress to other drugs.

14. Scientific evidence has clearly demonstrated that marijuana is not a narcotic drug, and the law should properly reflect this fact.

15. The Commission found no evidence of chromosome damage or teratogenic or mutagenic effects due to cannabis at doses used by man.

The National Commission on Marihuana and Drug Abuse then made these recommendations:

1. That possession of cannabis for personal use no longer be considered a crime.

2. That casual distribution of small amounts for no remuneration or for incidental remuneration not involving profit, no longer be considered a crime.

3. That the government give increased support for research on the value of cannabis in the treatment of diseases, including migraine, alcoholism, terminal cancer, and glaucoma.

4. That the twelve states which classify marijuana improperly as a narcotic, change this terminology.

President Nixon did not accept the first two of these recommendations.

Recent Reports on Dangers of Cannabis

On the other side of the controversy over the effects of cannabis, it should be mentioned that during the several years since the publication of the National Commission's *Report on Marihuana* there have been a number of isolated reports which suggest the possibility of several deleterious effects of the use of cannabis—especially the use of the more potent forms in large quantities over a prolonged period of time. These alleged effects include:

1. Interference with the body's mechanisms of immunity.

2. Decrease in male hormone levels, with the suggestion that in some cases femalelike breasts have developed in young males.

3. Reduction in sperm count.

4. Disruption of cell metabolism, specifically in the synthesis of DNA.

5. Increase in reaction time on the part of automobile drivers and a diminution in ability to concentrate. (Hence, the frequent warning about the danger of driving after smoking marijuana.)

Still other recent reports have raised the question of the presence of possible cancer-causing agents in marijuana cigarettes. Another legitimate area of concern is the fact that THC accumulates in fat tissue and thus it may be retained in the body for long periods of time—even two to three weeks.

As mentioned, these have been isolated reports often based on few observations or experiments. It remains to be seen whether the implications of these reports will be corroborated by additional research and subsequent evaluation of the results.

In view of the present very confused status of cannabis research, caution would seem to be advisable—caution both with respect to the use of cannabis in any of its forms and caution in advancing any particular claims in regard to the effects of such use.

Books on Marijuana

Since during the last few years we have been inundated with books and other publications on marijuana, many of which are unreliable, a comment or two is in order to furnish a guide to those seeking more and dependable information on the subject. The authoritative *The Botany and Chemistry of Hallucinogens* by Richard Schultes and Albert Hofmann has an excellent section on cannabis. Two other superior books are *Marihauna Reconsidered* by Dr. Lester Grinspoon of the Harvard Medical School and *Uses of Marijuana* by Dr. Solomon Snyder of The Johns Hopkins University School of Medicine. As mentioned, Solomon's *The Marihauna Papers* and Andrews and Vinkenoog's *The Book of Grass* are rich sources for earlier essays, papers, and reports. The latest extensive study is the official report of the National Commission on Marihuana and Drug Abuse, published under the title, *Marihuana: A Signal of Misunderstanding. Marijuana: The New Prohibition*, written by John Kaplan, professor of law at Stanford University, presents the case for legalizing marijuana —for those over 16.

A Final Personal Note

It should be abundantly clear by now that the marijuana story is a very complex one. Few if any of the over 2,000 publications provide conclusive answers to the question of marijuana's physical and psychological effects on humans. Adequate control groups are rare in these studies. The whole subject is clouded with emotion, distortion, pleading by special-interest groups, and mythology, despite the fact that cannabis has been used for over 8,000 years by millions of people. Then, too, in discussions of marijuana, there is a very misleading lumping together of marijuana with true narcotics such as opium and heroin and with cocaine as though all four have the same properties and dangers. Even the botany of the plant is poorly understood, an unpardonable condition when we consider that *Cannabis* is one of man's oldest economic plants and has had five major uses throughout its history.

Because of the highly controversial nature of the subject, perhaps the authors may be permitted the indulgence of this brief caveat: We are not physicians, pharmacologists, or toxicologists, but we are two botanists who have read the record, critically we think. We are not marijuana smokers, nor do we advocate the use of marijuana or hashish by anyone. We remain two old-fashioned straights who are convinced that any drug is potentially harmful to the individual. We do suggest, however, that the public and particularly the law-making and law-enforcement agencies have given a disproportionate amount of attention to marijuana (it is estimated, for example, that in 1968 the state of California spent $75 million in processing marijuana violations), and that instead more attention should be directed to alcohol and tobacco—two other plant products—for both of these substances are tissue killers. Furthermore, alcohol may be addictive and tobacco habit-forming, in the sense of psychological dependence. On the other hand, with marijuana, as Grinspoon (1971) puts it, "There has never in its long history been reported an adequately documented case of lethal overdosage. Nor is there any evidence of cellular damage to any organ."

Suggested Readings

Andrews, George, and Simon Vinkenoog, eds. *The Book of Grass.* New York: Grove Press, 1968. An anthology of some of the significant literary essays, historical accounts, and medical and scientific papers on marijuana.

Bloomquist, E.R. *Marijuana.* Beverly Hills, Calif.: Glencoe Press, 1968. A general popular paperback written by a physician and drug authority.

Goode, Erich, ed. *Marijuana*. Chicago: Aldine-Atherton, 1969. A collection of papers on the marijuana problem edited by a sociologist.

Grinspoon, Lester. *Marihauna Reconsidered*. Cambridge, Mass.: Harvard University Press, 1971. One of the best books on the subject—covers the history, botany, chemistry, pharmacology, medical uses of cannabis, as well as other topics. Written by a clinical professor of psychiatry at Harvard Medical School. Should be read by all persons who hithertofor have obtained their information on marijuana from newspapers and television.

Kaplan, John. *Marijuana: The New Prohibition*. Cleveland, Ohio: World Publishing, 1970. A professor of law at Stanford University presents the case for the legalization of marijuana.

Merlin, Mark D. *Man and Marijuana*. New York: A.S. Barnes, 1972. Another brief, general account which discusses the botany, ecology, geographical distribution of marijuana, as well as the cultural diffusion of the plant throughout Europe and Asia.

National Commission on Marihuana and Drug Abuse. *Marihuana: A Signal of Misunderstanding*. New York: New American Library, 1972. The official report of the National Commission on Marihuana and Drug Abuse appointed by President Richard Nixon. Represents the most recent comprehensive study in this country, including a review and evaluation of the research on marijuana published to date (1972).

Oursler, Will. *Marijuana*. New York: Ericksson, 1968. A popular account of the marijuana problem.

Schultes, Richard E., and Albert Hofmann. *The Botany and Chemistry of Hallucinogens*. Springfield, Ill.: Charles C. Thomas, 1973. A leading authority on the botany of hallucinogenic plants and an outstanding expert on the chemistry of hallucinogens have joined forces to produce this excellent volume.

Secretary of Health, Education, and Welfare. *Marihuana and Health*. Fifth Report to the U.S. Congress. Washington, D.C.: U.S. Government Printing Office, 1975. The annual report of the National Institute on Drug Abuse on marijuana and its effects on health. A good source for information on the latest research, some of which raises questions about the deleterious effects of marijuana.

Smith, David E., ed. *The New Social Drug*. Englewood Cliffs, N.J.: Prentice-Hall, 1970. A collection of essays on cultural, medical, political and legal perspectives on marijuana.

Snyder, Solomon H. *Uses of Marijuana*. New York: Oxford University Press, 1971. A brief and well-written book by a professor of psychiatry and pharmacology of Johns Hopkins University School of Medicine. The volume discusses the use of cannabis as medicine, history, behavioral effects, dangers, recent research, and legal aspects. A good introduction to a complex subject.

Solomon, David, ed. *The Marihuana Papers.* Indianapolis: Bobbs-Merrill, 1966. A valuable collection of the significant scientific papers, literary essays, and investigative reports on marijuana, including a generous selection from the famous LaGuardia report of 1944.

Opium oozing from the cuts made in
the young capsules of the opium
poppy (*Papaver somniferum*) growing
in Bulgaria.

1a

Plate 1

1a Autumnal coloration.
1b Goldenrod *(Solidago)*.
1c Yew *(Taxus)* seeds.
1d Nightshade *(Solanum dulcamara),* poisonous plant.

1c

1d

1b

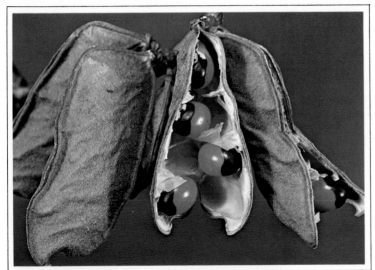

2a

Plate 2

2a Precatory bean *(Abrus precatorius)*, whose seeds are deadly.

2b St. John's wort *(Hypericum perforatum)*.

2c Poinsettia.

2b

2c

9
Medicinal Plants
Man's Great Blessings and Sometime Curse

Plants, Botany, and Medicine

People and plants have had a close association since the beginnings of the human species; this intimate relationship, involving plants as sources of food, clothing, shelter, fuel, weapons, and medicine, has continued throughout the development of man and of human culture. Similarly, botany and medicine have been closely linked throughout man's history—indeed until fairly recently the two were virtually one. The great physician Sir William Osler has said, "The desire to take medicine is perhaps the greatest feature which distinguishes man from animals." The earliest man who became knowledgeable about human disease and who took the first stumbling steps in therapy—be he called herb doctor, witch doctor (an inexcusable pejorative which ought to be eliminated), medicine man, sorcerer, or shaman—had to be a botanist of sorts, for most of his drugs came from plants. A substantial case can be made for the claim that the shaman is the oldest professional man in the evolution of human culture.

The legendary Chinese Emperor Shen Nung (about 2700 B.C.), according to tradition, studied the flora of his kingdom and reputedly knew some 365 plants of medicinal value, including opium and chaulmoogra oil. (The pharmacopoeia attributed to him, however, was not written until some centuries after his death.) The ancient Egyptians had a well-developed pharmacopoeia; the Ebers Papyrus dating back to 1500 B.C. lists approximately 800 principles or drugs. It is a startling thought that

Figure 9.1   Paracelsus (1493–1541), alchemist and physician, whose life and works led to the Faust legend. (Redrawn from a sixteenth-century woodcut by August Hirschvogel.)

if we had been able to read the Papyrus with understanding we would have reaped the rich benefits of antibiotics more than 100 years ago rather than having to wait until 1928 for a rediscovery of antibiotics.

In ancient Greece there existed a professional class of experts—the **rhizotomi** (literally, "root cutters")—who knew plants and where to find them. They gathered the plants with elaborate precautions and ceremonies; they muttered incantations and followed the practice of collecting certain plants in the dark of the moon ("slips of yew slivered in the moon's eclipse," *Macbeth*). Hippocrates (460?–377? B.C.), the Greek physician often hailed as the Father of Medicine and deviser of the well-known code of medical ethics, prepared a list of plants with their uses, including those of medicinal value. Theophrastus (374–287 B.C.), pupil of Aristotle, was responsible for extensive writings on botany, but unfortunately most of these have been lost. Dioscorides (64–120? A.D.), Greek physician, was the author of the five-volume *De Materia Medica* with references to several thousand botanicals or plant drugs. His was the first classification according to therapeutic use and his *De Materia Medica* was used as a reference for the next 15 centuries. Avicenna (980–1037), Arab physician and philosopher, wrote a book with 700 drugs; this volume became the chief guide for medical practice in Western Europe during the twelfth through the seventeenth centuries. The early medical teaching at the University of Bologna and other medieval universities was largely based on the writings of Avicenna.

The first steps toward a full *materia medica* were taken by the colorful and independent alchemist and physician, Theophrastus Bombastus von Hohenheim, commonly called Paracelsus (Figure 9.1), hailed in Robert Browning's poetic drama *Paracelsus* as

The wondrous Paracelsus, life's dispenser,
Fate's commissary, idol of the schools.

He was one of the early proponents of the **Doctrine of Signatures** whose lingering vestiges have persisted well into the twentieth century. You will recall that the Doctrine of Signatures is the belief that plants were created by God for man's use and that each plant bears a mark, or sign, indicating what it is good for. Thus a leaf or plant with a liverlike shape is good for liver trouble; a plant with red juice may be used to cure circulatory diseases; and the convoluted meat of the walnut, resembling the brain, is effective in the treatment of maladies of the head. Incidentally, Paracelsus, living up to his middle name of Bombastus, upon assuming the professorship of medicine at the University of Basel, stood before his class and dramatically burned the books of such earlier medical savants as Theophrastus, Dioscorides, Galen, and Avicenna (only the treatises of Hippocrates escaped).

The Medieval period and that immediately thereafter was the heyday of the herbalists. What might be considered the first true pharmacopoeia was the *Dispensatorium* (1535) of Cordus. In this period, too, there developed the physick gardens with the commonly used drug plants, a sort of living botanical drugstore.

Thus botany and medicine have been closely allied until well into the nineteenth century. Indeed, botanists were usually M.D.s and vice versa; you will recall that the great Swedish botanist of the eighteenth century, Linnaeus, had a medical degree and taught medicine, although he was primarily a botanist. The outstanding American botanist, Asa Gray, founder of Harvard's Gray Herbarium, was likewise a medical doctor.

The latter part of the nineteenth century witnessed the spectacular rise of organic chemistry. This development ushered in the age of coal tar, or the synthetic era, during the course of which many drugs were manufactured or synthesized. Up to about 1900, 80 percent of our drugs came from plants. In the following decades there was a decline in the pre-eminence of plant drugs, or botanicals. The first edition (1820) of the *United States Pharmacopeia* listed 650 drugs with 455, or 70 percent from plants; the eleventh edition (1936) had 570 drugs, 260 or 45 percent from plants.

Another dramatic shift but in the reverse direction took place about 45 years ago, just prior to World War II, when there developed a surge of renewed interest in medicinals of plant origin. A veritable revolution occurred with the appearance of the so-called wonder drugs, antibiotics such as penicillin, mostly from such plants as molds, lichens, and actinomycetes, a group of filamentous bacteria. The revolution was enhanced by the discovery, or better rediscovery, of muscle relaxants from South American arrow poisons; tranquilizers, such as reserpine from the Indian snakeroot or *Rauwolfia;* blood anticoagulants from sweet clover; cortisone precursors from the steroids of plants such as yams; hypertension agents from the false hellebore;

rutin to treat fragile capillaries and other hemorrhagic diseases; tumor-inhibiting agents from members of the dogbane family; and psychoactive plant drugs of great potential value in experimental and possibly therapeutic psychiatry.

In 1941 of the 10 most frequently prescribed drugs in the United States, 2 were from plants—codeine and digitalis. Nearly half of the 300 million new prescriptions written in 1961 in this country contained at least one ingredient of plant origin. In 1967, among the approximately 1 billion new and renewed prescriptions, 37 percent came from plants, 6 percent from animals, 7 percent from minerals, and the balance were synthetic. The sale of drugs from plant sources increased five times in the decade from 1950 to 1960, and the curve is still mounting sharply with a total annual sale volume of drugs from plants of over $1 billion. Small wonder that some have hailed this trend as a "botanical boom" or a "botanical renaissance." In 1961 more than $2 million were spent by 25 drug firms in seeking new medicinal plants. Some $10 million were expended in perfecting and developing such promising drugs as the steroids.

So we need to be reminded, in this age when our interest in synthetic materials is so pervasive, that many important drugs are still not synthesized but must be obtained from plants: digitalis, morphine, codeine, cocaine, ergotamine, podophylline, caffeine. Several others have been synthesized but the bulk of these medicines comes from plants, for the manufacturing process is still too expensive: quinine, atropine, reserpine, ephedrine. Of all the so-called wonder drugs of major importance only one class—the sulfa drugs—was wholly of synthetic discovery; all others, even those now synthesized, were discovered first from plant sources. Furthermore, Dr. Richard Schultes, the distinguished ethnobotanist at Harvard, offers the startling estimate that currently we know only about 10 percent of the organic constituents of the approximately 500,000 species of flowering plants, or angiosperms. Thus 90 percent of the organic components in plants still awaits discovery, investigation, and possible exploitation. The plant kingdom is virtually an untapped reservoir of tens of thousands of chemical compounds, many of which may be **biodynamic**—that is, have a marked effect on living organisms such as man.

How can one account for the fact that plants, in contrast to animals, are able to accumulate tens of thousands of organic compounds? One suggestion has arisen from circumstances discussed previously that plants, unlike animals, do not have excretory systems and hence the metabolic products accumulate in their cells and tissues. Among the more important of such compounds for medicine are the alkaloids and glycosides.

Alkaloids

You will recall from Chapter 7 on poisonous plants that alkaloids are important chemical compounds which are alkali-like, or basic, in reaction as opposed to acid; they are bitter in taste, organic, contain nitrogen, and have a marked physiological effect on animals including man. This effect is usually exerted on the nervous system. You will also recall that the names of alkaloids end in *-ine* as in morph*ine*. Over 5,000 alkaloids have been identified in plants, 90 percent of which occur in the angiosperms. Alkaloids tend to be found in certain families. All the members of one family, the poppy family, have alkaloids. Others rich in alkaloids are the dogbane, potato-tomato, coffee, and legume families. Some families such as the mints are completely devoid of alkaloids. A few years ago an American pharmaceutical firm in testing approximately 40,000 species for the presence of alkaloids, found that about 15 percent of them possess alkaloids.

Glycosides

In the discussion of poisonous plants we defined glycosides as compounds with one or more sugar molecules attached to one or more nonsugar compounds. Like alkaloids, glycosides are bitter and have a noticeable physiological effect on animals including humans. Among the various types of glycosides in plants are those that break down to form hydrocyanic acid (as in wilted cherry leaves), those that produce goiter, coumarin derived from sweet clover, and the **steroids.** It is difficult to give a nontechnical definition of steroids but it will serve our purpose to say that they are hydrocarbons with 17 carbon atoms in 4 rings and, further, they have roughly the solubility of fats. Later we will have occasion to mention a type of steroid known as **cardiac glycosides** (digitalis), and another kind of steroid found in arrow poisons, fish stunners, and in such plants as yams, agaves (century plants), and yucca (Spanish bayonet).

How Are Plants of Use in Medicine?

Given the vast array of organic compounds in plants, the question naturally arises as to how plants are employed in medicine. There are three ways in which plants are useful in medicine: First, plants or their chemicals may be used directly as drugs, as in the instances of digitalis, morphine, and atropine. Second, they may also be employed as precursors or starting materials for the synthesis of drugs. Steroids in plants such as yams are made into cortisone, sex hormones, and oral contraceptives. Finally, the organic molecules in plants—alkaloids, glycosides, or other compounds—may serve as models for the chemist. A chemist cannot simply go to his laboratory and decide to devise a chemical compound which will cure a specific disease; there is no a priori method of accomplishing this feat. Instead the chemist must first be furnished a plant or plant product which has been found to be effective as a drug. He then analyzes the responsible chemical compound, works out its chemical structure, and finally tries to synthesize the same or a related chemical. Thus when plants are discovered with chemicals that inhibit growth and tumor-formation (such as colchicine in the autumn crocus) the chemist, with these clues in hand, tries to synthesize a molecule similar to the natural antitumor agent in the plants. In a like fashion, the isolation of dicoumarin in moldy sweet clover led to the synthesis of other anticoagulants. In the words of Professor C. C. Albers of the University of Texas, "Plants provide blueprints for thousands of medical substances a chemist can synthesize. Plant explorers search for promising plants, then a valuable extract is produced and the chemists take over. They juggle and shuffle the molecules and come up with a variety of derivatives of natural products."

Methods Used in Discovering Medicinal Plants

Essentially there are three methods employed in discovering new plants of medicinal importance. First, there is the trial-and-error method, the random or semirandom approach, in which one begins to test all available plants. Because this shotgun method involves the expenditure of considerable time and money the method may be narrowed by limiting the testing to the native plants of a particular geographical area, say Cuba, or the study may be restricted to plants effective in the management of one disease such as cancer. (The Cancer Chemotherapy

National Service Center has tested approximately 26,000 plant extracts from 6,500 species in an effort to locate new drugs for cancer treatment.) Or the investigation may be focused on certain specific families known to be rich in alkaloids (for example, the potato-tomato family).

Second, there is the method of discovery in which one concentrates on the plants used in folk medicine as reported in both ancient and modern literature—histories, chronicles, accounts of exploration and travel, missionary reports, anthropological papers, and similar documents. We have already noted that reference was made to antibiotics in the Egyptian papyri and had we been receptive antibiotics might have come into modern use much sooner. Medieval and more recent European herbals are still rich sources; John Parkinson's herbal of 1640, for example, lists 3,800 medicinal plants. Other productive sources are the writings of the early explorer-naturalists and the physician-herbalists of the sixteenth and seventeenth centuries. Dr. Francisco Hernandez, physician to the king of Spain, traveled with the Spanish armies in Mexico in 1570–1575 and reported on many interesting plants, including the hallucinogenic sacred mushrooms and morning glories. The *Rig Veda,* the oral folk poetry tradition of India, traceable to 1500 B.C., refers to the medicinal properties of snakeroot or *Rauwolfia;* again we might have had the use of the valuable drug reserpine thousands of years ago had we but the wit to heed the words from ancient sources. The use of ephedra for asthma was known in folk medicine several thousand years ago in China, but ephedrine entered Western pharmacopoeias only in the 1920s. Pursuing this method, the Cancer Chemotherapy National Service Center has combed the literature since the beginning of writing—back to 2838 B.C.—for references to plants used as antitumor agents.

Because it is sometimes impossible to make a precise identification of a plant referred to by a common name especially since the locality of the plant often is not cited a recent modification of this method is to examine the data given on the labels of specimens in the **herbarium** (a collection of preserved plants, mostly dried and mounted on large white sheets of paper, which are then filed in cases). The labels not only reveal the name of the plant which the expert can check by direct examination, but its **habitat** (type of situation in which it grows, whether in a sandy soil, wet marsh, open field, etc.), geographi-

cal location, name of collector, and often notes on the folk uses of the plant including any medicinal uses. The considerable virtue of this method is that one can be absolutely certain of the identity of the plant and can learn the place of collection. Recently, a study of this nature at the Harvard University Herbaria involved the examination of over 2.5 million specimens which yielded 7,500 reports of medical or toxic properties.

A third method of discovering new plant drugs, and the best approach, is that requiring extensive ethnobotanical field work among intact but fast disappearing aboriginal societies; for example, field work in the Amazon region of South America. Drug companies, government agencies, botanical gardens, and universities regularly send out field expeditions for this purpose. In this way, for instance, new hallucinogens and muscle relaxants derived from native arrow poisons have been discovered by modern medicine.

Since ethnobotany is very much involved in such searches for drugs and toxic plants, we should pause and ponder the breadth of the subject. **Ethnobotany**, literally, ''people botany,'' is that part of botany which stresses the utility of plants, including the plant lore of the people and the uses of plants in their culture—in their festivals, their medicine, and their religion. Thus, it is an interdisciplinary study encompassing a core of botany but drawing upon chemistry, pharmacology, anthropology, archeology, linguistics, history, sociology, and comparative religion. And we should add that ethnobotany may not be restricted to the concerns and activities of primitive societies but can pertain to present-day, advanced peoples and nations as well.

A Few Representative and Important Medicinal Plants

Few plants have had such a powerful impact on human beings and civilization as the medicinal plants, some of which, in addition to being of value in medicine, are poisonous, others hallucinogenic, and still others are dangerous narcotics. Some have been used in the desperate struggles with such devastating diseases as malaria and leprosy. Others have been em-

Figure 9.2 Opium poppy (*Papaver somniferum*).

ployed to combat mental illness and cardiac disorders. The struggle for the control of these invaluable plants has led to international intrigue, smuggling, and warfare. Some of the plants have been so highly prized that they have been regarded as divine and even worshipped. In the pages that follow we shall not only discuss the medicinal virtues of these plants, but will also mention other ways in which they have made their impact felt on the human species.

Opium Poppy and Morphine

No plant is a greater blessing or boon, yet at the same time, no plant is a greater curse than the opium poppy. Similarly, it has been said that no plant has brought so much happiness and so much sorrow and tragedy. It is a blessing for those unfortunates who are enduring the agonies, the insufferable pain associated with extensive burns, ghastly battle wounds, body-shattering car accidents, and terminal cancer. It has given relief to millions in severe pain for it is the most effective painkiller the world has ever known. Sir William Osler has written, "Morphine is God's own medicine." But on the other hand, it is a most dangerous drug because of the peril of addiction. Millions have had their lives shattered because they became opium addicts.

The opium poppy *(Papaver somniferum,* Figure 9.2), a member of the poppy family, is an annual herb three to five feet tall with white to pink to purple flowers. It is a native of Turkey and adjacent Asia Minor but it has spread as a weed to other regions of the world with similar climates. Although it is illegal to grow it in the United States, it is now extensively cultivated in India, China, Vietnam, Burma, Indonesia, Turkey, the Balkans, and the Mediterranean region. The world production of opium is in the neighborhood of 10,000 tons, of which only 400 tons are used for medicinal purposes; the balance ends up in the drug trade. Other species of the poppy genus, devoid of opium or with only small quantities and hence without medicinal value are grown in our gardens as handsome ornamentals (examples, Oriental poppy, Iceland poppy, and corn poppy).

See Plate 3a, opium poppy.

Latex, a milky juice, is obtained from the fruit of the plant, the characteristic capsule of the poppy. The latex with the crude opium contains some 26 alkaloids, of which the medicinally most important are **morphine, codeine,** and **papaverine.** After the petals fall from the flower and before the capsule is quite mature, fairly shallow incisions, not deep enough to reach the

See photograph on page 208, opium poppy.

interior of the fruit, are made with a knife into the capsule. The crude opium is present only for a short period of eight to ten days and only in the cells of the thin layer of the capsule wall—it is not present in the seeds which are collected and used on poppy-seed rolls and for the extraction of a culinary oil.

In medical practice, morphine is administered orally, or more usually, by hypodermic needle. The alkaloid exerts its effects on the nervous system, first acting as a stimulant, then later as a depressant. It has the conspicuous property of relieving pain and hence is an analgesic—the best. It is also a **soporific,** or **hypnotic,** as it induces sleep (hence the name morphine from the Greek god of dreams, Morpheus)—first a pleasant drowsy euphoria, then dreamless, peaceful sleep. Additionally, it relaxes spasms. The Arabs have used it for centuries to dope race horses, stimulating them to greater effort.

Morphine or opium—eaten, snuffed, drunk, smoked, or injected—is a narcotic involving all the pleasant effects ascribed to its medicinal use; but it may also lead to addiction. Morphine is a classic narcotic with its danger of addiction involving the three elements of tolerance, severe physical withdrawal symptoms, and intense craving so overpowering in some cases that the victim may resort to violence to obtain the drug. William Emboden, in his beautifully illustrated *Narcotic Plants*, writes, "Withdrawal from physiological addiction caused by opiates is a nightmare of unparalleled horror: every mucous membrane releases a constant flow of mucous; chills, sweats and delusions overtake the victim; spasms of nausea and diarrhea become so severe that blood vessels can rupture in the stomach which sometimes leads to death." Or mark the graphic description given by Dr. Robert DeRopp in his classic *Drugs and the Mind:*

> God forbid that any reader of this book should ever know from direct experience what [the addict] suffered. "Withdrawal sickness" in one with a well-developed physical dependence on opiates is a shattering experience and even a physician, accustomed to the sight of suffering, finds it an ordeal to watch the agonies of patients in this condition. About twelve hours after the last dose of morphine or heroin the addict begins to grow uneasy. A sense of weakness overcomes him, he yawns, shivers, and sweats all at the same time while a watery discharge pours from the eyes and inside the nose which he compares to "hot water running up into the mouth." For a few hours he falls

into an abnormal tossing, restless sleep known among addicts as the "yen sleep." On awakening, eighteen to twenty-four hours after his last dose of the drug, the addict begins to enter the lower depths of his personal hell. The yawning may be so violent as to dislocate the jaw, watery mucous pours from the nose and copious tears from the eyes. The pupils are widely dilated, the hair on the skin stands up and the skin itself is cold and shows that typical goose flesh which in the parlance of the addict is called "cold turkey," a name also applied to the treatment of addiction by means of abrupt withdrawal.

Now to add further to the addict's miseries his bowels begin to act with fantastic violence; great waves of contraction pass over the walls of the stomach, causing explosive vomiting, the vomit being frequently stained with blood. So extreme are the contractions of the intestines that the surface of the abdomen appears corrugated and knotted as if a tangle of snakes were fighting beneath the skin. The abdominal pain is severe and rapidly increases. Constant purging takes place and as many as sixty large watery stools may be passed in a day.

Thirty-six hours after his last dose of the drug the addict presents a truly dreadful spectacle. In a desperate effort to gain comfort from the chills that rack his body he covers himself with every blanket he can find. His whole body is shaken by twitchings and his feet kick involuntarily, the origin of the addict's term, "kicking the habit."

Throughout this period of the withdrawal the unfortunate addict obtains neither sleep nor rest. His painful muscular cramps keep him ceaselessly tossing on his bed. Now, he rises and walks about. Now he lies down on the floor. Unless he is an exceptionally stoical individual (few addicts are, for stoics do not normally indulge in opiates) he fills the air with cries of misery. The quantity of watery secretion from eyes and nose is enormous, the amount of fluid expelled from stomach and intestines unbelievable. Profuse sweating alone is enough to keep bedding and mattress soaked. Filthy, unshaven, disheveled, befouled with his own vomit and feces, the addict at this stage presents an almost subhuman appearance. As he neither eats nor drinks he rapidly becomes emaciated and may lose as much as ten pounds in twenty-four hours. His weakness may become so great that he literally cannot raise his head. No wonder many physicians fear for the lives of their patients at this stage.

Opium has had a long history beginning with the legend that Buddha (563?–483 B.C.), Indian philosopher and founder of Buddhism, in order to prevent sleep from overtaking him, cut off his eyelids which fell to the ground, whereupon there sprang up an herb that produces sleep.

A Sumerian tablet dating back to 4000 B.C. mentions the opium poppy, referring to it as the "joy plant." The hieroglyphics of ancient Egypt make reference to it. Homer in his *Odyssey* sings of nepenthe (opium) which lulls pain and permits one to forget sorrow. The ancient medics—Hippocrates, Theophrastus, Pliny, Dioscorides, Galen, and Avicenna—all knew and discussed opium. The erratic genius Paracelsus was the first to dissolve opium in alcohol, producing tincture of opium, or **laudanum** (or ladanum). This was a considerable accomplishment, which gave physicians a better way to administer it than by offering the crude opium. In Germany in 1805 Friedrich Sertürner isolated **morphine** (the first alkaloid to be discovered) and henceforth it could be given in standardized, measured doses. Until fairly recently children who were teething and consequently crying excessively were given **paregoric**—tincture of opium to which camphor is added. Despite the fact that morphine has been known for 160 years, it has never been synthesized.

Opium has fascinated a number of major literary figures: Thomas De Quincey's *Confessions of an English Opium Eater* (1820) is well known, as is Samuel T. Coleridge's (1772–1836) "Kubla Khan," a poem written while the poet was under the influence of opium. Another prominent author who reputedly resorted to opium was Elizabeth Barrett Browning.

Opium and the opium trade have had considerable impact on history. The Chinese, contrary to common belief, began smoking opium fairly recently—in the seventeenth century. As a result of widespread abuse, the Chinese in the early 1800s forbade the importation of opium. This action threatened the lucrative British-dominated trade between India and China, resulting in the First Opium War (1839–1842) which ended in a peace treaty stipulating the opening to British trade of five treaty ports and the transfer of the island of Hong Kong to the British. A Second Opium War occurred in 1865, after which the Chinese were forced to legalize the importation of opium.

Figure 9.3 Coca (*Erythroxylon coca*) leaves.

In addition to morphine, opium also contains the alkaloid **codeine**, a sedative used in cough syrups and to treat the common cold, whooping cough, laryngitis, and mumps. Codeine is less toxic than morphine, having about a fifth of the pain-killing properties of morphine and less danger of addiction.

Heroin does not occur in nature but is a semisynthetic derivative of morphine and acetic acid. It is similar in its effects to morphine although it produces greater euphoria. It is reported to be six times as addictive as morphine.

Coca Plant and Cocaine

Like the opium poppy, the coca plant has been employed both in medicine and as a euphoric, and its use has often led to abuse. The small tree or shrub known as coca (not to be confused with cacao or cocoa, the chocolate tree, or the coconut) is a native of the eastern slopes of the Andes of Peru and Bolivia. The plant is cultivated throughout South America, and in Indonesia, Ceylon, and Taiwan. The leaves (Figure 9.3) which contain the alkaloid **cocaine** are harvested three to four times a year (Figure 9.4). The custom of chewing coca leaves goes back well before Francisco Pizarro conquered Peru (1531–1535). Pizarro observed the native Incas chewing the leaves (Figure 9.5) of the plant they referred to as "the Divine Plant" but which they did not worship as god. Somewhere in the mists of antiquity a venturesome pre-Inca discovered that the foliage of coca has the beneficial properties of stimulating, relieving fatigue, promoting endurance, causing one to forget hunger and thirst (the cocaine paralyzes the nerves that convey hunger pangs), and, in general making one feel better. We now know that the principle increases heart beat, rate of respiration, and blood pressure. For centuries Peruvian native laborers, porters, and guides, with little or no food or water, have climbed the steep Andean trails bearing large loads. Every hour or so they stop and replace the cud of leaves in their mouths with fresh leaves to which is added a bit of powdered lime. They use the term *cocada* for the length of time a cud will last and so cocadas are used to measure distances. Many natives live at elevations of 12,000 to 13,000 feet on the *altiplano*, and it appears that coca leaves help to make life at least sufferable in that wet, cold, bleak and altogether harsh environment. The sixteenth-century Spanish conquerers found it advantageous to provide coca leaves to the Inca slaves working the gold mines. Records show they distributed 2.5 million pounds of coca leaves per year. Currently,

Figure 9.4 Harvesting coca leaves in Bolivia. [Courtesy James A. Duke.]

Figure 9.5 Bolivian chewing coca leaves. [Courtesy James A. Duke.]

the peoples of Peru and Bolivia consume annually approximately 20 million pounds.

In the latter part of the nineteenth century coca was introduced into Europe; in Paris a coca wine became the rage, reaping a fortune for its promoters. In the United States extracts of coca leaves were used to prepare Coca-Cola (the cola portion of the combination is another plant product, the caffeine-containing cola nut of Africa). In 1904 the manufacturer of Coca-Cola was persuaded to remove the cocaine from the beverage. Five years later the U.S. Bureau of Food and Drugs, initiated a famous law suit (*United States v. Forty Barrels and Twenty Kegs of Coca-Cola*) in which the government charged the manufacturer with misbranding because, it was asserted, Coca-Cola now contained no coca. Today a few hundred tons of dealkaloidized coca leaves are imported each year into the country to flavor cola beverages.

Over the last few hundred years cocaine has come to be used as a euphoric. You will perhaps recall that Conan Doyle's famous detective Sherlock Holmes is described as injecting cocaine into his arms. Robert Louis Stevenson reputedly wrote his *The Strange Case of Dr. Jekyll and Mr. Hyde* in six days and six nights with the stimulus of cocaine which had been prescribed for his tuberculosis. In the nineteenth century Sigmund Freud advocated the use of cocaine to dissipate fatigue and to alleviate depression and only much later discovered the evils of the drug.

Even though the term *narcotic* is applied to cocaine, it differs from morphine in that in the former there are apparently no tolerance symptoms or withdrawal effects, although cocaine does evoke an intense craving, enough so that a desperate victim may resort to violence. Hence cocaine is considered a dangerous drug. It had a wave of popularity in the 1920s and its use is on the rise again. A 1972 news item reveals that cocaine was selling at $9,000 a pound in New York and Miami black markets.

Cocaine is used in medicine for eye surgery in the removal of cataracts—in spinal anesthesia, and formerly as a local anesthetic by dentists. The alkaloid was isolated in 1860, and it can be synthesized albeit the process is not commercially practical. Somewhat related synthetic substances such as **procaine** (trade name = Novacaine) are now employed commonly by dentists and doctors as local anesthetics.

Since there is so much misrepresentation of coca and cocaine, let us turn to the statements of Dr. Richard Schultes of Harvard for a distinction.

> I naturally learned to chew [the natives'] toasted coca leaves and, finding it to be a most helpful custom when one must work hard and there is little food, I used coca for eight years while in these remote areas, with absolutely no desire to continue upon my return. Cocaine, the powerful alkaloid extracted from the leaves is, of course, a very dangerous addicting drug. But coca leaves, as they are used by the South American Indians, particularly in the bleak Andean heights, are not addictive and they do serve a useful purpose enabling undernourished, debilitated persons to do a day's work and thus, at least, survive. The energy expended upon punitive international legislation against coca leaves might better be supplanted by an all-out attack upon the basic problems of malnutrition, disease, and a system which in many respects resembles paid slavery. . . .Unwise legal prohibitions in certain Andean areas aimed at extirpation of the coca custom have invariably driven the Indian, deprived in his inhospitable cold altitudes of the euphoric coca, to the dangerously poisonous local distilled drinks with an attendant rapid rise in crime.

It is obvious that Schultes follows the definition of narcotic that includes substances like cocaine which produce stupor or narcosis with intense craving but not necessarily tolerance or withdrawal effects.

Fever-Bark Tree, Quinine, and Malaria

The story of the fever-bark tree is an incredible history involving the suffering and death of millions; smuggling and other skulduggery; religious prejudice; discovery of a priceless medicinal plant by native peoples years before this knowledge penetrated the consciousness of so-called enlightened European man; intense struggles over plant products on the part of great nations; and, finally, impressive triumphs by medical and scientific research.

Malaria has been called the greatest killer in the world by Norman Taylor in his fascinating and eminently readable book *Plant Drugs That Changed the World.* Taylor goes on to say that this disease has killed more people than all the wars and all the plagues, including the Black Death. Still other millions spared death have been left a legacy of fevers, chills, weakness, lack of ambition, and misery. The effects of the disease encompass muscle soreness and backache, cold chills running up and down the spine, the appearance of goose flesh, the chattering of teeth, the involuntary shaking of arms and legs, violent vomiting, agonizing head pains, great thirst, drenching sweat, and finally the feeling of exhaustion and depression. And these seizures return again and again, with the spacing of the attacks dependent upon the type of malarial parasite; tertian fever occurs every third day and quartan is on a four-day cycle. Major permanent damage to the body may include liver malfunction and destruction of brain cells.

For thousands of years mankind suffered with but did not know the cause nor the cure for this dread disease (called variously malaria, ague, chills and fevers, and shakes). One persistent theory was that the malady represented emanations from the swamps or marshes—hence *mal-aire*, "bad air," as the name for the disease. It was held that night air was particularly dangerous; people were cautioned to stay indoors and keep their doors and windows closed. (As it happens, this was good advice.) Among the curative measures were such drastic procedures as the opening of skulls to allow the disease-producing demons to flee, fingers were amputated as sacrifices to the gods, and blood-letting was common until fairly recent times. (In retrospect we can see that this blood-letting merely accentuated the debilitation of the victims.)

Malaria depopulated whole regions—the plains around Rome, the Roman Campagna, is a case in point. The disease raised havoc with wars and military campaigns. Malaria killed thousands of troops on both sides during the Civil War. It is known that George Washington used fever-bark during the American Revolution. It has been estimated that in the Spanish-American War there were four American soldiers sick with malaria for every one wounded. In World War I, the Allied troops were immobilized in Greece because of malaria; in World War II over half a million of our troops suffered malaria, particularly in Africa and in the South Pacific. The whole continent of Africa was virtually rendered uninhabitable to early European settlers. History records terrible outbreaks of malaria in the fourth to fifth centuries B.C. and in the sixth to seventh, eleventh to twelfth, eighteenth to nineteenth centuries A.D. Cicero declared Rome "a pestilential city" and one section of the city was known as "the vale of Hell." No one escaped this dreadful malady, neither peasant nor king; Alexander the Great and Oliver Cromwell died of it. Some historians attribute the fall of Greece and Rome to the devastation brought on by malaria—at least as a contributing cause.

Nor has the North American continent been spared. Until quite recently—the 1950s—some 17 of our southeastern states were subject to it and at one time it was endemic as far north as New York City. In a mild year there might be 4 million cases, and as many as 6 million in a bad year. Approximately 5,000 people died each year.

In India for many years the death rate for malaria was 1 million. World mortality at present is approximately 3 million per year with some 800 million sufferers, most of whom are but half-alive. Even at this late date when medicaments to combat the disease are available and cheap, a third of the world population is threatened by malaria.

In 1880 a French army doctor, Charles Laveran, serving in Algeria, discovered that the disease is caused by an organism which destroys the red-blood cells in the human body. The parasite is a protozoan (one-celled animal) called *Plasmodium*, one species of which is *P. malariae*. Laveran's discovery is undoubtedly one of the great medical achievements of all times. He received a Nobel Prize in 1907. In 1897 a British doctor, Ronald Ross, working in India, found that the parasite is carried by mosquitoes. For this research he was knighted and awarded a Nobel Prize in 1902. In the same year Giovanni Grassi, an Italian zoologist, demonstrated that the malarial organism is transmitted by a particular kind of mosquito, the *Anopheles* mosquito, and only by the female insect.

Now we must backtrack to pick up the story of the developments in finding a cure for malaria. In the 1630s, word reached Europe, probably via Jesuit priests in Lima, Peru, that the bark of a tree (Figure 9.6) growing on the eastern slopes of the Andes was effective in treating malaria. The news electrified Europe —to appreciate the intensity of the feeling of hope aroused, imagine similar word flashed to us that cancer can be cured. The natives of the area had known of the tree and its virtues for sometime, although there is no evidence that the earlier Incas knew of it at the time of the Spanish conquest. The native name for bark is *quina* and this tree was called **quina quina,** "bark of barks."

Figure 9.6 Removing bark from a fever-bark tree (*Cinchona*) in Guatemala. [Courtesy U.S. Department of Agriculture.]

One intriguing question is how the natives ever discovered that the bark of this particular tree, among tens of thousands of species of trees, was effective in treating malaria. We can only speculate, but one plausible guess is that at some point a native with malaria chanced to refresh himself at a pool into which a quina quina tree had fallen. When he found that his fever was alleviated perhaps he was shrewd enough to attribute his cure to the water and then to the bark that was in the water. He then spread the word to others.

The quina quina tree, also called the fever-bark tree, was named *Cinchona* by Linnaeus for the Countess of Chinchon, wife of the Spanish ruler of Peru (with the misspelling you will have noted). Legend has it that she had been cured by the bark. The medicine was also known as contessa powder.

In Europe the Jesuits were the early users of the bark and hence it was often referred to as Jesuit's bark or powder, as well as Peruvian bark. The Jesuits stationed in South America, good ecologists and conservationists that they were, taught the natives to plant five new cinchona trees to replace each one cut down and stripped of bark, then with a religious flourish, they recommended that the five trees be planted in the shape of a cross.

Characteristically the seventeenth-century people as well as doctors were suspicious of the bark; for one thing it was new, and secondly it was sponsored by the Jesuits and hence some feared that the promotion of the use of the bark was a Catholic plot to kill all Protestants. Cromwell, although dying of malaria, refused to take the proffered medicine with the remark that he would not be "Jesuited to death."

About this time an apothecary's apprentice and engaging scoundrel named Robert Talbor came forth with a secret remedy which he claimed cured malaria. As a result he built up quite a reputation in his local area. In 1668 he came to London, and, since he was greatly sought after, he soon amassed a fortune. Charles II's malaria was cured by Talbor for which service he was appointed physician to the king and he became Sir Robert Talbor. Charles forced the Royal College of Physicians to elect Talbor a member. When the heir to the throne of Louis XIV, king of France, contracted malaria, Talbor was sent to Paris where he cured both the heir and the king. Later he went on to repeat his therapeutic triumphs in Vienna, Madrid, and other capitals of Europe.

Louis XIV wished desperately to buy Talbor's secret and finally he convinced Talbor to write the formula with the promise that it would be locked in a safe until Talbor's death. For this, the king provided 3,000 crowns and a pension for life for Talbor. When Talbor died in 1681, Louis revealed the secret—he found that Talbor's miraculous malarial cure consisted of lemon juice, rose leaves and—cinchona bark. Eventually cinchona was admitted to the British pharmacopoeia. Talbor received no Nobel Prize—it was not yet in existence, for one thing—but he did erect a monument to himself in Trinity Church, Cambridge, which bears the inscription written by himself,"The most honorable Robert Talbor, Knight and Singular Physician, unique in curing fevers of which he had delivered Charles II of England, Louis XIV, King of France, the Most Serene Dauphin, Princes, many a Duke, and a large number of lesser personages."

For nearly a century following the astonishing news of 1630 that quina quina was an effective drug, no European had yet seen a fever-bark tree. The French botanist Joseph de Jussieu came to South America to search for the tree and in 1737 he saw his first one which he described as the "most beautiful tree in the world," matching the lines from Erasmus Darwin's *The Botanic Garden*:

Cinchona, fairest of Peruvian maids,
To Health's bright goddess in the breezy glades
On Quito's temperate plain an altar rear'd.

He spent 30 years in the jungle searching for cinchona as well as other plants. On the night before his departure for Europe, a native stole all his specimens, whereupon de Jussieu disappeared in the jungle where he wandered in a bewildered state until he finally returned to France a deranged man.

A Dr. José Mutis finally sent Linnaeus some dried leaves and flowers of the tree, and on the basis of this material Linnaeus prepared the description and gave the scientific name *Cinchona officinalis*. We now know that there are also other species of cinchona which yield the drug. These several species are evergreen trees or shrubs native to the eastern slopes of the Andes ranging from Venezuela to Colombia to Ecuador to Peru to Bolivia, growing at elevations of 3,000 to 10,000 feet in locations with 90 to 125 inches of annual rainfall. They do not grow in groves or clumps but the individual trees are scattered—quite typical of tropical species as opposed to the temperate situation where trees may form extensive groves, as with pines, redwoods, and Douglas fir.

In 1777 the Spanish sent expeditions to locate and exploit cinchona trees. For nearly 200 years the medicine was taken in the form of the very bitter powdered bark. Two Frenchmen in Paris, Joseph Pelletier and Joseph Caventou, in 1820, discovered the alkaloid in the quina bark, which they named **quinine**, pronounced "quin éen" in every country but the United States where it is rendered "kwy' nine." The work of these two scientists is commemorated by a monument in Paris.

With the isolation of the alkaloid quinine, doctors could prescribe a measured, standardized dose to patients. Quinine is a remarkable drug since it is one of the few medicines which is specific for one disease or condition, namely malaria and related fevers. Sir William Osler in writing of the treatment of malaria in 1907 said there is only one word—quinine. It has been learned that in cinchona bark there are about 30 alkaloids including **quinidine,** used for cases of irregular and rapid heartbeat and other cardiac conditions, and **cinchonine.** **Totaquine**—the so-called poor man's quinine—is a mixture of several alkaloids, including quinine, but the latter is in small concentration.

The first factory in the United States to manufacture quinine was built in Philadelphia in 1823. A Dr. John Sappington of Missouri, through an error made by his son, acquired several pounds of the drug which he advertised as Dr. Sappington's Fever Pills. He persuaded ministers in the Mississippi Valley to ring their church bells every evening to remind the people to take their fever pills. Needless to say as a result, this ingenious entrepreneur became rich.

In the 1800s the struggle for cinchona bark became intense, with the result that in the wild greed to obtain the precious bark the standing trees were stripped of their bark and left to die. The producing countries of South America—Bolivia, Peru, Colombia, and Ecuador—in an effort to safeguard their monopoly, eventually prohibited the exportation of seeds, seedlings, and living plants. This action was of great concern to the British, who needed the drug for India and the rest of their tropical colonies, and to the Dutch who controlled the immense plant wealth of the East Indies. The Dutch sent a man to South America to collect seeds and plants in 1852—they even dispatched a Dutch warship to bring him out. The mission ended in failure, for most of the living plants were dead on arrival and the surviving seeds produced plants with very poor yields of the drug.

In 1859 the English commissioned Clements Markham for a similar mission. Markham was accompanied by the famous explorer and collector, Richard Spruce. This expedition was also a failure, for the plants proved to be poor yielders of quinine. Finally Charles Ledger, an English bark collector *(cascarillero)* and trader, living in a region of Peru near Lake Titicaca known for its high-yielding cinchona trees, persuaded Manuel Incra Mamani, an Indian worker, to collect seeds from the trees with the best yields. Manuel was discovered and thrown in jail, beaten, starved, and he finally died. Meanwhile, Ledger sent the seeds to London only to find that the government was not interested since it had had one disastrous experience with cinchona. However, the Dutch bought one pound of his seeds for a paltry 100 francs, or $20, and this single pound of seeds is the source of today's great cinchona plantations of Java and adjacent lands, plantations probably worth well over $50 million.

The Dutch exhibited great skill in horticulture—in the growing, selecting, and grafting of the plants. They grafted scions of high-yielding cinchona but with poor root growth on stocks of plants producing low concentrations of quinine and strong roots. As a result of these efforts the Dutch established a world monopoly based on this single pound of Ledger's seeds. This monopoly which lasted until World War II set quotas for planting, prices to be paid, amounts to be manufactured, and the ultimate world market price. The Dutch even built their own quinine factories in Java.

A number of events ultimately made the Dutch monopoly less effective, however. The enhanced commercial production of the insecticide DDT provided a powerful weapon with which to decimate the mosquito population, as a result of which the incidence of malaria decreased by approximately 90 percent in the United States. Then, too, various synthetic substitutes for quinine such as Paludrin and Aralen came on the market. Finally, the Japanese invasion of the Dutch East Indies in 1942 stopped the flow of quinine to the Allied countries—as it did the flow of tea, coffee, rubber, sugar, kapok for stuffing life-preservers, abaca fiber for rope, and palm oil. What made matters even more critical was that two years previously the Germans had captured Amsterdam and thus possessed Europe's reserve

Figure 9.7   Foxglove (*Digitalis purpurea*).

See Plate 3b, foxglove.

stock pile of quinine. As a result, 90 percent of the world's quinine supply was in the hands of the enemy.

The United States became concerned over the serious consequences of not being able to obtain a source of quinine in the Western Hemisphere. Accordingly, a top-priority program was instituted, one element of which was to send to the Andes, home of cinchona, such eminent botanists as William Steere, Raymond Fosberg, and Wendell Camp to locate new sites of cinchona and to find new species which might prove to be big-yielders of quinine. A new species was found near Lake Titicaca and La Paz, the quinine capital of the world, which has the highest-yielding bark discovered to date. In addition, the United States government had millions of seedlings planted in Guatemala with the thought that these would be harvested to furnish an emergency supply of quinine.

In 1944 quinine was synthesized by William Doering then of Columbia University and Robert Woodward of Harvard. However, the synthesis is complicated and much too expensive for large-scale production, costing about $1,000 a gram. A substitute for quinine, **Atabrine,** was synthesized from coal tar in 1928 in Germany. Unfortunately, it has side effects such as nausea, jaundice, and diarrhea. Other effective synthetic substitutes are chloroquine and primaquine. But the perfect substitute has not yet been found. For one thing, there are four different species of *Plasmodium* and each reacts differently to the various drugs. Then, too, the parasites are developing resistance to the substitutes, but this is less true of quinine.

Foxglove, Digitalis, and Heart Disease

Another important substance in the arsenal provided by medicinal plants is the drug **digitalis**, derived from the leaf blade of the garden foxglove (*Digitalis purpurea*, a member of the snapdragon family, Figure 9.7), a native of southern and central Europe although it has become naturalized in other parts of Europe and in North and highland South America. In this country it is often grown in our gardens as an ornamental, for it is an attractive herbaceous biennial, up to four feet tall and with handsome thimblelike, whitish or purplish flowers. Digitalis contains the glycoside **digitoxin** as well as about 30 other glycosides.

Digitalis is a heart stimulant and is the most important drug used for the treatment of certain heart diseases. It improves the tone and the rhythm of the heartbeat and better circulation results. In addition, it is employed in the treatment of muscular dystrophy and glaucoma where it reduces the pressure in the eyeball by decreasing the fluid content. Digitalis has never been synthesized and so we must rely on the plant for this invaluable drug.

Although digitalis is mentioned in the old manuscript herbals as early as 1250 it was not specified for heart disease. William Withering, an English doctor, is responsible for the modern use of digitalis by the medical profession. Dr. Withering was of the old school—he saw about 2,500 patients a year and in so doing had to ply the wretched country roads of the period in a horse-drawn carriage. Incidentally, he hated botany and it was only when he met a young lady fond of plants that he learned to love both botany and the damsel, so much so that in his spare time he wrote a popular book on botany (1776) in which he followed the Linnaean classification system. On one of his trips in the country, he heard of a woman on the brink of death with a severe case of dropsy, a disease characterized by the accumulation of liquids in the body cavities, both chest and abdomen, and a swelling of legs and ankles. A few weeks later, much to Withering's surprise, he learned that the woman had made a good recovery. Upon inquiry he found that she had resorted to the folk medicine of the region and had ingested a mixture of herbs, including foxglove.

Withering began a ten-year experimentation with the plant. His laboratory was his kitchen where he dried foxglove leaves in a frying pan over a coal fire. Somehow he managed to work out a safe dosage for digitalis. In 1758 he summarized his research in *An Account of the Foxglove and Some of its Medical Uses with Practical Remarks on Dropsy and Other Diseases.* This monograph is now considered one of the great medical classics.

We now know that digitalis acts as a **diuretic**; that is, it reduces the accumulation of liquids in the body by stimulating urination. We also know that dropsy is not a disease in itself, but a symptom of heart disease. Digitalis works by strengthening the heart which pumps more blood to the kidneys which, in turn, take up more water from the tissues. Millions of lives have been saved and prolonged by digitalis over the last couple hundred years. However, too heavy a dose is fatal, for digitalis is extremely toxic. As mentioned in the chapter on poisonous plants, there have been cases of deaths of children who either sucked the nectar of the flower or chewed the leaves. Again we see that the difference between a medicine and a poison is often merely a question of dosage.

Kalaw Tree, Chaulmoogra Oil, and Leprosy

Leprosy, from the earliest of times—and we have records of the disease in the Nile Valley as far back as 2,500 years ago—has been regarded as a dread, insidious, loathsome disease which is incurable. Apparently it first appeared in Europe in the eleventh century when the returning Crusaders brought it back from the Near East. Soon it became the custom to treat the victims of the disease as outcasts. They were required to wear bells to warn the healthy, and upon the sound of the telltale bell, the cry of "Unclean! Unclean!" would reverberate in the narrow streets of the old medieval cities and all would flee from the despised lepers. One of the duties of the priests of the Middle Ages was to cast out the lepers—to remove them to the miserable leper hovels at the edge of the cities. To this day we still have this association between the leper and the outcast, between the leper and sin, as in the expression moral leper.

The symptoms of the disease are dramatic: First, there is a lack of sensitivity of the skin—even cuts and bruises may cause no pain; the skin takes on a characteristic porcelainlike whiteness; later the skin becomes mottled with red, purple, or bronze spots, even yellowish or reddish-brown nodules may appear; the eyebrows fall off; there may be nasal ulcers and facial deformity; fever develops; and finally, the extremities such as fingers and toes, having become ennervated, may fall off.

Transmission of the disease is through skin contact. (We caution our students that they must not sleep with infected persons!) Virtually all advanced and untreated cases are fatal. Even today millions of people have leprosy, mostly people who live in warm, damp climates, many of whom are not safely isolated. In 1963 the United States Public Health Service published figures indicating that there were 15 million leprosy victims in the world, 80 percent in Africa and Asia. There were 5,000 cases in the United States.

Most of us have read about Father Damien (1840–1889), the courageous Belgian, who went as a missionary to the Pacific islands in 1863. He worked in a leper colony on Molokai in the Hawaiian Islands—"the island of the living dead," as Robert Louis Stevenson described it. Father Damien himself contracted leprosy and died in 1889. There is a leper colony in continental United States, the U.S. National Leprosarium in Carville, Louisiana; and there are leprosaria in the Philippines, India, Africa, and Malaya.

Dr. G. A. Hansen, a Norwegian physician, demonstrated in 1874 that leprosy is caused by a bacterium (*Mycobacterium leprae*). Hence, leprosy is also called Hansen's disease; many find this alternative name more acceptable than leprosy with all its past unfortunate connotations.

Although the natives of Asia were reputed to have some kind of cure for leprosy, this native drug was ignored by the rest of the world until 1853, when Dr. F. J. Mouat of the British Indian Medical Service became impressed with the stories of native successes. His feeling was reinforced when he had occasion to examine two ancient documents, the pharmacopoeia ascribed to Emperor Shen Nung (2700 B.C.) and the Indian *Veda* (1500 B.C.) in which there are references to the effectiveness of chaulmoogra oil in the treatment of leprosy.

Although the seeds of the chaulmoogra or kalaw tree, collected by tribesmen, were sold in the native markets in China, Burma, and India, no one seemed to know the identity of the tree, certainly no European. The tree was finally discovered—a word, in this field of plant drugs, meaning rediscovered or found by a European or American centuries or longer after a plant has been used successfully by native people—by the renowned botanical explorer and plant collector, Joseph Rock (1884–1962). Rock was a precocious youth who learned Arabic by the age of 16 and taught that language at the University of Vienna. By 1907 he was professor of botany and Chinese at the University of Hawaii. Then appeared on the scene Dr. David Fairchild, himself a respected botanical explorer and plant hunter, author of such enchanting books as *The World Was My Garden* and *Garden Islands of the Great East,* and the head of the United States Department of Agriculture's Division of Foreign Seed and Plant Introduction (which now employs some 90 explorers to collect seeds and plants for agriculture, industry, and medicine). Fairchild hired Rock and in effect pointed at the map of Asia in the general direction of Indochina, Siam, Burma, and India, telling him to go find the trees and collect seeds.

Rock knew only that the trees grew somewhere in that vast area and that from the descriptions filtering down from natives, they were probably members of the tropical family Flacour-

See Plate 3c, kalaw tree.

tiaceae. Armed with this meager information, Rock began an odyssey of thousands of miles by pony, bullock cart, canoe and raft, encountering jungle fever, malaria, bandits, communists, tigers, treacherous servants, and river rapids. He finally found the trees in Burma where fortunately they were bearing fruit—the size of tennis balls and covered with wooly hair. He soon learned that the monkeys were fond of the fruit and they became his competitors in his efforts to collect seeds.

The 80 to 90 foot trees are named chaulmoogra from the Burmese name. They are also known as kalaw trees. The chaulmoogra oil is extracted from the seeds. We now know that there are three species of *Hydnocarpus*, the genus name for the trees, which are native to Burma, Thailand, the East Indies, and other parts of southeast Asia.

Rock sent seeds to Hawaii where large kalaw tree plantations have subsequently been established, as they have in the Philippines. He then spent some 30 years in China and Tibet, during the course of which he was able to introduce approximately 700 different rhododendrons and azaleas, most of them to the Arnold Arboretum in Boston. The Chinese communists finally drove Rock out of China and he died in Hawaii in 1962 at the age of 78.

Subsequent to Rock's introduction of kalaw trees, it has been learned that chaulmoogra oil is very effective for incipient cases of leprosy, usually effecting a complete cure, although it does require three to five years of treatment in a leprosarium. On the negative side, the oil is rancid in odor and acrid in taste and hence nauseating and is even rejected by some patients. To overcome these difficulties, the oil is now often injected intravenously.

In 1946 there appeared synthetic substances, the sulfa drugs or sulfones, which are effective in curing leprosy. The synthetics, too, have negative aspects: They sometimes produce a skin rash, and they cause nausea, anemia, and bloody urine. The British have found that a combination of chaulmoogra oil and sulfa drugs is more effective than either used singly. It is rather interesting that for some time there has been a suspicion that leprosy and tuberculosis are rather similar. Both are caused by bacteria and the sulfa drugs are effective with both diseases.

One of the obstacles to better progress in developing more effective therapy for leprosy has been the inability to infect experimental animals with the disease. Some success has been obtained with mice but unfortunately for research they get only a mild form of the disease. In 1974 the journal *Science* carried a report that success has been achieved with the inoculation of armadillos with the leprosy bacterium.

Snakeroot, Reserpine, Lunacy, and Hypertension

Norman Taylor writes that for 35 centuries "Western man has ignored a whisper from the earth of India." He is referring to the fact that Western civilization has been blind to an important drug used for thousands of years as a folk medicine in India in the treatment of the mentally ill and those with high blood pressure. It was rediscovered some 25 years ago.

The ancient Indian *Veda* makes reference to the use of snakeroot in medicine. In the intervening 3,000 years this drug has been known to medicine men, bazaarkeepers, and Indian peasants, and it is referred to by them as the "insanity herb" (*pagal-ke-dawa*). In Hindi the plant is called *chandra*, the word for "moon." And indeed for centuries in India it has been used for moon disease or lunacy, or, as we would say, for the mentally ill. Long ago it was noted that the drug lowers blood pressure and that it may be employed as an antidote for snake bites and the stings of scorpions and other insects. The Dutch botanist and physician, G. E. Rumpf (or Rumphius; 1627–1702), called the "Pliny of India," and who published the first illustration of the plant, tells us, "Men seem to have learned the powers of this plant from the so-called mongoose or weasel. This little animal, before attacking a snake, fortifies itself by eating the leaves; or, injured in combat with a snake, seeks out this herb, eats the leaves, rolls itself around three or four times, then rests a little as if drugged, but soon afterwards regains its strength and rushes forward to re-attack. . . . It is said to cure the bite of most poisonous snakes, even the Cobra capella." If the account is true, one wonders how the mongoose learned that this plant has such a property.

The scientific name of snakeroot is *Rauwolfia serpentina*, a member of the dogbane family (Figure 9.8). The specific name refers to the snakelike roots and would appear to be an application of the Doctrine of Signatures, which in this case is valid. The plant is a low evergreen shrub, up to three feet tall. The medicine is derived from the roots, mostly from the bark of the roots, which is ground to a powder. The plant is a native of India, Ceylon, and the East Indies, but the present source of supply is India where it is cultivated on plantations in regions

Figure 9.8 Snakeroot (*Rauwolfia serpentina*).

with tropical heat and 100 to 150 inches of annual rainfall. The genus *Rauwolfia* with many species is found not only in the Old World tropics, but in all tropical parts of the world except Australia. The species native to the region from Mexico to Ecuador is used by the native people as an antidote against the bites of the fer-de-lance and coral snakes.

It was not until the last decade of the nineteenth century that two Dutchmen published accounts of this remarkable plant with notes on its chemistry and pharmacology. As a result it was planted in the famous botanical gardens in Buitenzorg, Java (now Bogor), but otherwise the plant was ignored for over 40 years. In 1943 an Indian doctor, R. N. Chopra, wrote about its hypnotic and sedative effects. In 1952 rauwolfia became front-page news with the isolation of the alkaloid **reserpine** which now made it possible to administer a standard dose with predictable effects.

Reserpine has in many respects revolutionized the treatment of nervous disorders. In the United States some quarter-million mental patients are admitted to hospitals each year; these hospitals cost the federal, state, and local governments $3 billion annually. Approximately 60 percent of the inmates are schizophrenics (have split personalities) and many of them have suicidal tendencies or show tendencies for other forms of violence. Formerly about the only relief which could be given was some sort of shock which made the patients less violent and easier to handle. Shock was induced by injecting insulin or metrazol which produced instant convulsions, or by the electroshock method which gave a charge of electricity just short of that which would produce permanent damage. The reactions were sometimes traumatic and the subsequent convulsive spasms occasionally caused the breaking of bones. Another method of treatment was a lobotomy in which part of the brain was destroyed—what Dr. DeRopp calls the "ice pick and mallet approach." Some relief was given but the patient was doomed to remain half-human for the rest of his life. Reserpine has changed all this and given relief to millions.

Its alkaloid acts on the central nervous system and the brain to produce a sedative effect. With continuing medication and sometimes without, many schizophrenics are able to return to their homes to lead nearly normal lives. Reserpine has been hailed as the most valuable tranquilizing drug ever to come from plants. It should be added that additional millions of people who are not mentally ill, or at least are not schizophrenics, but who may not be well adjusted to the stresses of modern life or otherwise may have emotional problems resort to the tranquilizer reserpine to calm them, to relieve anxiety, and to permit them to sleep. As a result, the sale of barbiturates has fallen off. And it should be emphasized that reserpine is not addictive—in no sense is it a narcotic.

In addition to its tranquilizing properties, reserpine reduces blood pressure; millions have had it prescribed for the treatment of hypertension. High blood pressure, or hypertension, is becoming an increasingly serious health problem in the United States with millions of people, particularly the middle-aged and elderly, affected by it. Most afflicted people are unaware of their potentially dangerous condition, for often there are no overt symptoms. High blood pressure is very important in diseases of the heart and circulatory system, the leading cause of death in the United States. The high pressure overburdens the heart and may impair the functioning of the kidneys and may eventually lead to a stroke. The use of reserpine reduces the blood pressure, often in three to six weeks. Thus reserpine has been a lifesaver and a life-prolonger, and what is remarkable is that all of this is a very recent development, with the first American paper on reserpine and blood pressure published in 1953.

In 1956 reserpine was synthesized by Dr. Robert B. Woodward of Harvard. So far this synthesis is little more than a scientific feat although a very important one, for the process is still too expensive to produce the drug commercially. Consequently, reserpine continues to be derived from plants.

By 1957 over 1,500 research and clinical papers had been published on rauwolfia and reserpine and its use in medicine for schizophrenia, paranoia, manic states, chronic alcoholism and to alleviate withdrawal symptoms in narcotic addiction. Some authorities hail reserpine as the most important development in the history of psychiatry, for it suggests that mental disturbances may have a purely chemical basis, pointing the way to the treatment of mental diseases with chemicals. In the words of biologist Ralph W. Gerard, "There can be no twisted thought without a twisted molecule."

In 1960 one of the largest of the pharmaceutical manufacturers reported prescriptions for reserpine in the amount of $30 million for the United States. Because of the enormous volume, it was possible to reduce the price from $45 a gram to $1. In 1965 despite the drastic reduction in price, $40 million of prescriptions were written for that year in this country. Reserpine is now sixth among all prescriptions written for natural products.

Plant Sources for Cortisone, Sex Hormones,
and Oral Contraceptives

Among the hormones produced by the cortex of the adrenal glands, located above the kidneys, is **cortisone** which raises the blood sugar level by increasing conversion of amino acids to carbohydrates. Extracted from animals, cortisone is used in the treatment of rheumatoid arthritis of which there are some 3 million cases in the United States. Among the other diseases treated with cortisone are Addison's disease (or adrenal insufficiency), rheumatic heart disease, bursitis, asthma, gout, hepatitis, leukemia, skin diseases, and over 90 other maladies. Cortisone can be made from the bile acids in the urine of oxen but the process involves some 32 to 40 separate steps and thus is complicated and expensive. Furthermore, the process requires 40 oxen in order to produce enough cortisone to treat one patient for one day. In 1938 one gram of cortisone cost $100.

Faced with this magnitude of cost, it became obvious that other sources of cortisone should be sought, sources which would produce substitutes or precursors of cortisone. Cortisone and other adrenal cortical hormones contain **steroids**. Naturally pharmaceutical houses, doctors, and researchers turned to plants, for some are rich in steroids. As early as 1925 a scientific paper was published indicating that there are steroids in the seeds of an African vine, *Strophanthus*, known formerly as a source of an arrow poison that works on heart muscle.

In 1949 there began one of the great plant hunts of all time, an expedition to Africa sponsored and staffed by two drug companies, the New York Botanical Garden, and botanists from the U.S. Department of Agriculture. Unfortunately the end results were disappointing, for only a few hundred pounds of seeds were collected. However, only 12 steps were required to convert the strophanthus seeds to cortisone. Thus a theoretical ton of seeds could produce the cortisone equivalent of that derived from 12,500 tons of beef cattle.

So the investigators and the pharmaceutical houses turned to other plant sources of steroids, in the course of which they realized that yams are a promising group, since it has been known for some time that natives of the tropics have added grated yam tubers into streams to stun fish. These are true yams (*Dioscorea*, Figure 9.9), not the sweet potatoes, erroneously called yams in the South. Yams are vines with enlarged tubers (enlarged tips of undergound stems, not roots as they are customarily referred to; Figure 9.10), which have supplied one of the main sources of starch to natives of the tropics for untold

Figure 9.9 Yam (*Dioscorea composita*). [Courtesy Edward S. Ayensu.]

Figure 9.10 Yam (*Dioscorea rotundata*) tubers piled up in a market place in Ghana. [Courtesy Edward S. Ayensu.]

millenia. On the average, a single tuber weighs 20 to 30 pounds, but some reach 100 pounds. Extensive investigation of yams revealed that there are four or five species with sufficient concentrations of steroids to provide precursors for the synthesis of cortisone.

Later the female sex hormones, estrogen and progesterone, and the male sex hormone, testosterone, were also manufactured from this plant material. In 1956 Dr. Gregory Pincus of the Worcester Foundation for Experimental Biology discovered that an extract from a Mexican yam stops ovulation in women and hence prevents conception. This and other research led to the present development of oral contraceptives.

A recent report indicates that approximately 60,000 tons of fresh yam tubers are used annually in the production of these valuable drugs. When these studies began, the cortisone produced cost $80 per gram; it is now down to $2 a gram. American pharmaceutical companies spend approximately $30 million a year for yam tubers and the finished products bring $100 million in return.

More recently, cortisone and related substances have been manufactured from the steroids of agaves (century plants of our Southwest and adjacent Mexico), yucca (Spanish bayonet), and soybeans—the latter a particularly promising source.

Figure 9.11 Belladonna (*Atropa belladonna*). [Courtesy U.S. Department of Agriculture.]

Plate 3

3a Flowers and capsules of opium poppy (*Papaver somniferum*).

3b Foxglove *(Digitalis purpurea).*

3c Kalaw tree *(Hydnocarpus),* source of chaulmoogra oil used in leprosy therapy.

3b

3a

3c

Plate 4   4c

4a Autumn crocus *(Colchicum autumnale)*, source of colchicine
    used to treat gout.

4b Madagascar periwinkle *(Vinca rosea)*, whose alkaloids are used to
    treat certain types of cancer.

4c Fly-agaric mushroom *(Amanita muscaria)*.

Belladonna and Atropine

A plant whose toxic properties were recognized and exploited as far back as the Medieval period is belladonna (*Atropa belladonna*, Figures 9.11 and 9.12), otherwise known as deadly nightshade, devil's herb, and sorcerer's herb. It is classified in

Figure 9.12   Belladonna (*Atropa belladonna*).

the potato-tomato family. It is a perennial herb, two to three feet in height, native to central and southern Europe and Asia Minor. It is now cultivated in the United States, Europe, and India. The plant is extremely poisonous—one berry may be fatal. This toxic property is reflected in the generic name *Atropa* which is derived from Atropos, in Greek mythology the Fate who cuts the thread of life. The specific name *belladonna*, or "beautiful lady," refers to the ancient practice by Italian and Spanish ladies of putting the juice of this plant in their eyes to enlarge the pupils to achieve a seductive look.

The drug is derived from the leaves, the tops, or even the roots. The plant has a number of alkaloids—known as the belladonna series: **Atropine,** synthesized but too costly to be practical; **hyoscyamine;** and **scopolamine.** Scopolamine, as mentioned, is used as an anesthetic in child birth; it is also the chemical used by police in some countries to assist in extracting confessions from accused persons. All three alkaloids are used in medicine to stimulate the sympathetic nervous system. Atropine, however, is the one best known, and it has a variety of medicinal uses: to relieve pain (analgesic); to dilate the pupils of the eye (by ophthalmologists); to reduce excessive perspiration and secretion of fluids since it dries up most tissues, in cases of hay fever, cough or colds; to treat shaking palsy or Parkinson's disease, and some 50 other ills.

Mandrake

A remarkable plant with a remarkable history is the celebrated mandrake (*Mandragora officinarum*, Figure 9.13), another member of the alkaloid-rich potato-tomato family. It is an herb native to the east Mediterranean region. The root is frequently forked with two leglike branches and at times it has protuberances which suggest male genitals, hence the name mandrake ("man"+"dragon," or "potent male"). With this remarkable appearance it is no wonder the Doctrine of Signatures was applied to it, giving rise to suggestions that the plant is efficacious in making the male virile, in insuring conception, in promoting sexual passion, and in thawing frigid females. Though the belief persists, mandrake is not an aphrodisiac. However, the juice of the plant will deaden pain and promote a dreamlike sleep and for this reason it was used as an anesthetic for over 2,000 years before the discovery of ether.

Figure 9.13   Mandrake (*Mandragora officinarum*).

The mandrake has had a long history and tradition. In the Bible the childless Rachel begs her sister, "Give me, I pray, of thy son's mandrake." Shakespeare makes frequent reference to the plant, "Shrieks like mandrake torn out of the earth" (*Romeo and Juliet*); "Would curses kill, as doth the mandrake's groan" (*Henry VI*); "Give me to drink mandragora,/That I might sleep out this great gap of time"(*Anthony and Cleopatra*).

Obviously a plant with all these remarkable virtues had to be protected, particularly against the common man, so to insure that only full-fledged herbalists collected this valuable plant, all sorts of legends were published in the herbals, among which is the following:

> Mandrakes are to be found under gallows, for they issue from the ground where semen of a hanged man has fallen. If a mandrake be pulled from the ground, it will come forth with such a shriek of horror that the collector upon hearing the cry will fall dead. However, if the herb be tied at the base of its rosette with a rope, and the other end of the rope be tied to the neck of a dog, the dog may be persuaded to run from the plant by his master's call. Upon lurching forward, the dog will pull the plant from the ground and as a consequence will fall dead from the terrible scream. Collectors, however, will have taken the precaution of stopping up their ears with wool, and to have cut around the plant with a double edged sword while murmuring incantations to protect them from harm.

Mandrake, which contains the alkaloids atropine and scopolamine, was used as a poison in the Medieval period and later, particularly by Lucrezia Borgia (1485–1519), a famous poisoner. It is reported that Hannibal triumphed over the African rebels by staging a fake retreat but leaving behind mandrake in his camp to stupify his enemies, after which he returned to slaughter them with ease. Caesar used the same ploy.

Ginseng

This plant resembles the mandrake in that in both the roots are forked and suggest the human figure (Figure 9.14). The Chinese hold the plant in reverence and it has been known to them for at least 5,000 years. Under the Doctrine of Signatures, this plant is good for the ills of man (ginseng = jen + shen, "man essence"). There is recorded at least one war between the Chinese and Tartars, fought over ginseng territory. One emperor is reputed to have offered the equivalent of $25,000 for one perfect specimen.

The Chinese species is *Panax ginseng* which, as suggested, is assumed to be a panacea for all diseases and ills. There is another species (*Panax quinquefolium*) growing in the forests of eastern North America which has long been used as a general tonic and a stimulant for the digestive tract. Ginseng contains a glycoside (panaquilon).

Interestingly, we have exported ginseng to China via Hong Kong—in 1858 about 360,000 pounds and in 1966 some 100 tons

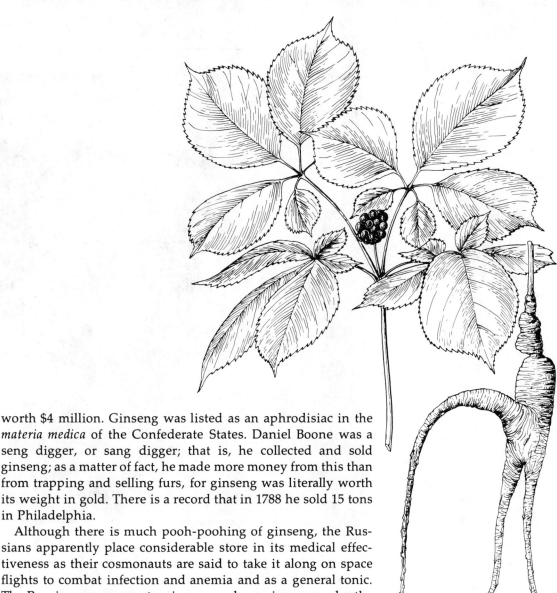

worth $4 million. Ginseng was listed as an aphrodisiac in the *materia medica* of the Confederate States. Daniel Boone was a seng digger, or sang digger; that is, he collected and sold ginseng; as a matter of fact, he made more money from this than from trapping and selling furs, for ginseng was literally worth its weight in gold. There is a record that in 1788 he sold 15 tons in Philadelphia.

Although there is much pooh-poohing of ginseng, the Russians apparently place considerable store in its medical effectiveness as their cosmonauts are said to take it along on space flights to combat infection and anemia and as a general tonic. The Russians sponsor extensive research on ginseng under the aegis of a Permanent Ginseng Committee.

In the United States, particularly in southern California, there is a new ginseng fad; advertisements singing its virtues have been carried in the national press including the *New York Times* (Figure 9.15).

Figure 9.14 American ginseng (*Panax quinquefolium*).

Curare and Arrow Poisons

Curare is the general name given to various South American arrow poisons made from several different plants. As early as 1540 the Spanish soldiers observed South American Indians

Figure 9.15 Newspaper advertisement describing the remarkable properties of ginseng (*Panax quinquefolium*).

using blowguns or shooting arrows tipped with poisons at game and at their enemies. Animals and humans are immobilized, for the curare causes them to lose muscular control including the muscles of respiration. The Indians called the arrows "flying death" and the poison is known as *woorai*, Indian for "he, to whom it comes, falls." The natives indicate the strength of the mixture by the expressions "one-tree curare," "two-tree curare," and so on, meaning in the first case that the curare is strong, since with it a wounded monkey can hop to but one tree before he falls, while with the second, he can make the greater distance to a second tree.

One of the frequent plant components of curare comes from

the bark of the moonseed vine (*Chondodendron*); it is an alkaloid (tubocurarine) which is used in medicine as a muscle relaxant—to relax muscles of the abdomen before an operation and in the treatment of rabies, lockjaw or tetanus, spastic conditions, St. Vitus's dance, epilepsy and nervous tics. It is also used as an anesthetic in throat surgery. The great French physiologist Claude Bernard, experimenting with frogs, worked on the effects of this alkaloid on the body. Among the other plants employed in the preparation of curare or arrow poisons is strychnos which produces the alkaloid strychnine.

Aspirin

It may come as a surprise to learn that even the common aspirin had its origin in plants. For centuries European peasants have utilized infusions of willow (*Salix*) trees to alleviate gout, rheumatism, neuralgia, toothache, earache, and other allied aches and pains. Later *salicin* was extracted from the willow. This chemical substance was then converted to salicylic acid which is still used for athlete's foot, dandruff, acne, greasy skin, warts, and corns. In 1899, in Germany, salicylic acid was combined with acetic acid to yield **acetyl-salicylic acid**, or aspirin. Aspirin, of course, is nearly the universal painkiller even though it is only a tenth as effective as morphine (which has, of course, its defect of possible addiction). Aspirin is used for over 40 diseases or maladies, including arthritis and rheumatic fever. It is the most widely prescribed drug in the pharmacopoeia, and yet we still know little about why it is effective or its mode of action other than that it reduces fever. Aspirin is not without its dangers as is attested by the fact that there are reports of 500 to 1,000 deaths from it annually in this country.

Autumn Crocus, Colchicine, and Gout

One of the myths which has persisted for centuries is the belief that gout is a disease resulting from overindulgence in high, rich living—too much food and alcohol. Others—usually those who have the disease—speak of it as a disease of genius, for many persons of fame have suffered from gout. Biochemically gout is caused by an excess of uric acid in the body; it usually begins as pain in a big toe and then proceeds to the ankles, to the knees, and to other parts of the body. As early as the sixth or seventh century the enlarged globose underground stem (corm) of the autumn crocus (*Colchicum*, a member of the lily family) was used to treat gout. The plant possesses an alkaloid,

See Plate 4a, autumn crocus.

colchicine, which is nearly specific for gout—it is also used for rheumatism. It has a special use in cytology; namely, to double the chromosome numbers of cells, a process of some importance as you will see in Chapters 17 and 19 on genetics and evolution respectively. Since colchicine interferes with the division of the nucleus, it is classified as an antimitotic or antitumor agent, and the hope is that it or some synthetic substance resembling it may eventually be developed to treat cancer.

Ephedra and Ephedrine

The Chinese *ma huang* is a medicinal plant known for over 5,000 years. It is an Asiatic species of the genus *Ephedra,* a vinelike shrub of the gymnosperms, with slender green stems and either without leaves, or almost leafless, growing in dry areas. The alkaloid **ephedrine** was isolated from it in 1887 and it is used to treat colds, asthma, and hay fever, in nose drops or inhalers. It is a **decongestant** which clears the nasal and bronchial passages by shrinking the mucous membranes of these regions. Ephedrine also increases the blood pressure and stimulates the central nervous system. You may recall that a few years ago an American athlete was disqualified at the Olympic Games because he had taken some ephedrine before a contest.

Ephedrine was synthesized in 1927 but the bulk of the drug is still derived from plants. The American species of *Ephedra,* growing in the Southwest and in Argentina, have no ephedrine but a North American species has been made into tea, called Mormon tea or Mexican tea.

Plant Laxatives

It may well be said that we as a people may not worship God, but we do pay daily homage to our bowels—for we must have that sacred one movement per day. Some 680 types of laxatives, or cathartics, are advertised in this country and annual sales total $100 million. Millions of our fellow citizens are habitual users of cathartic pills or laxative drugs.

It is interesting and possibly significant that in primitive societies purges or laxatives and **emetics** that provoke vomiting are among the oldest medicines since they cause visual expulsion from the body of the demons that lead to sickness. The earliest record of cathartic use appears in the Ebers Papyrus of the Egyptians where senna, castor oil, and aloes are listed. The Chinese of Emperor Shen Nung's period utilized rhubarb. The Spanish when they invaded California and Oregon observed that the Indians of this region used a bark, *cascara sagrada*, "sacred" or "holy bark." This material is now sold in every drugstore. The source of the bark is the cascara buckthorn tree (*Rhamnus purshiana*). Approximately four to five million pounds of the bark are gathered each year, and because it is bitter, the material is sugar-coated or covered with chocolate. The glycosides in the bark have never been synthesized.

Antibiotics, the Wonder Drugs

Antibiotics are substances found in such fungi as molds and actinomycetes (bacteria which form filaments, or threads), lichens, and other plants which destroy or inhibit the growth of other organisms such as bacteria. Some angiosperms, for example, have antibiotic properties, but usually they are much weaker than the lower plants and of little medicinal value. This remarkable property of some molds was known by the ancient Egyptians and Chinese who placed green molds on sores. The phenomenon was rediscovered by chance, another classic example of serendipity, when in 1928 Alexander Fleming (1881–1955) observed that in some contaminated culture dishes the bacteria in the vicinity of the blue-green mold (*Penicillium*, Figures 14.7 and 14.8) had been destroyed. He at once realized that this mold might be employed to combat bacterial parasites. Fleming was awarded a Nobel Prize for his research. Later the substance **penicillin** was extracted from the mold. One of the most productive strains of the mold was discovered growing on a cantaloupe in a market in Peoria, Illinois.

In the intervening years since the chance discovery of the antibiotic action of penicillin, many more antibiotics have been literally unearthed since many do come from the soil: streptomycin, Aureomycin, Chloromycetin (now synthesized), and Terramycin—all obtained from fungi known as actinomycetes.

As is well known, these antibiotics are utilized to combat infections in wounds and elsewhere, and penicillin is used in the treatment of a whole host of diseases caused by pathogenic bacteria; for example, anthrax, pneumonia, and various streptococcus infections.

Recent Advances

Research over the last decade has revealed many other promising plant drugs. For example, plant extracts with the glycoside rutin control hemorrhages and strengthen fragile capillaries. The early-spring American hellebore (*Veratrum*), which we cited

See photograph on page 164, hellebore.

earlier as a poisonous plant, has an alkaloid veratrine which lowers blood pressure. Several promising antitumor agents have been discovered: Our spring Mayapple has a substance which acts like colchicine in that it prevents cell division and so may be useful in cancer therapy. Another particularly promising tumor-inhibiting agent is derived from the Madagascar periwinkle *(Vinca rosea,* Figure 9.16), a woody tropical shrub related to our common creeping garden periwinkle. An alkaloid (vinblastine) is derived from the plant and it is used to treat leukemia and Hodgkin's disease, a condition characterized by the enlargement and/or inflammation of the lymph glands, spleen, and liver.

See Plate 4b, Madagascar periwinkle.

Conclusions

It is noteworthy that the inhabitants of several different parts of the world—the ancient peoples of Asia, the medieval Europeans, and the pre-Columbian American Indians—apparently developed independently the concept known as the **Doctrine of Signatures**. It does seem a natural inclination to assume that a plant with a snakelike root might be used to treat snake bites and that a plant with red juice might be good for circulatory or blood diseases. And in some cases (for example, snakeroot) the hunch paid off.

As you read all this material on plant drugs you must have marveled over the success which native people have had in finding plants that are effective against disease. Of course, one explanation is that millions of people have experimented with all kinds of plants over the millenia since man appeared on this globe, and we have no record of the vast numbers who lost their lives in tasting strange and unknown plants. An interesting suggestion has been made which might at least give a partial explanation why natives were able to discover so many medicinal plants with medically effective alkaloids and glycosides. Aboriginal peoples of various regions of the world, including the American Indians, believed that demons caused disease and that the way to drive the demons out of the body was to feed plants with a bitter taste to the ill. As you know, bitter plants have alkaloids and glycosides and, further, these substances are effective against many diseases and conditions. This may be one reason why aborigines have located so many medicinal plants.

Figure 9.16 Madagascar periwinkle *(Vinca rosea = Catharanthus roseus).*

You will also have been struck by a recurring phenomenon: The early knowledge of medicinal plants by native peoples was followed by a long period of neglect and indifference on the part of Western man; then a dramatic discovery (or rediscovery) by Western man in the same sense that Columbus discovered the New World. This was true of coca, cinchona, digitalis, chaulmoogra oil, reserpine, curare, and many others. You may well ask why this should be so. In part it is due to ethnocentric snobbery or ethnic arrogance, a scornful attitude toward aborigines, their culture and their folk medicine by Western man who all too often believes his civilization and culture, including his science and medicine, to be vastly superior. Western man has ignored the counsel of a Sudanese psychiatrist to "always stay on good terms with the local witch doctor. I've learned a lot from medicine men." But Dr. Robert DeRopp in his *Drugs and the Mind* (1957) describes the situation best of all:

> In fact the only people who seemed unaware of the virtues of Rauwolfia were the great omniscient scientists of the West. It is curious indeed that a remedy so ancient and one on which so much excellent research had been carried out by several Indian scientists should have been ignored by Western researchers until the year 1947. This situation resulted, in part at least, from the rather contemptuous attitude which certain chemists and pharmacologists in the West have developed toward both folk remedies and drugs of plant origin, regarding native medicines as the by-products of various old wives' tales and forgetting that we owe some of our most valued drugs (digitalis, ephedrine, and quinine, to name only a few) to just such "old wives' tales." They further fell into the error of supposing, because they had learned the trick of synthesizing certain substances, that they were better chemists than Mother Nature, who, besides creating compounds too numerous to mention, also synthesized the aforesaid chemists and pharmacologists. Needless to say, the more enlightened members of these professions avoided so crude an error, realizing that the humblest bacterium can synthesize, in the course of its brief existence, more organic compounds than can all the world's chemists combined.

Dr. Benjamin Rush (1745?–1813), one of the most distinguished American physicians of his time, in a speech before the American Philosophical Society in 1774, said he had "taken pains to inquire into the success of some of these Indian specifics and have never heard of one well attested case of their efficacy." He added that "we have no discoveries in the materia medica to hope for from the Indians of North America," because "it would be a reproach to our schools of physic if modern physicians were not more successful than the Indians even in the treatment of their own diseases." Yet, the facts are, as so eloquently described by Virgil J. Vogel in his *American Indian Medicine* (1970), that 200 drugs used by the Indians made the first edition of the U.S. *Pharmacopeia* (1820), and 170 of these original Indian remedies are still in the latest edition of that official work.

Suggested Readings

Claus, Edward P., Varro E. Tyler, and Lynn R. Brady. *Pharmacognosy.* 6th ed. Philadelphia: Lea and Febiger, 1970. A respected treatise on natural drugs—their collection, identification, preparation, botany, chemistry, properties, and uses.

DeRopp, Robert S. *Drugs and the Mind.* New York: St. Martin's Press, 1957. Rev. ed., 1975. A lively book for the generalist authored by a biochemist who writes with an engaging style.

Dodge, Bertha S. *Plants that Changed the World.* Boston: Little, Brown, 1959. An attractive, delightful book on the impact of several important plants on history.

Duran-Reynals, M. L. *The Fever Bark Tree.* Garden City, N.Y.: Doubleday, 1946. One of the best general accounts of malaria and cinchona.

Emboden, William A., Jr. *Narcotic Plants.* New York: Macmillan, 1972. Beautifully illustrated book on the chief narcotic plants.

Jaramillo-Arango, Jaime. *The Conquest of Malaria.* London: Heinemann, 1950. A scholarly treatment of the history of malaria.

Krieg, Margaret B. *Green Medicine.* Chicago: Rand McNally, 1964. A sprightly book on the search for plants of medicinal value, including recent investigations.

Schleiffer, Hedwig. *Sacred Narcotic Plants of the New World Indians.* New York: Hafner Press, 1973. A valuable collection of excerpts from texts on narcotic plants—from the sixteenth century to the present.

Schultes, Richard E. "The Plant Kingdom and Modern Medicine." *The Herbarist,* 1968. A brief paper on recent developments in the discovery of new plant drugs.

———, and Albert Hofmann. *The Botany and Chemistry of Hallucinogens.* Springfield, Ill.: Charles C. Thomas, 1973. See Suggested Readings, Chapter 8.

Stern, William L. "The Bond between Botany and Medicine." *Pacific*

Tropical Botanical Garden Bulletin 4, no.3 (1974), pp. 40–60. A paper on the early relationships between botany and medicine.

Swain, Tony, ed. *Plants in the Development of Modern Medicine.* Cambridge, Mass: Harvard University Press, 1972. An important collection of papers written by some of the world authorities on medicinal plants and plant drugs.

Taylor, Norman. *Cinchona in Java.* New York: Greenberg, 1945. A brief book on the history of cinchona.

———. *Narcotics: Nature's Dangerous Gifts.* New York: Dell, 1949. A popular exposition on narcotics derived from plants.

———. *Plant Drugs that Changed the World.* New York: Dodd, Mead, 1965. A very readable volume on the origin and uses of drugs derived from plants.

Vogel, Virgil J. *American Indian Medicine.* Norman: University of Oklahoma Press, 1970. Fascinating, scholarly discussion of the plants used by American Indians for medicinal purposes.

Woodson, Robert E., Jr., Heber W. Youngken, Emil Schlittler, and Jurg A. Schneider. *Rauwolfia: Botany, Pharmacognosy, Chemistry, and Pharmacology.* Boston: Little, Brown, 1957. A model monograph on the botany, pharmacology, chemistry, and pharmacognosy of snakeroot written by specialists representing these fields.

Plant Names

Common name	Scientific name	Family
autumn crocus	*Colchicum autumnale*	Liliaceae
belladonna	*Atropa belladonna*	Solanaceae
buckthorn, cascara sagrada	*Rhamnus purshiana*	Rhamnaceae
chaulmoogra, kalaw	*Hydnocarpus kurzii*	Flacourtiaceae
coca	*Erythroxylon coca*	Erythroxylaceae
curare	*Chondodendron* spp.	Menispermaceae
ephedra, ma huang	*Ephedra sinica, E. equisetina*	Gnetaceae (gymnosperm)
fever-bark tree	*Cinchona* spp.	Rubiaceae
foxglove	*Digitalis purpurea*	Scrophulariaceae
ginseng	*Panax ginseng, P. quinquefolium*	Araliaceae
hellebore	*Veratrum viride*	Liliaceae
Madagascar periwinkle	*Vinca rosea (= Catharanthus roseus)*	Apocynaceae
mandrake	*Mandragora officinarum*	Solanaceae
Mayapple	*Podophyllum peltatum*	Berberidaceae
moonseed vine	*Chondodendron* spp.	Menispermaceae
opium poppy	*Papaver somniferum*	Papaveraceae
snakeroot	*Rauwolfia serpentina*	Apocynaceae
strophanthus	*Strophanthus sarmentosus*	Apocynaceae
yam	*Dioscorea* spp.	Dioscoreaceae

Morning glory (*Ipomoea*), a source of
plant hallucinogens.

10
Plant Hallucinogens
Botanical Escapes from Reality

We might well begin this chapter with the well-known lines from *Hamlet*,

> There are more things in heaven and earth, Horatio,
> Than are dreamed of in your philosophy.

Needless to say we are not advocating the use of hallucinogens, but we do think that in a book which purports to be one on plants and man, it would be inexcusable if we were to ignore the plant hallucinogens, for they are commanding enormous interest at the present time. Our justification for including them in this book on humanistic botany is the same as that once offered by Dr. Robert Maynard Hutchins, former president of the University of Chicago. During the McCarthy era he was called before a committee of the Illinois state legislature investigating communism. When asked if communism were taught at the university, he replied, "of course we teach communism. We also teach cancer, but we do not advocate it."

Definition of Hallucinogens

Hallucinogens are nonaddictive substances which in nontoxic doses cause hallucinations and produce changes in perception (of time, space, and of self), changes in mood, and changes in thought. The changes referred to are usually temporary. Frequently the second part of this definition is stated in terms of alterations in states of consciousness. By **hallucinations** we mean perceiving or sensing things which have no reality; for

255

example, an alcoholic may "see" a pink elephant. These hallucinations may involve any or all the senses—visual, auditory, olfactory, taste, or tactile. Visual hallucinations may consist of brilliant colors in different forms and patterns which are constantly changing, as in a kaleidoscope.

Note that the definition excludes narcotics or addictive substances such as morphine and its derivatives and also cocaine. This is not to imply that hallucinogens are not potentially dangerous, for the reverse is true. One may have a bad trip or in some situations permanent psychic or possibly physical damage may result. The term *hallucinogen* does not include anesthetics (such as ether), analgesics (such as aspirin), nor hypnotics (such as barbiturates). Unlike other drugs which may calm (reserpine) or stimulate (ephedrine), hallucinogens act on the central nervous system, bringing about a dreamlike state, but they do not depress the brain functions, as do the barbiturates.

Recent research suggests that hallucinogens do not produce the indicated phenomena directly but rather that cultural factors are involved. These substances then act primarily as triggers which set off the phenomena; in other words, the responses are conditioned mainly by one's environment and cultural background.

Other Terminology

As you read about these biodynamic substances you will encounter not only the term *hallucinogen* but also **phantastica, psychedelic,** and **psychotomimetic.** The first term we have already defined, but it should be remembered that it means more than the mere creation of hallucinations; in addition, it connotes the production of changes in perception, mood, and thought—or alterations in states of consciousness. *Phantastica* is the term used by Louis Lewin (1850–1929), the distinguished pioneer in this field, in his classic work *Phantastica: Narcotic and Stimulating Drugs, Their Use and Abuse* (1924). He defines the word essentially as we have defined hallucinogen. Originally, *psychedelic* (literally, "mind manifesting") was used in the sense of hallucinogen or phantastica, but unfortunately the word has come to mean much more, especially in the United States. Hence, in the interest of precision, the word is usually avoided in most professional and scientific treatises. The term *psychotomimetic* is more precise in that it emphasizes the fact that these substances produce conditions which ape or mimic psychotic conditions or mental disorders. This word stresses the second part of the definition we gave for hallucinogen, that is, the production of changes in perception, mood, and thought, or the production of altered states of consciousness.

By and large, these four terms—*hallucinogen, phantastica, psychedelic,* and *psychotomimetic*—are at present used more or less synonymously despite their slight differences in emphasis. But we shall restrict ourselves here to the use of *hallucinogen.*

History

There is every indication that the use of hallucinogens extends back into prehistory. Early man believed—indeed, present primitive people believe—that sickness and death are due to supernatural forces. They use hallucinogens to reach or to have communion with these supernatural forces to obtain their counsel on diagnosis and treatment of diseases. This act of communion is not a matter for the layman or the common man but is carried out by an expert—the shaman or herb doctor, the witch doctor, medicine man, *curandero* (healer), or sorcerer —who acts as an intermediary between the sick and the spirit world. In a sense, in this situation it is the doctor who takes the medicine and not the patient. We hasten to add, however, that this is only partly true or only initially true, for later the subject too may be given drugs.

Some scholars in this field suggest that hallucinogens may be responsible for the earliest ideas of deity or gods. In effect, they are saying that the visions of some early religious leaders may have been due to the hallucinatory effects of plants or in some instances perhaps due to fasting or starvation, to sickness or fever, or to self-torture involving long periods of deprivation. It is their theory that hallucinogens or harsh conditions may have produced exceptional psychic states. In any case, hallucinogens have been associated for centuries with religion as well as with magic and medicine.

How Did Primitive Man Discover Hallucinogenic Plants?

It is likely that primitive man tasted all sorts of plants, particularly in periods of scarcity and deprivation. Thus, in the course of time, he somehow discovered that some plants nourished him, some made him ill, some reduced pain, some caused him to have visions, and some killed him. But let us turn to the vivid account of Dr. DeRopp's *Drugs and the Mind,*

> We do not know, nor are we likely to discover, by what accident some wanderer in the Mexican deserts first stumbled upon the secret of the plant's effects. We may assume that the discovery of the drug resulted from the usual causes, a quest for food on the part of the wanderer, reduced to extremity by hunger and thirst, devouring anything containing moisture and nourishment, however evil-tasting that something might be. We can envisage that long-forgotten man, Aztec or pre-Aztec, chewing the nauseous, bitter cactus tops and lying down to rest, then, in a rising tide of astonishment, finding himself ringed on all sides with fantastic visions, with shapes, colors, odors of which he had never even dreamed. Small wonder that, when he found his way back to his tribe, he informed them that a deity dwelt in the cactus and that those who devoured its flesh would behold the world of the gods.

As DeRopp suggests, it was natural to attribute these fantastic effects on the body and mind to a divinity or spirit residing in the plant. Thus, these hallucinogenic plants came to be regarded as sacred, as objects of worship, and they were reserved for special magicoreligious rites. To protect them for these special purposes, there developed taboos with respect to their use for mundane purposes by ordinary men. These plants were not for laymen; they were to be used exclusively by the professionals—the shamans. We now know that the supposed divinity in these plants responsible for hallucinogenic effects is chemical in substance.

Botany of Hallucinogens

It is significant that almost all hallucinogens are derived from the plant kingdom, although there is growing evidence that certain hallucinogens among primitive peoples are of animal origin—e.g., grubs, serotonin from toad venom, and a substance from a type of marine fish known as dream fish. Other, but minor, nonplant sources are the synthetic amphetamines. The most potent hallucinogen known, LSD or lysergic acid diethylamide, is synthesized but the major part of the compound, lysergic acid, is derived from plants, specifically the fungus ergot and morning glories. So it is more accurate to say that LSD is semisynthetic, since a large part of the molecule must be provided ready-made by plants.

Among the estimated 800,000 species of plants of which perhaps as many as 500,000 are angiosperms, or flowering plants, only 60 to 65 species are known to be employed as hallucinogens; of these only 10 or so are cultivated. Most of these hallucinogenic species are angiosperms (30 genera in 17 families). The only other members of the plant kingdom with hallucinogens are in the group known as the fungi, specifically the mushrooms and some Mexican puffballs (both belonging to the club fungi or Basidiomycetes) and ergot (belonging to the sac fungi or Ascomycetes), a fungus infecting grains such as rye.

Cultural Factors

Many more hallucinogenic plants are known and used in the New World than in the Old World. But this fact probably does not reflect differences in actual numbers of species of such plants in the two regions so much as differences in cultural and historical factors.

Few if any cultures have not discovered at least one plant with hallucinogenic effects. The renowned student of narcotics, Louis Lewin, expands on this same thought in his *Phantastica:* "The passionate desire which consciously or unconsciously leads man to flee from the monotony of everyday life, to allow his soul to lead a purely internal life even if it be only for a few short moments, has made him instinctively discover strange substances. He has done so, even where nature has been niggardly in producing them and where the products seem very far from possessing the property which would enable him to satisfy this desire." Or in the words of the philosopher and historian, Will Durant, "No civilization has found life tolerable without . . . the things that provide at least some brief escape from reality."

Hallucinogens and Psychiatry

Chemistry

There are two main groups of hallucinogenic substances found in plants: One, the larger category, consists of those with nitrogen, mostly the now-familiar alkaloids. It is significant that these substances have a chemical structure closely related to that of the neurohormones of the human brain which play an essential role in the biochemistry of that organ. Here perhaps is a suggestion as to how the hallucinogens affect the brain. The second group of hallucinogenic compounds are nonnitrogenous, such as THC in cannabis, or marijuana.

Some hallucinogenic substances have been isolated and a few synthesized. Whether natural or synthetic, they promise to be of considerable importance in experimental psychiatry, in psychoanalysis, and in psychotherapy. For one thing, hallucinogens free the mind from the everyday world, and, further, they call up forgotten or repressed subconscious thoughts, ideas, and conflicts. Thus there is suggested a parallelism between the drug-induced mental state and the true clinical psychotic condition.

Several authorities in the field have made the point that the twentieth century will be remembered as the period of growth in the use, misuse, and abuse of hallucinogens. Abram Hoffer and Humphry Osmond in their book _The Hallucinogens_ (1967) elaborate on this: "The use of hallucinogens has been described as one of the major advances of this century. There is little doubt that they have had a massive impact on psychiatry, and may produce changes in our society. The violent reaction for and against the hallucinogens suggests that even if these compounds are not universally understood and approved of they will neither be forgotten nor neglected." And Aldous Huxley (1894–1963), novelist and grandson of the great biologist and defender of evolution, Thomas H. Huxley, asserts that "the development of drugs that change behavior may well prove to be far more revolutionary than achievements in nuclear physics."

And so these hallucinogens are not only used by primitive people to communicate with the spirit world and by modern professionals in experimental psychiatry, but also by so-called sophisticated people to escape reality or to extend experience beyond earthbound reality, as in the instance of artists, writers, or philosophers who seek new horizons. However, it cannot be overstressed that these substances may be psychologically and physically dangerous and must be used with great care—most of them should not be used except under qualified medical supervision. These are not harmless condiments but powerful tools of therapy.

An additional idea is best expressed by Dr. Richard E. Schultes of Harvard, an outstanding authority on plant hallucinogens and coauthor of a recent book on the subject, *The Botany and Chemistry of Hallucinogens*:

> The use of narcotics is always in some way connected with escape from reality. From their most primitive uses to their applications in modern medicine or their abuse in modern society this is true. All narcotic plants have also, sometime in their history, been linked to religion or magic. This is so even of tobacco, coca, and opium, which have suffered secularization and are now used hedonistically. Some narcotics—peyote is an example—conserve even today this religious basis in their use. And it is interesting to note parenthetically that when problems do arise from the employment of narcotics, they arise after the narcotics have passed from ceremonial to purely hedonic or recreational use.

One final point before we turn to a consideration of a few of the major hallucinogenic plants: Most of our knowledge of hallucinogenic plants comes from primitive people, or aborigines, who are fast disappearing. Extensive ethnobotanical field work is needed to salvage this important plant knowledge and lore before these cultures are destroyed by the onslaughts of civilization.

The Major Plant Hallucinogens

Peyote, Peyotism, and the Native American Church

Peyote (*Lophophora williamsii*, Figure 10.1) is a small gray-green, spineless cactus with a carrotlike shape but with only a bit of the top exposed above ground; the part above the soil resembles a small pin cushion. It grows in calcareous deserts, either on rocky slopes or in dry river beds. It is a native of central and northern Mexico and the adjacent United States, especially in the Rio Grande Valley (southern Texas and New Mexico). It has now spread to Arizona, California, and to other parts of Mexico.

The Spanish conquerors of Mexico in the sixteenth century observed the use of peyote by Aztecs who considered it a sacred plant. They worshipped it and indeed their religion centered around peyote. This practice is certainly pre-Columbian and undoubtedly goes back thousands of years. The Spanish found the natives' worship of a plant offensive and referred to peyote as the "diabolic root." They tried to stamp it out, only to have

Figure 10.1 Peyote (*Lophophora williamsii*) with flower. [Photograph taken in Laredo, Texas; courtesy Richard E. Schultes.]

the natives go underground. A law prohibiting the worship of peyote was enacted in Mexico in 1720, but the natives continued their worship in secret. As a matter of fact, the peyote religion has withstood four centuries of civil and ecclesiastical opposition; it still persists in Mexico and has also spread to the United States.

The earliest record of peyote worship in this country is from Texas in 1760. We know that during the American Civil War the American Indians were using peyote and that by 1880 the custom had spread to some 30 tribes of plains Indians, including the Comanche, Kiowa, Omaha, and Mescalero Apache. Over the years the peyote religion incorporated some Christian elements; in Mexico in the late seventeenth century there was a mission called El Santo de Jesus Peyote. In the years 1917 through 1923 ten states, including Texas, Arizona, New Mexico, Oklahoma, and—strangely—Massachusetts, passed legislation aimed at the suppression of peyotism, the religion centering around peyote. Since that time a few states have repealed these restrictive laws, notably Texas, Oklahoma, Utah, and New Mexico. There was a long struggle in the courts over peyotism until a case was brought to the Supreme Court of the United States which found for the Indians and peyote. In effect, the Court gave its sanction to peyotism and as a result it is a legally organized religion, called the Native American Church. At the present time there are approximately a quarter of a million followers distributed among 60 to 70 tribes in the United States and Canada.

What Is the Religion of the Native American Church, or Peyotism?

In common with other religions it preaches brotherly love, espouses high moral principles, and urges abstention from alcohol. In addition, the members believe that peyote gives them the ability to foresee and predict events; for example, how a battle will turn out. It reveals to them the persons responsible for the theft of such items as utensils. They report that peyote produces visions of great beauty, and they hear the voices of the spirits of their divine ancestors who give them guidance. Peyote brings them into communion with the spirit world from whence comes sickness and death, and these spirits render them assistance in the diagnosis and treatment of diseases. Finally, peyote sustains them and gives them courage to fight, it alleviates the pangs of hunger and thirst, and in general protects them from all dangers.

Some Mexican Indians—the Hulchol especially—go on an annual pilgrimage to the sacred land of the peyote, occasionally walking for 40 or more days and covering up to 300 miles. The trek is taken in spring or in October and November after the rainy season. Before leaving on the pilgrimage, the participants stage a ceremony of confession and purification during which they are expected to confess all their sexual adventures from the beginning of adulthood to the present. (In the interests of saving time, older persons with rich experience are permitted to telescope the recitals of their peccadillos.) The leader of the group ties a knot in a cord for each love affair and thus he keeps a tally. Quite clearly this ritual is one involving the return to childhood innocence.

Once on the trek and upon discovery of peyote plants, the Indians shoot arrows in the vicinity of the plants, after which they cut off the tops, leaving the basal part to continue growth. The Indians chew some of the fresh peyote and they rub others on their bruised or cut bodies. Apparently the plant does aid healing and prevents infection—studies have shown that it has antibiotic properties. The pilgrims collect as many peyote tops as they can and these are dried to form the characteristic brown, disc-shaped tops, or **mescal buttons,** which are very bitter and have a nauseating odor.

On the site of the discovery or later upon return to their home base, they hold a special peyote ceremony of worship, an all-night ritual held in a tepee or in the open, but in either case there is a fire. The Indians chew mescal buttons; one individual may ingest as many as 30 or 40. There is singing, chanting, dancing, meditation, and prayer. There may be a short talk or sermon by the leader. In the morning the ceremony ends with a communal meal.

The intoxication experienced includes the appearance of indescribably brilliant colored visions in kaleidoscopic movement, accompanied by auditory, olfactory, tactile, and taste hallucinations. There is a feeling of weight loss and depersonalization, objects appear to be enlarged (macroscopia), and there is an alteration in the perception of time. Parenthetically, it should be noted that there is a vast difference between this type of intoxication by natives ingesting peyote and the type of intoxication by persons using the vision-producing chemical principle, **mescaline.** Although the former contains 30 or more alkaloids, the latter is only a single alkaloid, but this one when used alone, is of far greater strength. Mescaline, the chemical principle, has been isolated and can now be synthesized. The name mescal is derived from *mexcalli,* or "liquor." There is considerable confusion over the word *mescal,* for it is more properly used for the agaves (century plants) and their derivative alcoholic beverages, pulque and tequila. Sometimes a bit of peyote is added to tequila. The legume *Sophora,* or red bean, is also called the mescal bean. In Mexico peyote and the mescal bean (*Sophora*) are frequently mixed in a drink.

A recent trend in non-Indian circles has been the use of peyote for nonreligious purposes either for pleasure or merely to experiment with the effects of this hallucinogen. A news story of a year ago relates the arrest of several youths who were apprehended in New York with 70 pounds of peyote buttons brought in from Arizona. It is estimated that the haul consisted of 3,000 buttons worth $3 apiece. If convicted, the young men under these circumstances face a sentence of up to five years in prison and a $15,000 fine.

Aldous Huxley, noted writer and critic, used mescaline and then described his experiences in *The Doors of Perception* (1954).

Cacti other than peyote may have mescaline and a few of these are used in place of peyote. The large columnar San Pedro cactus is one.

Ergot, Ergotism, and LSD

Ergot (*Claviceps purpurea,* Figure 10.2) is a fungus parasite (belonging to the sac fungi or Ascomycetes) which infects grasses or grains such as wheat, but especially rye. The word *ergot* is derived from the French word meaning "spur," for the infected grain (fruit) is spurlike and black-brown to purple in color.

An Assyrian tablet of 600 B.C. mentions the noxious pustules on ears of grain. In the Middle Ages—particularly in the tenth, eleventh, and twelfth centuries—there occurred dreadful epidemics of madness which seemed to be associated in some way with the consumption of bread. We now know that the flour which was used in baking came from ergot-infested rye. The frightful symptoms of this disease include abortions in pregnant females; burning sensation in extremities; feelings of being consumed by fire; constriction of blood vessels leading to

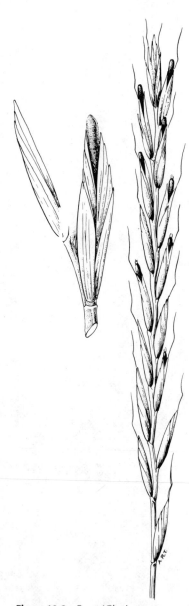

Figure 10.2 Ergot (*Claviceps purpurea*) on grain.

the blockage of circulation and resulting in the appearance of blue discolored areas on the body; onset of gangrene; shriveling and falling off of hands, arms, and legs; experiencing of hallucinations such as wild beasts in pursuit of the victim; madness; and, finally, convulsions leading to death.

During the Medieval period, tens of thousands of people died of this disease; in 994 in southern France, 40,000 were killed; in 1129 in northern France, 12,000 died. The disease became so devastating that in 1093 in southern France the people formed an order to take care of those afflicted and they chose St. Anthony as their patron saint. Hence the malady is called St. Anthony's fire as well as holy fire and ergotism. In desperation many victims made a pilgrimage to the shrine of St. Anthony in Egypt, and in truth this trek often helped—for one thing, the travelers relied on a different diet on the long journey.

In the early decades of this century there were epidemics in this country in New York, Ohio, and Kansas. A serious outbreak occurred in 1926 in the great Russian grain-producing region of the Ukraine.

An interesting fictionalized account of ergotism, given in John G. Fuller's *The Day of St. Anthony's Fire* (1968), is based on an actual episode occurring in a small French village in 1951 during which hundreds of townspeople went mad in a single night.

It is a sad commentary on man's intelligence that it was not until 1597—over 500 years after the first epidemic of holy fire—that physicians began to associate the disease with the ergot on the grain. We now know that a one percent infection of grain is enough to cause an outbreak of this plague.

About this same time, midwives in Europe began to use ergot in childbirth—to promote and strengthen uterine contractions. It is supposed that this use arose because someone was shrewd enough to take particular heed of the abortions that frequently occurred in pregnant women who contracted ergotism. In any case, ergot derivatives are now standard drugs in obstetrics. In 1935 the alkaloid **ergonovine** was isolated from ergot; it exerts a powerful effect on the pregnant uterus. Since it causes strong contractions, it is used in the third stage of labor and it has the added virtue that it controls hemorrhage. Needless to say this extremely potent drug may be dangerous and should never be used in the absence of medical supervision.

Strangely enough ergot derivatives are now used for migraine headaches, the cause of which is still unknown although we do know that blood vessels become dilated in connection with the disease. The alkaloid **ergotamine** has been isolated and when it is injected, 90 percent of all migraine sufferers obtain relief, although no cure is effected.

At the present time about one million pounds of raw ergot are used annually in the United States. Infected grains are cultivated in several states such as Minnesota, Wisconsin, North and South Dakota, Illinois, Indiana, and Nebraska.

A fabulous figure in the history of ergot is Dr. David Hosack (1769–1835), who in 1824 published a classic paper on ergot, one of the first American papers on the subject. In his article he warned against the use of the drug as a uterine stimulant but he did urge its use in the control of hemorrhage.

Hosack was the physician who attended the dying Alexander Hamilton after the latter was wounded in his duel with Aaron Burr. He was appointed professor of botany at Columbia University in 1795; later the institution added the title professor of physic, that is, medicine. Hosack started the first botanical garden in New York on land now occupied by the Rockefeller Center. His plan was to rival the botanic gardens at Kew and in Paris. He bought the land, 19 acres, in 1800 for $4,800 plus 16 bushels of wheat to be delivered every May first. This same land in the middle of Manhattan is now worth over $300 million. Hosack found the garden too big a burden, so he sold it to the state of New York in 1811. Three years later the legislature gave the property to Columbia University, which each year reaps an income of $9 to $15 million from rental of the land.

An important date in the history of hallucinogens is 1943 when the chemist Albert Hofmann was working in a laboratory of the Sandoz Chemical Works in Basel, Switzerland. He was giving his attention to the ergot alkaloids, all of whose nuclei are composed of lysergic acid, when he added diethylamide to lysergic acid and produced lysergic acid diethylamide—LSD. Let it be noted, as we mentioned above, that this process is a semisynthesis since it starts with a sizable molecule, lysergic acid, derived from the ergot fungus. Almost immediately upon producing the LSD, Hofmann began to feel peculiar effects:

> On the afternoon of 16 April 1943, when I was working on this problem, I was seized by a peculiar sensation of vertigo and restlessness. Objects appeared to undergo optical changes and I was unable to concentrate on my work. In a

dream-like state I left for home, where an irresistible urge to lie down overcame me. I immediately fell into a peculiar state similar to drunkenness, characterized by an exaggerated imagination. With my eyes closed, fantastic pictures of extraordinary plasticity and intensive color seemed to surge towards me. After two hours, this gradually wore off.
... I suspected that the lysergic acid diethylamide (LSD) with which I had been working that afternoon was responsible.

Hofmann later experimented with 250 milligrams of LSD, which he then regarded as a safe dose; we now know that this quantity is about 10 times the normal dosage. He experienced all the familiar effects of the drug. Subsequent research made it clear that LSD is the most potent hallucinogen ever discovered; it is approximately 10,000 times more potent than the same amount of mescaline.

Among the physical effects of LSD are restlessness, weakness or tiredness, tremors, and sweating. The psychological effects are feelings of irritation, hostility, and anxiety; a sense of being overcome by confusion; experiencing illusions of all the senses—visual, tactile, olfactory, for instance; loss of time sense—one "feels out of time"; perception of visions—some pleasant, some horrible (LSD "opens the gates of heaven or hell"); and finally, a feeling of removal from the world.

As is well known, LSD has been taken up by thrill seekers, by those who seek to expand consciousness, such as some artists, writers, and philosophers, and by those who hunger for a novel religious experience. In this connection LSD has been called "instant Zen" and "chemical mysticism." It must be emphasized that LSD is not a substance to be trifled with, for it can be very dangerous and lead to bad trips, especially by psychotics. Our mental hospitals are crowded with patients who have LSD-induced psychoses. There have been some reports that LSD use produces chromosome damage, though other investigators challenge this conclusion. Just as ergot was the great scourge of the Middle Ages, LSD may become the curse of the twentieth century.

A recent study (1976) suggests that the witches of Salem, Massachusetts, in 1692 were victims of the hallucinations produced by eating bread contaminated with ergot. You may recall that the trial resulted in the execution of 20 of the young girls.

On the positive side, LSD offers great promise for psychiatry, for LSD parallels some mental conditions and the drug thus may be an important tool for the psychiatric researcher. LSD also may be an aid in psychoanalysis and in psychotherapy. Finally, the LSD molecule may serve as a model for the synthesis of other molecules which may prove to be more effective and lack the drawbacks of LSD.

In 1960 Hofmann found that the **ololiuqui** seeds also contain lysergic acid alkaloids. Ololiuqui, an ancient hallucinogen, is a tropical and subtropical vine belonging to the morning glory family. The Aztecs used it as an analgesic in medicine and in their religious ceremonies. These Indians considered that the seeds gave one the power of prophecy and divination, and that they facilitated communion with the gods. We now know that some species of the common morning glory (*Ipomoea violacea*) have alkaloids which are hallucinogenic. Curiously, two of the varieties of morning glory which produce hallucinogens are called Heavenly Blue and Pearly Gates.

See photograph on page 254, morning glory.

Amanita, the Fly-Agaric, and the Divine Soma

See Plate 4c, fly-agaric mushroom.

The fly-agaric mushroom (*Amanita muscaria*, Figure 10.3) is a fungus belonging to the club fungi (Basidiomycetes). The common name comes from the fact that the mushroom if ingested by flies, kills them. It has been used for ages by country people as a sort of vegetable flypaper and fungal insecticide. One form of the mushroom, with a bright red cap and white spots, grows in deciduous and coniferous forests and in overgrown pastures in the temperate zone of Europe and Asia and in the Pacific Northwest. There is another form of the mushroom with a yellow cap which grows in the rest of temperate North America except for our northwestern states and adjacent British Columbia. The yellow form is not used as a hallucinogen but it is toxic, causing a severe but rarely fatal illness. However, the closely related but completely white or olive destroying angel (*Amanita phalloides* and related species) is deadly poisonous.

The red-capped *Amanita* is one of our oldest hallucinogenic plants. In 1658 a Polish youth who was a prisoner in Siberia reported the use of the fly-agaric by natives for purposes of intoxication. We now know that it had much earlier use as a shamanistic inebriant. It has been suggested that the ancient berserkers of Scandinavia who went on periodic orgies of killing first became intoxicated with *Amanita*, though some experts such as the distinguished ethnomycologist (one who studies the relationship between fungi and man and his cultures) Gordon Wasson questions this.

In any case, Siberian tribesmen living to the far north have used it as an inebriant for centuries. After the mushrooms have been gathered they are dried in the sun or over a fire. The Siberians then chew them dry, or they may be taken with water or reindeer milk or with the juice of a native berry. The mushroom is used in ritualistic drinking and it has a truly remarkable quality—the intoxicating principle passes through the kidneys unimpaired, so the partakers collect their urine and use it again and again as an inebriant. It is said to retain its quality through five passages, or to the fifth generation. In addition, the collected urine may be passed around among the individuals in the group. The first report of this bizarre ritual was made in 1730 by a Swedish officer who was a prisoner in Siberia. In 1762, Oliver Goldsmith (1728–1774), author of the novel *Vicar of Wakefield* and the poem *The Deserted Village,* wrote, ''The poorer [Tartars] post themselves around the huts of the rich and watch the opportunity of the ladies and gentlemen as they come down to pass their liquor, and holding a wooden bowl catch the delicious fluid. Of this they drink with the utmost satisfaction and thus they get as drunk and as jovial as their betters.''

The Siberian tribesmen, when going on a reindeer trek, take along a supply of the mushroom and suitable collecting utensils, very much as we would pack a case of beer before leaving on an outing. And we must concede that there are advantages in the former—the intoxicant can be used again and again. Indeed, it has been suggested that amanita would be ideal for astronauts.

We are also told that one to four mushrooms produce intoxication; a person thus intoxicated is said to be ''bemushroomed.'' The symptoms are twitching, trembling, and slight convulsions; a feeling of euphoria, manifested by a desire to dance, to shout, and to sing; experiencing of visual hallucinations; macroscopia; a strong impulse for violence and the need to rush around wildly; self-mutilation; and finally, exhaustion ending in sleep. On the other hand, used in moderation, the mushrooms raise the spirits and are said to increase one's strength so that, for example, a person can carry a 120 pound sack of flour for ten miles. Needless to say with such remarkable virtues, a high value is placed on the agarics; one mushroom

Figure 10.3 Fly-agaric mushroom (*Amanita muscaria*). [Courtesy R. Gordon Wasson.]

buys three to four reindeer. Incidentally, Wasson tells us that reindeer have two passions—amanita and human urine, and they, too, get intoxicated with both.

Gordon Wasson informs us that amanita has long played a vital religio-magical role in India. About 3,500 years ago, the Aryan people swept down from the north into the Indus Valley in India, bringing with them the cult of **soma,** the sacred plant or god-plant. The people worshipped this holy inebriant and/or plant as a god. Wasson is bold enough to suggest that the very idea of god may have arisen through the unearthly effects on someone who had accidentally eaten this mushroom, with the beautiful visions suggesting the idea of a deity. In the Indian legends and tales of the past which constitute the *Rig Veda,* soma refers to a god, or a plant, or the juice of a plant (the dark extract used in religious rites). In this collection of folk poetry dating back at least 3,000 years, there are 1,028 hymns, and 120 of them make major references to soma, the god plant. Wasson and his late wife Valentina have advanced the fascinating thesis that the original or divine soma was *Amanita muscaria.*

The Wassons have unusual backgrounds; he was a banker, a vice-president of J.P. Morgan & Company in New York, and she, a Russian pediatrician. They are both self-taught mycologists (students of the fungi), and their impressive two-volume *Mushrooms, Russia, and History* is now an expensive collectors' item. More recently (1968) Gordon Wasson published *Soma, Divine Mushroom of Immortality*, a beautiful book with handsome colored pictures of amanita. In another of his writings he gives a fascinating account of the manner in which he and his wife came to study mushrooms:

> Those who do not know the story will be interested in learning how it came about that my late wife, a pediatrician, and I, a banker, took up the study of mushrooms. She was a Great Russian and, like all of her countrymen, learned at her mother's knee a solid body of empirical knowledge about the common species and a love for them that is astonishing to us Americans. Like us, the Russians are fond of nature—of the forests and birds and wild flowers. But their love for mushrooms is of a different order, a visceral urge, a passion that passeth understanding. The worthless kinds, the poisonous mushrooms—in a way, the Russians are fond even of them. They call these "worthless ones" *paganki*, the "little pagans," and my wife would

make of them colorful centerpieces for the dining-room table, against a background of moss and stones and wood picked up in the forest. On the other hand, I, of Anglo-Saxon origin, had known nothing of mushrooms. By inheritance, I ignored them all; I rejected those repugnant fungal growths, manifestations of parasitism and decay. Before my marriage I had not once fixed my gaze on a mushroom, not once looked at a mushroom with a discriminating eye. Indeed, each of us, she and I, regarded the other as abnormal, or rather subnormal, in our contrasting responses to mushrooms.

A little thing, some will say, this difference in emotional attitude toward wild mushrooms. Yet my wife and I did not think so, and we devoted a part of our leisure hours for more than thirty years to dissecting it, defining it, and tracing it to its origin. Such discoveries as we have made, including the rediscovery of the religious role of the hallucinogenic mushrooms of Mexico, can be laid to our preoccupation with the cultural rift between my wife and me, between our respective peoples, between the mycophilia and mycophobia (words we devised for the two attitudes) that divide the Indo-European peoples into two camps.

But to return to the important thesis of the Wassons that the ancient divine soma was the fly-agaric, they enumerate evidence from the *Veda:*

1. The word *soma* is referred to as a plant without roots, leaves, flowers, and seeds—"born without seeds."
2. Soma also indicates an inebriant.
3. Reference is made even to the ceremonial drinking of urine; in fact, the priests are said to take amanita and the people receive the urine.

Since amanita is a sacred plant, if not a deity, taboos developed on its use, particularly since the plant is scarce in India. It came to be accepted that the mushroom was not to be used by lay people, only by professionals, the priests, or disaster would befall the transgressor. The Wassons raise the intriguing question as to whether these ancient taboos are not the basis of the strong Anglo-Saxon fear and abhorrence of mushrooms. As you know, the peoples of the English-speaking world customarily regard mushrooms as loathsome, unsavory, repulsive, decadent, sinister, and, in general, suggestive of decay, disease, evil, and death—all attitudes summarized in the word *mycophobia*. On the other hand, the people of Slavic stock characteristically love and venerate mushrooms (*mycophilia*)—they know them, they eat them, and they are comfortable with them. Apparently the Slavs never experienced the mushrooms as taboo.

For some reason, centuries ago the people of India gave up the use of amanita, probably because it could not be easily obtained. Since they were far from the source of the fly-agaric, they turned to substitutes, to such plants as *Ephedra*, and in the process they lost all direct knowledge of amanita—its identity, its history, and its uses. And there the story of soma ends for the present.

While we are dwelling on the fantastic relationship between mushroom and man, we are reminded of Lewis Carroll's *Alice in Wonderland* in which it is related that by eating a mushroom a person may become very large or very small. Carroll had previously read a review of Mordecai Cooke's manual of British fungi in which there is an account of *Amanita muscaria* and its strange properties.

The alkaloid **muscarine** was discovered in the mushroom in 1969. However, it apparently is not the main inebriating principle, but rather various ibotenic acid derivatives are. Ibotenic acid is related to certain amino acids.

Mushrooms other than amanita (*Psilocybe* and others) had a similar religious use in ancient Mexico. The Spanish conquistadors of Mexico observed with horror the Aztec religious cult based on the sacramental consumption of sacred hallucinogenic mushrooms called by the natives *teonanacatl*—"flesh of the gods." (A cynic has remarked that Christians always are intolerant of the use of any sacramental inebriant other than alcohol.) With the use of these sacred hallucinogens the Aztecs communed with the spirit world, thus permitting prophecy and obtaining counsel and divine guidance in the diagnosis and treatment of disease. We know that mushroom worship has deep roots, going back at least 3,000 years. The practice is depicted in frescoes and documented by "mushroom effigy stones" (small works of sculpture portraying mushrooms) found in Mayan sites in Guatemala, dating back to 1000 B.C. It is a historical fact that in 1502 inebriating mushrooms were consumed at the coronation of Montezuma II (1480?–1520), the last Aztec emperor of Mexico. For the last 400 years, however, since the advent of Christianity, this worship has been secret.

During past decades there have been a few sporadic reports of the practice but the research of the Wassons in the 1950s really provided the only major documentation. Gordon Wasson in his *Soma* remarks, "Until this very day no poet in the English language has ever sung the supernal beauties of the fly-agaric." We will leave to your judgment whether the following verse is poetry and whether it has even remote connection with beauty; but, in any case, it was written 40 years ago by an undergraduate (Archie H. Silver) in a Harvard botany class which had just learned of amanita and its beguiling virtues:

A sturdy folk—Siberians,
They like their liquor strong.
A mushroom wild supplies the drink
And they reply with song.
Amanita muscaria
Fly agaric makes them sing,
But it has also made them do
A strange unheard of thing!

This fungus "fly agaric"
Has properties quite strange—
It passes in and out of you
Sans alcoholic change.

Since it as urine keeps its kick
As in its native haunts,
These Russian drunkards carry cans
On bacchanalian jaunts!

Years later a Yale student, Leslie Epstein, challenged by the earlier Harvard effort, came forward with this contribution:

In the modern Soviet Union,
Ruled by Krushev and Nikol' Bulgunion
Sent away very far
Is the weary old Tsar
And those who wont live in communion.

They land in those parts to the East
Prepared to make merry and feast.
But the place is so freezin'
That nothing is pleasin'
And worse! There aint wimmin or yeast.

Now, one day Dimitri's fox terrier
Discovered a stone that was harrier

Said Dimitri, "You glungus!
Don't you know that's a fungus,"
And, indeed, 'twas *Amanita muscaria.*

No more do the exiles despond,
Of life they've grown quite fond—
Now the sewers are empty,
But not so the gentry,
They've got urine that's bottled in bond.

Other plant hallucinogens

Earlier we mentioned in other connections several hallucinogenic plants: marijuana *(Cannabis,* Figures 8.2 and 8.3),
belladonna *(Atropa,* Figures 9.11 and 9.12), mandrake (the *Hexenkraut* of the Germans, Figure 9.13), and thorn apple or jimson
weed *(Datura,* Figure 7.11). The Indians of eastern North
America used the jimson weed in their initiation rites marking
the passage of a boy to manhood. After taking *Datura* the initi-
ates became stark mad for 18 to 20 days in the course of which
they lost all memory of being boys. Another species was used
ceremonially by the Indians in the Southwest and called by
them *torna-loco,* the "maddening plant." A tree species of *Datura,* called angel's trumpet because of its long tubular white
flowers, was often an ingredient in the pre-Spanish Indians'
chicha, a fermented maize beverage administered to wives and
slaves of dead warriors or chieftains to induce stupor before they
were buried alive to accompany their dead husbands and masters on the long journey to heaven. This fortified chicha is a
powerful drink, for the datura part of it contains the belladonna
series of alkaloids—atropine, scopolamine, and hyoscyamine.

See Plate 5a, henbane.

Other hallucinogenic plants are henbane, a native of Europe
and now spread to this continent; caapi, a tropical vine of
northern South America; and yakee or yato, a tropical forest tree
of the Amazon Valley taken as snuff by Indians (Figure 10.4).

See Plate 5c, nutmeg.

The two spices of the common nutmeg (Figure 12.10), the seed
proper (the so-called nutmeg) and the fleshy aril or mace, are
both hallucinogenic. The former is taken orally or snuffed
by—in the words of Richard Schultes—"students, prisoners,
sailors, alcoholics, marijuana-smokers and others deprived of
their preferred drugs." Apparently nutmeg is commonly smuggled into prisons and has widespread use there.

As a final fascinating tidbit in this completely engaging subject of hallucinogens, we are charmed by the report that the

Figure 10.4 South American Indians snuffing hallucinogen.

traditional pacifier of cats, catnip *(Nepeta cataria),* is now being taken over by some artists, writers, and other bons vivants as hallucinogenic, although it is a dangerous drug.

Suggested Readings

DeRopp, Robert S. *Drugs and the Mind.* New York: St. Martin's Press, 1957. See Suggested Readings, Chapter 9.

Emboden, William. *Narcotic Plants*. New York: Macmillan, 1972. See Suggested Readings, Chapter 9.

Fuller, John G. *The Day of St. Anthony's Fire*. New York: Macmillan, 1968. A fictionalized version of an incident which occurred in a French village in 1951 during which hundreds of townspeople were afflicted with St. Anthony's fire.

Furst, Peter T., ed. *Flesh of the Gods*. New York: Praeger, 1972. A highly recommended collection of ten essays giving an up-to-date discussion of plant hallucinogens by outstanding scholars in the field.

Heiser, Charles B., Jr. *Nightshades: The Paradoxical Plants*. San Francisco: Freeman, 1969. A delightful little classic on the nightshades, some of which are hallucinogenic.

Hoffer, Abram, and Humphry Osmond. *The Hallucinogens*. New York: Academic Press, 1967. An authoritative, scientific treatise on the chemistry and related aspects of hallucinogens.

Huxley, Aldous. *The Doors of Perception*. New York: Harper & Row, 1954. The distinguished novelist's report on his experiences with mescaline.

LaBarre, Weston. *The Peyote Cult*. New York: Schocken, 1969. One of the best things written on the subject—scholarly yet of interest to the nonspecialist.

Lewin, Louis. *Phantastica: Narcotics and Stimulating Drugs, Their Use and Abuse*. New York: Dutton, 1964. 1st ed., 1924. The respected classic in the field by the great German toxicologist.

Schleiffer, Hedwig. *Sacred Narcotic Plants of the New World Indians*. New York: Hafner Press, 1973. See Suggested Readings, Chapter 9.

Schultes, Richard E., and Albert Hofmann. *The Botany and Chemistry of Hallucinogens*. Springfield, Ill.: Charles C. Thomas, 1973. See Suggested Readings, Chapter 8.

———. *Hallucinogenic Plants*. New York: Golden Press, 1976. Compact, beautifully illustrated book written by the authority in the field.

Taylor, Norman, *Narcotics: Nature's Dangerous Gifts*. New York: Dell, 1949. See Suggested Readings, Chapter 9.

———. *Plant Drugs that Changed the World*. New York: Dodd, Mead, 1965. See Suggested Readings, Chapter 9.

Wasson, R. Gordon. *Soma, Divine Mushroom of Immortality*. New York: Harcourt Brace Jovanovich, 1967. Handsome book with beautiful illustrations, some in color. A fascinating discussion of the long history of *Amanita*.

Plant Names

Common name	*Scientific name*	*Family or other group*
angel's trumpet	*Datura suaveolens*	Solanaceae
caapi	*Banisteriopsis caapi*	Malpighiaceae
catnip	*Nepeta cataria*	Labiatae
ergot	*Claviceps purpurea*	Ascomycetes (fungi)
fly-agaric	*Amanita muscaria*	Basidiomycetes (fungi)
henbane	*Hyoscyamus niger*	Solanaceae
jimson weed, thorn apple	*Datura stramonium*	Solanaceae
morning glory	*Ipomoea violacea*	Convolvulaceae
nutmeg	*Myristica fragrans*	Myristicaceae
ololiuqui	*Rivea corymbosa*	Convolvulaceae
peyote	*Lophophora williamsii*	Cactaceae
sacred Mexican mushroom, teonanacatl	*Psilocybe mexicana*, and other genera and species	Basidiomycetes (fungi)
San Pedro cactus	*Trichocereus pachanoi*	Cactaceae
torna-loco	*Datura ceratocaula*	Solanaceae
yakee, yato	*Virola calophylla*	Myristicaceae

Coconuts, split and spread to dry, in
Sri Lanka.

11
Food Plants

Twelve Plants Standing between Man and Starvation

It is no exaggeration to say that food is one of the central issues of our time and that the food situation—too little food, often of the wrong type, for too many people—will continue to worsen as time goes on. Two-thirds of the world's people are by modern nutritional standards inadequately fed and are suffering from chronic malnutrition. Every year 10 to 20 million people starve to death or die of related causes. To compound this, the world's population is increasing at the rate of 2 percent per year, or by about 75 million persons annually. If the current rate continues, our present world population of 4 billion will double in 35 years. The United Nations estimates that by the year 2000 there will be 6 to 7 billion people on the earth.

Two centuries ago, the Reverend Thomas R. Malthus (1766–1834), in his seminal book *An Essay on the Principle of Population* (1798), advanced the thesis that population when unchecked tends to increase in a geometric ratio (2 to 4 to 8 to 16) while means of subsistence (food, for instance) tend to increase only in an arithmetical ratio (1 to 2 to 3 to 4) and that positive steps to prevent an increase in population are necessary as alternatives to such natural and brutal checks as overcrowding, disease, war, poverty, and starvation.

To a significant degree many of our global problems—struggles for power, disputes over territory, war—have been historically and still are intimately related to the food supply of the world. Hunger is a powerful enemy of peace, or as the Roman philosopher Seneca (4 B.C.?–65 A.D.) put it, "A hungry people listens not to reason, nor cares for justice, nor is bent by any prayers."

279

Hunting and Agricultural Periods

It is significant in terms of emphasizing the key role which food plays in the life of man that all of man's history on this globe is divided into two periods, each based on how he obtained his food. First, there was the **hunting period** during which he searched for food—fish, other animals, fruits (berries and nuts), seeds, edible stems, and roots—and gathered and caught this food from day to day. He obtained sugar and vitamins from berries and other fleshy fruits, starch from roots and some fruits and seeds, oil from nuts, and proteins from the meat of animals as well as from plants. Since he had to hunt for his food he had to keep moving on to new territory; he was perforce a nomad. His method of obtaining food by hunting meant that even a relatively large territory could sustain only a small human population and that he had to spend full time in locating food.

This hunting period, also called the Paleolithic or Old Stone Age, probably lasted over one million years. During this long period man learned to use fire, he developed primitive tools and weapons, he built crude shelters, and he relied on animal skins for clothing. Significantly it was this Paleolithic period that also saw the evolution of herbs from trees. This development from trees to herbs is important because most of our food plants as well as many other plants of importance to man are herbs—the cereals such as wheat, rice, and corn; fiber plants such as flax, cotton, and hemp; scores of vegetables; and many drug plants.

The second and final period in man's history is termed the **agricultural period** (or Neolithic or New Stone Age) in which man learned to plant seeds, to cultivate the soil, and to harvest crops. This enormously significant turning point in man's evolution probably occurred about 9000 B.C.

With the onset of the agricultural period man stayed in one place from the time he planted his seeds until he harvested his crops. He had to tend his crops. In the process of becoming sedentary, of waiting for his crops to mature, he became civilized, for he now had some leisure since fewer people were needed to obtain food. He had time to talk and argue; to study the stars, the sun, and the seasons which led him to considerations of time and the calendar; to develop religion, art, and philosophy; and, unfortunately, he even had leisure for war. Because the cultivation of crops made more food available, more people could be fed, with the result that the population increased. Villages arose, then towns, and finally cities. Man learned not only to adapt wild plants to his needs, but he gradually began to domesticate animals.

Scholars from various disciplines have speculated on the question of how the transition from food hunting to the planting and cultivation of seeds took place. One theory holds that seeds from wild plants gathered as food accidentally dropped around the dwellings and then germinated in the nitrogen-rich rubbish of fish, excreta, and other garbage which accumulated near the hovels of primitive man. Someone among these early people must have been bright enough to notice these adventitious plants and to suggest that similar plants might be grown by deliberately sowing seeds. So we may say that our cultivated, or crop, plants originated as weeds on rubbish heaps, and indeed, this explanation is known as the Dump-Heap Theory of the origin of agriculture. Hemp, or cannabis, you will recall, was one of the earliest of these dump-heap plants.

. See illustration on page 186, dump heap.

Another theory to explain the change from the hunting to the agricultural stage suggests that the cultivation of crop plants began in connection with the graves used to bury the dead, along with the tools and a supply of food provided for the use of the deceased in the next world. In the preparation of the graves the ground was disturbed—in a sense cultivated—and the seeds on the buried food plants germinated. Again some canny observer noticed the relationship between this phenomenon and the possibility of deliberately planting seeds in cultivated soil to obtain food.

There is every reason to suppose that agriculture—the planting of seeds (as well as pieces of roots and stems) and the cultivation of the soil—developed independently in several different regions of the world, in the Near East in the Fertile Crescent between the Euphrates and Tigris rivers, in the Western Hemisphere in Mexico and Peru, in southeast Asia, and in northeast Africa.

What Is Food?

Since we are concerned with food in this chapter we need to define the word, for it is employed in different senses by different persons. Botanists define **foods** as organic compounds which provide energy to organisms or which are incorporated into living substance (protoplasm) and into cell walls. As we indicated in Chapter 1, there are three categories of foods:

1. **Carbohydrates,** consisting of the elements carbon, hydrogen, and oxygen, in which the ratio of hydrogen to oxygen is the same as that in water—2 to 1 (examples of carbohydrates: sugar, starch, cellulose).
2. **Fats or oils,** with the same three elements but in which the ratio of hydrogen to oxygen is usually much greater than 2 to 1.
3. **Proteins,** consisting of the three elements already named plus nitrogen; these four elements make up units known as **amino acids.**

There are some 20 naturally occurring amino acids, and of these, 8 known as the **essential amino acids,** must be supplied in the human diet. All other amino acids required by man are synthesized by the body. Man may obtain the 8 essential amino acids from the meat of other animals, which in turn obtain them from plants for only plants can synthesize the 8 essential amino acids. Actually human beings acquire three-fourths of their proteins directly from plants, but it should be noted that individual species of plants, with the exception of legumes, have relatively small amounts of protein and not a single plant species provides enough of all 8 essential amino acids—a fact which must be remembered by those persons on a vegetarian diet. Long ago it was learned in the Orient that rice must be supplemented by beans or soybeans or fish, and on this continent the Indians knew that with corn there must be beans or squash.

Meat is expensive, for animals consume large quantities of plant food before it is converted into flesh. It is estimated that seven times as many people could be maintained on grain as can be fed on meat produced by animals nourished on the same quantity of grain. On the other hand, it should not be forgotten that there are some range lands which are unsuitable for tillage and if cattle were not pastured there the potential for food production of these extensive tracts of land would be lost to man. A substantial share of the world beef supply is produced on land that cannot be cultivated.

In addition to food, that is, in addition to carbohydrates, fats, and proteins, humans require in the diet small amounts of certain minerals, large quantities of water, and rather minute amounts of vitamins—nearly all of which can be obtained from plants consumed by man.

The Biochemical Uniqueness of Plants

As we also pointed out in Chapters 1 and 2, only plants can carry on photosynthesis, so only green plants (and a few bacteria) can manufacture carbohydrates from simple raw materials such as water and the gas carbon dioxide. In addition to the eight essential amino acids, only plants can synthesize most of the vitamins. Only plants, and only a limited number at that, namely legumes (with their root nodules housing the nitrogen-fixing bacteria) and a few other plants such as certain algae and bacteria, can take atmospheric nitrogen and fix it (that is, combine it with other elements and produce compounds which then can be absorbed by the roots of plants). Only plants carry on the fundamental syntheses in nature; they hold the past, present, and future of man.

Reserve Food In Plants

Essentially what man does—and what all animals do—is to locate where plants store their reserve food in large quantities and then they steal the food from plants. Among these special storage structures of plants are seeds or fruits, such as in cereals and grains, legumes, and nuts. Because seeds and fruits such as nuts have little water they can be stored and transported easily by man. Roots, rhizomes, tubers, bulbs, corms, and typical stems, although bulky and containing some water, may supply large quantities of food, particularly carbohydrates. Finally, leaves such as the leafy vegetables used for green salads have little food value but they are rich in vitamins and minerals, and, of course, they have lots of water.

Vegetarianism

A bit earlier we remarked that those persons on a vegetarian diet must bear in mind that no single species of plant provides enough of all eight essential amino acids. And since vegetarianism is growing in popular appeal we should explore the concept further. In the first place there are a number of reasons why people choose not to eat meat, among these being philosophical or religious objections to consuming flesh taken from another living creature, aesthetic aversion to meat because of the presence of blood and the general unclean nature of meat, and health considerations because of the high levels of saturated fats and cholesterol in meat and the various meat additives which cause or are suspected of causing cancer. There are also degrees of vegetarianism—there are those who do not eat any food of animal origin and there are others who do not eat meat but who do consume eggs, milk, and milk products such as cheese. People in the latter group, of course, obtain the necessary proteins and the essential amino acids from the animal products just listed, as well as from the plants ingested. Even those individuals who eat nothing but plants may have an adequate diet, for plants do contain the necessary foods—carbohydrates, fats, and proteins—as well as minerals and vitamins. There are, however, one or two precautions which ought to be observed. Remember that no one plant species contains an adequate supply of the eight essential amino acids, so it is important to plan one's diet in such a way that two or more plants complement each other with respect to their amino acids (a nutritional principle known as the complementarity of amino acids). We have already mentioned that the American Indian early learned to use both beans and squash and that Orientals combine rice and soybeans. The New Englanders' baked beans and brown bread is another combination in which there is complementarity of amino acids.

The other precaution to those who adhere to a strictly vegetarian diet is a warning that most plants have little or no vitamin B_{12}, a deficiency which may cause pernicious anemia leading to the degeneration of parts of the brain and spinal cord. For this reason, persons who follow a strict vegetarian diet should take a B_{12} supplement.

Twelve Plants Standing between Man and Starvation

Since we earlier stressed the point that all our food is ultimately derived from plants, it may come as somewhat of a surprise to learn that relatively few species of plants are involved. Of the 800,000 kinds of plants estimated to be in existence only about 3,000 species have provided food, even in the form of nuts, berries, and other fleshy fruits. Virtually all of these food plants are angiosperms, or flowering plants. This is not surprising when you recall that only the angiosperms have seeds enclosed in a carpel and hence only they produce true fruits, many of which are used by man for food.

Of the 3,000 plants noted above, only 150 species have been extensively cultivated and have entered the commerce of the world. And of the 150, only 12 species are really important—indeed it can be said that these 12 plants stand between man and starvation. If all 12 or even if a few of these cultivated plants were eliminated from the earth, millions of people would starve.

Three of these all-important species are cereals—**wheat, corn, and rice;** the last alone supplies the energy required by 50 percent of the people of the world. It is a remarkable fact that each of these cereals, or grains, is associated with a different major culture or civilization—wheat with Europe and the Middle East, corn or maize with the Americas, and rice with the Far East. Three of the 12 food plants are so-called root crops—**white,** or **Irish, potato** (not a root but a **tuber,** an enlarged tip of a rhizome, or horizontal underground stem); **sweet potato;** and **cassava,** or **manioc** or **tapioca,** from which millions of people in the tropics of both hemispheres derive their basic food. Two of the 12 are sugar-producing plants—**sugar cane** and **sugar beet.** Another pair of species are legumes—the **common bean** and **soybean,** both important sources of vegetable protein and hence sometimes referred to as the "poor man's meat." The final two plants of this august company are tropical tree crops—**coconut** and **banana.**

Now let us examine these 12 plants to learn why each is an important food plant.

Cereals or Grains

First we turn to the cereals (all members of the grass family) which derive their name from Ceres, the Roman goddess of crops. The grain of cereals is really a one-seeded fruit (**caryopsis,** Figure 11.1) in which the fruit wall and the seed coat are fused into one structure. The **endosperm** (food-storing tissue) of the seed is mostly starch, although there is a special surface layer of the endosperm, the **aleurone layer,** which contains protein. The embryo, or **germ,** has some oil and protein. In addition, grains have some minerals (but are low in calcium) and vitamins (except for vitamin A, which is, however, present in yellow maize; dried grains have no vitamin C). Thus grains are nearly ideal sources of food, except that any one given species does not provide enough of all the eight essential amino acids required by man. Since grains are low in water content, they are easily transported and stored by man, and are rather resistant to spoilage. Above all, the yield of food from cereals per plant or per acre is very high.

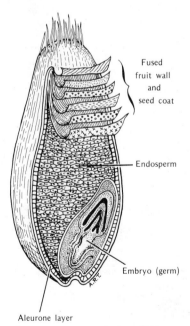

Fused fruit wall and seed coat

Endosperm

Embryo (germ)

Aleurone layer

Figure 11.1   Grain of wheat (*Triticum aestivum*).

Figure 11.2 Wheat (*Triticum aestivum*). [Courtesy U.S. Department of Agriculture.]

Wheat. The common, or bread, wheat is a member of the grass family and is the most widely cultivated plant in the world (Figures 11.1, 11.2, and 11.3). Unquestionably, it was the basis for the development of the early civilizations in the Near East. Wheat is one of the oldest cereals to be cultivated. Carbonized grains of wheat have been found in a prehistoric village (dating back to 7000 B.C.) in the Tigris-Euphrates basin.

Rice. The chief cereal of the Far East—China, Japan, India, the Philippines, and Indonesia—is rice, another grass (Figure 11.4). As noted before, an exclusively rice diet, although rich in carbohydrates and furnishing all the necessary calories, is still deficient in some of the essential amino acids. Energetic efforts are being made by plant scientists to improve the content of protein in rice, both in amount and with a better balance of the essential amino acids.

For centuries the Chinese have maintained fish ponds associated with their rice paddies; the fish not only furnished organic fertilizer for the rice and kept the mosquito population in check, but they provided the important protein supplement which is necessary to balance the rice diet. A rice diet can also be buttressed by legumes such as soybeans.

Polished rice is rice which in processing loses its bran layer and embryo, leaving only the starch-packed endosperm. Some of the most nutritious parts of the rice grain are thereby lost, including vitamin B, a deficiency of which causes beri-beri disease in humans.

Figure 11.3 Wheat (*Triticum aestivum*). [Courtesy U.S. Department of Agriculture.]

Figure 11.4 Rice (*Oryza sativa*). [Courtesy U.S. Department of Agriculture.]

Figure 11.5 Corn (*Zea mays*).

Corn. Indian corn, or corn or maize (*Zea mays*, Figure 11.5), belonging also to the grass family, is a plant in which the stamens and carpels are located in separate flowers but these flowers are borne on the same individual (a condition known as **monoecious**). The tassel of corn is made up of many male flowers and the ear consists of many female flowers. Each kernel on the ear was once the ovary of one flower and a single strand of

Figure 11.6 Sweet potato (*Ipomoea batatas*). [Courtesy U.S. Department of Agriculture.]

Figure 11.7 Cassava (*Manihot esculenta*). [Courtesy David J. Rogers.]

silk is the long style running from the ovary or kernel to a point outside the ear.

Corn, with starch from the endosperm and corn oil from the embryo, is an important food for man and animals but it is low in protein and certain vitamins.

There are several theories on the origin of corn, but apparently it evolved from some of the wild grasses of Central or South America. We have evidence that corn was cultivated in Mexico some 5,000 years ago. Columbus found that corn was cultivated by the Indians in Cuba as well as in Mexico and South America. Corn is presently the most important crop plant in the United States.

Roots or Rootlike Crops

White, or Irish potato. The white, or so-called Irish potato (*Solanum tuberosum*) is not a native of Ireland but of the Andes of Peru. It was introduced into Europe in 1570 but was slow in achieving acceptance as a food, partly no doubt because it is a member of the Solanaceae, a notorious family with several poisonous plants—henbane, deadly nightshade, and jimson weed. One preacher of the day is quoted as saying that if God had intended potatoes as food for man, he would have mentioned it in the Bible. And ludicrous as it seems, at one time the potato was thought to be an aphrodisiac. It is rich in starch, with some protein in a zone of cells located in the inner part of the skin; hence the old-fashioned advice to eat the skins of potatoes is nutritionally sound.

The potato was not commonly cultivated or eaten in Europe until the eighteenth century, and then its increased consumption was associated with a marked increase in population. It became the dominant food in Ireland in the early nineteenth century—indeed, almost the sole food for the peasants, who consumed 10 to 12 pounds a day. A blight caused by a fungus struck in 1845 and again in 1846, with the result that the entire potato crop was destroyed. It can be said that the lowly potato blight fungus was the direct cause of the devastating Irish famine of 1845–1846, of the death through starvation of 1.5 million Irish people, and the forced migration of a million Irishmen to the eastern seaboard of the United States where they became a dominant element in the political life of the big cities and the nation.

Sweet potato. The sweet potato (*Ipomoea batatas*, Figure 11.6), a native of tropical America, is a vine of the morning glory family. Columbus introduced this vegetable to Spain. In the United States it is often referred to as a yam but it is not a true yam (which belongs to the genus *Dioscorea*). The portion eaten is the root which is rich in carbohydrates—three to six percent is sugar and this amount increases in storage. The sweet potato yields 50 percent more calories than the white potato but the former has less protein. It is, however, a good source of vitamin A and of minerals.

The sweet potato is an important crop in the southeastern United States but it is more extensively cultivated in Africa, southeast Asia and Japan, which grow ten times as much as we do. In Japan and Taiwan it is grown as "typhoon insurance"—in case the rice crop is destroyed the people may fall back on the sweet potato.

Cassava, manioc, tapioca. This plant, also known as mandioca and yuca (Figure 11.7), is a native of South America from which it spread to the tropics of both hemispheres where it is the chief food for millions who depend on it for two meals a day. The tuberous roots (Figure 11.8), rich in starch, are sometimes a yard long and weigh several pounds. When freshly picked, the roots are bitter for they have a poisonous cyanic acid-producing glycoside which, being volatile, is driven off by heat or is expressed by pressure. The roots have little protein so natives depending on them are often subject to malnutrition. Farinha, a coarse meal prepared from cassava, is made into bread in Brazil. The tapioca we buy in northern stores is produced by gentle heating of the cassava which causes the starch to agglutinate into small spheres.

Figure 11.8   Cassava (*Manihot esculenta*) roots. [Courtesy U.S. Department of Agriculture.]

Sugars

Sugar cane. This perennial grass from whose stems sugar is extracted may reach a height of 15 feet (Figure 11.9). It is a native of the East Indies; Columbus—reversing the usual procedure—brought it to the New World where it is cultivated in Brazil and Cuba, Puerto Rico and the other Caribbean Islands, and in the United States in Louisiana, Florida, Hawaii, and Texas.

Sugar cane is one of the best possible energy sources, although it is said to provide empty calories since the nutritive element extracted from cane is pure sucrose, without any vitamins or minerals. The sugar babies of the West Indies suffer from protein malnutrition for their diet is mostly sugar.

Figure 11.9   Sugar cane (*Saccharum officinarum*).

Sugar beet. This important source of sugar is a variety of the common beet which in turn is a descendant of the wild beet still found on the seacoast of Europe (Figure 11.10). The sugar beet is a white-rooted biennial with an extensive root system often growing to a depth of six feet.

The sugar beet industry began in Europe about 1800. Napoleon was an early sponsor of this crop, for its cultivation in Europe assisted his embargo on English goods. At the time Napoleon was ridiculed for his support of this strange new plant; a cartoon of the period shows the emperor dipping a large sugar beet in his morning coffee.

Most of the world's sugar beets are grown in Russia, Germany, France, Poland, and in this country in Colorado, California, and Idaho. The sugar from sugar cane and the sugar beet is indistinguishable in taste although there is a slight difference in the proportion of two types of carbon atoms (isotopes).

Legumes

Common bean. This ubiquitous legume (*Phaseolus vulgaris*) is a native of the New World, probably originating in central Mexico. It is an ancient staple food of both North and South American Indians. The single species has over 1,000 varieties, among which the most common are the string, or snap, bean and the shell bean, the hallowed ingredient of Boston baked beans.

Soybean. This country is the major producer of soybeans (*Glycine max*, Figure 11.11) with 50 million acres devoted to the crop on which three-fourths of the world supply is grown. China is second in production. In the United States soybeans have become so important that they are beginning to rival wheat and corn in acreage. The reason is that soybeans have high protein content—40 to 45 percent of the dry weight—and they also contain a valuable oil—18 to 20 percent of the dry weight. (Large quantities of soybeans are also used in the plastics industry.)

The soybean is a native of China and is one of the oldest crops known; for thousands of years it has been, along with rice, a staple food of China, Japan, and India. It was not until the early part of the nineteenth century that the soybean was introduced into the United States but despite this late start it is already second in importance to corn in the Corn Belt. During World War II the soybean was given an added boost when the oil was first used in the manufacture of margarine. At the present time soybeans provide human food in the form of soybean sprouts, soybean sauce, salad oil, and shortening, to name just a few of the products of the plant.

One of the more interesting recent developments is the conversion of soybeans into artificial meat—synthetic beef, chicken, bacon, and ham. The soybean proteins are spun into fibers (textured vegetable protein) which are then fabricated into imitation bacon and used as meat extenders in hamburgers (soyburgers) and the like. However, soybeans do not provide enough of all eight of the essential amino acids and therefore some other food such as corn has to be added to the diet. On the other hand, soybeans are an economical method of supplying protein, in contrast to beef cattle which require 15 to 20 times as much land to produce the same amount of protein. All things

Figure 11.10 Sugar beet (*Beta vulgaris*). Note the extensive root system. [Courtesy Great Western Sugar Co.]

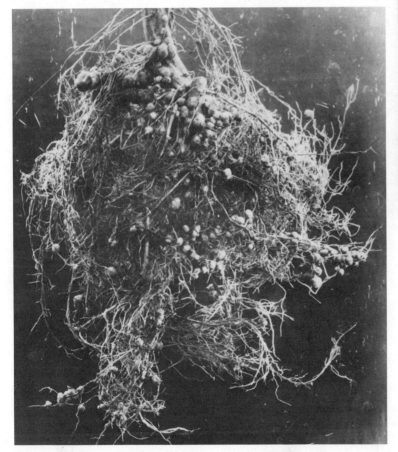

Figure 11.11 Nodules on soybean (*Glycine max*) roots. [Courtesy U.S. Department of Agriculture.]

Figure 11.12 Coconut (*Cocos nuci-fera*).

See photograph on page 278, coco-nuts.

considered, the soybean has been a spectacular success, so much so that it has been branded the "Cinderella crop" of American agriculture.

"Tree" Foods

Coconut. This beautiful, graceful palm tree (*Cocos nucifera*, Figures 11.12 and 11.13) of the tropics is undoubtedly man's most useful tree, at least in the tropics where it is called the tree of heaven and the tree of life. All parts of the plant are used for some human purpose: the nuts for food and oil, the large leaves for the thatching of houses and for the fashioning of baskets and hats, the fibrous coir of the outer shell for the making of mats, the shells for utensils and fuel, the young flower clusters for the extraction of a sweet juice (or toddy) which can be fermented into an alcoholic beverage, the stem for construction and for furniture, and occasionally the terminal bud (the palm heart or cabbage) for a delicious salad. There is an old Malayan proverb that no part of the coconut tree is wasted. Or in the words of Linnaeus, "Man *dwells* naturally within the tropics and lives on the fruit of the palm tree. He *exists* in other parts of the world and there makes shift to feed on corn and flesh." Truly it is one of the most important economic plants, for it is indispensable in the lives of millions of natives of the South Sea islands and other tropical lands such as those of the Caribbean. The plant has a pantropical distribution resulting no doubt from the fact that the nuts will float in sea water for as long as 100 days and remain viable.

One coconut tree may produce as many as 500 nuts a year, although 50 to 100 would be more normal. The fruit, the so-called nut, is technically a **drupe**. The typical drupe, as an olive or peach, has an outer zone which is fleshy and an inner wall which is tough and hard—the stone of the peach. The fruit of the coconut (Figure 11.14) is a dry drupe because the outer zone instead of being fleshy is less compact and fibrous (the coir). Actually, three layers can be identified in the coconut drupe: the outer smooth, rind; the middle, fibrous coir; and the hard stony shell. Inside the latter is the seed which consists of the endosperm and the embryo embedded in the outer endosperm. The endosperm is of two sorts: the outer white solid meat and the inner liquid milk. The white meat, or copra, yields the coconut oil of commerce and the coconut milk is a refreshing drink, rich in several vitamins. As a matter of fact, it is used by bota-

Figure 11.13 Fruits (coconuts) on coconut tree (*Cocos nucifera*). Note also the large pinnately compound leaves or fronds.

nists as a growth-promoting substance to culture plants or plant parts.

In former years the chief use of coconut oil was in the manufacture of soap but now most of the oil is used to make margarine, although 90 percent of the oil is made up of saturated fatty acids and hence not highly recommended. The meat is the main protein source for millions of people living on tropical islands; in Ceylon, for example, the annual consumption of coconuts is 140 per capita.

Banana. This plant (Figure 11.15) is often mistakenly referred to as a tree but actually it is a large perennial herb whose trunk is really made up of leaf stalks. Pliny called the banana the "plant of wise men" and hence Linnaeus gave it the specific name of *sapientum (Musa sapientum)* meaning wise.

It is of southeast Asian origin, particularly the Malayan region, but man early carried it to Africa and to other parts of the tropics, including the American tropics where it is a principal food.

There are two kinds of bananas: the sweet dessert banana, a familiar component of our northern fruit stands; and the cooking banana, or plantain, favorite food of the tropics. Although there are some 300 varieties of bananas, most of the better tasting ones do not reach northern markets for they do not ship well.

Figure 11.14 Section of coconut fruit, showing fibrous coir, hard, stony shell, and endosperm of the seed. [Courtesy Walter H. Hodge.]

The cultivated banana is seedless as the fruit develops without pollination (**parthenocarpy**). Technically, the fruit is a berry (fleshy fruit), specifically a leathery berry because of its outer rind or skin. And one could wax eloquent on the fact that the banana is one of the neatest and most convenient packages

Figure 11.15 Banana plant with fruit and large leaves. [Courtesy Walter H. Hodge.]

for food. It is certainly one of the best energy sources, for a daily intake of two dozen bananas will supply all the needed calories. Chemically, the fruit is mostly starch, with some sugar which increases as the fruit ripens, and some protein and oil. The banana plant is very productive: an area of land which will produce 33 pounds of wheat or 98 pounds of potatoes will yield 4,400 pounds of bananas.

To illustrate how conservative people are with respect to the introduction of new foods, we are reminded that when bananas were first brought to New England in 1690, the Yankees were uncertain as to how they should be prepared. So finally the bananas, skin and all, were put in the New England boiled dinner and cooked along with the meat and potatoes. It is reported that the resulting dish resembled thick soup.

Edible Wild Plants

Although edible wild plants lack the importance of the big 12
food plants, they do furnish a pleasant supplement to the diet.
We shall not, however, attempt a comprehensive treatment for
there are so many edible wild plants in any flora that if we were
to attempt a description of even the best, we would end up with
a long dreary inventory of hundreds of species. Consequently,
the best advice we can offer those readers who have an overwhelming urge to taste the many delicious wild plants is to turn
to the books on edible plants such as those by Merritt Fernald
and Alfred Kinsey, Oliver Medsger, and Euell Gibbons. We
suggest you start reading and start sampling, bearing in mind
that there are poisonous species to be avoided. The richness of
the possibilities is illustrated by a mere listing of the chapter
headings in Fernald and Kinsey's book: purees and soups;
starchy or root-vegetables, cereals, nuts and breadstuffs; cooked
green vegetables; salads; nibbles and relishes; pickles; condiments and seasoning; drinks; rennets; syrups and sugars;
confections; fresh or preserved fruit; jellies and marmalades;
table oils and butters; masticatories and chewing gums;
mushrooms, seaweeds and lichens; and emergency foods.

The Improvement of Cultivated Food Plants

During the tens of thousands of years that man has been associated with food and other useful plants, he has constantly
striven to improve the utility of these plants. Beginning virtually from the time man first planted seeds and cultivated the
soil, he has selected those plants best suited for his purposes. If
he were interested in binding materials, he selected those
plants of a particular species which produced the longest and
strongest fibers; on the other hand, if he sought to grow plants
for food, he selected those with large and numerous seeds, or
those plants with large, food-filled roots.

In addition to practicing **selection,** man discovered that it was
possible to combine the desirable traits of two plants by crossing, or **hybridizing,** the two. Thus **plant breeding** was born.
And this was more or less the state of the art at the time Gregor
Mendel, the great founder of genetics, began his research in
1856. As you will learn in Chapter 18, Mendel's work was ignored until 1900 when it was rediscovered. This revelation of

Mendel's principles of inheritance and the ensuing wave of research in genetics stimulated by it led to the widespread adoption of scientific breeding methods in agriculture. In the United States this development was spurred by the research, resident teaching, and extension activities of the land-grant agricultural colleges which, although they came into being soon after the Civil War, only began to hit their stride in the early decades of the twentieth century.

As a consequence of these several forces, agriculture in the United States made phenomenal progress in the decades between 1910 and 1940. Many new kinds of crop plants, such as soybeans and sorghum, were introduced, and at the same time rather remarkable improvement of the older crops was achieved. For example, early-ripening, frost-resistant varieties of corn extended the Corn Belt 500 miles northward and the spring wheat area spread even farther north and west, while the winter wheat growing zone was moved another 500 miles west to the Great Plains. The yields of many crops increased by 15 to 100 percent through the use of commercial fertilizer. More effective insecticides and fungicides were devised to wage battle against destructive insects and disease-producing fungi. (It has been estimated that from a third to a half of the crops in some regions of the world never reach the consumer because of the destruction caused by insects, fungi, rats, birds, and various other pests. And this does not take into account the equally great losses in the field while the crops are growing and maturing.) Herbicides were discovered in this period and they proved to be remarkably effective in controlling weeds. New varieties of crop plants resistant to plant diseases were developed. For example, wheat rust which formerly destroyed 300 million bushels of wheat annually in the United States and Canada was substantially checked by the breeding of rust-resistant wheat varieties.

Hybrid Corn

One of the spectacular successes of modern plant breeding—to choose but one among many—was the development of **hybrid corn,** in which two or more lines are crossed to produce a **hybrid** with not only a combination of the traits of the separate lines but an additional bonus in the form of more vigor and higher productivity, a phenomenon called **hybrid vigor** (see Chapter 17 for a more detailed account). As a result, the yield per acre of corn was increased by 100 percent; over 90 percent of the corn acreage in the United States is seeded with hybrid corn (some 65 million acres).

Green Revolution

Perhaps the most spectacular triumph of modern genetics and twentieth-century agriculture, however, is the so-called **Green Revolution** in which the production of cereals and other crops doubled and even tripled in the space of a few decades in some of the developing countries of the world.

This revolution began in Mexico in 1943 when the Mexican government invited several American plant scientists, financed by the Rockefeller Foundation, to come to Mexico to assist with the introduction of modern agricultural methods. In Mexico in the early 1940s the yield per acre of corn, the staff of life in that country, was only about 8 bushels, compared with 28 in the United States; the yield of wheat was 4 bushels less than that in the U.S. even though most of the Mexican wheat was grown on irrigated land; and the average yield of beans, the meat of the poor, was only a third of that in this country. As a consequence, millions of bushels had to be imported from other countries.

American botanists in close cooperation with Mexican colleagues gradually instituted modern agricultural practices. These included the selection and breeding of better adapted and higher yielding crop varieties, the wide use of manufactured fertilizer, the extension of irrigation in dry areas, and the control of plant diseases by breeding disease-resistant varieties as well as by the use of chemical pesticides in the case of certain crops. As a result, by 1963, corn and bean production was doubled, while wheat yield tripled.

Certainly this dramatic progress in agriculture deserves to be ranked with other triumphs of science which have occurred in the course of history. Jean Henri Fabre (1823–1925), French entomologist and popular writer on nature, tells us, "History records the battlefields on which we lose our lives, but it disdains to tell us of the cultivated fields by which we live: it can tell us the names of the kings' bastards, but it cannot tell us the origin of wheat. Such is human folly." In this instance, however, the leader of this extraordinary achievement in Mexico, Dr. Norman E. Borlaug (Figure 11.16), initially trained in plant pathology but by necessity turned plant breeder, was recognized

Figure 11.16 Norman E. Borlaug, major architect of the Green Revolution and recipient of Nobel Prize in 1970. [Courtesy Wide World Photos.]

for his leadership and scientific accomplishments by the award of a Nobel Prize in 1970.

Encouraged by the successes in Mexico the Rockefeller Foundation, joined now by the Ford Foundation, established in 1962 the International Rice Research Institute in the Philippines where soon there emerged a new dwarf rice, dubbed the "miracle rice," which was capable of doubling the rice yield. In the intervening years, the new improved wheat, rice, and corn varieties have been introduced to countries in South America and Asia with the result that production has increased dramatically. In India, for instance, within the space of four years wheat production was up 50 percent.

In the meantime, the population of the earth—particularly the population of the poorer, underdeveloped countries—has relentlessly increased at its alarming pace, adding 75 million additional persons to be fed each year. In the face of this frightening exponential growth of population, the Green Revolution certainly does not provide the ultimate solution to the food-population problem. While it is true that encouraging initial increases in crop production have been achieved, unfortunately these rates cannot be sustained.

Moreover, the Green Revolution has encountered other difficulties. There has been some resistance to the consumption of the introduced varieties for they are new and unfamiliar in taste. It should also be noted that the high-yielding varieties of wheat, rice, corn, and other crop plants require the application of large quantities of commercial fertilizer and ample supplies of water. The latter means irrigation in many parts of the world, and both irrigation and the commercial production of fertilizer require energy. Oil is needed for the pumping of water and for the operation of other farm machinery such as tractors, and oil or natural gas is essential for the manufacture of nitrogenous fertilizer. Not only is the element hydrogen provided by oil (or gas) in the chemical synthesis of fertilizer but the enormous energy needed to fix the nitrogen of the air is supplied by oil. In recent years, as we all know, oil shortages have developed and we hear alarming predictions that the oil supply of the world will be exhausted in the not too distant future. As a consequence the price of oil has increased enormously, so much so that the developing countries cannot afford to buy this fossil fuel with the result that they lack fertilizer and the power to operate irrigation systems. Thus since the new miracle seeds are of little value on the poor, dry soils of many parts of the impoverished countries of the world, the Green Revolution has not been an unqualified success.

However, it has at least bought time for us so that, if we but have the wisdom and the will, we may yet devise acceptable methods of population control before we are confronted by world starvation. Let it be noted that in the 1960–1965 period the rate of growth in food production in the poor countries was approximately half the rate of population growth. Obviously we are on a collision course and time is running out.

New research discoveries give some promise that further improvements in crop plants are possible even though these developments can never make up for the sharp increases in world population. Recently Purdue University scientists have found a mutant corn which has twice the normal amount of the essential amino acids lysine and tryptophane. This may be significant, for one of the deficiencies of corn protein is that it is low in these two essential amino acids. Thus, if these findings prove valid, corn, the staple food of most of South and Central America, could possibly supply not only all the calories needed by man but also all the protein. Only some vitamins and certain minerals would need to be added to provide a suitable diet.

Another cereal grain which has attracted a good deal of attention is *Triticale*, a man-made hybrid between wheat *(Triticum)* and rye *(Secale)*. Note that this is a cross involving two different genera even though it is usually difficult to hybridize two related species of the same genus. *Triticale* surpasses wheat in total protein as well as in the content of the essential amino acid lysine. In addition, it has the extreme hardiness and disease-resistance of rye.

What is really needed, however, is a successful cross between the new lysine-rich corn, with its abundant carbohydrate content and its otherwise adequate amino acids, and a plant which fixes the nitrogen of the air. In this way man could be supplied with the requisite calories and essential amino acids without the necessity of providing expensive and energy-demanding nitrogenous commercial fertilizer. Recently in Brazil it has been discovered that some strains of corn, growing under field conditions, have roots with the capacity to fix nitrogen. Apparently a bacterium present in the roots is responsible for the nitrogen fixation. So, what a few years ago seemed beyond the capacity of science now appears to be a distinct possibility.

Suggested Readings

Ames, Oakes. *Economic Annuals and Human Culture*. Cambridge, Mass.: Botanical Museum of Harvard University, 1939. A pioneering study of economic plants, their early history, and their significance to civilization.

Anderson, Edgar. *Plants, Man and Life*. Berkeley: University of California Press, 1969. A readable book on the origin and evolution of our crop plants by an iconoclastic botanist who was not afraid to think for himself.

Angier, Bradford. *Field Guide to Edible Wild Plants*. Harrisburg, Pa.: Stackpole Books, 1974. Useful manual with copious colored illustrations and notes on edibility of plants.

Appleman, Philip, ed. *Thomas Robert Malthus: An Essay on the Principle of Population: Text, Sources and Background Criticism*. New York: Norton, 1976. This admirable edition includes the text of the original (1798) Malthus essay, together with later revisions; also critical commentary by supporters and opponents of Malthus's doctrine.

Baker, Herbert G. *Plants and Civilization*. 2d ed. Belmont, Calif.: Wadsworth, 1970. A brief book on the plants of economic value and their bearing on civilization.

Brown, Lester R. *By Bread Alone*. New York: Praeger, 1974. Highly recommended book on the problems of food supply and population.

————. *Seeds of Change: The Green Revolution and Development in the 1970's*. New York: Praeger, 1970. The story of the Green Revolution and related developments in the 1970s.

Crosby, Alfred W., Jr. *The Columbian Exchange: Biological and Cultural Consequences of 1492*. Westport, Conn.: Greenwood Publishing Company, 1972. An impressive discussion of the plants introduced to Europe by Columbus and those brought to the New World from Europe.

Ehrlich, Paul R. *The Population Bomb*. New York: Ballantine, 1971. Well-known polemic on the dangers of population growth.

Fernald, Merritt L., and Alfred C. Kinsey (rev. Reed C. Rollins). *Edible Wild Plants*. New York: Harper & Row, 1958. Scholarly book on edible wild plants by the outstanding taxonomist Fernald and the equally distinguished entomologist and sexologist Kinsey.

Gibbons, Euell. *Stalking the Healthful Herbs*. New York: McKay, 1970. More of what's in the following entry.

————. *Stalking the Wild Asparagus*. New York: McKay, 1970. Popular account of adventures in finding and eating wild plants by an enthusiast.

Heiser, Charles B., Jr. *Seed to Civilization*. San Francisco: Freeman, 1973.

A little gem of a book by an accomplished scientific writer—on food plants and their role in the development of civilization.

Hill, Albert F. *Economic Botany*. 2d ed. New York: McGraw-Hill, 1952. The best, all-round, concise book on economic botany, which, however, needs revision since the last edition is dated 1952.

Mangelsdorf, Paul C. *Plants and Human Affairs*. Nieuwland Lectures, Notre Dame, Ind.: University of Notre Dame, 1952. A collection of lectures on the 12 most important food plants and their crucial significance to man.

———. "Biology, Food, and People." *Economic Botany* 15 (1961): 279–288. Thoughtful essay on the twin problems of population increase and food production, and the central importance of the 12 essential food plants.

Masefield, G. B., M. Wallis, S. G. Harrison, and B. E. Nicholson. *The Oxford Book of Food Plants*. London: Oxford University Press, 1969. A beautiful volume with color illustrations of food plants accompanied by a brief text.

Medsger, Oliver P. *Edible Wild Plants*. New York: Collier, 1972. A guide to the identification and preparation of North American edible wild plants.

Sax, Karl. *Standing Room Only*. Boston: Beacon Press, 1960. Exploration of problems of population growth by one of the country's eminent botanists turned demographer.

Schery, Robert W. *Plants for Man*. 2d ed., Englewood Cliffs, N.J.: Prentice-Hall, 1972. The most up-to-date, comprehensive book on economic botany. Richly illustrated.

Stakman, E. C., Richard Bradfield, and Paul C. Mangelsdorf. *Campaign against Hunger*. Cambridge, Mass.: Harvard University Press, 1967. A book on the early history of the Green Revolution written by some of the scientists who were pioneers in this movement.

Struever, Stuart, ed. *Prehistoric Agriculture*. Garden City, N.Y.: Natural History Press, 1971. A volume on the origins of agriculture and the role of agriculture in the development of civilization.

Plant Names

Common name	Scientific name	Family
banana	*Musa sapientum*	Musaceae
cassava	*Manihot esculenta*	Euphorbiaceae
coconut	*Cocos nucifera*	Palmae
common bean	*Phaseolus vulgaris*	Leguminosae
corn	*Zea mays*	Gramineae
rice	*Oryza sativa*	Gramineae
soybean	*Glycine max*	Leguminosae
sugar beet	*Beta vulgaris*	Chenopodiaceae
sugar cane	*Saccharum officinarum*	Gramineae
sweet potato	*Ipomoea batatas*	Convolvulaceae
wheat	*Triticum aestivum*	Gramineae
white potato	*Solanum tuberosum*	Solanaceae

Mosaic of sage (*Salvia*) leaves.

12
Spices
Botanical Treasure

Piquancy, zestiness, raciness, briskness, heat, pungency—all of these are wrapped up in **spice**. And who can deny the old adage that "Variety's the very spice of life/That gives it all its flavour"? But spice was not always synonymous with tang and relish, for the first uses of spices were probably in perfumery and fumigation.

The Great Disguisers

To Egyptians of the Pharaonic period unpleasant odors were associated with evil and incense was burned to banish malignant spirits and to ward off the foul aromas emanating from the masses. To satisfy the gods of death, and incidentally to disguise the fetid vapors of putrefaction, body cavities of noble Egyptians were cleansed with fragrant herbs and spices, with anise, cassia, and cinnamon during the embalming operation. One meaning of *embalm* is "to anoint with aromatic spices." The Testaments contain many references to the use of spices as aromatics and in Proverbs there is a tale of spices abetting a case of cuckoldry: "I have sprinkled my bed with *myrrh*, my clothes with *aloes* and *cassia*. Come! Let us drown ourselves in pleasure, let us spend a whole night of love; for the man of the house is away... until the moon is full he will not be home." It may be noted that the lady's rhapsody reflects ancient and questionable beliefs about the value of spices as **aphrodisiacs**.

305

Figure 12.1 *B'samim:* ceremonial, ornamented spice box used in the Jewish *havdalah* service which closes the sabbath observance. The delightful fragrance of spices is both wish and augury for a pleasant week.

The Hebrews always regarded cinnamon (Hebrew, *kinamon*) as a deliciously fragrant substance and valued it highly both as a flavoring and as a perfume. It was one of the principal ingredients used to make the precious ointments which Moses was commanded to use in the Tabernacle for anointing the officiating priests. Aromatic spices are symbolic of goodness, health, and happiness, and their use continues today in the Judaeo-Christian ritual, in the spice box (Hebrew, *b'samim*) ceremony (Figure 12.1) associated with the *havdalah* rite closing the Sabbath and in the censer of the Catholic High Mass.

It is difficult to say which group of people first used spices as food-flavoring materials: Egyptians, Hebrews, Indians, Arabians, Babylonians, Assyrians, Chinese. Archeological evidence has shown that some of the spices grown in India today—black pepper, cinnamon, turmeric, and cardamom—were known in the Indus Valley before 1000 B.C. The ancient Greeks imported Eastern spices like black pepper, cassia, cinnamon, and ginger into the Mediterranean arena following the extension of Greek conquest and influence during the empire-making days of Alexander the Great (356–323 B.C.). The Romans were profligate in their use of spices, both in the kitchen and for fumigants and cosmetics. It also seems clear that a major early use for spices was not just to enhance the flavors of good food, but rather, to cover up and change the flavors and odors of fouled and rotten fare (except perhaps for the Hebrews to whom aged food was proscribed) and to add interest and variety to the otherwise drab and monotonous diets characteristic of the Middle Ages in northern Europe. In days when food preservation techniques were primitive or nonexistent, unpalatable foods were made eatable through the use of spices. The wretched victuals of fifteenth-century Europe were camouflaged with spices and the hot curries of India and other Oriental regions are said to have developed from days when putrid flesh was the rule.

Before bathing was commonplace and associated with good health, spices were the body deodorants of the time. Roman men were customarily heavily perfumed and even the rugged legionaries reeked of the fragrances of the East. The poor quality wine of old Rome was spiced, supposedly to add heat to the bouquet. Chinese courtiers of the third century B.C. were required to hold cloves in their mouths when addressing the emperor. Distasteful medicines (and deadly poisons) were disguised with spices, a practice which continues today when extracts of coriander, cinnamon, and cloves are used for this purpose. In mid-seventeenth-century Europe physicians attending plague patients wore a heavy leather gown and a helmet sporting a long, beaklike nosepiece filled with aromatic spices to protect against the disease and ward off the foul odors of the sick (Figure 12.2).

Flavor Comes of Age

Consumption of spices as condiments, that is, as substances to stimulate the appetite and add relish to foods, seems also to have ancient origins. Seasoning from India and nutmeg and cloves from the Moluccas (Spice Islands) were introduced into China at a very early date. India must have been a center of spice lore, culture, and use in ancient times as it still is today. The Greeks, though they imported Eastern spices, made good use of kitchen herbs from neighboring Mediterranean lands: anise, caraway and poppy in the preparation of bread, fennel for seasoning vinegar sauces, coriander as an additive for wine, and mint as flavoring for meat sauces (mint jelly is still traditionally served with lamb). Provincial people in Greece used cheap and available garlic in their cooking. And the Romans were extravagant not only in their use of spices in perfumery but in their cuisine as well. Marcus Gavius Apicius (14–37 A.D.), gourmet and epicure, spent vast sums for exotic foods and spices. Among his various recipes it is said that he prepared desserts of poppy seed and honey and that his culinary talents included the use of black pepper, turmeric, and ginger from the East as well as many herbs and spices cultivated in parts of the Roman Empire nearer at hand: anise, basil, bay leaves, garlic, coriander. During the time of Emperor Constantine, about 330 A.D., cloves grown in the far-away Moluccas became known in the West as food seasonings. It would be rash of us to try to distinguish which spices were used as flavor enhancers and which were used as flavor hiders or to say during which periods of history either of these was first employed. It is probably true, however, that spices were used for both of these purposes simultaneously and that even the same spice may have served both ends depending upon the conditions of the time and the amounts employed.

Figure 12.2 Mid-seventeenth-century European costume worn by physicians attending plague victims. The gown was made of leather as were the shirt underneath, breeches, and boots, all of which fitted into one another. The long beak or nosepiece was filled with spices and the eyepieces of the helmet were covered with glass. [From a modern drawing derived from the seventeenth-century original in The Wellcome Institute of the History of Medicine and used by courtesy of The Wellcome Trustees.]

Companion to Exploration

It would be difficult to overestimate the role of spices in shaping the destiny of humanity. The lure of spices and their great value encouraged exploration of the globe: They led to opening up the East for exploitation by the West; they were responsible, at least in part, for the discovery of the New World and the subsequent systematic, ruthless decimation of the Aztecs, Mayans, and Incas, among other cultures. The search for spices stimulated the development of a sea route from western Europe around the Cape of Good Hope, across the Indian Ocean, to the Indian Peninsula. Spices were very much on Ferdinand Magellan's mind when he set out from Spain in 1519 to visit the Spice Islands and to circumnavigate the earth by traveling westward. Merchants risked life and fortune, wars were fought, populations enslaved—all for the sake of spices.

Hot tropical lands are the homes of all of our important spices and most of these come from the Orient: cinnamon and cassia, nutmeg and mace, black pepper, ginger, cloves, and cardamom. Only allspice, capsicum peppers and chilies, and vanilla are natives of the New World tropics. The Mediterranean region and Asia Minor provide some of the less important spices and culinary herbs and among these are bay leaves, saffron, anise seed, oregano, sage, rosemary, mustard seed, thyme, coriander, parsley, dill seed, and fennel. The cooler regions of Europe and Asia are almost bereft of native spices and herbs but we may count caraway seed, basil, tarragon, and mint as indigenous products of these areas. The most prized spices are those of the tropics, those for which risks were taken, lives lost, and empires threatened. It has been in pursuit of these that world history was fashioned.

See photograph page 304, sage.

Arabian Connection

Arabia stood at the crossroads of the ancient world, between Europe and Asia, between the Mediterranean and Arabian Seas. She took advantage of this fortunate position and thereby affected the course of world events for some hundreds of years. Cassia and cinnamon were highly favored spices in the countries of the Near East and in the Greek and Roman homelands. In the Biblical and classical periods spices of all kinds were among the most prized articles of commerce and ranked with precious metals, pearls, and jewels as items of highest esteem.

Figure 12.3 An old engraving depicting a transfer port in one of the spice trade routes; the ship of the desert meets the ship of the sea. [Redrawn from an American Spice Trade Association photograph of the original woodcut.]

Among the gifts the Queen of Sheba bestowed on Solomon, spices were of equal merit with gold and gem stones: "And she gave the king an hundred and twenty talents of gold, and of *spices* very great store, and of precious stones: There came no more such abundance of *spices* as these which the queen of Sheba gave to king Solomon" (I Kings).

Through their traditional trade routes and communications in the Orient, Arab merchants had virtually exclusive control over the purchase and transport of spices; in effect, they had a corner on the market (Figure 12.3). They were very jealous of their abilities and knowledge of the true sources of the spices and for centuries they told deceitful stories about the origins of these valuable commodities purposefully to maintain their stranglehold on the trade. They spread false tales about the habitats of cinnamon and cassia saying that they were gathered in Africa when in truth they came from Ceylon (now Sri Lanka) and southeastern Asia respectively. Arab traders related harrowing accounts about the difficulties of securing these much-coveted materials to demoralize competition, mislead purchasers, and to keep supplier and consumer apart. For example, Greek and Roman buyers were told that cinnamon grew on mountain peaks and that the twigs were used by large birds to build their nests. Only through great danger could the bark be collected, hence the scarcity and the high price. This was probably one of the best-kept trade secrets of all time, the original cover-up, the grandest subterfuge.

The Secret Is Out

About 40 A.D., just before the reign of Roman emperor Claudius I (10 B.C.–54 A.D.), a Greek merchant, Hippalus, made a startling discovery concerning wind patterns which swept the vast reaches of the Indian Ocean. First, he learned that they were seasonal, or monsoonal, and second, that they reversed their direction twice a year. Between April and October they blew from northwest to southeast and between October and April they came out of the east and blew toward the west. It was probable that the Arab traders had known of these shifty winds for centuries and had profited from it in their sea trading with India. Thus, Hippalus found, it would be possible for Roman ships to leave the port of Berenice on the west coast of the Red Sea and fetch up on the pepper-producing west coast of India, the fabled Malabar Coast. Then, later in the year, these same ships could return to their home port by following the west-blowing monsoons. Having learned the secrets of monsoonal direction, the Romans built an armada of merchant ships, regularized trade, eventually broke Arab domination of the Indian market, and lifted the veil of secrecy. Steady commerce with India enabled hedonistic Romans to wallow in spices to their hearts' content.

As Roman dominion gradually spread northward across the Alps, the so-called barbarian Goths, Vandals, and Huns, some of whom served in the Roman legions, became familiar with things Roman, including such spices as pepper. They were attracted to the pleasures of Rome and developed a taste for the refinements of Roman life. Between 375 and 476 A.D., there were repeated barbarian invasions into Roman territory to the south and in 476 the puppet emperor Romulus Augustulus was deposed, thus ending for all time the ascendancy of the Roman Empire in the West.

In 408, when the Gothic leader Alaric appeared with his barbarous hordes before the terrified people of Rome, he agreed to ransom the city for 5,000 pounds of gold, 30,000 pounds of silver, 4,000 silk tunics, 3,000 valuable skins, and *3,000 pounds of black pepper.* The barbarians had come into their own—they had learned the value of spices. This time Alaric spared the city; during the third siege in 410, however, he overwhelmed the defending forces and initiated the collapse of the Roman Empire.

Islam Conquers

The Arabs took advantage of Rome's weakness and, among other ventures, they reassumed their command of the spice trade. The Prophet Mohammed (570–632 A.D.) had been a spice dealer himself and was partner in a shop which traded in myrrh, frankincense, and Oriental spices. Following his teachings, Mohammedanism by the eighth century extended from Spain in the west to the borders of China in the east. Moslem influence was further expanded to India, Ceylon, and Java by the itinerant and ubiquitous Arab spice traders. Even some of the Moslem missionaries, who like their later Christian counterparts effected religious conversion by the sword, later settled on India's Malabar Coast to become peaceful spice dealers. Arabs of this era had accomplished what their forefathers had been unable to do—they now controlled the spice lands. They developed a flourishing civilization, built opulent cities, kept the writings of classical Greek scholars alive, established great libraries in all branches of learning, dominated science and medicine, and cultivated skillful trade and commerce in regions under their jurisdiction. All of this while Christian Europe endured the Dark Ages.

During the so-called Dark Ages (from about 476 to 1095, that is, roughly the 500 years between the collapse of the western Roman Empire and the First Crusade) the accessability of spices in western Europe north of the Alps was greatly curtailed. For the most part only small lots were obtainable and the Church was a favored recipient. Spices were so valuable that, as in biblical days, they were considered extravagant gifts. There is a record, for example, of Gemmulus, a Roman deacon, sending a present of pepper and cinnamon to Boniface, archbishop of Mainz. Traders from Germanic Hanseatic leagues were required to pay a tax in England that included ten pounds of black pepper just for the privilege of dealing with London merchants. The Church imported Oriental spices, and aromatic herbs were cultivated in monastery gardens, particularly of the Benedictine order. European trade with the Orient was minimal and the treasured spices of the East may have been brought to Europe through traveling Jewish merchants who were, to a limited extent, responsible for maintaining at least some commerce between East and West from the eighth to the tenth centuries.

Islam Deposed

Beginning with the First Crusade to the Holy Land toward the end of the eleventh century, Western Christendom came into direct collision with the civilizations to the East, namely with enlightened Arab culture. Latin feudal kingdoms and principalities were founded in Syria and Palestine and there was considerable social, intellectual, and economic interaction between the Christian West and the Moslem East. Doubtless because Islamic civilization was more stable and coherent than that of the West, at least until the end of the thirteenth century, the West was the net gainer. Along with the steady stream of commerce which developed, Oriental spices—pepper, nutmeg, cloves, and cardamom—became almost commonplace in the West. Increased availability of these commodities resulted in basic changes in European culinary habits and diets among not only the nobility but the rising middle class. What had been luxuries before became necessities.

European Spice Trade

Spices played an important role in the development and growth of the early European trading centers, particularly those of Italy—Venice and Genoa. The success of the Venetian and Genoese shipowners and factors in the East soon evolved into a European trade monopoly with a network of merchants throughout Europe. A pepperers' guild, later incorporated into a spicers' guild, was formed in London in 1180 to manage trade in spices, drugs, and dyestuffs. They had the responsibility to grade and select spices and medicinal products. Pepperers and spicers were the predecessors of apothecaries, herbalists, and physicians. Such was the early influence of spices and the spice trade.

In the latter part of the Middle Ages (arbitrarily, from the fall of the Western Roman Empire in 476 until the beginnings of the Renaissance about 1400) spices were still among the most expensive articles of trade: Peppercorns were counted out singly and were used as currency to pay bills and taxes; some European towns kept their accounts in pepper. Brides received pepper as part of their marriage portion. In the mid-sixteenth century the price of pepper on the Antwerp market served as a touch-stone for European business. A horse could be purchased for one pound of saffron and a pound of ginger was worth as much as a sheep. A cow could be bought for two pounds of mace. One pound of nutmeg bought seven oxen in fourteenth-century Germany. Even with our current rampant inflation, spices were relatively more expensive 500 years ago than they are today.

Tales of the incredible wealth of the Great East and the oppor-tunities for trade there brought back to Venice by the Polo brothers Nicolo and Maffeo whetted the insatiable appetites of Europeans for Oriental luxuries. Two years after their first ex-pedition (1260–1269), the Polos set out for Asia with Nicolo's young son Marco. They returned to Venice in 1297 laden with gem stones and pearls sewn into the linings of their threadbare garments, recounting fantastic stories about imperial cities and tales of the copious spices of Cathay and the islands of the South China Sea.

Marco Polo was imprisoned in Genoa following his capture in battle during the Venetian-Genoese war of 1298 and while jailed, he dictated his experiences in the East to a fellow prison-er. Among these memoirs were tantalizing references to the spice riches in the lands of the Great Khan. He asserted that 10,000 pounds of pepper were brought into Hangchow daily and that in the capital city of Kublai Khan, citizens drank a taste-tingling brew of rice wine and spice. Marco described plantations of pepper, nutmegs, and cloves on Java and the large quantities of cinnamon, pepper, and ginger raised along the Malabar Coast of India. Upon his release from prison and return to Venice, Marco was called upon continually to repeat his tales of spices and the magnificence of the East. Marco Polo was the first great public relations agent for China. And there is little doubt his vivid stories did much to initiate the great age of European discovery which was to begin in 1418 with the ex-ploratory voyages and navigational research encouraged and supported by Prince Henry of Portugal.

The World Divided

During the latter half of the fifteenth century Spain and Por-tugal emerged as the two major colonial powers. Bartholomeu Díaz of Portugal rounded the Cape of Good Hope in 1487 and

Christopher Columbus, sailing for Spain, stepped off on Watling's Island (which he named San Salvador) in the Bahamas in 1492. To keep these two fractious nations from squabbling, and incidentally to serve the purposes of the Church, in 1493 Pope Alexander VI divided the globe between Spain and Portugal merely by drawing an arbitrary line from pole to pole 100 leagues west of the Azores. Those lands to the east were to be the dominion of Portugal and those to the west were to be under the sway of Spain—as though there were no other nations in the world. In return for this great favor the Catholic monarchs of Spain and Portugal agreed to convert the conquered peoples to the Christian faith. João II of Portugal protested Alexander's arbitrariness (and possible bias since Alexander was born in Spain) and Spain and Portugal assented to divide the world between themselves (the Treaty of Tordesillas in 1494). Another line was drawn at 370 leagues west (about 46° west longitude) of the Azores. As in the 1493 papal Bull of Demarcation, the lands to the east were to be opened for Portuguese colonization and those to the west to Spanish exploration. Thus it was that Brazil, in all of South America, came under the heel of Portugal, while the remainder was available for the boot of Spain.

Earlier, but notably through the explorations of Vasco da Gama (beginning in 1497) and later navigators, enclaves in West and East Africa, India, Ceylon, and the East Indian Islands were established—over the violent protests of the residents—in the name of Portugal. Pedro Álvarez de Cabral took official possession of Brazil for Portugal in 1500 and then sailed eastward toward India. Spain embarked on her post-Columbian exploitation of the American continent.

Writer Jean Descola (*The Conquistadors*) observed that

The fifteenth century ended in a stirring atmosphere. Intoxicated by books with ink that had scarcely time to dry, following step by step the progress of the navigators, the minds of men could not distinguish between truth and legend. . . . Everyone marveled at how the discovered lands surpassed in splendor the lands that had been imagined. The icy glow of Samarkand silks; the scent of burning sandalwood in Java; the pepper and nutmeg [?] of Malabar; the glittering gems of Cipango [Japan]; were these not the means to intoxicate the contemporaries of Leonardo da Vinci. . . ? It was only a matter of renewing the alliance

with the Great Khan that had been outlined two centuries
earlier by the three Polos. . . . The first essential of this
grandiose plan was to find a way to the Great Khan.

And fanatic, adventure-hungry Columbus was bursting with all
of this when he set out to persuade Ferdinand and Isabella of
Spain that the key to world domination was theirs if only they
would support him on his westward voyage to Cathay and the
lands of the Great Khan. Although the monarchs vacillated in-
terminably, finally the reality of their needs triumphed over
their doubts about the dreams of Columbus. The gold and
spices of Cathay which would be theirs, their advisors coun-
seled, would more than replenish the depleted coffers and pay
the expenses of Columbus's projected voyage. Among other
perquisites, Columbus was promised a tenth of all gold, silver,
pearls, gems, and spices.

Spain's Spices

Although Columbus made four voyages to the Indies, he never
found gold in any great abundance, but he did discover two of
the three important New World spices. Martín Alonso Pinzón,
commander of the *Pinta* on Columbus's first voyage, is said by
historian Samuel Eliot Morison in his *Admiral of the Ocean Sea*
to have "brought in specimens [for Columbus to see] of the native creole pepper. . . which raised hopes of a lucrative trade in
spicery." Luckily, on his second voyage in 1493, Dr. Diego
Chanca accompanied the expedition. Chanca, a physician, was
well versed in botany. He observed the natives using the
pungent red fruits of *ají* to season their yams, meat, and fish.
This new spice, Morison's "native creole pepper," was indeed
hot and because its striking piquancy resembled that of the
pepper of the East with which they were familiar, ají was called
pimienta roja (red pepper) by the Spaniards. Actually it is in no
way related to the pepper of antiquity; rather, it is kin to the
sweet, or bell, pepper and to the tomato and potato. Nevertheless, this pepper was exhibited to the Spanish court as one of
the finds of Columbus's 1493 venture. Also reported from this
voyage by Dr. Chanca was a small tree which bore little round
fruits. These were pleasantly aromatic when dried and tasted like
a mixture of cinnamon, nutmeg, and cloves. None of the
Spaniards with Columbus was aware of the value and importance this pungent fruit was to gain. It was not until many years
after the death of the Admiral of the Ocean Sea that **allspice,** or

pimienta (pepper), as the Spaniards later called it, received acclaim as a valuable condiment. Thus the success of Columbus was a very mixed bag: He failed to return with the spices of the East; yet, indirectly through his efforts a great mountain of gold and other precious metals and jewels was about to be pillaged for the throne of Spain.

The third and last important spice from the Indies was discovered by the soldiers of the conquistador, Hernán Cortés. Cortés had taken command of an expedition during which he subdued Mexico between 1519 and 1521, destroyed the Aztec Empire, and eradicated Aztec culture on behalf of the Holy Roman Emperor of Spain. Nevertheless, and unknown to him, he contributed greatly to the world's store of spices, for in the humid coastal rain forests of southeastern Mexico, **vanilla** was discovered. This delicate and fragrant spice was used by the Aztecs to flavor their chocolate beverages. The Spanish conquistadors carried the vanilla pods to Europe and by the end of the sixteenth century the Spaniards had established factories to manufacture chocolate with vanilla flavoring.

Portuguese Property

Whereas the Spanish were to strike gold by sailing westward, the Portuguese were to strike spice by sailing eastward. Thus by chance, through the Treaty of Tordesillas, the Spaniards became heir to precious metal, the Portuguese to fantastic botanical treasure. The voyages of Díaz and da Gama opened for Portugal a practical seaway to the East, an accomplishment, says spice historian Frederic Rosengarten, which was "the most significant feat in the history of the spice trade." Venice and Genoa, which had monopolized the trade in spices, were deposed as leading commercial centers for the spice trade with the Orient. But the Portuguese were not content merely to trade in spices and through a series of battles and conquests under Alfonso de Albuquerque—Alfonso the Great—Portugal wrested an empire in the East from the Moslems. The Portuguese gained control of the Malabar Coast of India, Ceylon, the Sunda Islands, the important spice-trading center of Malacca and by 1514 they gained sovereignty over the Moluccas—the fabled Spice Islands of antiquity. The Portuguese maintained a despotic rule over the people of these newly won territories. Cheating and plundering the populace were their normal practices and any good will which might have existed melted away with the enslavement of Ceylonese cinnamon workers.

Early in the seventeenth century Britain and Holland became great international powers and each formed its own East India Company. The English and Dutch eyed the riches of the East which had been the sole province of Portugal for almost 100 years. They also cast jealous glances at Spain's New World empire. The Treaty of Tordesillas, whereby Spain and Portugal had divided the world between them, had become a presumption which could no longer be tolerated. Francis Drake's plunder of the Spanish West Indies and Panama and the destruction of the Spanish Armada in 1588, coupled with the arrival of powerful Dutch naval squadrons in the Indian Ocean, were destined to have calamitous effects on the imperial designs of Spain and Portugal. The gold and spice pie was about to be sliced several different ways.

Holland Takes Over

Dutch men-at-arms drove the Portuguese from the Spice Islands early in the seventeenth century and by 1621 Holland had world control of the nutmeg and clove business (Figure 12.4). By the end of the century the powerful Dutch had destroyed the Portuguese as an influence in the East and also had uprooted the English from their toeholds in the Orient. Through systematic destruction of native nutmeg and clove trees in the Spice Islands and concentration of these plants in controllable areas, the Dutch restricted the supply of spices, enabling them to regulate market prices. Dutch activity on Ceylon was parallel to that of the Portuguese, and they were at least as brutal to the cinnamon slaves as their predecessors had been. Quotas of bark were imposed on each village and default could mean torture and death to the inhabitants. The early eighteenth century saw the Dutch as masters of the spice trade—nutmeg, mace, cloves, cinnamon, black pepper, and ginger. The Dutch-held noose around the spice trade was cut toward the end of the eighteenth century when clove, nutmeg, and cinnamon plants were smuggled from Dutch-ruled areas and plantations were established by the French on their Indian Ocean islands and in other colonies. This, together with pressure exerted by the British naval blockade of the Dutch East Indian ports in 1780 and a decrease in profits, served to sound the death knell of Holland's monopoly over the spice trade. There

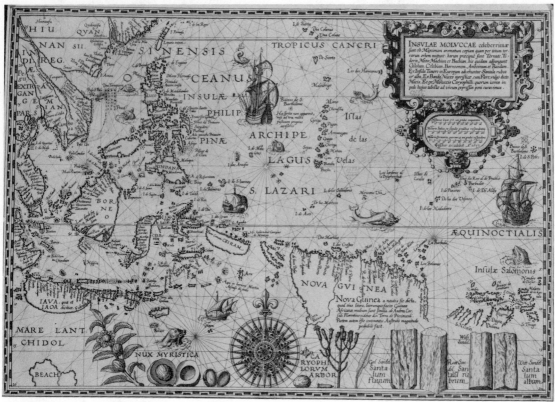

Figure 12.4 *Insulae moluccae:* Molucca Islands and surrounding spice isles are depicted in this Dutch map of 1617. On either side of the compass rose at the bottom are illustrations of nutmeg and mace, cloves, and three kinds of sandalwood. [Courtesy of and by permission British Library Board.]

were increasing losses from piracy and smuggling as well, and in 1799 the Dutch East India Company was disbanded, ending an unparalleled era in Dutch commercial supremacy.

The Spoils Are Split

Following a long period of fighting between Dutch and English forces, in 1824 these two nations concluded a treaty in which they carved up the East between them. The Dutch retained the islands of the East Indian Archipelago—Sumatra, Java, Celebes, the Moluccas—except for the northern part of Borneo, which was held by the English. The English also kept India, Ceylon, and the Malay peninsula northward to the edge of Siam. These colonial empires were to last virtually intact for almost 125 years. The British Indian Independence Act was signed in 1947 and Ceylon became sovereign in 1948. Local nationalists proclaimed the independence of Indonesia in 1945, but the stubborn Dutch did not withdraw from the East Indies until 1954. The spice lands of the East had been dominions of the West for about 450 years. Such has been the influence of botany on the affairs of nations.

Enter—The United States

The spice trade also added considerably to the coffers of the newly independent United States of America. Shortly after the Revolutionary War American ships were plying the lucrative China run. American goods—dried fish, tobacco, flour, soap, wooden articles, and candles—were traded for Oriental tea, dyes, ivory, lacquer ware, teak, ebony, rosewood, and spices. Headquarters for American shipping were centered in New England, in Boston, Salem, New Bedford, and New Haven. Voyages to the Orient were perilous; adding to the hazards of the sea voyage itself, there were Malay pirates and French privateers at sea and hostile natives ashore. In 1798 American merchant ships were authorized to arm themselves. The enormous profits which were to be gleaned from trade with the East made the dangers tolerable. It is said that some of the first millionaires in the United States owed their fortunes to these risky passages.

Of all the items of trade from the Orient, the most lucrative were the spices. And of these pepper was most profitable. According to the records, a Captain Jonathan Carnes of Salem, Massachusetts, had learned of the presence of pepper plantings on the north coast of Sumatra; during autumn of 1795 he left port bound on a secret voyage which lasted 18 months. In Sumatra he was able to purchase pepper at very favorable rates from local chiefs, avoiding the exorbitant prices charged by the Dutch on Java. He returned to New York harbor with a cargo of pepper which netted the ship's owner a profit of 700 percent. The success of this crossing set the stage for countless other voyages to the East by American skippers and it was not long before the Sumatra pepper trade was almost totally in the hands of American traders. The tremendous quantities of pepper which came into the United States through the port of Salem soon exceeded local demand and the surplus was exported either to Europe or redistributed to other places in the United States. The commercial importance of the pepper trade continued until the beginning of the Civil War in 1861.

Spice Trade Today—A Peaceful Pursuit

Modern spice trade is not today the highly centralized business it was during the sixteenth and seventeenth centuries when it was controlled by monopolistic interests. Although India and Indonesia together produce most of the world's pepper, Brazil produces substantial amounts as well. The best quality of cardamom is grown in Guatamala and the finest nutmegs and mace are shipped from Grenada in the Lesser Antilles. Allspice continues to be grown in the West Indies and true cinnamon still comes to us from Ceylon (Sri Lanka). Cloves are grown commercially in the Malagasy Republic (Madagascar) and Tanzania (Zanzibar and Pemba). Ginger is imported into the United States from Nigeria and Sierra Leone in Africa, and from Jamaica and India. The main source for vanilla is the Malagasy Republic although small quantities are grown in Mexico, Indonesia, and elsewhere. (Vanilla flavoring is manufactured chemically today and sold more cheaply than the natural product.) The most important trading centers for spices in the West are New York, Hamburg, and London while the Eastern market is dominated by Singapore. Spice giants of the past, Portugal and Holland, no longer appear in the top ranks of the today's spice trade.

Spices the World Over

Nose, nose, jolly red nose,
And what gave thee that jolly red nose?
Nutmeg and ginger, cinnamon and cloves,
That's what gave me this jolly red nose.

This refrain from a ballad popular in sixteenth- and seventeenth-century England appears in Thomas Ravenscroft's *Deuteromelia*, a collection of songs published in 1609. At about the same time, John Fletcher and Francis Beaumont published *The Knight of the Burning Pestle*, a play pointing out the evils of tobacco smoking, in which this bit of verse is incorporated. In the play, Merrythought blames spices for the sorry state of his florid nose which is actually inflamed by his love of strong liquor. Old Merrythought sings these stanzas to bamboozle his wife, after which she retorts, "If you would consider your state, you would have little lust to sing, I Wist." Merrythought's ruse has been discovered. Still, he did call attention to one of the basic qualities of spices: pungency.

Spices are pungent or aromatic substances of plant origin used as seasonings or flavorings in food; their discriminating use is associated today with gourmet cooking. They have little food value and are not eaten for their calories. Spices include such products as pepper, cloves, cinnamon, ginger, mace, nutmeg, allspice, and saffron. Closely akin to spices are the **culinary herbs** (also called **sweet herbs**), flavorings from plants such as dill, sage, coriander, basil, thyme, oregano, and parsley. It is very difficult to distinguish between spices and culinary herbs and such a distinction would only be artificial, for the latter may be considered as one group of spices. All of our important spices, however, are tropical in origin whereas the culinary herbs are mostly from temperate and subtropical plants. Although there are many spices, the world trade already described is concentrated in relatively few; only nine spices account for two-thirds of the commerce: allspice, capsicums and chilies, cardamom, cinnamon and cassia, cloves, ginger, nutmeg and mace, pepper, and vanilla. It would be difficult to pass a single day in which at least one of these spices did not pass our lips in some form. Because of this, the marked economic impact of the spice trade on world commerce, and the fascination of spice production, use, and lore, we feel a brief discussion of each of the big nine is called for.

Allspice, or Pimento

Allspice, widely known as pimento outside of the United States, is the only major spice grown on a commercial scale exclusively in the Western Hemisphere. The dried unripe fruits provide the spice of commerce which is said to combine the flavors of cinnamon, cloves, and nutmeg—hence the name. Whole berries are used for flavoring pickles, ketchup, sausages, and gravies; the ground product is incorporated in fruit cakes, pies, relishes, and preserves. In Jamaica a local drink, pimento dram, is made from the ripe berries and rum. Allspice is usually an important ingredient of the secret formulae from which Benedictine and Chartreuse liqueurs are compounded. Pimento berry oil is extracted from the dried spices and the leaf yields an oil employed in flavoring essences and perfumes. The pre-Columbian Mayans used allspice berries to embalm and help preserve the bodies of their leaders. Both spice and oil are stim-

Figure 12.5 Capsicum peppers, one of Columbus's American gifts to the Old World. [Courtesy American Spice Trade Association.]

See Plate 5b, red pepper.

ulant **carminatives,** that is, drugs which relieve flatulence. Years ago, pimento saplings from Jamaica were favored for walking sticks and umbrella handles; the plants were ruthlessly exploited before the trade was regulated in 1882 to save the young trees.

Allspice comes from a tree of the true myrtle family. It grows wild in the West Indies and Central America and is most abundant in Jamaica. Pimento was taken to Ceylon about 1824 and later to Singapore but the plantations did not thrive in either place. Today much of the crop in Jamaica is produced from semiwild trees although there is an increasing development of plantations.

Capsicum Peppers

This spice of many names all ending in pepper—bird, chili, cayenne, paprika, red, bell, sweet, devil—was called *pimienta,* "pepper," by the early Spanish explorers of the New World (Figure 12.5) because its fiery pungency reminded them of the Oriental black pepper with which they were familiar. However, capsicum peppers belong to the genus *Capsicum* of the tomato/potato family (Solanaceae); black pepper is *Piper nigrum* (Figures 12.12 and 12.13) of the piper, or pepper, family (Piperaceae). The many species of capsicum are natives of the New World and can be found in Mexico and Central America, the West Indies, and much of South America. Black pepper is Asiatic in origin. Capsicum peppers and black pepper are cultivated away from their homelands and sometimes the new growing conditions have encouraged changes in the quality and flavor of both these spices.

The capsicum spices are ground condiments made from the juiceless, ripe fruit, mainly of two species of *Capsicum (annuum* and *frutescens).* Piquancy, color, and fruit shape are exceedingly variable. Green and red sweet, or bell, peppers have the mildest flavor and contain little of the sharp principle. They are eaten raw in salads, cooked in various ways, stuffed with meat, and also pickled. Red, roundish Spanish paprikas (canned or bottled and sold as pimento) are rather bland; they are used as garnishes on salads and *paellas,* to stuff olives, and they are incorporated into cheese preparations. Hungarian paprika has long pointed fruits; it too is red but a bit more pungent than the Spanish varieties. The dried fruits are ground to produce powdered paprika which is employed as a condiment in cooking, as a garnish (on potato salad, for example), and as an essential ingredient of Hungarian goulash.

Chilies are the dried ripe fruits of pungent forms of *Capsicum annuum*. As a powdered condiment, they constitute red, or cayenne, pepper. Both chilies and cayenne pepper are used as seasonings. African chilies are very pungent; Japanese chilies are less strong. Chilies are used widely throughout the tropics, particularly in India. They are one of the hot components of curry powder, a preparation made by grinding roasted chilies with turmeric, coriander, cumin, cardamom, and other spices. An average curry powder may contain between 15 and 20 spices. Before the introduction of *Capsicum* into India black pepper *(Piper nigrum)* was used for this purpose.

Chilies are used exclusively in Central America and Mexico rather than black pepper and such dishes as hot tamales, tacos, enchiladas, and chili con carne are seasoned with this spice. Spaghetti, pizza, and barbecue sauces contain ground chilies as do some spicy sausages. Hot, or pepper, sauce preparations, such as "Tabasco," are made by pickling the fruit pulp of *Capsicum frutescens* in strong vinegar or brine and aging (Figure 12.6). Extracts of chilies are used in the manufacture of ginger beer, ginger ale, and other beverages. Cayenne pepper is added to poultry feed mixtures known as laying feeds.

Capsicum prepared as a drug from the ripe dried fruits of *Capsicum frutescens* has been used as a **counterirritant** (a drug applied in one place to relieve an irritation elsewhere in the body) in the treatment of rheumatism and as a gastric stimulant (carminative) for both man and livestock. Capsicum fruits are richer in vitamin C than citrus fruits. In 1937 Dr. Albert Szent-Györgi, a Hungarian biochemist, received a Nobel Prize for isolating vitamin C from paprika. The active ingredient in the highly pungent chilies is a crystalline substance, capsaicin. This compound is so potent as to be detectable in dilutions as great as one to one million. The hotter the pepper, the greater the content of capsaicin. Capsaicin is the active principle in commercially available aerosol animal repellents.

Figure 12.6 Pepper sauce is made by pickling the fruit pulp of *Capsicum frutescens* in vinegar and brine and allowing the mixture to age for three years in wooden casks before bottling. Shown is a scene in the plant of the McIlhenny Company of Avery Island, Louisiana, manufacturers for over 100 years of "Tabasco" Brand Pepper Sauce. [Courtesy McIlhenny Company and Walter S. McIlhenny.]

Cardamom

Cardamom seasoning comes from the seeds and fruits of a plant of the ginger family which resembles bamboo somewhat. The pea-sized fruits grow on long, branched shoots from near the base of the plant. The plants are native to the tropical evergreen rain forests of southern India and Ceylon. Before 1800 most of the spice crop was secured from wild plants which were encouraged to grow by thinning the surrounding forest to allow the sun to penetrate while providing some shade at the same time. Today, cardamom is grown in plantations but, as in nature, the plants need to be shaded. Most cardamom is produced commercially in India, in the southern states of Kerala, Mysore, and Madras; there is increasing production in Guatemala even though the spice is seldom used there.

The seeds have a pleasant aroma and a characteristic warm, slightly pungent flavor. In India cardamoms are used as a **masticatory** (a substance chewed to increase saliva flow) much as is chewing gum in the United States. It is said that the Vikings discovered cardamom during their voyages thousands of years ago and took it home with them to Scandanavia. Today genuine Danish pastries carry the faint aroma of this spice. Cardamoms give a delightful exotic flavor to baked goods, particularly to apple and pumpkin pies. They are one of the essential ingredients of Indian curry powders. Substantial amounts of cardamom are imported into the countries of the Near East where cardamom-flavored coffee is a symbol of Arab hospitality.

The whole fruits yield an oil which has been used in medicine as an aromatic stimulant and carminative. Apicius, the Roman gourmet, recommended cardamoms as a digestive aid for those who had indulged too heavily at the board. Oil of cardamom is used in perfumery, as flavoring in liqueurs and bitters, as well as to disguise ill-tasting medicines.

Cinnamon and Cassia

Bark from two species of the true laurel family provides cinnamon (*Cinnamomum zeylanicum*) and cassia (*Cinnamomum cassia*) spice. The former is native to the tropical evergreen forests of southern India and Ceylon; the latter grows in the eastern Himalayas of Burma and in South Vietnam. In the United States the spice purchased as cinnamon is usually cassia since the Food, Drug, and Cosmetic Act of 1938 allows the term *cinnamon* to be used for preparations from the bark of either or both species. In other countries it is possible to purchase both cinnamon and cassia labeled distinctively. Actually cassia bark resembles true cinnamon bark but it is coarser and thicker, has a more intense aroma, a higher oil content, and is not so delicately flavored as cinnamon. Cassia powder is reddish-brown while cinnamon powder is tan. Most of the true cinnamon imported into the United States is resold in Mexico.

Ceylon produces the best quality cinnamon bark and the bulk of the world supply. Other important cinnamon-producing countries include the Seychelles and the Malagasy Republic. Cassia bark has been supplied to the United States market from three principal sources: Saigon cassia, a variety indigenous to Vietnam; Padang cassia and Korintji cassia of Indonesian origin; and another variety of minor commercial importance from Malaysia. The best of the lot is the Saigon cassia owing to its high oil content.

Cinnamon and cassia are important baking spices and in powdered form they are used in cakes, buns, cookies, pies, fruit sauces, and puddings. Curry powder may contain cinnamon. Stick cinnamon, in the form of a quill (a roll of bark formed while drying) is an important pickling ingredient and it is used in preparing stewed and spiced fruits, baked apples, and in liqueurs. In Mexico hot chocolate is seasoned with cinnamon sticks. Cinnamon oil, extracted from the bark, is used for flavoring candies, chewing gum, dentifrices, and medicines and in the manufacture of incense, perfumes, soaps, aromatic sachets, and aerosol space deodorants.

Cloves

The name clove comes from the French *clou*, "nail," from the nail-shaped, dried, unopened flower bud (Figures 12.7 and 12.8). The spice is produced by trees of the true myrtle family. Clove trees are indigenous to the small volcanic islands of the Molucca group—the Spice Islands of old. In ancient times cloves were used to check tooth decay and to counter halitosis. Now, in the East, cloves are used as a table spice and in the manufacture of curry powders. By far the greatest use of cloves is in the manufacture of a peculiar Indonesian cigarette, the **kretek** (from the crackling of the burning product), and fully one-half of world production is consumed in this way. These cigarettes contain one-third shredded cloves and two-thirds tobacco. The smoke is strong, pungent, and aromatic. In the West cloves are available either ground or whole. Whole cloves are commonly used to decorate and flavor baked hams and pork roasts. They are added to pickled fruits, spiced hot drinks, cold punches, and meat gravies. Ground cloves may enliven bland puddings and add zest to fruit cakes and other desserts.

Figure 12.7 Harvesting cloves on Zanzibar. The dried unopened flower bud provides the spice of commerce. [Courtesy American Spice Trade Association.]

Figure 12.8 On Madagascar, harvested cloves are spread on mats to sun dry in dooryards of the clove workers' homes. [Courtesy Benjamin H. Kaestner, III, and McCormick & Company.]

Clove oil, produced by the distillation of cloves, flower stalks, and leaves, is used in the manufacture of perfumes (carnation odor), aromatic sachets, soaps, bath salts, and as flavorings. In dentistry it acts as an **astringent** (a drug which shrinks tissues); it flavors dentifrices, chewing gum, and candies. In medicine cloves are stimulative, **antispasmodic** (drugs with a sedative effect on the nervous system), and carminative.

Ginger

Ginger spice comes from the fleshy **rhizome** (rootstock which produces both aerial green shoots and roots) of a tropical plant which looks like bamboo (Figure 12.9). Ginger was one of the earliest spices, with black pepper, to have made its way to the West. The ginger plant can no longer be found in the wild state, so long has it been under cultivation. Even the exact region of origin is not known, but it is somewhere in southern Asia and it may have been India.

Ginger flavoring is one of the most penetratingly pungent of all spices. It is obtained from fresh or dried rhizomes which may be scraped, peeled, or boiled before drying. In Western countries, ginger is widely used for cooking purposes as in gingerbread (which was well known in Queen Elizabeth I's time), cakes, sauces, and soups, and in pickles. Ground ginger imparts a delightful flavor and bouquet when rubbed sparingly on meat, fowl, and fish before cooking. It is one of the frequent constituents of curry powder and is the most widely used spice in Chinese and Hawaiian/Polynesian cuisine. Ginger is used in the United States to flavor soft drinks and in England, ginger beer and porter.

Candies and preserves are also made from ginger. In the preparation of both, fresh, peeled and sliced ginger rhizomes are boiled in sugar syrup. Preserved ginger is bottled in thick sugar syrup, whereas in candymaking, the boiling process is allowed to continue until sugar crystals have formed around the strips of ginger. The strips are then dried and dusted with powdered sugar before sale.

Ginger oil is obtained by steam distillation from ground ginger. Until recent years, owing to its weak pungency, it has not been widely used. However, a growing market has recently been found for ginger oil in the preparation of men's toiletries. By contrast with the weakly pungent ginger oil, the **oleoresin** (natural product of a volatile oil and a resin) of ginger is very pungent and it is this product which is used to flavor soft drinks and ginger beer.

Ginger is widely used in local medicines in the Orient. Internally, it is a stimulating carminative and externally it acts as a counterirritant. It was used for similar purposes in Western medicine for man and livestock. Like so many other spices, ginger is supposed to be an aphrodisiac. (Urologists suggest that spices irritate the genitourinary system and may seem to stimulate the libido.) In seventeenth-century England, Nicholas Culpepper, an herbalist, prescribed ginger because it helps digestion, warms the stomach, clears the sight, and is profitable for old men; it heats the joints and is therefore useful against the gout; it expels wind. Henry VIII of England appears to have used ginger to ward off the plague. In the fifth century A.D., living ginger plants were carried aboard Oriental ships and the rhizomes were eaten to prevent **scurvy** (a disease resulting from an insufficiency of vitamin C) long before Western man had any ideas on the subject.

Ginger is available ground, cracked (broken bits), or whole, and whole ginger can be purchased either fresh or dried. India is the world's largest producer. Small amounts of the spice are

Figure 12.9 Ginger plant showing massive development of fleshy rhizomes from which the several ginger spice preparations are derived. [Courtesy U.S. Department of Agriculture.]

Figure 12.10 Dried whole fruits of the nutmeg tree. The upper two fruits still have the split fruit wall intact. Enclosed by the light-colored "blades of mace," is the seed proper, the nutmeg of commerce.

See Plate 5c, nutmeg.

Figure 12.11 Branchlet of nutmeg tree with two mature, apricotlike fruits each of which has only one seed. [Courtesy U.S. Department of Agriculture.]

imported into the United States from Jamaica, Nigeria, Sierra Leone, Haiti, and Taiwan. Jamaican ginger is the very finest available on the market.

Nutmeg and Mace

Both of these spices come from the same tropical evergreen tree of the nutmeg family. Nutmeg spice is the seed and mace is the fleshy, netted, red-to-orange membrane (**aril**) which surrounds the seed (Figure 12.10). There is just one seed in each apricotlike fruit (Figure 12.11). The original home of the nutmeg tree is, like cloves, in the Molucca Islands, and although they are rare, wild nutmeg trees may still be found there. Unlike ginger and black pepper, nutmeg and mace are relative newcomers to the West. They were not widely known in Europe much before 600 A.D. and their introduction is related to the spice-trading activities of the disciples of Mohammed. Grenada today produces the best nutmegs and mace, although substantial quantities are imported from Ceylon and from the island of Banda and others of the Molucca Islands, the native habitat of the tree.

Both nutmeg and mace are pleasantly aromatic and spicy but they taste different. They are used in small quantities to flavor bland milk dishes such as eggnog and custard, in cakes and cookies, and in puddings and fruit pies. Mace, however, is preferred for fish sauces, meat stuffings, and oyster stew. "Mace," says Rosengarten, "makes doughnuts taste like doughnuts."

Nutmeg is available whole or ground and mace is ordinarily only sold as a ground condiment; "blades of mace," the whole product, are not frequently marketed. Whole dried nutmegs are sometimes coated with powdered lime. This practice dates from the seventeenth century when the Dutch monopolists of the Moluccas soaked fresh nutmegs in milk of lime (calcium hydroxide in water) to kill the embryo in the seed to prevent purchasers from germinating seeds to start their own plantations. Strangely, though there is no longer any need for soaking the seeds in lime, many purchasers even today look for the lime coating as a symbol of authenticity and will only consider nutmegs so adorned.

The volatile oil extracted from nutmeg is used to flavor baked goods, table sauces, candies, dental preparations, perfumes, and toiletries. Nutmeg is sometimes used medicinally and is said to have stimulative, carminative, astringent, and aphrodisiac properties, although today it has a very limited place in Western medicine. In England, however, nutmeg is still carried in the *British Pharmacopoeia* as a drug for compounding certain tonics. Nutmeg butter, prepared from broken seeds and from mace which are not acceptable as spices, is used in ointments and perfumery.

Volatile oils of nutmeg and mace contain about 4 percent of a highly toxic substance, **myristicin,** and as little as 4 or 5 grams (454 grams equal 1 pound) are enough to induce symptoms of poisoning in man. Continued ingestion of large quantities can result in fatty degeneration of the liver. Powdered nutmeg is sometimes taken by adventurers looking for highs or kicks, since it has hallucinogenic properties (see Chapter 10). Nutmeg jags can cause headaches, nausea, dizziness, and other deleterious toxic side effects.

Figure 12.12 Vine of black pepper.

Pepper

Black and white pepper are products of the same tropical, woody vine (Figure 12.12), *Piper nigrum,* of the pepper family (Piperaceae; cf. *Capsicum* peppers). Pepper is native to the forest-clad slopes of the humid Malabar Coast of southwestern India where it is still grown commercially. Pepper fruits hang from the stem in narrow bunches on short branchlets (Figure 12.13). Without doubt, pepper is and has been the world's most important spice, the one around which empires were built and which was responsible for the rise and fall of the fortunes of important trading cities. Chefs say this is true because of the versatility of pepper; it may be added during three stages of food utilization: first, during the actual preparation of the food; second, during and after the cooking process; and finally, at the dinner table. Others attribute the popularity of pepper to its long storage life: Whole pepper, or peppercorns, can be stored for many years without losing their piquancy. The flavor of pepper is stimulatingly pungent and the aroma of freshly ground pepper has no parallel among the spices.

The main use of pepper has always been as a spice, that is, as a condiment to flavor food. Oil of pepper and oleoresin of pepper are used to flavor sausages and other preserved meats as well as in salad dressings, ketchup, and table sauces. Uses of dried pepper as a condiment—whole, ground, cracked—are numerous and there is scarcely a recipe, except those involving sweet foods, which does not call for pepper to improve and enhance the flavor of the food. Pepper is a major ingredient of

Figure 12.13 Cluster of ripening black pepper fruits.

pickling mixtures. The biting flavor of pepper provides a culinary diversion for those persons who must adhere to a salt-free diet.

Black pepper is prepared from the unripe, green fruits of the pepper vine. The fruits are picked and left in piles for a few days to ferment after which they are spread out for drying. The resulting product—the entire peppercorn—now dark brown or black, becomes the spice sold as black pepper. White pepper, on the other hand, is prepared from almost ripe fruits, fruits which are just at the point of turning red. Fruits are picked and placed in sacks suspended in slowly running water. The water-softened fruits are then rubbed to remove the outer layers. The now gray, dehulled peppercorns are washed once more and allowed to dry in the sun. The final product is creamy white. In the United States the robustly flavored black pepper is more popular than the delicately flavored white pepper and 11 times more of the former is imported than of the latter. Pepper is imported into the United States from southern Sumatra and other regions of Indonesia, from the Malabar Coast of India, from Sarawak on the island of Borneo, and recently, from the State of Pará in Brazil.

Vanilla

Vanilla flavoring has been called "the spice that is not a spice" because of the absence of volatile oils found in other spices and perhaps to the lack of a noticeably tingly sensation on the tongue. Nevertheless, vanilla is included in most general works on spices and is considered as a spice by the trade. Vanilla is a tropical green vine bearing thick leathery leaves. It is a member of the orchid family, the only one which has commercial importance other than as an ornamental plant (Figure 12.14). Botanically it is known as *Vanilla planifolia*, the generic name having been derived from the Spanish, *vainilla*, which means "little pod" and refers to the beanlike shape of the fruit. The vanilla of commerce is native in the humid lowland forests of southeastern Mexico, Central America, some Caribbean islands, and in parts of northern South America. In the wild it may become a huge plant climbing to the tops of tall forest trees. Rosengarten points out that although unknown outside of the Western Hemisphere until about 1520, "vanilla is the outstanding contribution of the Western Hemisphere to the spices of the world."

Figure 12.14 Flowers and flower buds of vanilla, a member of the orchid family. Vanilla flowers are pale yellow-green, aromatic, and remain open for less than one day. [Courtesy U.S. Department of Agriculture.]

The spice is obtained from the dried and cured fully grown but unripe fruits commercially called beans (Figure 12.15). The fruits are not aromatic nor flavorful when picked but gradually develop fragrance and flavor during the involved and lengthy curing process. Well-cured vanilla beans stored in tightly sealed containers will keep indefinitely.

Purists prefer to use the actual bean for flavoring foods rather than the extract but most vanilla flavoring is marketed, es-

Figure 12.15 Small-scale farmers on Madagascar grow vanilla beans and then sell them to curers in nearby towns. Here a curer's agent is purchasing locally produced beans. [Courtesy Vanilla Information Bureau.]

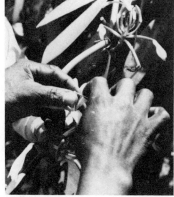

Figure 12.16 Vanilla flowers, like those of most orchids, are insect pollinated. The bees which naturally pollinate vanilla flowers, however, are indigenous to the native home of vanilla in the New World. Whenever vanilla is grown elsewhere, it must be artificially hand-pollinated in order for fruits (beans) to "set." In the picture, a deft-fingered Madagascan transfers a pollen mass to the pistil of a vanilla flower using a bamboo splinter. [Courtesy Benjamin H. Kaestner, III, and McCormick & Company.]

pecially in the United States, in the form of pure vanilla extract. This extract, made by dissolving out the savory principles from macerated fruit, is a favorite flavoring in ice cream, soft drinks, eggnogs, tobacco, baked goods, liqueurs, custards, and puddings. Vanilla is the key flavoring in most chocolates and it tends to reinforce the characteristic chocolate flavor. It is also used as a long-lasting, fragrant scent and as a base for face powder and soap perfumes.

The Malagasy Republic produces about 80 percent of the world crop of vanilla beans (Figure 12.16). Other producers are Réunion and the Seychelles in the Indian Ocean, Mexico, the French Pacific islands, Indonesia, and Uganda. Mexico, which was the first producer, still has the reputation of growing the best quality vanilla.

Unlike the flavor essences of most spices, vanilla flavoring has been manufactured synthetically (from **lignin,** a by-product of the paper pulp industry). In the United States manufacturers of vanilla flavoring are required to state on the container label whether the contents are artificial (imitation) or pure. Although artificial vanilla flavoring is far cheaper than pure extract of vanilla, it lacks the savory delicacy and delightful bouquet of the natural product.

Suggested Readings

American Spice Trade Association. *A Glossary of Spices.* New York: American Spice Trade Association, 1966. Contains brief write-ups of important spices and culinary herbs; pamphlet available from publisher.

1-212-420-8808

————. *A History of Spices.* Englewood Cliffs, N.J.: American Spice Trade Association, 1972. Concise story of development of spice trade; pamphlet available from publisher.

————. *Your Spice Shelf Cookbook.* Englewood Cliffs, N.J.: American Spice Trade Association, 1972. Pamphlet available from publisher.

Collins, Mary (pseudonym). *The McCormick Spices of the World Cookbook.* New York: McGraw-Hill, 1964.

Crosby, Alfred W., Jr. *The Columbian Exchange: Biological and Cultural Consequences of 1492.* Westport, Conn.: Greenwood Publishing Company, 1972. Well-written, scholarly approach which considers the two-way transfer of New World and Old World products including spices, drugs, edible plants, and diseases.

Day, Avanelle, and Lillie Stuckey. *The Spice Cookbook.* New York: David White Company, 1964. Comprehensive uses of spices in cookery.

Hewes, Agnes Danforth. *Spice Ho! A Story of Discovery.* 2d ed. New York: Knopf, 1947. Easy reading, good plot.

Norman, Barbara. *Tales of the Table: A History of Western Cuisine.* Englewood Cliffs, N.J.: Prentice-Hall, 1972.

Parry, John W. *Spices: Morphology, Histology, Chemistry.* 2d ed. New York: Chemical Publishing Company, 1969. Technical monograph.

————. *Spices: The Story of Spices.* 2d ed. New York: Chemical Publishing Company, 1969. Authoritative.

Ries, Maurice. *The 100 Year History of Tabasco.* Avery Island, La.: McIlhenny Company, 1968. An interesting success story of personal enterprise and commerce involving a single spice, the capsicum pepper.

Rosengarten, Frederic, Jr. *The Book of Spices.* Philadelphia: Livingston Publishing Company, 1969. Very best all-around book; contains gourmet recipes using each spice and culinary herb; beautiful pictures; complete; highly authoritative.

Vanilla Information Bureau. *Vanilla Desserts Cookbook.* New York: Vanilla Information Bureau (UNIVANILLE), 1972. Pamphlet available from publisher.

Verrill, A. Hyatt. *Perfumes and Spices Including an Account of Soaps and Cosmetics.* Boston: L. C. Page & Company, 1940.

Plant Names

Common name	Scientific name	Family	Part used
allspice	*Pimenta dioica*	Myrtaceae	fruits
aloes	{ *Aquilaria agallocha* or *Santalum album*	Thymelaeaceae Santalaceae	fragrant wood
anise	*Pimpinella anisum*	Umbelliferae	"seed"*
basil	*Ocimum basilicum*	Labiatae	leaves
bay	*Laurus nobilis*	Lauraceae	leaves
caraway	*Carum carvi*	Umbelliferae	"seed"
cardamom	*Elettaria cardamomum*	Zingiberaceae	seed and fruit
cassia	*Cinnamomum cassia*	Lauraceae	bark
cinnamon	*Cinnamomum zeylanicum*	Lauraceae	bark
clove	*Eugenia caryophyllus*	Myrtaceae	flower bud
coriander	*Coriandrum sativum*	Umbelliferae	"seed"
cumin	*Cuminum cyminum*	Umbelliferae	"seed"
dill	*Anethum graveolens*	Umbelliferae	"seed," leaves
fennel	*Foeniculum vulgare*	Umbelliferae	"seed," leaves
frankincense	*Boswellia* spp.	Burseraceae	bark resin
garlic	*Allium sativum*	Liliaceae	bulb
ginger	*Zingiber officinale*	Zingiberaceae	rhizome
mace	*Myristica fragrans*	Myristicaceae	aril
mint	*Mentha* spp.	Labiatae	leaves
mustard	*Sinapis alba*	Cruciferae	seed
myrrh	*Commiphora myrrha*	Burseraceae	bark resin
nutmeg	*Myristica fragrans*	Myristicaceae	seed
oregano	{ *Origanum* spp. and *Lippia* spp.	Labiatae Verbenaceae	leaves and flowering tops
parsley	*Petroselinum crispum*	Umbelliferae	leaves
pepper, black	*Piper nigrum*	Piperaceae	unripe fruits
pepper, capsicum	*Capsicum* spp.	Solanaceae	fruits
pepper, chili	*Capsicum* spp.	Solanaceae	fruits
pepper, red	*Capsicum* spp.	Solanaceae	fruits
pepper, white	*Piper nigrum*	Piperaceae	ripe fruits
poppy	*Papaver somniferum*	Papaveraceae	seed
rosemary	*Rosmarinus officinalis*	Labiatae	leaves
saffron	*Crocus sativus*	Iridaceae	stigmas
sage	*Salvia officinalis* and other species	Labiatae	leaves

*The "seed" of the Umbelliferae (carrot family) is botanically a fruit.

tarragon	*Artemisia dracunculus*	Compositae	leaves and tops
thyme	*Thymus vulgaris*	Labiatae	leaves and tops
turmeric	*Curcuma longa*	Zingiberaceae	rhizome
vanilla	*Vanilla planifolia*	Orchidaceae	fruits

Rockweed (*Fucus*), the common brown
alga found attached to rocky ledges
along the Atlantic coast. Note the
dichotomously branched thallus and
the floats or air bladders.

13
Algae
Grass of Many Waters

We borrow this subtitle from the late Professor Lewis Tiffany of Northwestern University, who many years ago wrote a book with this title. By it he wished to dramatize not only that algae are found in all sorts of waters—ponds, lakes, ditches, pools, swamps, puddles, brooks, rivers, and in the saline waters of oceans—but that algae serve the same purpose in aquatic environments as do grasses on land, that is, they are the chief source of food for animals.

In the listing of major plant groups given in Chapter 3, we stated that the thallophytes, defined as plants without true roots, stems, and leaves, are composed of two divisions—the **algae** (singular, **alga**) and the fungi. The algae differ from the fungi in that they have chlorophyll and therefore can carry on photosynthesis.

The algae, some of whose 21,000 species are called seaweeds, sea mosses, and by such unattractive names as pond scums, frog spittle, and frog slime, are a heterogeneous assemblage of mostly aquatic plants ranging all the way from simple, microscopic, swimming, unicellular forms to giant marine kelps which may attain a length of 200 feet and show considerable differentiation, including massive rootlike holdfasts, large blades resembling leaves, and stemlike stipes. The algae are classified on the basis of their pigments, nature of their motile cells, and type of food stored. We shall not be able to consider all the groups but will need to concentrate on a few representative types to elucidate the striking evolutionary developments in the algae; then we will try to show the importance of this group in terms of ecology and their human relevance.

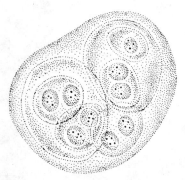

Figure 13.1 *Gloeocapsa* cells surrounded by jelly or gelatinous material.

Blue-Green Algae

As the name suggests these algae typically have chlorophyll plus a blue pigment and a red pigment. (The Red Sea derives its name from the circumstance that one of the blue-green algae has a high percentage of the red pigment and thus gives the water a red color.)

Most of the blue-greens occur in fresh water or in the soil and on damp stones and on the sides of flower pots. Several species grow in hot springs, such as those of Yellowstone National Park where the temperature of the spring water may reach 77 degrees centigrade. These thermal algae, as they are sometimes designated, cause the precipitation of calcium and potassium salts, forming travertine which becomes brilliantly colored by the algae present.

As you can see from Figure 13.1, these are extremely simple organisms consisting of but one cell. This single cell itself is simple, having a cell wall, cytoplasm in which the chlorophyll and the blue pigment are diffused, and finally, scattered chromatin material. There is no organized nucleus with a bounding nuclear membrane, there are no organized chloroplasts with membranes, and there are no mitochondria nor endoplasmic reticula. This unique and evolutionarily primitive cytological structure of the blue-green algae resembles that of the bacteria, and, in fact, these two groups are sometimes classified together for this reason.

Furthermore, as far as we know there is no sexual reproduction in the blue-green algae and even the method of asexual reproduction is a primitive type—simple cell division, or **fission,** in which a single cell divides and forms two new cells, or individuals. Sometimes the products of successive divisions stick together forming a spherical mass or in some species, a filament or thread. These loose associations of cells are designated **colonies,** by which we mean that all the cells are alike (i.e., there is no differentiation or specialization among them) and, further, any one of the cells may break free and lead an independent existence.

Green Algae

The green algae have a chlorophyll complement roughly comparable to that in the higher plants—in other words, there is no masking pigment such as in the blue-green algae and in some of the other groups we shall mention later. Sometimes the green algae are referred to as the grass-green algae for the reason just given.

Most green algae live in fresh water, although some are marine, while others occur in and on soil, and still others are found on tree trunks and branches and on rocks. Several are called snow or ice algae because of their habitats; others, strangely, are able to live in brine lakes with salt concentrations several times that in the oceans of the world. Some species have become funguslike in that they have lost their chlorophyll and have become parasites upon plants; one, for example, causes a rather serious disease of tea and pepper plants.

The group displays a considerable range of specialization, therefore, we will select three to illustrate the possible progression in specialization, or evolution.

A common green alga which grows on the bark of trees in temperate regions is known as *Protococcus*. (Because the algae rarely impinge directly on the lives of lay people, there are few common names for the various species and genera, except for some of the conspicuous marine algae or seaweeds. Hence we are forced to use the generic names.) *Protococcus* (Figure 13.2) is unicellular, sometimes forming loose clusters or colonies. Unlike the blue-green alga we previously described, *Protococcus* has a definite, organized nucleus surrounded by a nuclear membrane and each cell has a well-organized chloroplast also encased in a membrane. *Protococcus* resembles the blue-greens in that the sole method of reproduction is cell division.

An interesting green alga which grows in fresh water is *Ulothrix* (Figure 13.3), consisting of a filament of cells in which the basal one, the **holdfast cell,** functions to attach the plant to the substrate. The cells of the filament have organized nuclei and definite chloroplasts with membranes. At some time in the life of this alga, 2 to 32 bodies may develop in some of the cells of the filament. When the cell wall breaks down these smaller bodies, or cells, leave the filament. At this stage each one bears four whips, or **flagella** (singular, **flagellum**) by means of which they swim about. Eventually, these cells may lodge in favorable places and then each by repeated cell divisions produces a chain of cells resembling the parent filament. This process, of course, is **reproduction,** specifically **asexual reproduction** for there is no fusion of cells. The motile cells with four flagella are known as **zoospores. Spores** are asexual reproduc-

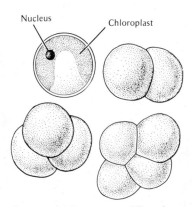

Figure 13.2 *Protococcus* cells and colonies.

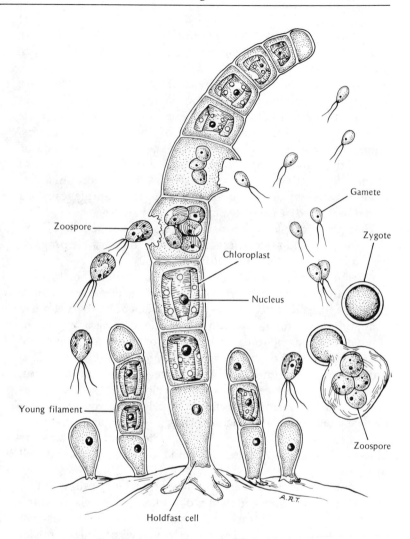

Figure 13.3 *Ulothrix.* Multicellular filament (in center) showing holdfast cell at base. To the right is shown the sexual cycle, and to the left, asexual reproduction by zoospores.

tive cells, and zoospores are so called because they swim, or are motile.

In addition, there is another type of reproduction in *Ulothrix.* At certain times, some of the cells of the plant form 8 to 64 small, internal bodies or cells. These too are released from the parent cell and they can be seen to resemble the zoospores except that they are smaller and each bears but two flagella. Furthermore, these cells do not produce new filaments directly, but two of them fuse. (The two cells that fuse may come from different filaments or from the same filament.) These two fusing cells are sex cells called **gametes** and the resulting cell is termed a **zygote.** The zygote eventually forms four zoospores which act like the other zoospores and thus each one forms a new individual. This process of fusing of the two gametes is **fertilization,** and, of course, is **sexual reproduction** since two cells unite, or fuse. But note that in *Ulothrix* the two gametes are exactly alike in size, appearance, and behavior; you cannot say that one is male and the other a female—there is no maleness or femaleness—there is no sexism, so to speak. This primitive type of sexual reproduction involving the union of two similar gametes is called **isogamy,** literally a "marriage of equals."

Previously, we called your attention to the similarity in appearance of the zoospores and gametes—the only differences are that the gametes are smaller and have only two flagella. Some botanists have suggested that originally the ancestors of *Ulothrix* or some such alga may have produced only zoospores. And then there came a time when the zoospores were so small, underdeveloped, and with so little food and protoplasm that they lacked the energy to produce new individuals directly. Rather, two underdeveloped—hungry, if you will—zoospores fused, thus pooling their resources, so to speak. This may have been the first case of sexual reproduction. This highly speculative explanation for the origin of sex has been called the hunger theory of sex—in case you may have wondered how it all began.

Ulothrix is considered not to be a colony but a true **multicellular individual** for there are differences among the cells of the filament—a holdfast cell, cells producing zoospores, and cells forming gametes.

Oedogonium (Figure 13.4) is another fresh-water alga which resembles *Ulothrix* in that it has a holdfast cell and the vegetative cells of the filament all have organized nuclei and chloroplasts. *Oedogonium* also produces zoospores which behave like the zoospores of *Ulothrix*. Sexual reproduction in this alga is a little more advanced than that of *Ulothrix*. Some of the cells in the filament produce two motile cells called male gametes, or **sperms,** which resemble the zoospores except that they are smaller. Other cells of the filament enlarge and each develops a large female gamete, or **egg,** which becomes packed with food. The sperm swims to the egg and unites with it to form a zygote. This process, of course, is fertilization but of a higher type than that in *Ulothrix*, since there is a definite male gamete, or sperm, and a distinct female gamete, or egg, which is larger than the sperm and is stationary. This type of fertilization in which there

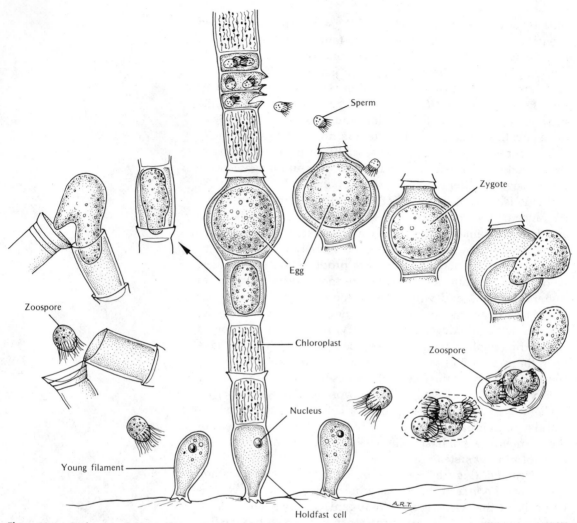

Figure 13.4 *Oedogonium.* Center filament shows basal holdfast cell. Circle to right shows the sexual cycle and the circle to the left depicts asexual reproduction by means of a zoospore.

is a union of unlike, or dissimilar gametes is called **heterogamy,** literally a "marriage of unequals." In some species of *Oedogonium* (Figure 13.5) there are separate male and female plants. Some zoospores when they germinate produce short filaments termed **dwarf males** because each is reduced to little more than a sperm-producing cell on a short spur or branch attached to the female plant. These dwarf males remind one of the marine worm *Bonellia* in which the male is reduced to a tiny, microscopic structure which spends its entire life in the kidneylike structure of the female and whose only function is to fertilize the eggs of the female.

Another form of green algae which we should at least mention are the **desmids,** favorite objects of study by the microscopists of past centuries who were strongly attracted to them by their infinite variety and their exquisite beauty (Figure 13.6). They are important constituents of the **plankton** (free-floating and swimming organisms) in acid bogs and lakes.

In this short discussion of several varieties of green algae you will have at least glimpsed what we mean by evolution, the progression from simple unicellular forms to colonies to true multicellular individuals. And with respect to reproduction, you will have observed the gradual specialization from plants which reproduce only by cell division, to those with zoospores, to others with isogamy, and finally to those with heterogamy. And later we shall see that this evolutionary process continues with the development of plants producing multicellular sex organs, to those bearing seeds, and finally to those which develop flowers.

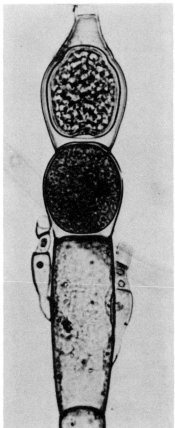

Figure 13.5 Female *Oedogonium* filament with two dwarf males attached. Lower enlarged, spherical cell contains an egg; the cell above has a zygote with thick wall. [Courtesy Turtox/Cambosco, Macmillan Science Co.]

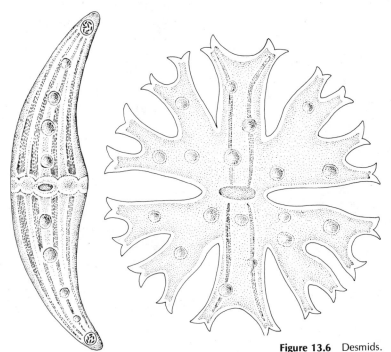

Figure 13.6 Desmids.

Brown Algae

An evolutionary line parallel to the green algae is the brown algae (Figure 13.7) which are, however, mostly marine, commonly denizens of cold waters although they are also found in warm marine waters. They are typically shore-inhabiting forms attached to rocks, reefs, and similar substrates. A few species are free floating. Even though these plants are thallophytes, among them are the largest plants known—some of the marine kelps are 200 feet long with massive **holdfasts** that remind one of roots, thick stemlike **stipes,** strap-shaped **blades** which function like leaves, and gas-filled **floats,** or **air bladders,** which give buoyancy to these huge plants (Figures 13.8, 13.9, and 13.10). In addition to these large kelps, the brown algae include the sea palms (Figure 13.11), and the long leathery straplike devil's aprons, or *Laminaria* (Figure 13.12).

Figure 13.7 Cells of a brown alga photographed with an electron microscope showing nucleus, nucleolus, chloroplasts, mitochondria, and other cellular bodies. [Courtesy Donald R. Markey.]

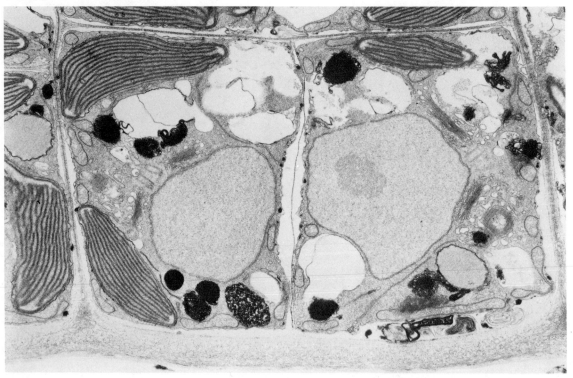

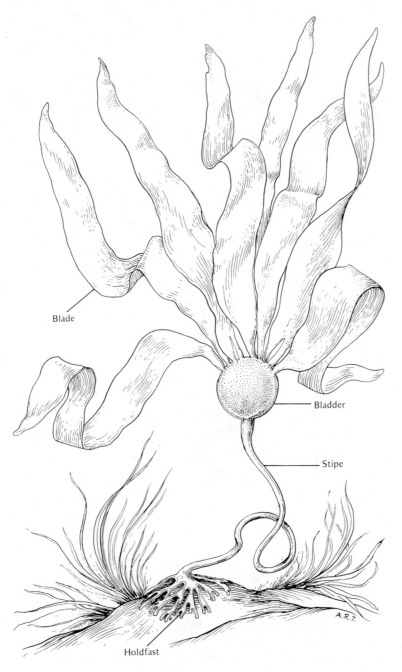

Blade

Bladder

Stipe

Holdfast

A.R.T.

Figure 13.8 Bull or bladder kelp
(*Nereocystis*).

Figure 13.9 Giant or vine kelp (*Macrocystis*).

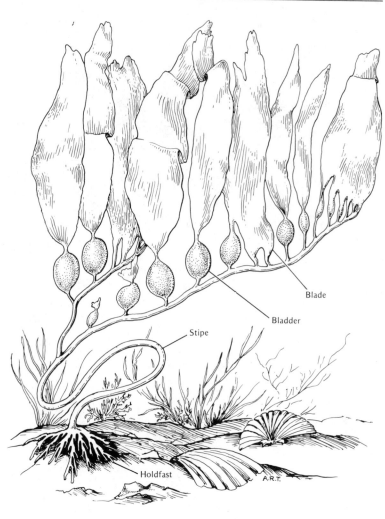

Figure 13.10 Elk kelp (*Pelagophycus*). [Courtesy Smithsonian Institution.]

See photograph on page 336, rockweed.

Rockweeds (*Fucus*, Figure 13.13) are familiar to those who have frequented the rocky shores of the North Atlantic. These shore-line or tidal-zone algae are attached to rocks by means of a basal disk and the plant itself is dichotomously branched (forked). In the enlarged tips of the plant are cavities in which are produced the male and female gametes. These are discharged into the open water where fertilization takes place (Fig-

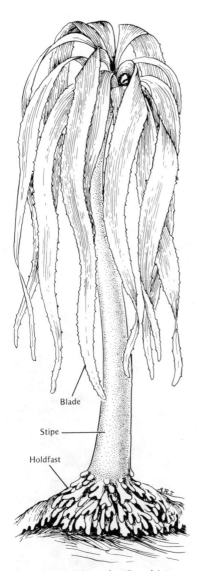

Figure 13.11 Sea palm (*Postelsia*) with holdfast, thick stipe, and crown of terminal blades.

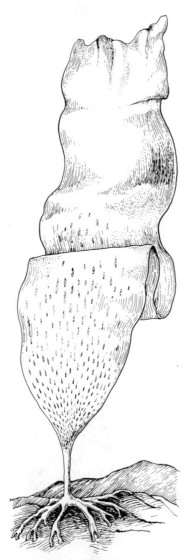

Figure 13.12 Devil's apron (*Laminaria*) with holdfast, stipe, and large straplike blade.

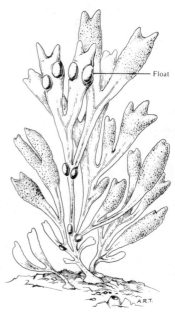

Figure 13.13 Rockweed (*Fucus*).

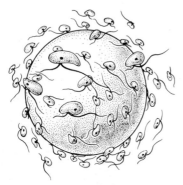

Figure 13.14 Fertilization of rock-weed (*Fucus*); large egg surrounded by a flock of small sperms.

ure 13.14). Since the male gametes are smaller than the eggs this process is a type of heterogamy. For decades *Fucus* has been used in college classes to demonstrate fertilization. Drops of sea water with male gametes and eggs are placed together under the microscope and soon clouds of sperms are seen hovering around the eggs. There is so much lashing of flagella that the egg is thrown into a fast spin. After a time, one sperm fuses with the egg and the other sperms swim away.

Figure 13.15 Gulfweed (*Sargassum*). [Courtesy Smithsonian Institution.]

Another brown alga is the gulfweed, or *Sargassum* (Figures 13.15 and 13.16), which derives its name from the Sargasso Sea where enormous numbers are found floating in those calm waters whence some may be distributed to the more northerly parts of the Atlantic by storms and by ocean currents. The Sargasso Sea, the home of the gulfweed, is a vast area of the Atlantic Ocean east of the West Indies roughly equivalent in size to the continental United States (approximately 2.5 million square miles). It is said that no other region of the earth produces so great an acreage of a single species of plant—the

Float

Figure 13.16 Gulfweed (*Sargassum*).

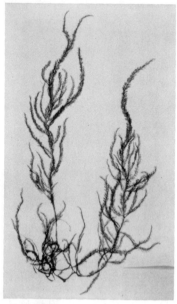

Figure 13.17 *Dasya,* a red alga.
[Courtesy Albert C. Smith.]

gulfweed. You may recall that Columbus in 1492 sailed through this sea, much to the terror of his sailors who were familiar with the legend that this sea was the mythical marine purgatory where ships became becalmed for months and eventually were doomed to circle endlessly in this naval graveyard. This alga bears a striking resemblance to a higher plant for it has what appear to be stems, leaves, and fruits. The putative stems and leaves are not true stems and leaves and the presumed fruits are bladders or floats.

Red Algae

A third evolutionary line parallel to the greens and browns is the red algae (Figures 13.17, 13.18, 13.19, and 13.20) which, as the name suggests, are forms with chlorophyll and a red pig-

Figure 13.18 Dulse (*Rhodymenia*), sold at seaside resorts and at seafood stores. [Courtesy Albert C. Smith.]

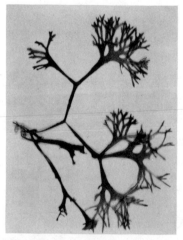

Figure 13.19 Irish moss (*Chondrus crispus*). [Courtesy Albert C. Smith.]

Figure 13.20 Red alga (*Gelidium*), one of the sources of agar. [Courtesy Albert C. Smith.]

ment. Most species are marine and typically inhabit warm waters where they may be some of the deepest growing plants. Some of these forms, frequently referred to as sea mosses, are brilliantly colored, delicately divided, suggesting feathers. They are one of the main attractions in the glass-bottomed sight-seeing boats around such islands as Bermuda and the Bahamas.

Diatoms

A fourth evolutionary line of algae is the **diatoms,** which are abundant in fresh and salt water as well as in the soil and belong to a group of algae known as the golden-brown algae. Diatoms may be said quite literally to live in glass houses for each of these unicellular organisms is encased in two glass, or silica, shells which fit together like two halves of a box. Diatoms occur in unbelievably diverse shapes and forms—disks, rods, wedges, boatlike objects and hundreds of other different configurations. As you can see in Figures 13.21, 13.22, 13.23, 13.24, and 13.25 they are objects of great beauty—indeed, they have been lauded as the "jewels of the plant world."

Impact of Algae on Man

Food for Fish and Other Aquatic Animals

As is emphasized by the title of this chapter—Algae: Grass of Many Waters—the main significance of these plants lies in the fact that they are the great food, and hence energy, source for fish and other aquatic animals. They occupy the basic and key position in the great food chains of the oceans and bodies of fresh water. Much of this food is provided by the algae in the **plankton** (Figure 21.10), the small, free-floating or swimming organisms (representing scores of species of plants and animals) at the surface of all bodies of water, fresh or salt. A blue whale measuring 75 feet and weighing 60 tons may have as much as 2 tons of plankton, mostly diatoms, in its gut at one time.

It is now well known that the quantity of algae present in a body of water is directly related to the size of the fish population of that body, and this in turn has a direct bearing on the size of the fishermen's catch. It has been observed that the most productive fishing areas are seldom very distant from fields of algae, particularly diatoms. For these reasons investigations of

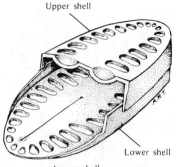

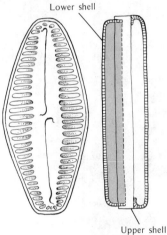

Figure 13.21 Diatoms. Top figure shows how the upper silica shell fits over the lower shell. Lower left figure depicts the top view of a diatom; lower right is a side view revealing the manner in which the two silica shells or halves fit together.

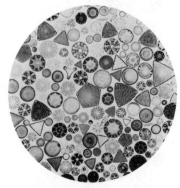

Figure 13.22 Several dozen species of diatoms, showing the diversity of form. [Courtesy Smithsonian Institution.]

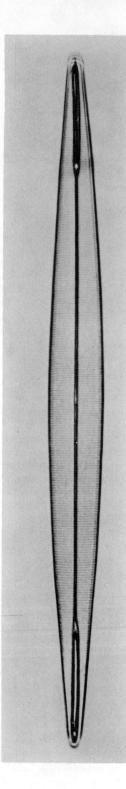

Figure 13.23 A bilateral diatom (*Amphipleura pellucida*). [Courtesy Bausch & Lomb Optical Co.]

all aspects of the lives of algae are important elements in the research programs of marine biological stations and government fisheries.

Algae as Human Food

Algae also furnish some human food—the red alga dulse (Figure 13.18) which is sold by the bag along with popcorn at seaside resorts, the green alga sea lettuce (Figure 13.26), and the red alga Irish moss (Figure 13.19) from which a dessert is made. All told some 100 species of algae are eaten by man, especially

Figure 13.24 A round diatom (*Arachnoidiscus ehrenbergii*). [Courtesy Bausch & Lomb Optical Co.]

5a

Plate 5

5a   Henbane *(Hyoscyamus niger)*, source of hallucinogens.

5b   Red pepper *(Capsicum)* fruits, source of the spice.

5c   Nutmeg *(Myristica fragrans)*, seed surrounded by red mace.

5c

5b

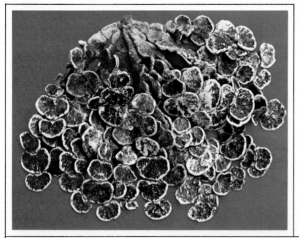

6a

6b

Plate 6

6a Coralline or calcareous algae, which by their activities build up coral or atoll reefs.

6b Cup fungus.

6c Queen Victoria water lily *(Victoria regia)*.

6c

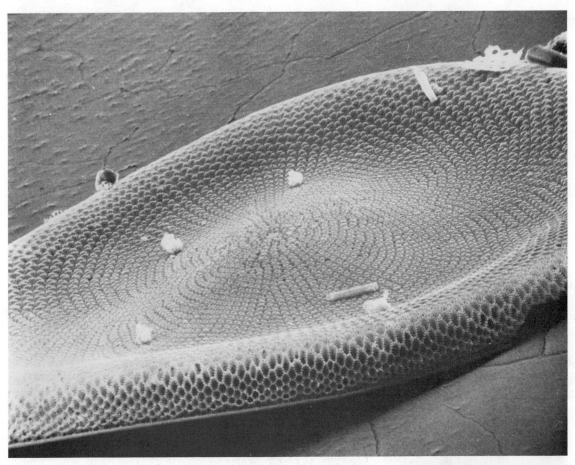

Figure 13.25   Diatom, as seen with the scanning electron microscope. [Courtesy Johns-Manville Co.]

by the Japanese, Chinese, Polynesians, and other inhabitants of the oceanic islands of the Pacific. The Japanese cultivate algae (Figure 13.27) by driving bamboo poles into shallow bays and hanging nets from these poles so that algae will attach themselves to the nets. At a later time the nets with the algae affixed are pulled up and the algae harvested. There is every indication that this type of marine agriculture will expand as the food

Figure 13.26   Sea lettuce (*Ulva*). [Courtesy Albert C. Smith.]

Figure 13.27 Drying the marine alga *Undaria* to prepare the food dish known as *wakame* in Japan. [Courtesy Walter H. Hodge.]

problem worsens. And much may be said in praise of algae as food, since they are well endowed with minerals (potassium, calcium, for instance), iodine (there is little or no goiter among algal feeders), vitamins (especially A and E but with some C and D), and finally there is a mild, built-in laxative in the form of the gelatin most of the algae possess.

Algae as Stock Feed

For centuries farmers have also gone down to the seas to gather seaweeds such as rockweed, *Sargassum*, dulse, and kelps which have washed up on the beaches, particularly after storms, and the collected algae have been fed to stock as a fodder additive. In some places such as the British Isles, Scandinavia, and on the coast of France, farmers drive their cattle to the seashore to allow the animals to graze on the seaweeds at low tide.

Algae as Fertilizer

Farms located in close proximity to oceans have been for thousands of years, and continue to be, fertilized with the algae collected from the beaches and spread on the fields where they add to the mineral content of the soil, function to retain water in the soil for long periods of time, and add to the humus of the soil through their slow disintegration. Catherine Bowen in her *Yankee from Olympus* tells us that John Adams, "staunch and stubborn, representative of a century that was past, rose to his feet, and turned his back on the White House and a world which had treated him unkindly, went home to his farm at Quincy, Massachusetts. In his barnyard, he found a hundred loads of seaweed. A fine load of manure, said Mr. Adams, paraphrasing Horace, was fair exchange for the honors and virtues of the world."

Diatomaceous Earth

Another valuable economic product derived from algae is **diatomaceous earth.** When diatoms die their empty silica shells sink to the bottom of the ocean or the lake or wherever they are growing. After millions of years large deposits of **diatomaceous earth** (Figure 13.28) may be built up, as in California where the deposits may be as extensive as 3 to 4 square miles and 700 feet deep, for instance, the White Hills of Lompoc. The material is harvested by power shovels, then used in the manufacture of scouring powders and of polishes for silver and other metals, for the production of insulating material, and for use as filters for oil and for syrup in refineries. Formerly it was incorporated in tooth pastes and powders but it is a little harsh on the enamel of the teeth. A special use is in the manufacture of light-weight brick utilized in the construction of massive domes and in other places where weight is a critical factor. As early as 532 A.D., Emperor Justinian ordered the dome of the Church of St. Sophia in Istanbul to be constructed from bricks fabricated from diatomaceous earth because of their light weight.

Formerly diatom shells were used to test the resolving power of microscope lenses, for their shells possess series of tiny dots. If the resolving power (the ability to distinguish detail) of the microscope is high the individual dots will be seen distinctly, but if the resolving power is poor the series of dots will merge as one line.

Figure 13.28 Ledge in the largest deposit of diatomaceous earth ever discovered—in Lompoc, California. [Courtesy Johns-Manville Co.]

Finally, it is thought that diatoms may have played a part, along with other photosynthetic algae, in producing the vast oil deposits of the world. We know that oil is elaborated in the metabolism of diatoms and that diatom remains are associated with oil fields.

Industrial Uses of Algae

In addition to the commercial uses of diatoms already described, other algae are harvested for their content of potassium, calcium, iodine, and algin, or algal jelly. In the Pacific Ocean specifically outfitted ships or barges are equipped with mechanical mowers which cut the kelps below the water line and then hoist them aboard. The algin is used to thicken soups and to smooth ice cream and puddings, and it has innumerable additional uses in polishes, paints, French salad dressing, and cosmetics. **Agar,** the gelatin derived from some red algae (Figure 13.20), has important biological and medical use as a culture medium on which to grow bacteria, fungi, and tissues of higher organisms.

Algae as Land-formers

See Plate 6a, coralline or calcareous algae.

The coralline, calcareous, or coral algae, belonging to the red and green algae, as well as to other algal groups, play a major role in building up so-called coral or atoll reefs. They absorb the calcium of the sea, incorporate it in their bodies, and when they die, they leave deposits of calcium carbonate or limestone which accumulate in large quantities and eventually build up land in the ocean. Formerly it was thought that the coral animals were exclusively responsible for the creation of coral islands but we now know that the role of the coral algae in these activities is a major one.

Ecological Role of Algae

Ecologically, algae are important not only because they furnish food to aquatic animals but they also give off oxygen in the process of photosynthesis which is used by animals in their respiration. The surplus oxygen purifies the water by oxidizing organic materials. In addition, the oxygen promotes the growth of certain bacteria (called **aerobic** bacteria since they require gaseous oxygen) which are active in the decomposition of organic materials such as sewage. Of course, if the algae grow too profusely, as under conditions of overfertilization with nitrates and phosphates, the floating masses of algae which result may prevent light from reaching the algae growing at lower water levels and so exert a deleterious effect. These algal mats may also use up so much oxygen in their respiration at night that fish and other aquatic organisms suffocate. Finally, the accumulation of dead algae may further overburden the water with organic materials. It should be noted, however, that such extreme conditions of algal growth are usually the result of overfertilization, or **eutrophication.**

Harmful Aspects of Algae

Also on the negative side of the ledger, algae may contaminate water supplies in reservoirs, lakes, ponds, and pools. Blue-green algae, particularly, may form **water blooms,** or **algal blooms,** which are extensive accumulations of algae that develop in ponds and lakes during the warm days of summer. These algae, and other algae such as some green and golden-brown algae, elaborate oils which are foul smelling (having a pigpenlike odor) and give the water a fishy taste. Besides rendering the water unfit for drinking purposes and unattractive for swimming, occasionally the algae in water blooms poison cattle. The offending algae may be eradicated by treating the water with dilute solutions of copper sulfate.

Reports of the **red tide,** the consequent death of millions of fish, and the contamination of shellfish so that they are unfit for human consumption occur every year. The red tide is caused by an overabundance of swimming unicellular algae known as **dinoflagellates** (Figure 13.29). These motile, red-pigmented algae are usually present in sea water in fairly small numbers but under favorable growth conditions they may suddenly multiply at a furious rate, so that a single quart of water may have as many as one million of them. Each cell elaborates a powerful poison which, like curare, produces paralysis, and death results because the muscles needed for breathing cease to function. As a consequence, the dinoflagellates cause serious plagues among fish and other marine creatures, killing millions of them, with the result that huge, stinking masses are often washed up on beaches.

Algae also contribute to the **fouling** of ships—the growth of algae, barnacles, oysters, and other marine life on the hulls of ships. Within a year following the launching of a ship, it may

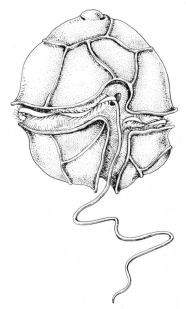

Figure 13.29 Dinoflagellate (*Gonyaulax*) which causes red tide.

have a growth of this material to a depth of three to four inches and weighing hundreds of tons. The speed of the vessel may thus be retarded by as much as 50 percent and the fuel bill increased markedly. Owners of large ocean liners of the *Queen Elizabeth* class are often forced to spend over $100,000 a year for defouling.

Summary

The **algae** play a significant role in the ecology of oceans and of fresh water in that they are the ultimate food-suppliers in **aquatic food chains.** They have certain economic uses as we have seen, as well as ways in which they lead to economic loss—contamination of water, destruction of fish by the red tide, and fouling of ships.

From an evolutionary standpoint algae are extremely reveal-ing for they include primitive **blue-green unicells** with little cellular differentiation—no organized nuclei and chloroplasts, no mitochondria and endoplasmic reticula. There is **no sexual reproduction** in these forms and the only method of reproduc-tion is the very simple asexual method of **cell divison.** The **higher algae** (greens, browns, and reds) have organized nuclei and chloroplasts as well as mitochondria and endoplasmic re-ticula. Some of the greens form loose aggregations of cells called **colonies** and still others achieve the **multicellular state.** They have a higher type of **asexual reproduction,** namely by **zoo-spores.** Some of the greens reveal a primitive type of **sexual reproduction—isogamy**—while others have attained the level of sexual reproduction known as **heterogamy.** Thus, a great deal of **evolution** has taken place, we think, in the vast assemblage of diverse forms known as the algae. And it was from the algae —probably the green algae—that the land plants had their origin. Significantly the blue-green algae which show every morphological reason for being considered primitive plants have been discovered as fossils in Precambrian rocks which are over 3 billion years old.

Suggested Readings

Alexopoulos, Constantine J., and Harold C. Bold. *Algae and Fungi.* New York: Macmillan, 1967. A good general treatment of the algae and fungi, particularly their structure and life histories, by two recognized scholars in their respective fields.

Bold, Harold C. *The Plant Kingdom*. 4th ed. Englewood Cliffs, N. J.: Prentice-Hall, 1977. A brief but fairly comprehensive coverage of the plant kingdom with a particularly good section on the algae. Highly recommended for the student who seeks to broaden his knowledge of the structure and evolutionary development of plants.

Dawson, E. Yale. *Marine Botany*. New York: Holt, Rinehart and Winston, 1966. Especially recommended for its able exposition on marine algae—structure, ecology, geographical distribution, and uses.

Fuller, Harry J., and Oswald Tippo. *College Botany*. 2d ed. New York: Holt, 1954. A general botany textbook with an extensive section on algae.

Guberlet, Muriel L. *Seaweeds at Ebb Tide*. Seattle: University of Washington Press, 1956. An attractive handbook for the amateur who seeks to identify seaweeds encountered on the Pacific Coast, particularly the Pacific Northwest. Well-executed drawings.

Kingsbury, John M. *Seaweeds of Cape Cod and the Islands*. Chatham, Mass.: Chatham Press, 1969. An excellent field guide for the beginner who wants to know the Atlantic Coast seaweeds, especially those found on Cape Cod. Handsome drawings.

Petry, Loren C. *A Beachcomber's Botany*. Chatham, Mass.: Chatham Conservation Foundation, 1968. Deals with the common plants encountered at the seashore, including conspicuous marine algae. Focused on Cape Cod but useful anywhere along the New England coast. Well illustrated, and written by a renowned Cornell botany professor.

Tiffany, Lewis H. *Algae: The Grass of Many Waters*. 2d ed. Springfield, Ill.: Charles C. Thomas, 1958. A nontechnical introduction to various facets of algae, including their structure, physiology, ecology, and utility.

A group of gill or agaric mushrooms.

14
Fungi
Microbes, Molds, Mildews,
and Mushrooms

The **fungi** are a fascinating group of organisms which have great economic importance and thus have had and continue to have a profound impact on man. Indeed, this galaxy of plants is of such import that three separate branches of botany focus on fungi—**mycology,** the study of fungi; **plant pathology,** the study of plant diseases; and **bacteriology,** or **microbiology,** the study of bacteria, viruses, and similar microscopic or even smaller structures. The last, microbiology, is of such consequence that it is usually segregated as a separate science, distinct from botany.

In the list of plant groups given in Chapter 3, we indicated that the thallophytes, defined as plants without roots, stems, and leaves, encompass the algae and **fungi** (singular, **fungus**). Whereas the algae have chlorophyll and can manufacture carbohydrates, the fungi lack chlorophyll and therefore they are either **parasites** or **saprophytes** or both.

By a **parasite** is meant an organism which derives its food from another living organism, called a **host**; examples of fungal parasites are the fungi which cause corn smut, wheat rust, and Dutch elm disease. A **saprophyte** is a plant which obtains its food from a dead organism or from nonliving organic food such as the humus in the forest floor or the cellulose and/or lignin in a dead log; examples of fungal saprophytes are mushrooms, puffballs, and most yeasts.

Some fungi may be either parasite or saprophyte. The blue mold *(Penicillium)* which grows on citrus fruits may begin as a

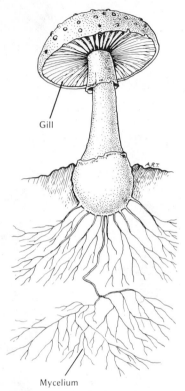

Gill

Mycelium

Figure 14.1 Mushroom with extensive underground mycelium.

parasite as it attacks the living cells of the fruit, but when the host cells die, the mold takes up a saprophytic mode of existence. Likewise the fungus causing the Dutch elm disease is a parasite while the elm tree is alive; when the tree dies, the fungus lives on the dead wood as a saprophyte. In either case—parasite or saprophyte—the fungus secretes enzymes which carry on **digestion** outside the body of the fungus; that is to say, foods in the substrate are rendered soluble so that they may be absorbed by the fungus.

Plant Body

The bodies of most fungi consist of threads or filaments which collectively make up the **mycelium.** In some of the higher fungi the mycelium forms a definite, easily visible, **fruiting body,** such as the familiar mushroom or puffball or cup fungus. It should be noted that the mushroom of the market, the puffball, or the cup fungus is only a small fraction of the whole body, for most of the fungus consists of an extensive, ramifying mycelial system below the ground or embedded in a log (Figure 14.1). The mycelial system has enormous surface area through which absorption takes place.

Reproduction

As might be expected in a group of organisms with such a high proportion of parasites, the fungi have well-developed, efficient reproductive methods, including the production of very large numbers of reproductive cells, particularly **spores** (generally one-celled, asexual reproductive structures). It is estimated that a single puffball may contain seven trillion spores. Some spores have thick walls and contain little water, consequently they are very resistant to both high and low temperatures. They require no water and so may lie dormant on a dusty shelf for years and then when the proper conditions of moisture and temperature occur, they germinate.

Spores, being tiny, are light. Many are dry and hence airborne; we know that they can travel thousands of miles and that they may reach altitudes of at least 13 miles above the earth. Other spores are sticky and are carried principally by insects. Some fungi, such as the rusts, produce as many as four different kinds of spores in their life cycles. All in all, spores play a large part in the lives of fungi and doubtless this may explain why the fungi are so successful—measured in terms of numbers of species, numbers of individuals, and their wide distribution. Fungi are truly ubiquitous, for there is virtually no place on earth where some species of fungi do not grow.

Fungi reproduce by another asexual method, too, namely by **fragmentation.** A piece of thread or filament breaks off the parent plant and this fragment regenerates another fungus plant.

Fungi also reproduce sexually—by isogamy, in many of the lower forms, and by heterogamy.

Groups of Fungi

The fungi are conservatively estimated as having at least 100,000 described species, with probably a total of 250,000 species in nature. Some 1,500 to 2,000 new species are added each year as the result of research and exploration. Fungi are classified in a variety of ways; indeed, some students of the group hold that they constitute a separate kingdom coordinate with the plant and animal kingdoms. For the purposes of this book we shall refer to 4 groups of fungi: bacteria (Schizomycetes), algal-fungi (Phycomycetes), sac fungi (Ascomycetes), and club fungi (Basidiomycetes). The last 3 groups, exclusive of the bacteria, are frequently referred to as the true fungi.

Bacteria

The bacteria (or Schizomycetes, Figure 14.2) are often classified as a separate group of organisms—sometimes with the blue-green algae because both groups are primitive, unicellular organisms which reproduce by simple cell division and cytologically both are alike in that they lack nuclear membranes.

Bacteria have become so important in modern biological research, as well as in agriculture, industry, and medicine, that their study constitutes a separate biological science, bacteriology or microbiology. We shall therefore not tarry long with bacteriology. Suffice it to say that bacteria are unicellular organisms, although some species form filaments or threads (i.e., Actinomycetes, several of which produce antibiotics of importance) suggestive of some of the higher fungi.

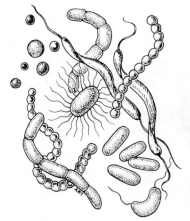

Figure 14.2 Bacteria: sphere, rod, spiral, and filamentous types.

Their usual method of reproduction is by cell division, although some produce spores. (Since only one spore is formed in each bacterial cell, it may be questioned whether spore formation in bacteria is a type of reproduction. Spores may be formed when conditions are unfavorable for growth, and thus may be merely a resistant or dormant stage.) In recent years it has been discovered that some bacteria exchange genes, thereby constituting a primitive type of sexual reproduction.

Bacterial fission may occur at a very rapid rate so that enormous numbers of bacteria may be produced under favorable circumstances. Some bacteria divide every 20 to 30 minutes; at this rate, at the end of 24 hours, there would be hundreds of trillions of cells. It has been estimated that one bacterium reproducing at this rate could in 5 days produce sufficient progeny to fill all the oceans of the world. Of course, this does not come close to actually happening because the food supply is limited and other conditions may not be favorable—there may be competition from other organisms such as algae, fungi, and other bacteria. Finally, the accumulation by the bacteria of toxic substances from their own excreted waste products also prevents the attainment of this theoretical number of bacteria.

Nevertheless, bacteria are found everywhere—in the water, in the soil, in the air, and in and on all organisms. In fact, it is sometimes said that if everything were removed from the earth but bacteria, we would still have the outlines of everything on the globe—bodies of water, sewers, plowed fields, intestines of people, tabletops, and so on.

While most bacteria are either parasites or saprophytes, there are two groups which are able to manufacture their own food. The purple bacteria, for example, have a chlorophyll-like pigment which makes it possible for them to carry on photosynthesis. The other category of bacteria oxidizes inorganic compounds such as nitrates, ammonia, and hydrogen sulfide, and then uses the energy thus derived to synthesize organic materials. This latter process is called **chemosynthesis.**

Paradoxically, bacteria are of enormous benefit to man, as well as of great detriment to him and his activities. It can almost be said that we cannot easily live with them nor can we live without them. Bacteria are of course one of the chief causes of human diseases (other causes include viruses, protozoa, worms, and higher fungi). Examples of bacteria-caused human diseases are diphtheria, tuberculosis, typhoid fever, pneumonia, syphilis, and tetanus (or lockjaw). Bacteria also cause diseases of domestic animals—tuberculosis of cattle, blackleg of cattle and sheep, and chicken cholera, merely to name a few. Although many plant diseases are brought about by higher fungi, some very important ones are induced by bacteria—fire blight of pears and of apples and bacterial wilt of corn, for instance. Some bacteria rob the soil of nitrogen in a process called **denitrification.** In addition, extraordinary quantities of food are spoiled by bacteria and have to be discarded. Further, because of activities of bacteria and fungi man must take the precaution of drying or canning or freezing to preserve his foods.

On the other hand, bacteria are of great utility to us, for they are instrumental in causing **decay** of dead plant and animal bodies. Were it not for bacterial activity, and the activity of other fungi, the earth would be covered with dead plant bodies and the carcasses of animals—not to mention the fact that we would soon lack enough raw materials from which more plants and animals could be formed. Fortunately bacteria and other fungi break down proteins, carbohydrates, and fats into simple compounds such as carbon dioxide, water, and nitrates, compounds which can be absorbed and used again by plants. Some free-living bacteria and others living in a symbiotic relationship in the nodules of legumes and other plants have the ability to take free, gaseous nitrogen from the air, combine it with other elements, and thus render it usable by plants. This is the process called **nitrogen-fixation.**

Bacteria play a key role in a number of industrial and agricultural processes including the manufacture of vinegar, the ripening of cream to form butter, the flavoring of some cheese, the production of silage, the manufacture of sauerkraut from cabbage, as well as the production of countless organic chemicals such as acetic, butyric, and lactic acids. Some bacteria, chiefly the filamentous types, or actinomycetes, are the source of valuable antibiotics such as streptomycin, Aureomycin, and Chloromycetin. Selman A. Waksman (1888–1974), a Rutgers University microbiologist, received a Nobel Prize in 1952 for his discovery of streptomycin.

Algal-Fungi

The first group of true fungi is the algal-fungi (or Phycomycetes), molds consisting of filaments forming a loose mycelium rather than being in the form of definite, compact bodies as is true of the fruiting bodies of mushrooms, puffballs, and cup fungi. The name algal-fungi alludes to the fact that they resemble the algae in reproductive methods—some have swimming zoospores and motile gametes and some forms reproduce by isogamy or heterogamy, quite reminiscent of the algae.

A common algal-fungus is the saprophytic bread mold (Figure 14.3)—or at least it was common until bakers put preserva-

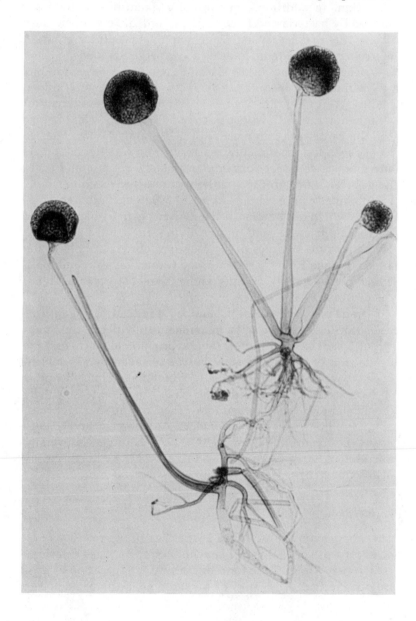

Figure 14.3 Bread mold (*Rhizopus nigricans*) with terminal, black spore cases. [Courtesy Carolina Biological Supply Co.]

tives or fungicides in bread and other bakery products. The mold forms a white cottony growth on the surface of the bread; later, black spots may appear—these are the black spore cases containing numerous spores. There are also many genera of water molds which grow saprophytically on dead fish, insects, and other aquatic animals in fresh and salt water. Some species attack fish as in the home goldfish bowl and some cause epidemics of fish cholera in fish hatcheries.

One of the troublesome plant parasites in this group is the very destructive potato blight fungus about which we shall write in greater detail later in this chapter.

Figure 14.4 Cup fungus (*Sarcocypha occidentalis*). [Courtesy Leland Shanor.]
See Plate 6b, cup fungus.

Sac fungi

A second group of true fungi is the sac fungi (or Ascomycetes) which bear this name because they produce a sac (or ascus) containing spores. Representative examples of saprophytes in this group are the cup fungi (Figure 14.4), the edible morels (Figure 14.5), and the yeasts (Figure 14.6) of baking, wine-making, and brewing fame. The green and black molds (*Aspergillus*) and the blue molds (*Penicillium*, Figures 14.7 and 14.8) are common forms growing on citrus fruits, vegetables, leather, and a variety of other materials. The fungi causing chestnut blight and the Dutch elm disease are two very destructive parasites among the sac fungi.

Many sac fungi (as well as club fungi) form an association between their mycelium and the roots of higher plants, especially trees. This root-mycelium combination is called a **mycorrhiza** (plural, **mycorrhizae**). This intimate relationship between the higher plant and a fungus is considered to be **symbiosis,** an association between two species in which there is mutual benefit. The higher plant, in this instance, supplies carbohydrate to the fungus and the latter provides miles of hairlike mycelium which absorbs water and nutrients from the soil and then passes these materials along to the root system of the higher plant. It is estimated that over 90 percent of our trees are at least partially dependent on mycorrhizae.

Club Fungi

The last group of true fungi comprises the club fungi (or Basidiomycetes). They have this designation because somewhere in their life cycles they produce characteristically a club-shaped structure (or basidium) which usually bears four spores on

Figure 14.5 Morel (*Morchella esculenta*), a fleshy, edible sac fungus. [Courtesy Howard E. Bigelow.]

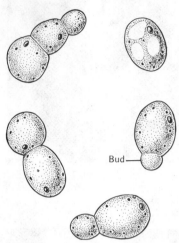

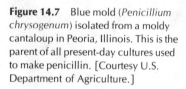

Figure 14.6   Yeast; some with buds.

Figure 14.7   Blue mold (*Penicillium chrysogenum*) isolated from a moldy cantaloup in Peoria, Illinois. This is the parent of all present-day cultures used to make penicillin. [Courtesy U.S. Department of Agriculture.]

See photograph on page 360, mushrooms.

short pegs. The common saprophytes of this group are the mushrooms (Figures 14.9 and 14.10), puffballs (Figure 14.11), coral fungi (Figure 14.12), bird's nest fungus (Figure 14.13), earthstars (Figure 14.15), and stinkhorns (Phallales, Figure 14.14). Some of our most destructive fungal parasites are club fungi—smuts on corn (Figure 14.16), wheat, oats and other cereals and rusts on wheat, pine, coffee, and apple. In addition, the shelf, or bracket, fungi (Figure 14.17) belong here; some of them are saprophytes which cause the decay of enormous quantities of logs, timber, and lumber while others are parasites which are equally destructive of living trees.

Lichens

While we are discussing the various types of fungi, we need to mention a group of unique organisms which are not strictly fungi but they do have a fungal component. These **lichens,**

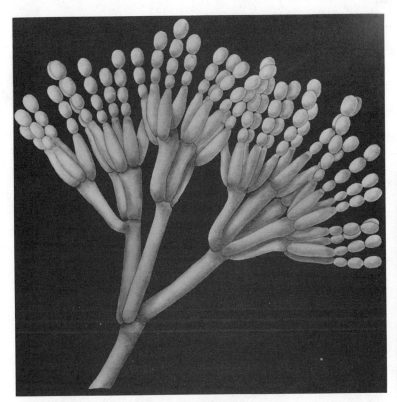

Figure 14.8 Blue mold (*Penicillium chrysogenum*); tips of filaments producing chains of spores. [Courtesy U.S. Department of Agriculture.]

Figure 14.9 Destroying angel or death angel (*Amanita virosa*), one of the deadliest of the toxic mushrooms. [Courtesy Howard E. Bigelow.]

Figure 14.10 Mushroom (*Lepiota*) "fairy ring"; the mycelium grows outward from an original inoculation center, producing successive circles of fruiting bodies. [Courtesy Henry Aldrich.]

Figure 14.11   Puffballs (*Calvatia craniformis*). [Courtesy Howard E. Bigelow.]

Figure 14.12   Coral fungus (*Clavaria*).

Figure 14.13   Bird's nest fungus (*Crucibulum vulgare*). [Courtesy Leland Shanor.]

Figure 14.14   Stinkhorn (*Phallus impudicus*). [Courtesy Henry Aldrich.]

Figure 14.15   Earthstar (*Geastrum triplex*). [Courtesy Howard E. Bigelow.]

Figure 14.16 Corn smut fungus (*Usti-lago maydis*); the large tumorlike growths are filled with great masses of black smut spores. [Courtesy U.S. Department of Agriculture.]

Figure 14.17 Shelf or bracket fungus (*Fomes applanatus*).

Figure 14.18 Lichens on tree trunk.

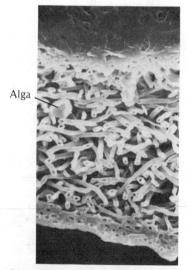

Figure 14.19 Scanning electron microscope photograph of section of lichen showing spherical algal cells and the threads of the fungal mycelium. [Courtesy Mason E. Hale, Jr.]

commonly seen as green-gray growths on the sides of trees and on rocks (Figures 14.18, 14.19, and 21.14), are not simple or single organisms but are combinations of two species—an alga and a fungus. Such a relationship is sometimes described as **symbiosis.** In this instance, the alga supplies the food and the fungus absorbs water and transmits it to the alga. In addition, the fungus affords a certain amount of physical protection to the alga. Some botanists regard this relationship in which the alga furnishes the food as one closer to parasitism rather than true symbiosis. A popular botany book of a century ago, refers to a lichen as an "unnatural union between a captive algal damsel and a tyrant fungal master." The algal (usually green or blue-green algae) and fungal (usually sac fungi) components can be separated and cultured apart, and certain algae and fungi may be brought together to form synthetic lichens.

Lichens play a conspicuous role in ecology for they are among the first plants to colonize, or to establish a beachhead, on bare rocks, cliffs, and mountains. After they have etched the rocks and accumulated a certain amount of minerals and organic matter, other plants such as mosses and wiry grasses come in; later, various tough herbs and small shrubs, and finally trees complete this **succession** of vegetational types.

In the far north lichens known as reindeer moss form carpetlike masses to a depth of eight inches and cover hundreds of square miles. This material is an essential source of food for reindeer and other animals. Another lichen of boreal North America, known as rock tripe, was often eaten by Indians and French trappers and explorers. One explanation for the manna of the Bible which descended from the sky in response to the prayers of the Israelites is that lichens were blown off the mountains by strong winds—a phenomenon which occurs at the present time.

Various pigments are derived from lichens, including the pigment found in litmus paper used in chemistry to determine the acidity or alkalinity of a solution and the pigment used to dye Harris Tweeds. In earlier days, lichen dyes were dissolved in human urine and then the yarns were immersed in this mixture. The salts in the urine functioned as mordants and fixed the dyes.

In recent decades evidence has been accumulating that some of the lichens produce antibiotics.

Because lichens are sensitive, they are reliable indicators of atmospheric pollution. Indeed, a few years ago the startling dis-

Alga

covery was made that even though Lapland is 10,000 miles from the site of the early atomic bomb explosions in the Pacific Ocean, Laplanders absorb more radiation than other people of the earth. This is traceable to the fact that these people subsist largely on reindeer and caribou meat which, upon investigation, was found to have high concentrations of radioactive chemicals, or isotopes. The reindeer and caribou, in turn, acquire the radioactive substances from reindeer moss, the chief food of the animals. It has been pointed out that since lichens do not have roots they obtain much of their mineral nutrients from the dust of the air. Thus they are easy victims of atomic fallout for they are not protected by the dilution which takes place in the soil, nor by the selective absorption and further dilution which occurs in the roots. It is significant that the reindeer and caribou as well as the Lapps accumulate radioactive substances in their tissues; reindeer and caribou may have 4 times the concentration of isotopes found in lichens, while the Lapps may have 100 times the concentration in the lichens.

Harmful Activities of Fungi

Spoilage of Food and Destruction of Other Materials

We remarked earlier that an extraordinary quantity of food is destroyed each year by the true fungi (fungi exclusive of bacteria). Everyone has observed molds on citrus and other fruits, on vegetables of all types, and on bread and other bakery products. In addition, fungi grow on flour, meat, and on dairy products such as milk, cream, butter, and cheese. As a result of the threat of fungal growth, we have to go to the trouble and expense of food preservation. Bread and other bakery goods commonly have chemical mold inhibitors added to them to protect them from fungi.

In addition to foods, all sorts of other materials are attacked and sometimes destroyed by fungi. During World War II when so many of our military operations were staged in the humid tropics, we learned anew that virtually nothing is safe from the ravages of fungi. Indeed, a whole new field of research in **tropical deterioration** sprang up in response to the serious problems of the armed forces. Among the materials attacked by fungi are rope, cloth and other fabrics, sacks or bags, tents, paper, books, leather, glue, paint, rubber, plastics, electrical insulation (including that in radios), photographic supplies, and optical equipment such as binoculars, gun sights, range finders, telescopes, and microscopes. The fungal mycelium grows over the lenses of optical equipment and clouds them thus rendering them ineffective. In some instances the enzymes secreted by the fungi actually etch the lenses so that they are permanently damaged.

Destruction of Wood

Another great source of economic loss attributable to the fungi is the destruction of wood in standing trees, in the logs of felled timber, in piled and stored lumber, and in the wood finally installed in place in houses or other structures. It is estimated that this loss in the United States reaches $9 billion a year.

There are several thousand species of wood-destroying fungi which belong to the club fungi. They often form fruiting bodies (Figure 14.17) on the sides of tree trunks and on logs which resemble shelves or brackets, hence they are frequently referred to as shelf or bracket fungi. These fungi secrete enzymes which dissolve the cellulose or the lignin or both in the cell walls of the wood. In this fashion the fungi derive their carbohydrates. But as a result of the action of the enzymes, the cell walls of the wood are weakened, if not completely destroyed, and there is thus produced a condition which is known as **wood decay** or **wood rot.**

To protect against wood-destroying fungi, wood is usually dried, or **seasoned,** to remove enough water so that fungal growth is inhibited; it is also treated with chemicals known to be poisonous, such as creosote, pentachlorophenol, and copper naphthenate. In this connection, it should be remarked that paint in itself does not eliminate fungal growth unless a fungicide has been added to the paint. Paint does help to keep the wood dry and in this indirect manner may help to minimize fungal growth and decay.

Plant Diseases

One of the chief sources of the devastation wrought by fungi is their role in causing thousands of plant diseases, variously referred to as wilts, blights, rusts, smuts (Figure 14.16), rots, and mildews. Virtually every species of seed plant is subject to one or more diseases induced by fungi; some plants—potato, bean, and cotton—are subject to 30 or more diseases. There are some 200 infectious diseases of maples, aside from insects, weather, and injuries related to modern life (e.g., winter salting of highways). Some fungi parasitize a number of different hosts (e.g., the damping-off fungi which attack young seedlings), while others are restricted to but one host species or genus (e.g., wheat rust, corn smut, and Dutch elm disease).

On a world-wide basis fungi are responsible for crop losses amounting to billions of dollars each year. In the United States, plant diseases during the decade 1951–1960 cost an estimated $4.25 billion plus an additional $.25 billion expended for disease-control programs. Generally losses amount to one percent of the gross national product, or 10 percent of the annual agricultural production.

We have already noted the havoc wrought by the terrible potato famine caused by the potato blight in Ireland in the middle of the nineteenth century. Here we have a dramatic illustration of the profound impact a single plant, in this instance a humble algal-fungus, can have on the lives of untold millions of people and, indeed, on the course of history.

The people of the time were perplexed by the disease and particularly mystified by a possible cause of the malady. Prizes were offered to anyone who could furnish proof for the cause of the disease and provide effective recommendations for its control. One person suggested that the disease was induced by the electricity from the locomotives which tore through the Irish countryside at the frightening speed of 20 miles an hour. The Reverend Miles J. Berkeley, who became interested in fungi, cautiously advanced the theory that the blight was brought about by a fungus—for which he was ridiculed. It was not until 1855 that the German mycologist Anton De Bary proved that potato blight was caused by an algal-fungus, or Phycomycete (*Phytophthora infestans*).

Chestnut blight is another extremely destructive disease caused by a sac fungus which infects the chestnut, a valuable lumber-producing tree. It was first introduced into this country from the Orient in 1904 and soon the disease was detected on trees in New York. Within four decades most of the chestnut trees in the eastern United States were destroyed.Doubtless one reason for the rapid spread and the resulting devastation wrought by the fungus is that it produces two kinds of spores. One type is adapted to dissemination by insects, birds, rodents, and even splashing water, whereas the other type of spore is carried by the wind. Both types of spores are produced in vast numbers.

The cluster of plant diseases known as the rusts are produced by some 4,000 species of club fungi (Basidiomycetes) which infect many of our major cereals as well as scores of other plants causing untold millions of dollars of damage each year.

Wheat rust is one of the more important members of this group. For thousands of years it has been responsible for plagues or devastating famines which swept the great wheat-growing regions of the world. The Romans even had a god of rust to whom they offered sacrifices in an attempt to restrain the disease. In this country there have been serious epidemics of wheat rust in the Great Plains States, notably in 1904 and again in 1916.

Wheat rust, like some of the other rusts, is exceptional in that it lives on two hosts—wheat and the common, or wild, barberry (but not the cultivated or Japanese barberry). In a sense it resembles the malarial parasite which infects both man and mosquito. The wheat rust life cycle is a complex one involving four different kinds of spores—quite literally a spore for every season, so to speak.

Since the rust life cycle involves two hosts, an obvious method of control is to eradicate the wild barberry. Many a youth in the 1920s and 1930s earned his way through college by working on the barberry eradication crews in the summer. Although elimination of the barberry helps, it was soon found that it was not the complete answer, for spores may be carried by wind into the wheat states from as far as Texas and other southern states. The control method now employed is breeding wheat plants resistant to rust. This program has had some success but it too has a catch, namely, no sooner do the plant breeders and plant pathologists develop a strain or race of wheat resistant to rust, than the wheat rust fungus changes or mutates so that it adapts to the new putatively resistant wheats in such a way that it is able to infect them. And so the race goes on between the plant breeders and the mutating rust fungi—usually with the former but a season or two ahead of the changing rusts.

Other important diseases caused by fungi are corn smut (Figure 14.16) and the Dutch elm disease. The former is a club fungus which produces large unsightly black tumors, or galls, on the ears and other parts of the corn plant. Each gall, or pustule, is packed with black spores; it is estimated that an average-sized tumor contains about 25 billion spores.

Currently the most destructive shade tree disease is the Dutch elm disease, induced by a member of the sac fungi, which was introduced into this country in the 1930s on some logs imported from Europe. (Ironically, the imported logs were being shipped in partial payment of World War I debts owed to this country.) Since then it has killed millions of American elm trees; at the present time the rate is about 400,000 trees per year. The fungus, disseminated by elm bark beetles, grows into the vessels of the wood where spores are formed which course through the vessels and infect other parts of the tree. Despite massive research efforts including applications of chemotherapy, disappointing progress has been made in finding effective control measures. Spraying with DDT succeeded in controlling the beetles and hence the dispersal of the disease, so that losses were cut to only .5 percent per year, which could be endured, but now, with a ban on DDT use, this avenue too has been closed. Once a tree is infected it should be destroyed to prevent the further spread of the disease. A complicating factor in controlling the disease is that the roots of adjacent trees sometimes grow together in the form of a **root graft** and hence the disease may be spread from tree to tree via their roots.

Human and Animal Diseases

Not only are fungi important causal agents for numerous plant diseases but they also produce scores of human and animal diseases of the skin, hair, nails, ears, and even internal organs. Indeed, the fungi are so important as **pathogens** (disease-producing organisms) that there is one branch of medicine known as **medical mycology** which concerns itself with the human diseases caused by higher fungi.

Athlete's foot is, of course, the best known malady and it is brought about by several species of fungi. Various conditions of the scalp referred to colloquially as ringworm are not, despite the name, induced by worms but by many different species of fungi. Other fungi, particularly in the humid tropics, attack the ears and the skin and produce unsightly pustules or ulcers (Figures 14.20, 14.21, 14.22, and 14.23).

Fungal pathogens are not always superficial for some species may invade deep-seated organs such as lungs, liver, spleen, and other internal organs.

We have already reported on ergotism, or St. Anthony's fire, a

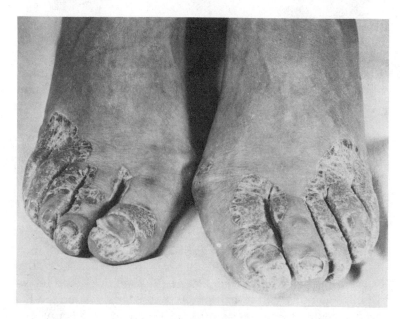

Figure 14.20 Fungal infection of toes and nails (candidiasis caused by species of the fungus *Candida,* usually *C. albicans*). [Courtesy Carmen C. Thomas and Norman F. Conant.]

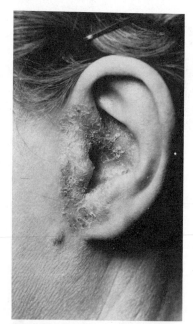

Figure 14.21 Fungal infection of the ear (otomycosis). [Courtesy Norman F. Conant.]

condition produced by the ergot fungus (a sac fungus, or Ascomycete) infecting rye as well as other cereals (Figure 10.2). Persons who consume bread baked from flour derived from infected grain may experience hallucinations and in severe cases may be driven to madness, while abortions may be induced in pregnant women.

Many people are allergic to the spores of molds and other fungi and hence suffer the same effects experienced by those persons with hay fever. An ironic aspect is that the researchers of fungi—mycologists and plant pathologists—occasionally become allergic to the very fungi they are investigating—like herpetologists who are bitten by the reptiles they are studying.

Poisonous Fungi

As noted previously, some fungi also affect humans because they are poisonous. Most of these belong to a group of the club fungi known as the agarics or gill fungi—the mushrooms or toadstools of popular usage. There are several thousand species of gill fungi of which only 30 or 40 are toxic. But these poisonous species are plentiful enough so that each year the newspapers carry stories of poisonings and in some instances deaths brought about by toxic mushrooms.

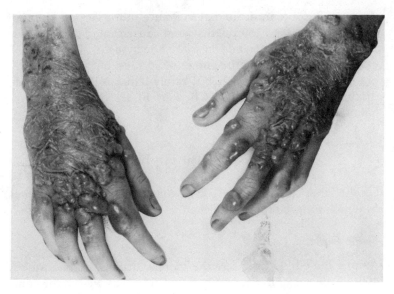

Figure 14.22 Fungal infection of hands (dermatomycosis). [Courtesy Norman F. Conant.]

It is amazing that even to this day one hears it said that the test of a poisonous specimen is to insert a silver spoon or silver coin in the pot where the mushrooms are being cooked; if the silver becomes tarnished or blackened, the mushroom is poisonous; if not, the mushroom is safe. Many a person has died like a dog for trusting that ancient shibboleth. The fact is that there is no simple test to distinguish between edible and poisonous mushrooms or toadstools. (Incidentally, these two terms *mushroom* and *toadstool* are often used interchangeably, although there is a tendency among lay people to use the former for the edible types and the latter, for the toxic kinds.) If you wish to identify the two types, you must learn to recognize the specific characteristics of the various poisonous species, and conversely, those of the edible species. Actually, mushrooms, despite the claims of gourmets, have little food value beyond a few minerals and some vitamin B.

Among the deadliest of the toxic mushrooms are several species of pure white or olive amanitas (*Amanita phalloides; A. verna; A. virosa,* Figure 14.9; and *A. bisporigera*), called destroying angels and death angels. The toxin in these mushrooms attacks the liver, causing it to atrophy and to cease functioning. It is estimated that 90 percent of the deaths from poisonous mushrooms in this country are attributable to these species of

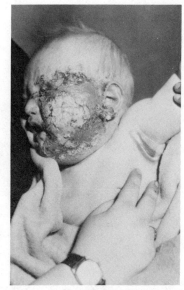

Figure 14.23 Fungal infection of face and armpit (candidiasis caused by species of the fungus *Candida,* usually *C. albicans*). [Courtesy John H. Stokes and Norman F. Conant.]

Amanita. Records indicate that in France in the early decades of this century 100 to 150 deaths were caused annually by these destroying angels. *Amanita muscaria,* the fly-agaric (Figure 10.3), a close relative of the white and olive species, but with a yellow, orange, or red cap, is toxic but rarely lethal. We have already discussed this species in Chapter 10 in connection with hallucinogenic plants.

Useful Aspects of Higher Fungi

On the other side of the ledger we may point to the many ways in which fungi are useful to man.

Edible Fungi

Among the edible fungi are the morels, truffles, and a number of wild species of mushrooms (Figure 14.24) as well as the commercially grown agaric or gill fungus (*Agaricus bisporus*). The

Figure 14.24   Common field mushroom (*Agaricus campestris*). [Courtesy Howard E. Bigelow.]

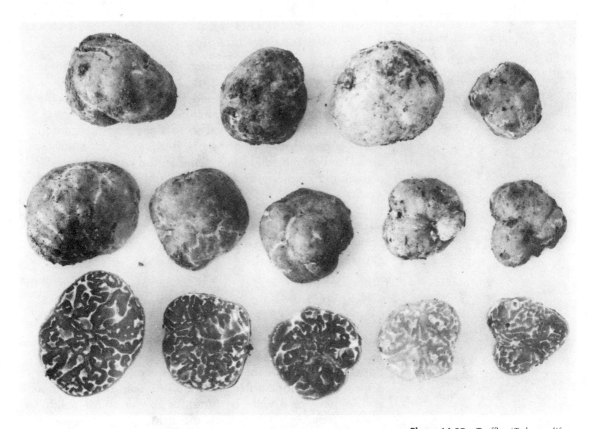

Figure 14.25 Truffles (*Tuber califor-nicum*), the subterranean, fruiting bodies of sac fungi which grow in symbiotic association with the roots of trees. [Courtesy James M. Trappe, U.S. Forest Service.]

morels (Figure 14.5), saprophytes found growing in woods in the spring, resemble mushrooms in that they have stalks and enlarged tops. However, the tops look like a sponge and the morels have spores borne in sacs, or asci, and hence they are members of the sac fungi.

Truffles (Figure 14.25) are the spherical fruiting bodies of certain sac fungi; they are subterranean and grow in symbiotic association with the roots of such trees as oak and beech. Because they are underground they are often located by their scent, which ranges from the pungent odor of the spicy-garlicky-cheesy tasting gourmet truffles to those that smell like rancid bacon or even sewer gas. Specially trained dogs or pigs, particularly pregnant sows for they apparently have a heightened sense of smell, are sometimes used to locate the truffles. A good truffle hound is said to sell for $400 in France.

Clyde Christensen in his sprightly little book, *The Molds and Man*, describes the procedure of hunting truffles:

> On a quiet evening of the truffle season, when the scent is likely to be most heavy and not blown about, the pig is taken under the arm or carried in a wheelbarrow to the wood where experience has shown the hunting to be good. The pig is carried or wheeled so that she may not get too tired—a good truffle-hunting pig is a wage earner and an artist, and is treated as such. Once in the woods, a rope is put around her neck, and she is given her head. When she smells a truffle she starts to root it out. She is pulled up, tied, and the hunter digs out the truffle, rewarding the pig with an acorn or some special tidbit. This continues until both partners are tired or the evening's quota has been gathered.

Truffles are not only highly prized delicacies of the gourmet but are highly priced—a small jar with three or four sells for $12; $200 for a pound of fresh truffles. But as Christensen puts it,

> The odor and flavor of truffles are something out of this world, and they are every bit as attractive to most people as they are to rodents, insects, and pigs. You do not have to acquire a taste for truffles, as you do for some cheeses that are ripened—or rotted—by fungi, or as you do for "high" meat, or the fish ripened by the Eskimos. The flavor of truffles is not "high" it is altogether different: all-permeating, mouth-watering, tantalizing, with the promise of Elysian enjoyment, a condensation of all that is noble and good. One need be neither a sophisticate nor a pig to enjoy truffles.

Fungal Cheeses

Several types of cheese owe their attractive flavors to the activities of fungi—specifically blue, Roquefort, Camembert, and Gorgonzola cheese. The green strands one observes in these cheeses (except in Camembert) are fungal threads or the mycelium of molds belonging to the sac fungi. In the ripening of cheese the fungi secrete enzymes which break down the proteins and carbohydrates in the cheese in a process akin to decay or putrefaction and the resulting disintegrative products furnish the zest and tang which is so appealing to cheese connoisseurs.

Fungi as Scavengers

Like the bacteria, the higher fungi play a very significant ecological role in nature in that they act as scavengers and recycle the basic elements of carbon, hydrogen, oxygen, and nitrogen. They break down the large organic molecules in proteins, carbohydrates, and fats and transform them into simple compounds such as carbon dioxide, water, and nitrates which then can be used again by plants to manufacture new organic compounds.

Industrial Fungi

Fungi produce valuable chemicals—organic acids such as citric and gluconic acids and enzymes such as diastase. Indeed the importance of fungi in industry is such that one branch of applied science is called **industrial mycology.**

Medicinal Fungi

We have already noted that the ergot fungus yields several alkaloids which are employed in gynecology and in the treatment of migraine headaches and that ergot produces the precursor molecule lysergic acid for the synthesis of LSD. And we have mentioned that fungi produce antibiotics, such as penicillin, streptomycin, Chloromycetin, Terramycin, and Aureomycin.

Yeast

The baking industry is beholden to the humble yeasts, sac fungi which are unicellular but sometimes form loose chains. They carry on a special type of respiration called **anaerobic respiration,** or **fermentation,** in which gaseous oxygen is not required. In this process, carbohydrates are broken down and ethyl alcohol and carbon dioxide are produced. It is the gas carbon dioxide which causes the dough of the bread to rise. The alcohol is driven off by the heat of the baking process—and thus produces the pleasant aroma of baking and bakeries.

The brewing and wine-making industries too are based on yeast, specifically on the fermentation process we have just described in which carbohydrates produce ethyl alcohol and carbon dioxide. Whereas carbon dioxide is the end product desired in baking, it is the alcohol which is the object in brewing and wine making.

Plant Pathology

Since fungi are such important **pathogens,** or agents causing disease, we should consider at least briefly the subject of **plant pathology**—the study of plant diseases, their causes, their transmission, and their control. By a **disease** we mean a marked deviation from the normal or average condition or physiological functioning of an organism.

Causal Agents of Plant Diseases

Plant diseases are not only induced by true fungi and bacteria (pear blight, bacterial wilt of corn), but by a number of other agencies and causes such as insects (gypsy moth, Japanese beetle), worms (nematodes), viruses (tobacco mosaic), flowering plants (dodder, mistletoe), chemicals (household gas, salt from roads, sulfur from smelting plants, smog), and malnutrition (lack of essential elements such as iron or magnesium causing a yellowing known as **chlorosis**).

Dispersal of Plant Diseases

The transmission of diseases or their causal agents is accomplished by wind (carrying spores), insects (which transmit viruses and fungi), water (as in the case of nematodes), birds (e.g., chestnut blight spores), and other animals, including especially man who in this jet age is particularly effective in disseminating plant diseases. Agents for disease transmittal, or **vectors,** as they are known, receive attention from plant pathologists because one way to check the spread of certain diseases is to eliminate, incapacitate, or at least to suppress the populations of the vectors. This is the only way yet known effectively to control epidemics of Dutch elm disease.

Control of Plant Diseases

In the management of plant diseases it is well to bear in mind that there is a fundamental difference in philosophy between those who treat plant diseases and the doctors who specialize in human medicine. In the latter there is emphasis on the individual patient, his welfare, and his survival, whereas in plant pathology the usual emphasis is on the crop or the totality of

Plate 7

7b

7a   Breadfruit *(Artocarpus altilis)* from the Pacific, the quest for which resulted in mutiny on the *Bounty*.

7b. Flowers of tea *(Camellia sinensis)*; sought after in China as a beverage plant during the 1840s by Robert Fortune, tea was grown in Western gardens as an ornamental in the eighteenth century.

7c   Chinese holly *(Ilex cornuta)*, introduced into cultivation in England by Robert Fortune in 1846.

7a

7c

Plate 8

8a Skimmia, brought from China into European cultivation by Robert Fortune in 1849.

8b Oriental dogwood (*Cornus kousa* variety *chinensis*), introduced from China into Western gardens in 1907 by Ernest H. Wilson.

8c Dove tree *(Davidia involucrata)* from China, one of Ernest H. Wilson's garden introductions of 1904.

8b

8a

8c

plants—except in the instance of valued shade trees or favorite shrubs and garden plants where the same stress may be placed on the individual. In other words, before measures are taken to control a plant disease, an assessment is made of the cost of the therapy relative to the value of the crop or the individual ornamental. If the first is greater than the second, the crop or individual is sacrificed.

Among the chief control measures employed in the battle against plant diseases are:

1. **Spraying** with **fungicides,** or chemicals toxic to fungi, such as Bordeaux mixture. (Parenthetically, the discovery of Bordeaux mixture is another classic example of serendipity. In the nineteenth century a French farmer undertook to discourage the theft of grapes by boys by slapping together a number of miscellaneous chemicals which he happened to have at hand; by chance these included lime, copper sulfate, and, of course, water. He sprayed this haphazard solution on his grapevines. Professor Pierre Millardet of the University of Bordeaux subsequently noted that these sprayed grape vines were free of mildew.)

2. **Dusting,** or applying dry poisons. Often this is done by airplanes, although planes are also used for spraying.

3. **Seed treatment,** by applying chemicals such as copper salts to seeds to kill or inhibit fungal growth.

4. **Sanitation,** by destroying diseased plants or parts of plants, as in the control of Dutch elm disease.

5. **Eradication of alternate hosts,** as in the management of wheat rust where the barberry is destroyed.

6. **Checking insect carriers of pathogens,** particularly essential with viral diseases.

7. **Quarantine,** by attempting to restrict specific diseases to certain regions by means of inspection posts on main highways and at entry ports.

8. **Crop rotation,** which is used with nematodes and with diseases where the causal fungus is restricted to certain specific hosts, as in corn smut.

9. **Breeding for disease resistance,** as in the example of wheat rust.

10. **Chemotherapy,** treating with chemicals which are absorbed by the plant or injected into the plant and then these chemical substances are translocated within the

plant. This method has been used in the attempt to deal with the Dutch elm disease.

11. **Biological control,** employing other organisms to parasitize the parasite or in some way to inhibit the activities of the pathogen. Various viruses which destroy bacteria have been used against fire blight of pear and crown gall, both diseases induced by bacteria. Some fungi are effective in killing nematodes (nematodes crawl through fungal loops which are then drawn tight; in other words, the nematodes are lassoed); other soil-inhabiting fungi attack the fungi which cause damping-off, a serious disease of seedlings.

Suggested Readings

Agrios, George N. *Plant Pathology.* New York: Academic Press, 1969. Good, solid scientific treatise.

Alexopoulos, Constantine J. *Introductory Mycology.* 2d ed. New York: Wiley, 1962. One of the best textbooks on fungi by an able mycologist.

————,and Harold C. Bold. *Algae and Fungi.* New York: Macmillan, 1967. See Suggested Readings, Chapter 13.

Bigelow, Howard E. *Mushroom Pocket Field Guide.* New York: Macmillan, 1974. Excellent, compact field guide with superb color photographs.

Bold, Harold C. *The Plant Kingdom.* 3d ed. Englewood Cliffs, N. J. : Prentice-Hall, 1970. See Suggested Readings, Chapter 13.

Christensen, Clyde M. *The Molds and Man.* 3d ed. New York: McGraw-Hill, 1965. Fortunate indeed is he (or she) who has his (or her) introduction to fungi via this lively, humorous gem of a book.

Conant, Norman F., David T. Smith, Roger D. Baker, and Jasper L. Callaway. *Manual of Clinical Mycology.* 3d ed. Philadelphia: Saunders, 1971. The standard, respected text in medical mycology.

Emerson, Ralph. "Molds and Men." *Scientific American* 186 (January 1952): 28–32. A lucid general treatment of the fungi, particularly of their importance to humans.

Gray, William D. *The Relation of Fungi to Human Affairs.* New York: Holt, 1959. A very comprehensive account of the infinite ways in which fungi affect the lives of humans.

Hale, Mason E., Jr. *The Biology of Lichens.* 2d ed. London: Arnold, 1974. A modern treatment of all aspects of lichens by a leader in the field.

Large, E. C. *The Advance of the Fungi*. New York: Dover, 1962. An admirable, scholarly discourse on the fungi and the constant battle man must wage to control the multitudinous diseases caused by fungi.

Zinsser, Hans. *Rats, Lice and History*. Boston: Little, Brown, 1935. A brilliant book about bacteria, particularly the microbe causing typhus fever, but with considerable history and some philosophical observations, all presented with charm and wit by a humanistic biologist.

The exquisite tracery of a fern (*Dicksonia*) frond.

15
Mosses and Ferns
Amphibians of the Plant Kingdom

The next group of plants in our listing from Chapter 3, and a group coordinate with the thallophytes, is the **embryophytes,** whose main diagnostic characteristic is reflected in its name. The embryophytes include two cohorts: the division known as the **true mosses and liverworts** (Bryophytes) and the group designated the **vascular plants.**

Mosses and Liverworts

The mosses are small plants (measuring a few inches) usually growing in dense mats (Figures 15.1 and 15.2) and forming carpets in fairly wet locations such as marshes, bogs, damp places on rocks and the sides of standing and fallen trees, and damp, cool woods. Liverworts—at least many of them—have rather flat, lobed thalli, or bodies, hence the name liverwort.

Because of the extensive mats or carpets formed by mosses, they play a role in nature in holding soil in place thereby preventing erosion. By their impressive water-holding capacity they slow down runoff in times of heavy rainfall and consequently are a factor in flood control. Mosses are ecologically significant for they are among the first plants, close on the heels of lichens, to colonize rocky ledges on hills and mountainsides. **Sphagnum,** or **bog moss,** is used by florists as a packing material to keep cut flowers, seedlings, and other nursery stock moist and fresh while in transit. The leaves of the bog moss are able to absorb and store large quantities of water. Dried sphagnum or **peat moss** is widely used by gardeners and landscape architects

389

Figure 15.1 Mosses forming a characteristic mat or carpet of vegetation.

Figure 15.2 Spore cases of mosses borne by stalks above the leafy shoots of the plants.

to provide a **mulch,** a material which retains water and thus keeps the soil porous. Among aborigines and in times of war, sphagnum has been used as a surgical dressing—here again its considerable absorptive powers are important. Absorptive cotton, for example, holds 5 or 6 times its weight in blood, while sphagnum absorbs 16 to 18 times its weight. In addition, sphagnum has antiseptic properties. **Peat,** a valuable fuel in Ireland and Scotland, is made up of mosses, largely sphagnum, which have decomposed slowly, carbonized, and then become compacted over thousands of years.

Vascular Plants

Vascular plants have the following characteristics which, in addition, represent important evolutionary advances over the thallophytes:

1. They all develop embryos.
2. They have true roots, stems, and leaves.
3. They possess the vascular tissues xylem and phloem. (Actually, these last two statements are different ways of saying the same thing, because true roots, stems, and leaves are defined as organs with vascular tissue.)

Figure 15.3 Tropical tree fern (*Cyathea*). [Courtesy Field Museum of Natural History.]

4. Most of them are land plants; or if not, there is indication they have gone back to the water secondarily (e.g., water ferns and water lilies).

The first group of living vascular plants we will consider is the **ferns,** an assemblage of some 9,000 species. Typically they grow in moist, shady situations. Most ferns are only a few feet tall, although there are some tree ferns in the humid rain forests of the tropics which attain a height of 50 to 75 feet (Figure 15.3).

Life History of a Fern

While we do not intend to make a fetish of life histories in this book, the fern life cycle not only is simple and clean but it may be used also to illustrate several important concepts. We start with the familiar mature fern plant (Figure 15.4) consisting of

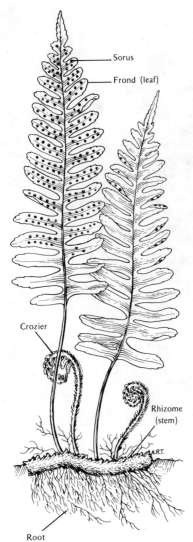

Sorus

Frond (leaf)

Crozier

Rhizome (stem)

A.R.T.

Root

Figure 15.4   Common polypody fern (*Polypodium*).

large, handsome leaves, or **fronds** (Figure 15.5), an underground stem (rhizome), and roots. (These are true roots, stem, and leaves for they all have the vascular tissues xylem and phloem.) At certain times there may appear on the lower sides of the leaves, brown spots which are referred to as **fruit dots** (or **sori,** Figure 15.6). They consist of clusters of **spore sacs** (Figure 15.7). Each spore sac is borne on a stalk; the spore case contains **spores** which are dispersed by the action of a row of cells which have differentially thickened cell walls. This special band of cells flips back and then snaps forward under certain conditions of moisture, with the result that the spores are hurled out with some force, and may thus be disseminated some distance from the parent plant.

When and if a spore chances to land in a favorable spot, it germinates and produces a small ($\frac{1}{8}$ to $\frac{1}{2}$ inch), green, membranous, heart-shaped **prothallus** (Figure 15.8). On the underside of the prothallus there are rootlike structures (called **rhizoids),** and microscopic but multicellular **male sex organs** (Figure 15.9) and **female sex organs** (Figure 15.10). The former produce motile **sperms** with flagella and each female sex organ contains a single **egg.** The sperms swim to the egg (ferns, you recall, usually grow in moist, shady places, or at least in places where there are temporary accumulations of water such as those which occur after rainstorms) and one sperm unites with the egg to produce a **zygote.** This process of fertilization, involving the union of a large, stationary egg and a smaller, motile sperm you will recall is heterogamy. The zygote develops inside the multicellular female sex organ and by means of a number of cell divisions produces a multicellular **embryo.** You will doubtless remember that in the green algae, the fertilized egg or zygote develops in the water and outside the parent filament, whereas in the fern the zygote remains in the female sex organ—much as a fertilized egg in a mammal develops in the womb—and produces a multicellular structure called the embryo—much like the embryo, or fetus, in higher animals.

The fern embryo, at first little more than a spherical mass of similar cells, gradually differentiates so that roots, a stem, and leaves are formed. The prothallus which, up to this point has been supplying food, water, and minerals to the developing plant, disintegrates and the young fern plant through further growth matures into a typical adult fern plant with large leaves, underground stem, and roots (Figure 15.11).

Figure 15.5 Polypody fern (*Polypodium*) leaf with sori (fruit dots) on lower surface of leaf.

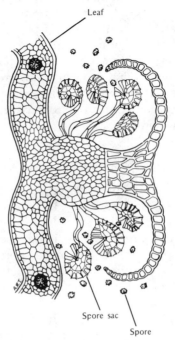

Figure 15.6 Cross-section of fern leaf with a sorus.

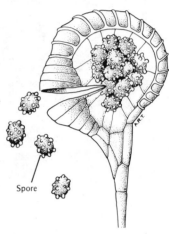

Figure 15.7 Fern spore sac with spores.

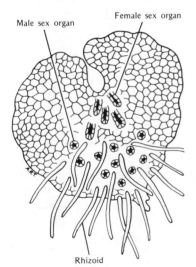

Figure 15.8 Fern prothallus or gametophyte.

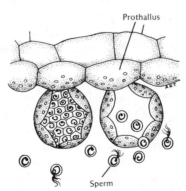

Figure 15.9 Fern male sex organs with sperms.

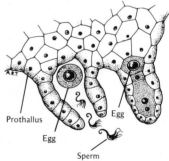

Figure 15.10 Fern female sex organs; each with one egg.

Figure 15.11 Fern prothallus with young sporophyte attached.

You will note that in the fern, sexual reproduction is still dependent upon water—the sperms must swim to the egg. This archaic method of transport in a land plant is doubtless a legacy from its aquatic ancestry. In any case, ferns are sometimes referred to as the "amphibians of the plant kingdom," for although they grow on land, sexual reproduction is dependent on a certain amount of free water. For this same reason, the ferns are sometimes said to have one foot on land and one foot in the water.

The Two Generations, or Phases, of Ferns

Botanists over 100 years ago discovered that the fern life cycle, as described above, is divided into two phases, or generations. The typical mature fern plant with roots, stem, and leaves is the **sporophyte**—it is the **asexual generation** which produces spores (hence the name sporophyte) and its cells have double the chromosome number found in the cells of the prothallus, egg, and sperm. This double number is referred to as the **2n**, or **diploid, number.**

The small, heart-shaped prothallus with its sex organs and gametes is designated the **gametophyte**—it is the **sexual generation** which produces gametes (hence the name gametophyte) and its cells have half the number of chromosomes found in the cells of the sporophyte. This lower number is termed the **n**, or **haploid, number.**

Alternation of Generations

In the life cycle of the fern the sporophyte produces spores which germinate to form the prothallus. The gametes from the sex organs unite to produce a zygote which develops into an embryo. The embryo matures and forms the fern plant with roots, stem, and leaves. The spores on the latter fall to the ground and the cycle begins again. The point is that sporophytes normally produce gametophytes, and gametophytes typically produce sporophytes. This phenomenon in which there is an alternation of the two phases is called **alternation of generations.** It is an important concept in botany for all plants reproducing sexually show this phenomenon. Those algae which reproduce sexually possess it, but the phenomenon becomes a regular and conspicuous feature in all embryophytes.

Two Critical Points in Life Cycles

We have already said that the prothallus with its sex organs and gametes has the lower number of chromosomes, or is in the *n*, or haploid, condition. When the egg and sperm, each bearing *n* chromosomes, unite in fertilization, the resulting zygote, of course, is 2*n*. And when the zygote divides to form the embryo, all the resulting cells are 2*n*, or diploid. The same is true of all the cells of the fern plant with roots, stem, and leaves. However, in the formation of the spores in the spore sacs, there is a special type of division of the nuclei in which the diploid chromosome number is changed to the haploid condition. This special nuclear division is called **meiosis,** or **reduction division,** the details of which will be briefly elucidated in Chapter 17 on genetics. Suffice it to say here that the spores are haploid and hence form haploid prothalli.

Thus in any plant, indeed in any organism which reproduces sexually there are two critical stages in its life history when the chromosome number is altered—at **fertilization** when the chromosome number is changed from haploid to diploid and at the time of **spore formation** in plants when the process of **meiosis** or **reduction division** takes place in which the 2*n* chromosome number is changed to *n*.

Fruit Dots (or Sori)

Earlier, in describing the life history of the fern, we mentioned the sori. These structures have long mystified the casual observer. For example, the people of the seventeenth and eighteenth centuries were puzzled by the circumstance that they could find no flowers or seeds on ferns. Therefore they believed that ferns reproduce at night or in some clandestine fashion. Curiously, at the same time and even earlier the old herbals were graced with fine drawings of fern leaves with conspicuous fruit dots. It simply never occurred to the people of this period to associate fruit dots with reproduction. People thought that if they could find fern seeds they would have unusual properties. Thus Shakespeare in *King Henry IV* writes, "We have the receipt of fern seed, we walk invisible." Or as his contemporary playwright Ben Jonson says, "I have no medicine, sir, to walk invisible,/ No fern seed in my pocket."

Strangely, we have similar manifestations of misunderstanding even today when furious customers storm into florist shops and demand their money back because their ferns have never flowered or they complain that the leaves of their ferns are covered with "brown bugs" or "disease spots" (really the sori).

So-called Fern Allies

In some of the older classifications the ferns were grouped with the **club-mosses** (not true mosses but they resemble the mosses in appearance; the club refers to the **cones** which some of these plants bear, Figure 15.12) and the **horsetails** (their bushy aspect suggests the tails of horses; they also have cones, Figure 15.13). We now believe that these two cohorts of vascular plants are not closely related to the ferns but represent independent lines of evolution in which these plants have attained about the same level of specialization as the ferns and which they generally resemble in their life cycles.

The club-mosses and horsetails are of interest because at one time—during the Carboniferous period, or the Age of Coal (some 345 million years ago, Figure 15.14)—they were represented by arboreal, or tree, forms. These giant club-mosses and huge horsetails have sometimes been referred to as the vegetable counterparts of the dinosaurs. Apparently the climate was warmer during the Carboniferous period than it is at the present time, hence more carbon dioxide was forced out of the seas and more of this gas was available for photosynthesis. In any case, these ancient club-mosses and horsetails, as well as ferns are important because their vegetative bodies and their spores, produced in prodigious quantities, formed the **coal** we are now burning and which earlier fueled the Industrial Revolution.

Other than in their role in the formation of coal, the ferns and the so-called fern allies are of little significance or human relevance—except that because fern fronds are of great beauty and variety ferns are often grown in gardens. Indeed, Thoreau once declared, "God made ferns to show what He could do with leaves."

See illustration on page 44, horse-tails.

Figure 15.12   Club-moss (*Lycopodium*).

See photograph on page 388, fern frond.

Origin of Land Plants

Having outlined the life history of a fern, we should now back-track to consider the giant evolutionary step from algae to ferns—from aquatic plants to land organisms. If you pause for a moment and reflect you will be impressed with the fact that aquatic plants such as algae live a rather salubrious existence; they grow in the water which gives them physical support or buoyancy and provides them not only with the water for photosynthesis but with mineral salts. There is no problem of conduction because the plants are bathed in water with dissolved salts allowing these materials to be obtained directly by most algal cells. The water of their habitats even provides the vehicle by which the zoospores are dispersed and the sperm reaches the egg. Finally, there is usually no danger of the plants becoming desiccated, or drying out, for they are surrounded by water.

In contrast, consider the situation when such aquatic algae invade the land, as we believe that ancestral algae did: They are at once faced with the danger of drying out; thus the evolution of a surface **cuticle** (waxlike layer) must have been one of the first and most critical developments in the history of land plants. These fragile algae also lacked support, a problem which was eventually met by the gradual evolution of a root system which serves to anchor the plant in place and by the evolution of the xylem which renders support to the aerial parts of the plant. At the same time, the root provides a means by which water and mineral salts can be absorbed from the soil. Since the source of the raw materials was some distance from the photosynthetic units, the leaves, there developed tissues for the conduction of water and dissolved salts—the xylem—and tissues for the transport of manufactured food—the phloem. Finally, lacking water, these first adventurous land plants were confronted with the problem of disseminating their reproductive cells. Spores, of course, are adapted to land existence and can be propelled by air currents. The Achilles' heel of the early land plants was the requirement of water through which the sperm can swim to the egg. The fern, for example, is still essentially wedded to the water or at least to wet places. After a long period of time land plants eventually evolved **pollen** which can be transported by wind, insects, or other animals to the female structure.

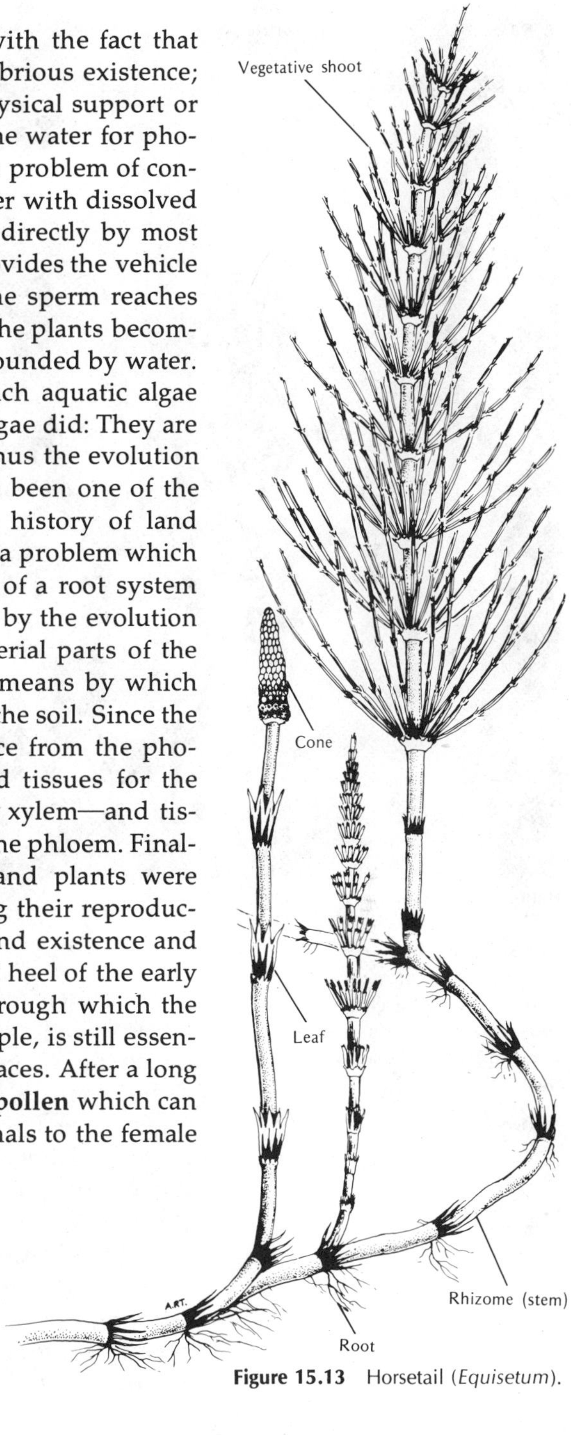

Figure 15.13 Horsetail (*Equisetum*).

Figure 15.14 Restoration of a Carboniferous coal swamp. Plants with fernlike foliage are seed ferns (seeds are shown at left margin). Arboreal club-mosses (to the left) and arboreal horesetails (to the right) are also shown. [Courtesy Field Museum of Natural History.]

It is rather interesting that as early as 1903 a French paleobotanist, O. Lignier, promulgated a theory of land plant origin in which he suggested that the ancestors of land plants were dichotomously branching algae resembling *Fucus*, the rockweed, except that they were probably green. Then Lignier postulated that one of the dichotomous branches penetrated the soil to form a root, some of the ends of other branches flattened out to fashion leaves, and some other dichotomies straightened out a bit to produce the main axis, or stem.

Amazingly enough, abundant fossil plants known as **psilophytes** (literally, "naked plants"; Figures 15.15 and 15.16) have been found in Silurian and Devonian rocks (390–440 million years old) which have a striking resemblance to Lignier's hypothetical transitional land plant (Figure 15.17). Some of these simple, fossil vascular plants are little more than dichotomous stems, for they lack or have just the beginnings of roots and some lack leaves or have only the merest suspicions of leaves.

It is now thought that the psilophytes represent a transitional group—a sort of missing link—between the algae and the vascular land plants (Figure 19.4). Some of the psilophytes evolved along the lines of club-mosses, others in the direction of horsetails, and still others in the direction of ferns. This latter line probably furnished the ancestors of the seed plants.

Since the finding of the psilophytes is one of the major discoveries in plant morphology, it would be appropriate to quote the words of a botanist turned poet, Donald Culross Peattie, from his book *Flowering Earth:*

> Among these detectives of the vanished, these pioneers into the remote past, a great name is that of Sir John William Dawson. Eighty years ago Sir John was cracking rocks and pawing over the fragments on the Gaspé peninsula of Canada, when he came on a fossil fragment in a stratum of early Devonian age, that gave him a start. He was a God-fearing, Bible-swearing gentleman who did not, in that year of grace 1859, take any stock in Mr. Darwin's blasphemy about the descent of man. But he was a good paleobotanist, for all of that, and when he found a land plant square in the middle of the Age of Seaweeds, he knew he had made a discovery.
>
> He took his stony fragment home to Nova Scotia, where he was born, and went to work on it. Neither mad nor a magician, he dared to look back three hundred and fifty million years, and see what must have been growing then. He was so sure of what he saw that he could take up a pencil and draw it. I have that picture before me. It is a picture of the earliest known plant upon the earth. Sir John called it Psilophyton, which means "naked plant." Very naked it looks, very new for all it is so old—a skinny, wiry, straggling thing, no more than the dim beginning of an idea for a plant. Which is just about what it was.
>
> The shoot seems to have been scarcely a foot in height; it had a bit of underground stem without roots; it had branches, but without leaves, and at the tips of them it bore spore cases (for it was to be ages before seeds fell upon the

Figure 15.15 Two fossil psilophytes: *Horneophyton* (left) and *Rhynia.*

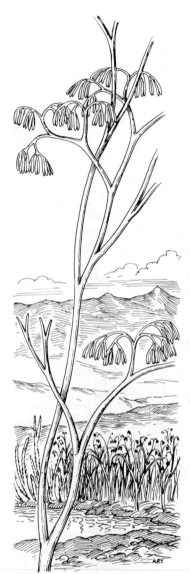

Figure 15.16 *Psilophyton,* fossil psilophyte, of Devonian age. [From original specimen, courtesy Francis M. Hueber.]

ready earth). This thing, this meagre, venturesome, growing and certainly green thing, lost in the interminable darknesses of time gone by, came alive again in the mind of Sir John William Dawson.

Too lively, his imagination! said his colleagues to one another. Psilophyton, it was smilingly decided, never grew anywhere outside of his head. For more than fifty years the drawing was thought of as a curiosity, a scribbling without scientific value.

One day, in the terrible year of 1915, when the English and Germans were dying at Ypres and the French and Germans at Artois, two British paleobotanists, over-age for service, were plying their peaceable if unappreciated trade in the mountains of Aberdeenshire, when they unearthed a Devonian marsh, turned by time into a dark chippy sort of flint called chert, and full of fossils. This bog, when it was a bog, must have been close to the ocean, although the village of Rhynie, hard by, is now thirty miles from the North Sea and well up in the hills. So Robert Kidston and William Lang called the first of their plants to be described, Rhynia.

They saw that Rhynia must have grown very thickly in the bog, in a green swale like rushes in a marsh today; they saw it stood about eight inches high, that it had neither leaves nor roots but only underground stems and rootlets, that it bore spore cases—that it was, indeed, so like Sir John William Dawson's drawing of the imaginary Psilophyton that Psilophyton must have been very real indeed.

And in the years since, it has turned up in fossils at points so far scattered as Connecticut, Maine, Scotland, Wales, Germany, and Victoria in Australia. No doubt any more of Dawson's bold guess, no doubt of the importance of Psilophyton, the "naked plant," the first known plant citizen in the land. Spores like a fern's give hint, in this bleak tentative little ancestor, of great things to come.

Suggested Readings

Andrews, Henry W. *Ancient Plants and the World They Lived In.* Ithaca, N.Y.: Comstock, 1947. A general exposition on fossil plants.

———. *Studies in Paleobotany.* New York: Wiley, 1961. The standard text authored by a distinguished scholar in the field.

Bierhorst, David W. *Morphology of Vascular Plants.* New York: Macmillan, 1971. A scholarly advanced text with many original ideas.

Bold, Harold C. *Morphology of Plants.* 3d ed. New York: Harper & Row, 1973. The best all-around, modern plant morphology which covers all plant groups—algae, fungi, liverworts, mosses, as well as vascular plants.

———. *The Plant Kingdom.* 3d ed. Englewood Cliffs, N. J.: Prentice-Hall, 1970. See Suggested Readings, Chapter 13.

Coulter, Merle C., and Howard J. Dittmer. *The Story of the Plant Kingdom.* 3d ed. Chicago: University of Chicago Press, 1964. A good, readable general exposition on the evolution of the plant kingdom.

Delevoryas, Theodore. *Morphology and Evolution of Fossil Plants.* New York: Holt, Rinehart and Winston, 1962. A short introduction to paleobotany.

———. *Plant Diversification.* New York: Holt, Rinehart and Winston, 1966. A good, brief book on the evolution of the plant kingdom.

Foster, Adriance S., and Ernest M. Gifford. *Comparative Morphology of Vascular Plants.* 2d ed. San Francisco: Freeman, 1974. Comprehensive, scholarly treatise by two able botanists who write with clarity and grace. Profusely illustrated.

Fuller, Harry J., and Oswald Tippo. *College Botany.* 2d ed. New York: Holt, 1954. See Suggested Readings, Chapter 13.

Peattie, Donald C. *Flowering Earth.* New York: Putnam's Sons, 1939. A charming exposition on selected botanical topics by a professional humanistic botanist.

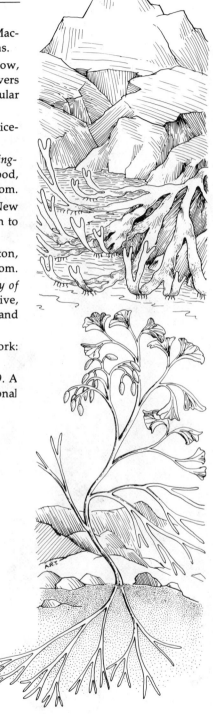

Figure 15.17 Sketch illustrating one theory (that originating with O. Lignier) to explain the origin of vascular land plants from aquatic algae.

Flowers of *Allamanda cathartica* from
Brazil.

16
Seed Plants
Key to Man's Survival

It is significant that the 12 food plants which may be said to stand between man and starvation are all seed plants, specifically flowering plants (see Chapter 11 on food plants). Furthermore, wood for fuel and shelter, fibers for clothing, drugs, spices, rubber, gums, resins, oils, tannins, dyes, perfumes, tobacco, waxes, narcotics, beverages such as coffee, tea, cocoa, and chocolate, and many other economic products are derived largely from seed plants, particularly angiosperms. Thus we are not indulging in hyperbole when declaring that the seed plants hold the key to man's survival. Only the fungi, including the bacteria, with their hallucinogens, antibiotics, industrial chemicals, alcohol, scavengers, and pathogens come close to the seed plants in their economic impact on human beings.

There is no question but that the seed plants, with an estimated 500,000 species of the total of 800,000 species estimated in the plant kingdom, are the dominant plant group on the earth at the present time. Seed plants are found in virtually all parts of the world where they dominate the landscape and occupy almost every type of ecological niche. While they are basically land plants, some of their members have apparently returned to fresh water (water lilies, Figure 16.1; water hyacinth, Figure 16.2; elodea; duckweed) and to the sea (salt water eel grass), some have taken to the air as **epiphytes** (plants which receive physical but not nutritional support from other plants; examples: orchids and Spanish moss), some have become parasites (dodder, mistletoe), a few are saprophytes, and a goodly number have become adapted to living in deserts (cacti, Figure 19.5; agaves, Figure 19.6; spurges, Figure 19.7; aloes, Figure 19.8).

See Plate 6c, Queen Victoria water lily.

403

Figure 16.1   Queen Victoria water lily (*Victoria regia*). The leaves may reach diameters of six feet.

Figure 16.2   Water hyacinth (*Eichhornia crassipes*), a very troublesome weed in the watercourses of Florida, in parts of Africa, and in Australia. Note the swollen petioles which provide buoyancy for these floating plants.

Figure 16.3   Indian pipe (*Monotropa uniflora*), one of the few flowering plants lacking chlorophyll.

Place in the Plant Kingdom

In the listing given in Chapter 3 the seed plants are classified with the embryophytes and vascular plants—in fact, they constitute a coordinate group with the ferns in the larger assemblage of vascular plants. The distinguishing characteristic of this cohort is the possession of **seeds,** reflected in the name of the group. According to our classification, two groups make up the seed plants: the **gymnosperms** and the **angiosperms.**

Gymnosperms

This group is small in terms of numbers of living species—approximately 800 species—but large in numbers of individuals which occupy vast regions of the world where they dominate the landscape, particularly in temperate mountainous regions and in the swampy wastes of the north. As the name indicates, these plants have naked seeds—they are not enclosed in a carpel as they are in the flowering plants. Most of the gymno-

Figure 16.4 Seed fern (*Medullosa noei*) with fernlike leaves and seeds. [Courtesy Theodore Delevoryas.]

sperms have **cones,** reproductive structures which bear seeds or pollen sacs with pollen. Almost all are large woody plants, usually trees. Most, but not all gymnosperms are **evergreen,** that is they retain their leaves year after year and the leaves are shed a few at a time rather than all at one season as with our familiar **deciduous** trees.

Among the gymnosperms are the extinct **seed ferns** (Figure 16.4), **cycads** (Figure 16.5), **ginkgo** (Figures 16.6 and 16.7), **ephedra** and its relatives, and the largest group, the living **conifers**.

The seed ferns are known only as fossils (Carboniferous period) but they are significant for although they have the large leaves or fronds of ferns, they also have true seeds and hence this may suggest common ancestry for the ferns and the higher seed plants.

The cycads are plants whose large fronds resemble palm leaves, so much so that they are often used on Palm Sunday as a

Figure 16.5 Cycad (*Dioon edule*) with large pollen cone.

substitute for palms. They are natives of tropical and subtropical regions—some are found in the West Indies, Mexico, and Florida. They are often cultivated in northern greenhouses where the very large seed cones of some species attract attention.

Figure 16.6 Maidenhair tree or ginkgo (*Ginkgo biloba*). A "living fossil" and yet a tough street tree.

Figure 16.7 Fan-shaped leaves and fleshy seeds of ginkgo (*Ginkgo biloba*).

The ginkgo, or the maidenhair tree (Figures 16.6 and 16.7) is a deciduous tree with fan-shaped leaves. The species has male and female individuals (dioecious); the seeds on the female trees have a foul, rancid smell—"like that of raw, dog vomit," Professor M. L. Fernald of Harvard used to say to startle his classes. Ginkgo is of particular interest because it has been called a living fossil in that it is not known in the wild, and the only reason we still have living trees is that they were cultivated in Chinese temple gardens where they have survived even though they have disappeared elsewhere. In the eighteenth century Westerners brought seeds of the ginkgo to Europe and to America, where it is now often grown as a street tree for it seems to be able to tolerate smoke and is quite resistant to the usual tree diseases.

Ephedra, which we have mentioned before in connection with the drug ephedrine, belongs to a group of shrubs growing in arid parts of the world, including our own Southwest. One species of *Ephedra* is a much publicized weed that is growing on, and possibly destroying, the Wailing Wall in Israel. Possibly related to *Ephedra* is one of the most bizarre plants in the plant kingdom—*Welwitschia mirabilis* (Figure 16.8), of the arid regions of southwestern Africa. It has a large (4 to 6 feet in diameter at

Figure 16.8 *Welwitschia* of southwestern Africa, with squat, woody, tuberous stem from which arise two long, straplike leaves. [Courtesy Field Museum of Natural History.]

Figure 16.9 Pine (*Pinus strobus*) cones which bear ovules, and later seeds.

Figure 16.11 Redwoods (*Sequoia sempervirens*), one of our tallest trees. [Courtesy Field Museum of Natural History.]

Pollen cone

Figure 16.10 Cluster of pollen cones of pine.

the apex) squat, tuberous stem, attached to a long root, which bears only two long, straplike leaves, sometimes reaching a length of 18 feet. Thus it richly merits the specific name *mirabilis*—"wonderful." Only a few thousand plants of *Welwitschia* are still extant and these are protected by law which provides a fine and a prison term for anyone destroying one.

Conifers

The **conifers** constitute a large group of living tree species, typically of temperate mountainous regions. They are mostly evergreen trees, from which so much of our timber and lumber is derived—pine, spruce, fir, Douglas fir, hemlock, redwood, cedar, cypress, and larch. As the name conifer indicates, these plants all have the reproductive structures designated cones —large seed, or "female," cones (Figure 16.9) and smaller pollen, or "male," cones (Figure 16.10).

Spectacular trees in this group are the Douglas fir, the redwood, and the giant sequoia. The Douglas fir, one of our most valuable timber and lumber-producing trees, is a native of the Rocky Mountains and our Pacific Coast, ranging from British Columbia to central California and thence along the high mountains to northern Mexico. Some of these trees reach a height of 300 feet, have diameters up to 15 feet, and may be as old as 400 years.

The redwood (Figure 16.11) is another valuable timber tree which grows on the Pacific slopes of the Coast Range from southern Oregon to northern California, always within reach of coastal fogs. The largest tree on record is one which grew to 380 feet, 26 feet in diameter, and was approximately 2,200 years old. It is estimated that such a tree would yield 500,000 board feet of lumber.

The closely related big tree, or giant sequoia (Figure 16.12) is not as tall but has more bulk, or volume. There is one record of a tree 320 feet tall, 37 feet in diameter, with bark 2 feet thick, and 4,000 years old. The largest living giant sequoia is the General Sherman tree which is 275 feet tall, 84 feet in circumference at the base, and is estimated to be approximately 4,000 years old. Giant sequoias are found in scattered groves at altitudes of 5,000 to 8,000 feet on the western slopes of the Sierra Nevada Mountains.

A close relative of the redwood and big tree is the dawn redwood which has had a remarkable history. It was first discovered as a fossil and then much later (1946) it was found growing in central China. Thus the designation living fossil is particularly apt. Seeds have been sent to this country and the dawn redwood is now rather widely grown, particularly on university campuses.

Finally, the conifers include the longest living organisms— plant or animal—the bristlecone pine (Figure 6.29) of eastern

Figure 16.12 Big tree or giant sequoia (*Sequoiadendron giganteum*) in the Sequoia National Forest, California. [Courtesy U. S. Department of Agriculture.]

California and adjacent Nevada, Arizona, and New Mexico (which we discussed in Chapter 6). The annual rings of the oldest tree of the species, fittingly dubbed Methuselah, have been counted and the number of rings tallied gives the startling figure of 4,600 years—no other living organism is as old. Not only are these individual living trees venerable in age but the fossil record of the conifers extends back to the Paleozoic geological era, about 280 million years ago. We are reminded of a remark that Professor E. C. Jeffrey of Harvard was fond of making: "I have a lot of respect for the pine tree, it is older than the rocks it grows on and the birds that sit in its branches."

Angiosperms

See photograph on page 402, flowers of *Allamanda*.

The angiosperms, or flowering plants, with an estimated 500,000 species, differ from the gymnosperms in that the former have covered seeds enclosed in a carpel (hence, the name angiosperm), flowers, vessels in the wood (usually), and the unique phenomenon of double fertilization. There are two subdivisions of the angiosperms: the **dicotyledons** and the **monocotyledons.**

Flowers

One of the questions about angiosperms and their flowers which has occupied the attention of botanists is the problem of what conditions bring on flowering. There is general agreement that a number of factors are involved in inducing flowering; there usually must be an accumulation of reserve food in the plant, the temperature must be suitable, and, for some plants, the length of day is critical. You have doubtlessly heard of **long-day plants** such as corn, wheat, clover, gladiolus, and larkspur and **short-day plants** such as chrysanthemums, asters, and poinsettia. The former require long daily spans of light (13 hours or longer) in order to flower; the latter need short durations of light (less than 13 hours). Still other plants are neutral, or indifferent, to the duration of light (tomato). This response of plants to length of day is known as **photoperiodism.** These light periods may be manipulated experimentally or on a commercial scale so that the desired flowers may be produced at the proper season, for example, Christmas and Easter. There is some evidence that floral **hormones** also play a role in the initiation of flowering.

You will recall that in Chapter 2 on form and function, we described what might be called a typical flower—at least a complete one (Figure 16.13). The outer whorl, or circle, of members—often green or sometimes another color—consists of the **sepals** which protect the flower in the bud stage. The next whorl, usually brightly colored, consists of the **petals** which attract insects by means of their color. The next series of structures, resembling clubs, are the **stamens** which produce pollen (Figures 7.6 and 16.14) in terminal **pollen sacs.** Finally, occupy

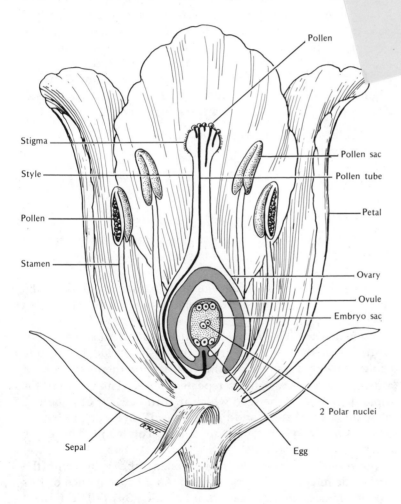

Figure 16.13 Flower.

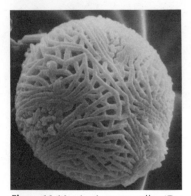

Figure 16.14 Angiosperm pollen (*Tetracentron sinense*) photographed with scanning electron microscope. [Courtesy James W. Walker.]

ing the center of the flower are the **carpels** or **pistils,** each one consisting of the neck, or **style;** the receptive tip, or **stigma;** and the enlarged base, or **ovary,** in which there are one or more **ovules.**

Pollination

The first step in the reproductive process in the flower is **pollination,** in which the pollen from the stamen is transferred to the stigma. If this occurs in the same flower or between flowers on the same plant, we say the plant is **self-pollinated** (garden peas, wheat). If the pollen is carried from the stamen in a flower on one plant to the stigma in a flower on another plant, we have **cross-pollination** (orchids, apples). Various agencies, such as wind, insects (bees, wasps, flies, gnats, butterflies, moths, carrion flies), water, bats, birds, man, and even snails and slugs are responsible for carrying the pollen from stamen to stigma (Figures 16.15, 16.16, and 16.17). Emily Dickinson alludes to the process in a charming little verse:

> To make a prairie it takes a clover and one bee,—
> And revery.
> The revery alone will do
> If bees are few.

Double Fertilization

Once the pollen lands on the stigma it sends down a **pollen tube** which grows through the tissues of the stigma, style, and ovary like a fungal filament.

Inside the ovule there develops a structure designated the **embryo sac** with eight cells, or nuclei (Figure 16.18). The pollen tube, containing three nuclei at this stage, grows to the ovule and one of the nuclei, termed a **male,** or **sperm, nucleus,** unites with one of the nuclei in the embryo sac, called the **female gamete,** or **egg.** As a result of this **fertilization** there is produced a diploid **zygote** which by repeated cell divisions forms the diploid **embryo** of the seed which in turn consists of a rootlike segment, a short stem, and two tiny seed leaves, or **cotyledons** (two in a **dicotyledon,** one in a **monocotyledon,** hence the names of the two groups).

The other male nucleus in the pollen tube unites with the two **polar nuclei** in the embryo sac. As a consequence of this second process of fertilization, a triploid ($3n$) cell is formed

Figure 16.15 Monarch butterflies pollinating a milkweed. [Courtesy Kjell B. Sandved.]

Figure 16.16 Nectar-feeding bat pollinating an agave. [Courtesy U.S. Department of Agriculture.]

Figure 16.17 Whitewing dove pollinating saguaro cactus. [Courtesy U.S. Department of Agriculture.]

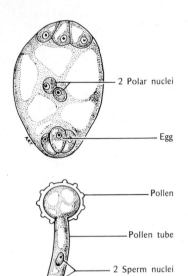

2 Polar nuclei

Egg

Pollen

Pollen tube

2 Sperm nuclei

Tube nucleus

Figure 16.18 Embryo sac or female gametophyte (above) and pollen and pollen tube or male gametophyte (below) of angiosperms.

which by successive divisions produces the triploid **endosperm,** or food-storage, tissue of the seed.

Gradually the outer layers of the ovule are transformed into **seed coats** and the whole **ovule** now becomes the **seed.** The **carpel** or **pistil** matures at the same time and forms the **fruit.**

It is important to note that in this process of fertilization, two male gametes are involved and we thus have what is called **double fertilization:** One sperm unites with the egg to form the zygote and the other sperm nucleus fuses with two polar nuclei to produce the endosperm. This angiospermic process of double fertilization is unique in the entire biological world—nowhere else does it occur—no where else in the plant kingdom, nor anywhere in the animal kingdom.

The Significance of Double Fertilization to Civilization

Double fertilization is of immense significance for it is through this process that the tissues containing most of the food used by the world is produced. The union of the second male gamete nucleus with the two polar nuclei produces the endosperm. And you will remember that it is the endosperm, rich in carbohydrates and with some proteins and fats, which man eats when he consumes cereals or grains such as rice, wheat, corn, barley, rye, and oats or when he drinks coconut milk or eats coconut meat or when he dines on legumes. In this latter case the foods in the endosperm have already been absorbed by the cotyledons which now are gorged with their content.

Another important fact is that the endosperm is triploid, or $3n$, and that in its formation, the pollen tube supplies one male gamete and the embryo sac provides two polar nuclei. As you might expect, this means that the female wields more control over the endosperm than the male—a detail of some practical significance when one is breeding cereals where one is interested in producing the best type of endosperm-rich foods.

Pollination versus Fertilization

Unfortunately, many people, including biologists, confuse the two processes of pollination and fertilization. You frequently hear and read that insects or birds fertilize the flowers. The accepted gambit in teaching children the facts of life is to talk about the role of the birds and the bees in fertilizing flowers. We are inclined to agree with Henry L. Mencken that this approach "does not make sex simple, it merely serves to make botany obscene."

Pollination, we remind you, is the transfer of pollen from the stamen to the stigma. Period. **Fertilization,** on the other hand, is the actual union of the male gamete with the egg to produce the zygote, and the fusion of the other male gamete with the two polar nuclei to form the endosperm.

Fruit versus Seed

Speaking of confusion, it should now be clear to you why we make a distinction between fruits and seeds; the former are mature carpels or pistils, the latter are mature ovules. In the peas you buy at the market, the **pod,** or **legume,** is the fruit which developed from a carpel. You can see a short projection at one end which is the remnant of the style and stigma. The pea seeds inside the pod are the ripened ovules.

Gametophyte and Sporophyte in the Angiosperms

The fern life cycle, you will remember, was divided into two phases, or generations, the gametophyte and the sporophyte. The fern prothallus is the gametophyte, and the sporophyte is the plant with roots, stem, and leaves.

In a similar fashion, the life history of a flowering plant consists of a gametophyte and a sporophyte. As a check on your understanding of the material discussed to this point, you might think for a moment and decide what in the angiosperm is sporophyte and what is gametophyte, remembering that the former is $2n$ and produces spores and the latter is n and forms gametes.

We trust you will come to the conclusion that the familiar flowering plant, be it an oak tree or a buttercup, is the sporophyte—it produces spores (the young pollen grains) and is diploid. The gametophyte generation is represented by two structures—the embryo sac with eight nuclei, one of which is the female gamete, plus the mature pollen grain with its pollen tube enclosing three nuclei, two of which are male gametes. These two structures are haploid and both produce gametes (Figure 16.18).

Ferns versus Angiosperms

If evolution and morphology—the science Charles Darwin called the "soul of biology"—intrigue you, we suggest you will be interested in the next three paragraphs.

In the fern life cycle the gametophyte (prothallus) is small, free-living, and independent—it is green and hence makes its own food; the sporophyte is much larger and after a brief embryonic period it is also independent, for the mature plant possesses roots, stem, and leaves. In the angiosperms, the sporophyte is the larger and independent generation while the gametophyte is smaller (reduced to 11 cells, or nuclei) and completely dependent on the sporophyte. The gametophyte is not green; indeed, the embryo sac is buried in the ovule and never sees the light of day. The fern gametophyte bears multicellular male and female sex organs; in the angiosperms, the female sex "organ" is reduced to the egg and possibly two additional cells (synergids) and the male sex "organ" is reduced to two sperm nuclei.

You may ask, why? We really don't know, but one theory is that the progenitors of the vascular plants started out with two equal generations—same size and both equally independent. The gametophyte happens to be a generation which is especially adapted to water—the sperm swims to the egg, while the sporophyte is better suited for land existence—its spores may be carried by the wind. And so when plants came on land, the sporophyte was the generation which was favored, with a concomitant reduction in the gametophyte. Had we considered the life cycles of some of the plants which stand in an intermediate position to ferns and angiosperms—the cycads and the conifers—you would have been able to follow the very gradual reduction in the gametophyte and in their sex organs as well as the increasing supremacy of the sporophyte.

Whether this speculation is valid or not, we do end up with flowering plants which have a type of reproduction suitable for land existence, with the male element traveling to the stigma by means of some land agency such as the wind, insects, or other animals. The rest of the journey to the egg is traversed by means of the pollen tube. You will recall that earlier we said a fern is really an amphibian, that it is wedded to the water because of the need for this medium for the sperm to swim to the egg. In the angiosperms we have plants which are no longer wedded to the water—at least so far as sperm transport is concerned.

Early Recognition of Sex in Plants

After this discussion of comparative morphology and **phylogeny** (study of the evolutionary relationships among plants), we turn to a brief reference to the fact that as early as

2,800 years ago man was aware of sexuality in plants, particularly in such two-sexed plants (dioecious) as date palms. Mesopotamian reliefs dating back to approximately 850 B.C. show deities in the process of pollinating female date palms with clusters of flowers from male trees.

Diversity in Flowers

Since these ancient times man has wondered at the endless diversity among the flowers of the estimated 500,000 species of angiosperms. Whereas all flowers are built on the fundamental plan of the flower we described earlier in this chapter, there is great variation in color, numbers of parts, presence or absence of some parts, fusion of some parts, and segregation of stamens and carpels to different flowers on the same plant (monoecious) or to different plants (dioecious). Or, in the words of Thomas H. Huxley, "Flowers are the primers of the morphologist; those who run may read in them uniformity of type amidst endless diversity, singleness of plan with complex multiplicity of detail. As a musician might say: every natural group of flowering plants is a sort of visible fugue wandering about a central theme which is never forsaken, however it may momentarily cease to be apparent."

Flowers also differ greatly in size—from the tiny flowers of the floating aquatic *Wolffia* (or water-meal) whose entire body is only $^1/_{25}$ of an inch long, the smallest living angiosperm, to the flowers of *Rafflesia arnoldii* (Figure 16.19) which may be as large as washtubs (up to 3 feet in diameter). *Rafflesia* is a tropical parasite which grows on roots or underground stems of trees in Sumatra. Its huge, orange with yellow spotted flowers may weigh as much as 16 pounds. The petals are an inch thick.

The hundreds of families of flowering plants are pretty largely characterized by different types of flowers. At the generic and species levels, these cohorts are also distinguished on the basis of floral characters, including those of the resulting fruits and seeds.

Even the botanical beginner recognizes that there is something distinctive about the flowers of monocotyledons and dicotyledons. The former (lily; tulip, Figure 16.20; iris) are built on a plan of three—three sepals, three petals, three or six stamens, and three carpels; the latter (snapdragon; pea, Figure 16.21; petunia; daisy) are usually constructed on a formula of four or five, or some multiple of these numbers. Everyone

Figure 16.19 Largest angiosperm
flower, of *Rafflesia arnoldii,* in Sumatra.
Flowers may reach 3 feet in diameter
and weigh as much as 16 pounds.
[Courtesy W. Meijer.]

recognizes the characteristic gestalt, or form, of legume flowers,
such as those of peas, beans, locust, clover, and sweet pea, with
their distinct right and left halves (bilateral symmetry) and with
a keel-like structure on which bees and other insects land.

The flowers of the fall season such as daisies, chrysanthemums, sunflowers, marigolds, and the year-round dandelion are recognized by all as a special kind of flower. These
plants belong to the composite family for they have composite
flowers (Figures 16.22 and 16.23)—that is, the structure which
appears to be a flower, with large peripheral "petals" and central "stamens," is in reality a large collection, or aggregation, of
hundreds of flowers. In one type of composite flower, represented by the sunflowers, the showy peripheral "petals" are
sterile **ray flowers** specialized for attraction of insects and the
relatively inconspicuous central structures are tiny but complete **disc flowers,** with a full complement of sepals, petals in
the form of a tube, stamens fused together to form a ring, and a
style connecting the basal ovary with two stigmas. The disc
flowers are the fertile flowers which carry on pollination, double fertilization, and ultimately produce fruits and seeds. Thus,
there is a division of labor between the ray and disc flowers.
From the standpoint of evolution, the composite family is

regarded as the most specialized and advanced in the dicotyledons.

There is a striking relationship between the type of flower structure and the kind of pollination carried on by a specific species—whether by wind, insects, or water. In the wind-pollinated flowers like the grasses (Figure 16.25), ragweed (Figure 7.1), and catkin-bearing trees as oak, birch (Figure 16.24), alder, which are so often involved in causing hay fever, or allergic rhinitis, there may be such modifications in the flower as reduction in the size of the flower, green or colorless sepals and petals, and production of large quantities of light, powdery pollen. In some wind-pollinated plants—the grasses for example—the stigmas are large and feathery and so are effectively adapted to intercept pollen as it is carried by air currents, and the stamens are thrust out some distance from the flower (dangling stamens) where the wind picks up the pollen.

On the other hand, insect-pollinated flowers are often large, highly colored, and with abundant sticky pollen, along with honey or nectar as well as attractive aromas. Some insect-pollinated flowers, such as orchids, have special devices to guide the insect pollinator in such a way that it must brush against the stamens and the stigmas. Some have adhesive pollen sacs which stick to the heads of the insects, and others even possess trigger mechanisms to insure pollination. Small wonder that Charles Darwin was fascinated by the ingenious devices employed by the orchids to insure that pollination takes place.

In the yucca, or Spanish bayonet, the pollinator, the pronuba moth, rolls up a ball of pollen from the stamen and carries it to the stigma. It then crawls to the ovary in which it deposits its eggs. When the ovules mature as a result of the stimuli provided by pollination and fertilization, some of them are eaten by the larvae of the moth; but some seeds survive and so the plant reproduces itself and nourishes the larvae as well—all in all, a fascinating partnership between a plant and an insect.

Some flowers are specialized to accomplish water pollination. The fresh-water eel grass (*Vallisneria spiralis*, Figure 16.26) is rooted in the soil at the bottom of shallow ponds and its female flowers are borne on long spiral stalks which reach to the sur-

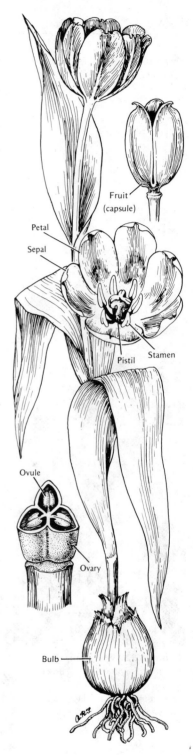

Figure 16.20 Tulip (*Tulipa*).

Figure 16.21 Sweet-pea (*Lathyrus odoratus*).

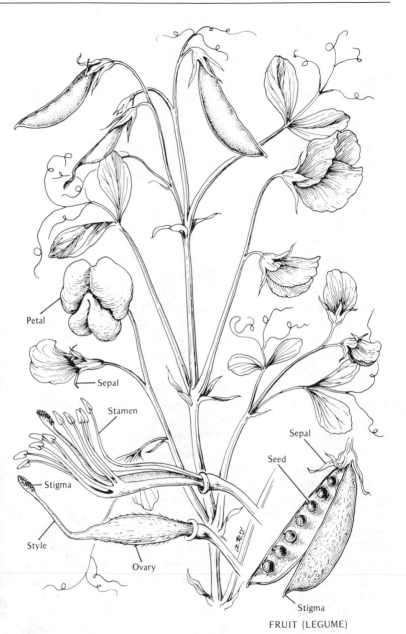

Figure 16.22 Pyrethrum (*Chrysanthemum cinerariaefolium*) flowers, showing nature of composite flowers. These flowers are used to make the well-known insecticide pyrethrum. [Courtesy U.S. Department of Agriculture.]

FRUIT (LEGUME)

Ray flower

Disc flower

Stamen

Stigma

Petals

Sepal

Ovary

RAY FLOWER   DISC FLOWER

Figure 16.23 Sunflower (*Helianthus annuus*) showing the nature of the head ("flower" of nonbotanists) and individual disc and ray flowers.

Figure 16.24 Catkins (long clusters of flowers) of paper birch (*Betula papyrifera*). [Courtesy U.S. Department of Agriculture.]

face of the water. The flowers with stamens break off from the parent plant and float on the surface of the water by means of air-filled pontoons (inflated petals). Since the female flowers float in slight depressions caused by surface tension, the boatlike male flowers are swept close to them. The pollen on the overhanging stamens brushes against the stigmas of the female flowers and pollination is accomplished. Whereupon the long floral stalk bearing the female flower recoils and pulls the female flower back into the mud of the pond where the fruit and seeds develop. You may be beguiled by a comparison of our prosaic scientific account of the remarkable reproduction in the eel grass with that of Maurice Maeterlinck (1862–1949), poet, dramatist, Nobel Laureate in literature (1911), and noted writer of essays on nature. This passage is taken from his essay "The Intelligence of Flowers":

We must not leave the aquatic plants without briefly mentioning the life of the most romantic of them all: the legendary Vallisneria, an hydrocharad whose nuptials form the most tragic episode in the love-history of the flowers. The Vallisneria is a rather insignificant herb, possessing none of the strange grace of the Water-lily or of certain submersed verdant tresses. But it would seem as though nature had delighted in imbuing it with a beautiful idea. Its whole existence is spent at the bottom of the water, in a sort of half-slumber, until dawns the wedding-hour, when it aspires to a new life. Then the female plant slowly uncoils its long peduncular spiral, rises, emerges and floats and blossoms on the surface of the pond. From a neighbouring stem, the male flowers, which see it through the sunlit water, rise in their turn, full of hope, towards the one that rocks, that awaits them, that calls them to a fairer world. But, when they have come half-way, they feel themselves suddenly held back: their stalk, the very source of their life, is too short; they will never reach the abode of light, the only spot in which the union of the stamens and the pistil can be achieved! . . .

It would be insoluble, like our own tragedy upon this earth, were it not that an unexpected element is mingled with it. Did the males foresee the disappointment with which they would meet? One thing is certain, that they have locked in their hearts a bubble of air, even as we lock in our souls a thought of desperate deliverance. It is as though for a moment they hesitated; then, with a magnificent effort, the finest, the most supernatural that I know of in all the pageantry of the insects and the flowers, in order to rise to happiness they deliberately break the bond that attaches them to life. They tear themselves from their stalk and, with an incomparable flight, amid bubbles of gladness, their petals dart up and break the surface of the water. Wounded to death, but radiant and free, they float for a moment beside their heedless brides and the union is accomplished, whereupon the victims drift away to perish, while the wife, already a mother, closes her corolla, in which lives their last breath, rolls up her spiral and descends to the depths, there to ripen the fruit of the heroic kiss.

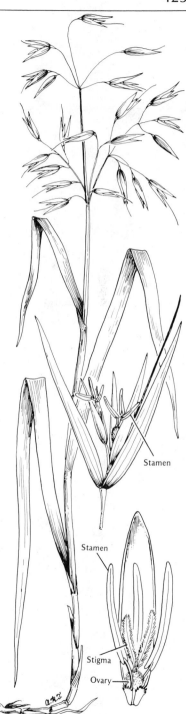

Figure 16.25 Oat (*Avena sativa*), an example of a grass.

Stamen

Stamen

Stigma

Ovary

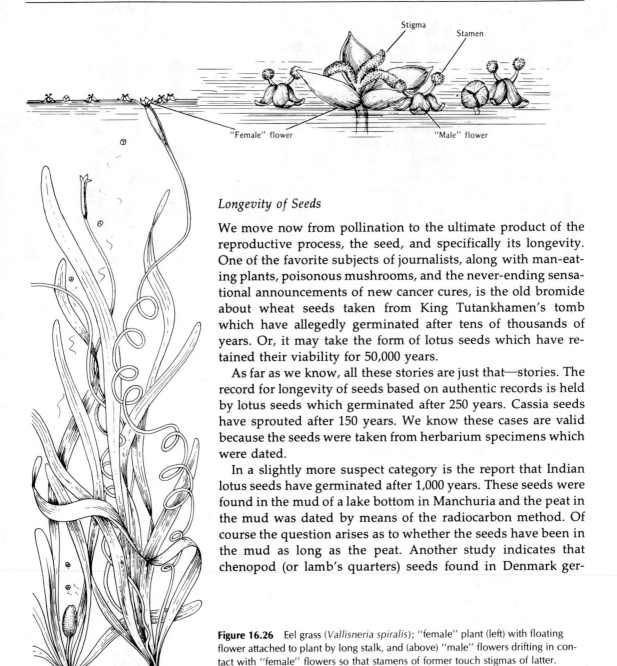

Stigma

Stamen

"Female" flower

"Male" flower

Longevity of Seeds

We move now from pollination to the ultimate product of the reproductive process, the seed, and specifically its longevity. One of the favorite subjects of journalists, along with man-eating plants, poisonous mushrooms, and the never-ending sensational announcements of new cancer cures, is the old bromide about wheat seeds taken from King Tutankhamen's tomb which have allegedly germinated after tens of thousands of years. Or, it may take the form of lotus seeds which have retained their viability for 50,000 years.

As far as we know, all these stories are just that—stories. The record for longevity of seeds based on authentic records is held by lotus seeds which germinated after 250 years. Cassia seeds have sprouted after 150 years. We know these cases are valid because the seeds were taken from herbarium specimens which were dated.

In a slightly more suspect category is the report that Indian lotus seeds have germinated after 1,000 years. These seeds were found in the mud of a lake bottom in Manchuria and the peat in the mud was dated by means of the radiocarbon method. Of course the question arises as to whether the seeds have been in the mud as long as the peat. Another study indicates that chenopod (or lamb's quarters) seeds found in Denmark ger-

Figure 16.26 Eel grass (*Vallisneria spiralis*); "female" plant (left) with floating flower attached to plant by long stalk, and (above) "male" flowers drifting in contact with "female" flowers so that stamens of former touch stigmas of latter.

minated after 1,700 years. The date was determined by archeological study of artifacts found at the same site. It will be noted that in both of these cases the age of the seeds themselves was not determined directly; only material associated with the seeds was dated. It remains to be seen whether in the future we shall find authentically dated seeds which are more ancient than 250 years and yet retain their viability.

Most seeds of garden and wild plants retain their viability for an average of 3 to 10 years, at most 25 years. There is a famous experiment at Michigan State University which is still being continued. In 1879 Professor William J. Beal of that university buried 20 bottles with seeds of various weeds and wild plants including clover. The original plan was to dig up a bottle every 5 years and run germination tests on the seeds. However, in order to prolong the study, bottles are now being lifted at 10-year intervals. After 90 years the seeds of only a few weed species such as evening primrose, curly dock, and mullein, or velvet leaf, are still viable.

Many years ago, a similar experiment was set up by a professor in a neighboring Midwestern state university, but unfortunately the professor forgot the precise spot where the seeds were buried, and so they have never been located. Doubtless some time in the future in excavating for a new building, the bottles will be discovered, and then we shall be able to compare the results with those of Dr. Beal whose memory did not fail him.

Goethe's Study of the Flower

No account of the flower and flowering plants is complete without reference to the contributions of the great German poet Johann Wolfgang von Goethe (1749–1832), author of the epic *Faust,* and one who devoted considerable time to the study of botany. Indeed, he coined the word *morphology* for the study of form and structure, and some botanists regard him as the founder of this science. He was intrigued by Linnaeus's system of classification and in fact writes of Linnaeus, "Except Shakespeare and Spinoza, I am not aware that any man of the past has had such an influence upon me." Goethe was fascinated by the concept of **homology,** the similarity in structure between organs due to common evolutionary origin. In his essay *Metamorphosis of Plants* (1790) he advanced the thesis that sepals, petals, stamens, and carpels are all transformed, or metamorphosed, leaves. Modern morphological, particularly paleobotanical research growing out of the discovery of the psilophytes, supports Goethe with respect to his astute conclusion that the floral organs and leaves are homologous. These more recent studies further indicate that the leaves of ferns and seed plants are themselves modified branches.

Suggested Readings

(See also the Suggested Readings for Chapter 15)

Arber, Agnes. *Goethe's Botany*. Waltham, Mass.: Chronica Botanica, 1946. Essay on the great poet's contributions to botany written by a remarkable English botanist. The book also includes a translation of Goethe's famous essay on the metamorphosis of plants.

Cronquist, Arthur. *The Evolution and Classification of Flowering Plants*. Boston: Houghton Mifflin, 1968. A recent, up-to-date synthesis.

Emboden, William A. *Bizarre Plants*. New York: Macmillan, 1974. See Suggested Readings, Chapter 2.

Lewes, G. H. *The Life and Works of Goethe*. New York: Dutton, 1908. Distinguished biography with a valuable chapter on the poet as a man of science.

Maeterlinck, Maurice. *News of Spring*. New York: Dodd, Mead, 1917. A collection of his essays on nature, written in colorful, purple prose.

Meeuse, B. J. D. *The Story of Pollination*. New York: Ronald, 1961. One of the best books on pollination.

Taylor, Norman. *The Ageless Relics: The Story of Sequoia*. New York: St. Martin's Press, 1962. A short, lively account of the redwood and the big tree—discovery, distribution, and history.

Plant Names

Common name	Scientific name	Family
bristlecone pine	*Pinus aristata*	Pinaceae
dawn redwood	*Metasequoia glyptostroboides*	Taxodiaceae
dodder	*Cuscuta* spp.	Cuscutaceae
Douglas fir	*Pseudotsuga menziesii*	Pinaceae
duckweed	*Lemna minor*	Lemnaceae
eel grass, fresh water	*Vallisneria spiralis*	Hydrocharitaceae
eel grass, salt water	*Zostera marina*	Zosteraceae
elodea, waterweed	*Elodea canadensis*	Hydrocharitaceae
giant sequoia, big tree	*Sequoiadendron giganteum*	Taxodiaceae
ginkgo, maidenhair tree	*Ginkgo biloba*	Ginkgoaceae
Indian pipe	*Monotropa uniflora*	Monotropaceae
mistletoe	*Viscum album*	Loranthaceae
Queen Victoria water lily	*Victoria regia*	Nymphaeaceae
redwood	*Sequoia sempervirens*	Taxodiaceae
Spanish bayonet, yucca	*Yucca* spp.	Agavaceae
Spanish moss	*Tillandsia usneoides*	Bromeliaceae
sunflower	*Helianthus annuus*	Compositae
water hyacinth	*Eichhornia crassipes*	Pontederiaceae
water-meal	*Wolffia* spp.	Lemnaceae
water lily	*Nymphaea* spp.	Nymphaeaceae

Spiny fruit of jimson weed (*Datura stramonium*), a classic plant for the study of genetics.

17
Genetics
The Elegant Science

Why Study Genetics?

There are a number of cogent reasons why we think it essential
to know something about genetics—at least the fundamentals
of the subject. For one thing, many people experience the process of heredity as parents and it would seem useful to know
what the process is all about. Fortunately the same genetic principles apply to man as to plants and lower animals.

A further reason to have a working knowledge of genetics is
that many of the great public questions of the day—population
growth, health hazards, radiation damage, atomic fallout,
nuclear energy, and numerous diseases such as diabetes, rheumatic heart disease, hemophilia, and some forms of cancer—require some knowledge of genetics just to understand
them, let alone to solve them.

Another reason for including the subject of genetics here is
that it is such an excellent illustration of the scientific method—how science goes about tackling a problem or unknown situation; how it unfolds facts and interpretations; how it makes
its halting progress; how it constantly must modify its conclusions; how scientists interact; and so forth.

And finally, the development of genetics is one of the great
chapters in the intellectual history of man. The formulation of
the broad generalizations of genetics represents one of the most
impressive triumphs of the human mind.

For these reasons we present some of the fundamental principles of genetics so that you will have a basic understanding of

429

the science and so that you will have an appreciation of the essential contributions which genetics has made and can continue to make. We cannot hope to achieve comprehensive coverage of this vast field, particularly we cannot consider all the latest research findings. We can only try to lay a foundation of the basic facts and their history with the thought that you will be stimulated sufficiently to pursue this subject in other books and publications, a guide to which we provide by listing some of the useful titles in the Suggested Readings at the end of the chapter.

What Is Genetics?

Let us begin with two definitions. **Genetics** is the science of inheritance, or heredity. By **heredity** we mean the transmission of traits—such as flower color, seed color, and eye color in man—from parents to offspring.

Brief History

Genetics is a relatively young science; indeed we can say that it began as a science in 1900, at least as far as most of the world is concerned. To be sure, there were some preliminary glimmerings before the end of the nineteenth century but these isolated facts and observations hardly constituted a science.

Before 1900 some general statements were made such as, "an individual inherits roughly $1/2$ of his traits from his parents, $1/4$ from his grandparents, and the other $1/4$ from more remote ancestors." An individual was regarded as a blend or compromise between his parents. Indeed, this concept is sometimes called the **blending theory of inheritance.** The vehicle for the transmission of traits from one generation to another was thought to be the blood. Thus we have such statements as he "comes from good blood," she is of "royal blood," and he is "related by blood." Sometimes this concept is known as the **blood theory of inheritance.** Curiously, to this day you will encounter in legal documents and other archaic spheres references to blood relationships, despite the fact that all these ideas of blending, of compromising, and of blood as the carrier of traits have been shown to be without foundation. Instead, at the present time we have what is called the **particulate theory of inheritance,** or the **theory of the gene.** But we are getting ahead of our story.

Mendel

The scientific study of genetics begins with the work of Gregor Mendel (1822–1884), an Austrian monk, who carried on his historic experiments with garden peas in the monastery garden in Brünn, Austria (now Czechoslovakia). In these simple surroundings he developed the fundamental principles of heredity, even though, as he himself states, he was hampered by lack of time when he was young and by his corpulence as he grew older. But despite these obstacles he was able to spend several years on his classic experiments with peas.

Mendel published a paper summarizing his research in 1866 in the *Proceedings of the Brünn Society for the Study of Natural History*. The result: dead silence—no one paid any attention to his work and findings. Truly, Mendel's paper with its epoch-making discoveries in genetics had a remarkable history for it was disregarded by all for 34 years—until 1900—when another remarkable series of events took place. Three botanists—Hugo de Vries of Holland, Carl Correns of Germany, and Erich von Tschermak of Austria—working in different countries came independently to the same conclusions as had Mendel; then in checking back into the scientific literature—as all good scientists do—each of the three found Mendel's original paper.

Scientists and historians of science have speculated on the reasons for the long period during which Mendel's work was ignored. One suggestion has been that Mendel published his research in an obscure journal of a local natural history society; who reads the *Proceedings of the Brünn Society for the Study of Natural History?* it was asked. But we now know that Mendel sent copies of his paper to two of the leading botanists of the day and that other copies were sent to the great libraries in London and to the United States.

Another explanation offered is that Mendel's ideas were not understood because they were too advanced. A third apologia —and the one probably closest to the truth—is that the scientific world was completely preoccupied with the revolutionary and frightening generalizations in Charles Darwin's *Origin of Species*, published in 1859.

There has also been discussion of the question of why Mendel was successful whereas his predecessors were not. Some answers have been advanced to explain his accomplishments; where others studied inheritance in terms of whole individuals, he concentrated on single, isolated characters, like flower color,

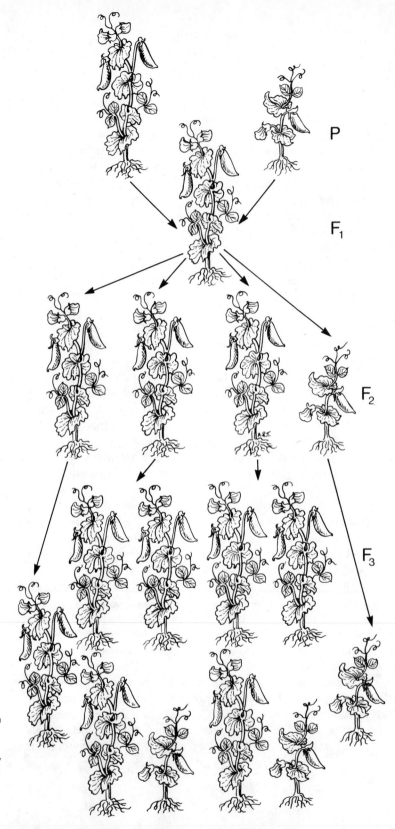

P

F₁

F₂

F₃

Figure 17.1 Diagram illustrating one of Mendel's cross. Tall pea plant crossed with short pea plant resulted in all tall pea plants in the F₁ generation. When the latter individuals were permitted to carry on self-pollination, they produced 3 tall to 1 short in the F₂. The F₃ generation is also shown.

seed color, and so forth. He counted all the individuals produced in all his crosses, and he kept accurate and complete pedigree records. Finally, he was very shrewd in the choice of material to work with, or perhaps, more likely, very lucky in this choice.

Mendel's Basic Cross

Mendel crossed tall garden peas (6 to 7 feet tall) with short or dwarf, pea plants ($^3/_4$ to $1^1/_2$ feet). These peas are designated as the parental generation (*P*). Since peas are self-pollinated (the pollen from the stamens in one flower pollinates the stigmas of carpels in the same flower), he cut off the stamens from one parent and then manually pollinated these emasculated flowers with pollen from the other parent. He found that the seeds resulting from this cross always produced tall plants. This rather surprised him for he expected that the next generation would be intermediate in size.

He permitted the tall plants of the first filial generation, or F_1, to carry on self-pollination. The seeds from the resulting cross produced the second filial generation, or F_2 (Figure 17.1). He found that some of the F_2 individuals were tall and some dwarf—specifically, in the ratio of 3 to 1. (The actual count was 787 tall to 277 dwarf.)

When he permitted the F_2 pea plants to carry on self-pollination, he found that in the third filial generation, or F_3, the dwarf plants always produced short plants. In the tall plant group or population, he found that $^1/_3$ of them always gave tall but $^2/_3$ of them produced tall and short plants in a 3:1 ratio.

Law of Unit Characters

With the results of this cross and others like it before him, Mendel reasoned that there must be something inside the tall pea plant which makes it tall and something inside the dwarf plant which makes it short. He called this something a **factor**. Further, he reasoned that there must be two factors in each plant, for all the F_1 plants were tall but upon subsequent self-pollination they produced some tall and some dwarf in the F_2. So the F_1 individuals must have a tall factor and a dwarf factor. These various statements we have just made constitute Mendel's first law, or principle, of heredity, namely the **law of unit characters,** which may be rendered as: *Factors control the inheritance of various characters and these factors occur in pairs.* Later these factors came to be called **genes**.

Law of Dominance

In the experiment previously described, Mendel considered that one factor of a given pair may prevent the expression of the other. The F_1 plants obviously have a tall factor and a dwarf factor since they are the product of a tall parent and a dwarf plant. Later the F_1 plants, upon self-pollination, produce some talls and some dwarfs. Yet all the F_1 individuals are tall. These facts led to Mendel's second law of genetics, **the law of dominance,** by which is meant that *in a given pair of factors, one factor may inhibit or mask the expression of the other.* In the example given, in the F_1, the tall factor masks the dwarf factor and so all the F_1 plants are tall. We call the factor which expresses itself the **dominant**—here the tall factor; and the factor which is masked or inhibited is designated the **recessive**—here the dwarf factor.

With these facts and principles before us, let us analyze the crosses we described before (Figure 17.2). We use the capital letter T to designate the tall factor, or gene, the capital indicating dominance; we employ the small letter t to indicate the dwarf factor, or gene, the small letter signifying the recessive. The original parents are shown as TT and tt, since the factors or genes occur in pairs. The tall parent produces spores and eventually gametes with T; the dwarf parent yields gametes with t. At the time of fertilization, the gamete with T unites with the gamete with t producing the F_1 plant, Tt. Referring to Figure 17.2, we see that the F_1 plants were permitted to carry on self-pollination, which is equivalent to saying that Tt plants crossed with Tt plants. In any case, the stamens of the F_1 plants produce spores or pollen grains which eventually yield T and t gametes; likewise the carpels eventually produce gametes with T and t. As shown in Figure 17.2, these gametes combine at random to produce the F_2: TT, Tt, Tt, and tt. Of these plants three are tall and one is dwarf, thus giving the 3:1 ratio in the F_2. When the tt plants are self-pollinated they will produce dwarf plants; when the TT individuals are self-pollinated they will always produce tall plants. The Tt plants will behave just like the Tt F_1 plants, namely they will produce tall and dwarf individuals in a 3:1 ratio.

Some Useful Terms

You will note that in the cross just described there is a distinction between the outer appearance of an individual and its inner genetic make-up. We use the term **phenotype** to refer to

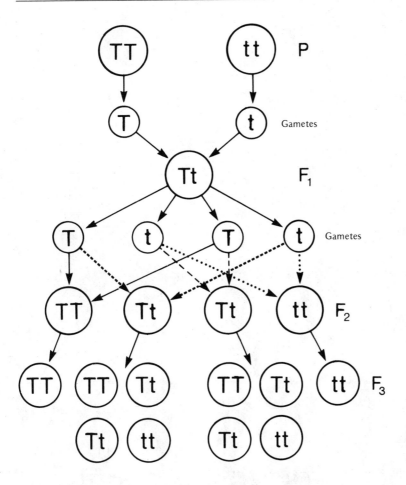

Figure 17.2 Analysis of a cross between tall and dwarf pea plants. The gene for tallness is shown as *T*; the gene for the dwarf condition, by *t*.

the external appearance of the organism; thus we say that *TT* and *Tt* individuals are tall. **Genotype** signifies the genetic make-up of the organism or the actual genes which are present; thus, although *TT* and *Tt* belong to the same phenotype, they are of different genotypes. By **homozygous** we mean that the factors, or genes, of a given pair are alike, as in *TT* or *tt*; **heterozygous** indicates that the factors, or genes, of a pair are unlike, as in *Tt*.

Law of Segregation

If you will refer to Figure 17.2 you will see that the F_1 *Tt* plants form gametes, some of which are *T* and others *t*. In other words the factors separate out in spore formation and so eventually the

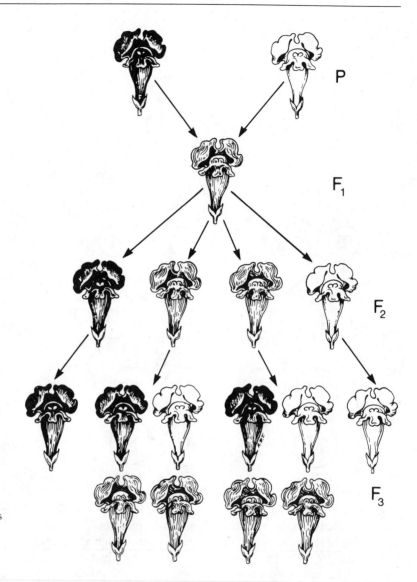

Figure 17.3 Cross between red-flowered snapdragons and white-flowered snapdragons, illustrating absence of dominance. All the F_1 plants have pink flowers, while in the F_2 the ratio is 1 red: 2 pink: 1 white. The F_3 generation is also shown.

gametes are either *T* or *t*. We may now turn to Mendel's third principle of heredity, the **law of segregation:** *The paired factors or genes separate into different daughter cells*—first spores are produced in plants and then later gametes are formed.

Crosses without Dominance

Since Mendel's time it has been learned that most traits do not show dominance, but that an intermediate condition may be produced. For example, four o'clock, snapdragon, and sweet pea flowers may be either red or white. When red and white flowered snapdragons (Figure 17.3) are crossed, they produce pink flowers in the F_1. When the F_1 plants are crossed they provide the F_2 in which there are: 1 red: 2 pinks: 1 white, an F_2 ratio of 1:2:1 (Figure 17.4).

Hybrid

In the crosses described above, we have been discussing the mating of different kinds of parents resulting in progeny which may be designated **hybrids.** In genetics, the term *hybrid* means the product of a union of two individuals differing in one or more pairs of characters; thus, when a tall pea plant, *TT,* is crossed with a dwarf plant, *tt,* the F_1 individuals are hybrids, *Tt.*

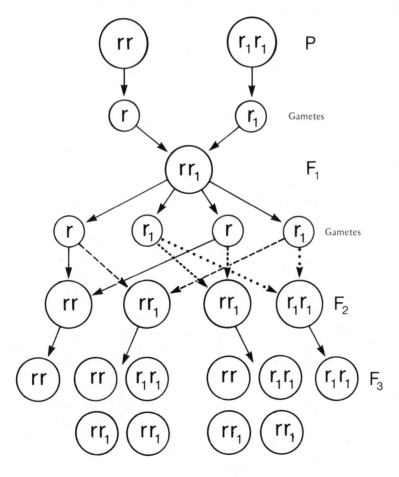

Figure 17.4 Analysis of a cross between red-flowered snapdragons and white-flowered snapdragons. The gene for red is represented by *r*, the gene for white by r_1. Plants homozygous for *r* have red flowers (*rr*); plants homozygous for r_1 are white (r_1r_1); and heterozygous individuals (rr_1) have pink flowers.

The term *hybrid* is also used in taxonomy to denote the product of a cross between two different species, two varieties, or even two genera.

Dihybrid Cross

So far we have been considering what are called **monohybrid crosses**—crosses between two individuals differing in only one set of characters, that is tall × dwarf, or red flowers × white flowers. We need to go to the next level, the **dihybrid cross,** to understand the meaning of Mendel's fourth law of heredity. If you will study Figure 17.5, you will note that we start with the

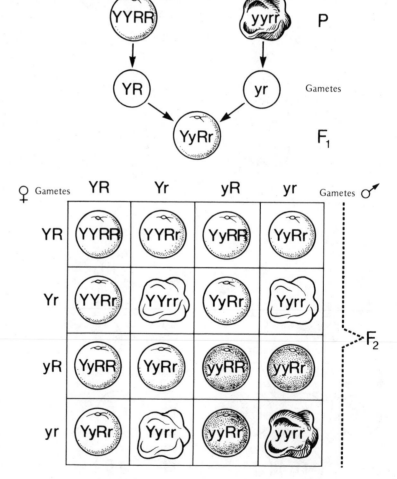

Figure 17.5 Diagram of a cross between a pea plant with yellow and round seeds and one with green and wrinkled seeds. The genes are depicted as follows: *Y* for yellow, *y* for green, *R* for round, and *r* for wrinkled. Because of dominance, all F_1 individuals are yellow and round. When the latter individuals are permitted to carry on self-pollination, the F_2 phenotypic ratio is 9:3:3:1.

parents (*P*), one with yellow and round seeds and the other, green and wrinkled seeds. Yellow and round are dominant. The various letters used signify the following: *Y*=dominant yellow gene; *y*=recessive green gene; *R*=dominant round gene; and *r*=recessive wrinkled gene. The parents are shown as *YYRR* and *yyrr* and their respective gametes as *YR* and *yr*.

Thus the resulting F_1 is *YyRr* and phenotypically all the seeds are yellow and round because of dominance.

The F_1 individuals are allowed to self-pollinate, which is to say we have the equivalent of *YyRr* individuals hybridizing with other *YyRr* plants. Each of the *YyRr* individuals will produce four different kinds of gametes: *YR, Yr, yR,* and *yr*. In order to work out all the possible combinations we use a checkerboard with the male ($\male$) gametes at the top and female ($\female$) gametes at the side, or vice versa. As you can see there are 16 different possible combinations, so we end with the F_2 ratio of 9:3:3:1, or with 9 yellow, round; 3 yellow, wrinkled; 3 green, round; and 1 green, wrinkled.

It should be emphasized that these ratios of 3:1, 1:2:1, and 9:3:3:1 are based on large numbers of individuals involved in crosses. If you were to count just a few individuals you might not achieve these ratios, any more than you would find that in all human families there are an equal number of sons and daughters even though the over-all sex ratio is 1:1.

Law of Independent Assortment

The fact that the gene *Y* and the gene *R* are together in one of the parents and *y* and *r* in the other parent, does not mean that these genes will stick together when the gametes are formed by the F_1 plants and in subsequent crosses. On the contrary, the genes of the two sets separate out and then combine at random. These ideas are incorporated in Mendel's fourth law of genetics—**the law of independent assortment,** which states that *the genes representing two or more contrasting pairs of characters are segregated to the spores (to the gametes in animals) independently of one another and then the gametes combine at random with respect to one another.*

If we were to go on to the next level—which we won't—we would consider a **trihybrid cross,** a cross between two individuals differing in three sets of characters. Merely to indicate how complicated this cross is, let us just report that the F_2 ratio is 27:9:9:9:3:3:3:1, if there are three dominants.

Summary of Mendel's Four Laws of Genetics

Mendel's important contributions to genetics may be summarized as follows:

1. *Law of unit characters:* Factors, or genes, control the inheritance of characters; these factors, or genes, occur in pairs.
2. *Law of dominance:* One factor, or gene, in a pair may mask, or inhibit, the expression of the other factor.
3. *Law of segregation:* Only one factor, or gene, of each pair goes into a spore or gamete.
4. *Law of independent assortment:* The factors or genes representing two or more pairs of characters are distributed to the spores (or gametes in animals) independently of one another; then the gametes combine at random with respect to one another.

A Few Problems

It is suggested that at this point and before we turn to a discussion of the various post-Mendelian aspects of genetics, that you review the meanings of the following terms: *dominant, recessive, phenotype, genotype, homozygous, heterozygous,* and *hybrid.*

It is also recommended that you attempt the following problems as a test of your understanding of the principles of genetics before you go on to the next section:

1. A pea plant which is heterozygous tall and heterozygous round-seeded is crossed with a pea plant which is heterozygous tall and heterozygous round. Tall and round are dominant. Describe the resulting phenotypes, giving the numbers of each type. Describe the genotypes and give the numbers of each type.
2. A homozygous round-seeded and heterozygous yellow-seeded pea plant is hybridized with one which is heterozygous round-seeded and heterozygous yellow-seeded. Describe and give the numbers of the resulting phenotypes and genotypes.
3. A pea plant which is homozygous yellow-seeded and heterozygous round-seeded is crossed with a plant homozygous yellow-seeded and homozygous wrin-

kled-seeded. Describe and give the numbers for the resulting phenotypes and genotypes.

Meiosis, or Reduction Division

Having discussed several types of crosses, we should now link the genetic phenomena with the events actually observed in cells. In Chapter 5 on cells we described the process by which cells divide and hence reproduce themselves. Ignoring the details and the technical terms applied to the several stages, the important events in this process are:

1. Formation of threads, or rods, called **chromosomes** from the scattered chromatin in the nucleus.
2. Duplication of each chromosome.
3. Separation of chromosome pairs and movement of chromosomes to the two poles of the cell.
4. Formation of the cell plate in the middle of the cell with eventually the appearance of a complete separating cell wall.
5. Reconstitution of two nuclei in the two new cells.

The end result is that we now have two new cells which are exactly alike and also like the parent cell—similar with respect to both numbers of chromosomes and in the kinds of chromosomes.

Somewhere in the life history of every plant that reproduces sexually is a special kind of nuclear division which is known as **reduction division,** or **meiosis.** In this particular type of division the chromosome number is halved, or changed from the diploid (*2n*) condition to the haploid (*n*) number. Whereas in animals meiosis occurs at the time of gamete formation, in plants it takes place in the formation of spores; for example, at the time of pollen formation in the flowering plants.

It is not our intent to give a detailed description of this important but complicated process of meiosis, nor to burden you with the technical terminology. However, by studying Figure 17.6 we hope that you will understand the essential events which take place:

1. Similar, or homologous, chromosomes pair—in this case, the long chromosome from the male parent pairs with the long chromosome from the female parent.

Figure 17.6   Comparison of mitosis (ordinary nuclear division) and meiosis (reduction division). One set of chromosomes (shown in black) came originally from one parent, and the other set (in white) came from the other parent. (A) Diagram of mitosis, shows the duplication of each chromosome and the distribution of six chromosomes to each of the daughter cells. (B) Diagram of meiosis, showing the pairing of homologous chromosomes and the duplication of each of these chromosomes, forming four chromatids (tetrads). In a later stage, two chromatids of each tetrad go to one cell and the other two to the other cell. In the next division the paired chromatids separate and migrate to different cells, thus producing cells with three chromosomes (haploid condtion). Note that not all the chromosomes that came from one parent end up in the same cell—instead some cells have black and white chromosomes.

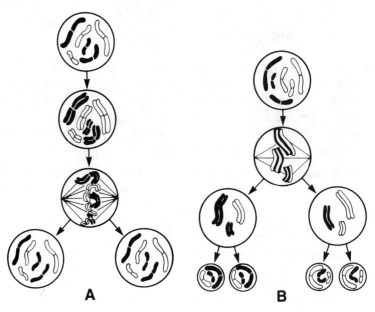

2. Each of the chromosomes duplicates itself—each of the resulting structures is called a **chromatid;** thus where we had but a pair of chromosomes, we now have a **tetrad** (group of four chromatids).

3. Two chromatids of each set move to one pole and the other two chromatids of the tetrad move to the other pole.

4. There is a random assortment of the chromosomes from the parents; that is, not all the chromosomes from one parent migrate to the same pole nor do the chromosomes from the other parent go to the other pole.

5. There is a second division of the two cells in which the chromatids of each pair now separate and go to different cells.

6. The four new cells end up with half the original number of chromosomes, or the haploid number.

The consequence of this elaborate process of meiosis is that in the four resulting cells the chromosome number is haploid (*n*) and the chromosomes are different in the four cells.

Similarity between Mendel's Factors (Genes) and Chromosome Behavior

Let us now consider the similarity between the behavior of the chromosomes and the genes. The modern view is that various characters or traits are regulated or controlled by genes which are located on the chromosomes (Figure 17.7). You will note the resemblance between the theoretical genes and the chromosomes, which, of course, can be observed with the microscope:

1. The genes are in pairs and so are the chromosomes. In each pair of chromosomes, one comes from the male parent and the other from the female.
2. There is segregation of genes at the time of spore formation in plants (at gamete formation in animals) and there is a similar segregation of chromosomes—one chromosome of each pair goes to a given spore.
3. There is independent assortment of genes and the same is true of chromosomes—it is a matter of chance which chromosomes or chromatids go into which cells in meiosis.

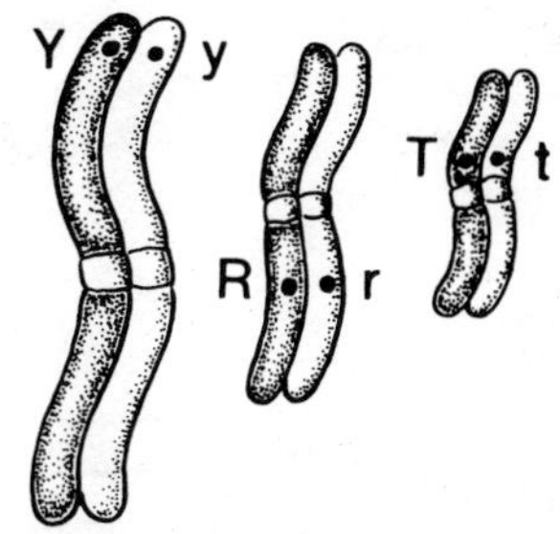

Figure 17.7 Diagram showing the location of genes on chromosomes. The gene for yellow seeds (Y) is located on one of the paired chromosomes, while the gene for green seeds (y) is found on the homologous chromosome. Similarly, the genes for roundness and wrinkled conditions of seeds are located on another set of chromosomes.

The explanation for this similarity in the behavior of genes and chromosomes is clear—the genes are located on the chromosomes, so naturally they will behave as do the chromosomes. Thus the prevalent theory to explain heredity is the **chromosome theory** or, if you prefer, the **gene theory of inheritance.**

Developments in Genetics since Mendel

Linkage

We have said that Mendel found that the various factors act independently of one another, or are independently assorted. Since the time of the rediscovery of Mendel's work in 1900, it has been learned that certain characters are inherited as a unit, or in a block. This phenomenon is termed **linkage.** How is it explained? The genes controlling these linked characters are located on the same chromosome and hence would be inherited as a block (Figure 17.8). If there are four sets of chromosomes, there are four blocks, or units, of inheritance. In retrospect, it seems remarkable that all the characters Mendel dealt with happened to be located on different chromosomes.

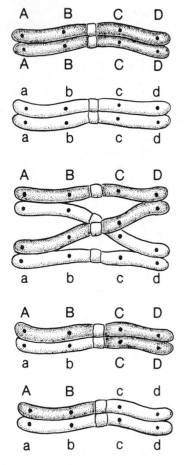

Figure 17.8 Diagram depicting crossing-over. At the top are two homologous chromosomes, each consisting of two chromatids. The letters *A, B, C,* and *D* indicate genes with homologous genes *a, b, c,* and *d.* In the middle figure the homologous chromosomes are paired with one stippled chromatid twisted over a white chromatid. The figure at the bottom shows the next stage in which a break has taken place in the two twisted chromosomes, and as a result a portion of the stippled chromatid becomes attached to a white chromatid, and a comparable portion of the first chromatid becomes associated with the remaining part of the white chromatid. Thus, although the original chromatids carried genes *A, B, C, D,* and *a, b, c, d,* they now carry *a, b, C, D, A, B, c, d,* respectively.

Crossing-over

No sooner had linkage been established when it was found that sometimes the characters which are linked do not stay linked. Why not? When the chromatids pair in meiosis, some of them may twist around their counterparts, or homologous chromatids; further, a break may occur at this point with one part of a chromatid attaching itself to another and hence there is an exchange of pieces of chromatids. The result is that some of the genes linked on one chromatid are now located on the other chromatid and vice versa (Figure 17.8).

Chromosome Maps

One of the impressive achievements of modern genetics is that geneticists are able actually to locate genes on chromosomes, and thus make chromosome maps (Figure 17.9). Hundreds of genes of the fruit fly (*Drosophila*) and of corn (Figure 17.10) have been mapped. The method of mapping is a simple one—the percentages of crossing-over are determined and if these percentages are high for two pairs of genes, they are placed far apart. On the other hand, if the percentage is small, the genes are located close together. The rationale is that if the genes are separated by some distance there will be more opportunity for twisting and crossing-over; on the other hand, if two genes are close, there will be less physical opportunity for crossing-over.

Number and Interaction of Genes

So far we may have given the impression that there are relatively few genes and that these operate pretty independently. The facts are that there are thousands of genes in higher organisms—more than 2,500 genes have been studied in the fruit fly and undoubtedly there are far more. Furthermore, not

Figure 17.9 Chromosome map of one of the ten corn chromosomes, showing the location of various genes. The relative distances between the genes are determined by the percentage of crossing-over between the genes. [Courtesy Edward H. Coe, Jr.]

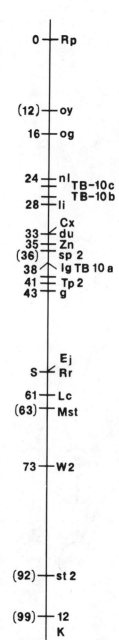

all characters are controlled by one gene, but several genes may be involved. Also genes interact and affect other characters.

Sex Inheritance

With all these revelations about genes and their role in heredity it was logical to suppose that there must be a gene for sex. However, this is not true. Instead there are sex chromosomes in animals and in some plants where there are separate sexes (dioecious).

Let us consider the situation in man which has been worked out with thoroughness. *Homo sapiens* has 46 chromosomes in all body cells. In the female there are 44 ordinary chromosomes and two so-called sex chromosomes designated as X chromosomes; the male has 44 ordinary chromosomes and two sex chromosomes but one differs from the other, and so they are styled X and Y chromosomes. If you will refer to Figure 17.11 you will see that an XX female parent produces X and X gametes, while the XY male parent forms X and Y gametes. The various types of gametes combine at random, producing the F_1: XX, XY, XY, and XX, or two males and two females—a 1:1 ratio. So sex in *Homo sapiens* is determined at the time of fertilization by the chance union of two gametes.

Sex-Linked Characters

There is a curious pattern of inheritance in which certain conditions or maladies occur in the males but skip the female members of the family or line. Color blindness and hemophilia, or bleeder's disease, are examples. In some royal families, the males may be bleeders but most of the females are not. The explanation (Figure 17.12) is that the gene controlling this condition is located on the sex chromosomes, specifically on the X chromosome and this gene is recessive; in other words the normal, or nonbleeding, condition is dominant. Thus a female with a single gene for hemophilia on the X chromosome does not develop the disease because the dominant gene may be on the other X chromosome; but a male with a single gene for hemo-

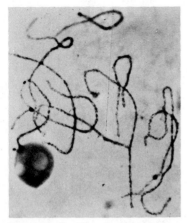

Figure 17.10 Chromosomes of corn. The large dark object is the nucleolus. [Courtesy Delbert T. Morgan, Jr.]

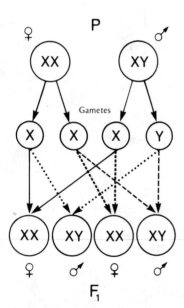

Figure 17.11 Diagram illustrating sex inheritance in humans and in certain plants. The female has 2 *X* chromosomes, and the male has an *X* and a *Y* chromosome.

philia will have the malady for there is no dominant gene on the *Y* chromosome. To produce a female with hemophilia we would have to cross a female with one gene for hemophilia with a male hemophiliac; in this cross some of the females would be homozygous for hemophilia and would hence develop the disease. Thus we say that such conditions as hemophilia and color blindness are **sex-linked characters.**

Apparently Queen Victoria of Great Britain was the original carrier of the recessive gene for hemophilia. It is thought that a mutation occurred in Victoria or in one of the gametes of her parents. We know that one of Victoria's sons was afflicted with the disease and that two of her five daughters carried the recessive gene. It was through these two daughters that hemophilia was introduced into the Russian and Spanish royal families. Alexis, the last czarevitch of Russia and the two sons of Alfonso XIII, former king of Spain, suffered from hemophilia. As far as is known the recessive gene has not been transmitted to the present British royal family.

Mutations

The concept of a mutation such as that which may have affected Queen Victoria, is basic in genetics and evolution. A **mutation** is defined as a change in the make-up of a line of organisms which cannot be explained on the basis of past breeding nor by a change in the environment. Furthermore, the change, or new feature, is passed on to the next generation; in other words, a mutation is inheritable—it is thus a genetic change. Mutations play an important role in the production of new and desirable plants in horticulture and agriculture, as they do in evolution, for they introduce new features.

We now know that mutations may be caused by chemical changes in a single gene or there may be a doubling or tripling of whole chromosome sets and thus we have plants with $4n$ and $6n$ chromosome conditions. Plants with extra sets of chromosomes beyond the diploid number $(2n)$ are designated **polyploids.** Many of our economic crop plants are polyploids, for example wheat and potatoes. Mutations may also be caused by the addition of one extra chromosome, a condition brought about by an imperfect reduction division. We should make clear that mutations are constantly being produced in nature but at a relatively low rate.

It is now possible to induce mutations in plants artificially,

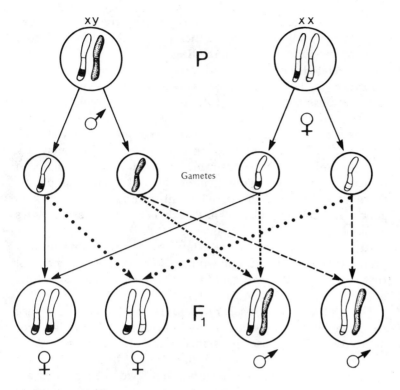

Figure 17.12 Diagram to show inheritance of sex-linked characters. In humans, the recessive gene for hemophilia is carried on the *X* chromosome, as is the dominant gene for the normal condition or nonhemophilia. The black band on the *X* chromosome represents the gene for hemophilia and the blank band stands for the normal gene.

but we hasten to add that in the present state of the art experimental geneticists cannot produce the kind of mutations they want; instead the mutations they produce are haphazard. Exposure to X rays may induce mutations—hence the operator of the X-ray machine in the physician's office is protected by a thick lead shield. Radiations produced by atomic explosions may induce mutations, as will radioactive minerals such as uranium. These phenomena are matters of real concern in the world at the present time, for it is an alarming fact that most mutations induced in man are deleterious. In addition, there are some chemicals, such as the alkaloid colchicine derived from the autumn crocus and used in gout therapy which induce mutations.

Plant Breeding

How are all these facts, theories, and principles employed in the practical breeding of plants? Suppose you want to develop a very productive wheat plant which is also resistant to the wheat rust fungus. You would first **select** those wheat plants with many, large grains. You would then proceed to establish a **pure line** for productivity by **inbreeding;** that is, you would cross closely related individuals and thus establish the homozygous condition for productivity, or as nearly a homozygous condition as possible. In wheat this inbreeding would be accomplished by self-pollination of very productive plants. Once you have a line of plants homozygous for high productivity, the offspring produced will also be high yielding. You may ask whether inbreeding is desirable since it is frowned on in humans. The answer is that genetically, and certainly in plants, there is not much wrong with inbreeding if the stock is good—if there are no bad genes, such as those for certain types of feeble-mindedness in man.

At the same time you are establishing a pure line of very productive wheat plants you would also be inbreeding the most rust-resistant plants you could identify to establish a pure line, or the homozygous condition, for resistance.

The next step is to cross, or hybridize, individuals from these two lines, with the result that the hybrids have both high productivity and disease resistance. And there is an added bonus—increased vigor, something we call **hybrid vigor** (see Chapter 11), which often results when two inbred lines are crossed. The method we have just described, that is, the crossing of two inbred lines, is the method used to produce **hybrid corn** (Figure 17.13). As is well known, hybrid corn is unusually productive, yielding as much as 35 percent more than the old strains of the grain.

There are other methods and variations of methods of plant breeding which may also be used or combined with the procedures just described. For example, new and desirable genes may be introduced into cultivated plants from wild relatives of these plants. Another method is to be constantly on the alert for the appearance of desirable mutations in a collection of plants or population. These favorable mutations may then be incorporated in the lines you are developing. Double flowers in a number of ornamental species and pink dogwood (which arose first in the wild) are examples of mutations which appeared and were then exploited.

Sometimes we have what are called **bud mutations,** a change involving only one branch of a plant since the mutation occurred in only one bud. Quite understandably these bud mutations must be perpetuated by grafting. The California navel

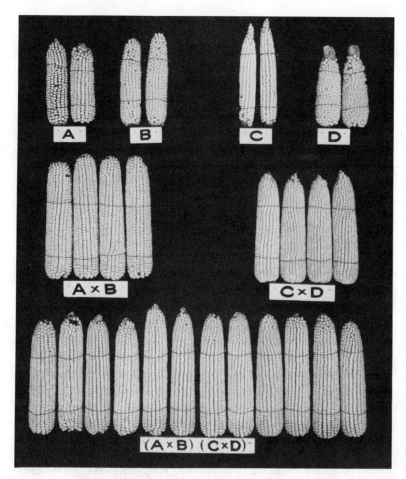

Figure 17.13 Method of producing hybrid corn. The ears marked *A, B, C,* and *D* represent the products of four different inbred lines. Strain *A* is crossed with *B,* and strain *C* with *D.* Then the products of these two lines are crossed to produce the ears of corn shown in the bottom row. Note the increase in the size of the ears and in the number of kernels on the ears. [Courtesy Funk Brothers Seed Co.]

orange and the nectarine (peach with a smooth skin) are examples of fruits which arose through spontaneous bud mutations.

The Nucleic Acids, DNA and RNA

In Chapter 5 on cells we said that the nucleic acid DNA (deoxyribonucleic acid) is found in the chromosomes and that the DNA molecule is a double spiral, or double helix. We further went on to state that the nucleic acid RNA (ribonucleic acid) serves as a messenger for the DNA to the ribosomes where the RNA determines the order or sequence of amino acids in protein manufacture on the ribosomes.

Now let us consider the bearing of these facts on genetics. In the first place the gene is a code unit—it bears information, specifically information on how to order the amino acids in the long protein chains. The gene is composed of DNA and thus consists of a double strand, or double helix, made up of thousands of atoms. The information, or code, of the DNA is transferred to the messenger RNA which takes this information to the ribosomes where proteins, particularly enzymes, are manufactured. As explained before, the information on the RNA controls the sequence of the amino acids in the chains of protein molecules (specifically, the base pairs in the RNA molecule determine the ordering of the amino acids). Enzymes control all chemical reactions, and in turn these chemical reactions are responsible for the characters and traits of organisms. It is in this manner that the DNA transmits bits of information from parent to offspring.

Scientific Method as Illustrated by Genetics

As we have learned, Mendel performed a number of experiments from which he derived a number of facts, or **data.** He next advanced a **hypothesis** (tentative explanation or guess) to explain these facts. He reasoned that there must be something in the plant which controls the inheritance of the various traits, or characters, such as tallness, flower color, and the like. He called each of these somethings *Merkmal*, which came to be translated as "**factor.**"

When he crossed tall and dwarf pea plants only tall plants were produced in the F_1, but when the F_1 generation was self-pollinated, the F_2 had some tall and some short plants. From these facts he reasoned that there must be two factors in each plant (**law of unit characters**).

Mendel next formulated the hypothesis that all the F_1 individuals are tall because, in a given pair of factors, one may mask or inhibit the other (**law of dominance**). Further research revealed that dominance does not always operate, hence the original hypothesis of dominance had to be modified to the extent of saying that it occurs only in certain plants and with certain characters in the plants.

To explain the results he obtained with dihybrid crosses Mendel postulated the **law of independent assortment;** that is, that the various genes representing two or more characters are distributed to the spores (or gametes in animals) independently of one another and then the gametes combine at random. After Mendel's time it was learned that this principle does not always hold, for certain characters are inherited in a group, or block. The hypothesis of **linkage** was then advanced to explain this, to wit, the genes controlling these characters which are inherited in a block are located on the same chromosome and so, of course, they would stay together.

Later it was discovered that not all linked characters stay linked. To explain this phenomenon the hypothesis of **crossing-over** was advanced; that is, the chromatids sometimes twist, break, and exchange segments.

As we have said, Mendel hypothesized theoretical factors to explain the control of the inheritance of characters. Later the word *factor* was changed to *gene* (1909). After Mendel's paper was published, chromosomes were discovered in nuclei of cells (1875), and their behavior described with the aid of the microscope. Then came the suggestion that the theoretical units, the genes, are located on chromosomes, and the parallelism in behavior of genes and chromosomes was noted (1903). Finally, the nucleic acid DNA was discovered and this led much later to the suggestion that this material bore the genetic code and passed it on to the RNA which delivered the message to the ribosomes where the amino acids are ordered in protein chains.

You will note that in science we first gather a series of facts, or accumulate **data,** by observation and/or experimentation. Then a tentative explanation, or **hypothesis** is formulated to explain the facts. With additional data derived from experimentation or by observation, it may be concluded that the hypothesis is a valid one and that there seem to be no exceptions. At this point the hypothesis may be considered a **theory.** After considerable more experimentation and data gathering by many different individuals working on different organisms in different parts of the world, the theory may be considered to be well enough established to be referred to as a **law.** You will observe that there are no strict or rigid lines of demarcation between hypothesis and theory and between theory and law—rather it is a matter of degree, and it must be admitted that biologists are rather casual in the use of these terms.

So, you see the halting manner in which science progresses. The original hypothesis is constantly being modified and refined to take into consideration new facts and new knowledge. And there is no reason to suppose that our present concepts are wholly true and that they will not have to be modified. A medical dean a few years ago announced to the entering first year class that 50 percent of what they would be taught in medical school would prove subsequently to be false—the only trouble, he said, is that we don't know which 50 percent.

In connection with experimentation we should say a word about the role of the **control.** In an experiment we usually modify a single condition—let us say that we expose a group of plants to red light in an attempt to determine if and how red light affects the growth of plants. This group of plants is known as the **experimental group;** another group, the **control group,** are plants similar in every particular except that the one condition is not modified; in this instance these plants are not exposed to red light. Then, after a period of time, we compare growth in both groups of plants. If the experimental plants show some effect which is not present in the controls, we reason that the effect was caused by the modified condition; here, the red light.

What separates great scientists from the pedestrian investigator or mere data-gatherer is the ability to develop fruitful hypotheses. This requires the same kind of genius, the same kind of insight, the same kind of imagination as that demanded to create great literature, great art, and great music. It can be said that an elegant or brilliant hypothesis is a thing of beauty comparable to a sonnet, a sculpture, or a sonata.

The role of chance discovery, or **serendipity,** is important; in a sense it plays the same role in research as do mutations in evolution, for both introduce the striking new element. But it usually takes a person of rare perception with a background of appropriate knowledge to appreciate the significance of a chance occurrence or observation. "Chance," Charles Nicolle tells us, "favors only those who know how to court her."

If you wish to investigate these matters further we recommend W. I. B. Beveridge's *The Art of Scientific Investigation* and Carl Swanson's admirable book *The Natural History of Man.*

Suggested Readings

Beveridge, W. I. B. *The Art of Scientific Investigation.* New York: Norton, 1950. A highly recommended, stimulating, and informative book on research as a process.

Levine, Robert P. *Genetics.* 2d ed. New York: Holt, Rinehart and Winston, 1968. A lucid exposition on modern genetics.

Merrell, David. *Introduction to Genetics.* New York: Norton, 1975. A good, solid text.

Rosenberg, Eugene. *Cell and Molecular Biology.* New York: Holt, Rinehart and Winston, 1971. A good introduction to molecular biology.

Sayre, Anne. *Rosalind Franklin and DNA.* New York: Norton, 1975. Watson's account of the discovery of the structure of DNA is corrected here with a description of the important but neglected contributions of Rosalind Franklin. Anyone who reads *The Double Helix* should also read this book.

Swanson, Carl P., and Peter L. Webster. *The Cell.* 4th ed. Englewood Cliffs, N. J.: Prentice-Hall, 1977. A brief book on the structure of cells.

———. *The Natural History of Man.* Englewood Cliffs, N. J.: Prentice-Hall, 1973. A beautiful book on the influence of scientific discoveries on man's changing concept of himself and his place in the universe.

Wallace, Bruce. *Genetics, Evolution, Race.* Englewood Cliffs, N. J.: Prentice-Hall, 1972. A series of essays on contemporary biology with emphasis on topics of social importance.

Watson, James D. *The Double Helix.* New York: Atheneum, 1968. The story of the discovery of the structure of DNA by one of the discoverers. A personal account written with unusual frankness.

———. *Molecular Biology of the Gene.* 2d ed. New York: Benjamin, 1970. A sophisticated but lucid exposition on the subject by one of the founders of molecular biology.

Gregor Mendel is portrayed by Professor Richard M. Eakin of the University of California, Berkeley. Note the pot of peas and the cigar in the dish. When Dr. Eakin lectures to his class on Mendel he dresses for the part and plays the role of Mendel. [Courtesy Richard M. Eakin.]

18
Mendel
Founder of Genetics

Who was this man who sired the science of genetics? What manner of human being was he? These and other questions spring to mind as one marvels at the seminal discoveries of this renowned botanist.

Formative Years

Gregor Johann Mendel (Figure 18.1) was born in 1822 near Brünn, Austria (now a part of Czechoslovakia). He came of peasant stock in which there was a mingling of German and Slavic genes—his biographer says blood! Mendel's father was a poor farmer who was forced to devote brutally long days to work on his own farm and, according to the custom of the day, he was then required to contribute three days a week of service to the local duke. But his father had a genuine fondness for gardening and fruit-growing, and it was from him that the boy Johann developed his deep love for plants, for gardening, and for nature in general. Certainly his father's example was one of the important influences in young Mendel's life that helped to stimulate his profound interest in living things and to shape the kind of man he became.

In due time the boy was sent to the village school where he rose to the top of his class. Again in high school he was one of the best pupils, in striking contrast to both Linnaeus and Darwin, who were such indifferent students that their teachers

Figure 18.1 Gregor Johann Mendel (1822–84). Photograph taken at the time of his genetic experiments. [Courtesy Moravian Museum, Brno.]

455

and their respective fathers despaired of them. Because of his outstanding academic performance, Mendel was sent for two years to the local Philosophical Institute, despite the considerable sacrifice this imposed on his impoverished family. At the institute he studied philosophy and some science.

Mendel Becomes a Monk

At this point in his career he was faced with a choice of vocation: he could be a farmer, which meant that he was destined for a life of poverty like his father, or he could enter the Church and be guaranteed a comfortable albeit a simple living. The decision was one of anguish, for Mendel was an only son whose father wished fervently that he join him and eventually take over the family farm. On the other hand, his mother, impressed with his academic promise, dreamed that he might have the opportunity to improve himself. After much soul-searching, Mendel joined the Augustinian monastery in Brünn as a novice in 1843; he became a priest in 1847.

The monastery in Brünn was the second great influence on his life, for here he had recourse to a library with books on science, a herbarium of plants representative of the local flora, and a small botanical garden. Coming from the simple and impoverished background of his father's farm, Mendel was attracted to these facilities for scholarship and he made good use of them. He literally trained himself in science, particularly botany, by reading, by studying the identified and classified herbarium specimens, and by making observations in the botanical garden.

For a while he served as a substitute teacher in the local secondary school but when he took the qualifying examination for a regular teaching post he failed. Stung by this defeat, he managed to persuade his ecclesiastical superiors to send him to the University of Vienna for two years (1851–53) where he studied botany and other sciences. He returned to the monastery and served as a substitute teacher in the local schools for 14 years. From all reports he was a very good teacher as he had the ability to make complex matters clear and understandable. Surprisingly, in view of his excellent academic record as a student and his fine performance as a teacher, he failed his second qualifying examination for a permanent teaching position —indeed, he never passed this examination.

Botanical Research

When teaching and clerical duties permitted, he carried on botanical investigations. We know that he had the use of a microscope and that he bought and read all of Charles Darwin's books as they appeared. One of the stimulating influences in this period of his life was the Brünn Society for the Study of Natural Science of which he was an active member. He derived intellectual stimulus from the kindred spirits who met regularly, read papers on their simple investigations, and then discussed the implications of their observations. It was all new and it was exciting to be exploring the unknown with colleagues of similar interests.

Figure 18.2 The garden of the monastery in Brünn (Brno) where Mendel performed his experiments with peas; to the left is the monument to Mendel. [Courtesy Moravian Museum, Brno.]

In 1856, when he was already 34 years old, Mendel embarked on his experiments involving the hybridization of pea plants. He devoted 7 years to these activities, growing his plants in a modest plot in the monastery garden (Figure 18.2).

Mendel summarized the results of his various crosses and he read a paper on the subject in 1865 to the Brünn Society. As was the custom in those halcyon days, his paper was published in the Society's *Proceedings* (1866) under the title of "Experiments in Plant Hybridization" (translated from the German). As we previously indicated in Chapter 17 on genetics, this paper, which has since proven to be one of the classic papers of all times in science, was met with dead silence, until de Vries, Correns, and Tschermak reached the same conclusions and rediscovered Mendel's work in 1900. Here we have an illustration of a recurring phenomenon in science, as well as elsewhere, described as "an idea whose time has come." It does seem that at certain periods all the data, observations, and experimental results accumulate to make it inevitable that a major conceptual breakthrough will occur. We see it here, and we shall see it again in the near simultaneous discovery by Charles Darwin and Alfred Wallace of the role of natural selection in the origin of species.

See photograph on page 454, Mendel as portrayed by Professor Richard Eakin.

His Later Years

Mendel was elected abbot of his monastery (Figure 18.3) in 1868 and after that he had little time for science because his administrative and religious duties demanded nearly all his time, particularly since he was soon engaged in a long and strenuous

Figure 18.3 The monastery in Brünn (Brno) where Mendel lived and worked for 40 years. [Courtesy Moravian Museum, Brno.]

fight with the government over its attempt to tax monasteries. He developed a kidney disease which was said to be due to nicotine poisoning—he reputedly smoked 20 cigars a day. He finally contracted dropsy and died in 1884. Since there was no suspicion of his future fame, all his papers and notes were burned except for his bound books, thus there are in existence few letters and documents written by him. The pity of it is that only 16 years after his death, his work was rediscovered and soon thereafter his greatness was recognized.

What are the characteristics of the man which might possibly help to explain Mendel's success in research? First, his peasant background probably contributed to his practicality, caution, tenacity, and great patience. In addition, he was thorough, methodical, and, most of all, he had a penetrating mind which cut through all the minutiae and details of crosses and experiments to focus on the major trends and generalizations.

Contributions

Any appraisal or evaluation of Gregor Mendel would certainly acknowledge him as the founder of genetics, as the person who gave us classical, or Mendelian genetics, as it is called. We still speak of Mendelian ratios and Mendelian inheritance. Who else can claim the discovery of four laws of science—unit characters, dominance, segregation, and independent assortment? Accordingly, most scholars and scientists judge Mendel to be a great botanist and one worthy of taking a place alongside the other great botanists or biologists such as Linnaeus and Charles Darwin.

Suggested Readings

Eakin, Richard M. *Great Scientists Speak Again*. Berkeley: University of California Press, 1975. When Professor Eakin lectures to his University of California classes on Mendel, he dresses for the part and delivers the lecture as he imagines Mendel might. This book summarizes the lectures Eakin gives on Mendel, Darwin, Pasteur, Harvey, Beaumont, and Spemann.

Iltis, Hugo. *Life of Mendel*. London: Allen & Unwin, 1932. The definitive Mendel biography.

Mendel, Gregor. *Experiments in Plant Hybridization*. Cambridge, Mass.: Harvard University Press, 1963. A translation of the original, epoch-making paper published in 1865 which founded genetics.

Stern, Curt, and Eva R. Sherwood, eds. *The Origin of Genetics*. San Francisco: Freeman, 1966. A collection of the important early writings on genetics, beginning with Mendel's original paper.

Sturtevant, A. H. *A History of Genetics*. New York: Harper & Row, 1965. An excellent account of the genesis and development of genetics.

Golden barrel cactus (*Echinocactus grusonii*), depicting the products of a line of evolution involving modification of stems for water storage in a desert habitat and the development of elaborate, ornate spines.

19
Evolution
Unifying Principle of Life

It would be as unthinkable to omit consideration of evolution from any book on general botany as it would be to write of English literature and leave out Shakespeare or to publish a volume on religion without mention of the soul. Evolution is the great central principle in all of biology—it permeates every nook and cranny of the life sciences. It is the unifying thread which links all aspects of the biological sciences.

The Evolution Controversy

Evolution has been a controversial subject for over a century. In the latter part of the nineteenth and the first part of the twentieth century a number of professors were dismissed or were embroiled in controversy because they taught evolution in their college classes. High school teachers were even more vulnerable. Indeed, the struggle over the teaching of evolution was one of the major forces in the development of academic freedom in this country, for out of this struggle emerged the concept of tenure to protect professors from those who would attempt to suppress their teaching.

Scopes Case

During the last century there were numerous battles over evolution but perhaps the best known case is the celebrated Scopes trial which took place in Dayton, Tennessee, in 1925. The State of Tennessee had some years previous to this date enacted a law forbidding the teaching of evolution in the schools and colleges

461

of the state. A group opposing the law persuaded John Scopes, a young biology teacher in the local high school, to consent to arrest for teaching evolution so that the law could be tested in the courts. And so the scene was set for one of the great trials of history, the so-called Monkey Trial.

To buttress the legal staff of the prosecution the state brought in William Jennings Bryan, renowned lawyer and orator, fundamentalist, advocate of free silver, and thrice Democratic candidate for the presidency of the United States. The defense staff in turn reinforced itself with the addition of that great defender of lost causes, Clarence Darrow.

One of the strategies of the defense was to have outstanding experts in various fields of science, such as biology and geology, testify as to the validity of evolution. The zoologists, for instance, stated that man was considered to be an animal and was classified as a mammal, defining a mammal as a creature with hair and mammary glands. A few days later when Bryan was inveigled to take the stand, he absolutely refused to be a mammal. The next day a reporter made the point that obviously Bryan was right, for the bald Bryan had little hair on his head and he certainly did not suckle his young.

Despite the learned testimony and the great legal skills of Darrow, Scopes was found guilty and fined $100. However, upon appeal to the supreme court of the state the case was thrown out on a technicality. A few days after the trial, Bryan died in Dayton and the community later established a college, Bryan College, in his honor.

Other Evolution Cases

In 1967 Tennessee abolished its evolution law but as late as 1973 there were attempts to reinstitute the antievolution statute in one guise or another. In 1972 a poll of the high school students in Dayton revealed that 75 percent of them believed in the biblical version of creation. On the occasion of the poll, a local minister was quoted as saying that Darwin's theory "breeds corruption, lust, immorality, greed and such acts of criminal depravity as drug addiction, war and atrocious acts of genocide."

In recent years there has been occasional resistance to the teaching of evolution in Texas and California. In 1965 there was a concerted drive in Texas to prevent the adoption of three high school biology texts which allegedly "teach evolution as a fact." All three books had been prepared by panels of outstanding high school and college teachers under the auspices of the respected American Institute of Biological Sciences. In California, in 1972, there was a struggle involving the state board of education which approves all textbooks for the elementary schools of the state. A strenuous effort was made to change the "scientific dogmatism" allegedly involved in the treatment of evolution in school texts and to force equivalent treatment of the biblical account of creation. Finally a compromise was reached in which it was agreed that the question of the philosophy of man's origin should be left to the social science textbooks.

An intriguing episode occurred in Illinois during the 1940s. A high school textbook appeared with fairly extensive coverage of evolution. As a result it was soon branded as an "evolution text," and schools were urged not to adopt it for this reason. Finally the publishers persuaded the authors to prepare another version of their text with a watered-down account of evolution, particularly with respect to the evolution of man. One could buy either version. They were soon labeled the "liberal edition," and the "fundamentalist edition." Both versions carried the same title but there was one additional difference: The earlier edition had for a frontispiece a color plate showing a scene from the West; the later version has a picture of some stunted trees growing in a rocky mountainside. Accompanying the picture are the words, "Trees, dwarfed and distorted by an unfavorable environment."

In the late 1950s the most widely used high school textbook of biology also came in two editions—a standard edition and a special edition, called the Gregor Mendel edition, which carried the imprimatur of a Catholic bishop. The special edition, by quotation from an encyclical letter, *Humani Generis*, of Pope Pius XII explains the Catholic position with respect to evolution. All this reminds one of the authors of this book of his high school days when there were two editions of a popular history of the United States. The only difference was in the chapter on the Civil War—one was slanted toward the position of the Union, and the other toward the sentiments of the Confederacy. Verily, truth is relative.

Misconceptions

In a sense it is unfortunate that evolution became linked with the question of the origin of man, for it is likely that had the discussion been restricted to the evolution of plants, no one would have raised an objection. And the same is probably true if consideration had been limited to the animal kingdom, exclusive of

man. And it certainly is unfortunate that from the first the
evolution theory came to be regarded as one which holds that
man originated from monkeys, for to many people this suggestion is repugnant. The theory itself came to be known as the
"monkey theory" and any legislation on the matter, as the
"monkey law." This gross distortion of evolutionary thought is
incorporated in a little rhyme that goes,

> First he was a tadpole, just beginning to begin.
> Then he was a bullfrog with tail tucked in.
> Then he was a monkey, swinging from a tree.
> Now he's a professor with a Ph.D.

Of course no reputable biologist or evolutionist believes that
monkeys gave rise to man; they do suggest, however, that *Homo
sapiens* and various anthropoid groups may have shared common ancestors way back in the dim mists of antiquity.

In recent years it has been suggested whimsically that the
monkeys find the suggestion that man descended from them as
abhorrent as many people do. Thus these lines from a poem
entitled "The Monkey's Viewpoint":

> Three monkeys sat in a coconut tree
> Discussing things as they're said to be.
> Said one to the other, "Now listen, you two,
> There's a certain rumor that can't be true,
> That man descended from our noble race.
> The very idea! It's a dire disgrace;
> No monkey ever deserted his wife,
> Starved her baby, and ruined her life
> And you've never known a mother monk
> To leave the babies with others to bunk,
> Or pass them on from one to another
> 'Til they scarcely know who is their mother.
> And another thing! You'll never see
> A monk build a fence round a coconut tree,
> And let the coconuts go to waste.
> Forbidding all other monks a taste.
> Why, if I put a fence round this tree
> Starvation would force you to steal from me.
> Here's another thing a monk won't do;
> Go out at night and get a stew;
> Or use a gun, or club, or knife
> Yes, man descended, the ornery cuss,
> But, brother, he didn't descend from us!

Charles Erskine Scott Wood (1852–1944) in his *Heavenly Discourse* (1927) devoted a chapter entitled "The Monkeys Complain" to the same thesis. (Parenthetically, if you don't know Wood and his books, both are worth investigating. He was a graduate of West Point who later fought in the Indian wars of the West and emerged as a colonel. He settled in Portland, Oregon, where he began to write and to practice law. In the latter connection he maintained two offices—one for the wealthy and for corporation clients, and another, a secret chamber, to which he welcomed poets and artists, hoboes, dreamers, cranks, fanatics, sinners and saints, and scientists.)

Strange Contradictions

It is a strange anomaly that some people who react most violently to the thought that man might have evolved from lower animals have no trouble with the belief that bedbugs come from dirt and that mice develop from old rags.

On a higher intellectual plane, there are those who say they cannot see how evolution could have taken place, they cannot see how lower animals might have developed into higher animals, because so many profound changes are involved—the development of a heart, of eyes, and the brain, merely to mention a few of the more complicated organs. They are persuaded that these changes are too complex to have taken place even over a long period of time. Yet these same persons should be reminded that a human being begins as a single-celled zygote with little more than cytoplasm and a nucleus with DNA; it then becomes two-celled, then multicellular, then tissues and organs form, such as the heart, lungs, and the brain. All this from a single cell—and all these changes within a nine-month period. Surely if these profound changes can take place in a period of less than a year, similar developments can occur over millions of years.

Organic Evolution

In view of the confusion over the meaning of evolution, we should define the word as we use it in biology. By **organic evolution** we mean the historic process of change by which existing species have reached their present state.

The significant date in the history of evolution is 1859 when Charles Darwin published his *Origin of Species*. In this book he did two things: He brought together and summarized the evidence for evolution and, secondly, he presented his own theory to explain evolution, the theory of natural selection. Unquestionably, his *Origin* is one of the great classics of all science, indeed of all intellectual endeavor. We should hasten to add that the idea of evolution did not originate with Darwin; on the contrary, the concept is a very ancient one going back to the Greeks. Henry Fairfield Osborn, for example, has written a sizable book *From the Greeks to Darwin* in which he brings together the scores of different ideas about evolution which have emerged during 24 centuries.

One of the sources of confusion in popular discussions of evolution is the failure to distinguish among three separate questions:

1. Is evolution a fact?
2. What has been the course of evolution? Which groups gave rise to which organisms?
3. How is evolution to be explained?

One may answer the first in the affirmative and yet be in doubt as to the second and more particularly the third question. An overwhelming majority of biologists say yes to the first question, yet there is considerable debate about the second—that is, the precise relationships among the various groups of plants and animals. The third query is still under active investigation although there is general agreement over the main outlines of the explanations of evolution. In subsequent sections, let us pursue each of these three questions in turn.

Evidence for Evolution

The evidence for evolution will be discussed—following the precedent set by Darwin—under the rubrics of comparative morphology, comparative physiology, geographical distribution, fossils, vestigial organs, recapitulation, and changes in cultivated plants and domesticated animals.

Comparative Morphology

All plants in the plant kingdom can be arranged in a number of series resembling a branching tree in which the simplest forms are at the base and the more complex plants are at the extremities of the branches. Each one of the series is a continuous progressive sequence with some gaps.

Then too we have the striking circumstance that although there are approximately 500,000 species of flowering plants, all the flowers of these plants are fundamentally the same. They are all built on the same basic plan even though there is endless variation in the number and precise placement of floral parts and in the color of the flowers. Again, the ferns constitute a group of some 9,000 species, yet all have essentially the same life history with variations.

How else but on the basis that evolution has taken place can we explain the continuum of simple to intermediate to complex forms of plants, and the fact that hundreds of thousands of angiosperms have the same basic flower structure, and that thousands of fern life cycles are essentially the same?

Comparative Physiology

It is a remarkable truth that photosynthesis is fundamentally the same in all green plants whether we are dealing with an alga, a fern, or a lily. The same is true of other physiological processes such as the formation of proteins from amino acids and the role of DNA in providing the genetic code. Indeed, going beyond physiology to genetics, which of course is based on physiological processes, it is an extraordinary fact that all organisms follow the same genetic laws. To the botanist all these facts suggest that all plants are related and have common ancestors.

Geographical Distribution

Under this rubric we have a large collection of situations which seem incomprehensible unless evolution has taken place. A given genus (Figure 19.1) may have four closely related species—one growing in New England, another in the New Jersey area, another in Georgia, and the fourth in Florida. We can explain this situation by hypothesizing that this entire area along the eastern seaboard was once occupied by a single ancestral species which over a long period of time evolved along four different lines in response to different environmental conditions.

Or take the often observed circumstance that islands off the coasts of continents usually have similar but not identical floras with those of the adjacent mainland. Some of these cases can be explained by postulating that the land masses were once continuous and therefore shared a common ancestral flora. Then there occurred a separation of the islands from the mainland

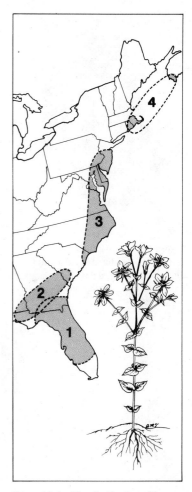

Figure 19.1 The distribution of four closely related species of one genus (*Sabatia*, rose pink). Presumably all four evolved from a common ancestor which once was distributed from Maine to Florida.

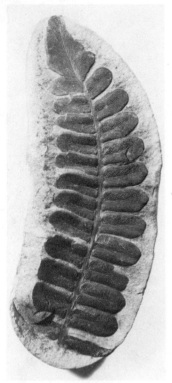

Figure 19.2 Fossil seed fern leaf (*Neuropteris*) embedded in an ironstone nodule. Note the resemblance to fern foliage. [Courtesy Theodore Delevoryas.]

with the result that the plants of the two regions diverged in response to different climatic and other conditions.

Similarly, the plants on any large land mass will be fairly uniform unless the area is divided by high mountains or by large bodies of water which act as barriers. In such circumstances, the plants on opposite sides of the barriers may be different.

The point here is that we have thousands of observations of geographical distribution of plants which make no sense unless evolution has occurred.

Fossils

Fossils are the remains or impressions of plants embedded in rock or in the crust of the earth (Figure 19.2). Fossils have been known to man for centuries and from the beginning they perplexed him. They were regarded variously as freaks of nature, the results of spontaneous generation, the molds used in creating species and discarded by the Creator and, finally, as something deliberately placed in the rocks to test the faith of man.

The significant point about fossil plants is that in general they are like modern forms but usually simpler; the simplest fossils such as those of algae are found in the deepest and oldest rock strata while the complex plants such as angiosperms are found in the recent and more superficial layers of the earth. Both of these facts argue strongly that evolution has taken place. As a matter of fact, the evidence from fossil plants, or from **paleobotany,** as the study of fossil plants is called, is among the most compelling we have in support of evolution.

Vestigial Organs

This term **vestigial organ** is applied to such structures as the human appendix, which has no apparent function. The evolutionist interprets this situation by saying that though this structure had a function in the ancestral forms, it has now been lost, though the structure persists for a time. It is significant that there are some 70 vestigial structures in the mature human body and as many as 180 in the human embryo.

Vestigial structures are also present in plants. You will recall that the angiosperm embryo sac has eight nuclei, only three of which participate in the process of double fertilization. The other five once had a function but this has been lost, yet the structures persist.

Recapitulation

By **recapitulation** we mean that in the course of embryo development, an individual may pass through some of the stages its ancestors passed through during evolution. Sometimes this is stated as ontogeny recapitulates phylogeny. **Ontogeny** refers to the development of the individual from an egg, **phylogeny** to the development of the race or group of organisms. The human embryo has remnants of gill slits, and in the development of the blood system and the kidneys of man there is first a fishlike stage, then a froglike stage, and finally that of man.

Some plants have sperms with whips, or flagella—this suggests some of the primitive algae which are unicellular and bear flagella. When the moss spore germinates it first produces a green thread made up of a chain of cells reminiscent of the green filamentous algae, so much so that early botanists thought this structure was an alga. When the fern spore germinates it produces a flat prothallus which resembles some of the platelike algae. Some adult cacti have no leaves but seedlings often bear leaves for a time and then lose them.

How can we explain these and hundreds of other similar situations unless evolution has occurred?

Changes in Cultivated Plants and Domesticated Animals

Another critical body of evidence in support of evolution is that man has actually observed evolution during the course of recorded history. We know that all the common breeds of poultry—Rhode Island Red, White Leghorn, Plymouth Rock, etc.—have developed from the jungle fowl in the last few thousand years. The same is true of the many types of present-day pigeons and the scores of breeds of dogs; both groups developed from their respective wild types during the few thousands of years that man has written history.

The same situation obtains in plants. The cabbage is a good example. The various types of cabbage and cabbagelike forms—head cabbage, red cabbage, cauliflower, broccoli, Brussels sprouts, and kohlrabi—have all evolved from the colewort, a wild type of cabbage which resembles a leafy lettuce (Figure 19.3). And all these profound changes took place before the eyes of man—he has literally seen evolution unfold.

In the laboratory geneticists have produced new types of plants and animals which could be considered new species if they occurred in nature. For instance, they have produced a new form of the fruit fly, *Drosophila artificialis* which in-

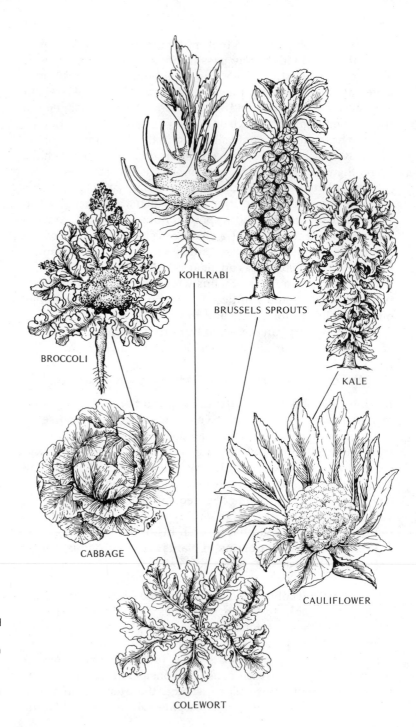

Figure 19.3 Evolution of *Brassica oleracea*. From a wild leafy ancestral plant (colewort) there have developed through selection plants with edible leaves (cabbage and kale), plants with specialized buds (Brussels sprouts), plants with clusters of flower buds (cauliflower and broccoli), and plants with enlarged stems (kohlrabi).

KOHLRABI

BRUSSELS SPROUTS

BROCCOLI

KALE

CABBAGE

CAULIFLOWER

COLEWORT

terbreeds with others of the same type and produces fertile off-spring. Thus *D. artificialis* fits the definition of a species.

On the plant side two different genera, the radish and the cabbage, have been crossed to produce the rabage or cabbish, which amusingly enough frequently has the roots of the cabbage and the tops of the radish—the worst of both vegetables. In any case, the new form interbreeds and produces fertile off-spring.

Course of Evolution

The second of the three questions we set out to explore is one involving the course of evolution. There are dozens of schemes to show the probable evolution of the plant kingdom and we show a simple one in Figure 19.4. The explanation for the diversity of opinion is that much research remains to be done. Tens of thousands of plants have not yet been discovered and named and additional thousands of species have not been studied critically. In the absence of all this information we can make only provisional guesses on the relationships, or phylogeny, of the plant kingdom.

Ignoring the names of the groups of plants, we can say that in general there has been a progression from single-celled to multicellular plants; from asexual reproduction as by cell division and zoospores to sexual reproduction—first isogamy, then heterogamy, and then on to multicellular sex organs, seeds, and flowers; from aquatic organisms to land plants; from thallus plants to vascular plants with roots, stems, and leaves; from plants with life histories with two independent, free-living generations, gametophyte and sporophyte, to the type of life cycle in the angiosperms where the sporophyte is large and dominant and the gametophyte reduced to 11 nuclei.

Causes of Evolution

The third question we promised to explore is the problem of the cause or causes of evolution.

Lamarck's Theory of the Inheritance of Acquired Characteristics

Jean Baptiste Lamarck (1744–1829) was a French botanist, who after devoting most of his life to botany, including the publica-

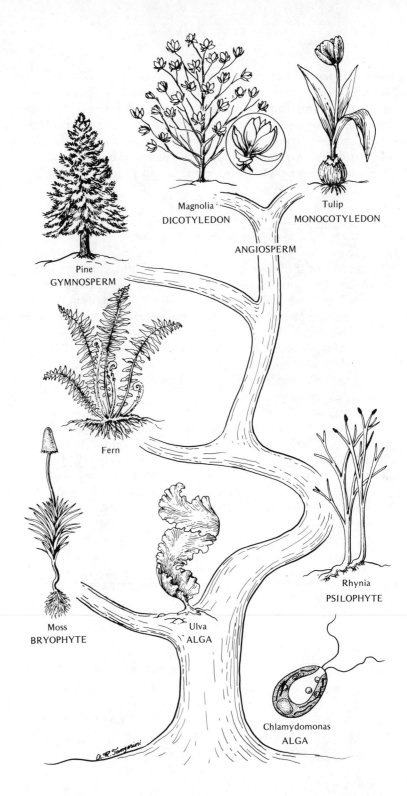

Figure 19.4 Phylogenetic diagram depicting possible relationships among major groups of plants.

tion of a flora of France, shifted his interests to zoology when he became 50 years of age. In 1809 he presented his theory to explain evolution—**the theory of the inheritance of acquired characteristics.** He pointed out that blacksmiths use the muscles of their arms a good deal and therefore these muscles develop and enlarge. Characteristically, at least in those days, the sons of blacksmiths would take up the fathers' vocation and the sons in turn would use their arm muscles so that they would enlarge and become stronger. Hence over a succession of generations of blacksmiths the arm muscles would get larger and larger. Lamarck reasoned that organs and structures grow and develop when used, and this enlargement is then passed on to the next generation. Thus, according to this theory, the long necks of giraffes could be explained by saying that by stretching for the leaves on trees over many generations, their necks became the elongated structures they are today. This notion is reflected in a ditty of the day:

A deer with a neck which was longer by half
Than the rest of his family's—try not to laugh
By stretching and stretching became a giraffe,
Which nobody can deny.

According to Lamarck's theory of the inheritance of acquired characteristics, use leads to development of structures and organs, and conversely disuse leads to the atrophying of such structures. This development or lack of development then is passed on to the next generation, and hence there is, according to Lamarck, inheritance of the characteristics developed or acquired during the lifetime of the organism. By extrapolation, a change in the environment can be substituted for use or disuse. When the climate changed as a result of the southward movement of the continental ice sheet, trees responded by developing thicker bark which functioned to prevent excessive water loss during the cold winter when little or no water can be absorbed from the soil. The thick bark character was transmitted from generation to generation and augmented in each, with the result that over a long period of time temperate trees developed a bark of considerable thickness.

A German biologist, August Weismann (1834–1914), undertook an experiment to test the validity of Lamarck's theory. He cut off the tails of mice and reasoned that if Lamarck were correct the progeny would have no tails. However, he found that the F_1 mice were born with tails. He continued the experiment for 22 generations, each time snipping off the tails of the animals and then permitting them to reproduce—with the result that the mice were always born with tails. Weismann concluded on the basis of these experiments that acquired characteristics are not inherited. A wit at the time said that this just goes to show that Shakespeare was right when he said, "There's a divinity that shapes our ends,/ Rough-hew them how we will." Another folk philosopher described his reaction: "Wooden legs do not run in families, although wooden heads do."

Most biologists give very little credence to Lamarck's theory although now and then there is a revival of interest in the concept, as in the instance of the Russian Trofim Lysenko, who a few years ago managed to acquire the official support of the Russian government and thereby to attract world-wide attention.

Darwin's Theory of Natural Selection

Earlier we said that Charles Darwin in his *Origin of Species* (1859) made two contributions to evolutionary thought: He marshaled the evidence for evolution and he put forward his own theory to explain evolution, namely, **the theory of natural selection.** This theory is based on five tenets:

1. **Overproduction.** Everywhere we observe a tremendous overproduction of progeny and reproductive cells—for example, the spores of ferns and puffballs. In the latter there may be several trillion spores. It has been estimated that a single woodland fern plant, such as the Christmas fern, produces 50 million spores each season. If each spore survived and produced a new plant and occupied a square foot of space and if each of these ferns in turn formed 50 million spores, it would not be too many generations before the entire land mass of North America would be covered with the progeny of this one fern plant. And, of course, there are some 9,000 other species of ferns doing the same thing, not to mention some 500,000 species of flowering plants producing enormous quantities of seeds.

2. **Struggle for existence.** This great overproduction means that there is not enough room, not enough light, and not enough food for all organisms; therefore, there is a struggle for the essentials of life or, as Darwin said, a struggle for existence, with competition especially keen among similar plants which are struggling for the same environment.

3. **Variation.** It is a fact that no two organisms are exactly alike even though they have the same parents, with the single exception of the rare instances of identical twins.

4. **Survival of the fittest.** Those organisms which best fit or are best adapted to the environment will survive. Take a number of seedlings produced by the same parents growing in a dry habitat. Those individuals which have the capacity for producing long roots will survive and the others will be eliminated.

5. **Heredity.** The particular variations which have been of survival value will be transmitted to the next generation and so these desirable variations will be built up over many generations, while the variations of little or no survival value will be eliminated. To refer back to our previous example, the long-root character will be transmitted to successive generations and only the longest of them will survive. The end result is that over thousands of years of time there will be produced in this dry habitat a race of long-rooted plants.

To summarize, Darwin argued that a process of natural selection goes on in nature. All organisms overproduce their progeny and this leads to a struggle for existence. Since there is great diversity, or variation, among offspring, those organisms that are best adapted to the environment will survive (and reproduce) and the characteristics which make it possible for them to survive will be perpetuated through heredity. Over a long period of time there will be a gradual development of new types or new species.

De Vries's Mutation Theory

One of the criticisms of Darwin's theory on the origin of species is that he did not explain how variations originated. Hugo de Vries (1848–1935) supplied one answer. You will recall that de Vries was the Dutch botanist who along with two other botanists rediscovered Mendel's work. De Vries noticed in populations of evening primroses the occasional appearance of **sports** —that is, marked variants which breed true. He called these sports **mutations** and he suggested that evolution was brought about by the variations produced by mutations, rather than by the minor variations which Darwin envisioned. This concept of de Vries is his **mutation theory** (1901).

The Modern View of Evolution—a Synthesis

The present-day concept of evolution incorporates the theories of Darwin and those of de Vries and then augments them with a few more recent ideas. We say that change, or variability, comes

Figure 19.5 Fleshy-stemmed cactus (*Myrtillocactus geometrizans*) with spines.

Figure 19.6 Tequila agave (*Agave tequilana*) with fleshy leaves ending in spines.

about through mutations—both gene mutations and the mutations caused by changes in chromosome number—as well as by the recombination of characters in hybridization. Natural selection then operates on the populations made up of these variants, selecting those best suited for a particular environment. Thus over a long period of time there will develop new types or new species.

It should be noted that survival of the fittest implies not only the physical survival of individuals but their ability to leave offspring. Since an important element of fitness is reproductive effectiveness, natural selection may be regarded as **differential reproduction** in a population.

Another important process in the origin of species is **reproductive isolation** by which is meant the separation of populations of plants of the same species by barriers to gene exchange so that the different populations gradually differentiate into distinct species. According to this concept we start with a **gene pool,** or all the genes, dominant and recessive, in a given population of one species, and there then develop various **physical and biological barriers.** An example of the former are changes in the environment in a vast area so that there are local differences with the result that the different variants occupy different habitats and therefore may not exchange genes with plants of the same species in other localized habitats. An example of a biological barrier is the situation where the plants in a given area are of the same species but do not exchange genes because their flowers mature at different times. Thus the two sets of plants are effectively isolated from each other even though they grow side by side. Eventually they will evolve into two different types, or species, as will the populations separated by physical barriers.

Types of Evolution

Most people when they think of evolution regard it as change or development from simple organisms or structures to complex organisms or organs. This is not always so, and this type of change is only one kind of evolution, which we term **progressive evolution.**

We may also have **retrogressive evolution** which is evolution from complex to simple structures. (This does not mean or imply retracing the exact steps of evolution.) Flowers lose sepals or petals or both over time. During the course of evolution plants may lose leaves, as in the cacti.

In those instances where the same type of structure is produced in two different and unrelated groups of organisms we have **parallel evolution.** Seeds, for example, evolved independently in some of the extinct arboreal club-mosses as well as in the group of higher plants designated the seed plants. Likewise, the vessel cell developed in some ferns and gymnosperms as well as in the angiosperms.

Sometimes the whole make-up or appearance of two or more groups of organisms, growing under the same conditions, is similar although the groups are not related. The process leading to this condition is known as **convergent evolution, or convergence.** In deserts we observe plants which have small leaves or no leaves, enlarged fleshy leaves or stems, and spines. These may be unrelated plants belonging to such groups as the cacti (Figure 19.5), agaves (Figure 19.6), the spurges (Figure 19.7), and the aloes (Figure 19.8). Although their vegetative bodies, or external appearances, are similar—an obvious adaptation to the xeric, or dry habitat—their flower structure shows that they belong to unrelated families.

Figure 19.7 Fleshy-stemmed spurge (*Euphorbia canariensis*) with spines.

See photograph on page 460, barrel cactus.

Impact of Evolution on Society and the Intellectual World

As we remarked at the outset of this chapter, evolution permeates and saturates all aspects and facets of biology. It is the central unifying thread which forms the background of all concepts, ideas, and generalizations in all branches or subdivisions of the life sciences. To a large extent the same is true of the related fields of anthropology and psychology and the other social and behavioral sciences.

Evolution and Religion

Evolutionary thought has had a sharp impact on religion and theology. Indeed, it is not too extravagant a statement to make that all hell broke loose in ecclesiastical circles soon after 1859, the date of the publication of Darwin's *Origin of Species,* for allegedly the concept of evolution called into question such ancient beliefs as the Genesis account of creation involving Adam and Eve and the creation of all creatures at one time. The fossil evidence does suggest that man's origin took place a million

Figure 19.8 Aloe (*Aloe rupestris*) with fleshy, spiny leaves.

years or more ago and that lower plants and animals had their origins not only at different times but hundreds of millions of years ago. (Archbishop James Ussher, 1581–1656, and Dr. John Lightfoot of Cambridge University by means of a set of calculations based on the Bible set the time of creation at 9 A.M., Sunday October 23, 4004 B.C., and this remarkable finding was often published in the Bibles of the time and much later.)

To some minds the concept of evolution seemed to question the ancient belief of design and purpose in the universe. And the last straw was the revolting suggestion that man evolved from lower animals. Particularly objectionable was the notion that man sprang from the monkeys instead of being created in God's image. Disraeli in a speech at Oxford in 1864 threw down the gauntlet: "What is the question now placed before society with glib assurance the most astounding? The question is this—Is man an ape or an angel? My Lord, I am on the side of the angels."

It is thus not surprising that the clergy were hostile to the disturbing concept of evolution. There was a celebrated debate between Samuel Wilberforce, bishop of Oxford, and biologist Thomas Henry Huxley at the annual meetings of the British Association for the Advancement of Science in Oxford in 1860. Bishop Wilberforce in his presentation ridiculed Darwin's theory and turning to Huxley "begged to know, was it through his grandfather or his grandmother that he claimed his descent from a monkey?" When it came Huxley's turn on the platform, he gave a scientific justification for Darwin's ideas, and then said he would not be ashamed to have a monkey for his ancestor but he would be "ashamed to be connected with a man who used great gifts to obscure the truth."

Another famous exchange took place at the founding of the Johns Hopkins University in Baltimore in 1876. Huxley was invited as the inaugural speaker and as the university wished to emphasize its nonsectarian nature the customary opening prayer was omitted. This omission and the presence of Huxley was too much for some clergy. One minister was quoted as saying, "It was bad enough to invite Huxley. It were better to have asked God to be present. It would have been absurd to ask them both."

Misuse of Darwinism

As the ideas of evolution permeated the various strata of society, they began to be used to justify the ruthless competition of business and the cruelty and inhumanity of the Industrial Revolution. Such phrases as "struggle for existence" and "survival of the fittest" were picked up and used glibly as descriptions of what takes place in industry and business. Just as nature was characterized as being "red in tooth and claw," so were commercial enterprises. "Might makes right" was another slogan of the day. In general, evolutionary thought was prostituted to justify ruthless competition in business, the unscrupulous entrepreneur, and laissez-faire capitalism. For example, John D. Rockefeller, in speaking to a Sunday school class argued, "The growth of a large business is merely a survival of the fittest. . . . The American Beauty rose can be produced in the splendor and fragrance which brings cheer to its beholder only by sacrificing the early buds which grow up around it. This is not an evil tendency in business. It is merely the working-out of a law of nature and a law of God." Andrew Carnegie also employed evolutionary thought for similar purposes. Darwin was taken aback by the misuse of his concepts and at one point remarked; "I have received in a Manchester newspaper rather a good squib, showing that I have proved 'might is right,' and therefore that Napoleon is right, and every cheating tradesman is also right."

The new evolutionary ideas were also used to justify the slow progress or change in the social and political spheres. After all, it was argued, evolution in nature is exceedingly slow. Conservatives not only borrowed from Darwinism to buttress their philosophical positions but persons on the left turned to it for support. For instance, Karl Marx wrote, "Darwin's book is very important and serves me as a basis in natural science for the class struggle in history."

Evolution was utilized in defense of imperialism and the subjugation of putative weaker races. There was much talk of manifest destiny, especially Anglo-Saxon manifest destiny, and the survival of the fittest. During the debate over our annexation of the Philippines, orators invoked the law of progress or evolution and the inevitable tendency of populations in nature to expand.

Evolutionary concepts were used, or rather misused, to justify militarism and war with the argument that armed conflict eliminates the weak and unfit as in nature. Not that these pronouncements were allowed to pass unchallenged, for David Starr Jordan (1851–1931), eminent biologist and later president of Stanford University, made a forceful argument for the position that war is a biological evil and rather than eliminating the halt and the blind, it all too often carries off the physically and mentally fit and leaves behind the least fit.

We would not, however, be completely accurate if we were to leave you with the impression that all scientists and members of the clergy were squared off in opposing camps. Indeed, there were thinkers and writers in both spheres who undertook to reconcile religion and the Bible with science and evolution. They agreed that there was no fundamental conflict between the two, and they reminded us that the Bible is a volume of religious truths, whereas evolutionary principles are concepts valid in the realm of science. It was explained that the Bible speaks in poetical language when it refers to creation in six days. Furthermore, evolutionary ideas are not degrading; on the contrary the grandeur and sweep of evolution enhances the nobility of man. Asa Gray (1810–1888), the distinguished botanist, and Charles W. Eliot (1834–1926), the respected president of Harvard and a chemist, were two scientists who were active reconcilers of science and religion, while the celebrated preacher, Henry Ward Beecher (1813–1887) maintained a similar position from the ranks of the clergy.

Social Darwinism

As time went on, the salient features of evolutionary thought permeated philosophy as well as the emerging science of society, sociology, where they were grouped under the heading of **social Darwinism.** Herbert Spencer (1820–1903), indeed, was the person from whom Darwin borrowed the expression "survival of the fittest," and Spencer was one of the pioneers in applying evolution to the social sciences. He borrowed the ideas and evidence of organic evolution to support his **theory of social selection,** by which he meant that the struggle for subsistence—for food, shelter, clothes, and fuel—is the force which is responsible for social progress or change in society. He reasoned that this pressure, by placing a premium upon skills and ability to adapt, has stimulated human advancement and selected the best of each generation for survival.

William Graham Sumner (1840–1910) of Yale, an early sociologist and disciple of Spencer's, was another social Darwinist. He was a pessimist who used Darwinism to justify the hardships of life, the necessity for labor, and the inevitability of suffering. He rationalized that competition is good and that success is the reward of virtue. Further, Sumner taught that the progress of civilization depends on the selection process which in turn depends on the operation of unrestricted competition. To him competition was a law of nature like gravitation, and therefore he opposed any restraints on the economic system, such as tariffs. He was confident that courage, enterprise, good education, intelligence, and perseverance were qualities which would ultimately emerge at the top. In his view millionaires might be regarded as the bloom of competitive civilization.

At the present time social Darwinism has been largely displaced, at least in its grosser aspects and in its open advocacy. We leave to the reader the determination as to how much social Darwinism and the abuse of evolutionary thought still linger on in society.

Suggested Readings

Darwin, Charles. *On the Origin of Species.* Facsimile 1st ed. New York: Atheneum, 1967. A reproduction of the famous 1859 edition, one of the great scientific classics of all time.

Eaton, Theodore H., Jr. *Evolution.* New York: Norton, 1970. A lucid, crisply written textbook.

Gray, Asa. *Darwiniana.* A. Hunter Dupree, ed. Cambridge, Mass.: Harvard University Press, 1963. A collection of essays on evolution and related topics by Darwin's contemporary and America's leading botanist of the time.

Greene, John C. *The Death of Adam: Evolution and Its Impact on Western Thought.* New York: New American Library, 1961. A vigorous account of evolution and its impact on Western thought—written by a historian.

Hofstadter, Richard. *Social Darwinism in American Thought.* Rev. ed. Boston: Beacon, 1955. A vivid exposition of the subject by a historian who writes with a lucid, robust style.

Huxley, Julian. *Evolution: The Modern Synthesis.* New York: Harper, 1943. The grandson of Darwin's "bulldog" brings the subject of evolution up to date (as of the 1940s).

Osborn, Henry F. *From the Greeks to Darwin.* New York: Scribner's, 1929. A history of evolutionary ideas from the early ones of ancient Greece to those of Darwin.

Stebbins, G. Ledyard. *Processes of Organic Evolution.* 2d ed. Englewood Cliffs, N. J.: Prentice-Hall, 1971. Excellent brief book on our present understanding of evolution by one of the leading evolutionary thinkers of our time.

Volpe, Peter E. *Understanding Evolution.* 2d ed. Dubuque, Iowa: Brown, 1970. A well-balanced, readable introduction to the subject.

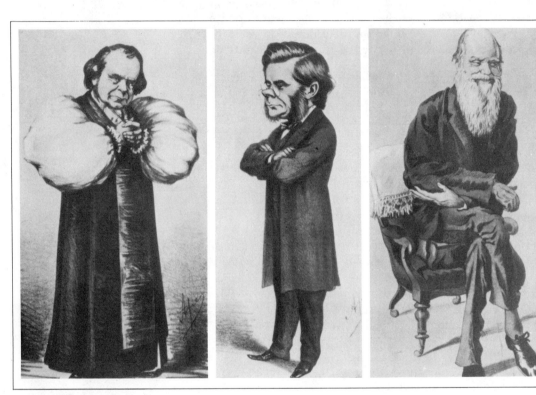

Caricatures of Bishop Samuel Wilber-
force, Thomas H. Huxley, and Charles
Darwin, as they appeared in *Vanity
Fair* in 1871.

20
Darwin
The Great Synthesizer of Biology

We consider that Charles Darwin and his work merit a chapter in a book of this character. In the first place he is universally recognized as the greatest of biologists and the person responsible in large part for the elucidation of the great unifying principle of biology—evolution. In addition, in the course of these pages you may achieve further insight into the manner in which scientists conduct their work. Finally, the unfolding of the evolutionary concept and the controversies surrounding it constitute another important chapter in intellectual history.

Forebears

Charles Robert Darwin was born in Shrewsbury, England, on February 12, 1809, on the same day as Abraham Lincoln. Charles's father, Dr. Robert Darwin, was a prosperous country physician, and his grandfather was the celebrated Dr. Erasmus Darwin (1731–1802), physician, poet, and amateur scientist. Erasmus was one of the early persons to speculate on evolution, and you will recall that he put Linnaeus's system of plant classification to verse in "The loves of the plants." Charles Darwin's mother was a Wedgwood, the famous family of potters and creators of Wedgwood china. Thus genetically Charles came from good stock as measured by the accomplishments of his forebears; certainly the Darwins and Wedgwoods were highly respected English families.

Early Life

It is reported that Charles showed a taste for natural history and collecting insects, plants, and birds long before he went to school.

He was sent to the Shrewsbury Day School for his ninth to sixteenth years. The curriculum was classical with emphasis on languages in which Charles did not do very well. He once remarked, "During my whole life I have been singularly incapable of mastering any language."

His father and his teachers considered young Charles to be a very ordinary boy—if anything, rather below the common standard of intellect. Indeed, some of his teachers thought of him as not far removed from a dunce. His father once said in exasperation, "You care for nothing but shooting, dogs, and rat-catching, and you will be a disgrace to yourself and all your family." Never did parental prediction fall so far short of fulfillment.

Darwin's father was a huge man physically—6 feet 2 inches, weighing 328 pounds—energetic and dominating. He liked to finish a day's work as physician with a two-hour monologue delivered to his awe-stricken children. He was severe with young Charles and this may have contributed to the impression that the boy gave of being timid, immature, and quietly rebellious.

University Days

Charles was sent in 1825 to the University of Edinburgh to study medicine. But he found the lectures intolerably dull except for those in chemistry. Upon first witnessing an operation on a human subject, he rushed away in anguish for he could not bear the sight of blood. After two years he left Edinburgh, as what in these days we would call a dropout.

The family decided that since Charles did not wish to be a physician, he should become a clergyman. And so he was sent off to Cambridge University even though his academic record thus far was mediocre. Julian Huxley has opined that with present-day standards, Darwin would not have been able to obtain admission to any modern university.

Charles always considered the time spent at the university as wasted as far as his academic program was concerned, except for one bright spot—John Henslow, professor of botany, whose lectures in botany he liked for their lucidity and for their admirable illustrations. He also delighted in the field excursions. As time went on, he developed a close relationship with Henslow, and Darwin later acknowledged that Henslow had influenced his career more than anyone else. At Cambridge he was known as "the man who walks with Henslow."

One of his favorite pastimes was collecting insects, plants, birds, and geological specimens. He later wrote of his pride in being cited in a book on English beetles with the words "captured by C. Darwin, Esq." in reference to some of the insects he had collected. He said that at the time he had a feeling akin to the joy of a poet who had just had his first poem published. His ardor for collecting was unique: It is related that once he was out in the field where he collected two rare beetles which he held one in each hand. He then saw another rare beetle and in his anxiety to capture it, poked one of the original beetles in his mouth with the result that the ejected acid from the animal forced him to spit out the insect.

Another passion of his university days was hunting and he became a very good marksman. Despite his lack of interest in his academic studies, he always felt that the three years spent at Cambridge were the happiest of his life, for during this period he was in excellent health and in the highest spirits. In 1831 he received the B. A., having scraped through with a bare pass.

The Voyage of the *Beagle*

About this time the British government was in the process of organizing the surveying voyage of H.M.S. *Beagle* (Figure 20.1), which was to chart the coasts of South America and other lands. It was Professor Henslow who called Darwin's attention to the fact that the expedition was looking for an unpaid naturalist. Darwin's father objected to the whole scheme, but said, "If you can find any man of common sense who advises you to go, I will give my consent." Fortunately Uncle Wedgwood sided with Charles and so the young man arranged for an interview with the captain of the *Beagle*, Robert Fitzroy. At first, Fitzroy did not like Darwin's looks, particularly the shape of his nose, but in the end he agreed to have Darwin on board.

So finally Charles Darwin at age 22 embarked on a voyage which was to take five years (1831–1836) and which would en-

Figure 20.1 H. M. S. *Beagle* in the Straits of Magellan. [Courtesy Down House Museum.]

tail the exploration of both coasts of South America as well as the shores of New Zealand and Australia.

On the frequent stops of the ship, Darwin investigated the geology of the islands and the coastal regions of the mainlands visited. He had taken with him Charles Lyell's *Principles of Geology*, a book which was destined to have a profound influence on his thinking, particularly his ideas on evolution. Darwin also collected animals; it was said of him that he "tried to put all of South America in a specimen bottle." He led a strenuous life, for he often spent as many as ten hours in the saddle on his collecting forays. He was not content with mere collecting; when he got back on board ship he devoted endless hours to dissecting the new and strange organisms.

In the course of the voyage the ship circumnavigated the world, and this long exposure to tropical waters gave Darwin the opportunity to unravel the complex factors responsible for the origin and development of coral islands. He also worked out the relationships between the plants and animals on the Galapagos Islands and those on the mainland of South America. The voyage was the most important event in his life and it determined his subsequent career. Certainly the expedition was his first real education in the biological sciences.

The five years spent on the *Beagle* represented Darwin's creative period during which he was exposed to completely new floras and faunas and strange geological formations, and since he was alone much of the time, he had the opportunity to brood and to think. In many ways Darwin's period on the *Beagle* is comparable to Linnaeus's journey to Lapland where Linnaeus, too, was exposed to a new flora and enjoyed weeks of solitude. At any rate, for Darwin this was the period when many of his creative ideas emerged, at least in germ form.

Darwin kept a daily journal of his observations and reflections. He combined enormous energy with concentrated attention in his work despite the fact that he was almost constantly seasick on board ship. He once remarked, "I hate every wave of the ocean, with a fervour, which you who have only seen the green waters of the shore, can never understand." And it was in South America that he contracted a tropical disease which led to a long and severe illness and which plagued him the rest of his life.

Figure 20.2 Charles Darwin at age 30. [Courtesy Down House Museum.]

London

Upon his return from this five-year voyage he took lodgings in London where he began to work on his journal and on his extensive collections. In 1837 he started his first notebook in which he recorded facts and observations on the origin of species, or evolution, a project he continued for 20 years. When he embarked on the *Beagle* he was a Bible-quoting Christian with complete belief in Genesis, but what he saw in South America shook his faith. His study of the distribution of plants and animals and the fossils of past organisms disturbed him deeply, and it was with some reluctance that he began to explore the evolutionary implications of his data.

In 1839 he married his cousin, Emma Wedgwood (Figures 20.2 and 20.3). Being a systematic sort of person, before taking this momentous step he prepared a chart with the reasons he should marry and then the counterarguments. The young couple lived in London for three years before moving to the country where Darwin spent the rest of his life.

Figure 20.3 Emma Wedgwood Darwin. Photograph taken at about the time of her marriage to Charles Darwin. [Courtesy Down House Museum.]

Down

Darwin's father bought a house in Downe (Figure 20.4) for the young Darwins and indeed supported Darwin for the balance of his life. Interestingly enough, Darwin never in his lifetime held a position or job, except for the unpaid post as naturalist on

Figure 20.4　Down House. [Courtesy Down House Museum.]

Figure 20.5　Darwin's laboratory table in his study at Down House. Note the microscope on the window ledge.

the *Beagle*. It was at this point in his life that Darwin began to suffer from ill health, characterized by weakness, fatigue, headache, insomnia, and dizziness, and he was destined to be a semi-invalid for the rest of his life. He could work only a few hours a day and most of his intellectual life was spent on a sofa. He found that he could not even bear the weight of a book and hence resorted to the expedient of tearing out sections of books and reading them in this form. He tells us that "I never pass 24 hours without many hours of discomfort, when I can do nothing whatever."

It seems extraordinary that after his strenuous explorations while with the *Beagle* he now became virtually a recluse and hardly ever left Down even for a visit to neighboring London. He did not attend scientific meetings and saw only his close friends, who included John Henslow, Charles Lyell, Joseph Hooker, and later Thomas H. Huxley.

There has been speculation on the nature of Darwin's lifelong illness; one theory is that the source of his difficulty was the tropical disease he was exposed to in South America, while another suggestion is that he inherited a neurotic condition, or melancholia.

Despite his illness, he managed to write and to publish his *Journal* of the voyage of the *Beagle* (1839) which is universally recognized as one of the classics on travel and exploration. He also devoted several years to dissecting (Figures 20.5 and 20.6) and studying the barnacles he had collected, work which culminated in a four-volume monograph on this important group of marine organisms. These years spent in dissecting barnacles and the ensuing comparative studies he made on their anatomy were invaluable from the standpoint of his scientific development.

The Evolution Project

As we have mentioned, Darwin began his first notebook on evolution in 1837. After accumulating a mass of observations and reflections on the subject, he wrote a brief abstract of 35 pages in 1842. By 1844 he had enlarged his account to 230 pages. He discussed his tentative conclusions set forth in this version with his close friends, the geologist Charles Lyell, the botanist Joseph Hooker, the Harvard botanist Asa Gray (by correspondence), and later with Thomas H. Huxley. After receiving their counsel he began to prepare an extensive treatise on evolution which was intended to be three or four times the scale of the eventual *Origin*; by 1856, he had finished ten chapters.

Figure 20.6 Darwin's microscope.

In the process of developing and refining his thoughts on the origin of species, he was greatly influenced by the works of two men: Lyell's *Principles of Geology* (1830–1833) with its lucid account of geological change over time, and Thomas Malthus's *An Essay on the Principle of Population* (1798). You will recall that Malthus emphasized the extreme fertility of animals and man, and drew the conclusion that they increase geometrically while food and other essentials increase arithmetically on a globe whose space is finite.

In 1858 came a bolt from the blue. Alfred Wallace (1823–1913, Figure 20.7), a naturalist and traveler and a man who on occasion had corresponded with Darwin, sent the latter an essay entitled *On the Tendency of Varieties to Depart Indefinitely from the Original Type* which, to Darwin's astonishment, described the same theory of the origin of species as Darwin's. As Darwin tells us, "I never saw a more striking coincidence; if Wallace had my ms. sketch written out in 1842, he could not have made a better short abstract! Even his terms now stand as heads of my chapters. . . . So all my originality, whatever it may amount to, will be smashed."

While ill with malaria in the jungles of Malaya, Wallace wrote his essay in one week, although he did base his writing on

Figure 20.7 Alfred Russel Wallace. [Courtesy Mansell Collection.]

Figure 20.8 Charles Darwin at age 51. [Courtesy Down House Museum.]

See illustrations on page 482, caricatures of Darwin, Huxley, and Wilberforce.

three years of intermittent thought on the subject. In contrast, Darwin had brooded over the evidence, the theory, and the implications of evolution for over 20 years. This striking example of "parallel evolution" in the realm of thought—the independent genesis of the theory of natural selection to explain the origin of species in the minds of Darwin and Wallace—reminds one of the simultaneous rediscovery of Mendel's epochal genetic laws by de Vries, Correns, and Tschermak.

With the receipt of the Wallace communication, Darwin was faced with a moral dilemma. On the one hand he had Wallace's sketch of his ideas on evolution which Darwin was rather expected to espouse, and yet he felt he could not ignore his own 20 years of effort on the development of his theory of evolution. He consulted his friends Lyell and Hooker who urged that both concepts be presented in the form of joint papers. And so on July 1, 1858, at a meeting of the Linnean Society of London the Wallace paper was read as well as Darwin's abstract. The priority is clearly with Darwin for he wrote an abstract in 1842 and a more extensive version in 1844, followed by ten chapters in 1856.

In any event, the Wallace incident spurred Darwin on to renewed effort as a result of which he wrote the *Origin of Species* in 13 months and it was published in November 1859 (Figure 20.8). It was an instant success; the first edition of 1,250 copies was sold out the first day. In all, the book passed through six editions, the latest in 1872.

As related in Chapter 19, the publication of the *Origin* had the effect of a bombshell dropped in religious and other intellectual circles as well as in the world-wide scientific community. Because of his poor health, Darwin did not appear in public or participate in the controversy, rather the case for evolution was upheld by his surrogates, Lyell, Hooker, Asa Gray in this country, and especially Thomas Henry Huxley (Figure 20.9) who joined the battle with great gusto. For his prominent part in the fight, Huxley came to be known as "Darwin's bulldog."

Other Books

Had Darwin merely published the *Origin*, he would have made his mark in biology, but he wrote many other books, which in turn would have made him a leading figure in science had he never written the *Origin*. Indeed, had he only published his

T. H. Huxley

Figure 20.9 Thomas Henry Huxley. [Courtesy Mansell Collection.]

books on botany, he would today be accepted as a leader in the field. A mere listing of his major books other than the *Origin* and the *Journal* gives some notion of the extraordinary breadth of his work, covering as it does botany, zoology, and geology: *The Zoology of the Voyage of the H.M.S. Beagle** (three volumes, 1838–1843), *The Structure and Distribution of Coral Reefs* (1842), *The Various Contrivances by Which Orchids Are Fertilized by Insects* (1862), *On the Movement and Habits of Climbing Plants* (1865), *The Variation of Animals and Plants under Domestication* (1868), *The Descent of Man* (1871), *Insectivorous Plants* (1875), *Cross and Self Fertilization in the Vegetable Kingdom* (1876), *The Different Forms of Flowers on Plants of the Same Species* (1877), *The Power of Movements in Plants* (1880), and *The Formation of Vegetable Mould Through the Action of Worms* (1881).

Charles Darwin died in 1882 at the age of 73 (Figure 20.10). He was buried in Westminster Abbey, and it will come as no surprise to learn that three of his pallbearers were his old friends and supporters, Hooker, Huxley, and Wallace. His university, Cambridge, conferred an honorary LL. D. on him in 1877; but strangely in view of his eminence as a scientist, the British government made no move to knight him or bestow any other official honor on him. Some have suggested that this lack of recognition was due to the influence of the church. As if to make amends for past lapses, the British government eventually knighted three of Darwin's sons.

Figure 20.10 Charles Darwin at age 71. [Courtesy Down House Museum.]

Qualities of the Man

It is instructive to examine the qualities of Darwin which may have contributed to his achievements. In the first place he was a keen observer, a characteristic without which no one can go very far in science, particularly biology. Accompanying his fine sense of observation was the circumstance that he was an avid collector from boyhood, and collectors absorb an enormous amount of field biology, or ecology. One of his rare qualities was the ability to ask searching questions of nature. Thomas H. Huxley stressed Darwin's "intense and passionate honesty." Certainly he had a vivid imagination, and most important of all he was blessed with great speculative powers. He himself writes in the *Autobiography*, "My mind seems to have become a kind

*The titles have been abbreviated where they are unduly long.

of machine for grinding general laws out of large collections of facts." And indeed his methods are exemplars of inductive reasoning.

Personally, Darwin was genial, simple, and generous. With respect to the qualities of his mind he once wrote, "At no time am I a quick thinker or writer: whatever I have done in science has solely been by long pondering, patience and industry." His writing is not always clear, for he wrote clumsy sentences and poorly formulated phrases. He claimed that because he had so much difficulty in expressing himself lucidly and precisely, he was forced to think long and intently, but let us turn to his own words in the *Autobiography:*

> I have as much difficulty as ever in expressing myself clearly and concisely; and this difficulty has caused me a very great loss of time; but it has had the compensating advantage of forcing me to think long and intently about every sentence, and thus I have been often led to see errors in reasoning and in my own observations or those of others. There seems to be a sort of fatality in my mind leading me to put at first my statement and proposition in a wrong or awkward form. Formerly I used to think about my sentences before writing them down; but for several years I have found that it saves time to scribble in a vile hand whole pages as quickly as I possibly can, contracting half the words; and then correct deliberately. Sentences thus scribbled down are often better ones than I could have written deliberately.

Contributions

There is no question but that Charles Darwin would be included in any listing of the great men in all history. He played a prominent part in the formulation of the most important generalization in biology—the concept of evolution. Before him there were avalanches of isolated facts and observations on plants and animals; his concept of evolution tied these facts and observations together and made sense out of chaos. His concept of evolution forms the foundation for the entire structure of modern biology.

His *Origin of Species* literally is the book that shook the world. It is undeniably one of the authentic classics and would be included in any selection of great books.

His evolutionary thought not only initiated an intellectual revolution in science but it forced the re-examination of theology, philosophy, sociology, anthropology, and psychology. The magnitude of the upheaval of thought in these several disciplines is such that had he lived but a few hundred years earlier, he would surely have been burned at the stake.

Suggested Readings

Appleman, Philip, ed. *Darwin: A Norton Critical Edition.* New York: Norton, 1970. A valuable collection of writings on Darwin and evolution, including those of Lyell, Hooker, and Huxley. Other essays emphasize the influence of evolutionary thought on science, theology, philosophy, and society.

Darwin, Charles. *The Autobiography of Charles Darwin.* Nora Barlow, ed. New York: Norton, 1969. A must if you really want to understand Darwin.

de Beer, Gavin, ed. *Autobiographies: Charles Darwin, Thomas Henry Huxley.* London: Oxford University Press, 1974. A handsome volume with both Darwin's autobiography and Huxley's.

Huxley, Julian. *The Living Thoughts of Darwin.* New York: Longmans, Green, 1939. A summary of Darwin's ideas on evolution and other biological subjects.

Irvine, William. *Apes, Angels, and Victorians: The Story of Darwin, Huxley, and Evolution.* New York: McGraw-Hill, 1955. A beautiful exposition on Darwin, Huxley, and evolution by a scholar who writes with a lively style. A good way to recapture the flavor of the early battle over evolution.

Moorehead, Alan. *Darwin and the Beagle.* New York: Harper & Row, 1969. A truly superb account of Darwin's adventures on the famous voyage of H.M.S. *Beagle.* Handsomely illustrated.

Sears, Paul B. *Charles Darwin: The Naturalist as a Cultural Force.* New York: Scribner's, 1950. A thoughtful interpretation of Darwin's contributions to science and to intellectual life in general.

On shifting dunes, the graceful *Am-mophila,* a salt-tolerant sea grass, may play a critical role in binding the sand during plant succession.

21
Ecology
Unifying Science

There are those to whom ecology is an emotional state, the mere mention of which sets adrenalin coursing through blood vessels, raises blood pressure, quickens the pulse, causes eyes to flash and tempers to flare. In less inflammatory times, biologists understood **ecology** to be the study of the interrelationships and interactions among plants, animals, and the environment. It still means this today, but some of the more recently added connotations have so warped this basic definition as to create a detrimental polarization of our political, economic, and social approaches to questions about the environment.

To biologists who draw on all branches of science in their attempts to understand the highly complex system that is the environment, ecology is a "unifying science." To the industrialist or the manufacturer ecology may be the "subversive science," a reference to the restraints placed by governmental agencies on the exercise of unfettered enterprise. To the enthusiast, ecology is a crusade, a rallying ground for various well-meant socioecological activities and sometimes ill-considered moves against different branches of the entrenched establishment. The concerned citizen sees ecology as a hope for the future, a process, a movement through which the environment can be returned to Edenlike purity. Then there is government, yielding to pressures from all sides, bending this way and that, trying to satisfy opposing forces, sometimes initiating new and untried measures, while at the same time (it is to be hoped) headed toward the establishment of programs dedicated to the maintenance of an ecologically secure balance between man and his environment.

495

Somewhere in all this pushing and pulling is the reason and understanding which must lead to action based upon the sincere desire for the common welfare of man and the other organisms with which he shares his earthly home. Although the very vastness of ecology and its parameters gives us pause, we are going to present a few basic principles with examples of their applications to the possible solution of environmental problems. We are reminded in this instance of Alexander Pope's oft-quoted phrase from *An Essay on Criticism*, "For fools rush in where angels fear to tread." Like Disraeli, we would like to be on the side of the angels.

In previous chapters, we have already discussed many aspects of ecology—that is, relationships between organism and environment: organic gardening, roots and soil, insectivorous plants, symbiosis, lichens and their role in soil formation, fungi and bacteria and their activities as decomposers of organic material and causers of disease. For a moment, however, let us look a bit more closely into what constitutes environment.

Understanding Our Environment: Vital Cycles of Life

We can define **environment** as the total of all external forces acting together which influences the lives of organisms (Figure 21.1). Such elements as soil, atmosphere, water, fire, minerals, other organisms, barometric pressure, wind, altitude, latitude, insolation (exposure to the sun's rays), and temperature are all factors of the environment. Soil, for example, is an intricate environment in itself, partly organic, partly inorganic, and teeming with an infinity of life. It is important to grasp that no one of these factors acts independently of the others, and herein lies one of the main impediments in studying and understanding the environment. None of the factors operates in isolation. For example, the temperature of any environment at any time is conditioned by geography, altitude, latitude, insolation, soil, atmospheric water vapor, slope of land, and wind. To investigate and interpret the total effect of temperature on the ecology of plants in the field, at least these elements would have to be considered.

One way to think of the environment is as a series of interacting cycles: the "Great Cycles of Nature," we could call them. Some cycles are basically biological, others physical, and some-

Figure 21.1 Biotic and abiotic elements of the tropical rain forest are interdependent in a tightly knit balanced ecological system. [Courtesy Chicago Natural History Museum.]

times these overlap and influence each other. Within the biological series of cycles, factors of the environment certainly do affect and influence one another. These cycles are the modern results of countless ages of previous natural experimentation, of trial and error, of the elimination from each cycle of unproductive and detrimental segments and the retention of productive and beneficial segments. The end products, then, are those which have been tested by time and proven in nature's laboratory to be efficient and economical.

Environment and earth are inseparable from one another. One view of environment shows a system of interrelated cycles in which the components have been and are in a state of "dynamic equilibrium"; components may intensify, moderate, enter and leave cycles: Primeval seas gave way to dry land; lifelessness was replaced by life; dinosaurs and pterodactyls became extinct; birds dominated the air, flowering plants the forests, and fish the seas. Natural environmental changes such as these were not sudden and violent; rather, they were gradual, allowing for mutual adjustments among all the ingredients of the environment over long periods of time. Thus the factors composing the environment are delicately and harmoniously balanced; all the cogs mesh nicely but they are tenuously fitted together. Disturb one part and you disturb another.

What man has done in some cases since his technological capabilities have multiplied, is to disturb convulsively this finely tuned, long-evolving balance of nature; he has disrupted or dislodged some of the segments in some of the cycles of nature, those very cycles which took so many hundreds of millions of years to evolve and which work so coherently when left alone (Figure 21.2). Although there are probably more of these natural cycles than we will ever know, there are some that are well known and ecologically significant. These deserve closer inspection.

Figure 21.2 Overlogging and fire, followed by erosion, have resulted in this devastated landscape near Damascus, Virginia. [Courtesy U.S. Department of Agriculture.]

Carbon, Essential Ingredient of the Organic World

Carbon is the fundamental chemical ingredient of all forms of life; it is intrinsic to the meaning of *organic*. All carbon comes from the gas carbon dioxide, a constituent of the air, or from carbon-containing compounds in the seas and in fresh water. Carbon from carbon dioxide is manufactured into food by green plants during the process of photosynthesis. It is because of this unique ability of green plants that other forms of life which cannot manufacture their own food (animals and non-green plants) can exist.

In both plants and animals carbon is the basic building block of organic molecules. In both plants and animals carbon-containing compounds are sources of the energy used to propel the chemical reactions necessary to assemble other organic molecules and to drive vital processes. Green plants, however, have an additional source of energy available to them: They are able to capture and use solar energy to charge the photosynthetic apparatus. All forms of life are dependent upon the ability of green plants to remove carbon from the atmosphere during photosynthesis and to build that element into plant substance. This phenomenon is sometimes called **carbon fixation.**

Figure 21.3 shows one of the great cycles of nature in which atmospheric carbon in the form of carbon dioxide is fixed into food by photosynthetic plants; the food is utilized by these plants and by other organisms and the carbon in it is eventually returned as gaseous carbon dioxide to the air. The organisms that inhabit the earth can be segregated into three groups depending upon whether they **produce, consume,** or **decompose** food. Producers, consumers, and decomposers all break down foods, but only producers manufacture it in addition to breaking it down. Some ecologists consider that there are only consumers and producers but that there are two kinds of consumers: **macroconsumers** and **microconsumers.** The macroconsumers are chiefly animals which eat or ingest particles of organic matter directly. Microconsumers, on the other hand, must decompose particles of organic matter into soluble substances which can then be absorbed through the cell walls of these organisms. Fungi and bacteria are the major microconsumers and we call these organisms, decomposers. Organisms in each of these groups contribute to the return of carbon dioxide to the atmosphere, but only the producers are able to remove it from the air and synthesize food from it. Let us, then,

Carbon Dioxide of the Atmosphere

Figure 21.3 Carbon cycle. Carbon is extracted from the atmosphere by photosynthesizing green plants, used by all forms of life, and eventually returned to the air as carbon dioxide through respiration and combustion.

look at the kinds of organisms which compose each of the three groups involved in the economics of carbon utilization.

Air contains about .03 percent carbon dioxide, a very small proportion of the total, most of which is nitrogen and oxygen. The producers of food are, of course, green plants. In addition to producing food, like all other organisms, green plants also respire, that is, they use food and give off, as a by-product, carbon dioxide. During daylight hours, green plants utilize more carbon dioxide in photosynthesis (food manufacture) than they give off through respiration; in the dark, respiration continues to produce carbon dioxide but none is removed from the air since photosynthesis has been temporarily curtailed.

On the left-hand side of the diagram of the carbon cycle, are the consumers. These include the animals and man. In the final analysis, all animals subsist on plants, either directly or through the medium of other animals which do subsist on plants. Consumers do not produce food, they only use it, and in doing so they respire and give off carbon dioxide which is recycled into the atmosphere to be reutilized by the producer green plants.

At the end of life, both producers and consumers become substrates for the decomposers. These are mostly micro-organisms, the fungi and bacteria of the soil, the "sanitary engineers of the organic world." They are unable to manufacture their own food and subsist entirely on the carcasses of consumers and producers and on the dead bodies of their own kind as well. During this process they too release carbon dioxide to the air and, through a series of complex enzymatic activities, they are able to reduce organic molecules to water-soluble compounds some of which they absorb and use in their own metabolic processes. If we reflect a bit on the activities of decomposers, we realize the crucial role they play in the economy of life. Were it not for their abilities to break down organic materials these would remain locked up and inaccessible to other organisms; they could not be recycled again into the system of life and reutilized to build new life; the earth would become one vast mausoleum of dead and undecomposed bodies. In short, life on this planet would become impossible.

Carbon dioxide is also released into the atmosphere by the combustion of organic materials—wood, coal, oil, gas, peat—and through volcanic and geothermal activities. Natural combustion of organic products has been a continuing event on earth. Lightning storms did and still do set fire to forest lands and to grasslands; man has not been the only setter of fires in nature. We know from fire scars left in the wood of ancient tree trunks (see Chapter 6), that forest fires occurred before the advent of man in certain localities or in places where there has never been evidence of man's residence.

Modern man accelerates the release of carbon dioxide to the atmosphere by burning carbon-containing fuels for different purposes. Actually, though, this carbon was at one time a part of the carbon dioxide of the atmosphere, stored through photosynthesis, and manufactured into different organic compounds by green plants. All man does by burning is to restore that carbon to the air in gaseous form.

Another source of carbon dioxide is from eruptions of geysers, jets of hot water and steam which are intermittently and forcefully ejected into the atmosphere through vents in the earth's surface. Besides superheated steam, some carbon dioxide and other gases are emitted during these eruptions. Carbon dioxide is also among the various gaseous ejecta of active volcanoes (Figure 21.4). It is produced during the actual eruption

Figure 21.4 Carbon enters the atmosphere as carbon dioxide gas through volcanic eruptions. Gases are being ejected into the air from Volcán Santiaguito in Guatemala. [Courtesy U.S. Department of Agriculture.]

and given off gradually from lava as it cools and hardens after extrusion. These phenomena contributed to the original supply of carbon dioxide in the atmosphere of the newly formed planet earth—before the advent of green plants and photosynthesis.

"He Leadeth Me Beside the Still Waters. He Restoreth My Soul."

Let us now consider **water,** that common substance and universal solvent, so taken for granted and abundant in some parts of the earth, so closely guarded and scarce in others. Water is an essential constituent of every living organism. Over 90 percent of protoplasm is water; the sapwood of trees is saturated with water; cell sap is predominantly water; human tissues contain between 75 and 90 percent water. (Someone once said, irreverently, even the Archbishop of Canterbury is 90 percent water.) The water in cells helps to maintain the turgidity and stiffness of some plant parts, particularly in herbs. Minerals of the soil are dissolved in the water which is absorbed through the roots; the sap stream carries this mineral solution to every extremity of the plant where the minerals are utilized in various ways to make plant substance.

The oxygen given off as a by-product during photosynthesis comes from water. This plant-produced oxygen is the major source of oxygen in the atmosphere, the necessary gas for the existence of most forms of life. Water is the oxygen-bearing medium which supports the lives of the countless inhabitants of seas, lakes, and watercourses. Clearly water is the *sine qua non* of life on earth, that which helps to distinguish earth from its partner planets in the solar system, that which has made earth a green and vital globe among other celestial bodies.

The never-ending circulation of water on earth is called the **water,** or **hydrologic, cycle** (Figure 21.5). Our oceans and lakes are the banks from which water is withdrawn through evaporation by the heat of the sun's rays, raised into the clouds, inserted as precipitation into the terrestrial part of the water cycle, and eventually redeposited—with interest in terms of the life it has stimulated among the earth's inhabitants—into the lakes and seas. Although about three fourths of the earth's surface is covered by waters of the oceans, and most of the water in precipitation—rainfall, snow, sleet, dew, fog, hail—comes from that source, this precipitation is unevenly distributed to the land masses, both geographically and seasonally.

It is estimated that 80,000 cubic miles of water are annually

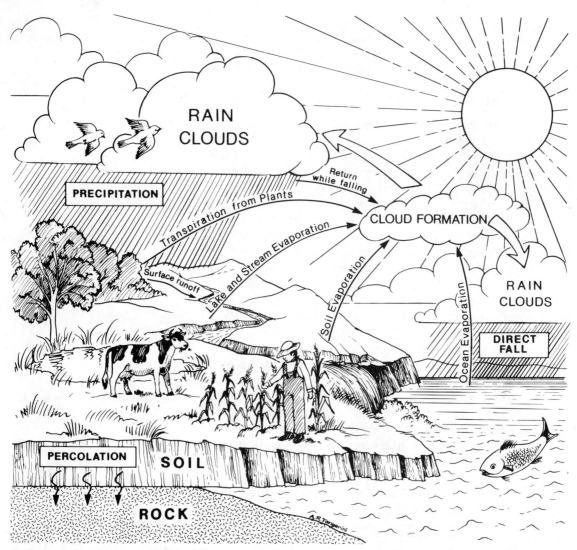

Figure 21.5 Hydrologic cycle. Water reaching the earth as precipitation is returned to the atmosphere by evaporation from the surfaces of organisms, earth, and water and by transpiration from green plants.

evaporated from the seas and 15,000 cubic miles of water from lakes and continental land surfaces. Of this amount 24,000 cubic miles are returned to earth each year as precipitation on land surfaces (equivalent to a column of water 475 feet deep over all of Texas). And yet the average annual precipitation at Arica, Chile, is only .03 inch per year, making this the driest spot on earth. Two thousand miles to the northwest, at Quibdó, Colombia, the average annual precipitation is 364 inches. And 7,000 miles from Arica, Mt. Waialeale (5,000 feet elevation) rises cloud-capped on the Island of Kauai in the Hawaiian Archipelago; there, at the boggy summit, the average annual precipitation is 460 inches, the world's highest.

Seasonal precipitation cycles are significant too and the growth of plants is delicately tuned to these sequences. The deserts of the American Southwest are sere, brown or dull gray-green most of the year, but the winter rains—when they come—enliven these desolate regions with spring color, as though the plants knew that this was their moment of glory and it was to be brief. Botanists and other naturalists in that part of the world know the phenomenon well and eagerly await the possibility of a blooming desert each year.

We might at this point recall the story of tree rings from Chapter 6 and the fact that its value in archeology and climatology is critically related to seasonally and annually variable precipitation. In the arid Southwest, you will remember, water is the limiting factor to growth.

Precipitation, as can be seen in Figure 21.5, is a product of the atmosphere. It falls on forest, farm, grassland, desert, lake, and river. Much of this precipitation immediately finds its way to streams over the soil surface (where it may cause erosion) or underground and it flows back to the sea. Some water infiltrates the upper levels of the soil where it is absorbed by growing plants; some percolates to lower levels to become part of the ground-water reserve. Most of this ground water is unavailable to plants.

Although there is only a single source of precipitation, the atmosphere, there are several sources through which this moisture is restored to the atmosphere to fall once again as precipitation. Water is returned to the seas by stream flow, and during episodes of precipitation, it falls directly into the oceans from which it is evaporated into the atmosphere. Some precipitation never reaches the earth's surface and is recycled directly to the atmosphere. Evaporation from the soil, from bodies of fresh water, and from the surfaces of plants also returns water to the air. Of special interest to botanists is the water vapor lost from the internal tissues of green plant parts through stomata and cuticles during the process of transpiration.

Between 97 and 99 percent of the water which enters the plant from the soil is lost by transpiration from the leaves. (For every gram [$1/454$ pound] of carbon dioxide fixed during photosynthesis, 100 grams [about $1/4$ pound] of water are removed by plants from the soil.) Nevertheless, the small percentage of water which is retained is essential for the life of the plant in ways noted earlier in this section. Transpiration rates—loss of water vapor from plant tissues over a given time period—vary considerably from one kind of plant to another. A large apple tree gives off about 1,800 gallons of water in a growing season of six months. From these figures, it is not difficult to apprehend the astronomical amounts of water which must be transpired by the extensive vegetation mass of Amazonian rain forest. Plants, vegetation, play a very significant role then in restoring vital water to the atmosphere so that it can once again be recycled and redeposited on earth to make life possible.

Nitrogen, Gaseous Basis of Proteins

In the *Yearbook* on food and life produced by the United States Department of Agriculture, a department chemist has written, "If there were any one 'secret of life,' protein might be considered at the heart of it, since protein is the essential stuff of which all living tissue is made." As you know from previous sections of this book, proteins are one of the three basic foods, the other two being carbohydrates and fats (and oils). Also you know that the building stones of all proteins are amino acids, which are nitrogen-containing compounds. We think by this time, you also realize that the primal source for these three basic foods resides in the food-making abilities of green plants. Ultimately it is upon these organisms that animals and nongreen plants must rely for sustenance if they are to survive. The genetic mechanism, you will recall, is situated in large measure in the nucleic acids, and the nucleotides comprising them contain the all-important nitrogenous bases. The amino acids of protein, however, are the sources of most nitrogen compounds in organisms.

The fundamental chemical substance which characterizes protoplasm is protein. Proteins are utilized to build protoplasm in relatively large quantities by plants during cell division, a fundamental step in the process of growth. During the cell enlargement which follows cell division proteins continue to be used. Proteins are also required to replace diseased and injured tissues and for other purposes. Plants which are not supplied with adequate amounts of nitrogen are not able to manufacture the protein requisite for normal growth; hence, they become stunted, malformed, and they show other symptoms of protein (nitrogen) deficiency. Nitrogen deficiency also limits the synthesis of the nucleic acids DNA and RNA, and thus impairs cell division and functioning of the genetic apparatus.

About 18 percent of the dry matter of the human body consists of protein. Hair, skin, nails, and muscle tissue are made up almost entirely of protein. In the human body, as in other animals, not only is protein required to build new cells and tissues but also to restore tissues wasted by disease or damaged through injury. Continual protein deficiency in humans, one of several forms of malnutrition, results in debilitation and it may be a major factor contributing to death.

It is customary for plant physiologists, gardeners, and farmers to speak of "nitrogen deficiencies" in plants. Because gaseous nitrogen (about 80 percent of the air) cannot be used directly by green plants, ordinarily nitrogen must reach plants in a water-soluble form so that it can be absorbed by the roots and shunted to amino acid manufacturing centers in the protoplasm of cells. The **nitrogen cycle** (Figure 21.6), by which this gaseous chemical element becomes available to plants in a utilizable form, is another of the great cycles of nature.

Microscopic plants play a major role in this cycle: They capture and harness some of the vast supply of atmospheric nitrogen and turn it into a form which green plants can use. Ecologist Eugene P. Odum stresses that the microscopic nitrogen-fixers provide "the chief mechanism for moving atmospheric nitrogen from the air reservoir into the productivity cycle." Furthermore, the fungi and bacteria of decay—the decomposers—and certain other specialized groups of bacteria carry on sophisticated chemical transformations by which the nitrogen in the remains of dead plants and animals is converted into mineral forms of nitrogen and recycled back into plants for the manufacture of proteins and nucleic acids. These microscopic plants are really the hinges upon which the gates of life swing. Without them, well-balanced diets would be impossible to provide on an economically practical level.

The nitrogen cycle is really a series of cycles and reciprocal activities, among the most complex of the great cycles of nature. There are many steps, numerous participants, and several variables in the cycle and we can only present here a shortened version. For ease of reference, the several stages of activity have been numbered in Figure 21.6.

Cycles can be entered at any stage and we may start ours at stage 1 which accounts for the inevitable death and decomposi-

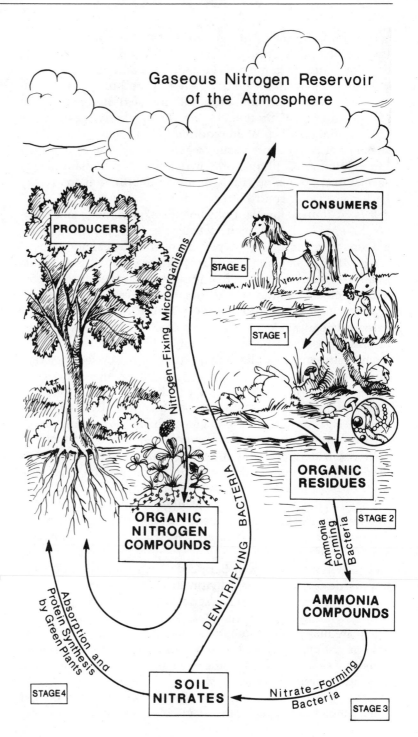

Figure 21.6 Nitrogen cycle. Nitrogen is removed from the atmosphere by symbiotic and nonsymbiotic microorganisms, and from organic residues by the microorganisms of decay acting together with certain specialized bacteria; the nitrogen-containing compounds formed in each case are utilized by green plants for protein synthesis and eventually for food by animals.

Figure 21.7 Decomposing organic debris on the forest floor. Twigs, leaves, animals—all are prey to the enzymes of microorganisms which eventually break down complex molecules to release their chemicals which are reused by living green plants.

tion of plants and animals. The organic remains of plants and animals (Figure 21.7) are acted upon by the enzymes of the decomposing fungi and bacteria of the soil and are reduced to less complex organic residues. Certain specialized soil bacteria are able to use these partially broken-down organic residues as sources of energy and in doing so they release ammonia, an inorganic nitrogen-containing compound (stage 2). Ammonia, through the activities of two distinctive groups of soil bacteria, is converted to water-soluble mineral salts called nitrates (stage 3). Nitrate salts contain nitrogen in the form most readily utilized by green plants. Nitrate-containing solutions of the soil are absorbed into the roots and the nitrogen is used in the manufacture of amino acids and the nitrogen bases of DNA and RNA nucleotides (stage 4). These are compounded in the plant into the proteins and nucleic acids of protoplasm. Thus green plants are producer organisms, just as you saw previously in the discussion of the carbon cycle. When plants are consumed (stage 5) by animals, plant proteins are converted into animal proteins. Simply stated, a juicy beefsteak or a succulent flounder fillet is ultimately only converted grass or algal plankton, humble beginnings for elegant fare.

The rather neat system just described is only one part of the nitrogen cycle and we ought to look at some other activities which involve the biological cycling of this gas. There is a group of bacterial thieves called the **denitrifying bacteria.** These or-

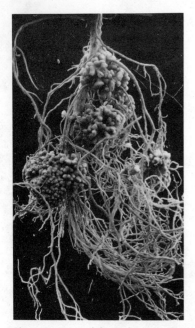

Figure 21.8 Nodules on legume roots. Symbiotic bacteria living in these root swellings convert or "fix" gaseous nitrogen into organic nitrogen compounds which can be used by the green plant host to manufacture proteins and nucleic acids. [Courtesy U.S. Department of Agriculture.]

ganisms are able to utilize the nitrate salts formed in stage 3 for their own purposes, removing them from the main run of the cycle through a shorted circuit. They turn this nitrate into gaseous nitrogen which is released into the air and becomes useless as such to green plants. Growth of these nitrate robbers is favored by flooded ground and prolonged wet weather, by compaction of the soil and depletion of its oxygen. Conditions which encourage the growth of the denitrifying bacteria can be overcome for the most part by preventive or remedial agricultural practices. In nature these bacteria probably do not represent a widespread threat because conditions which favor their growth are of relatively limited extent and duration.

Among the most unusual groups of bacteria associated with nitrogen assimilation by green plants are those harbored in tissue swellings (**nodules**) on rootlets (Figure 21.8). These bacteria are restricted to this form of life in a symbiotic relationship with the green plant. They are able to fix or stabilize gaseous nitrogen from the soil atmosphere (which is continuous, of course, with the air above) and to transform it into organic nitrogen compounds right in the roots of the host plant. These nitrogenous compounds become immediately available to the host green plants and are used in the manufacture of proteins and nucleic acids.

Among the important agricultural crops which shelter **symbiotic nitrogen-fixing bacteria** in root nodules are members of the legume family, peas and beans, vetch and alfalfa, soybeans and clover. Besides the organic nitrogen compounds used directly by these plants, some leaches out from the nodules into the soil solution and can be absorbed by nearby plants; also bits and pieces of root nodule tissue flake off into the soil and their nitrogen is released for use by other (or the same) plants. Thus it has been a long-standing agricultural practice, in keeping with sound ecological principles, for farmers to plant these bacteria-housing legumes as green manure. These plants are grown alternately with other crops and plowed back into the soil for their organic contents and soil-building properties as well as to release the nitrogen compounds formed by the bacteria in their roots.

Symbiotic nitrogen-fixing bacteria occur in the roots of wild as well as domesticated legumes and in the roots of other kinds of plants as well. Nitrogen-fixing microorganisms have been reported in roots of alder, bayberry, Russian olive, and ginkgo, for example. Several groups of **nonsymbiotic nitrogen-fixing bacteria** also inhabit the soil. These exist on dead and decaying organic residues and are able to combine gaseous nitrogen with carbohydrates.

Certain forms of fresh water and marine blue-green algae can fix gaseous nitrogen into forms useful in the growth of higher plants. Nitrogen-fixing blue-green algae occur naturally in the rice paddies of the Orient, and it has been shown that increased production of grain results if the waters are sown with additional blue-green algae.

Blue-green algae, symbiotic and nonsymbiotic bacteria are able to transform sizable amounts of atmospheric nitrogen into compounds beneficial to green plants. Some of the symbiotic nodule-inhabiting legume bacteria have been found to fix as much as 250 pounds of nitrogen per acre each year. An estimate of 5.5 million tons has been made for the nitrogen thus added to the agricultural soils of the United States. Nonsymbiotic nitrogen-fixing bacteria add less nitrogen to soils than symbiotic nitrogen-fixing bacteria. However, nonsymbiotic nitrogen-fixers are ubiquitous in soils whereas symbiotic nitrogen-fixers require the presence of certain host plants to perform their transformations. Fixation of nitrogen by microorganisms is certainly a good argument in favor of the proponents of organic gardening in which commercial fertilizers are proscribed. And what is more, bacterially-fixed nitrogen does not contribute to the runoff of excess nitrogen fertilizer reported to pollute streams in some of our intensively cultivated farmlands of the Midwest.

Any crimp in or deletion from one of the great cycles of nature is bound to have an effect on the wheel of life. As noted earlier in this chapter, these cyclic phenomena are not haphazard conglomerations of organisms and activities; rather, they are tightly engineered systems easily shoved out of phase by the slightest jarring to become linear sequences. Some of man's technologies interfere with and disrupt these cycles and when this happens, not only is man's existence threatened, but so are the lives of other organisms dependent upon the components and activities of the cycle. For convenience, we speak of these natural cycles as though they existed alone, but this is not true as a little reflection will plainly show. In Chapter 22, we intend to give you a few examples of what happens when man, through carelessness or greed, affronts the laws of nature.

Links of Life: The Food Chain

Brobdingnagian Jonathan Swift turned out what may be the first printed description of a food chain in his, "On Poetry: A Rhapsody":

So, Nat'ralists observe, a Flea
　　Hath smaller Fleas that on him prey;
And these have smaller still to bite 'em,
　　And so proceed *ad infinitum.*

Witty and catchy, yes, but not necessarily good biology. In biological terms, a **food chain** refers to the transfer of food energy from producer organisms to successive levels of consumer organisms, from plants to animals which are eaten by other animals, which may in turn be eaten by other animals—but not *ad infinitum.* During the transfer of food energy at each successive level, or link, in a food chain there is an 80 or 90 percent loss of potential energy, mostly in the form of heat from respiration. It is plain that this eat and be eaten chain cannot continue through many stages and still be productive of energy. Usually there are only four or five levels, although some food chains may be longer. At each successive level in the food chain there are fewer and fewer organisms to occupy that stage. Thus short food chains bring consumers closer to producers, closer to the original source of potential energy—the plant.

Among the shortest food chains are those which involve man as a consumer. Early man, with some exceptions of course, was the same terminal consumer he is today; for the most part he coped successfully with the animals for which he was potential prey. But his food options were limited to such as the wilds yielded: cereal grains, tubers, fruits and seeds, tender leafy vegetables, and animals (including insects and their larvae). Man cannot digest cellulose, so the massive potential energy residing in the herbage of grasses, for example, was not available to him, except where he was successful in killing wild animals which had fed on grasses. The use of fire to prepare food increased the variety of his diet for by cooking plants he was able to make some of them more palatable and digestible than before. And this was probably true for some of his animal cuisine as well. (Dr. Bassett Maguire, plant explorer, says that toasted, certain large South American spiders taste like crab meat.)

During the so-called Neolithic Revolution ancient man

changed from a food taker to a food maker, from collecting plants and hunting animals to growing and raising them. Eventually, he domesticated animals—the sheep, goat, pig, and later cattle—and he learned horticulture, the tending of gardens; he became less dependent on the whims of nature; village life began in earnest. Green leaves and stems of grasses, which had previously been unavailable to him as food, could now be eaten in the form of flesh. The culture of plants and animals eased man's burden in life and hastened his civilization; he now had greater control over his dietary requirements and the substances he could utilize as food were expanded.

For the most part, omnivorous man stands as a first- and second-level consumer and fortunately for him he is fairly close in the food chain to the source of potential energy in plants. Thus we have an arguable platform for vegetarianism, for vegetarians are as close as possible—as first-level consumers—to the source of plant energy. Biologically speaking, vegetarians are more economical in their utilization of food energy than other humans.

There are many kinds of food chains; some are terrestrial and some aquatic. Of the latter, some are fresh water and others marine. Some food chains, such as the one described for man, are short; others are longer. Some involve a single linear series of links, others are interconnected with related food chains to become **food webs.** One of the well-studied food chains occurs in abandoned fields in the Midwest. The participants are red clover, field mice, weasels, and eagles or other birds of prey. The producer plant is red clover; field mice eat red clover fruits to become first-level consumers. Weasels prey on field mice and they are in turn preyed upon by eagles or large hawks. These birds-of-prey could as well eat the field mice directly, which they sometimes do. Owls, which may not be able to manage a weasel, could also eat the field mice.

Figure 21.9 consists of a so-called **biomass** (living weight of organisms) **pyramid,** or **pyramid of numbers,** which accounts for energy levels and relative numbers of organisms occupying each level. Using the red clover-eagle example, you will see that the broad base of the pyramid consists of red clover, the producer level. Mice, weasels, and eagles successively occupy the next three energy levels. The tapering of the pyramid indicates a lessening of available energy at each level and a corresponding decrease in the population of organisms at each level. Continual loss of available energy at each successively higher

Figure 21.9 Biomass pyramid. There is a progressive loss of energy from the producer level at the base, through the consumer levels, to the summit of the pyramid.

level limits the numbers of organisms which can subsist at that level. There are fewer eagles than field mice in any given area. The organisms at any of these levels are subject to decomposer fungi and bacteria which act interpositionally. Plants, mice, and weasels may die without having been eaten and are exposed at each respective level to the activities of the decomposers.

Fallen red mangrove leaves and bits and pieces of marine algae are decomposed by fungi, bacteria, and protozoa (one-celled animals) in the warm, sloshing, brackish waters of muddy river estuaries in southern Florida. This debris from chlorophyll-containing plants, plus the decomposing micro-organisms, is ingested by a large group of **detritus** (debris) consumers including several species of crustaceans (shrimp, crabs), insect larvae, nematodes (a kind of worm), bivalve mollusks (mussels, clams, oysters), and even by small, bottom-feeding fish. Feces from some of these organisms are recycled and ingested by other organisms at the same level (nothing is wasted). The next consumer level consists of small carnivores, minnows and small game fish. These are eaten by large carnivores at the apex of the pyramid, top-feeding game fish and fish-eating birds such as the fish hawk or osprey.

Other marine food chains begin with phytoplankton (Figure 21.10), the myriad microscopic algae of the seas (and fresh waters) which live together in what has been called "meadows of the oceans." These in turn are eaten by the zooplankton, which are food for small fish. (The largest mammals, whales, subsist directly on plankton.) Small fish are eaten by larger fish and these may be eaten by man, by still larger fish, by fish-eating birds, or by sharks.

Plant Succession

If in springtime you were to look closely at the soil surface of a newly vacated city lot, your garden which had not been planted, or the cornfield yet to be sown with seed for the summer's crop, you would see all kinds of sprouting plantlets, "adventurous hopefuls," weeds. Untended the vacant city lot would range with a multitude of weeds by the end of summer and a productive garden would be impossible. And if the farmer did not cultivate his fields, did not keep the earthy rows between the corn free from weeds, these would compete with his

See photograph on page 524, mangrove root thickets.

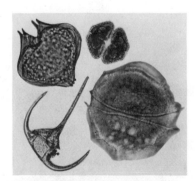

Figure 21.10 Some forms of phytoplankton, highly magnified. These unicellular chlorophyll-containing algae live in countless numbers in the upper layers of the marine seas and fresh water where they manufacture food and produce oxygen. They constitute the lowest level in aquatic food chains, the producer organisms. [Courtesy Shirley D. Van Valkenburg.]

crop for moisture and nutrients to the disadvantage of the crop. This growth of volunteer plants on almost any tenantable piece of earth's surface, dry land or water, goes on in nature continuously. If left undisturbed there would be a continual and regular replacement of vegetation on any given parcel of land or farm pond, season after season, year after year, until the plants on that land or in that pond reached a state of equilibrium with the local climate. Such a change in vegetation in any locality over any period of time is called **plant succession.**

Plant succession is not a random or chaotic change in vegetation; rather, it is a phenomenon marked by regular alternations of plant life reflected in a temporal continuum of vegetational form. The direction and speed of change depend upon many factors, for example, the original condition of the site, climate (precipitation, temperature), soil structure and nutrients, and the plants and animals on nearby sites. Some of the changes are initiated within the plant community itself; others are imported from outside the community. A common feature in the progress of any plant succession is the modifying influence of previous tenants on the site. Thus plants growing on a site at any one time during the course of succession modify that site toward two ends: they make the site untenantable by their own kind at the same time that they make it receptive to the plants which will replace them. This concept is nicely exemplified by the well-studied vegetational succession in the Piedmont of North Carolina.

Originally the North Carolina Piedmont was forested and the major large trees were oaks and hickories. Much of this forest was cut for farms during settlement of the country by Europeans early in the eighteenth century. In some places, this land has been cropped more or less continually; in other places it has been abandoned for one reason or another. Abandoned farmland is subject to a veritable invasion by seeds and fruits from plants growing on surrounding, vegetated land. Seeds and fruits arrive by wind, some are carried by water, and others inevitably come in on the fur, feet, and in the guts of mammals and in the feathers and guts of birds.

On these recently plowed fields the first plants to sprout are herbaceous weeds of various kinds, annual grasses and biennials like the horseweed (Figure 21.11). During the next season the horseweed flowers and plants of perennial white aster begin to grow among the horseweeds and annual grasses. The asters grow rapidly, crowd out the horseweed, and flower

See photograph on page 494, sand dunes.

Figure 21.11 An early stage in secondary plant succession. In this recently abandoned weedy field, the land has been occupied by herbaceous annuals and a few kinds of biennial plants.

themselves during the next summer. By this time, tough perennial grasses have invaded the region and forced the aster from
the ground; the aster is not able to compete with these sturdy
grasses.

At about this stage, sometime during the ascendancy of the
perennial grasses, young pine seedlings appear among the
grass tufts (Figure 21.12). Pine seeds are adapted to germinate
on a mineral seedbed, a soil surface not much covered by leaf
litter and open to the sun. Within a few years, the pines overtop
the herbaceous plants and shade the area making it unsuitable
for their further growth.

The pines continue to grow rapidly and eventually they compete with each other for available resources, mineral nutrients
and water. Weaker and less vigorous pines are crowded out;
they die, fall to the ground, rot, and contribute to the accumulating layer of needle litter on the forest floor. At about
this point the forest is completely dominated by pines and the
upper layer of the forest floor is clothed with plant remains—a
mat of leaves, bits of bark and wood—in various stages of
decomposition. The pines have in reality put themselves out of
business by this time, since pine seeds require a mineral
seedbed for successful germination and pine seedlings need almost full sunlight if they are to thrive. The maturing pine trees
are rooted in the top layers of the soil and there is intense competition for moisture; new seedlings just do not have a chance
to survive, let alone to compete successfully with their parents.

But the seeds and seedlings of other trees are not at a disadvantage under these conditions and those of sweetgum and oak
are more tolerant of shade than those of pine. Their roots, particularly the stout taproots of oak seedlings, are deeper-pene-
trating and can reach water supplies not available to the
shallow-rooted pine seedlings. Soon, a stand of young
sweetgum trees rises under the pines followed by an upward
invasion of oak saplings and later, sturdy-rooted hickories. The
establishment of these broad-leaved trees spells the demise of
the pine forest, for oaks and hickories are potentially overstory
trees and can grow upward, through the pines, eventually to
overtop and shade them (Figure 21.13). This does indeed occur
and about 80 to 140 years after abandonment of the cultivated
field, the old pines begin to die little by little and their places
are taken by the oaks and hickories.

In about 200 years, the old farm field becomes an oak-hickory
forest, much as it was in the days before the European settlers

Figure 21.12 Tough perennial
grasses have taken over from the annual and biennial plants shown in Figure
21.11; pine saplings and other young
trees are now evident.

Figure 21.13 Toward the end of the
secondary succession, a few aged
pines remain. These will soon be
squeezed out by the vigorous oaks and
hickories; no new pines will appear in
this forest for the heavy leaf litter covering the floor prevents the germination of pine seeds. Eventually, the
climax forest vegetation will achieve
equilibrium with the local climate and
a balanced ecological system will
ensue.

first felled the original forest and plowed the virgin soils. This oak-hickory forest in the Piedmont of North Carolina is in equilibrium with the climate and as long as it remains undisturbed by felling, fire, or other catastrophe, it will continue on in the same form for an indefinite period.

Any vegetation form which has reached an equilibrium with the local climate represents the **ecological climax vegetation** for the locality; it is no longer part of an ecological succession. The oak-hickory forest is the climax vegetation in the Piedmont of North Carolina; chaparral vegetation represents the climax in certain arid regions of California; the tropical rain forest is the climax in parts of the Amazon River Basin in Brazil; and the original prairie grassland stood as the climax on the deep soils of the Central Plains before the advent there of the European. Climax vegetation is dynamic; it continues to change and to grow while the general appearance of the vegetation—forest, grassland, chaparral—remains essentially the same. The new seedlings and saplings which come up in it to replace senile dominant plants are of the same species, oaks and hickories, grasses, scrubby chaparral shrubs. Thus, the pattern of vegetation is maintained during the climax stage and ecological succession, with its related changes in vegetational aspect, is terminated.

The oak-hickory forest succession just described is an example of **secondary succession;** it took place on a site that had been vegetated previously. An important feature of secondary succession, wherever it takes place on the land surfaces of earth, is that it occurs in places where soil has already been formed. For this reason, secondary succession on land is a relatively rapid phenomenon in contrast to **primary succession** during which an initial stage must be the actual formation of soil.

Primary succession occurs on new areas, bare rock, sand bars, faces of landslide slopes, and lava flows. Although the species of plants which may colonize such areas differ in different places on earth, the general pattern of succession is much the same overall. Bare rock probably represents the most extreme environment on which primary succession may occur; bare rock has little if any capacity to retain water; its surface is barren of organic matter; mineral nutrients are scarce; it is exposed to the shriveling heat of the sun and the drying drafts of the wind. On such a sere and sterile environment, pioneer lichens and certain mosses appear to be the only forms of plant life which can take hold and grow (Figure 21.14). Mosses and crusty lichens on

Figure 21.14 In this early stage of primary succession on bare rock, lichens have become established on exposed surfaces and mosses in the crevices and cracks. Bits and pieces of twigs and leaves are already beginning to accumulate and decompose in the moss mat, first steps in the process of soil formation.

rocks probably get their first mineral nutrients and organic bits from wind-born dust, from particles of debris washed out of the air by rain, and from water which runs over the rock from nearby soils. Gradually, and patiently slow, the plants grow; parts die and accumulate. Bit by bit, the mass of lichen and moss increases as does the mineral and organic matter (humus) entrapped in the meshes of vegetation.

Seeds of herbaceous vascular plants may find niches in the lichen-moss mat and a little moisture held in the intricacies of this curious seedbed may be just enough for germination to take place and to sustain life (Figure 21.15). As the mat grows, it continues to accumulate mineral sediments and humus at a somewhat more rapid pace and the building plants provide ever more places for particles to lodge. Little by little some of the humus thus snared begins to decompose because of the workings of fungi and bacteria and minute grains of mineral matter mix with the partially decayed organic stuff. A very thin layer of soil commences to form and seeds may germinate and seedlings grow more successfully in this improved environment. Slowly the rocky environment becomes increasingly hospitable to more plants and succession accelerates somewhat. Finally, in a manner resembling the stages of secondary succession, the vegetation reaches the climax typical of the area.

Actually the most rapid succession on bare rock occurs where there are deep cracks in the rock. Organic debris and mineral matter readily accumulate and moisture is retained in these clefts. Seeds and spores are easily caught in the cracks where they germinate and grow more rapidly than those captured by the lichen-moss environment on the bare surfaces of the same rock. Alternate freezing and thawing (in cold climates) and pressure from expanding roots, serve to widen the crevices and to increase the holding capacity of these microenvironments. Given sufficient time, soil develops, plant succession proceeds ever more rapidly, the plants creep out of their niches, and the rock is ultimately covered with the vegetation characteristic of the region.

Figure 21.15 Advanced stage in primary succession on rock indicates the presence of considerable soil, at least sufficient to permit the establishment of two species of flowering plants, pokeberry and poison ivy.

Summary

Ecology is the science of the environment which considers the interrelationships and interactions among plants, animals, and the conditions under which they live. This science can be viewed as a series of intermeshing cycles among which are those involving **carbon, water,** and **nitrogen.**

Carbon, from the carbon dioxide of the atmosphere, is incorporated into the bodies of plants in a large number of essential compounds, initially through **photosynthesis.** Sooner or later, through the **respiration** of plants and animals, through **combustion,** and through **industrial processing,** this carbon is returned again and again to the atmosphere where it is recycled through plants during the photosynthetic process in the manufacture of organic compounds. In a sense, some of the carbon dioxide reaching the air is **fossil carbon dioxide** which has been released during the combustion of fossil plant substance (coal, oil, gas, peat) to produce heat energy. Additionally, carbon dioxide gets into the atmosphere from the geological phenomena involved in vulcanism and geothermal action.

Plants and animals utilize **water** in the economy of life. For one thing, their very substance comprises water in a high degree. Importantly, water is brought together with carbon dioxide in cells of green plants where it becomes an intrinsic component of the food-making process. While photosynthesis is going on, **oxygen** is produced as a by-product. The oxygen in the atmosphere comes largely from this plant source. Bodies of water on earth, particularly the oceans, are the reservoirs impounding our water supply. This water reaches the land surfaces of earth by precipitation from the atmosphere. Through various means—stream flow, transpiration from plants, evaporation from soil surfaces and from seas and lakes—water is restored to the atmosphere and recycled, to fall once more on earth where it is reused to replenish and to sustain life.

Proteins comprise the fundamental stuff of life, the essential components of which are **amino acids,** nitrogen-containing compounds. Proteins manufactured by green plants are consumed by animals, utilized by nongreen plants, and converted into the proteins of their own bodies. The **nitrogen** in proteins and **nucleic acids** comes from two major sources: dead bodies of plants and animals and from the nitrogen reservoir of the air. Through a complex series of chemical transformations, the tissues of dead organisms are decomposed by fungi and bacteria into organic residues. These are further acted upon by certain specialized bacteria which transform organic nitrogen-containing residues into **inorganic nitrates,** a form of nitrogen which is soluble in the soil water and absorbable by the roots of living green plants. In these plants the nitrate nitrogen is reutilized in the manufacture of protein and amino and nucleic acids. Free-living **denitrifying bacteria** may circumvent the use of nitrate nitrogen in green plants by converting it back into gaseous nitrogen. Gaseous nitrogen of the atmosphere is changed into organic nitrogen compounds by **nitrogen-fixing, nodule-inhabiting bacteria** which live symbiotically in the root tissues of legumes and other plants, by **nonsymbiotic soil bacteria,** and by **nitrogen-fixing blue-green algae.**

Food chains comprise a series of organismal links in which there is a transfer of food-derived energy from link to link. Important points to remember about food chains are:

1. All start with **producers** which are chlorophyll-bearing plants that have the ability to manufacture food through photosynthesis.
2. Successive levels in the food chain above the producer level are **consumer** levels.
3. At each successive level, only 10 to 20 percent of the potential energy available from the previous level is passed on.
4. The population or organisms (**biomass**) at each successive level diminishes as the distance from the producer level increases. Food chains which are interdependent comprise **food webs.** Food chains may be terrestrial, aquatic, marine, fresh water, and combinations of these major types.

Plant succession may be viewed as a change in the composition of vegetation at any one place over a period of time. If it occurs on a site which was never vegetated and where there is no soil, it is a **primary succession.** Primary succession proceeds very slowly and soil-making is an integral part of the process. **Secondary succession,** on the other hand, takes place in previously vegetated localities where there is an already-formed soil. Progress is more rapid than in primary succession. In either case, the final stage of succession leads to the formation of **climax vegetation,** a self-regenerating assemblage of plants conditioned by the climate of the area and by other factors within the plant community itself and imported into the community from the outside. Plants at each stage of a succession prepare the site to favor plants of the next stage while at the same time creating conditions which make their own perpetuation impossible. Any catastrophic interference by man or nature—felling, fire, farming, windstorm, or disease—may change the course of succession into unpredictable channels which lead to unknown ends.

Suggested Readings

Ackermann, William C., E. A. Colman, and Harold O. Ogrosky. "Where We Get Our Water." In *Water, The Yearbook of Agriculture 1955*. Washington, D.C.: U.S. Department of Agriculture, 1955.

Billings, W. D. *Plants, Man, and the Ecosystem*. 2d ed. Belmont, Calif.: Wadsworth, 1970. Readable, but somewhat technical account about selected ecological topics.

Dawson, E. Yale. *Marine Botany*. New York: Holt, Rinehart and Winston, 1966. Technical to semitechnical; well-written chapters on plant life of the seas; contains sections on interactions between algae and marine seed-plants and the environment.

Jones, D. Breese. "Protein Requirements of Man." In *Food and Life, Yearbook of Agriculture 1939*. Washington, D.C.: U.S. Department of Agriculture, 1939.

Odum, Eugene P. *Fundamentals of Ecology*. 3d ed. Philadelphia: Saunders, 1971. Authoritative, comprehensive, standard textbook.

Wagner, Richard H. *Environment and Man*. 2d ed. New York: Norton, 1974.

Plant Names

Common name	Scientific name	Family
alder	*Alnus* spp.	Betulaceae
alfalfa	*Medicago sativa*	Leguminosae
apple	*Pyrus malus*	Rosaceae
bayberry	*Myrica* spp.	Myricaceae
bean	*Phaseolus vulgaris*	Leguminosae
clover	*Trifolium* spp.	Leguminosae
corn	*Zea mays*	Gramineae
ginkgo	*Ginkgo biloba*	Ginkgoaceae
hickory	*Carya* spp.	Juglandaceae
horseweed	*Erigeron canadensis*	Compositae
maize	*Zea mays*	Gramineae
oak	*Quercus* spp.	Fagaceae
pea	*Pisum sativum*	Leguminosae
pine	*Pinus* spp.	Pinaceae
red clover	*Trifolium pratense*	Leguminosae
red mangrove	*Rhizophora mangle*	Rhizophoraceae
rice	*Oryza sativa*	Gramineae
Russian olive	*Elaeagnus angustifolia*	Elaeagnaceae
soybean	*Glycine max*	Leguminosae
sweetgum	*Liquidambar styraciflua*	Hamamelidaceae
vetch	*Vicia sativa*	Leguminosae
white aster	*Aster pilosus*	Compositae

Mangrove (*Rhizophora*) root thickets
along warm marine shores host
myriads of sea creatures, some of
which may participate in the process
of food-chain concentration.

22
Man's Influence over His Environment

Compared with Western Europe, the Middle East, and the Orient, the North American continent has seemed until recently a cornucopia, an endlessly bountiful land of limitless production. Settlers from the cramped cities and used-up farms of the Old World flocked to the shores of Columbia for different reasons and with different goals. But all were imbued with the opportunities the new land afforded and impressed with its broad expanses of forest and plain, its teeming wildlife, its freshness, and its over-all abundance. Coming from straitened circumstances of all kinds, they gorged themselves on its plenteousness, heedless that it too could become exhausted and misused, weakened and sterile. A list of those who warned against this profligacy and who argued in the nineteenth century for the preservation of natural resources is not long—Henry David Thoreau, Francis Parkman, Frederick Law Olmsted, John Muir, and others could be mentioned—and their motives and objectives differed in detail.

The science of ecology as a distinct discipline which seeks to measure, describe, and understand the interacting elements of the environment, is a child of the waning years of the nineteenth century. Early ecologists were conscious of the degradation of natural resources which was going on, but for the most part their admonitions were as those of Isaiah, voices "that crieth in the wilderness." Deterioration of land and its productive capacity is subtle; it is not sudden and it does not at once meet the eye (Figure 22.1). Similarly, air and water pollution

525

Figure 22.1 Deterioration of land through neglect and ignorance of the processes of nature. Failure to use ecologically sound methods of tillage have resulted in severe erosion of this formerly productive farmland and reduction of its owner to penury. [Courtesy U.S. Department of Agriculture.]

Figure 22.2 Paul Bigelow Sears, ecologist and humanist, who has urged that the way to use land successfully is to share the responsibility for that use with nature. [Courtesy Paul B. Sears; photographed in East Africa, 1971.]

have grown gradually with industrial expansion and population increase to a level where now they seem to have reached critical proportions. But this did not happen all at once either. What we call environmental problems, are not problems of the environment; rather, they are problems of man: his failure to introduce sound programs of environmental education into the curricula of his schools, his poor understanding of the environment and callousness about its quality. Paul B. Sears's (Figure 22.2) *Deserts on the March* sounded the clarion call in 1935:

> Nature is not to be conquered save on her own terms. She is not conciliated by cleverness or industry in devising means to defeat the operation of one of her laws through the workings of another. She is a very business-like old lady, who plays no favorites. Man is welcome to outnumber and dominate the other forms of life, provided he can maintain order among the relentless forces whose balanced operation he has disturbed. But this hard condition is one which, to date, he has scarcely met. His own past is full of clear and somber warnings—vanished civilizations buried, like dead flies in lacquer, beneath their own dust and mud. . . . For man, who fancies himself the conqueror

of it, is at once the maker and the victim of the wilderness [in the biblical sense].

Environmental mismanagement is nothing new; it has only intensified with our ever-growing capacity to tamper with nature's neatly dovetailing cycles (Figure 22.3). Robbing Peter to pay Paul has been a maxim of Western civilization with a long history.

After God had made heaven and earth, dry land and sea, and populated them with plants and animals, according to the Hebrew Bible he made "male and female," which Linnaeus called *Homo sapiens*. God said, "Let us make man in our image. . . and let them have dominion over the fish of the sea, and over the fowl of the air, and over the cattle, and over all the earth, and over every creeping thing. . . . Be fruitful and multiply, and replenish the earth, and subdue it. . . . I have given you every herb yielding seed. . . and every tree, in which is the fruit of a tree yielding seed—to you it shall be for food." These statements have been bases for countless arguments: Did God give these things to man as a trust, to be appreciated and husbanded? Or did God give them to man to squander and plunder entirely to suit his own ends? Too often, it appears, the latter in-

Figure 22.3 Environmental mismanagement occurs in urban as well as rural areas. In this Manoa Valley scene, not far from the campus of the University of Hawaii, vegetation was removed from a steep slope later used as a homesite. High rainfall, saturated soil, and a subsequent landslide dislocated the house foundation and nearby structures. [Courtesy Soil Conservation Service, U.S. Department of Agriculture.]

terpretation was accepted by followers of the Judaeo-Christian faiths. This is not the place to dwell on biblical interpretation, but rather to point out that the dichotomy of Western man's attitude toward nature has ancient beginnings. In the light of what we have told you in preceding pages, we can take a look at a few of the more obvious man-caused abuses of nature, his sometimes arrogant indifference to, naïve disregard or simple ignorance of the orderly process and over-all benignity of the environment, to see if we can pinpoint some of the reasons for our problems with the environment.

Despoiling the Land

The road was cut with furrows where dust had slid and settled back into the wheel tracks. Joad took a few steps, and the flour-like dust spurted up in front of his new yellow shoes, and the yellowness was disappearing under gray dust. . . .

The owners of the land came onto the land, or more often a spokesman for the owners came. They came in closed cars, and they felt the dry earth with their fingers, and sometimes they drove big earth augers into the ground for soil tests. The tenants, from their sun-beaten dooryards, watched uneasily when the closed cars drove along the fields. . . . Yes, he can do that until his crops fail one day and he has to borrow money from the bank. But—you see, a bank or a company can't do that, because those creatures don't breathe air, don't eat side-meat. They breathe profits; they eat the interest on money. If they don't get it, they die the way you die without air. . . . The squatting men looked down again. What do you want us to do? We can't take less share of the crop—we're half starved now. The kids are hungry all the time. We got no clothes, torn an' ragged. If all the neighbors weren't the same, we'd be ashamed to go the meeting. . . . In the little houses the tenant people sifted their belongings and the belongings of their fathers and of their grandfathers. Picked over their possessions for the journey to the west. The men were ruthless because the past had been spoiled, but the women knew how the past would cry to them in the coming days. . . . Maybe we can start again, in the new rich land—in California, where the fruit grows. We'll start over. But you can't start. Only a baby can start.

Tenderly, pathetically, John Steinbeck described the plight of an entire population, forced to move on because the land had blown away. It was not quite this simple but *The Grapes of Wrath* gives eloquent testimony to the wages earned from mismanagement of the earth.

The ecological events which led to the catastrophe and human misery of the Dust Bowl in Texas, Oklahoma, and other Plains States, have been vividly portrayed by the ecologist Paul Sears in his *Deserts on the March*. The climax vegetation in the Plains States is grass, long grass in the east and short grass in the west, depending upon precipitation. During the opening up of the West, cattlemen ranged their herds over this endless sea of pasturage, year after year. Most of the cattlemen did not own the land on which their beasts grazed; they did not care for it like the treasure it was; instead they permitted overgrazing and then moved the cattle on to richer pastures. Homesteaders and tenant farmers settled on the abandoned cattle lands and cleaved the now sparse sod with their plows. The process of ecological succession which had formed the rich sod was undone—overturned—and the land, already weakened by overgrazing, was destroyed in a relatively short time.

Cyclic climatic changes brought periods of drought and the wind blew, as it always does over the wide sweep of plains. Crops are no match for the wild wind and they could not perform the soil-holding feats of the original prairie sod (Figure 22.4). Great blowouts appeared, first on the knolls, later in the valleys. Soon, the whole landscape was one continuous blowout. Hampered by drought, even the minor soil-holding ability of the crops was ineffective and the sand and dust drifted over everything—over crops, fences, barns, houses, and the trees and shrubs of the windbreaks. The land became a profitless, wasted desert which would support neither man nor beast (Figure 22.5).

Grass, even when close cropped, has remarkable recuperative powers (as any lawn-mowing homeowner ought to know); its growing apices are below the level where grazing animals (except for sheep and goats) usually reach. Thus grasslands can be grazed, but grasses cannot be scoured, year after year, and at the same time manufacture and store food to tide the plants

Figure 22.4 A "sand-blow" area in North Dakota. Rows of corn do not have the soil-holding power of grass sod. [Courtesy U.S. Department of Agriculture.]

through a drought. Overgrazing offends nature and she replies by diminishing or withholding her bounty. If then, after overgrazing, the sod is broken and scattered by the plow, if the thick grass root layer is sundered, it can no longer hold the soil and moisture in the face of wind and sun and these two, beneficent on other occasions, become scourges. They destroy

Figure 22.5 The great Dust Bowl. Remains of a South Dakota farm and homesite in 1936. [Courtesy U.S. Department of Agriculture.]

the climax grassland so thoroughly that a generations-long secondary succession is required to reform the sod and to favor, once again, the equilibrium which permits the climax vegetation to flourish.

Food Chains and Poisoned Food

In Chapter 21, we described food chains and the way in which the energy stored in plants is passed on to other organisms by the eat-and-be-eaten pathway. You will remember that only 10 to 20 percent of the energy is transmitted from level to level as the organisms become larger and the population smaller. This general scheme is what experience has taught us to expect of food chains. We have discovered more recently, however, that products other than food energy sometimes tend to accumulate rather than to diminish as the pyramid of numbers is traversed from base to apex. This phenomenon is known as **food-chain concentration** or **magnification.** Attention was focused on this process and popularized with special reference to DDT by Rachel Carson (*Silent Spring,* 1962) when it was realized that toxic concentrations of chemicals could reach man and other animals in this manner through diet. The several variables which influence food-chain concentration are still not completely understood and this active area of research frequently brings new information to light. Thus our ideas are continuously being reconsidered and revised as new data surface to refute long-held beliefs; this is a way of life in science. The example below will serve as a case in point.

See photograph on page 524, mangrove root thicket.

One of the great boons to insect control was the introduction of DDT to agriculture and public health during World War II. This compound is a synthetic insecticide, one of a group technically known as **chlorinated hydrocarbons** (compounds of hydrogen, carbon, and chlorine) or **organochlorines.** There is no doubt that by destroying the mosquito vectors of the malarial parasite DDT has had more influence than any other chemical in history on the reduction of malaria and saving of lives. Among other applications, DDT has been used in strictly controlled doses to limit the mosquito population in the salt water marshes along the shores of Long Island, New York, a region very close to large centers of human population. When it was learned that DDT could be toxic to fish and wildlife, the spray preparation was carefully diluted and kept below the toxic level.

But the mosquito control specialists were not completely aware of all the factors comprising the food-chain apparatus in the salt marsh environment, nor did they entirely understand the toxic residual effects of DDT, nor that it could continue to accumulate and build up in animal tissues.

The DDT, which was supposed to have been diluted, detoxified, and washed out to sea by the tides, dropped to the bottom of the shallow marsh waters where it became adsorbed onto surfaces of the organic particles (detritus) making up a portion of the sediments. Through the food-chain apparatus, the toxic DDT residues were concentrated in tissues of the many animals which feed on detritus—small fishes, crabs, mussels, snails. Small amounts of DDT are soluble in water (solubility may be as low as 1.2 parts DDT per billion parts of water) and fish absorb some of this through their gills while breathing. As little animals became food for larger animals, and eventually for fish-eating birds such as ospreys, the DDT residues continued to pile up in the fatty tissues of the top-level feeders. DDT, it was learned, accumulates in the fatty tissues of animals, including man, and contrary to its low solubility in water, it is highly soluble in fat (about 9 percent in oleic acid, one of the important constituents of certain fats). It is known that chlorinated hydrocarbons such as DDT are physiologically active in a deleterious way. They are not lethal, as are the nerve gases for example, but they insidiously interfere with important biochemical processes in animals, which could lead, it was feared, to a variety of unnatural symptoms including cancer. Thus, as the various levels in the food chain (technically known as **trophic levels**) are traversed, the chemical could continue to concentrate within the bodies of the organisms nearer and nearer to the top of the food chain. With man being at the apex of some of these food chains, naturally there was considerable concern that he would become the greatest accumulator of DDT and could suffer harm.

These fears were not without foundation for it had been suspected that entire communities of predatory birds had been wiped out by the effects of continually increasing concentrations of DDT; that fiddler crabs accumulate large quantities of DDT much to their detriment; that the young of ospreys and brown pelicans do not hatch because the egg shells are rendered thin and weak because of the disruption by DDT of the shell-forming processes. It was learned too that DDT residues may reach rivers, lakes, and seas as runoff from croplands where the insecticide has been used. Thus there was ample cause for concern, not so much because of the death of the graceful osprey or of some unseen fiddler crabs along our coastlines, but because of the potential hazard to man.

The seemingly cut-and-dried case against DDT and Rachel Carson's call to arms were basically responsible for marshaling the public, through the Environmental Defense Fund, against the continued use of DDT. This resulted in laws which now ban the sale and use of DDT and similar chlorinated hydrocarbons in the United States. But the DDT story is still far from complete. There is continuing controversy about the effects of DDT on humans and other animals, and proponents of the ban have been accused of misrepresenting the facts and exaggerating the toxicity of the chemical to achieve their own ends.

If DDT were prohibited from use in countries where today malaria is still endemic and still one of the great scourges of the people, it would result in untold hardship and greater human death rates than are already present. (In 1975 it is estimated there were 20 million victims of malaria in south Asia alone.) Other insect-borne diseases would flourish as would insects themselves and crop production would undoubtedly wane. A 1971 report of the World Health Organization (an agency of the United Nations) on DDT and its influence on the reduction of malaria encourages its continuing use for this purpose. Because of the considerable adverse publicity given DDT and in order to present a more balanced picture of the pros and cons of DDT toxicity, especially in humans, we think the quotation below from the World Health Organization report germane to the subject:

> The safety record of DDT for man is truly remarkable. At the height of its production, over 400,000 tons per year were used for agriculture, forestry, public health and other purposes, all involving some human contact. For typhus control, whole populations have had 10% DDT powder blown into their clothing as they wore it. For malaria control, millions of men, women and children have had the interior walls of their homes sprayed year after year, in some cases for more than 20 years. For control of yellow fever, DDT has been added directly to drinking water. For food protection, many plants and animals eaten by man have been sprayed with this insecticide. Yet, in spite of the prolonged exposure of the population of the world and the

heavy occupational exposure of a substantial number of people, the only confirmed cases of injury have been the result of massive accidental or suicidal ingestion.

Those who oppose the use of DDT suggest that it may present a hazard as a carcinogen [cancer-producing substance] and a mutagen [mutation-producing substance]. The limited experimental data relating to the mutagenicity of DDT are inconclusive. Although there is definite evidence that, in mice, DDT in large doses increased the incidence of hepatomas [liver tumors], the significance of this finding in relation to man cannot be assessed as yet. In view of this, and in the light of the evidence available on the health of individuals most heavily exposed to DDT, there is at present no sound reason to believe that the millions of people protected against vector-borne diseases are at tangible risk from their small exposure to DDT.

There is other evidence cited in an article by Thomas H. Jukes, well-known scientist and Professor of Medical Physics at the University of California, Berkeley, that within a group of "35 workers in a DDT factory who, for periods ranging from 9 to 19 years, absorbed daily up to 400 times as much DDT as the general population," there have been no cases of cancer. He concludes from these and other extensive data that "there is no epidemiological evidence connecting DDT with cancer in human beings."

We know more each day about the ways in which animals handle DDT in their metabolism and the position of the DDT in the food-chain concentration apparatus. Some of these phenomena were not known when the possibility of cumulative deleterious effects of DDT were first pointed out. For example, evidence for the continual stepwise increase in the concentration of DDT in the food chain is best demonstrated in terrestrial food chains. Evidence from intensive studies on aquatic food chains, on the other hand, supports the view that the residue concentration in each food-chain level depends on the net amount of DDT actually retained by the organisms involved since all the DDT absorbed or ingested does not concentrate indefinitely; some is metabolized, changed into harmless compounds and excreted, and some is excreted directly; neither of these portions remains to be concentrated in fatty tissues. Furthermore, it is known that not all kinds of organisms (especially fish which have been well studied) exposed to the same concentrations of DDT retain, metabolize, or excrete the same amounts of the chemical. That is, not all organisms respond to DDT in the same way. Laboratory experiments have shown, for example, that DDT in high dosage produced little effect against the desert locust, cockroach, and the Mexican bean beetle and that other insecticides must be used to control them on crops. We can assume then that DDT in the concentrations used in insecticides is not toxic to these particular insects.

There are data which show that DDT is not as persistent in the marine environment as once believed. Research has proven that the half-life of DDT (period of time necessary for half a given quantity of DDT to undergo disintegration) in naturally illuminated sea water is about ten days. In the presence of ultraviolet radiation, such as occurs in the sun's rays, DDT is decomposed into harmless compounds.

Nevertheless, caution must continue to be exercised in the use of DDT and other unnatural chemical compounds which we insert into the food chain. We must continue to examine and monitor the biological effects of these substances—before we use them and while they are being used (Figure 22.6). The article by Professor Jukes gives an overview of the DDT con-

Figure 22.6 A monitoring team in Mississippi collects soil samples, specimens of potato tubers and upper plant parts for analyses to determine the presence of pesticide residues. [Courtesy U.S. Department of Agriculture.]

troversy from the scientific, social, and moral points of view. He sums up by writing, "A dilemma of our times is the 'environmental-chic' movement that is fashionable among prosperous urban dwellers whose way of life depends on a high rate of consumption of natural resources. . . . The inarticulate majority of the world's people have never enjoyed the technological amenities of a prosperous and industrialized civilization. Instead, they are struggling against disease and hunger. Cheap insecticides are needed by these people. Whether one supports their cause, as I do, or is instead oriented more towards wild animals and birds, will depend largely upon conditioning and preferences." Clearly the issues involved in DDT use are at the same time emotional, moral, and scientific. Only after intensive dispassionate experimentation, observation, and testing can the effects of DDT on and between humans and other animals be fully assessed and evaluated.

It should also be pointed out that synthetic compounds with a potential for human toxicity do not always have to be used to control or extinguish man's insect enemies. Granted, mosquitoes and other insects carry disease-producing organisms and are in themselves pestiferous nuisances which must be controlled; admitted, crops can be ravaged by the unchecked preying of some insects. But at times there are other ways to accomplish insect control than by exposing whole food chains to the possibility of poisoning. Biological control employing predators and parasites of offending organisms is sometimes effective; changes in our systems of cropping and use of land and water may help; pyrethrum and derris (Figure 22.7) from which rotenone is obtained, are insecticides which are not toxic to humans. These methods are always worth trying and where they will work effectively and economically they are preferable to the use of toxic substances. An excellent volume by Eugene P. Odum contains several alternative methods to the use of synthetic, toxic chemicals as insecticides (see Suggested Readings).

Figure 22.7 Plantation of derris in El Salvador. The insecticide rotenone is extracted from roots of these legume vines. [Courtesy U.S. Department of Agriculture.]

The Car and the Air

We need not remind you that the oxygen in the air you breathe comes from green plants and that it comprises about 20 percent of the atmosphere. This very same atmosphere contains nearly 80 percent nitrogen, a gas which cannot be used by most plants and animals until it is converted into another form. Yet one of the underlying causes of air pollution is involved in the union of these two biologically critical gases —oxygen and nitrogen—into compounds known as oxides of nitrogen. This conversion actually occurs in nature to some extent but it is greatly intensified when the gases are heated together as they are in power generating plants and in internal combustion gasoline engines. Taken alone, **nitrogen (nitric) oxide** is comparatively harmless; however, its chemical relative, **nitrogen dioxide** is potentially highly poisonous to humans and plants.

Exhaust fumes from engines burning gasoline contain quantities of unburned gasoline and other **hydrocarbons** (compounds of hydrogen and carbon), carbon monoxide, carbon dioxide, water vapor, sulfur compounds, and other substances which are vented into the air. Additionally, hydrocarbon emissions are products of manufacturing, oil fields, oil refineries, gasoline pumping stations, and other activities involving the petroleum industry. It is not the direct effect of the gaseous hydrocarbons and nitrogen oxides on plants and animals which causes concern, rather, it is the reaction products of these two classes of compounds. In the presence of solar energy, the hydrocarbons combine with the nitrogen oxides to produce a poisonous visible product containing a mixture of formaldehyde, peroxyacylnitrates, and other gaseous compounds which together comprise **photochemical smog** (*smog = sm*, from smoke and *-og*, from fog; **London smog** results primarily from the sulfur oxides and particles which come from burning coal). Nitrogen dioxide is a brownish gas and contributes its share to the overall color and toxicity of smog. Thus there may be an abundance of material in the atmosphere which has the potential to create photochemical smog—the eye-watering, throat-scratching anathema to normal breathing and good health—to depress the production of oxygen by green plants, to reduce visibility, and to produce objectionable odors.

A 1953 survey of the Los Angeles area showed that while the petroleum industry was emitting about 500 tons of hydrocarbons a day, about 1,300 tons were being produced by the internal combustion engines of road vehicles: cars, buses, and trucks. Four years later it was estimated that motor vehicles were responsible for the production of some 80 percent of the hydrocarbons in the atmosphere. Although Los Angeles in particular has become associated in the United States with air

Figure 22.8 Smog over a Southern California city. [Courtesy Bethlehem Steel Corporation.]

pollution, nearly every major city in the world today is affected by photochemical or London smog or both (Figure 22.8).

To limit the emission of hydrocarbons by automotive engines manufacturers reluctantly began research on pollution-control devices. California was first to institute a program of control for vehicular emissions in 1961, and in 1968 the federal government established an agency to oversee the activities of the automobile industry (among other responsibilities) to develop and install pollution control devices on their products. By 1970 manufacturers had reduced carbon monoxide 70 percent and hydrocarbons 80 percent from uncontrolled levels. The year 1974 was set as the time for stringent standards to go into effect, but our multi-billion-dollar automotive industry claimed it could not meet this unrealistic deadline. The energy crisis of 1974 highlighted the fact that the addition of effective pollution-control devices to automotive engines necessary to meet federal standards could lead to fuel economy penalties of up to 30 percent. Pollution-control devices increase gasoline consumption and decrease the efficiency of engines—twin evils which could limit the lucrative market for the gas-guzzling behemoths of the American highway. (The trend toward building smaller, lighter cars in this country is one result of the critical shortage of petroleum.)

To complicate matters still further, the catalytic converters being installed into pollution-control systems on gasoline engines were found to be deactivated by the lead from tetraethyl lead, a commonly used antiknock additive in high-octane gasoline mixtures. Again the automobile and the related petroleum industry were required to modify their technologies. It has been necessary for the petroleum industry to retool in response to government intervention, and to begin regular production of nonleaded, high-octane gasolines so that the catalytic converters could effectively control emissions. These fuel mixtures are somewhat more expensive to the consumer but well worth it when we realize that lead in itself is toxic to all life and that it escapes into the atmosphere as gaseous lead bromide from automobile exhaust. Joseph Priest in his book, *Problems of Our Physical Environment, Energy, Transportation, and Pollution,* has a fine chapter which explains the workings of the internal combustion engine, the production of air pollutants by these engines, the several devices used to reduce or eliminate these products, and alternative engines for use in road vehicles.

The fact of the matter is that here and elsewhere we must be our own watchdogs. Continuing vigilance is necessary if we are to have any influence over our own destinies and well-being in the face of the sometimes self-seeking interests of a small but powerful and vocal minority in industry and in the government. Paul Sears has put it well:

> Once the public knows that machinery has been established to correct an evil, it settles back to a condition of complacency, assuming that Uncle Sam will do the job. Partly this is due to inertia, of course, but more largely to a misunderstanding of how government must work in a democracy.
>
> While the people regard their task as completed with the passage of good legislation, predatory interests which are hampered by the legislation look upon their own task as being nicely started. They are immediately put in a position of knowing all the rules under which their enemy, society, must carry on the combat. Although actually representing minorities, they are powerful, and they never settle back to sleep. The stakes in the game are high, and justify unceasing attention. Ceaselessly, therefore, they look for loopholes, applying pressure here, craft and stealth there, until the program which had seemed adequate to protect the well-being of the people for all time is as full of holes as a sieve.

As long ago as 1790, John Philpot Curran put it another way: "It is the common fate of the indolent to see their rights become a prey to the active. The condition upon which God hath given liberty to man is eternal vigilance; which condition if he break, servitude is at once the consequence of his crime and the punishment of his guilt." And Demosthenes wrote on this subject: "There is one safeguard known generally to the wise, which is an advantage and security to all, but especially to democracies as against despots. What is it? Distrust."

Rules and Ethics for Ecology

We could go on at considerable length with a series of examples showing all the different kinds of abuses of nature: water pollution, fertilizer runoff, eutrophication of ponds and lakes, radiation pollution. Much of this, though, has been well expressed in books and articles; some of these have already been noted and others appear in the Suggested Readings at the end of this chapter. We would like to call to your attention especially *The Closing Circle* by botanist Barry Commoner. Professor Commoner enumerates four generalizations which he calls "laws of ecology." We think these are practical and we want to tell you about them. They are not new. They have been stated before, but Commoner's presentation is especially geared to today's ecological perspectives.

1. *Everything is connected to everything else.* This statement reflects the view of an elaborate network of intercommunications in the natural world, among different living organisms and their physiochemical surroundings. Food chains, successional regimes, the nitrogen, carbon, and hydrologic cycles each contains elements which are interdependent. If we disturb one element, another is likely to be dislocated or to become impotent. Francis Thompson speaks to this idea poetically in lines from *The Mistress of Vision:*

To each other linked are,
That thou canst not stir a flower
Without troubling of a star.

Disturbances of ecological phenomena are brought about in many ways by different agents. Fire, flood, lava flows, and disease are among the natural disturbances which affect the regular progress of biological cycles. Man introduces exotic plants and animals, clears land, builds dams, adds excess nutrients to waters, and these too upset the processes of nature. The course of man's disruptions is sometimes unpredictable; almost always, though, it is preventable.

Examples of man-made disturbances are road building and other forms of land clearing. These activities destroy native vegetation and interrupt normal cycles of plant and animal succession. Open land invites invasion by weeds, some of which, like ragweed and poison ivy, are noxious to man himself. Colonization of a site by rampant exotic vines like Japanese honeysuckle and kudzu is favored by land clearing. In the warmer parts of the eastern United States, these plants sometimes mantle the tops of native forest trees and shade them so effectively that they decline and sometimes die (Figure 22.9). At the same time they eliminate indigenous shrubs and herbs. Premature death

Figure 22.9 Kudzu, a rampant exotic vine, drapes over native trees and shrubs in Washington, D.C. [Courtesy Paul Elihu Stern.]

of the trees and other native plants prepares the way for an aberrant plant succession which not only affects native plants and normal vegetation cycles, but also animals whose very lives are dependent on these plants.

In Hawaii, with its unique flora, the exotic guava, lantana, and fountain grass compete so successfully with the native flora in some areas that entire populations of indigenous plant species are threatened with extinction. Guavas were introduced for their edible fruits, lantanas and fountain grass for their ornamental value. Lantana and fountain grass are especially pernicious invaders; on some dry sites on the Island of Hawaii they grow in almost pure stands, dominating native plants and persisting where almost nothing else will grow.

2. *Everything must go somewhere.* This is a simplified version of a physical law which states that matter can neither be created nor destroyed. In the biological world, as you well know by this time, one organism's waste is another organism's dinner. Solid waste from cattle is rolled into balls by the dung beetle; the female deposits an egg in each ball, buries it, and the larvae are provided with a ready-made meal when they hatch. Carbon dioxide respired by animals is used as raw material by plants during photosynthesis. The balanced aquarium is a well-known system involving the oscillation of carbon dioxide between respiring fish and photosynthetic aquatic plants. In natural systems, everything is used and reused, and then used again. Nothing is truly wasted.

Man produces materials, however, which sometimes do not decompose to become productive again in another of nature's transformations. Barry Commoner gives an example of this in the discarded flashlight battery. After it is used up, the battery is discarded into the trash can. The battery may contain elemental mercury which is vaporized when the trash is burned in the municipal incinerator. The mercury vapor is emitted from the incinerator stack, carried by the wind, and eventually brought down to earth again by rain or snow. The mercury, which may now be in the soil, is washed into a lake where it condenses into elemental mercury, sinks to the bottom, and accumulates. Certain bacteria decompose mercury into methyl mercury, a water-soluble organic compound which is absorbed by fish and other aquatic animals. The mercury accumulates in the tissues of fish which may be eaten by man, by other fish, or by fish-eating birds. This is another example of food-chain concentration which we discussed earlier in this chapter. Mercury is not healthy for man; it may cause severe nausea and vomiting, abdominal pain, loosening of teeth, kidney damage, muscle tremors, jerky gait, personality changes, and other evils. The mere fact that we throw away an exhausted dry cell does not mean that the mercury in it goes away; it merely goes out of sight—for the time being.

3. *Nature knows best.* The cycles and substances of nature have been tried repeatedly in the crucible of time. They are the results of an incalculable number of biological experiments; they are viable or they would have been rejected as untenable for life. In the words of the evolutionist, the mechanisms of evolution are geared to select for advantageous changes and against those which are disadvantageous. Thus, we are on pretty safe grounds to assume that the productions of nature which we now have are the best possible alternatives to the hundreds of millions which must have been tested over the millenia.

For each naturally produced organic substance, there is a corresponding enzyme system capable of decomposing that substance. Barry Commoner notes that "the varieties of chemical substances actually found in living things are vastly more restricted than the *possible* varieties [of chemical substances which can be formulated in the laboratory.]" Chemists can make many compounds which do not occur in nature and some of these may be active biologically—that is, they may affect animal or plant function. Some of the synthetic drug preparations which we commonly use—aspirin, for example—fall into this category. Commoner goes one step further; he says of these man-made compounds, "It is probable that no degradative enzyme exists, and the material tends to accumulate." The important point here is that biologically active synthetic compounds ought to be treated as we do drugs—"prudently, cautiously." Commoner says, discouragingly, this is "impossible when billions of pounds of the substance are produced and broadly disseminated. . . where it can reach and affect numerous organisms not under our observation. Yet this is precisely what we have done with detergents, insecticides, and herbicides. The often catastrophic results lend considerable force to the view that 'Nature knows best.'"

4. *There is no such thing as a free lunch.* This is one of the basic tenets of economics: You get nothing for nothing. If we mine our natural resources they never come back. Once we use up all the coal, gas, and oil there won't be any more.

Someone will suffer sometime if we are profligate in our use of these resources today. Someone will have to pay sometime.

Industry seems to find it convenient and economical to dump manufacturing wastes into nearby streams. Cities do similar damage by pouring untreated sewage into rivers. Effects of these activities on the stream and on the life in and along the stream will depend on the amount and kind of materials dumped. Pollution upstream may adversely affect the water supply of towns downstream; beaches may be rendered unsafe for swimming and shellfish unfit for food. Industrial convenience and economy upstream exact payment downstream.

Flood plains are favored places for building and agriculture: They are relatively level, rock-free, and the alluvial soils are generally rich and easily worked. But streams flood periodically, houses are torn loose and floated away, crops are drowned, soil is lost, and the form of the land may be sharply altered. Payment cannot be avoided; it can only be shifted or delayed, but not denied.

Solutions to problems of the deteriorating environment we face today are not based so much on our inability to understand the problems, but rather on our hesitancy over coming to grips with the solutions which usually involve individual and collective sacrifice. This reluctance, in turn, may involve ethics or moral duty, individual choice or preference versus the collective good. The noted conservationist Aldo Leopold (1887–1948) thought of ethics as the acceptance of the realization "that the individual is a member of a community of interdependent parts. His instincts prompt him to compete for his place in that community, but his ethics prompt him also to co-operate (perhaps in order that there may be a place to compete for)." Leopold believed that "an ethic, ecologically, is a limitation on freedom of action in the struggle for existence. . . . philosophically [it is] a differentiation of social from anti-social conduct."

Every entrepreneur would probably always be willing to practice ecologically sound management in running his enterprises if it did not limit his profits, that is, if sacrifice could be reduced to a minimum or to zero. And entrepreneurs are not alone; most of us would like to enjoy a life without sacrifice. When forest industries reforest their own logged off land, their basic motive is to restock the land with a marketable crop for the future (Figure 22.10). Incidentally, however, reforestation prevents soil erosion, provides habitat and sustenance for

Figure 22.10 Commercial plantation of slash pine (*Pinus elliottii*) in Florida. These trees are about ten years old and are ready to be harvested for conversion into wood pulp. [Courtesy Soil Conservation Service, U.S. Department of Agriculture.]

wildlife, and regenerates recreational and scenic areas for society. The motivation behind replanting the forest does not necessarily rest on an ethical basis; rather, it may rest on an economic basis—future profit. Here, fortunately, what happens to be good for industry coincides with what is also good for society and the environment. But this is not always so.

Witness the use of toxic plasticizers in the manufacture of polyvinyl automobile seat covers. These chemicals are good for industry because they enable it to make a product which is attractive to the consumer, durable, and which will help sales of cars, for example. At the same time, the product emits vapors which are reported to be deleterious, that is, they have been shown to result in the development of abnormal tissues in experimental animals. This fact was reported several times before 1970 after industry testing both in the United States and abroad. Laboratory results published in 1961, for example, showed that upon repeated exposure to vinyl chloride (a gaseous constituent of polyvinyl plastics) there were "micropathological changes in the livers of rabbits and statistically significant increases in the average weight of the livers of male and female rats." The authors of this report did not see any possibility of human danger resulting from exposure to vinyl chloride and they concluded that "it is doubtful whether it would be possible for humans to be exposed continuously at 500 ppm [parts of vinyl chloride per million of air] in production plants since this high a general concentration would indicate severe leaks in the equipment and extremely high concentrations adjacent to the leaks."

This and later studies on experimental animals did not set off any major alarm until cases of cancer in factory workers exposed to the vinyl chloride vapors began to be reported. Ethical motivation—that is, an overriding concern for the common good —should have prompted manufacturers to halt production and use of vinyl chloride at the slightest suspicion of pathogenicity and until further thorough evaluation could be conducted to determine if humans could exist safely in an atmosphere containing any concentration of vinyl chloride. It is not ethical to wait for the appearance of cancer in humans before taking action to modify an environment containing a suspected carcinogenic substance. These substances usually take years to produce an effect, which is too often irreversible.

Aldo Leopold pleaded for an ethical relation of people to the land, that is, of people working in partnership with the land. He viewed such a desirable relationship as inconceivable, though, "without love, respect, and admiration for land, and a high regard for its value. By value," he explained, is meant "something far broader than mere economic value; I mean value in the philosophical sense. . . . No important change in ethics was ever accomplished without an internal change in our intellectual emphasis, loyalties, affections, and convictions." He urged us to "quit thinking about decent land-use as solely an economic problem. Examine each question in terms of what is ethically and esthetically right, as well as what is economically expedient." There is nothing intrinsically wrong or socially bad about economic expediency and profit-making, provided they are tempered with fairness, do not infringe on the collective rights of society, nor, ecologically speaking, upon the rights of the land and the rest of the environment.

These sentiments and beliefs which Leopold applied specifically to the land and called "The Land Ethic" apply equally to the whole of the environment. They comprise the motivation which can result in steady and lasting progress to protect and enhance the quality of our environment. Ethical concern and economic advantage must be equal partners in all of man's efforts to better his life. The pressure of economic advantage must not be allowed to overcome the social good of ethical concern. Government has legislated and will continue to legislate to protect the environment—it must—but permanent protection can only issue from moral obligation among all of us, from love, respect, and admiration for our environment.

Following an extended tour in the late 1930s to study soil erosion and land use in Western Europe, North Africa, and the Middle East, Walter Clay Lowdermilk of the United States Soil Conservation Service formulated the "Eleventh Commandment," his addition to the Mosaic Decalogue. Whereas the Decalogue deals primarily with interpersonal relationships, the "Eleventh Commandment" is founded on the moral principle of common good. It says, "Thou shalt inherit the Holy Earth as a faithful steward, conserving its resources and productivity from generation to generation. Thou shalt safeguard thy fields from soil erosion, thy living waters from drying up, thy forests from desolation, and protect thy hills from overgrazing by thy herds, that thy descendants may have abundance forever. If any shall fail in this stewardship of the land, thy fruitful fields shall become sterile stony ground and wasting gullies, and thy descendants shall decrease and live in poverty or perish from off the face of the earth."

To recapitulate this chapter on man's influence over his environment, we would like to turn again to the words of Paul Sears and quote from the chapter of his *Deserts on the March* entitled, "Man, Maker of Wilderness." These lines contain the embodiment and lesson of ecology:

The face of earth is a graveyard, and so it has always been. To earth each living thing restores when it dies that which has been borrowed to give form and substance to its brief day in the sun. From earth, in due course, each new living being receives back again a loan of that which sustains life. What is lent by earth has been used by countless generations of plants and animals now dead and will be required by countless others in the future. . . . No plant or animal, nor any sort of either, can establish permanent right of possession to the materials which compose its physical body. Left to herself, nature manages these loans and redemptions in not unkindly fashion. She maintains a balance which will permit the briefest time to elapse between burial and renewal. The turnover of material for new generations to use is steady and regular. Wind and water, those twin sextons, do their work gently. Each type of plant and animal, so far as it is fit, has its segment of activity and can bring forth its own kind to the limits of subsistence. The red rule of tooth and claw is less harsh in fact than in seeming. There is a balance in undisturbed nature between food and feeder, hunter and prey, so that the resources of the earth are never idle. Some plants or animals may seem to dominate the rest, but they do so only so long as the general balance is maintained. The whole world of living things exists as a series of communities whose order and permanance shame all.

Suggested Readings

Adler, Cy A. *Ecological Fantasies.* New York: Green Eagle Press, 1973. A review of ecological "red herrings."

Billings, W. D. *Plants, Man, and the Ecosystem.* 2d ed. Belmont, Calif.: Wadsworth, 1970. See Suggested Readings, Chapter 21.

Carson, Rachel. *Silent Spring.* Boston: Houghton Mifflin, 1962. Probably the single most influential book to bring ecology to the popular attention.

Commoner, Barry. *The Closing Circle.* New York: Knopf, 1971. (Reprinted New York: Bantam Books, 1972.) Economic, social, and hygienic consequences of environmental abuse; "rules" of ecology and how to get along with nature; nontechnical.

———. *Science and Survival.* New York: Viking, 1967.

Crosby, Alfred W., Jr. *The Columbian Exchange: Biological and Cultural Consequences of 1492.* Westport, Conn.: Greenwood Publishing Company, 1972.

Ehrenfeld, David W. *Biological Conservation.* New York: Holt, Rinehart and Winston, 1970.

Enthoven, Alain C., and A. Myrick Freeman, III, eds. *Pollution, Resources, and the Environment.* New York: Norton, 1973.

Grosvenor, Gilbert W., François Leydet, and Joseph Judge. "America's Wilderness: How Much Can We Save?" *National Geographic Magazine* 145 (February 1974): 151–205. Pictorial travelogue with descriptions of wilderness areas in the United States.

Jukes, Thomas H. "Insecticides in Health, Agriculture and the Environment." *Naturwissenschaften* 61(1974): 6–16. A review of the DDT controversy by a respected scientist.

Leopold, Aldo. *A Sand County Almanac and Sketches Here and There.* London: Oxford University Press, 1949. A collection of essays on the land and ethics of land use; philosophical/biological.

Lowdermilk, W. C. *Conquest of the Land through Seven Thousand Years.* Agriculture Information Bulletin 99, Washington, D. C.: U.S. Department of Agriculture, 1953. A soil scientist's view of land use, past, present, and future; nontechnical.

Nash, Roderick. *Wilderness and the American Mind.* New Haven: Yale University Press, 1967. Historically based evaluation of wilderness and what it has meant and still means to the people of the United States; scholarly but quite readable.

North, Douglass C., and Robert Leroy Miller. *The Economics of Public Issues.* 2d ed. New York: Harper & Row, 1973.

Odum, Eugene P. *Fundamentals of Ecology.* 3d ed. Philadelphia: Saunders, 1971.

Priest, Joseph. *Problems of our Physical Environment, Energy, Transportation, Pollution.* Reading, Mass.: Addison-Wesley, 1973. Excellent review of practical physics for the nonphysicist with special reference to the influence of physical phenomena on the environment; semitechnical.

Sax, Karl. *Standing Room Only: The World's Exploding Population.* 2d ed. Boston: Beacon Press, 1960. A world-renowned Harvard geneticist's view of expanding population. Professor Sax lost some friends with the publication of this book.

Sears, Paul B. *Deserts on the March.* 3d ed. Norman: University of

Oklahoma Press, 1959. First popularly written modern book to call attention to use and abuse of the land and their consequences; eloquent; almost poetic; emotionally charged; scientifically authoritative.

Steinbeck, John. *The Grapes of Wrath.* New York: Viking, 1939. A Nobel-Prize-winning novelist's story of the people actually caught up in the catastrophe that was America's Dust Bowl of the 1930s; poignant, heart-rending, stimulating.

Wagner, Richard H. *Environment and Man.* 2d ed. New York: Norton, 1974.

World Health Organization. "The Place of DDT in Operations against Malaria and Other Vector-Borne Diseases." *Official Records of the World Health Organization* 190 (1971): 176–182. An internationally based assessment of the use of various pesticides, their benefits and potential harm to man.

Plant Names

Common name	Scientific name	Family
derris	*Derris elliptica* and other species	Leguminosae
fountain grass	*Pennisetum setaceum*	Gramineae
guava	*Psidium guajava*	Myrtaceae
Japanese honeysuckle	*Lonicera japonica*	Caprifoliaceae
kudzu vine	*Pueraria lobata*	Leguminosae
lantana	*Lantana camara*	Verbenaceae
poison ivy	*Toxicodendron radicans* (= *Rhus toxicondendron*)	Anacardiaceae
pyrethrum	*Chrysanthemum coccineum* and other species	Compositae
ragweed	*Ambrosia* spp.	Compositae

Egyptian Queen Hatshepsut's plant explorations to the Land of Punt are commemorated in bas-relief on the walls of her temple near Thebes.

23
Exploring for Plants

Few think of botanists as explorers and adventurers cast in the same mold as Christopher Columbus, Robert E. Peary, James Cook, David Livingstone, and Thor Heyerdahl. Yet there were some, mostly unsung, who ventured into distant wilds in search of new plants, whose tales of discovery tingle with excitement, whose privations rivaled those of Coleridge's Ancient Mariner, and whose treasure trove exceeded Pizarro's glittering gold of the Inca. Whether for the sheer love of discovery, the need for a living, or the selfless desire to help mankind, these botanists—Richard Spruce, Alexander von Humboldt, Hipólito Ruiz and José Antonio Pavón, Peter Kalm, John and William Bartram, David Douglas, Frank Kingdon-Ward, Joseph F. Rock, Frank Ludlow and George Sherriff, and many others—deserve higher acclaim and recognition for their discoveries than an indifferent public has awarded them. Exploration for plants continues today; its direction and emphases have changed over the years, but its goals, to broaden the usefulness of plants and to learn about them as forms of life, remain unaltered.

Too seldom do we contemplate the origins of plants we grow in our gardens, eat, or use for their fibers, or value for their medicinal properties. But some of even the commonest plants were introduced from the wild at great personal sacrifice, usually from remote places, and often at considerable expense. Our garden camellias, forsythias, tulips, flowering cherries, lilacs, crocuses, and chrysanthemums were once really at home only in faraway lands. As we have discussed, rauwolfia root for tranquilizers, cinchona bark for quinine, coca leaves for cocaine, vinca for antileukemia drugs, dioscorea tubers for the

551

steroids important for birth control, together with cinnamon and cloves, coffee, tea, rubber, cocoa, banana, and a host of other plants as we know them today were brought into our lives originally through the efforts of plant explorers. Edible plants from one region have been introduced into others: mango, avocado, papaya, and macadamia nut, for example, have been striking successes; while soursop, carambola, and bael fruit are notable failures as table fruits in the United States. It should be emphasized, however, that some botanical expeditions do not necessarily have plant usefulness as an immediate goal; rather botanists search for plants to inventory and learn about the different kinds, to establish records of the natural resources of an area, to trace plant distribution, and to study plants as living organisms in their natural habitats.

Botanical expeditions have been supported variously. Some explorations were sponsored by broad-visioned commercial nurserymen, such as the old British firm of James Veitch & Son, and others by public and private botanical gardens and arboreta. In this country the Arnold Arboretum of Harvard University, Longwood Gardens of Pennsylvania in cooperation with the United States Department of Agriculture, and the New York Botanical Garden have been leaders. The Royal Horticultural Society of Great Britain hired collectors and sent them around the world to gather botanical rarities.

Joseph Banks (1743–1820, Figure 23.1), later knighted and a wealthy patron of botany and who for over 40 years would be president of the prestigious Royal Society of London, as a young man of 28 accompanied Lieutenant James Cook (Figure 23.2) on H.M.S. *Endeavour* during his circumnavigation of the globe between 1768 and 1771. Banks and one of Linnaeus's favorite students, Daniel Carlesson Solander, served botany nobly during the voyage. Between them they collected 17,000 plant specimens "of a kind never before seen in this kingdom [England]." Throughout his long life, Banks continued to put his wealth to work for botany: He equipped the scientists aboard the *Endeavour* and supported botany on Cook's later voyages, urged the transplantation of the breadfruit tree from Tahiti in the Pacific to the British islands in the Caribbean, and sponsored the work of plant collectors in India, China, Australia, Africa, and North America.

The search for plants has been supported also by royal patronage. The travels of Hipólito Ruiz and José Pavón in the viceroyalty of Peru were carried out by command of Charles III

Figure 23.1 Joseph Banks, from an engraving by John Raphael Smith. [Courtesy The National Maritime Museum, London.]

of Spain, king from 1759 to 1788. These two young pharmacists sailed from Cádiz in 1777 to seek seeds and plant specimens in South America; for more than a decade they explored the parched deserts of Chile, the frozen heights of the Andes, and the debilitating steamy forests of eastern Peru to bring back flowers for their king. Theirs was the first attempt to provide a comprehensively documented study of the plants of Spain's colonies in the New World.

Plant collecting has at times been a national objective. The Dutch and British enterprises of the mid-nineteenth century to bring cinchona from South America into cultivation in their Asian colonies is an example. Chapter 9 on medicinal plants outlines the Dutch efforts to introduce the fever-bark tree into Java. Clements R. Markham and Richard Spruce sought to bring cinchona to India and Ceylon for the English. These trials failed, but later attempts were to prove successful. Similarly, we have described how Joseph F. Rock was sent by the United States Department of Agriculture to Indochina, Siam, India, and Burma in the early 1920s to hunt for seeds of the chaulmoogra tree. At that time the oil expressed from them, was used as a cure for leprosy. Plantations were established successfully in Hawaii and studies begun on the life cycle and cultural requirements of the trees, the chemical composition, and active ingredients of the oil, and the best means to administer the drug to leprous patients.

Lest the false impression be had that plant hunting is a concern only of the last 200 years, one should know about the oldest botanical expeditions on record. The Egyptian Queen Hatshepsut, about 1500 B.C., mounted an expedition to the Land of Punt, the thumb which juts from Africa into the Indian Ocean. From this dry and forbidding land, Prince Nehasi, leader of the expedition, returned to Egypt with 31 young frankincense (or myrrh) trees, source of the precious balm used to sanctify bodies of deceased royalty. The trees were potted for the trip in wicker baskets and, slung on poles, were carried by slaves. Then they were transplanted to the terraced gardens of the Temple of Amon at Karnak on the banks of the Nile River in Upper Egypt. It is also known that the queen's husband and half-brother, Thutmose III, the Napoleon of Egypt who later deposed his wife by a *coup d' état*, introduced a large number of plants from Syria.

Results of these early botanical explorations can be seen today in relief on walls of old Egypt. At Karnak, for example, 275

Figure 23.2 James Cook, oil painting by Nathaniel Dance. [Courtesy The National Maritime, London—Greenwich Hospital Collection.]

See illustration on page 550, Queen Hatshepsut's plant explorations.

Figure 23.3 William Bligh, from an engraving by John Conde. [Courtesy The National Maritime Museum, London.]

See Plate 7a, breadfruit.

Figure 23.4 Breadfruit, object of William Bligh's voyages [Courtesy John J. Fay.]

plants are engraved on the sides of the "Botanic Chamber" of Thutmose's temple. The queen's expedition to Punt is commemorated pictorially on the walls of her temple at Deir el-Bahri near Thebes. Evidently the queen's expedition was a commercial venture, for besides the useful plants, her ships returned laden with ivory, gold, ebony, cinnamon, monkeys, baboons, and skins. Of the plants brought back from Syria by Thutmose and depicted in his temple, few can be identified; none, however, appears to have had economic value. Alice M. Coats, horticultural writer, thinks Thutmose's botanical effort "almost appears scientific"; that is, he returned with the plants as specimens of Syria's flora.

The Breadfruit Voyages

"Bread-fruit Bligh." Who would imagine that a distinguished vice-admiral in the British Royal Navy and governor of the Colony of New South Wales in Australia could be known to history by such an inelegant epithet? But William Bligh's name has been inextricably combined with the breadfruit since his fateful voyage to Tahiti (then called Otaheite) as captain of H.M.S. *Bounty* in 1787 (Figure 23.3). Bligh could not have known, when as a youth of 23 years he shipped with Captain James Cook on H.M.S. *Resolution*, that his first taste of breadfruit on Tahiti in 1777 was only a foretaste of events which were to remain with him in one way or another for most of his life.

In prehistoric times ancestors of the Tahitians carried the breadfruit with them, along with their other cultivated food plants, on their migrations among the islands of the tropical Pacific Ocean. Breadfruit trees (Figure 23.4) were already thriving on Tahiti when James Cook, Joseph Banks, and botanist Daniel Solander arrived there in 1769 aboard the exploring ship H.M.S. *Endeavour*. Solander later praised the starchy fruit, writing that it was "by us during several months daily eaten as a substitute for bread and was universally esteemed as palatable and nourishing as bread itself. No one of the whole ship's Company complained when served with bread-fruit in lieu of biscuit; and from the health and strength of whole nations [i.e., the South Sea islanders], whose principal food it is, I do not scruple to call it one of the most useful vegetables in the world." Small wonder, then, with such a glowing recommendation, that planters in the British West Indies were moved to explore the possibilities of introducing this marvelous food plant from the Pacific to the Caribbean. Valentine Morris, captain-general of the British West Indies, wrote to Joseph Banks in 1772 saying, "as the [Negro slave] population of these islands often suffered from lack of food, the introduction of the bread-fruit would certainly prove a great blessing to all the inhabitants."

In the eighteenth century, Great Britain's sugar came largely from its West Indian possessions and the labor employed in growing, harvesting, and processing the cane was provided by Negro slaves. Thus planters saw in the breadfruit a cheap and readily available food source for their slaves and they welcomed the possibility of a decrease in their dependence for food on supplies which had to be purchased from North America. These ideas impressed the influential and botanically minded Banks, who was, of course, already familiar with the breadfruit. He used his good offices to propose a scheme to King George III whereby the breadfruit could be transplanted from Tahiti in the Pacific to the British West Indies for the great benefit of all concerned.

In 1787 the King approved plans to enrich the West Indian colonies with the breadfruit and the indefatigable Banks undertook to organize and supervise the dispatch of an expedition for this purpose. The Royal Society for Promoting Arts and Commerce offered the prize of a gold medal to the first person to convey "from the islands in the South Sea to the islands in the West Indies, six plants of one or both species of the bread-fruit tree, in a growing state." The stage was thus set for a saga which was to feature crime on the high seas, an astounding feat of marine navigation and seamanship, the successful transportation of hundreds of growing plants across thousands of miles of ocean in a sailing ship, and the permanent introduction of a new species of edible plant from one part of the world to another. As an epic test of human endurance and tenacity, William Bligh's breadfruit voyages would have few competitors.

After the return to England of Cook's final expedition in 1780 (Cook himself was murdered by natives on the Island of Hawaii in February 1779), William Bligh, Cook's sailing master, was relieved from active naval service until he was returned to duty in February 1781. When the War of American Independence came to its humiliating conclusion (for the British), Bligh was furloughed at half-pay in 1783 (at two shillings a day). Sometime later that year he entered the West Indian mercantile trade,

Figure 23.5 H.M.S. *Bounty,* water-color by Gregory Robinson. [Courtesy The National Maritime Museum, London.]

sailing between England and Jamaican ports. He was in this business in 1787 when Banks recommended him as commander and purser of H.M.S. *Bounty* (Figure 23.5), a former West Indiaman, to be outfitted for the South Seas as a "floating garden." Bligh was only 33 years old at the time.

The *Bounty* was fitted out by Bligh with meticulous care for the special purpose of transporting breadfruit plants from Tahiti to the West Indies. He took considerable advantage of Banks's botanical knowledge and we read among Bligh's notes that "the great cabin was appropriated for the preservation of the plants. . . . It has two large sky lights and on each side three scuttles for air, and was fitted with a false floor cut full of holes to contain the garden pots in which the plants were to be brought home." David Nelson, a Kew gardener (i.e., at the Royal Botanic Gardens, Kew) who had been botanist and plant collector with Cook on his third voyage, when Bligh served as sailing master and when Cook was killed, was selected as chief botanist in whose care the breadfruit plants would be trusted. On Banks's nomination, Nelson was assisted by gardener William Brown. The *Bounty,* with its complement of 46 men and officers, left England for the South Seas on December 23,1787.

Her original route was to have been west, across the Atlantic, around Cape Horn at the stormy foot of South America, and over the South Pacific to Tahiti. But the tempestuous seas of Tierra del Fuego were too wild for *Bounty;* buffeted and beaten, her men irritable and suffering from "rheumatic complaints," she was ordered around and headed east. *Bounty* recrossed the South Atlantic, reprovisioned at Cape Town, South Africa, and sailed the Indian Ocean to Van Diemen's Land (now Tasmania) where she anchored to take on wood and water. Bligh navigated his ship south of New Zealand, northeast to Tahiti, and moored in Matavai Bay on October 26, 1788, ten months after leaving England.

Botanist Nelson and his assistant collected and propagated breadfruit plants. Bligh and his crew remained six months on Tahiti until the plants became well enough established to endure the sea voyage to the West Indies. The idled crew, lulled by warm breezes, relaxed discipline, and compliant women, fell willing prey to the amusements of island life. It was with great reluctance, on April 4, 1789, that they had finally to leave the friendliness of Tahiti for the loneliness of the sea, fresh with memories of delectable dalliances. To this point, Bligh had achieved his mission: *Bounty* carried 1,015 thrifty breadfruit plants in 774 pots, 39 tubs, and 24 boxes.

Events to follow created world-wide interest, not only in themselves but for the breadfruit as well. On April 28, off the Friendly Islands (now Tonga), Bligh's ship was seized by members of the crew led by Fletcher Christian, officer of the watch. Bligh and 18 crew members were cast adrift in *Bounty's* open longboat with scant rations of food and water, canvas, twine, sails, a chest of carpenter's tools, a quadrant, and a compass, but no map, sextant, or timekeeper of any kind (Figure 23.6). Bligh pointed his little craft unerringly westward, 3,618 miles, to the Dutch-held island of Timor in the East Indies. He arrived on June 14 without so much as the loss of one man (Figure 23.7). Bligh eventually landed in Portsmouth, England, aboard the Dutch vessel *Vlydte* on March 14, 1789.

The mutineers returned to Tahiti, gathered up their Polynesian belles and sailed to Pitcairn Island, a tiny uninhabited speck of a volcanic island in the southeast Pacific Ocean. There they burned *Bounty* after retrieving all useful materials and settled down for what they had hoped would be an unalloyed idyllic existence, but ever fearful of discovery and retribution by British naval authorities. Mutiny was an atrocious crime akin to piracy and convicted mutineers were subject to death. Life on Pitcairn Island did not provide the hoped-for idyllic ex-

Figure 23.6 Artist's conception of "The Mutineers turning Lieut. Bligh and part of the Officers and Crew adrift from His Majesty's Ship the Bounty," hand-colored aquatint by Robert Dodd. [Courtesy The National Maritime Museum, London.]

istence and the mutineers, their wives, and offspring (Figure 23.8) returned to Tahiti in 1831. In 1856 the *Bounty* descendants migrated westward to far distant Norfolk Island. Some later left Norfolk Island and settled once more on Pitcairn Island where today's inhabitants are all related to the original *Bounty* mutineers and their Tahitian wives.

Figure 23.7 Artist's version of "Lieut. Bligh and his Crew of the Ship Bounty hospitably received by the Governor of Timor," engraving by William Bromley. [Courtesy The National Maritime Museum, London.]

Neither William Bligh nor Joseph Banks was easily discouraged and in March 1791, a new breadfruit expedition was sanctioned by the British Admiralty. Bligh chose a trading vessel for the voyage, H.M.S. *Providence*, with a second, H.M.S. *Assistant*, assigned as consort. Two skilled botanists, James Wiles and Christopher Smith, joined the company. *Providence* and *Assistant* sailed from England on August 3, 1791, bound for Tahiti via the Cape of Good Hope and Van Diemen's Land. They entered Matavai Bay, Tahiti, on April 10, 1792.

Bligh refitted his ships and botanists Wiles and Smith assembled a collection of growing breadfruit trees. Three months later the ships set sail for the journey westward to the Caribbean. Aboard *Providence* were more than 2,000 breadfruit plants, twice the number carried by the *Bounty*, gathered and grown in half the time it had taken Nelson and Brown. On January 23, 1793, Bligh's vessels arrived safely in Kingstown Harbour, St. Vincent, where he left 544 breadfruit plants for introduction into the economy of that island. A week later the ships proceeded to Port Royal, Jamaica, where the remainder of the breadfruit trees were off-loaded on February 5. Thus after five years two months, two trips to the South Pacific, a mutiny at sea, and an epic voyage of over 3,000 miles in an open boat, the breadfruit venture was successfully concluded with the introduction of plants from Tahiti in the South Pacific to St. Vincent and Jamaica in the Caribbean.

Sir Joseph received a letter from "the Botanic gardener in Jamaica; dated December 1793" which noted "All the trees under my charge are thriving with the greatest luxuriance. Some of the Bread Fruit are upwards of eleven feet high, with leaves thirty-six inches long; and my success in cultivating them has exceeded my most sanguine expectations." An early nineteenth century historian of the British West Indies wrote that "the Cultivation of these valuable exoticks will, without doubt, in a course of years, lessen the dependence of the Sugar Islands on North America for food and necessaries." Disappointingly, the hopes of Sir Joseph, King George, William Bligh, the Royal Society for Promoting Arts and Commerce, and the West Indian planters never materialized for they all failed to reckon with the vagaries of human taste: The breadruit trees did thrive indeed; they produced bountiful crops of fruit. For their part, however, the Negro slaves, perversely, refused to eat these alien products preferring the more familiar yams and plantains. Breadfruit was fed to pigs for 50 years and it was not

Figure 23.8 Thursday October Christian, son of Fletcher Christian and Maimiti, a Tahitian, born on Pitcairn Island, from an engraving by Henry Adlard. [Courtesy The National Maritime Museum, London.]

until after emancipation, in the middle of the nineteenth century, that it came to be widely adopted for human food in the British West Indies. An original breadfruit tree planted by William Bligh in 1793 still stands in the botanical gardens on St. Vincent, mute testimony to the capriciousness of human nature, on the one hand, and the doggedness of the human spirit on the other.

Tea, the Gentle Brew

The antique volumes with yellowed pages are musty and tattered. Their tales of pirates in rake-masted junks recall a fabulous age and their queued Chinese gentlemen speak to us from the fairyland of pagoda-dotted islands with humped wooden bridges better known from willow-patterned Nanking blue porcelain. But the books tell us about the real-life China known to Robert Fortune (1813–1880; Figure 23.9), Scottish plant collector for the British East India Company, the Horticultural Society of London, and at one time, for the U.S. Department of Agriculture. Britain had been victorious in its shameful Opium War; proud Emperor Tao Kuang on the Dragon Throne was humiliated and forced to open the treaty ports of Canton, Amoy, Foochow, Ningpo, and Shanghai to general trade and to cede Hong Kong to the English in 1842. But the ever-cautious Chinese restricted travel of foreigners to the immediate vicinity of these coastal cities. A few of the more adventuresome, like Robert Fortune, roamed a considerable distance beyond the permitted limits, sometimes dressed in native garb, shaven-headed and queued, and accompanied by native interpreters. Throughout 18 years, most of which he spent in China, Fortune surveyed tea estates and methods of production, smuggled out tea plants and seed for trial in British Indian plantations, visited nurseries to gather new blooms for English gardens, and scoured the countryside for plants as far as he dared venture in those perilous times.

Although the span of Fortune's travels was limited, he was a keen observer and took advantage of every opportunity to move about the country. He reflected that "the manners and customs of the people, and the strange formation of the country, are indeed striking when viewed by the stranger's eye—the pagodas, like monuments to departed greatness, towering on the hills; the strange dresses and long tails of the men, and the small deformed feet of the women. Added to which, this is the

Figure 23.9 Robert Fortune, Scottish plant explorer. [Courtesy Royal Botanic Garden, Edinburgh.]

land of tea,—a beverage which in the eyes of Englishmen is enough to immortalise any country, had it nothing else besides."

Tea has been cultivated for so long that its original home is a matter of doubt and it is not known where tea plants grow wild today. Considering the present localities in Southeast Asia where the several kinds are now grown, it seems likely that tea was dispersed in very early times from near the sources of the Irrawaddy River in northern Burma. Its first use was probably medicinal, but it has been used as a beverage in China for between 2,000 and 3,000 years. Tea had been imported into Britain since the seventeenth century, beginning the now-famous association between tea-drinking and the English; but not until 1839 did they attempt to cultivate tea on a plantation scale in the Assam estates of their own colony, India. Thus, when the treaty ports of China were opened to the British a few years later, they were naturally keen to learn about Chinese tea varieties and methods of cultivation and processing with a view to improving the newly founded enterprise in India. The Chinese were understandably less than cooperative.

In 1845, the last full year of his first residence in China, Fortune sailed south along the coast from Shanghai to the treaty port of Foochow on the Min River. From there he hoped to penetrate to the Bohea Hills, to examine the celebrated black tea plantations of the district. Whether he was a paranoiac we shall never know, but it seems he always interpreted Chinese reluctance to allow him free passage as a personal affront, and in this instance he wrote that the mandarins (public officials, hence, any influential persons) "did everything in their power to dissuade me from making the attempt. . . . that their only reason for wishing to prevent my going into the interior was, that the natives were in a state which made it unsafe for a foreigner to trust himself among them. . . . they declared that no tea was grown in this district; being fully persuaded that an Englishman could have no other object in exploring the country than to see the cultivation of his favourite beverage." Despite the roadblocks he overcame their objections and, with coolies and interpreter, tramped westward into the Bohea Hills. There, among mountains between 2,000 and 3,000 feet high, he beheld with delight the sought-for tea plantations.

He was elated with his luck: "I was now fortunate enough not only to find an extensive tea district, but also to be present when the natives were picking and preparing the leaves [Figure

Figure 23.10 Harvesting tea in China. [Redrawn from an engraving in J.-G. Houssaye, *Monographie du Thé*. Published by the author, Paris, 1843.]

See Plate 7b, flowers of tea.

23.10]; and I not only procured specimens for my herbarium, but also a living plant." These he took with him on his return to the northern green tea districts, and found "on minute comparison, that it [Bohea tea, a black tea] was identical with the *Thea viridis*," the species which produced green tea. Fortune observed and recounted for posterity that green and black teas came from the same species—now called *Camellia sinensis*—and that the differences were in the processing of the leaves and buds after plucking. Black tea is a fermented product whereas green tea is unfermented.

Finally, his collections assembled, and after considerable wrangling with the vessel's master, Fortune gained passage on a wood-carrying junk bound north for Ningpo and Shanghai. The coastal waters of the South China Sea and Straits of Formosa teemed with pirates in those days and junks usually sailed in fleets for safety. The mandarins, fearful that armed junks might turn their guns on government installations, would not allow them to carry cannon for defense. Thus captains and crews sailed with considerable fear and trepidation through pirate-infested waters.

Fortune himself was well armed with both pistols and a double-barreled shotgun (i.e., "fowling piece"). When the anchor was weighed Fortune took to his bunk with a raging fever (malaria?) never dreaming that in his weakened state he would have to confront singlehandedly a junkload of murderous freebooters. Fifty or sixty miles from the Min Fortune's unarmed junk was set upon by *jan-dous* (pirates) and he was roused from his sickbed, "ill and feverish," to defend the vessel. Cleverly he allowed the pirate ship to approach within gunshot and when it seemed the pirates were certain of their prize—they "came down upon us hooting and yelling like demons" and firing willy-nilly—he jerked himself up from behind the gunwales, sighted, and blasted the pirate's deck with his shotgun. The pirate helmsman was killed and their junk slid off captainless, sails flapping uselessly, while Fortune's boat, sail still crowded on, soon left the pirates astern, no doubt pondering the remarkable effectiveness of the Englishman's guns.

All in all, Fortune was pleased with his first stay in China. He packed his many collections in Shanghai and shipped from Hong Kong for England. As he left Shanghai harbor, he "could not but look around. . . with pride and satisfaction; for in this part of the country. . . [he] had found the finest plants in. . . [his] collections. . . . Eighteen glazed cases, filled with the most beautiful plants of northern China, were placed upon the poop of the ship." In May 1846, Fortune arrived in England with what was then the richest assemblage of Chinese plants ever to reach Western Europe. The plants, Fortune observed, "arrived in excellent order, and were immediately conveyed to the garden of the Horticultural Society at Chiswick. . . as luxuriant and beautiful" as ever.

During Robert Fortune's first sojourn in the Celestial Empire (1843–1846) he was seldom able to venture inland more than 30 miles from treaty ports. Political conditions were unsettled and no European knew the interior of the country well enough even to recommend areas of special importance to the plant collector. Yet Fortune made a critical examination of tea cultivation and manufacture and reported his findings to the Western World. Fortune's ornamental plants were, for the most part, gathered from private gardens and nurseries in the country in and around the treaty ports. But, it must be added, most of these plants, especially the tree peonies which he assembled from gardens near Canton, came originally from other areas of China.

We owe some of our most treasured ornamental plants to the good horticultural judgement of Robert Fortune; the plants resulting from his first trip alone would make up a handsome garden. Among them were the winter jasmine, which in late winter bears cascades of yellow flowers on slender green leafless branches; the golden-flowered *Forsythia viridissima*, whose early blossoming is looked for in winter-bleak temperate lands as a harbinger of spring; Chinese holly, a shrub sporting stiff, spiny, glistening green leaves and red fruits; winter honeysuckle, whose deliciously fragrant white flowers have earned it the name *Lonicera fragrantissima*, "most fragrant lonicera"; and *Weigela florida*, a shrub which bears masses of rosy pink, trumpet flowers during mid-spring.

See Plates 7c, Chinese holly, and 8a, skimmia.

This trip was the first of four that Fortune made to the East between 1843 and 1861. He was to pave the way for others; his plants were to whet the botanical appetites of such men as George Forrest and Ernest H. Wilson who, in somewhat more settled times, sallied into the interior to regions only dreamed of by Robert Fortune.

Royal Lily

Central China's rivers have gouged some of the most ruggedly spectacular gorges on the face of the earth. There are lofty mountains, rocky precipices, and a climate hot enough in summer to melt the hinges on the gates of hell and cold enough in the winter to freeze the tail off a brass monkey. The valleys at all seasons "are subject to sudden and violent windstorms against which neither man nor beast can make headway." This country of the middle Yangtze River drainage between Ich'ang and Ch'engtu belonged to Ernest H. Wilson (1876–1930), dean of modern plant collectors (Figure 23.11). It was not country to be entered without courage and strength of mission; it demanded respect from those who wished to survive its wildness. But it held then, and probably still does, a botanical wealth and beauty surpassing all measure. And Wilson was determined to wrest some of that from the crags and crevices and take it back with him for the gardens of temperate Europe and America. For about ten years, beginning in 1899, first under the sponsorship of the famous but now defunct English nursery firm of Veitch, and later under the auspices of Charles Sprague Sargent, found-

Figure 23.11   Ernest H. Wilson, dean of modern plant collectors, in Changyang Hsien, China, 1909. [Courtesy The Arnold Arboretum.]

er and first director of Harvard's Arnold Arboretum, Wilson made his way along the river bottoms and clung to the sides of ravines, driven ever onward toward the next flaming rhododendron, a golden yellow poppy, another crimson primrose.

Of all his floral conquests, Wilson was most proud of the regal lily which had won his heart (Figure 23.12). He was determined "that it should grace the gardens of the western world . . . Its slender stems . . . flexible and tense as steel . . . crowned with one to several large funnel-shaped flowers . . . [and] laden with delicious perfume exhaled from every blossom."

Wilson left Boston on his fourth trip to China toward the end of March 1910. Once there, he headed for the military town of Sungpang Ting at the headwaters of the Min-kiang, a major tributary of the mighty Yangtze River, on the very edge of the grasslands of northeastern Tibet. Sungpang Ting in those days was an important outpost of Chinese civilization, a crossroad through which native medicines, hides, deer horns, and musk passed on their way to the wealthy towns of Szechuan and through which brick-tea and cotton cloth reached isolated hamlets along the farthest reaches of the Tibet-China border. At Sungpang Ting, Wilson, his bearers, and coolies rested, and after provisioning they "sallied forth and for seven consecutive days plunged down the seemingly interminable gorge of the Min-kiang [Figure 23.13]. The mountains on either side are so high," he marveled, "that the summits were usually hidden from view. . . It was frightfully hot and travelling most fatiguing." The slender trail being followed was actually the main road and Wilson noted, matter-of-factly, "the narrow track is hewn and blasted from the solid rock and here and there tunnelling has been necessary." He saw huge Chinese characters etched on the rocky slopes to warn travelers of the dangers and urge them to move on in some places where landslides could be expected. The road skirted "the edge of the river's turbulent waters but more usually ribbon-like it winds from fifty to 300 feet above."

The greatest potential danger along these trails occurs when two mule trains meet from opposite directions; passing is only possible at particular places and one caravan must stop to allow the other through. On the seventh day of the trek, Wilson noted in his diary, "A bad road through barren, desolate country. . . . barring absolute desert no more . . . repelling country could be imagined. . . . A fierce up-river wind blows regularly . . . and it is difficult to make headway against it. The leaves on the Maize

Figure 23.12 Regal lilies. [Courtesy U.S. Department of Agriculture.]

Figure 23.13 Valley of upper Min-kiang, home of the regal lily. [Photo by E. H. Wilson. Courtesy The Arnold Arboretum.]

Figure 23.14 Packing bulbs of regal lily at Ich'ang, China for shipment to the United States. [Courtesy The Arnold Arboretum.]

plants are torn to shreds by the wind's violence." It was in this inhospitable environment that Wilson was to find the regal lily "here and there in abundance on the well-nigh stark slate and mudstone cliffs."

Wilson and his train camped one evening, after eight days of travel, and made arrangements with local inhabitants to collect 6,000 or 7,000 bulbs in October, months after the flowering season when the bulbs had fully matured (Figure 23.14). It had taken Wilson four months from his arrival at Peking in May to reach the place where the regal lily grew. Exhausted and suffering from dysentery, he decided to return to Ch'engtu for medical treatment and its relative comforts.

Returning by the narrow trail, in cheerful mood and in anticipation of the rest and pleasure awaiting them, Wilson's party made good progress; the warning signs carved on the rocks did not frighten them and, he gloried, "Song was in our hearts." Suddenly a piece of rock struck the path in front of them, bounced, and plunged into the river 300 feet below. The bearers were ordered to speed up, to pass the area. Then the full fury of the rockslide crashed upon his caravan. Ducking and dipping,

Wilson sprinted along the path headed for a safe area in the lee of some hard rocks when he felt something rip his leg "as if a hot wire passed through. . . . I was bowled over, tried to jump up, found my right leg was useless, so crawled forward to the shelter of the cliff."

Wilson at first dismissed the adventure as "only a small slide and our lives had had a providential escape." But a glance at his bloody leg shocked him into the realization that his boot had been sliced, the toe cap torn off and along with it the nail of his big toe, and worse, his right leg had been broken in two places below the knee and the calf severely lacerated. He described his state as "not a pleasant situation to find oneself in alone with Chinese and four days from the nearest medical assistance." A splint was improvised from the legs of his camera tripod and strapped to his injured limb.

About this time, he was startled to spot a mule caravan heading his way along the precipice trail in a place too narrow for them to turn back. They dared not stand still for fear of another rockslide. Gritting his teeth, Wilson had only one alternative: to lay crosswise on the narrow ledge and allow the mules to step over his prone form. Wracked with pain, quivering with fright, he remained motionless while some 50 of the heavily-laden beasts stepped over his prostrate body. "Then it was that I realized the size of a mule's hoof. . . . I do not know with mathematical exactness," he observed later, but "the hoof seemed enormous, blotting out my view of the heavens. The instinctive surefootedness of the mule is well-known and I realized it with my gratitude as these animals one by one passed over me and not one even frayed my clothing."

Breathing somewhat more freely, but still aching with pain and wholly debilitated by amoebic dysentery, Wilson was hoisted into a carrying chair, his mutilated leg lashed to the right pole. In this manner, agonizing with every bump and jog, Wilson endured the journey to Ch'engtu arriving in three days. At the Friends' Mission there, his badly infected leg was looked after by a physician and amputation was recommended. With the stubbornness that characterized his life as a plant collector, Wilson would not allow the operation. "Somehow," he said, "I never felt this would be necessary." Three months later, on crutches, he hired a boat for Ich'ang on the Yangtze where there were steamers shipping for Shanghai from which he could sail to America. He crossed the Pacific and the continent and arrived in Boston to spend weeks in the hospital. For a year he limped about with a cane; 12 months from the date of the accident, he discarded the cane and walked freely once again. The bones never did set correctly and Wilson walked the rest of his life on a crooked right leg, shorter by almost an inch than his left. He proudly wrote that the once-injured leg with the "lily limp . . . has since carried me many, many thousands of miles."

Amazingly, Wilson thought the permanent infirmity of a leg a small price to pay for introducing to the world a wonder like the regal lily. He noted that the bulbs collected in China arrived safely in Boston a few days after he had himself. From this stock "has sprung the millions [of regal lilies] now happily acclimated in American gardens and other gardens across the seas. Its beauty captured all hearts at sight."

Euan H. M. Cox, author of *Plant-Hunting in China,* believed that Wilson "probably introduced more first-class ligneous [woody] plants to cultivation than any other individual collector." Wilson was a collector's collector, a systematic, perspicacious, professional plant explorer who, unlike Robert Fortune who was born too early, had access to the plant-rich heartland of western China. He combed the countryside for potentially worthy ornamentals, often returning to previously seen plants weeks or months later, after the flowering season, to gather seeds, bulbs, or roots. Beside gathering living materials for gardens, he pressed and dried plant specimens as vouchers for his living collections and for use in the detailed botanical studies necessary to classify his plants accurately. These pressed specimens were mounted on sheets of heavy paper and permanently placed in the herbaria of botanical gardens, museums, and universities throughout the world.

Because Wilson made four expeditions to China betwen 1899 and 1910 he became closely identified with China and the nickname "Chinese" Wilson was pinned on him which name, Cox says, he secretly disliked but publicly tolerated. His association with China is commemorated in the generic name, *Sinowilsonia* (*sinae* = the Chinese), a shrub of only marginal ornamental interest. Following his China years, Wilson continued his explorations under less rigorous circumstances and he visited Japan, Korea, Formosa, and South Africa always on the lookout for attractive garden plants. There is hardly a garden or park in temperate America, Britain, or Europe that does not feature plants from Wilson's work as a collector. His introductions of ornamental plants are thoroughly appreciated by the community of gardeners and in "a walk round the nurseries with Ernest

Wilson, it seemed impossible to find a tree, shrub or herbaceous plant with which he was not familiar. A first class botanist, perhaps the greatest of the plant hunters." Wilson is credited with bringing more than 1,000 plants into cultivation; there are dozens of species of rhododendrons, viburnums, lilies, primroses and gentians, maples and magnolias, hydrangeas and roses in our gardens which we owe to his unusual imagination and perception. Wilson's books sparkle with the excitement of his adventures as plant explorer; he wrote proudly of his successful introductions and of the wild glories of some plants which, transplanted, failed to thrive in the alien environment of the garden. Ironically, the man who battled the raw forces of nature and had been crippled deep in the mountain fastnesses of China was killed with his wife on October 15, 1930, in an automobile accident near Worcester, Massachusetts when he was but 54 years of age.

See Plates 8b, Oriental dogwood, and 8c, dove tree.

The Future

These few tales of plant collecting are only skimmings, mere fragments from a rich lore awaiting the curious reader (see Suggested Readings). Although some accounts of plant exploration are interesting solely as tales of adventure, the real importance of exploration must be judged in terms of the plants gathered and their potential value in medicine, horticulture, agronomy, and pure botany.

At this point it is reasonable to ask, Is plant exploration at an end? What is its future? Do we know all the kinds of plants, the places where they grow, how they exist? Have we apprised science of all useful and harmful botanical products? Are all human diseases which might be cured by drugs of plant origin known to us? Have we experimented with these plants to see if they are therapeutically valuable? What genes exist in wild plants that may be incorporated beneficially into crop and ornamental plants to impart disease resistance or to increase yields? In a broader sense, are we satisfied that the balance of payments directed toward earth exploration is commensurate with that directed toward extraterrestrial exploration? "No one regards what is before his feet; we all gaze at the stars" (Quintus Ennius, 239–169 B.C.).

It is true that the pioneering days of plant exploration are finished. We have made a fair survey of our plants; we know what plants to expect in most regions of the world. But who would be so rash as to assure us that the hidden valleys of The Himalaya, the serrated ridges of the Owen Stanley Range of New Guinea, and the sandstone monoliths of South America's Guayana Highland do not conceal rich botanical treasures? Explorer Bassett Maguire knows from his 20 years' experience, "involving much field work, herbarium study, and collaboration by many competent taxonomists, [that] some 10,000 Guayana plant collections remain to be identified and interpreted." And who will venture to guess the number of new plants still to be collected in that area of 400,000 square miles or in any area of tropical rain forest?

With the many advantages we now have—the helicopter, rapid and safe transportation, new navigational devices, techniques using polyethylene collecting containers, refrigeration, improved preserving fluids, speedy means for shipping live plants and for drying herbarium specimens—we may be on the threshold of even greater discoveries than those wonders managed by the plant collectors of old. We are at the brink of a new era of study such as was inconceivable to the pioneer plant explorers. The future still holds botanical bounty for those who would seek it. By no means have we used up our raw plant resources or exhausted possibilities for further inquiry.

Critical questions which demand firm answers do remain, however. Will we have the sense to use our wild plants wisely? And perhaps even more germane, will we have the wisdom and foresight to preserve what is left of our vegetation and flora so they can be explored in the field, grown in gardens, and investigated in the laboratory? In the final analysis, answers to these questions will determine whether or not plant exploration is at an end.

Suggested Readings

Anderson, A. W. *How We Got Our Flowers*. New York: Dover Publications, 1966. (Originally published as *The Coming of the Flowers*. London: Williams and Norgate, 1950.) Popular stories on the collection from the wild and introduction into gardens of some of our common flowering plants; nontechnical.

Berkeley, Edmund, and Dorothy Smith Berkeley. *John Clayton: Pioneer of American Botany*. Chapel Hill: University of North Carolina Press, 1963. A glimpse into early botany and plant collecting in North

America and their relationship to the botanists and horticulturists of Europe.

Coats, Alice M. *The Plant Hunters*. New York: McGraw-Hill, 1969. Comprehensive, well-researched series of exploits of collectors of horticultural plants; semitechnical; a bit heavy going in places; unillustrated.

Coats, Peter. *Flowers in History*. New York: Viking, 1970. Nontechnical; art history and botany; profusely illustrated.

Cox, E. H. M. *Plant-Hunting in China*. London: Collins, 1945. Very readable histories of some of the great horticultural plant explorers in China.

Fairchild, David. *The World Was My Garden*. New York: Scribner's, 1938. Probably the best of Fairchild's several books on plant explorations; semiautobiographical; well illustrated. Fairchild was one of the founders of the Bureau of Plant Introduction, U.S. Department of Agriculture.

Fletcher, Harold R. *A Quest of Flowers: The Plant Explorations of Frank Ludlow and George Sherriff*. Edinburgh: Edinburgh University Press, 1975. Punctilious; scholarly; illustrated.

————.*The Story of the Royal Horticultural Society 1804–1968*. London: Oxford University Press, 1969. Exhaustive, scholarly.

Foley, Daniel J., ed. *The Flowering World of "Chinese" Wilson*. London: Macmillan, 1969. A selection of E. H. Wilson's exploits as plant collector; interestingly written.

Fortune, Robert. *Three Years' Wanderings in the Northern Provinces of China. . .* 2d ed. London: John Murray, 1847. What it was like to be a foreigner in an inhospitable land and how it was possible to collect plants there for Western gardens.

Gardner, William. "Robert Fortune and the Cultivation of Tea and Other Chinese Plants in the United States." *Journal of the Royal Horticultural Society* 97 (1972): 401–409.

Harper, Francis, ed. *The Travels of William Bartram*. New Haven: Yale University Press, 1958. John and William Bartram of Philadelphia were among the first serious plant collectors and gardeners in eastern North America.

Jaramillo-Arango, Jaime. *The Conquest of Malaria*. London: William Heinemann, 1950. The introduction of cinchona bark (quinine) from its native haunts in the Andes to cultivation in the East Indies; semitechnical.

Kingdon-Ward, F. *Plant Hunter's Paradise*. New York: Macmillan, 1938. Another of Kingdon-Ward's exciting books on plant exploration.

Mackaness, George. *The Life of Vice-Admiral William Bligh R. N., F. R. S.* Rev. ed. London: Angus and Robertson, 1951. The standard modern biography.

Merrill, Elmer Drew. "The Botany of Cook's Voyages." *Chronica Bo-*

tanica 14, nos. 5 and 6 (1954): 161–384. A scholarly monograph; technical.

Nordhoff, Charles, and James Norman Hall. *The Bounty Trilogy: Mutiny on the Bounty, Men against the Sea, Pitcairn's Island.* Boston: Little, Brown, 1951. Novelized account of William Bligh's first breadfruit voyage and its aftermath; captivating; historically based.

Powell, Dulcie. "The Voyage of the Plant Nursery, H. M. S. *Providence, 1791–1793.*" *Bulletin of the Institute of Jamaica. Science Series* 15, no. 2 (1973): 1–70. Scholarly; well documented; readable.

Royal Horticultural Society. *Journal Kept by David Douglas during His Travels in North America, 1823–1827* . . . New York: Antiquarian Press, 1959. (Originally published, London: Royal Horticultural Society, 1914.)

Spruce, Richard. *Notes of a Botanist on the Amazon & Andes.* London: Macmillan, 1908. Based on Spruce's letters to the Royal Botanic Gardens, Kew, England; ponderous and detailed but with some exciting episodes; outstanding cultural notes on native societies some of which are probably extinct now.

Stern, William L. "Plant Collecting in the Land of Balboa." *The Garden Journal* 10, no. 2 (1960): 44–49, 64. Popularly written tale of exploration for plants in the forests of Darien Province, Panama.

Sutton, S. B. *Charles Sprague Sargent and the Arnold Arboretum.* Cambridge, Mass.: Harvard University Press, 1970. Details the founding and early history of one of America's great botanical gardens; biographical.

———. *In China's Border Provinces: The Turbulent Career of Joseph Rock, Botanist-Explorer.* New York: Hastings House, 1974.

Taylor, Norman. *Plant Drugs that Changed the World.* New York: Dodd, Mead, 1965. Lucid tales of the exploration for and use of plant-based medicines; popularly written.

Tyler-Whittle, Michael. *The Plant Hunters.* Philadelphia: Chilton, 1970. Lively stories of the exploits of some of the great plant explorers; interestingly written and accurate.

Villiers, Alan. *Captain James Cook.* New York: Scribner's, 1967. Captain Cook as a seaman and navigator.

Wilson, Ernest H. *Plant Hunting.* Boston: Stratford, 1927. A two-volume, popular account of some of Wilson's exciting stories of his own plant collecting. He was truly one of the finest of all the plant hunters.

Plant Names

Common name	Scientific name	Family
avocado	*Persea americana*	Lauraceae
bael fruit	*Aegle marmelos*	Rutaceae
banana	*Musa sapientum*	Musaceae

Common name	Scientific name	Family
breadfruit	*Artocarpus altilis*	Moraceae
camellia	*Camellia* spp.	Theaceae
carambola	*Averrhoa carambola*	Oxalidaceae
chaulmoogra	*Hydnocarpus kurzii*	Flacourtiaceae
Chinese holly	*Ilex cornuta*	Aquifoliaceae
chrysanthemum	*Chrysanthemum* spp.	Compositae
cinchona	*Cinchona* spp.	Rubiaceae
cinnamon	*Cinnamomum zeylanicum*	Lauraceae
cloves	*Eugenia caryophyllus*	Myrtaceae
coca	*Erythroxylon coca*	Erythroxylaceae
cocoa	*Theobroma cacao*	Sterculiaceae
coffee	*Coffea arabica*	Rubiaceae
crocus	*Crocus* spp.	Iridaceae
dioscorea	*Dioscorea* spp.	Dioscoreaceae
fever-bark tree	*Cinchona* spp.	Rubiaceae
flowering cherry	*Prunus* spp.	Rosaceae
forsythia	*Forsythia* spp.	Oleaceae
frankincense	*Boswellia* spp.	Burseraceae
gentian	*Gentiana* spp.	Gentianaceae
hydrangea	*Hydrangea* spp.	Hydrangeaceae
lilac	*Syringa* spp.	Oleaceae
lily	*Lilium* spp.	Liliaceae
macadamia nut	*Macadamia integrifolia*	Proteaceae
magnolia	*Magnolia* spp.	Magnoliaceae
mango	*Mangifera indica*	Anacardiaceae
maple	*Acer* spp.	Aceraceae
myrrh	*Commiphora myrrha*	Burseraceae
papaya	*Carica papaya*	Caricaceae
plantain	*Musa* sp.	Musaceae
primrose	*Primula* spp.	Primulaceae
rauwolfia	*Rauwolfia* spp.	Apocynaceae
regal lily	*Lilium regale*	Liliaceae
rhododendron	*Rhododendron* spp.	Ericaceae
rose	*Rosa* spp.	Rosaceae
soursop	*Annona muricata*	Annonaceae
rubber	*Hevea brasiliensis*	Euphorbiaceae
tea	*Camellia sinensis*	Theaceae
tree peony	*Paeonia suffruticosa*	Paeoniaceae
tulip	*Tulipa* spp.	Liliaceae
viburnum	*Viburnum* spp.	Caprifoliaceae
winter jasmine	*Jasminum nudiflorum*	Oleaceae
yam	*Dioscorea* spp.	Dioscoreaceae
yellow poppy	*Meconopsis integrifolia*	Papaveracae

Glossary

A

abiotic. Condition characterized by absence of life or living organisms.

Actinomycetes. Group of filamentous bacteria.

addiction. Condition involving intense craving, tolerance, and withdrawal symptoms.

adventitious bud. A bud formed in some place other than in a leaf axil or at the tip of the stem or one of its branches; for example, a bud produced at the site of a wound on a stem.

aerobic bacteria. Bacteria which require gaseous oxygen.

agar. A gelatinous substance derived from some red algae; used as a culture medium to grow bacteria, fungi, and tissues of higher organisms.

agricultural period. Cultural era which began about 9000 B.C. when man learned to cultivate soil, plant seeds, and harvest resulting crops; also called Neolithic or New Stone Age.

alga. Thallophyte with chlorophyll and hence capable of photosynthesis; fresh-water forms variously called pond scums, frog spittle, and frog slime, while some of the marine forms are referred to as seaweeds, sea mosses, and kelps.

algal bloom. Extensive accumulation of algae, especially blue-green algae, which develops in ponds and lakes during the warm days of summer; same as water bloom.

algal-fungi. Group of thallophytes without chlorophyll, often called molds, which resemble the algae in their reproduction. They consist of filaments forming a loose mycelium rather than a definite compact body; also called Phycomycetes. Example: common bread mold.

alkaloid. Organic chemical which is alkaline, or basic, in reaction, bitter, nitrogenous, and produces a marked physiological effect in animals including man. Names customarily end in *-ine* as in morphine, nicotine, cocaine, and caffeine.

allergic rhinitis. Disorder of humans caused by wind-blown pollen or spores of fungi whose symptoms include inflammation of mucous membranes of nose and related structures, continuous or intermittent obstruction of the nasal passages, accompanied by wheezing, sneezing, coughing, copious flow of watery discharges, itching of nose, mouth, and pharynx, excessive flow of tears, light-sensitivity, headache, irritability, and insomnia; also called hay fever and pollenosis.

alternate arrangement of leaves. That condition where only one leaf is attached at each node and the leaves are disposed in a spiral fashion about the stem; same as spiral arrangement.

alternation of generations. A life cycle in which there is an alternation of the two generations, gametophyte and sporophyte, i.e., the gametophyte produces the sporophyte and the latter produces the gametophyte.

amino acid. Chemical compound composed of carbon, hydrogen, oxygen, and nitrogen; amino acids form the building blocks from which proteins are made. Example: lysine.

anaerobic respiration. Respiration in the absence of gaseous oxygen or in the presence of limited atmospheric oxygen; also called fermentation. Example: process carried on by yeast in which sugar is converted into alcohol and carbon dioxide in the manufacture of wine.

analgesic. Substance which relieves pain. Example: aspirin.

anesthetic. Substance used to numb or eliminate feeling temporarily, especially of pain. Examples: ether, procaine.

angiosperm. Flowering plant whose seeds are enclosed in a carpel and characterized further by double fertilization and usually vessels in the xylem. Examples: roses, buttercups, elms, orchids.

angstrom unit. A unit of length equal to $1/10,000$ of a micron or $1/10,000,000$ of a millimeter (there are about 25 millimeters in an inch).

annual. Plant which completes its life cycle from seed to seed in one year or less. Examples: petunia, marigold, ragweed.

annual ring. A layer of wood formed by the vascular cambium in one year in those parts of the world where there is normally one growing season per annum.

anthocyanin. A red, blue, or violet pigment dissolved in the cell sap of vacuoles of cells in flowers, leaves, and other plant parts.

antibiotic. A substance produced by such fungi as molds and Actinomycetes (bacteria which form filaments), by lichens, and by other plants, which destroys or inhibits the growth of other organisms such as bacteria. Examples: penicillin, Terramycin.

anticonvulsant. Muscle relaxant or remedy for convulsions. Example: curare.

antihistamine. A drug used to slow the release of histamines and thus decrease the discharge of liquids from nose and eyes.

antisomniac. Substance used to treat insomnia or inability to sleep. Examples: barbiturates of various kinds, scopolamine.

antispasmodic. A drug which relieves spasms and has a sedative effect on the nerves. Examples: phenobarbital, valerian (*Valeriana officinalis*), *Cannabis*, paregoric (camphorated tincture of opium).

aphrodisiac. A drug or potion which arouses sexual desire. Examples: *Cannabis* (presumed), damiana, *Turnera aphrodisiaca* (reputed); yohimbe bark, *Pausinystalia yohimbe* (presumed).

apical meristem. A meristem at the tip of a stem or root or their branches whose dividing cells are responsible for the growth in length of the plant part.

Aralen. Synthetic substitute for quinine; proprietary name.

aril. An outer covering of the seed which is sometimes fleshy and brightly colored.

Ascomycetes. *See* sac fungi.

asexual reproduction. Formation of similar offspring in which there is no fusion of sex cells or gametes; for example, by spores, fission, cuttings, and bulbs.

aspirin. Acetylsalicylic acid; originally derived from salicin (from *Salix*, or willow) which was converted to salicylic acid and then combined with acetic acid to produce acetylsalicylic acid, or aspirin.

astringent. A medicinal substance which shrinks and hardens tissues. Examples: witch hazel lotion, camphor, oil of wintergreen.

atropine. Alkaloid derived from belladonna (*Atropa belladonna*) and other members of the nightshade, or potato-tomato, family; used as an analgesic, to dilate pupils of the eyes, to reduce excessive perspiration and secretion of fluids, and to treat palsy and dozens of other maladies.

Aureomycin. Antibiotic derived from Actinomycetes; proprietary name.

autumnal coloration. Fall coloring of leaves which occurs predominantly in trees of temperate eastern Asia and eastern North America.

auxin. Plant hormone, or growth-regulating, substance which promotes cell enlargement. Example: indoleacetic acid (IAA).

axillary bud. Bud produced in a leaf axil; also called lateral bud.

B

bacteria (singular, bacterium). Unicellular thallophytes which commonly lack chlorophyll and usually reproduce by cell division; also called Schizomycetes.

bacteriology. The science, or study, of bacteria.

bark. Collective name for all the tissues of root and stem from the outside surface of the plant in to the cambium; hence, includes epidermis, cork, cortex, and phloem.

Basidiomycetes. *See* club fungi.

belladonna series of alkaloids. The three alkaloids, atropine, scopolamine, and hyoscyamine, found in several members of the potato-tomato family such as belladonna and jimson weed.

berry. Fleshy, several-to-many-seeded fruit. Examples: tomato, grape, blueberry, cucumber.

bhang. A weak *Cannabis* preparation made from dried plants, gathered green, powdered, and converted into a drink with water or milk, or into candy with sugar and spices.

biennial. Plant which completes its life cycle from seed to seed in two years. Examples: carrot, beet, turnip.

biological barrier. Condition where, for example, plants of the same species do not exchange genes because their flowers mature at different times.

biological control. The use of other organisms which are natural enemies to combat insect pests and other parasites.

biomass. Weight of living organisms in any community of plants or animals.

biomass pyramid. Graphic convention to illustrate relative weight or numbers of organisms present at any level in a food chain.

binomial. The two-word scientific name of a plant or animal consisting of a generic noun (genus) and specific adjective, or genetive (specific name). Examples: *Quercus suber, Homo sapiens.*

binomial system of nomenclature. The manner of naming plants and animals whereby a two-word name is assigned to each.

biotic. Pertaining to life.

blade. That portion of the leaf which consists of a broad expanse of green tissue in contrast to the narrowed petiole, or leaf stalk.

blood theory of inheritance. The ancient and discredited belief that traits are inherited via the blood; not employed at present except in tradition-bound professions such as law.

blue-green algae. Unicellular thallophytes, sometimes forming colonies, which have chlorophyll plus red and blue pigments.

bordered pit. A recess in the wall of a tracheid or vessel cell in which a part of the wall overhangs the depression; in face view, commonly appears as two concentric circles; valvelike structure which permits passage of water and dissolved materials from cell to cell.

botany. The science devoted to the study of plants.

brown algae. Mostly marine thallophytes of cold waters that have chlorophyll plus a brown pigment. Examples: kelp, sea palm, rockweed, gulfweed, and devil's apron.

bryophytes. Mosses, liverworts, and their relatives.

bud. In vascular plants, a mass of cells either actively dividing or at least having the potential for division, and the whole mass surrounded by modified or overlapping leaves or bud scales in some cases.

bud mutation. Inheritable change which occurs in a single bud. If the novelty associated with this change is desirable, some form of vegetative reproduction, such as grafting, must be employed to perpetuate it.

bud scale. Tough, sometimes thickened, modified leaf, one or more of which cover and protect buds, chiefly against excessive water loss.

bundle scar. Dot-like mark within a leaf scar; consists of the remnant of a conducting strand which was broken off at leaf fall.

C

caffeine. Alkaloid derived from coffee and tea plants; used as a stimulant and diuretic (drug which increases urination).

cambium. *See* vascular cambium.

carbohydrate. Organic compound containing carbon, hydrogen, and oxygen, in which the ratio of hydrogen to oxygen is 2:1, as in water. Examples: starch, sugar, cellulose.

carbon fixation. *See* photosynthesis.

Carboniferous period. Interval of geological time, about 350 million years ago, during which the vegetative parts of plants (mostly arboreal clubmosses, horsetails, ferns, and conifers) and their spores were transformed into coal; also called Age of Coal. In North America the Carboniferous period is divided into the Mississippian and Pennsylvanian periods.

carcinogen. Any substance that tends to produce a cancer. Examples: tobacco smoke, coal tars and related hydrocarbons, asbestos.

carminative. Substance which promotes expulsion from or reduced formation of gas in the body. Examples: ginger, peppermint.

carnivorous plant. *See* insectivorous plant.

carotenoid. Yellow or orange pigment found in cells of carrot roots and chloroplasts of leaves.

carpel. Part of flower enclosing ovules which eventually produce the eggs; same as pistil.

cascara sagrada. Literally, "sacred," or "holy bark"; laxative derived from the buckthorn tree (*Rhamnus purshiana*).

cathartic. A fairly powerful purgative (agent used to evacuate the bowels). Example: castor oil.

cell. The smallest structural unit of plants and animals which has organized protoplasm and which in plants is surrounded by a cellulose cell wall.

cell cavity. The interior space of the cell surrounded by the cell wall.

cell doctrine. *See* cell theory.

cell sap. The fluid content of the vacuole consisting mostly of water. Dissolved in the cell sap may be salts, sugars, organic acids, and pigments; suspended in it may be crystals, fats, alkaloids, and rubber.

cell theory. Generalization developed by Schleiden and Schwann that all living things are constructed of cells, all cells come from pre-existing cells, and all activities of organisms are the sum total of the specific actions of their individual cells.

cellulose. A complex carbohydrate consisting of long strands of glucose molecules; makes up 40 to 55 percent by weight of plant cell wall substance.

cell wall. The outermost layer or boundary of the cell composed predominantly of cellulose in plants.

central dogma. Doctrine which holds that the information, or code, carried by the DNA in chromosomes is transmitted by RNA to the ribosomes where the amino acids are ordered in a particular fashion to produce specific proteins, such as enzymes.

cereals. Grains or fruits of the grass family, such as wheat, corn, rye, barley, and rice; also used for the plants themselves.

charas. Pure resin of *Cannabis*; ten times as strong as bhang; same as hashish.

chaulmoogra oil. Oil derived from seeds of the kalaw tree, or *Hydnocarpus*; used to treat leprosy.

chemosynthesis. Process of food manufacture in certain bacteria which utilize the energy derived from the oxidation of inorganic compounds such as nitrates, ammonia, and hydrogen sulfide.

chemotherapy. Treatment of diseases with chemicals which are absorbed by the plant, or injected into the plant, and which are then translocated throughout the plant.

chicha. Fermented maize beverage.

Chloromycetin. Antibiotic derived originally from Actinomycetes but now synthesized; proprietary name.

chlorophyll. Green pigment, usually located in chloroplasts, which makes it possible for plants to manufacture food or carry on photosynthesis.

chloroplast. A plastid containing chlorophyll and in which photosynthesis occurs.

chromatid. One of the two daughter strands in a chromosome.

chromatin. Readily stainable chromosomal substance; the complex of DNA and proteins.

chromosome. Nuclear body containing protein and DNA and bearing genes in linear order.

chromosome map. Diagram showing the probable location of genes on chromosomes.

chromosome number. The specific numerical complement of chromosomes contained in the nuclei of cells in each species of plant and animal.

class. A unit of classification, above the order and below the division, consisting of one or more related orders. Example: Dicotyledoneae.

climax vegetation. The plants present on any site in which an equilibrium is reached with the climate; succession has terminated and the pattern of vegetation occupying the site remains more or less stable.

club fungi. Non-chlorophyll-bearing thallophytes which characteristically produce a club-shaped structure (basidium) usually bearing four spores on short pegs; also called Basidiomycetes. Examples: mushrooms, puffballs, stinkhorns, shelf fungi, rust fungi, and smut fungi.

club-mosses. Small plants somewhat resembling mosses in size but possessing vascular tissue and often bearing cones (suggesting the name club).

cocaine. Alkaloid derived from the coca plant (*Erythroxylon coca*).

codeine. Alkaloid derived from the opium poppy (*Papaver somniferum*); used as a sedative in cough syrups, for example.

colchicine. Alkaloid derived from *Colchicum*, the autumn crocus; used to treat gout and as an antitumor agent; in cytology and genetics, used to double the chromosome number of cells.

colony. A loose association of similar cells with little or no specialization, and, furthermore, any one of the cells may break free and lead an independent existence.

complementarity of amino acids (or proteins). Nutritional principle under which one food (or plant) provides some of the essential eight amino acids while the diet is supplemented with another food (or plant) containing the missing essential amino acids. Thus all eight essential amino acids are made avialable in the diet.

composite family. Compositae (Asteraceae); characterized by tightly compressed aggregations of tiny flowers forming a floral head as in daisy, black-eyed Susan, and sunflower. The floral head may consist of an outer ring of ray flowers (the white "petals" of the daisy) and an inner center comprising disc flowers (the golden middle of the daisy).

compound leaf. Leaf in which the blade is divided into two or more parts called leaflets.

cone. Reproductive structure composed of a central axis to which are attached a number of scales bearing spore sacs, as in club-mosses or horsetails; pollen sacs, or ovules (or seeds), as in pines, spruces, and firs.

conifer. A cone-bearing tree belonging to the gymnosperms. Examples: pines, hemlocks, larches, spruces.

consumer organism. Animals, including man, which ingest particulate foods by eating. *See* decomposer organism.

control. In an experiment, the part of an organism, the whole organism, or set of organisms not manipulated, as opposed to the experimental part, plant, or group which is exposed to the manipulation or treatment.

convergence. *See* convergent evolution.

convergent evolution. Development in which the appearance of two or more unrelated groups of plants, growing in a similar environment, is alike; also called convergence. Example: desert plants often have small leaves or no leaves, or thickened, succulent leaves or stems, and spines; yet these similar appearing plants may be unrelated as cacti, spurges, agaves, and aloes.

coralline algae. Red algae, green algae, as well as other algae, which by their activities build up so-called coral, or atoll, reefs; same as calcareous, or coral, algae.

cork. Layer(s) of cells which replace(s) the epidermis of stem and root and which has a waxlike material in its cell walls, thus functioning to reduce the loss of water from the plant.

cortex. Region of the stem and root located under the epidermis which stores food and, if green, may also manufacture food.

cortisone. Hormone derived from the cortex of the adrenal glands of animals; used to treat a number of maladies including rheumatic heart disease, bursitis, hepatitis, and leukemia; also manufactured from steroids of such plants as yams, agaves (century plant), yuccas (Spanish bayonet), and soybean.

cotyledon. The seed leaf; one is present in embryos of monocotyledons, two occur in dicotyledons, and two to several in conifers.

coumarin. Glycoside found in grass and other plants which gives freshly cut vegetation that characteristic vanillalike odor of newly mowed hay.

counterirritant. A drug or agent which produces irritation in one part of the body to relieve pain or inflammation elsewhere. Example: mustard plaster.

cross-dating. The comparison of annual ring sequences in ancient timber artifacts or fallen tree trunks with those in standing trees to produce a backward stretching datable chronology.

crossing-over. Genetic or breeding phenomenon in which traits which are linked do not stay linked because chromatid parts from two homologous chromosomes have interchanged during meiosis.

cross-pollination. Transport of pollen from stamens in the flowers of one plant to stigmas in flowers of another plant in angiosperms, or from pollen cones of one plant to seed cones of another plant in gymnosperms.

culinary herb (sweet herb). A plant whose green parts, ripe seeds or fruits, or tender roots are sweetly fragrant; used with foods because of their characteristic flavors; mostly derived from temperate and subtropical regions. Examples: basil, marjoram, tarragon.

curandero. Healer, or medicine man.

curare. General name applied to several different South American arrow poisons and to the muscle relaxants derived from these mixtures; also, a plant yielding this substance.

cuticle. Waxlike layer covering the surfaces of epidermal cells of the shoot system; functions to minimize water evaporation.

cycad. Tropical and subtropical gymnosperm with palmlike leaves and typically bearing cones.

cytokinin. Plant hormone or growth-regulating substance which incites cell division.

cytologist. One who specializes in cell study.

cytology. The science, or study, of the cell.

cytoplasm. The protoplasm, or living substance of the cell, with the exception of the nucleus.

D

Darwinism. In the strict sense, Darwin's theory of natural selection; in the broad sense, a term equated with evolution.

data. Facts or information, such as those produced by measurements or observations.

decay. Process carried on by bacteria and fungi in which the proteins, carbohydrates, and fats in dead plants and animals are converted into simpler compounds such as carbon dioxide, water, and nitrates.

deciduous trees. Woody plants which shed all leaves at regular times, for example, in the autumn in the case of temperate trees, or during the dry season in the tropics.

decomposer organism. Microorganisms, mainly fungi and bacteria, which break down organic matter into soluble substances which are then absorbed through the cell walls of these organisms. *See* consumer organism.

decongestant. Substance used to clear nasal and bronchial passages by shrinking the mucous membranes of these regions. Example: ephedrine.

dendrochronology. The science, or study, of time and related events as deduced from variations in the annual rings of trees.

dendroclimatology. The science, or study, of past climatic variations through their influence on the formation and diversity of annual-ring patterns.

denitrification. Process in which nitrogenous compounds are converted into gaseous nitrogen by denitrifying bacteria.

deoxyribonucleic acid, DNA. One of two nucleic acids found chiefly in the nucleus; characterized by the sugar deoxyribose and constituting the genic substance of plants and animals.

dermatitis. Skin disease manifested by irritation and rash. Example: condition produced by contact with poison ivy.

desmid. A kind of single-celled green alga commonly found floating in bogs and lakes.

detritus. Minute organic or inorganic particles; disintegrated material; debris.

diatom. A kind of unicellular golden-brown alga in which the protoplast is enclosed in two glass or silica shells, fitting together like two halves of an old-fashioned pillbox.

diatomaceous earth. A fine siliceous material made up of empty shells of diatoms.

dichotomous branching. A type of branching in which the main axis, or stem, or leaves of a plant fork repeatedly into two divisions of equal size, as in the thallus of *Fucus* (rockweed), in stems of the primitive psilophytes, and in leaves of the staghorn fern.

dicotyledons. Flowering plants with two cotyledons, or seed leaves, in the seed; also, these plants have pinnately and palmately veined leaves in which the minor veins form a conspicuous network, or reticulum; floral parts commonly number in the fours and fives or multiples thereof.

dicoumarin. Glycoside, originally obtained from wet or moldy sweet clover, now synthesized, which prevents coagulation of blood.

digestion. Process in which insoluble (or complex) foods are transformed into soluble (or simpler) substances through the actions of enzymes.

digitalis. Glycoside derived from *Digitalis*, or foxglove; used to treat various heart disorders.

dihybrid. In genetics, a cross between two individuals differing in two sets of characters.

diploid. Having two sets of chromosomes as in zygotes and in the body cells of higher plants; same as $2n$ number.

disc flower. One of the individual flowers which comprises the center of the floral head in those members of the composite family, such as sunflower and daisy; it usually has a full complement of floral parts and is capable of producing seed.

disease. Marked deviation from the normal, or average, condition or physiological functioning of an organism.

divine soma. The fly-agaric mushroom (*Amanita muscaria*), according to Gordon Wasson.

DNA. *See* deoxyribonucleic acid.

doctrine of signatures. The old belief that plants were created by God for man's use and that each plant bears a mark or sign indicating what it is good for. Examples: bloodroot good for treatment of diseases of the blood, liverwort for liver maladies, lungwort for consumption.

dominance. Genetic principle developed by Mendel which states that in a given pair of factors (genes), one factor (gene) may inhibit or mask the expression of the other.

dominant. In genetics, the gene in a pair which expresses itself.

double fertilization. In angiosperms, the process involving two sperms (male gametes), whereby one fuses with the egg to form the zygote and the other sperm unites with the two polar nuclei of the embryo sac to form the triploid endosperm.

double helix. The twisted, two-stranded chains of nucleotides comprising the framework of the DNA molecule.

drug. Has several different usages. (1) *In the broad sense:* Any chemical substance which alters structure or function in a living organism—a biodynamic agent. (2) *By the physician:* Any substance employed as a medicine in the treatment of physical or mental disease. (3) *By the layman:* A substance used as a medicine or one which is habit-forming or leads to addiction.

drupe. Type of single-seeded (usually) fruit in which the outer layer of the fruit wall is fleshy and the inner layer is hard and stony. Examples: peach, olive, plum.

dump-heap theory of the origin of agriculture. Seeds from plants brought by primitive man to his crude hovels dropped and grew in the nitrogen-rich rubbish of fish, excreta, and other garbage accumulated around these huts. This suggested to someone that plants could be grown near home base rather than being gathered from a distance.

E

early wood. In an annual ring, the first layer of wood produced in the growing season by the vascular cambium; also called spring wood.

ecology. The science, or study, of the interrelationships and interactions among plants, animals, and the environment.

egg. Female gamete.

electron. A negatively charged atomic particle.

electron microscope. An instrument which uses beams of electrons and magnetic fields to produce magnification.

embryo. A multicellular structure in bryophytes and vascular plants which develops within the female sex organ from the zygote by a series of cell divisions; the young sporophyte; in seeds, the embryo consists of a short axis (the lower part of which produces the root and the upper part of which forms the stem) bearing one or more cotyledons (seed leaves).

embryophytes. Plants which form embryos; include bryophytes (mosses and liverworts) and vascular plants.

embryo sac. Structure in the ovule of an angiosperm with eight nuclei or cells—one egg, two polar nuclei, and five others; the female gametophyte of the angiosperm.

emetic. Substance which induces vomiting. Examples: mustard, ipecac.

endemic. Restricted to a given region, e.g., to an island, mountain top, valley.

endoplasmic reticulum. An elaborate cytoplasmic network of flattened tubules related to the manufacture of cellular products and transfer of cellular materials.

endosperm. The food-storing tissue in seeds; originates from the double fertilization process in angiosperms in which one sperm nucleus unites with two polar nuclei of the embryo sac—thus the endosperm is triploid (has three sets of chromosomes).

environment. In the biological sense, the total of all external factors, biotic and abiotic, acting together which influences the lives and behavior of organisms.

enzyme. Organic catalyst, or substance, which facilitates a chemical reaction, often speeding up the reaction, while not itself being used up in the process. Examples: diastase, papain from papaya (*Carica papaya*).

ephedrine. Alkaloid derived from *Ephedra,* a genus of gymnosperm shrubs; used as a decongestant to treat colds, asthma, and hay fever.

epidermis. Layer of surface cells which by virtue of its waxlike outer surface (cuticle) in shoot systems cuts down the amount of water lost by evaporation, and which by virtue of the hairlike prolongations of its cells in roots increases the absorptive surfaces of these structures.

epiphyte. Plant which grows on another plant (or pole, wire, or other structure) but receives only mechanical support from the latter and not nutritional maintenance. Examples: Spanish moss, many orchids.

ergonovine. Alkaloid isolated from the fungus ergot, which exerts powerful effect on the pregnant uterus causing strong contractions.

ergot. Fungus parasite infecting grasses and grains, such as wheat and rye.

ergotamine. Alkaloid, derived from the fungus ergot, used to treat migraine headaches.

ergotism. Disease produced by consumption of bread infected with the parasitic fungus ergot; symptoms include burning sensation in extremities, hallucinations, induction of abortions; same as St. Anthony's fire.

erosion. Removal of soil and rock by action of water, wind, glaciers, land and mud slides.

essential amino acids. The eight amino acids which must be supplied to man since he cannot synthesize these eight compounds (lysine, tryptophan, phenylalanine, leucine, isoleucine, threonine, methionine, and valine).

ethnobotany. Literally, "people botany"; division of botany which concerns itself with the utility of plants, including the plant lore of peoples and the use of plants in their cultures—their festivals, their agriculture, their medicine, and their religion.

eutrophication. In ponds, lakes, streams, and oceans, the process of enrichment, or overfertilization, with mineral nutrients or organic materials, resulting in excess growth of algae which reduces light at lower water levels, encourages growth of decomposer organisms resulting in oxygen depletion and often death to other aquatic plants and animals, including fish.

evergreen. Popular name for a plant which retains its leaves season after season and loses them a few at a time. Examples: pines, spruces, firs, mountain laurel, some rhododendrons.

evolution (organic or biologic evolution). Historic process of change by which existing species have reached their present state.

F

factor. In genetics, something which controls the inheritance of a trait or characteristic; same as gene.

family. A unit of classification, above genus and below the order, consisting of one or more related genera. Examples: Rosaceae (rose family), Compositae (daisy family), Fagaceae (oak family).

fat (oil). Organic compound containing carbon, hydrogen, and oxygen, in which the ratio of hydrogen to oxygen is not 2:1, as in carbohydrates, but usually much greater.

female sex organ. Structure which produces the egg cell (female gamete).

fermentation: *See* anaerobic respiration.

fern. Vascular plant with usually large leaves (fronds) but no seeds. Examples: staghorn fern, Boston fern, common polypody.

fertilization. Process in which two gametes fuse or unite.

fiber. Narrow, elongated cell with pointed ends and thick walls; the main kind of supporting cell in the wood and some other tissues of angiosperms.

figure. The markings or patterns seen in wood; often mistakenly called grain.

fission. A type of asexual reproduction in which a one-celled organism divides to form two new one-celled organisms. Examples: in blue-green algae and bacteria.

flagellum. Whip, or lash, on zoospores, some sperm cells, and some other gametes, by means of which they swim about.

flat-cut board. Board sawn from a log perpendicularly to the radius or diameter.

floriculture. The study and/or cultivation of ornamental flowering plants.

flower. The characteristic reproductive structure of angiosperms, or flowering plants; when complete, flowers consist of sepals, petals, stamens, and carpels (pistils).

food. Organic compound which furnishes energy or is used to form new cells. Examples: carbohydrates, fats (oils), and proteins.

food chain. A series of organisms in which there is a transfer of food energy from producer organisms to successive levels (trophic levels) of consumer organisms.

food chain concentration. The accumulation of nonfood products at each higher trophic level of the biomass pyramid.

food web. Interconnected food chains.

forestry. Study and/or care of forests, particularly as they concern the production of timber and other tree products.

fossil. Any evidence, remains, or impressions of prehistoric plants (or animals) embedded in rock or in the crust of the earth.

fouling. Accumulations of algae, barnacles, oysters, and other marine organisms on the hulls of ships, piling, or dockage.

fragmentation. Type of asexual reproduction in which a segment of thread, or filament, or some other part breaks off the parent plant and this piece regenerates another plant.

frond. The large leaf characteristic of many ferns, cycads, palms, and some other plants.

fruit. In angiosperms, the structure produced by the maturation of the ovary, the whole carpel (or pistil), and sometimes other portions of the plant adjacent to these parts.

fruit dot. Popular term for the collection of spore sacs which appears to the naked eye like a dot on a fern leaf; same as sorus.

fungicide. Substance used to kill or retard growth of fungi. Example: Bordeaux mixture.

fungus. Thallophyte without chlorophyll and hence food secured saprophytically or parasitically, or both ways.

G

gamete. Sex cell; may be male (sperm) or female (egg) or with no sexual differentiation.

gametophyte. The sexual, or gamete-producing, generation characterized by the haploid (*n*) chromosome number.

ganja. Substance prepared from dried tops with the exuded resin from *Cannabis* plants; may be two or three times as strong as bhang; it is smoked, eaten, or drunk.

gene. Factor which controls the inheritance of a character or trait; located on a chromosome; a section of a DNA molecule consisting of many nucleotides.

gene pool. All the genes, dominant and recessive, in a given population of a species.

gene theory of inheritance. Concept that the inheritance of traits is controlled by genes located on the chromosomes.

genetics. Science, or study, of inheritance, or heredity.

genotype. Term which refers to the genetic make-up of the organism, or the actual genes which are present.

genus (plural, genera). The first word in a binomial; a group of closely related species which are more alike among themselves than they are like any other group of plants or animals. Examples: *Cocos* (coconut), *Saccharum* (sugar cane), *Hevea* (Pará rubber plant), *Acer* (maple).

gibberellin. A kind of plant hormone, or growth-regulating substance, which promotes cell enlargement.

glucose. A kind of simple sugar containing six carbon atoms.

glycoside. Organic chemical consisting of one or more sugar molecules attached to one or more nonsugar molecules; often bitter and exerts a marked physiological effect on animals and man. Example: dicoumarin.

grafting. Process by which a bud or small twig (scion) is affixed to the stem (stock) and root system of another plant in such a way that the cambial layers of both stock and scion are in contact. (Some herbs are grafted with little or no involvement of cambial layers.)

grain. Refers to the prevailing direction of fibers and tracheids in wood, for example, straight grain, spiral grain, interlocked grain; frequently misused for the term *figure*.

grain. The fruit of cereals; actually a one-seeded fruit, technically termed a caryopsis, in which the fruit wall and the seed coat are fused into one structure.

green algae. Thallophytes with the same chlorophyll complement as in the higher plants.

Green Revolution. Agricultural movement resulting in the doubling and even tripling of the production of cereals and other crops within a few decades (1940–70) in some developing countries of the world (e.g., Mexico, Philippines).

growth. Irreversible increase in size.

guard cells. In leaves and other green parts of vascular plants, the two cells which surround each stoma and by their action either enlarge the opening or diminish the size of the pore.

gymnosperm. Plant whose seeds are not enclosed as in a carpel; many have cones. Examples: pines, spruces, redwood, *Ephedra*, *Ginkgo*, and cycads.

H

habitat. Place where a plant grows.

habituation. Refers to the intense desire, or hunger, for a particular drug; also called psychological dependence or craving.

hallucinations. State of perceiving or sensing things which have no reality; for example, an alcoholic may "see" a pink elephant; may involve any or all the senses—visual, auditory, olfactory, taste, and tactile.

hallucinogen. A nonaddictive substance which in nontoxic doses causes hallucinations and produces alterations in states of consciousness, that is, produces changes in perception (of time, space, and of self), changes in mood, and changes in thought. The changes are usually temporary. Example: mescaline.

haploid. Having one set of chromosomes, as in gametes; same as *n* number.

hardwood. The commercial, or trade, name for the timber of dicotyledonous trees; characterized by the presence of vessels and often thick-walled wood fibers.

hashish. Resin from *Cannabis* flowers and adjacent parts.

heartwood. The dark-colored wood of the interior parts of tree trunks.

hemorrhagic. To cause to bleed, or hemorrhage.

hepatoma. A cancer of the liver.

herb. Soft-stemmed plant with little wood, low in stature or climbing, usually living for a year, or a few years at most. Examples: petunia, impatiens, marigold, zinnia, morning glory.

herbal. Botany book of the Medieval and Renaissance periods, sometimes with illustrations, and consisting of descriptions of plants (and even animals and rocks) with particular emphasis on their utility, medicinal importance, poisonous, and edible qualities.

herbarium. A collection of preserved plants, mostly dried and mounted on large white sheets of paper, which are filed systematically in steel or wooden cases.

herbicide. Substance used to kill weeds and other undesirable plants. Example: 2, 4-D.

heredity. Transmission of traits from parents to offspring.

heroin. A white, crystalline powder which does not occur in nature but is a semisynthetic derivative of morphine and acetic acid.

heterogamy. Union of two dissimilar, or unlike, gametes.

heterozygous. Condition where the genes of a pair are unlike.

histamine. Organic base with carbon, hydrogen, and nitrogen; produced by damaged membranes of nose, throat, and bronchial passages exposed to the proteins in pollen and fungal spores.

holdfast. As on brown algae, rootlike structure which attaches the plant to the substrate. Examples: in *Laminaria, Nereocystis.*

holdfast cell. Basal cell of an algal filament, or thread, which functions to anchor the plant to the substrate. Examples: in *Ulothrix, Oedogonium.*

homology. Similarity in structure between organs or parts due to common evolutionary origin. Example: sepals, stamens, and leaves are thought by some botanists to be similar in origin, being ultimately derived from branches or branching systems.

homozygous. Condition where the genes of a pair are alike.

hormone. Chemical substance manufactured in small quantities in one part of the plant and then usually transported to another part where it exerts its special effects; chemical messenger. Example: indoleacetic acid (IAA).

horsetail. Lower, living vascular plant lacking seeds and whose bushy aspect suggests the name; bears cones; has jointed stems.

horticulture. The study and/or cultivation of vegetables, fruitbearing plants, and ornamental plants.

host. The living organism from which a parasite derives its food. Examples: elm tree is host for Dutch elm disease fungus, chestnut tree for chestnut blight fungus.

humanistic botany. Botany with primary emphasis on plants used by humans, and the impact of plants on people, their civilization, their history.

humus. Organic material in the soil arising from the decomposition of vegetable and animal matter.

hunger theory of the origin of sex. Concerns the speculation that eons ago two underdeveloped, or "hungry," zoospores fused to produce a new individual.

hunting period. Cultural period extending for a million years until approximately 9,000 B.C., during which early humans obtained their food by searching for edible plants, fish, and other animals; also called Paleolithic or Old Stone Age.

hybrid. In genetics, the product of a union of two individuals differing in one or more pairs of characters; in taxonomy, the product of a cross between two different species, or more rarely, two genera.

hybrid corn. Corn plant resulting from a cross between two inbred lines; characterized by increased vigor and productivity.

hybrid vigor. Increased vitality and productivity in the offspring of a cross between two inbred lines, as in hybrid corn.

hyoscyamine. Alkaloid derived from belladonna (*Atropa belladonna*) and other members of the potato-tomato family; along with atropine and scopolamine, makes up belladonna series of alkaloids.

hypertension. High blood pressure.

hypnotic. *See* soporific.

hypothesis. Tentative explanation advanced to explain a set of facts or observations.

I

ibotenic acid. The principle, or compound, in the fly-agaric mushroom (*Amanita muscaria*) which is responsible for its hallucinogenic effects.

inbreeding. Crossing closely related individuals.

independent assortment. Principle elucidated by Mendel, which states that the factors (genes) representing two or more contrasting pairs of characters are segregated to the spores (gametes in animals) independently of one another, and then the gametes combine at random with respect to one another.

indicator plant. Plant which grows only in the presence of certain minerals (or other environmental factors) and hence serves as a sign that such chemicals (or other environmental factors) are present. Example: some species of *Astragalus*, or poison vetch, indicate presence of the chemical element selenium.

industrial mycology. Applied science which deals with the fungi of importance in industry.

inheritance of acquired characters. Theory developed by Lamarck, stating that through use structures and organs develop (conversely, through disuse organs atrophy), and this development is then passed on to the next generation.

insecticide. Substance used to kill insects. Examples: pyrethrum, rotenone, DDT, chlordane.

insectivorous plant. One which traps insects or other small animals; same as carnivorous plant. Examples: pitcher plant, Venus's flytrap, sundew.

internode. Segment of stem between two nodes.

isogamy. Union of two similar, or like, gametes.

isolation. Separation of populations of the same species by physical or biological barriers to gene exchange so that different populations gradually differentiate into distinct species.

K

kelps. General name for large, marine brown algae, such as *Laminaria* or devil's apron, sea palm, *Macrocystis*, and *Nereocystis*.

L

lateral bud. *See* axillary bud.

late wood. In an annual ring, the final layer of wood produced during the growing season by the vascular cambium; also called summer wood.

laudanum (or ladanum). Opium dissolved in alcohol; tincture of opium.

law. A generalization, or statement of a process, which is not known to vary under a given set of conditions. Example: law of independent assortment.

laxative. A mild purgative, or substance used to evacuate the bowels. Example: mineral oil.

leaf axil. Upper angle formed by the petiole and stem.

leaflet. One of the parts of the blade in a compound leaf.

leaf scar. Mark left on the stem when the leaf falls off.

lenticel. Opening or pore in the cork, or bark, which permits gaseous exchange between the environment and the interior of the stem or root.

leprosy. Disease of the skin and deeper tissues, including nerves, caused by the bacterium *Mycobacterium leprae*; also called Hansen's disease.

lichen. Symbiotic association between an alga and a fungus; the former supplies the food and the latter, water and perhaps protection.

light microscope. An instrument which uses glass lenses and ordinary light to produce magnification.

lignin. Noncellulosic constituent of plant cell walls, particularly in woody plants, which amounts to 15 to 30 percent by weight of the cell-wall substance; lignin stiffens and supports the cellulose foundation of the cell wall.

linkage. In genetics, the inheritance of traits as a unit or block because the genes controlling these traits are located on the same chromosome.

liverwort. A group of bryophytes, many of which consist of rather flat, lobed thalli, or bodies, hence the name.

London smog. A dense, visible toxic mixture of sulfur oxides, particulate matter, and other airborne products resulting from the combustion of coal.

long-day plant. Refers to the photoperiodic response in which plants require long spans of light (13 hours or longer) in order to initiate flowering. Examples: corn, gladiolus, larkspur.

LSD. _See_ lysergic acid diethylamide.

lysergic acid diethylamide. LSD; compound derived by semisynthesis from alkaloids of ergot, some morning glories, and other plants.

M

macroconsumer organism. _See_ consumer organism.

malaria. Disease involving recurring fever, caused by the destruction of red blood cells by protozoa belonging to several species of _Plasmodium_ which are carried and disseminated by the female _Anopheles_ mosquito.

male sex organ. Structure which produces sperms (male gametes).

marijuana. Dried, crushed leaves and flowering tops of _Cannabis_; also refers to the _Cannabis_ plant.

masticatory. A substance, sometimes medicinal, which when chewed improves condition of the mouth, including increase in the flow of saliva. Examples: betel nut, chewing gum.

materia medica. Materials of medicine or drugs; also used as title of treatises on medicinal drugs and courses of study.

medical mycology. Study of human diseases caused by fungi.

meiosis. Process of nuclear division during which, among other things, the chromosome number is reduced or changed from diploid ($2n$) to haploid (n); process occurs in plants at the time of spore formation; same as reduction division.

meristem. A restricted region in plants in which cell division is more or less continuous during the growing season; located at tips of stems and their branches, tips of roots and their branches, and between wood and phloem (the vascular cambium).

mescal buttons. Dried, disc-shaped tops of peyote.

mescaline. Alkaloid derived from peyote; a hallucinogen.

metabolism. The collective name for all the chemical reactions which go on in the living organism; includes respiration and food manufacture.

microconsumer organism. _See_ decomposer organism.

micron. A unit of measure; $1/1,000$ of a millimeter; $1/25,000$ of an inch; also called a micrometer.

microscope. See electron microscope; light microscope.

millimeter. A unit of measure; $1/1,000$ of a meter; about $1/25$ of an inch.

mitochondrion (plural, mitochondria). A cytoplasmic particle which captures, converts, and transfers energy during the process of respiration.

mitosis. Process of nuclear division.

monocotyledon. Flowering plants with one cotyledon, or seed leaf, in the seed; also, the main veins in the leaves are usually parallel; floral parts usually in threes or multiples thereof.

monohybrid cross. In genetics, a cross between two individuals differing in one set of characters.

morphine. Alkaloid derived from opium poppy (_Papaver somniferum_); a true narcotic; used as analgesic in case of great pain, as with severe wounds and cancer.

morphology. Study of form and structure.

moss. Small plant (measuring a few inches at most), usually growing with others in dense mats in fairly wet situations such as marshes, bogs, damp places on rocks, in moist, cool woods, and on trees in cloud forests of tropics; forms embryos; bryophyte.

mulching. Operation of placing a layer of organic material such as bark and wood chips, leaves, or lawn clippings over surface of the soil to retard water loss and weed growth.

muscarine. Alkaloid derived from the fly-agaric (_Amanita muscaria_); probably not the substance responsible for the hallucinogenic effects of _Amanita_.

mutagen. A substance, preparation, or radiation

capable of producing a mutation. Examples: colchicine, X rays.

mutation. Inheritable change produced by an alteration in a gene or chromosome or in chromosome number.

mutation theory. De Vries's suggestion that evolution is brought about through variations produced by mutations.

mycelium. The mass of threads, or filaments, forming the body of a fungus.

mycology. Study, or science, of fungi.

mycophilia. Love of mushrooms, or fungi.

mycophobia. Dislike or distrust of mushrooms, or fungi.

mycorrhiza. Symbiotic association between the mycelium of a fungus and the roots of a higher plant in which the roots supply carbohydrates to the fungus and the mycelium absorbs water and nutrients from the soil and passes these on to the higher plant.

N

narcotic. Has several meanings: (1) *Etymological meaning:* Any agent capable of causing a depressive state (narcosis) in the central nervous system. (2) *Popular:* A dangerously addictive drug or presumed addictive drug. (3) *Legally:* Any drug listed as a narcotic. (4) *Strict sense:* Substance which produces addiction. Example: morphine.

natural selection. Darwin's theory to explain evolution, involving the overproduction of organisms and the resulting struggle for existence; because of variation, some forms will be better fitted for survival and their desirable traits will be passed on to the next generation.

nicotine. Alkaloid derived from tobacco (*Nicotiana tabacum*) and other species of *Nicotiana*.

nitrogen-fixation. Process during which atmospheric or gaseous nitrogen is combined with other elements to produce nitrogenous compounds; carried on by bacteria and blue-green algae, which may be free-living in the soil, or by symbiotic bacteria in nodules on the roots of legumes and other plants.

nitrogen-fixing algae. Certain blue-green algae which, besides manufacturing sugar by photosynthesis, also convert gaseous nitrogen into organic nitrogen compounds in their own bodies.

nitrogen-fixing bacteria, nonsymbiotic. Bacteria which exist on dead and decaying organic residues in the soil and are able to transform atmospheric nitrogen into organic nitrogen compounds in their own bodies.

nitrogen-fixing bacteria, symbiotic. Bacteria which live in the root tissues of legumes and some other plants and are able to transform atmospheric nitrogen into organic nitrogen compounds in their own bodies.

nitrogenous base. Organic compound, containing atoms of nitrogen, hydrogen, carbon, and sometimes oxygen, which is a constituent of nucleotides.

node. Place on a stem where a leaf is or was attached.

nodule. In legumes and some other plants, irregular swelling on the roots inhabited by symbiotic nitrogen-fixing bacteria.

nuclear membrane. The outermost layer of the nucleus which the electron microscope reveals as a multiple-layered membrane.

nucleic acid. DNA and RNA; compound constructed of long series of molecular groupings called nucleotides concerned with the storage and replication of hereditary information (DNA) and protein manufacture (RNA).

nucleolus (plural, nucleoli). A specialized body within the nucleus related to the formation of ribosomes.

nucleotide. Molecular building block of DNA and RNA consisting of a sugar (deoxyribose or ribose), a phosphate, and a nitrogenous base.

nucleus (plural, nuclei). A protoplasmic body in the cell which controls all cellular activities including heredity.

O

Old Stone Age. *See* hunting period.

oleoresin. Natural product consisting of a volatile oil and a resin. Example: turpentine.

olericulture. Cultivation and/or study of vegetables.

ontogeny. Development of an individual from zygote to adulthood.

opposite arrangement of leaves. Condition where two leaves are attached to the stem at each node.

order. A unit of classification, above the family and below the class, consisting of one or more related families. Examples: Magnoliales, Orchidales, Liliales.

organ. One of the main parts of a plant, such as root, stem, and leaf; an organ is composed of tissues.

organic compound. Chemical substance containing carbon.

organic gardening. Horticulture or gardening without the use of commercial fertilizers and synthetic insecticides, fungicides, or herbicides.

organism. An individual plant or animal.

ovary. Enlarged base of carpel (pistil) which encloses ovules.

ovule. Structure in flowering plants, located inside the ovary, which eventually becomes the seed; also present in gymnosperms but not enclosed.

oxidation. Addition of oxygen to a compound; process in which there is a loss of electrons from a molecule or atom.

P

paleobotany. The science, or study, of fossil plants.

Paleolithic Age. *See* hunting period.

palisade layer. Tissue in leaves consisting of a file, or row(s), of elongated cells usually beneath the upper epidermis, well supplied with chloroplasts and hence photosynthesis takes place here.

palmately compound leaf. Condition where leaflets are attached to tip of the petiole and arranged like the fingers of the hand.

palmately veined leaf. Arrangement of the veins in a leaf blade where the chief veins spread out from the tip of the petiole like the fingers on the hand.

Paludrin. Synthetic substitute for quinine; proprietary name.

papaverine. Alkaloid derived from opium poppy (*Papaver somniferum*); smooth muscle relaxant.

parallel evolution. Development of same type of structure in two different and unrelated groups of organisms. Examples: seeds in seed plants and in some of the extinct arboreal club-mosses; vessels in angiosperms (flowering plants) as well as in some gymnosperms (e.g., *Ephedra*).

parallel-veined leaf. Condition where the chief veins run parallel with one another, as in many monocotyledons.

parasite. Organism which derives its food from another living organism called the host. Examples: corn smut fungus, wheat rust fungus, mistletoe, dodder.

paregoric. Tincture of opium to which camphor is added.

parthenocarpy. Development of fruit without pollination resulting in seedless fruit, as in banana, some grapes, navel orange.

pathogen. Disease-producing organism. Example: fungus causing chestnut blight.

peat. Organic material made up of mosses (largely *Sphagnum* or bog moss) which has decomposed slowly, carbonized, and then become compacted over thousands of years; used as fuel in countries like Ireland and Scotland where there are large deposits.

penicillin. Antibiotic derived from the blue-green mold *Penicillium;* used to combat bacterial infection.

perennial. Plant whose life cycle is three or more years long. Examples: elms, apple, maples, irises, peonies.

pesticide. Agent used to kill insects, fungi, bacteria; general term which includes insecticides and fungicides.

petal. In flowers, one member of the whorl situated between the sepals and stamens; usually colored and functions in attracting insects.

petiole. Leaf stalk connecting the stem with the leaf blade.

peyotism. Religion revolving around use of peyote. Example: Native American Church.

phantastica. Essentially equivalent to hallucinogen.

pharmacology. Science that deals with the action of drugs on animals and man (and plants).

pharmacopoeia. Treatise listing officially approved drugs.

phenotype. Refers to the external appearance of an organism.

phloem. Food-transporting part of the conductive tissue in all vascular plants; the inner part of the bark of trees and shrubs; also present in herbs.

phosphate. A chemical grouping derived from phosphoric acid consisting of atoms of phosphorus and oxygen.

photochemical smog. An unstable, visible, toxic mixture of various hydrocarbons, formaldehyde, peroxyacyl nitrates, and other chemicals which forms in the presence of solar energy.

photoperiodism. Growth and reproductive responses of plants to different lengths of exposure to light during a 24-hour period.

photosensitivity. In connection with poisonous plants, phenomenon in which some substance becomes poisonous to an animal upon exposure of the animal to light.

photosynthesis. The process by which green plants manufacture food. In this process, carbon dioxide and water react in the presence of light and chlorophyll at a suitable temperature to yield sugar and oxygen.

Phycomycetes. *See* algal-fungi.

phylogeny. The evolutionary relationships among organisms.

physical barrier. An environmental obstacle, such as a high mountain range or extensive body of water, which prevents the easy exchange of genes among the members of the same species growing on opposite sides of the obstacle.

physiology. Study of functions and processes.

pinnately compound leaf. Condition where the leaflets are arranged along the petiole in the fashion of a feather.

pinnately veined leaf. Arrangement of the veins in a leaf blade where there is a single central vein with branch veins arising from either side of this central vein.

pistil. *See* carpel.

pit. Thin place or recess in a cell wall which permits the passage of water and materials in solution.

pith. Usually small core of tissue running through the center of a stem; cells store food.

plain-sawn board. *See* flat-cut board.

plankton. Small, free-floating or swimming organisms found near the surface of fresh or salt water.

plant pathology. Study or science of plant diseases—their causes, transmission, and control.

plant succession. On a given area of land or in any aquatic habitat, the orderly sequence of plants which occupy the site until a state of balance is reached with the local environment.

plasma membrane. The outermost layer (three-layered as seen by electron microscope) of the cytoplasm of a cell; encloses the living matter of the cell and controls the passage of materials to and from the protoplasm.

plastid. Specialized cytoplasmic body concerned with food manufacture and storage of food.

poisonous plant. One containing some substance which when taken even in small or moderate amounts produces deleterious or harmful reaction in man or animal.

polar nuclei. Two nuclei of the embryo sac in angiosperms.

pollen. Dustlike particles produced by stamens and similar structures of seed plants. Young pollen grains may be equivalent to spores; older pollen grains are male gametophytes.

pollination. Transfer of pollen from stamen to stigma in angiosperms or from pollen cone to seed cone in gymnosperms.

polyploid. A plant with three or more sets of chromosomes, i.e., $3n$, $4n$, $5n$, etc.; that condition in cells where there are three or more sets of chromosomes.

pomology. Study of fruits and fruit growing.

primary succession. Sequence of vegetational changes on a site which has not previously been tenanted and where soil has to be formed.

principle. As used in connection with poisonous plants, medicinal plants, etc., the chemical compound which causes the effect, be it toxicity, intoxication, sleep, nausea, or whatever.

procaine. Synthetic substitute for cocaine used by dentists and physicians as local anesthetic; trade name for procaine is Novocaine.

producer organism. Green plants which manufacture food through photosynthesis.

progressive evolution. Development from simple structures (or organisms) to complex structures (or organisms). Examples: isogamy to heterogamy; algae to vascular plants.

protein. Organic compound containing carbon, hydrogen, oxygen, and nitrogen; made up of chains of amino acids.

prothallus. Small, green, membranous, often heart-shaped structure produced by the germinating fern spore; bears sex organs which produce sperms and eggs; the gametophyte of the fern.

protoplasm. The living substance of the cell; cytoplasm plus nucleus.

protoplast. The protoplasm within a cell considered as an individual entity.

pruning. Cutting of stems, roots, and their branches usually for cultural enhancement.

psilophytes. Fossil vascular plants found in Devonian and Silurian rocks (formed some 390 to 440 million years ago) which are characterized by their simplicity—often lack roots and leaves (or have the merest suggestions of roots and leaves) and consist of dichotomous or forking stems.

psychedelic. Literally, "mind-manifesting"; originally used in the sense of hallucinogen, but now usage has broadened to mean much more.

psychological dependence. Condition in which there is intense craving or hunger for a particular drug; sometimes referred to as habituation.

psychotomimetic. Substance which produces conditions that ape or mimic psychotic conditions or mental disorders; essentially equivalent to the word *hallucinogen*.

pure line. A series of organisms (the offspring of several generations) which is homozygous for one or more sets of characters.

purgative. Substance employed to evacuate the bowels; includes laxatives (mild purgative like mineral oil) and cathartics (powerful purgative like castor oil).

pyramid of numbers. *See* biomass pyramid.

Q

quarter-sawn board. Board sawn from a log along a radius or a diameter.

quill. A roll of bark, particularly of cinnamon, formed while drying.

quinidine. Alkaloid derived from *Cinchona*, or fever-bark tree; used to treat irregular and rapid heart beat.

quinine. Alkaloid derived from *Cinchona*, or fever-bark tree; used to treat malaria.

R

ray cell. A unit, or cell, of the vascular rays.

ray flower. One of the individual, showy flowers radiating from the margin of the floral head in those members of the composite family, such as sunflower and daisy; it attracts insects and is usually sterile.

recapitulation. In the course of embryo development, an individual may pass through some of the stages its supposed ancestors passed through during evolution; ontogeny recapitulates phylogeny. Example: Cacti, whose stems are leafless when fully mature, produce leaves as seedlings.

recessive. In genetics, the gene in a pair whose expression is masked or inhibited.

red algae. Thallophytes with chlorophyll plus a red pigment; mostly marine, typically of warm waters. Examples: dulse, Irish moss.

red tide. Marine condition caused by an overabundance of swimming unicellular algae known as dinoflagellates, which elaborate a powerful poison that paralyzes fish and other animals, as well as humans when they consume contaminated seafood.

reduction division. *See* meiosis.

replication. The process of duplication of the DNA molecule.

reproduction. Formation of similar offspring.

reserpine. Alkaloid derived from snakeroot, or *Rauwolfia*; used to treat various nervous disorders and hypertension (high blood pressure); used as a tranquilizer.

respiration. Chemical process in which foods are broken down and energy is released.

resolution. The property of a lens which enables it to discriminate as separate entities any two adjacent points or objects.

responsiveness. Ability to react to stimuli or changes in the environment.

retrogressive evolution. Trend of development from complex structures (or organisms) to simple structures (or organisms). Example: loss of sepals and petals from flowers of some species.

rhizome. Frequently fleshy, usually horizontal underground stem; sometimes called a rootstock.

ribonucleic acid, RNA. One of two nucleic acids; found in nucleoli and cytoplasm; characterized by the sugar ribose and concerned with the manufacture of specific proteins; RNA carries code from DNA to ribosomes.

ribosome. A cytoplasmic particle which cannot be seen with the light microscope (i.e., submicroscopic); composed of nucleic acid and protein; intimately concerned with protein formation.

RNA. *See* ribonucleic acid.

root graft. The union or growing together of the roots of adjacent trees.

root-hair cell. T-shaped cell in the epidermis of roots which projects out into the soil in a fingerlike fashion and absorbs water and dissolved mineral elements.

rotenone. Active ingredient of certain insecticides obtained from derris (*Derris* spp.) root which is not harmful to humans.

S

sac fungi. Thallophytes without chlorophyll which produce a sac, or ascus, containing spores; also called Ascomycetes. Examples: cup fungi, morels, yeasts, truffles, Dutch elm disease fungus.

St. Anthony's fire. *See* ergotism.

saprophyte. Plant which obtains its food from a dead organism or from nonliving organic matter such as the humus in forest soil. Examples: mushrooms, puffballs, yeasts.

sapwood. The light-colored wood of the outer layers of tree trunks immediately inside the vascular cambium of the living tree through which most of the upward water movement takes place.

Schizomycetes. *See* bacteria.

scion. In grafting, the small twig or bud which is affixed to the stock.

scopolamine. Alkaloid derived from belladonna (*Atropa belladonna*) and several other members of the potato-tomato family; used to treat insomnia; mixed with morphine, constitutes twilight sleep or anesthetic for child birth; used by police in some countries to extract confessions; along with atropine and hyoscyamine make up the belladonna series of alkaloids.

scurvy. A disease produced by the deficiency of vitamin C and marked by swollen and bleeding gums, red skin blotches, prostration.

seasoning of wood. Removal of water from wood so that growth of decay-producing organisms, such as fungi, is inhibited.

secondary succession. Sequence of vegetational changes on a site which has previously been tenanted and where soil is already formed.

sedative. Substance used to calm or soothe a person. Example: reserpine.

seed. Reproductive structure formed from ovule; composed of one or two seed coats, endosperm present or absent, and an embryo consisting of stem-root axis with one or more cotyledons.

seed fern. Fossil gymnosperm of the Carboniferous period which had fernlike leaves (fronds) but which bore true seeds.

seed plant. Plant which produces seeds; includes gymnosperms and angiosperms (flowering plants).

segregation. Principle developed by Mendel stating that one of each of the paired factors (genes) separates into different daughter cells.

selection. The process of picking the most desirable members of a population, the breeding or crossing of these chosen individuals, the further picking of the most desirable individuals from among the offspring, and so on for any number of generations.

self-pollination. Transport of pollen from stamen to stigma in same flower or to the stigma of another flower on the same plant in angiosperms, or from pollen cone to seed cone in same plant in gymnosperms.

semisynthesis. Chemical manufacturing process in which a large part of the resulting molecule is provided ready-made by plants. Example: manufacture of LSD from lysergic acid of plants.

sepal. One member of the outer whorl of parts of a flower; may be green or colored; protects flower in bud stage and, if colored, serves to attract insects.

serendipity. Discovery by chance, or by accident.

sex-linked character. In genetics, a trait which appears more often in one sex than in the other because the genes controlling it are located on the X chromosome.

sexual reproduction. Production of offspring involving the fusion of two cells or gametes.

shaman. Herb doctor, medicine man.

shoot system. That part of the plant consisting of the stem and its branches with their attached leaves.

short-day plant. Refers to the photoperiodic response in which plants require short durations of light (less than 13 hours) in order to initiate flowering. Examples: asters, chrysanthemums, poinsettia.

shrub. Plant which occupies an intermediate position between herbs and trees, having more wood than herbs, taller than herbs, usually lives longer than herbs, and finally, usually has several trunks or stems arising from the ground line rather than a single trunk as in most trees. Examples: forsythias, privets, lilacs, hydrangeas.

sieve tube. In flowering plants, a chain or series of sieve-tube cells forming a pipeline in the phloem for the conduction of food.

sieve-tube cell. Chief food-conducting cell in the phloem of flowering plants; end walls bear numerous small openings which match similar openings in super- and subadjacent cells, thus forming a pipeline called a sieve tube.

simple leaf. Leaf with a single, undivided blade.

smog. *See* London smog; photochemical smog.

social Darwinism. Encompasses evolutionary concepts transferred from biology to the social sphere, for example, to sociology and philosophy.

softwood. The commercial, or trade, name for the

timber of a conifer; characterized by the absence of vessels.

soma. *Amanita muscaria,* the fly-agaric mushroom, according to Gordon Wasson.

soporific. Substance used to induce sleep; same as hypnotic. Examples: opium, tetrahydrocannibnol (THC) of *Cannabis.*

sorcerer. Medicine man, magician, wizard.

sorus. *See* fruit dot.

species. The binomial of a plant or animal; the smallest unit of classification; a kind of plant or animal; the members of a species share similar structural characteristics; all the members of a species have the potential to interbreed and to produce fertile offspring; members of a species are related by descent—they come from the same ancestors. Examples: white oak, red maple, bloodroot, sugar cane.

specific epithet. *See* specific name.

specific gravity of wood. The ratio of the weight of a piece of wood in air to the weight of an equal volume of water.

specific name. The second word in a binomial.

sperm. Male gamete.

spice. Pungent, aromatic, flavor-giving plant product mainly derived from tropical regions; bark, fruits, flower buds, rhizomes, seeds used to season and flavor foods; of little or no food value.

spiral arrangement of leaves. *See* alternate arrangement of leaves.

spongy layer. Tissue in leaves consisting of isodiametric to irregularly shaped cells among which are many, large intercellular spaces; usually situated below the palisade layer; cells have chloroplasts and hence photosynthesis occurs here.

spore. One-celled (generally), asexual reproductive structure.

sporophyte. The asexual, spore-producing generation characterized by the diploid (2*n*) chromosome number.

stamen. Clublike to slender structure of the flower which bears at its apex sacs containing pollen.

steroid. Fat-related compound; for example, it has roughly the solubility of a fat; hydrocarbon with seventeen carbon atoms arranged in four rings.

stigma. Place on the carpel (pistil), usually at the tip, where pollen is received.

stimulus. An environmental factor or change in the environment which induces a reaction in a living organism.

stipe. Stemlike part of a brown alga or mushroom.

stipule. Basal appendage of petioles in some plants; usually green; may be large and more or less persistent (as in roses) or small and short-lived (as in elms).

stock. In grafting, the stem into which the scion is inserted.

stoma. Opening or pore between two guard cells which permits the passage of water vapor, carbon dioxide, oxygen, and other gases, between the internal environment of the plant and the external environment of the air; usually located in leaves.

streptomycin. Antibiotic derived from certain species of Actinomycetes.

strychnine. Alkaloid derived from strychnos plant; a frequent component of curare.

style. Neck connecting the ovary and the stigma of the carpel (pistil).

submicroscopic. Term used to indicate an object smaller than can be seen through a light microscope, i.e., magnification with the electron microscope is required.

succession: *See* plant succession.

symbiosis. Association between two species in which there is mutual benefit. Examples: lichen, in which the alga supplies food and the fungus supplies water; mycorrhiza, in which the roots supply carbohydrates to the fungus and the fungus absorbs water and nutrients from the soil and passes these on to the roots.

T

taxonomist. One who specializes in the study of classification.

taxonomy. The science, or study, of classification.

teonanacatl. Aztec name for hallucinogenic mushrooms; literally, "flesh of the gods."

terminal bud. Bud formed at the tip of the main axis of the stem or at the tips of its branches.

terminal bud scale scar. Mark left on the stem when bud scale falls off. Group of terminal bud scale scars comprises the terminal bud scar; represents place where terminal bud was located at one time.

Terramycin. Antibiotic derived from certain species of Actinomycetes; proprietary name.

tetrad. Group of four, as in cluster of four chromatids or four pollen grains.

tetrahydrocannabinol. The intoxicant, or psychoactive, principle, or chemical compound, in *Cannabis,* or marijuana; THC.

textured vegetable protein. Soybean proteins spun into fibers and then fabricated into imitation bacon or used for meat extenders as in hamburgers ("soyburgers").

thallophyte. Plant without roots, stems, leaves, and flowers. Examples: alga, fungus.

thallus. A simple plant body with relatively little differentiation and lacking true roots, stems, and leaves; characteristic of algae and fungi, i.e., of thallophytes.

THC. *See* tetrahydrocannabinol.

theory. A hypothesis supported by considerable data.

theory of social selection. Herbert Spencer's concept that the struggle for subsistence, like natural selection, is the force responsible for social progress, or change, in society.

thermal algae. Group of algal species which grow in places with extremely high temperatures as in hot springs and geyser pools.

tissue. A group of cells usually similar in origin, structure, and function.

tolerance. The physiological state whereby progressively larger doses of a drug must be taken in order to achieve a given effect.

torna-loco. The maddening plant of the Indians of the American Southwest; a species of jimson weed (*Datura*).

totaquine. Mixture of several alkaloids, including quinine, from the bark of the *Cinchona,* or feverbark tree; called the poor man's quinine.

toxicology. The science, or study, of poisons, or toxic substances.

toxin. Poisonous substance.

tracheid. The major water-conducting and supportive cell of conifers; also occurs in other vascular plants including ferns and angiosperms. Cells are long, tapering at both ends, more or less thick walled and commonly bear bordered pits in their walls.

tranquilizer. A drug, or medicine, used to calm, or soothe, a person without directly inducing sleep. Example: reserpine.

transcription. The formation of RNA by one strand of the DNA molecule.

transpiration. Evaporation of water from the plant, or the loss of water vapor from the plant.

travertine. A type of rocklike material found in and around hot springs (e.g., Yellowstone National Park), formed in part by the precipitation of calcium and potassium salts through the activities of algae, especially certain blue-green algae.

tree. Plant composed of considerable wood, much taller than herbs or shrubs, and which lives longer than either herbs or shrubs; usually has one main trunk, or stem, arising from the root. Examples: pines, oaks, elms, mahoganies.

trihybrid cross. In genetics, a cross between two individuals differing in three sets of characters.

triploid. Having three sets of chromosomes; same as $3n$ number.

Triticale. Man-made hybrid between wheat (*Triticum*) and rye (*Secale*) showing desirable properties of both.

trophic level. A stage in the movement of food energy through the biomass pyramid.

truffle. Sac fungus with relatively spherical, subterranean fruiting body growing in symbiotic association with the roots of such trees as oaks and beeches.

tuber. Enlarged tip of a rhizome, or horizontal underground stem. Example: white, or "Irish" potato.

tubocurarine. Alkaloid derived from moonseed vine (*Chondodendron*) and used as a muscle relaxant in preparation for abdominal surgery and in the treatment of rabies; lockjaw, or tetanus; and epilepsy.

U

unit character, principle of. In genetics, a principle established by Mendel that factors (genes) control inheritance of characters, or traits, and these factors (genes) occur in pairs.

V

vacuolar membrane. The innermost layer of the cytoplasm which surrounds the vacuole(s); a triple-layered membrane as seen with the electron microscope; regulates passage of materials between cytoplasm and vacuole.

vacuole. The cavity or cavities within the cytoplasm containing cell sap in which the principal component is water.

vascular cambium. A sheath, or layer, of meristematic cells situated between phloem and wood in stems, roots, and some leaves whose dividing cells are responsible for the addition of new xylem and new phloem and thus for the increase in diameter, or thickness, of the plant part.

vascular plant. Plant with xylem and phloem.

vascular ray. Radially oriented sheets, or ribbons, of cells in stems and roots of woody plants; the portion in the wood (wood ray) is continuous across the vascular cambium with the portion in the phloem (phloem ray); conducts materials laterally and stores food.

vascular tissue. Conductive cells of higher plants, specifically, xylem (wood) and phloem.

vector. Agent responsible for transmission of disease-producing organisms such as bacteria and fungi. Examples: wind, water, insects (as the *Anopheles* mosquito in malaria), and other organisms.

vegetarianism. Mode of existence involving the consumption of plants and the exclusion of animals from the diet. Some forms of vegetarianism countenance the consumption of animal products such as eggs, milk, and cheese.

vein. Prominent line, or ridge, on surface of a leaf blade which consists internally of xylem and phloem cells. The vein conducts water, mineral salts, and food and furnishes support to the leaf.

vessel. In flowering plants, a row of vessel cells which transports water and dissolved mineral compounds through the wood.

vessel cell. The chief water-conducting cell in the wood of flowering plants; each cell is open at the top and bottom ends and is linked in rows with similar cells to form vessels.

vestigial organ, or structure. A structure, such as the human appendix, which seems to have no present function in the body, but which perhaps had a function in the ancestors of the organism. Example: five cells in embryo sac other than egg and two polar nuclei.

vinblastine. Alkaloid derived from Madagascar periwinkle (*Vinca rosea*); used as a tumor-inhibiting agent in treatment of leukemia and Hodgkin's disease.

virus. Noncellular particle which cannot be seen with the light microscope (i.e., submicroscopic) which infects plants (including bacteria) and animals and causes diseases; unable to reproduce outside the host; consists of protein shell and a nucleic acid core; has some properties of living things, such as ability to reproduce and mutate.

vitamin. Organic substance which must be added to the diet of some organisms in minute quantities for proper functioning of the organism.

W

water bloom. *See* algal bloom.

weed. In the broadest sense, a plant which is growing in a place it is not wanted. Usually weeds are aggressive, colonize disturbed habitats, are frequently introduced, or foreign; abundant; noxious, or troublesome; and are of little or no economic value. Examples: dandelion, ragweed, bindweed, poison ivy, kudzu, Japanese honeysuckle.

whorled arrangement of leaves. Condition where three or more leaves are attached to the stem at each node. Examples: *Equisetum*, bedstraw (*Galium*).

withdrawal symptoms. Severe physical reactions which occur when a person who has developed tolerance to a drug abruptly stops taking the drug. Example: delirium tremens (DTs).

wood. Water-conducting part of the vascular tissue and supportive framework of vascular plants; the tree trunk less the bark and pith; same as xylem.

wood anatomy. Science, or study, of the microscopic structure of wood.

wood decay. Destruction of cell walls of wood by enzymes secreted by wood-destroying fungi belonging to the shelf, or bracket fungi; also called wood rot.

X

xylem. *See* wood.

Z

zoospore. Motile, or swimming, spore.

zygote. The cell ($2n$) which results from the fusion of two gametes.

Index

acanthus, 1
acetyl-salicylic acid, 247
achene, 187
Actinomycetes, 249, 363, 365
addiction, 198
agar, 350, 356
agaric, 360, 378, 380, 381
Agaricus, 380, 381
agave, 240, 253, 264, 403, 476, 477
agricultural period, 280, 281
agriculture, 280, 281, 296–300
   origin, 281
air bladder, 344, 345–349
Albertus Magnus, 153
alcohol
   effects, 200, 205
   production by yeasts, 383
aleurone layer, 285
algae, 64, 336–359
   cultivation, 353, 354
   ecological role, 356, 357
   evolution, 343, 358
   harmful aspects, 357, 358
   human food, 352–354
   impact on man, 351–358
   industrial uses, 355, 356
   land-formers, 356
   oil deposits, 356
algal bloom, 357
algal-fungi, 363, 365–367
algin, 356
alkali disease, 179
alkaloid, 172–175, 213, 250
   belladonna series, 242, 274
allergic rhinitis, 168–170, 419
allergy-producing plants, 168–170
allspice, 308, 320, 321
aloe, 403, 477
alternate arrangement, 14
alternation of generations, 394, 395
Amanita, 268–274, 277, 379, 380, color
   plate 4c

Ambrosia, 168–170, 185
amino acid(s), 26, 119, 120, 506
   complementarity, 284
   essential, 282–284, 300
ammonia, 508, 509
amygdalin, 175
analgesic, 190, 247
anesthetic, 222, 242
angel's trumpet, 274, 277
angiosperm, 64, 404, 410–427
anise seed, 308
annual, 32
annual ring, 140, 141, 145, 146,
   151–161
   archeology, 157–161
   complacent ring series, 156–158
   history of man, 157–161
   radioactive carbon dating, 161
   seasons, 153–161
   sensitive ring series, 156–158
   sunspots, 157
   timber dating, 157–161
   tree growth, 151–161
   width, 155–157
anthocyanin, 35
antibiotic, 190, 249, 363–365, 383
anticonvulsant, 190
antidepressant, 190
antihistamine, 170
antispasmodic, 326
aphrodisiac, 193, 242, 327, 328
apical dominance, 30, 31
apical meristem, 108–111
   root, 110
   stem, 109
Aralen, 229
aril, 328, color plate 5c
Aristotle, 23, 24
Arrow poison, 245–247
Ascomycetes, 363, 367
ascus, 367
Aspergillus, 367

aspirin, 247
assassin, 192
Astragalus, 179, 180, 185
astringent, 326, 328
Atabrine, 230
athlete's foot, 377
atoll reefs, 356
Atropa belladonna, 240–242, 253, 274
atropine, 173, 241, 242
Aureomycin, 249
autumn crocus, 247, 248, 253, color
   plate 4a
autumnal coloration, 34, 35, color
   plate 1a
auxin, 31
Avicenna, 210

bacteria, 338, 361, 363–365, 384
   aerobic, 356
   denitrifying, 508–510
   harmful aspects, 364, 365
   nonsymbiotic nitrogen-fixing, 511
   photosynthetic, 364
   purple, 364
   symbiotic nitrogen-fixing, 508, 510
bacteriology, 5, 361, 363
banana, 285, 293–295, 303
Banks, Sir Joseph, 552
barberry, 376
bark, 22, 30, 136, 137
barrier
   biological, 476
   physical, 476
Basidiomycetes, 363, 367–371
basidium, 367
basil, 308, 321
bay leaf, 308
Beagle, voyage, 485, 487, 488, 491
Beal, William J., 425
bean, 285, 290, 303
belladonna, 240–242, 253, 274
beri-beri, 286

595

berry, 294
bhang, 192
Bibliotheca Botanica, 76
biennial, 32
big tree, 409, 427
bilateral symmetry, 418, 420
biodynamic agent, 197, 212
binomial, 51, 57; *see also* nomenclature, binomial system
biomass pyramid, 513–515
bird's nest fungus, 367, 370
bittersweet, 175, 185
black mold, 367
bladder kelp, 345
blade, 12, 344, 346, 347
Bligh, William, 554–560
blight, 374
blind staggers, 179
blue-green algae, 338, 357
blue mold, 361, 362
bog moss, 389, 390
Bonellia, marine worm, 342
Bordeaux mixture, 385
Borlaug, Norman E., 298, 299
botany, 4, 5
   medicine, 209–213
Bounty, 554–559
bracken fern, 183, 185
bracket fungus, 368, 371, 374
branching, dichotomous, 346
bread mold, 366, 367
breadfruit, 552, 554–560, color plate 7a
   Pacific native, 554
   West Indian success, 559, 560
breeding for disease resistance, 376, 385
bristlecone pine, 159, 160, 409, 410, 427
brown algae, 344–350
bryophyte, 64, 389, 390
buckthorn, 249, 253
buckwheat, 181, 185
bud, 12, 30, 31
   adventitious, 12
   axillary, 12, 30
   lateral, 12, 30
   mutation, 448, 449
   scale, 30
   terminal, 12, 30, 31
bull kelp, 345
bundle scar, 30

caapi, 274, 277
cabbage, evolution, 469, 470
cabbish, 471
cactus, 403, 460, 476, 477

calcareous algae, 356, color plate 6a
cambium, vascular, 8, 9, 16, 22, 23, 33, 34, 108, 109, 136, 137, 153, 154
   action, 136, 137, 153, 154
Cannabis, 187–207, 274
   effects, 196, 197
   fibers, 187, 189, 194
   history, 191, 192, 194–196
   indica, 189
   literary associations, 193, 194
   medicinal uses, 189–191, 203
   sativa, 189
   types, 192, 193
   U.S. experience, 194–196
   uses by man, 189–191
capsaicin, 323
capsicum, 322
caraway seed, 308
carbohydrate, 6, 282, 283
carbon, 499
   cycle, 499–503
   dioxide, 14, 15, 499, 501–503
   fixation, 499
   monoxide, 537
Carboniferous period, 25, 396, 398, 405
cardamom, 308, 320, 321, 323
carminative, 322, 324, 326, 327, 328
carnivorous plant, 35–40, 43
   human-eating, 39
   "man-eating tree," 38–40
carotenoid, 35
carpel, 14, 411, 412
Carson, Rachel, 531–533
caryopsis, 285
cascara sagrada, 249, 253
cascarillero, 229
cassava, 175, 185, 285, 289, 303
cassia, 308, 321, 324, 325
castor bean, 178, 179, 185
castor oil, 178
catalyst, organic, 23
Catharanthus roseus, 250, 253, color plate 4b
cathartic, 248, 249
catkin-bearing tree, 419, 422
catnip, 275
cell, 7, 88–125
   cavity, 104, 137
   discovery, 92–94
   division, 108–113
   doctrine, 95
   fine structure, 106–108
   green, 99, 100, 102
   guard, 17, 18
   position in life, 94
   ray, 138

cell (*continued*)
   root-hair, 20, 21
   sap, 103
   sieve-tube, 22, 23
   size, 95, 96
   structure, 96–108
   summary, 120–123
   theory, 95
   vessel, 22, 141–143
   wall, 100, 101, 147
cellulose, 9, 100, 101
century plant, 240, 253, 476, 477
cereal, 285–288, 296–300, 303
charas, 193
chaulmoogra oil, 232–235, 253
chemistry of plants, unique, 26
chemosynthesis, 364
chemotherapy, 377, 385
chestnut blight fungus, 367, 375, 376
chicha, 274
chilies, 323
Chinese holly, color plate 7c
chlorinated hydrocarbon, 531
Chloromycetin, 249
chloroquine, 230
chlorophyll, 8, 14, 15, 101, 107
chloroplast, 15, 16, 17, 99, 100, 102, 107
chlorosis, 384
Chondrus crispus, 350, 352
Christian, Fletcher, 557–559
chromatid, 442, 444
chromatin, 102, 103
chromosome, 111–114, 118, 119, 441, 451
   number, 113, 114
   map, 444, 445
   theory of inheritance, 443
Cinchona, 223–230, 253
cinchonine, 228
cinnamon, 308, 320, 321, 324
class, 61
classification, 60–65
   sexual system, 63, 72, 74, 83
Claviceps purpurea, 264–268, 277
Clifford, George, 75
climax vegetation, 518
Closing Circle, 540
cloves, 308, 317, 318, 320, 321, 325, 326
club fungi, 363, 367–371
club-moss, 396
coal, 25, 396, 398
   Age of, 396, 398
cobra lily, 36, 37, 43
cobra plant, 36, 37, 43
coca, 221–223, 253
Coca-Cola, 222

cocada, 221
cocaine, 221–223
coconut, 278, 285, 291–294, 303
Cocos nucifera, 278, 285, 291–294, 303
codeine, 212, 217, 221
coir, 291, 292, 294
colchicine, 247, 248, 447
Colchicum, 247, 248, 253, color plate 4a
colony, 338
Columbus, Christopher, 315
Commoner, Barry, 540–543
Commoner's laws, 540–543
complacent ring series, 156–158
complementary pair, 118–120
composite family, 418–420
composite flower, 418–420
compound, organic, 6
Comprehensive Drug Abuse Prevention and Control Act of 1970, 196
cone, 396, 397, 405–408
Confessions of an English Opium Eater, 220
conifer, 405, 408–410
consumer, 499–501
contessa powder, 226
control, 452
    biological, 27, 386, 536
    plant diseases, 384–386
convergence, 460, 476, 477
converter, catalytic, 538
Cook, James, 552, 553
copra, 278, 291–294
coral fungus, 369, 370
coral reef, 356
coralline algae, 356, color plate 6a
coriander, 308, 321
cork, 22, 30
corn, 285, 287, 288, 297–301, 303
    chromosomes, 446
    hybrid, 297, 298, 448, 449
    lysine-rich, 300
    smut, 368, 371, 376, 377
    tryptophane-rich, 300
Correns, Carl, 431, 457
Cortés, Hernán, 316
cortex, 21, 22
cortisone, 238–240
cotyledon, 412
coumarin, 176
counterirritant, 323, 327
craving, 198
Crick, Francis F. H. C. , 113–118
Critica Botanica, 76
crop rotation, 385
cross-breeding, 448
cross-dating, 159, 160

cross-pollination, flowers, 412
cross(es)
    dihybrid, 438
    without dominance, 436, 437
crossing-over, 444, 451
cultivated plants, changes in, 469–471
cumin, 323
cup fungus, 367, color plate 6b
curandero, 257
curare, 245–247, 253
curry powder, 323
cuticle, 16, 17, 18, 397
cycad, 405, 406
cycles of life, 496–511
cytokinin, 31, 32
cytologist, 96
cytology, 97
cytoplasm, 101–103, 106–108

daisy, 418, 420
damping-off fungus, 375, 386
Darlingtonia, 36, 37, 43
Darwin, Charles, 38, 41, 58, 63, 415, 419, 457, 465, 466, 474, 475, 477–481, 482–493
Darwin, Erasmus, 75, 227, 483
Darwinism
    misuse, 478–481
    social, 480, 481
Darwin's books, 490, 491
Dasya, 350, 352
data, 450, 451
Datura, 173–175, 185, 274, 277, 428
dawn redwood, 409, 427
Dawson, Sir William, 399, 400
DDT, 229, 377, 531–536
    accumulation in tissues, 532, 534, 535
    animal metabolism, 534, 535
    danger, 534–536
    disintegration, 535
    food-chain concentration, 532
    malaria control, 533, 534
    man, 531–536
death angel, 379
decay, 147–149, 365, 382
deciduous, 29, 405
decomposer, 499–501
decongestant, 248
dendrochronology, 157–161
dendroclimatology, 160, 161
denitrification, 365, 508–510
deoxyribonucleic acid, *see* DNA
deoxyribose, 118–120
dermatitis, 170–172
dermatomycosis, 379
derris, 27, 536

Deserts on the March, 526, 529, 539, 546
desmid, 343
destroying angel, 369, 379
devil's apron, 344, 347
devil's herb, 240–242, 253
diabolic root, 261
diatom, 351–353, 355, 356
diatomaceous earth, 355, 356
dicotyledon, 13, 64, 410, 412
    flower, 417
dicoumarin, 176
Dieffenbachia, 179, 185
diffusion, 15
digestion, 362
digitalis, 176, 185, 212, 230–232, 253
Digitalis purpurea, 230–232, 253, color plate 3b
digitoxin, 230–232
dill seed, 308, 321
dinoflagellate, 357
dioecious, 188
Dionaea, 37, 38, 43
Dioscorea, 239, 240, 253, 289
Dioscorides, 210
diploid, 394, 441
disc flower, 418, 421
disease(s), 384
    caused by bacteria, 364, 365
distribution, geographical, 467, 468
diuretic, 231
DNA, 113–120, 449–451
    inheritance, 113–120
    replication, 118–120
doctrine of signatures, *see* signatures
doctrine of special creation, *see* special creation
dodder, 384, 403, 427
dominance, law of, 434, 450
double fertilization, 410, 412–414
    significance, 414
double helix, 114–120
Douglas fir, 409, 427
Douglass, Andrew Ellicott, 157, 158, 160, 161
dove tree, color plate 8c
dropsy, 231
Drosera, 37, 38, 43
Drosophila artificialis, 469–471
drug, 197
drupe, 278, 291–294
duckweed, 403, 427
dulse, 350, 352
dumb cane, 179, 185
dump-heap theory, 186, 281
Dust Bowl, 528–531

dusting, 385
Dutch elm disease fungus, 362, 367,
    376, 377
dwarf male, 342, 343

Eakin, Richard M., 454, 459
early wood, 152, 154
earthstar, 368, 370
Ebers Papyrus, 209, 248
ecology, 5, 494–523
    Bible, 527, 528
    climax vegetation, 518
    Dust Bowl, 529–531
    ethics, 539–546
    interrelationships, 539–543
    introduced plants, 540, 541
    laws, 540–543
    man, 525
    summary, 519–521
    synthetic chemicals, 542
    waste disposal, 541, 542
eel grass
    fresh water, 419–424, 427
    salt-water, 403, 427
egg, 341, 348, 412
Eichhornia, 403, 404, 427
electron gun, 105
electron microscope, invention, 105
"Eleventh Commandment," 545
elk kelp, 346
elodea, 403, 427
embryo, 285, 390, 392, 412
embryo sac, 411–415
embryophyte, 64, 389
emetic, 248
Endeavour, 552
endemic, 37
endoplasmic reticulum, 102, 107, 108
endosperm, 285–288, 414
energy, absorption and use, 7
environment, 494–549
    Bible, 527, 528
    ethics, 543–546
    land, 528–531
    man, 498, 524–549
    pollution, 536–539
Environmental Defense Fund, 533
enzyme, 23, 116–120, 362, 374, 450
Ephedra, 248, 253, 406, 407
ephedrine, 170, 248
epidermis, 16, 17
    leaf, 100
epiphyte, 403
equilibrium, dynamic, 498
Equisetum, 44, 183, 185, 396, 397
ergonovine, 265
ergot, 264–268, 277

ergotamine, 266
ergotism, 264–268
erosion, 20, 498, 526, 527–531
estrogen, 240
ethnobotany, 216
ethylene, 31, 32
Euphorbia, 403, 477
euphoric, 221, 222
eutrophication, 357
evergreen, 30, 405
evolution, 59, 63, 460–481
    algae, 343, 358
    biologic, 465
    cabbage, 469, 470
    causes, 471–476
    controversy, 461–465
    convergent, 460, 476, 477
    course, 471, 472
    evidence, 466–471
    ferns and seed plants, 415, 416
    impact on society and intellectual
        world, 477–481
    land plants, 396–401, 415, 416
    misconceptions, 463–465
    parallel, 477
    plant kingdom, 471, 472
    progressive, 476
    religion, 477–479
    types, 476, 477
excretory system, lack in plants, 213
exotic plants, 540, 541
experimental group, 452

factor, 433, 450, 451
fagopyrism, 181
Fagopyrum, 181, 185
Fairchild, David, 233
fairy ring, 369
family, 61
farinha, 289
fat, 7, 282, 283
fennel, 308
fermentation, 383
fern, 388–401
    allies, so-called, 396
    life history, 391–396
fertilization, 341, 346–348, 392, 395,
    412
    double, 410, 412–414
fever-bark tree, 223–230, 253
fiber, 100, 141, 142
figure, 144–146
    plain-sawn board, 144–146
    quarter-sawn board, 144, 145
fish cholera, 367
fission, 338, 364
flagellum, 339

flat-cut board, 144–146
Fleming, Alexander, 249
flesh of the gods, 272
float, 344, 347, 349
flora, 165
Flora Lapponica, 73, 76
Flora Virginica, 76
Flora Zeylanica, 81
floral hormone, 411
floriculture, 5
flower, 14, 402, 410–426
    cross-pollinated, 412
    dicotyledon, 417
    disc, 418, 421
    diversity in structure, 417–426
    insect-pollinated, 412, 413,
        419–421
    monocotyledon, 417–424
    ray, 418, 421
    self-pollinated, 412
    wind-pollinated, 419, 422, 423
flowering plant, 11–14, 402,
    410–427
fly-agaric mushroom, 268–274, 277,
    color plate 4c
flying death, 246
food, 7, 279, 281–284
food chain, 351, 352, 358, 512–515,
    531–536
    aquatic, 351, 352, 358
    concentration, 524, 531–536
    energy levels, 512
    magnification, 531–536
    man, 512
    marine, 515
    terrestrial, 513
food plants, 278–303
    improvement of, cultivated,
        296–300
food preservation, 373
food web, 513
fool's parsley, 173, 185
forestry, 5
form and function, 11
formaldehyde, 537
Fortune, Robert, 560–564
    Chinese pirates, 562, 563
    plant introductions, 563, 564
    status as plant explorer, 563, 564
fossil plants, 398–401, 405, 468
fouling, 357, 358
foxglove, 176, 185, 230–232, 253,
    color plate 3b
fragmentation, 363
Franklin, Rosalind, 113, 114, 117, 118
fresh-water eel grass, 419–424, 427
Friendly Islands, 557
frog slime, 337

frog spittle, 337
frond, 388, 392
fruit, 283, 285, 414, 415
    versus seed, 415
fruit dot, 392, 393, 395, 396
fruiting body, 362
Fucus, 336, 346–348
Fundamenta Botanica, 76
fungi, 64, 337, 360–387
    causes of animal diseases, 377,
        378
    causes of human diseases,
        377–379
    edible, 380–382
    groups, 363
    harmful activities, 373–380
    industrial, 383
    medicinal, 383
    role in cheese ripening, 382
    role in spoiling food, 373
    scavengers, 383
    true, 363, 365–371
    useful aspects, 380–383
fungicide, 385

gamete, 340–343, 346–348
    female, 341, 346, 412
    male, 341, 346
gametophyte, 394, 395
    angiosperms, 414, 415
ganja, 192, 193
gas, 25
gelatin, 350, 354, 356
Gelidium, 350, 356
gene, 111–120, 433, 449–451
    theory of inheritance, 430, 443
gene pool, 476
Genera Plantarum, 76
genetics, 428–453
    brief history, 430–433
    problems for students, 440,
        441
genotype, 435
genus, 51, 52, 60
George III, 555
Gerard, John, 47
germ, 285
giant kelp, 346
giant sequoia, 409, 427
gibberellin, 31
gill fungus, 360, 378, 380, 381
ginger, 308, 320, 321, 326–328
ginkgo, 405–407, 427
ginseng, 244–246, 253
glucose, 101
glycoside, 175–177, 213, 250
    cardiac, 176, 177, 185, 213

Goethe, Johann Wolfgang von, 425,
    426
goiter, 176
goldenrod, 169, 170, color plate 1b
Gonyaulax, 357
gout, 247, 248
grafting, 33, 34
grain, 285–288, 296–300, 303
grain (wood), 144
Grapes of Wrath, 528, 529
grass, 168
grass-green algae, 339
Grassi, Giovanni, 225
gravity, specific, 145, 146
great cycles of nature, 496–511
green algae, 338–344
green mold, 367
Green Revolution, 298–300
Grew, Nehemiah, 98, 131, 153
Gronovius, Johann Friedrich, 74
growth, 7
    continuous, 8
    localized, 8
    substance, synthetic, 31, 32
guard cell, 17, 18
gulfweed, 348–350
gymnosperm, 64, 404–410

habitat, 215
habituation, 198
hallucination, 173, 197, 255–257
hallucinogens, 254–277
    botany, 258, 259
    chemistry, 259, 260
    definition, 255–257
    discovery, 257, 258
    history, 257, 258
    psychiatry, 259, 260
Hammarby, 2, 83
Hansen, G. Armauer, 233
Hansen's disease, 232–235
haploid, 394, 441
hardwood, 140–143
Hartekamp, 76
Hasan-Ibn-Sabbah, 191, 192
hashish, 187, 191, 192, 202
hashish club, 193, 194
hashishins, 192
Hatshepsut, Queen, 550, 553, 554
Hauptmann, Bruno Richard,
    131–135
hay fever, 168–170, 419
heartwood, 136, 143
Helianthus, 418, 421, 427
hellebore, 173, 185, 249, 253
Helmont, Jean-Baptiste van, 24
hemophilia, inheritance, 445–447

hemp, 187, 189
    fiber, 187, 189, 194
henbane, 274, 277, color plate 5a
Henslow, John, 485
herb, 29
    culinary, 321
    sweet, 321
herbal, 168, 215
herbalist, 47, 62
herbarium, 215, 456
herbicide, 27, 32
heredity, 430, 475
heroin, 221
heterogamy, 342, 348
heterozygous, 435
Hexenkraut, 242–244, 253, 274
Hippocrates, 210
histamine, 169, 170
Hofmann, Albert, 226, 267
holdfast, 337, 344, 345–347
    cell, 339, 341
holy bark, 249
holy fire, 265
homology, 425
homozygous, 435
Hooke, Robert, 91–94
hormones, 30–32
    use in agriculture and horticul-
        ture, 32
Horneophyton, 399
horse chestnut, 30
horsetail, 44, 183, 185, 396, 397
horticulture, 5
Hortus Cliffortianus, 76, 77
Hortus Uplandicus, 72
Hosack, David, 266
host, 361
    alternate, eradication, 385
Humboldt, Alexander von, 153
humus theory, 23, 24
hunger theory of sex, 341
hunting period, 280, 281
Huxley, Aldous, 260, 264, 276
Huxley, Thomas Henry, 478, 482,
    488–491, 493
hybrid, 297, 437, 438
    corn, 297, 298, 448, 449
    vigor, 297, 298, 448
hybridizing, 296, 448
Hydnocarpus, 232–235, 253, color
    plate 3c
hydrocarbon, 537
hydrocyanic acid, 175, 176
hydrologic cycle, 503–506
hyoscyamine, 173, 242
hypertension, 235, 237
hypnotic, 190, 218
hypothesis, 450, 451

ibotenic acid, 272
ice algae, 339
inbreeding, 448
incense trees, 553
independent assortment, law, 439,
    450, 451
Indian hemp, 187
Indian Hemp Commission report,
    198, 199
Indian pipe, 403, 404, 427
indicator plant, 180
indoleacetic acid, 31
inheritance, 430
    acquired characteristics theory,
        471–474
    blending theory, 430
    blood theory, 430
    particulate theory, 430
insect carriers of pathogens, check-
    ing, 385
insecticide, 27
insectivorous plant, 35–40, 43
insect-pollinated flower, 412, 413,
    419–421
intercellular space, 16, 18
*International Code of Botanical No-
    menclature*, 58
internode, 12, 30
Ipomoea, 254, 268, 277
    batatas, 285, 288, 289, 303
Irish moss, 350, 352
isogamy, 341
Iter Lapponicum, 73

Jack-in-the-pulpit, 179, 185
Janssen, Hans and Zacharias, 90
Jesuit's bark, 226
jewels of the plant world, 351
jimson weed, 173–175, 185, 274, 277,
    428
Johannsen, Wilhelm Ludvig, 113
Jukes, Thomas H., 534–536

kalaw tree, 232–235, 253, color plate
    3c
kelp, 337, 344–347
Koehler, Arthur, 132–135
kretek, 325
kudzu, 540

Laboratory of Tree-Ring Research,
    157–161
lacquer tree, 172
LaGuardia report, 199, 200
Lamarck, Jean Baptiste, 471–474
lambkill, 181, 185
Laminaria, 344, 347

"Land Ethic," 544, 545
land plants, orgin, 396–401
Land of Punt, 550, 553
late wood, 152, 154
lateral meristem, 108, 109, 136, 137
laudanum (ladanum), 220
laurel
    mountain, 181, 185
    sheep, 181, 185
Laveran, Charles, 225
law, 450, 451
laxative, 248, 249
lead, toxicity, 538
leaf, 12, 14–18
    axil, 12
    compound, 12
    internal structure, 15–18, 100
    palmately compound, 12
    palmately veined, 13
    parallel-veined, 14
    pinnately compound, 12
    pinnately veined, 13
    scar, 30
    simple, 12
leaflet, 12
Ledger, Charles, 229
Leeuwenhoek, Antony van, 91, 153
legume, 283, 285, 290, 291, 303, 415
    flower, 418, 420
    nitrogen fixation, 510
Lemna, 403, 427
lenticel, 30
Leopold, Aldo, 543–545
leprosarium, 233
leprosy, 232–235
Lewin, Louis, 256, 259, 276
lichen, 368–373
    indicator of atmospheric pollu-
        tion, 372, 373
    radioactive chemicals, 373
    role in colonizing, 372, 518, 519
    succession, 372, 518, 519
life cycle
    critical stages in, 395
life, definition, 6, 7
life history of a fern, 391–396
light energy, 15
Lignier, O., theory of land plant ori-
    gin, 398, 401
lignin, 101, 332
limnoria, 149–151
Lincoln, Almira H., 1, 58
Lindbergh kidnap case, 131–135
Link, K. P., 176
linkage, 443, 444, 451
Linnaeus, Carl, 2, 51, 58, 62, 68–87
    birth, 70

Linnaeus, Carl (*continued*)
    contributions to science, 85
    education, Netherlands, 73
    education, Sweden, 70
    Hammarby, 83
    journey to England, 76
    Lapland journey, 72
    old age, 84
    physician in Stockholm, 78
    Prince of Botanists, 85
    professor, Uppsala, 79
    venereologist, 78
Linnean Society of London, 86
litmus pigment, 372
liverwort, 389, 390
living fossil, 407, 409
living thing, characteristics, 6, 7
loco disease, 180
loco weed, 180, 185
London smog, 537
long-day plant, 410
longevity of seeds, 424, 425
"Loves of the Plants," 75, 227, 483
Lowdermilk, Walter Clay, 545
LSD, *see* lysergic acid diethylamide
lunacy, 235–238
Lycopodium, 396
Lyell, Charles, 486, 489
Lysenko, Trofim, 474
lysergic acid, 258, 259, 266
lysergic acid diethylamide, 258, 259,
    264–268
lysine, 300

ma huang, 248
mace, 274, 308, 318, 320, 321, 328,
    329, color plate 5c
macroconsumer, 499
Macrocystis, 346
Madagascar periwinkle, 250, 253,
    color plate 4b
maddening plant, 274
Maeterlinck, Maurice, 422, 423
magnification, empty, 104, 105
maidenhair tree, 405–407, 427
maize, 285, 287, 288, 296–300, 303
malaria, 223–230, 533, 534
malnutrition, 384
Malpighi, Marcello, 131, 153
Malthus, Thomas R., 279, 301, 489
man
    ecology, 525
    enviromnent, 525
    land, 528–531
Mandragora, 47, 242–244, 253, 274
mandrake, 47, 242–244, 253, 274
Manihot, 285, 289, 303

manioc, 175, 185, 285, 289, 303
manna, 372
marijuana (also marihuana),
        187–207, 274
    botany, 187–189
    dangers, 203–204
    major studies, 198–204
Marijuana Act of 1937, 195
marine borers, 147, 149–151
Markham, Clements R., 229, 553
master chronology, 159, 160
masticatory, 324
Mayapple, 181, 182, 185, 250, 253
medicinal plants, 208–253
    discovery, 214–216
meiosis, 395, 441, 442
membrane, 106–108
Mendel, Gregor Johann, 431–439,
        454–459, 463
Mendel's basic cross, 432–436
Mendel's factors and chromosome
        behavior, 443
Mendel's four laws, 440, 450, 451
mercury pollution, 541, 542
meristem, 30, 31, 108, 109, 136, 137
mescal, 264
    button, 253
mescaline, 264
metabolism, 26
metamorphosis, 425, 426
Metasequoia, 409, 427
microbe, 361
microbiology, 361, 363
microconsumer, 499
Micrographia, 92–94
microscope, 90, 91, 93, 97, 98
    electron, 98, 104–106
    invention, 90
    light, 97, 98
mildew, 361, 374
milk sickness, 181–183
mineral nutrition, 26–29
mint, 308
mistletoe, 384, 403, 427
mitochondrion, 102, 106
mitosis, 111–113
mitotic series, 112
Mohl, Hugo von, 97, 101
mold, 361, 365, 366, 367, 373
Molucca Islands, 316–318
monocotyledon, 14, 65, 410, 412,
        417–424
    flower, 417–424
monoecious, 287
monohybrid cross, 438
Montaigne, Michel, 153
moonseed vine, 247, 253

morel, 367
morning glory, 254, 268, 277
morphine, 217–221
morphology, 11, 415, 425
mosses, 389, 390
    colonizers of rocks, 389, 518, 519
    ecological significance, 389, 518,
        519
mulch, 390
mulching, 27
multicellular individual, 341
Musa sapientum, 285, 293–295, 303
muscarine, 272
mushroom, 361, 368, 369, 378–381
    effigy stones, 272
    field, 380
    sacred hallucinogenic, 272, 277
mustard seed, 308
mutation, 376, 446, 447, 448, 475, 476
    theory, 475, 476
mycelium, 362
Mycobacterium leprae, 233
mycology, 361
    industrial, 383
    medical, 377
mycophilia, 271, 272
mycophobia, 271, 272
mycorrhiza, 367
myristicin, 329

name
    botanical, 46
    common, 45
    folk, 45
    generic, 52
    plant, 45
    species, 51
    specific, 51, 55
    valid, 57
    vernacular, 45, 49
naming, 45
narcotic, 197, 198
National Commission on Mari-
        huana and Drug Abuse, report,
        200–203
Native American Church, 261–264
natural selection, theory, 474, 475
Nelson, David, 556, 557
nematode, 384, 385
Neolithic Age, 280, 281
Nepenthes, 36, 37, 43
Nereocystis, 345
nettle, 172, 185
New Stone Age, 280, 281
nightshade, 175, 185, color plate 1d
nitrate, 508, 509
nitric oxide, 537

nitrogen, 506–511
    cycle, 506–511
    deficiency, 507
    dioxide, 537
    -fixation, 26, 283, 300, 365,
        507–511
    -fixer, 507–511
    -fixing bacteria, 26, 283, 300, 508,
        510, 511
    -fixing blue-green algae, 511
    -fixing higher plants, 510
    oxide, 537
nitrogenous base, 118–120
node, 12, 30
nodules, legumes, 283, 365, 510
nomenclature, binomial system,
        52, 81–83
Novacaine, 222
nuclear membrane, 99, 102, 103
nucleic acids, 116–120, 449–451
nucleolus, 99, 103, 113
nucleotide, 118–120
nucleus, 99–103
    male, 412, 414
nutmeg, 274, 277, 308, 317, 318, 320,
        321, 328, 329, color plate 5c

Oedogonium, 341–343
oil, 25, 282, 283
Old Stone Age, 280, 281
oleander, 176, 177, 185
olericulture, 5
ololiuqui, 268, 277
ontogeny, 469
opium, 216–221, 253
opium poppy, 216–221, 253, color
        plate 3a
opium wars, 220
opposite arrangement, 14, 30
oral contraceptive, 240
orchid, 403
order, 61
oregano, 308, 321
organ, 12
organic, 499
    catalyst, 23
    compound, 6
    evolution, 465
    gardening, 27–29
organism, 6
    consumer 499
    decomposer, 499
    producer, 499
organochlorine, 531
oriental dogwood, color plate 8b
Origin of Species, 58, 63, 431, 465, 474,
        475, 477, 481, 489, 490, 492, 493

Osler, Sir William, 190, 209, 217, 228
otomycosis, 378
ovary, 14, 411, 412
ovule, 14, 411, 412
oxygen, 14, 15, 503

paleobotany, 468
Paleolithic Age, 280, 281
palisade layer, 16, 17, 100
Paludrin, 229
panaquilon, 244
Papaver somniferum, 216–221, 253,
    color plate 3a
papaverine, 217
paprika, 322, 323
Paracelsus, 210, 211, 220
parasite, 361, 362
paregoric, 220
parsley, 308, 321
parsnip, 172, 185
parthenocarpy, 294
pathogen(s), 377
    checking insect carriers, 385
pea, genetics, 432–441
peat, 25, 390
peat moss, 389, 390
Peattie, Donald Culross, 2, 3
Pelagophycus, 346
penicillin, 249
Penicillium, 249, 361, 362, 367–369
pepper, 308, 319, 320, 321, 322, 329,
    color plate 5b
    black, 308, 320, 321, 322, 330
    red, 322, 323
    white, 308, 320, 321, 329
peppercorn, 329
perennial, 32
peroxyacylnitrates, 537
Peruvian bark, 226
pesticide, 27
petal, 14, 411
petiole, 12
peyote, 261–264, 277
    ceremony, 263
peyotism, 261–264
Phallales, 368, 370
phantastica, 256, 257
pharmacology, 196, 197
pharmacopoeia, 190, 211, 252
phenotype, 434
Philosophia Botanica, 86
phloem, 15, 16, 17, 21, 22, 23, 136–139
phosphate, 118–120
photochemical smog, 537, 538
photoperiodism, 410
photosensitivity, 181

photosynthesis, 8, 14, 15, 102, 107,
    364, 499
    bacteria, 364
    removal of carbon dioxide from
        atmosphere, 499
    significance, 24–26
Phycomycetes, 363, 365–367
phylogenetic diagram of plant king-
    dom, 472
phylogeny, 416, 469
physiology, 11–43
Phytolacca, 183, 185
phytoplankton, 343, 351, 515
pimento, 322
pimienta, 322
Pincus, Gregory, 240
pine, 408–410
Pinus aristata, 159, 160, 409, 410, 427
pistil, 14, 412
Pitcairn Island, 557, 558
pitcher plant, 35, 36, 37, 43
pith, 22, 136
plain-sawn board, 144–146
plankton, 343, 351, 515
plant breeding, 296, 447–449
plant(s)
    versus animals, 8, 9
    biochemical uniqueness, 283
    characteristics, 8, 9
    definition, 5–9
    usefulness in medicine, 214
plant diseases (pathology), 361,
    374–377, 384–386
    causal agents, 384
    dispersal, 384
plant exploration, 550–573
    first records, 550, 553
    future, 569, 570
    objectives, 551–554
    sponsorship, 551–554
plant kingdom, relationships
    within, 472
plant naming, 44–67
    class, 61
    family, 61
    order, 61
plasma membrane, 99, 101, 102, 106
plastid, 99–103, 107
poinsettia, 183, 185, color plate 2c
poison, arrow, 245–247
poison control center, 183
poison hemlock, 173, 185
poison ivy, 170–172, 185
poison oak, 170–172, 185
poison, role of in plants, 167
poison sumac, 170–172, 185

poison vetch, 179, 180, 185
poisoned food, 531–536
poisoning, what to do, 183, 184
poisonous plants, 165–185
    definition, 166
    fungi, 378–380
    history, 167, 168
    types, 168–185
poisonwood tree, 172, 185
pokeberry, 183, 185
pokeweed, 183, 185
polar nuclei, 411–414
polished rice, 286
pollen, 14, 397, 411
    sac, 411, 412
    tube, 411–414
pollination, 412–415, 419–423
    versus fertilization, 414, 415
pollution, atmospheric
    federal regulations, 537, 538
    indicator, 372, 373
pollution-control system, automo-
    tive, 538
Polo, Marco, 313
polyploid, 446
Polypodium, 392, 393
pomology, 5
pond scum, 337
population, 279, 299
Postelsia, 344, 347
potato
    sweet, 285, 288, 289, 303
    white, or Irish, 285, 288, 303
potato blight fungus, 288, 367, 375
potato famine, 288, 367, 375
precatory bean, 177, 178, 185, color
    plate 2a
primaquine, 230
principle of priority, 52
procaine, 222
producer, 499–501
progesterone, 240
protein, 7, 116–120, 282–284, 300,
    506, 507
    synthesis, 116, 119, 120
    synthetic meat, 291
    textured vegetable, 291
prothallus, 392, 394
Protococcus, 339
protoplasm, 7, 97, 101–103, 106–108
Providence, 559
pruning, 34, 35
Psilocybe, 272, 277
psilophyte, 398–400
Psilophyton, 399, 400
psychedelic, 256, 257

psychological dependence, 198
psychotomimetic, 256, 257
puffball, 367, 370
pulque, 264
pure line, 448
purple bacteria, 364
putrefaction, 382
pyramid of numbers, 513–515
pyrethrum, 27, 420, 536

quarantine, 385
quarter-sawn board, 144, 145
Queen Victoria water lily, 404,
    427, color plate 6c
quina quina, 225
Quincey, Thomas De, 220
quinidine, 228
quinine, 223–230, 253

rabage, 471
Rafflesia arnoldi, 417, 418
ragweed, 168–170, 185
rain forest, tropical, 497
Rauwolfia serpentina, 235–238, 253
ray, 138
ray cell, 138
ray flower, 418, 421
Ray, John, 58, 63
recapitulation, 469
recessive, 434
red algae, 350, 351
red bean, 264
red tide, 357
reduction division, 395, 441, 442
redwood, 408, 409, 427
reforestation, 543, 544
regal lily, 564–569
reindeer moss, 372, 373
replication, 118–120
reproduction, 7, 339–343, 346–348
    asexual, 339
    differential, 476
    fungi, 362, 363
    sexual, 341, 346–348
reproductive isolation, 476
reserpine, 235–238
reserve food, 283
resolution, 104, 105
Resolution, 554
resolving power, 104, 105, 355
respiration, 7, 106, 501
    anaerobic, 383
responsiveness, 7
retrogressive evolution, 476, 477
rhizoid, 392, 393
rhizome, 285

rhizotomi, 210
rhubarb, 178, 179
Rhus, 170–172, 185
Rhynia, 399, 400
ribonucleic acid, *see* RNA
ribosome, 102, 107
rice, 285, 286, 287, 296–300, 303
Rig Veda, 192, 215, 233, 270, 271
ringworm, 377
RNA, 120, 449–451
    messenger, 120
    ribosomal, 120
    transfer, 120
Rock, Joseph F., 233, 234, 553
rock tripe, 372
rockweed, 336, 346–348
root, 12, 19–22
    graft, 377
    internal structure, 21, 22, 110
    nodule, 50, 283, 365
    system, 19
root-hair, 20, 21
Ropp, Robert De, 218–220, 237, 251,
    252, 258
rosary pea, 177, 178, 185
rose fever, 168
rosemary, 308
Ross, Ronald, 225
rot, 374
rotenone, 27, 536
royal lily, 564–569
rust, 368

sac fungi, 363, 367
sacred bark, 249
saffron, 308
sage, 304, 308, 321
St. Anthony's fire, 265
St. John's wort, 181, 185, color plate
    2b
Salem witches, 267
salicin, 247
salicylic acid, 247
salt-water eel grass, 403, 427
San Pedro cactus, 264
sanitation, 385
Sappington, John, 228
saprophyte, 361, 362
sapwood, 136, 143
Sargassum, 348–350
Sarracenia, 35, 36, 43
Schizomycetes, 363–365
Schleiden, Matthias Jakob, 95
Schulman, Edmund, 159
Schultes, Richard E., 206, 212, 223,
    252, 260, 261, 274

Schwann, Theodor, 95
science, 6
scientific method, 450–452
scion, 33
Scopes case, 461, 462
scopolamine, 173, 242
scurvy, 327
sea lettuce, 352, 353
sea moss, 337, 351
sea palm, 344, 347
Sears, Paul B., 20, 526, 527, 539, 546
seasoning, 374
seaweed, 337, 344–353
seed, 14, 280, 281, 283, 285, 404, 414,
    415, 424
    coat, 414
    fern, 405
    longevity, 424, 425
    plant, 64, 402–427
    treatment, 385
segregation, law, 435, 436
selection, 296, 448
selenium, 179, 180, 185
    indicator plant, 180
self-pollinated flower, 412
sensitive ring series, 156–158
sepal, 14
Sequoia, 408, 409, 427
Sequoiadendron, 409, 427
serendipity, 176, 249, 385, 452
Sertürner, Friedrich, 220
sex hormones (male and female),
    humans, 240
sex inheritance, 445, 446
sex organs (male and female),
    392, 393
sex reversal, 188
sex-linked character, 445–447
shaman, 257
shelf fungus, 368, 371, 374
Shen Nung, Emperor, 209, 233, 248
shipworm, 150, 151
shoot system, 19
short-day plant, 410
shrub, 29
sieve tube, 22, 23
signatures, doctrine of, 47, 210, 211,
    235, 242, 244, 250
Silent Spring, 531
skimmia, color plate 8a
skunk cabbage, 179, 185
Smith, James E., 86
smog, 537, 538
    London, 537
    photochemical, 537, 538
smut, 368, 371

snakeroot, 235–238, 253
white, 181–183, 185
snapdragon, genetics, 436, 437
snow algae, 339
social selection, theory, 480
Socrates, 173
softwood, 137–141
Solander, Daniel Carlesson, 552, 554
solanine, 175
Solanum tuberosum, 285, 288, 303
Solidago, 169, 170, color plate 1b
soma, 268–274
Sophora, 264
soporific, 190, 218
sorcerer's herb, 240–242, 253
sorrel, 178
sorus, 392, 393, 395, 396
soybean, 240, 285, 290, 291, 303
Spanish bayonet, 240, 253, 419, 427
Spanish moss, 403, 427
special creation, doctrine, 59
species, 58, 59
Species Plantarum, 52, 59, 81–83
specific gravity, 145, 146
Spencer, Herbert, 480
sperm, 341, 348
nucleus, 412, 414
Sphagnum, 389, 390
spice guild, 312
Spice Islands, 316–318
spice trade
Arab, 308, 309, 311
English, 318
European, 312–319
modern, 320
Roman, 310
United States, 319
spices, 304–335
aphrodisiacs, 305
aromatics, 305, 306
Bible, 306, 309
Christopher Columbus, 315
condiments, 307
deodorants, 306
Dutch East Indies, 317
economic value, 308, 312
flavor disguisers, 306
flavorings, 306
Marco Polo, 313
Portuguese exploration, 316
Spanish exploration, 315
world exploration, 308–319
spiral arrangement, 14
spongy layer, 16, 17
spore, 339, 362–364
formation, 395
sac, 392, 393

sporophyte, 394, 395, 415
spraying, 385
Spruce, Richard, 553
spurge, 403, 477
stamen, 14, 411
Steinbeck, John, 20, 528, 529
stem, 12, 22, 23, 29–31
internal structure, 22, 23
steroid, 213
stigma, 14, 411, 412
stinkhorn, 368, 370
stipe, 337, 344, 345–347
stipule, 12
stock, 33
stoma, 17, 18
streptomycin, 249, 365
strophanthus, 239, 253
struggle for existence, 474
strychnine, 247
strychnos, 247, 253
style, 14, 411, 412
succession, 494, 515–519
lichen, 372, 518, 519
primary, 518, 519
secondary 516–518
terrestrial, 516–519
succession powders, 167
sugar, 14, 15
beet, 285, 290, 291, 303
cane, 285, 289, 290, 303
sulfur compounds, 537
sundew, 37, 38, 43
sunflower, 418, 421, 427
survival of the fittest, 475, 480
sweet clover, 176, 185
symbiosis, 375, 367, 372, 381
synthetic meat, 291
system, biological, 115, 116
Systema Naturae, 74, 82
Szent-Györgi, Albert, 323

"Tabasco," 323
Tahiti, 554–559
Talbor, Robert, 226, 227
tapioca, 175, 185, 285, 289, 303
tarragon, 308
taxonomist, 61
taxonomy, 61
Taxus, 173, 185, color plate 1c
tea, 560–564, color plate 7b
cultivated in India, 561
green and black, 562
introduction to Britain, 561
native in southeastern Asia,
561
teonanacatl, 272, 277
tequila, 265, 476

teredo, 150, 151
terminal-bud
dominance, 30, 31
scale scar, 30
scar, 30
Terramycin, 249
testosterone, 240
tetrad, 442
tetrahydrocannabinol, *see* THC
thallophyte, 64, 337, 361
thallus, 64, 337, 361
THC, 188, 191, 201, 203, 204
Theophrastus, 62, 210
theory, 450, 451
thermal algae, 338
thiaminase, 183
thiamine, 183
thorn apple, 173–175, 185, 274, 277,
428
thyme, 308, 321
Tillandsia, 403, 427
Timor, 557, 558
tissue, 99, 100
toadstool, 379
tobacco, effects, 200, 205
tolerance, 198
torna-loco, 274, 277
totaquine, 228
Tournefort, Joseph Pitton de, 63
Toxicodendron, 170–172, 185
toxicology, 173
toxin, 177
tracheid, 22, 137, 138, 140, 141
tranquilizer, 190, 236, 237
transcription, 120
transpiration, 18, 505, 506
travertine, 338
tree, 29
age, 151–161
fern, 391
wind-pollinated, 168
tree growth
environment, 155–157
increase in diameter, 153, 154
trembles, 181
trihybrid cross, 439
triploid, 412
Triticale, 300
trophic level, 532
tropical deterioration, 373, 374
truffle, 381, 382
tryptophane, 300
Tschermak, Erich von, 431, 457
tuber, 239, 285
tubocurarine, 247
tulip, 417–419
tumor-inhibiting agent, 250

turmeric, 323
twelve plants standing between
    man and starvation, 284–295
twilight sleep, 173
2, 4–D, 32

Ulothrix, 339–341
ultramicrotome, 105, 106
Ulva, 352, 353
unit characters, law, 433, 450
U.S. Army Panama study, 199
Ussher, Archbishop James, 478

vacuolar fluid, 103
vacuolar membrane, 99, 102, 103
vacuole, 99, 100, 102–104
Vallisneria spiralis, 419–424, 427
vanilla, 308, 316, 320, 321, 330–333
vascular plant, 64, 390
    characteristics, 390
    seedless, 64
vascular ray, 22, 136, 138, 140–142
vector, 384
Veda, see Rig Veda
vegetarianism, 283, 284
vegetative body, 33
vein, 16, 17, 18
Venus's flytrap, 37, 38, 43
veratrine, 249, 250
Veratrum, 164, 173, 185, 249, 253
vessel, 22, 141–143
vestigial organ, 468
Victoria regia, 404, 427, color plate 6c
vinblastine, 250
Vinca rosea, 250, 253, color plate 4b
Vinci, Leonardo da, 153
vine kelp, 346
virus, 384
vitamin, 26, 183, 283, 284
    B$_1$, 183
    B$_{12}$, 284
    C, 323, 327
Vries, Hugo de, 58, 431, 457, 475

wakame, 354
Waksman, Selman A., 365

Wallace, Alfred Russell, 457, 489–491
Warfarin, 176
Wasson, R. Gordon, 269, 270, 271,
    273, 276
water, 14, 15, 503
    bloom, 357
    cycle, 503–506
    hemlock, 181, 185
    hyacinth, 403, 404, 427
    lily, 403, 404, 427
    -meal, 417, 427
    mold, 367
    oxygen and photosynthesis, 503
    precipitation, 503
    transpiration, 505, 506
    tree growth, 155–157, 505
    world distribution, 503–505
Watson, James D., 113–118
Wedgwood family, 483, 487
weed, 33
    killer, 32
Weismann, August, 473, 474
Welwitschia mirabilis, 407, 408
wheat, 285–287, 296–300, 303
    rust, 368, 376
whorled arrangement, 14
Wilberforce, Bishop Samuel, 478,
    482
wild plants, edible, 296
Wiles, James, 559
Wilkins, Maurice H. F., 113, 117
Wilson, Ernest H., 564–569
    adventurous return from royal lily
        trip, 566–568
    explorations in China for royal
        lily, 565–568
    plant introductions, 568, 569
    status as plant collector, 568, 569
wilt, 374
wind-pollinated flower, 419, 422, 423
wind-pollinated tree, 168
withdrawal symptoms, 198
Withering, William, 231
Wolffia, 417, 427
wonder drugs, 249
wood, 15, 16, 21, 22, 126–163
    anatomy, 131

wood (*continued*)
    -boring insects, 147, 149, 150
    color, 143
    decay, 147–149, 374
    -destroying fungi, 147, 148, 374
    deterioration, 147–151
    economic value, 128, 129
    fiber, 141, 142
    figure, 126, 144–146
    grain, 144
    hardness, 147
    -inhabiting fungi, 147–149
    marine borers, 147, 149–151
    molds, 147, 148
    ornamental value, 126, 127
    plant product, 129–143
    preservation, 148, 149
    properties, 145–147
    rotting, 147–149, 374
    specific gravity, 145–147
    -staining fungi, 147, 148
    strength, 146, 147
    structure and origin, 135–147
    structure and properties, 145–147
    uses, 128, 129
Woodward, Robert, 230, 238
woody twig in winter, 29–31
woorai, 246
World Health Organization and
    DDT, 533, 534
Wright, Frank Lloyd, 127

xylem, 15, 16, 21, 22, 136
    ray, 136
    see wood

yakee, 274, 277
yam, 239, 240, 253, 289
yato, 274, 277
yeast, 367, 368, 383
yew, 173, 185, color plate 1c
yucca, 240, 253, 419, 427

Zea mays, 285, 287, 288, 297–301, 303
zoospore, 339–342
Zostera, 403, 427
zygote, 340–343, 412